STUDENT'S GUIDE TO THE
Presidency

Student's Guides to the U.S. Government Series

STUDENT'S GUIDE TO THE

★ ★ ★ ★ ★ ★ ★ ★ ★ ★ ★ ★

Presidency

ADVISORY Editor

Bruce J. Schulman, Ph.D.

Boston University

CQ PRESS

A Division of SAGE

Washington, D.C.

DEVELOPED, DESIGNED, AND PRODUCED BY

DWJ BOOKS LLC

CQ Press
2300 N Street, NW, Suite 800
Washington, DC 20037

Phone: 202-729-1900; toll free, 1-866-4CQ-PRESS (1-866-427-7737)

Web: www.cqpress.com

Cover design: Matthew Simmons/www.MyselfIncluded.com

Photo acknowledgments for the Primary Source Library: Library of Congress: pp. 340, 343, 344, 345, 346, 348, 351; The Granger Collection, New York: p. 342; Montgomery C. Meigs Papers, Manuscript Div., Library of Congress, Washington, D.C.: p. 347; Theodore Roosevelt Collection, Harvard College Library: p. 354; Ralph E. Becker Collection, Smithsonian Institution: p. 356; Herbert Orth, Time Life Pictures, Getty Images: p. 359; MPI, Getty Images: p. 362; AP Images: pp. 363, 365, 367, 368, 371; Scott J. Ferrell, CQ: p. 375.

♾ The paper used in this publication exceeds the requirements of the American National Standard for Information Sciences—Permanence of Paper for Printed Library Materials, ANSI Z39.48–1992.

Printed and bound in the United States of America

12 11 10 09 08   1 2 3 4 5

Library of Congress Cataloging-in-Publication Data

Student's guide to the presidency
    p. cm. — (Student's guides to the U.S. Government series)
  Includes bibliographical references and index.
  ISBN 978-0-87289-555-3
  1. Presidents—United States. 2. Executive power—United States.
I. Schulman, Bruce J. II. Title. III. Series.
  JK516.S8 2009
  352.230973—dc22   2008050731

CONTENTS

Part Three: PRIMARY SOURCE LIBRARY

LIST OF ILLUSTRATIONS

READER'S GUIDE

The list that follows is provided as an aid to readers in locating articles on related topics. The Reader's Guide arranges all of the A–Z entries in the Guide according to 11 key concepts of the curriculum in American Government: Administrations, Presidential; Amendments; Elections and the Electoral Process; Executive Branch; Federalism and Politics; Political Parties; Presidential Benefits and Perks; Presidential Duties and Responsibilities; Principles of Government; The Constitution; and Vice Presidents and the Vice Presidency. Some articles appear in more than one category.

Administrations, Presidential

Adams, John, Administration of (1797–1801).

Adams, John Quincy, Administration of (1825–1829)

Arthur, Chester A., Administration of (1881–1885)

Buchanan, James, Administration of (1857–1861)

Bush, George H.W., Administration of (1989–1993)

Bush, George W., Administration of (2001–2009)

Carter, Jimmy, Administration of (1977–1981)

Cleveland, Grover, Administrations of (1885–1889, 1893–1897)

Clinton, William J., Administration of (1993–2001)

Coolidge, Calvin, Administration of (1923–1929)

Eisenhower, Dwight D., Administration of (1953–1961)

Fillmore, Millard, Administration of (1850–1853)

Ford, Gerald R., Administration of (1974–1977)

Garfield, James A., Administration of (1881)

Grant, Ulysses S., Administration of (1869–1877)

Harding, Warren, Administration of (1921–1923)

Harrison, Benjamin, Administration of (1889–1893)

Harrison, William Henry, Administration of (1841)

Hayes, Rutherford B., Administration of (1877–1881)

Hoover, Herbert, Administration of (1929–1933)

Jackson, Andrew, Administration of (1829–1837)

Jefferson, Thomas, Administration of (1801–1809)

Johnson, Andrew, Administration of (1865–1869)

Johnson, Lyndon B., Administration of (1963–1969)

Kennedy, John F., Administration of (1961–1963)

Lincoln, Abraham, Administration of (1861–1865)

Madison, James, Administration of (1809–1817)

McKinley, William, Administration of (1897–1901)

Monroe, James, Administration of (1817–1825)

Nixon, Richard M., Administration of (1969–1974)

Pierce, Franklin, Administration of (1853–1857)

Polk, James, Administration of (1845–1849)

Reagan, Ronald, Administration of (1981–1989)

Roosevelt, Franklin D., Administration of (1933–1945)

Roosevelt, Theodore, Administration of (1901–1909)

Taft, William H., Administration of (1909–1913)

Taylor, Zachary, Administration of (1849–1850)

Truman, Harry S., Administration of (1945–1953)

Tyler, John, Administration of (1841–1845)

Van Buren, Martin, Administration of (1837–1841)

Washington, George, Administration of (1789–1797)

Wilson, Woodrow, Administration of (1913–1921)

Amendments

Twelfth Amendment (1804)

Twentieth Amendment (1933)

Twenty-fifth Amendment (1967)

Twenty-fourth Amendment (1964)

Twenty-second Amendment (1951)

Twenty-third Amendment (1961)

Elections and the Electoral Process

Bush v. Gore (2000)

Conventions, Presidential Nominating

Democratic Party (1828–)

Election of 2008

Elections, Presidential

Electoral College

Federalist Party (1792–1816)

First Lady

PACs (Political Action Committees)

Political Parties and the President

Presidency and the Media

Presidency, Qualifications for

Presidential Appearances and Public Appeals

Presidential Campaigns

Presidential Debates

Presidential Primaries

ABOUT THE ADVISORY EDITOR

Bruce J. Schulman is The William E. Huntington professor of History at Boston University, a position he has held since 2007. Dr. Schulman has also served as the Director of the American and New England Studies Program at Boston University. Prior to moving to Boston University, Dr. Schulman was associate professor of History at the University of California, Los Angeles. Dr. Schulman received his Ph.D. and M.A. from Stanford University; he received his B.A., Summa Cum Laude with Distinction, in history from Yale University.

Since the 1980s, Dr. Schulman has been teaching and writing about the political face of the United States. He has taken an active role in education at the high school level as well as serving as the Principal Investigator for the Teaching American History Grant program with the Boston Public Schools. He also worked with the History Alive program, a curriculum-based interactive instructional program. In addition, Dr. Schulman served as director of The History Project in California, a joint effort of the University of California and the California State Department of Education to improve history education in the public primary and secondary schools.

Dr. Schulman is the author of several award-winning and notable books that combine his interest in history and politics. Among them are: *From Cotton Belt to Sunbelt: Federal Policy, Economic Development, and the Transformation of the South, 1938–1980; Lyndon B. Johnson and American Liberalism; The Seventies: The Great Shift in American Culture, Politics, and Society;* and *Rightward Bound: Making America Conservative in the 1970s* (co-edited with Julian Zelizer). Dr. Schulman's published books and numerous essays have examined and scrutinized the fabric of America's political and socioeconomic life and its direct impact on today's citizens.

PREFACE

As British Prime Minister Winston Churchill once remarked, "It has been said that democracy is the worst form of government except for all those others that have been tried." In CQ Press's new series, *Student's Guides to the U.S. Government,* librarians, educators, students, and other researchers will find essential resources for understanding the strange wonder, alternately inspiring and frustrating, that is American democracy.

In the *Student's Guide to the Presidency,* the third volume in the *Student's Guides* series, both young and experienced researchers, especially students and teachers, will find all they need to know about America's chief executive—the constitutional provisions and legal procedures, the pivotal campaigns and the outrageous scandals, the key players and the watershed policy changes—the pure pageantry of American presidential politics. The office is part royalty—the nation's ceremonial head of state as well as its head of government—and part democracy—the only office, along with the vice presidency, elected by all of the people, this most dynamic and most scrutinized branch of the federal government has always been a bundle of contradictions. As the presidency grew from a relatively weak office with almost no staff and few prerogatives into the office held by the unchallenged leader of the government's strongest branch, its inhabitants have become sources of fascination and controversy. One president, Lyndon B. Johnson (1963–1969), barely exaggerated when he suggested that, "being president is like being a jackass in a hailstorm. There's nothing to do but to stand there and take it." Although critics have seen danger in the concentration of power in the White House, partisans of freedom the world over have also hailed the office as a beacon of hope, a symbol of democratic values, an institution that makes even the most powerful leader subject to the aspirations and values of the people.

The *Student's Guide to the Presidency* unravels the historical development of the American presidency—the ways in which the office has changed over the past two-and-a-half centuries as well as its current status, unlocking the mysteries surrounding such contemporary issues as campaign finance reform, the qualifications for the nation's highest office, and the separation of powers. Each of the three parts of the *Student's Guide to the Presidency* takes a unique approach to enhancing users' understanding of the national executive branch. Part One features three essays, each of which addresses a provocative issue or question about America's highest office: "The Executive Branch: Behind the Scenes Since 1789"; "Power Trip? How Presidents Have Increased the Power of the Office"; and "Is the U.S. President the Most Powerful Leader in the World?"

Part Two features more than 125 A–Z entries spanning the administration of John Adams—the nation's second president and first vice president, the latter position described by him as "the most insignificant office that ever the invention of man contrived or his imagination conceived"—to the administration of Woodrow Wilson. Entries address the major Cabinet posts; executive departments; the instruments of presidential power, the ways that members of the executive branch take office and what sort of Americans have occupied the White House; the relationship between the presidency and other institutions, including the Congress, the Supreme Court, the political parties, the states, and the federal bureaucracy; as well as the historic election in 2008 of America's first African American president, Barack Obama. Special features within Part Two abound: "Point/Counterpoint" highlights opposing views on the same issue using primary evidence and concludes with a thought-provoking "Document-Based Question." "Spotlight" focuses on unique situations and events. "Decision Makers" takes a closer look at notable individuals, and "Justice for All" examines important moments in the long journey to extend the fundamental rights of citizens to all Americans.

Part Three contains a "Primary Source Library" of key documents, including inaugural addresses and constitutional amendments involving the election of the president and presidential succession; photos; and political cartoons that are essential to understanding the history of the American Presidency. These documents complement the information highlighted in both the essays in Part One and the A–Z entries in Part Two. Part Three also includes guidelines for using the Primary Source Library and for general research. The guidelines offer direction on Researching with Primary and Secondary Sources, Developing Research Questions, Identifying Sources of Information, Planning and Organizing research for use in a paper or report, Documenting Sources for the Bibliography, and Citing Sources.

Other helpful tools include a List of Illustrations, a Reader's Guide that arranges material thematically according to the key concepts of the American Government curriculum, and a timeline of Historical Milestones of the U.S. Presidency. The *Guide* concludes with a Glossary of political and elections terminology, a Selected Bibliography, and an Index.

An eye-catching, user-friendly design enhances the text. Throughout, numerous charts, graphs, tables, maps, cross-references, sources for further reading, and images illustrate concepts.

The Student's Guides to the U.S. Government Series

Additional titles in the *Student's Guides to the U.S. Government* series include the *Student's Guide to Elections,* the *Student's Guide to Congress,* and the *Student's Guide to the Supreme Court.* Collectively, these titles will offer indispensable data drawn from CQ Press's collections and presented in a manner accessible to secondary level students of American history and government. The volumes will place at the reader's fingertips essential information about the evolution of American politics from the struggles to create the United States government in the late eighteenth century through the ongoing controversies and dramatic strides of the early twenty-first century.

For study in American history, the *Student's Guides to the U.S. Government* collect a treasury of useful, often hard-to-find facts and present them in the context of the political environment for easy use in research projects, answering document-based questions, and writing essays or reports.

The *Student's Guides* offer valuable tools for civics education and for the study of American politics and government. They introduce young people to the institutions, procedures, and rules that form the foundations of American government. They assemble for students and teachers the essential material for understanding the workings of American politics and the nature of political participation in the United States. The *Guides* explain the roots and development of representative democracy, the system of federalism, the separation of powers, and the specific roles of legislators, executives, and judges in the American system of governance. The *Guides* provide immediate access to the details about the changing nature of political participation by ordinary Americans and the essential role of citizens in a representative democracy.

At the heart of the *Student's Guides to the U.S. Government* is the conviction that the continued success of the American experiment in self-government and the survival of democratic ideals depend on a knowledgeable and engaged citizenry—on educating the next generation of American citizens. Understanding American government and history is essential to that crucial education process, for freedom depends on knowing how our system of governance evolved and how we are governed.

By learning the rudiments of American government—the policies, procedures, and processes that built the modern United States—young people can fulfill the promise of American life. By placing at hand—in comprehensive essays, in easily recovered alphabetical format, and in pivotal primary source documents—the essential information needed by student researchers and all educators, the *Student's Guides to the U.S. Government* offer valuable, authoritative resources for civics and history education.

Bruce J. Schulman, Ph.D., Advisory Editor
The William E. Huntington Professor of
History, Boston University

1788: The United States Constitution is ratified by nine of the thirteen states and becomes the law of the land.

1789: George Washington wins the first presidential election on February 4.

1796: John Adams is elected president.

1800: Thomas Jefferson and Aaron Burr tie in the electoral college; the House of Representatives selects Jefferson after 36 ballots.

1804: The Twelfth Amendment is passed, requiring that electors vote separately for president and vice president.

1808: Jefferson continues Washington's two-term precedent for presidents, declining to run for a third term; James Madison is elected president.

1812: James Madison asks Congress to declare war on Great Britain.

1824: Andrew Jackson wins the popular vote but does not gain an electoral vote majority. The election must be decided by the House of Representatives, which elects John Quincy Adams.

1828: Andrew Jackson is elected president.

1831: The first national party convention is held in Baltimore.

1832: Andrew Jackson is reelected.

1836: Vice President Martin Van Buren is elected president.

1837: For the first and only time, the Senate decides the vice-presidential election, selecting Richard M. Johnson.

1840: Van Buren looses to Whig William Henry Harrison.

1841: William Henry Harrison dies after one month in office; John Tyler becomes first president to succeed to the office after the death of a sitting president.

1844: The Democrats nominate the first presidential dark-horse candidate, James K. Polk, who wins the election.

1846: Mexican-American War begins.

1848: Mexican-American War ends with the Treaty of Guadalupe Hidalgo.

1854: Anti-slavery supporters gather at Ripon, Wisconsin, and form the Republican Party.

1856: Democrat Franklin Pierce becomes the only elected president denied renomination by his party. James Buchanan wins the presidency.

1860: The new Republican Party elects its first president, Abraham Lincoln.

1861: Civil War (1861–1865) begins.

1863: Lincoln, using his power as commander in chief, issues the Emancipation Proclamation.

1865: President Lincoln is assassinated six weeks after the start of his second term. Andrew Johnson succeeds to the presidency and comes into conflict with Congressional Radical Republicans over Reconstruction policy.

1868: Johnson is impeached by the House of Representatives but is acquitted in the Senate.

1870: The Fifteenth Amendment, enfranchising newly freed slaves, is ratified on February 3.

1876: Democrat Samuel J. Tilden wins the popular vote against Republican Rutherford B. Hayes, but Republicans challenge the results in three states. A special electoral commission chooses Hayes.

1881: President James A. Garfield is shot by Charles J. Guiteau in Washington, D.C.; Chester A. Arthur succeeds to the presidency.

1884: Grover Cleveland is elected to the presidency, becoming the first Democrat to win the White House since before the Civil War.

1888: Benjamin Harrison becomes the third president elected without winning the popular vote.

1892: Grover Cleveland wins a second term as president, becoming the only president to serve two non-consecutive terms.

1898: Spanish-American War; United States acquires Puerto Rico, the Philippines, and Guam.

1901: President William McKinley is shot in Buffalo, New York; Theodore Roosevelt succeeds to the presidency.

1904: Theodore Roosevelt is elected president.

1908: William H. Taft is elected president.

1912: Roosevelt leaves the Republican Party and forms the Progressive—or Bull Moose—Party. With

Republican supporters split between incumbent Taft and Roosevelt, Woodrow Wilson is elected president.

1916: Wilson is reelected with the campaign slogan, "He kept us out of war."

1917: Woodrow Wilson asks Congress for a declaration of war against Germany to "make the world safe for democracy."

1920: Republican Warren G. Harding elected president; first presidential election in which women are permitted to vote nationwide.

1923: President Harding dies in office. Calvin Coolidge becomes president.

1924: Coolidge elected to the presidency.

1928: Republican Herbert Hoover is elected president over Democratic liberal Alfred E. Smith.

1929: Stock market crash leads to **Great Depression.**

1932: Democrat Franklin D. Roosevelt promises a "new deal" for the American people and wins an election landslide.

1933: Twentieth Amendment is ratified, moving the beginning of the president's term of office to January 20 of the year following the election.

1936: Roosevelt is reelected.

1937: Roosevelt proposes the Judiciary Reorganization Act of 1937 to increase the number of Supreme Court Justices to 15; Congress defeats the bill.

1939: Germany invades Poland; France and Great Britain declare war on Germany.

1940: President Roosevelt breaks the two-term precedent and is elected to a third term.

1941: Japanese bomb Pearl Harbor, Hawaii; President Roosevelt asks Congress to declare war on Japan. United States enters World War II.

1944: President Roosevelt is elected to an unprecedented fourth term.

1945: Roosevelt dies in office on April 12 and Harry S. Truman becomes president; World War II ends.

1948: President Truman defeats Thomas E. Dewey.

1951: The Twenty-second Amendment, setting a two-term limit on the presidency, is ratified.

1960: The first presidential debate between John F. Kennedy and Richard M. Nixon is televised from Chicago; Kennedy wins a close election in November.

1961: The Twenty-third Amendment is ratified, giving residents of Washington, D.C., the right to vote in presidential elections.

1963: President Kennedy is assassinated in Dallas, Texas; Lyndon B. Johnson succeeds to the presidency.

1964: The Twenty-fourth Amendment is ratified, abolishing the poll tax. Lyndon Johnson wins the presidency by the largest landslide in history.

1965: The Voting Rights Act, protecting African Americans' right to vote, is passed.

1967: The Twenty-fifth Amendment is passed, providing procedures in case the president is ill.

1968: Civil rights leader Martin Luther King Jr. is assassinated; Richard Nixon is elected president in a close contest.

1972: Richard Nixon wins a landslide reelection.

1973: Vice President Spiro T. Agnew resigns because of corruption and Nixon nominates Gerald Ford to replace him.

1974: President Nixon resigns because of the Watergate scandal; Ford succeeds to the presidency; Ford nominates Nelson A. Rockefeller for vice president.

1976: The first debate between vice-presidential candidates, Walter F. Mondale and Bob Dole, is televised from Houston, Texas.

1977: Jimmy Carter is inaugurated as the thirty-ninth president.

1981: Ronald Reagan is inaugurated as the fortieth president; in March, he is wounded in an assassination attempt.

1984: Democratic vice-presidential nominee Geraldine Ferraro becomes the first woman on a major party ticket, running with presidential nominee Walter Mondale.

1988: Republican George H.W. Bush becomes the first sitting vice president to be elected president since 1836.

1991: Persian Gulf War

1992: Bush loses reelection due at least in part to H. Ross Perot, a billionaire who mounts the strongest ever individual campaign, which splits the Republican vote; Democrat Bill Clinton is elected president with 43 percent of the popular vote.

1994: The Republican Party wins control of Congress.

1996 President Clinton is easily elected to a second term.

1998: A sex scandal threatens the Clinton presidency, the House of Representatives votes for impeachment.

1999: The Senate acquits Clinton of all charges, having failed to get the two-thirds majority needed for conviction.

2000: The Supreme Court settles disputed presidential election between Democrat Al Gore, who wins the popular vote, and Republican George W. Bush, giving the election to Bush.

2001: Al-Qaeda attacks on New York City and Washington D.C., as well as a hijacked plane crash in Somerset County, Pennsylvania, kill thousands of innocent Americans.

2003: United States and Allied forces invade Iraq and topple Iraqi dictator Saddam Hussein.

2004: President George W. Bush wins reelection with 51 percent of the popular vote.

2007: Former First Lady and New York senator Hillary Rodham Clinton announces her candidacy for the 2008 Democratic presidential nomination.

2008: In an April Gallup poll, 69 percent of Americans say they disapprove of Bush's performance in office, the highest negative rating recorded for a president since the firm began asking the question in 1938.

2008: Democratic presidential nominee Barack Obama of Illinois becomes first African American to head a major party ticket; Obama chooses Senator Joseph Biden of Delaware as his running mate. Republican nominee John McCain of Arizona selects Alaska Governor Sarah Palin as his vice-presidential running mate; she is the first woman on a Republican ticket.

2009: Barack Obama is inaugurated as the forty-fourth president of the United States.

PART ONE

Essays

The Executive Branch: Behind the Scenes Since 1789

 The executive branch of the U.S. government centers on the office of the president of the United States. In today's world, the title *President of the United States* speaks of power and influence. Americans look to the president as their leader, one who will guide them during times of crisis and change and who will protect them and keep their best interests at heart.

Presidents may not always fulfill these requirements; yet the people still expect them to do so. This expectation is born from a long line of influential presidents—those who have pushed the limits of their presidential powers both behind the scenes and before the people—and have made a profound impact on their country, if not the world. To understand this expectation, it is necessary to go back to the birth of the presidency in 1789.

Outlining the Presidency

During the summer of 1787, when the country's Framers were creating the Constitution, they saw the need to have an executive who would enforce the laws that are made by Congress and interpreted by the Supreme Court. Yet, having just fought their way out from under a tyrannical British monarch, the people of the colonies were wary of giving so much power to one individual. Realizing the problem, the Framers set out to develop a system that would allow each branch of government to counter the actions of the other two, thereby limiting the power of all three branches of government. In this way, while the people could have a strong leader who would enforce the laws, that leader would be kept from abusing power by the built-in system of **checks and balances.**

The actual job description for the presidency, as it is found in the Constitution, is rather vague. It states that the president will make sure "that the laws be faithfully executed." The Constitution also states that the president is the commander in chief of the United States armed forces, and has the authority to grant pardons, make treaties, **veto bills,** and appoint government officials. Yet, many of these powers are subject to the approval of Congress. The authority to declare war lies with the **legislative** branch. Treaties made by the president and many official appointments issued by the president are subject to the approval of Congress. In addition, the president's veto of a bill can be overridden with a two-thirds vote from Congress.

George Washington (1789–1797) and the Birth of the Presidency

After becoming president in 1789, George Washington set many **precedents** for the American presidency and for foreign policy. He established the custom of a two-term limit for presidents, and he initiated the formation of the cabinet. Washington's cabinet consisted of the Departments of State, War, and Treasury, and the office of the attorney general. Washington appointed trusted advisers to lead these departments. He also appointed the first five Supreme Court justices, naming John Jay to the position of chief justice.

Washington also the initiated America's **isolationist** foreign policy. He tried and failed to establish friendly relationships with France and Great Britain. As for domestic policy, Washington established his power as commander in chief of the U.S. military and the enforcer of federal laws when he led a militia into Pennsylvania to stop the Whisky Rebellion, a violent protest against a tax on whiskey. Under the advisement of his secretary of treasury, Alexander Hamilton, Washington supported the creation of a national bank and the creation of a tax system. Hamilton, who favored a strong federal government, was often at odds with Washington's secretary of state, Thomas Jefferson (1801–1809). Washington often took Hamilton's side, leading Jefferson to resign. The rivalry between the two cabinet members would ultimately lead to the formation of the first American political parties, the Federalists and the Democratic-Republicans.

During Washington's presidency, Congress set the president's salary at $25,000 a year. Washington refused the payment, claiming that he wanted to preserve his image as a selfless public servant. Congress insisted he take it anyway, so as not to set a **precedent** of the president's being unpaid, which would have only allowed wealthy individuals to run for president.

Andrew Jackson (1829–1837) and Jacksonian Democracy

The First **Bank of the United States** that was created under Washington was left to expire in 1811 by President James Madison (1809–1817). After discovering the benefits of having a national bank during the War of 1812 (1812–1814), Madison supported the creation of the Second Bank of the United States in 1815. This bank only survived until the early 1830s when President Andrew Jackson (1829–1837) instigated its removal, claiming that it benefited the rich rather than the common people. The bank would later become an issue in Jackson's reelection campaign, in which he would run against Kentucky senator Henry Clay, a bank supporter and one of Jackson's biggest rivals.

Jackson's decision to destroy the bank was one of several steps taken toward establishing Jacksonian democracy. Jacksonian democracy was a political philosophy that supported the increased involvement of citizens in the government, manifest destiny, the spoils system, and a central government with

limited power. The popularity of this philosophy spread after most white male citizens were given the right to vote in the 1820s. Jacksonian presidents continued to control the White House until Zachary Taylor (1849–1850) took over the presidency in 1849.

Along with introducing what became known as Jacksonian democracy, Jackson tried to increase the power of the presidency. He was the first president to veto a bill for reasons other than questioning its constitutionality, thereby expanding the president's veto rights. He also expressed his belief that each branch of the government should be able to interpret the Constitution as it sees fit. By making this comment, Jackson implied that Supreme Court decisions could be ignored. During his presidency, Jackson appointed six Supreme Court justices, all of them supporters of his policies. Congress resisted the appointment of Roger B. Taney, who as Jackson secretary of the treasury had helped him in his effort to close the Second Bank of the United States. Yet Jackson was able to pressure them into approving the appointment. With a majority of Jacksonian supporters on the Supreme Court, Jackson had essentially taken control of the judicial branch.

Although Jackson supported a central government with limited power, he still stood up for the Union and the authority of the presidency. In the late 1820s, southern states complained about high **tariffs** on products from Europe, which hurt southern plantation owners but helped northern industry. South Carolina officials claimed that they could nullify the legislation. By doing so, they were implying that they could choose which federal laws they would follow based on the interests of their state. While Vice President John Calhoun supported the **nullification** claim, Jackson threatened to enforce the federal tariff laws by sending troops to South Carolina.

Congress passed a Force Bill in 1833 that gave the president the authority to enforce tariff laws by use of military force. With South Carolinians unable to find allies among the other states, they agreed to a compromise. South Carolina repealed its nullification laws in exchange for federal legislation that would require tariffs to be lowered over the next ten years. Calhoun resigned from the office of the vice president before the compromise to retake his Senate seat. By engaging the military in order to oppose nullification rights, Jackson reinforced federal law and his position as the enforcer of federal law.

James K. Polk (1845–1849) and Manifest Destiny

In 1845, another Jacksonian president, James K. Polk, took office with an agenda that included four main points: re-establish the independent treasury system, reduce tariffs, acquire some or all of the Oregon Country, and buy California from Mexico. Polk was able to complete this entire agenda in one term. He also formed the Department of the Interior, which became a part of the cabinet.

As a Jacksonian, Polk was an enthusiastic supporter of manifest destiny. Therefore, it was no surprise when Polk supported his predecessor, John Tyler's (1841–1845) attempt to **annex** Texas. Polk would later lead the country through the Mexican-American War (1846–1848) to defend Texas's status as an American state. The war started over a boundary dispute between Mexico

Essays

and Texas regarding the southern border of Texas; Mexico said that the border was at the Nueces River, and Texas claimed that it was the more southern Rio Grande.

Polk sent troops, led by General Zachary Taylor (1849–1850), to Texas while he tried to settle the dispute through diplomacy. However, upon seeing the American troops near the Rio Grande, the Mexicans attacked, killing 16 American soldiers. Polk used this incident to convince Congress to declare war on Mexico. This war, which lasted for two years, was widely unsupported by northerners due to the possibility that Texas would become a slave state. Yet Polk went ahead with his war plans, leading to U.S. victory. This win, in addition to reinforcing Texas's claim that the Rio Grande was its southern border, led to the acquisition of the Mexican Cession, a vast territory that included present-day California and Nevada as well as parts of New Mexico, Utah, Arizona, Colorado, and Wyoming. Polk's secretary of state, Nicholas P. Trist, negotiated the Treaty of Guadalupe Hidalgo (1848) that was signed at the end of the war.

Earlier in his presidency, Polk had also acquired the Oregon Territory through negotiations with Great Britain, which also had claims to the region. This territory included the present-day states of Washington, Oregon, and Idaho, along with parts of Montana and Wyoming.

Abraham Lincoln (1861–1865) and the Civil War

Abraham Lincoln won the Election of 1860 as the nominee of the newly formed Republican Party. Not long after Lincoln was elected, many Southern states, believing that Lincoln would abolish slavery, seceded from the Union and formed the Confederate States of America. This led to the Civil War (1861–1865). Lincoln, a firm supporter of the Union, made an effort to reunite the states, and he was able to keep the slave states of Missouri, Kentucky, Maryland, and Delaware from seceding. During the war, these states were known as "border states." Not accepting the **secession** of the Southern states, Lincoln waited for the Confederacy to make the first attack, which it did in 1861 at Fort Sumter, South Carolina. After this first battle, Lincoln called on troops to "preserve the Union."

Despite increasing pressure from **abolitionist** groups, Lincoln did not move to end slavery until late 1862, when he issued the Emancipation Proclamation, a document containing two executive orders that freed all slaves in the states that had seceded from the Union. Lincoln, calling the proclamation a strategy for hurting the enemy, argued that his powers as commander in chief gave him the authority to issue the document. Soon after, he started laying the groundwork for the Constitution's Thirteenth **Amendment,** which would free all slaves in the United States. This Amendment was **ratified** in late 1865.

The war effectively finally ended when Confederate general Robert E. Lee surrendered to Union general Ulysses S. Grant (1869–1877) at Appomattox Court House in Virginia on April 9, 1865. Despite the protests of some northerners, Lincoln preferred to show the former Confederate states leniency when reinstating them into the Union. Unfortunately, in April 1865, just before **Reconstruction** could get underway Lincoln was assassinated by John Wilkes Booth.

Theodore Roosevelt (1901–1909): Progressivism and Foreign Policy

In 1901, the assassination of William McKinley (1897–1901) led to the succession of Theodore Roosevelt to the presidency. A supporter of the **progressive** movement and one who did not agree with the laissez-faire, or "hands-off" policy followed by previous presidents, Roosevelt cracked down on industry by setting regulations to make industry safer for workers and to make products safer for consumers. He issued lawsuits against trusts—business organizations designed to form monopolies, restrain trade, and fix prices. Roosevelt also helped to pass the Hepburn Act and the Elkins Anti-Rebate Act, both of which helped regulate the railroad industry. In addition, he supported the Pure Food and Drug Act and the Meat Inspection Act, which called for the labeling of food, required sanitary conditions in meat-packing plants, and allowed for the inspection of livestock. He also helped many Americans acquire a living wage through his "Square Deal" initiative.

While he fought to regulate industry, Roosevelt was heavily involved in internationalist foreign policy, as opposed to his predecessors, who generally supported an isolationist foreign policy. Roosevelt became known as a negotiator after he helped to settle the Russo-Japanese War (1904–1905), an effort that won him a Nobel Peace Prize in 1906. He also helped to negotiate disputes over territory in Venezuela, the Dominican Republic, and Morocco. Unfortunately, not all of Roosevelt's negotiations were successful. After negotiations with Colombia on acquiring land to build a canal failed, Roosevelt supported Panama's separation from Colombia. When the new Republic of Panama was formed in late 1903, the United States secured the necessary land to build the Panama Canal, which opened in 1914. In 1906, Roosevelt and his wife traveled to Panama to inspect the canal construction, making Roosevelt the first American president to travel abroad while in office.

Roosevelt also became involved in the affairs of other Latin American countries. For example, when a rebellion broke out in Cuba, President Tomás Palma requested the assistance of American troops, which Roosevelt agreed to provide. The U.S. military took control of Cuba a month later. This event came after Roosevelt issued the Roosevelt Corollary to the Monroe Doctrine (1823), giving him authorization to use the American military as an "international police power" in the Western Hemisphere. In 1907, Roosevelt, who had built up a large military force during his presidency, decided to show off the power of the U.S. Navy to the Japanese. He sent a fleet, called the Great White Fleet, to circumnavigate the globe and make a stop in Japan along the way. The trip was successful but may have inadvertently encouraged Japan to build up its navy.

Woodrow Wilson (1913–1921): Economics, Labor, and Peacemaking

The next influential president to win the White House was Democrat Woodrow Wilson, who was elected in 1912. In the early years of his presidency, Wilson exerted great control over Congress, including influence over committee membership. This allowed Wilson to enact major policies that affected

American industry, labor, and foreign policy. One of the main problems that he had to face during his presidency was the unfair business practices used by trusts and monopolies. In order to combat trusts, Wilson supported the creation of the Federal Trade Commission, which was given the responsibility of protecting consumers from unfair business practices such as price discrimination. The Clayton Antitrust Act, which went through Congress in 1914, shortly after the establishment of the Federal Trade Commission, made such practices illegal and recognized labor unions' right to strike.

While Wilson made major steps in the world of labor and economics, he took even bigger steps in the world of foreign policy. During his administration, Wilson was faced with the crisis of trying to maintain the isolationist policy established by George Washington, while several world powers engaged in World War I (1914–1918). Wilson even sent a representative to Europe to initiate peace talks, but this venture ended in failure. Attacks made by German submarines on American ships and the revelation of a possible alliance between Mexico and Germany made **neutrality** impossible to maintain. The United States declared war against Germany and its allies in 1917.

❝ *According to President Wilson:*

[**T**he United States entered the war] to make the world safe for democracy.

After the United States entered the war, Wilson supported the passing of the Espionage Act of 1917 and the Sedition Act of 1918. These pieces of legislation made it illegal for anyone to express antiwar, anti-British, or pro-German sentiments. He also authorized the creation of the American Protective League, a police force authorized to conduct interrogations and searches without warrants in order to expose those who practiced unpatriotic behavior.

Wilson did not play a major decision-making part in the war itself, preferring to leave strategy up to military leaders, but he was very influential in the negotiations for a peace treaty that would end the war. In 1918, as the war was ending, Wilson presented his Fourteen Points to Congress. These Fourteen Points were guidelines that the nations involved in the war were to follow to establish and maintain peace. Included in the plan was the establishment of a League of Nations that would enforce the peace. Wilson traveled to Paris, where he argued for his plan at the Paris Peace Conference, thus making him the first president to lead an American delegation at a peace conference. The Germans were willing to agree to the terms of the Fourteen Points, but Britain and France opposed the plan because it did not require Germany to pay reparations, or monetary compensation, and it gave away much of Britain's control over the seas. In the end, the plan was used as a base for a peace treaty, but only a few of the points survived in the final draft of the Treaty of Versailles, ending the war. Wilson played a large part in seeing the plans to establish the League of Nations come to fruition, but Congress refused to let the United States. join. Despite this setback, Wilson's proposal of the League and his involvement in making it a reality were major steps in moving the nation to an internationalist foreign policy.

★ ★ ★ ★ ★ ★ ★ ★ ★ ★ ★ ★ ★ ★ ★ ★ ★ ★ ★ ★

Franklin D. Roosevelt (1933–1945): The New Deal and World War II

Wilson's steps toward establishing an internationalist foreign policy were taken further by Franklin D. Roosevelt, who was elected to the presidency in 1932. However, Roosevelt spent most of his first term focused on domestic policy. With his New Deal he worked to end the **Great Depression** in the United States. This plan involved establishing relief through a variety of federal programs that provided jobs and helped citizens to reduce their debt. For example, the Federal Trade Commission (FTC) was given more authority in regulating **commerce** and the National Industrial Recovery Act (NIRA) was established in order to set codes on prices and production in industry.

The NIRA, however, was declared **unconstitutional** in 1935 by the Supreme Court, and ultimately the Court would become one of the biggest opponents to New Deal legislation. In 1937, Roosevelt presented Congress with a plan that would add several new justices to the Court, thus allow him to nominate justices who would support New Deal legislation. Congress did not pass this so-called "court packing" legislation. Despite the trouble he faced with the Supreme Court, Roosevelt still held the confidence of Congress after the success of his New Deal programs became increasingly apparent.

Other New Deal initiatives pushed by Roosevelt included legislation that allowed for government regulation of Wall Street and banks. Roosevelt also supported the repeal of Prohibition—the laws that prevented the manufacture, sale, and consumption of alcoholic beverages. One of Roosevelt's most successful New Deal programs was the Works Progress Administration (WPA), which provided jobs for thousands of Americans. His more drastic actions included an executive order that required Americans hand over their gold to the government. Many claimed this to be unconstitutional, but the War Time Powers Act of 1917 gave Roosevelt's executive order the ultimate authority.

In the late 1930s, Roosevelt, like Wilson, was faced with a brewing world war, while governing a nation that, in general, wished to follow an isolationist foreign policy. At the first signs of war in Europe, in 1935, Congress passed the Neutrality Acts, making it illegal for Americans to provide aide to any combatant nation. Roosevelt strongly protested the acts. As the war grew worse and the Allied powers lost battles, public opinion began to change, allowing Roosevelt to make his move. Roosevelt went around the Neutrality Acts in 1940, providing Great Britain with 50 American destroyers in exchange for military base rights in British colonies. Congress then passed the Lend-Lease Act in 1941, allowing the United States to provide material and financial aide to Britain, China, and the Soviet Union.

Before Japan's attack on Pearl Harbor, Hawaii, on December 7, 1941, an action that solidified America's full military involvement in the war, Roosevelt was already preparing the nation for war. He began building up the military in 1938 and convinced Congress to start the first peacetime draft in 1940. During this time, American military forces were providing aide to Allied military forces, by protecting their ships in U.S. waters and by providing noncombative aid such as transporting fighter planes. Despite the slowly shifting public opinion, Roosevelt still faced strong opposition from isolationists in Congress.

After the United States entered the World War II, Americans became suspicious of the loyalty of native Japanese and Japanese Americans who resided in the United States, especially on the West Coast. Roosevelt once again pushed the limits of his presidential power, issuing an executive order in 1942 that called for the internment of first-generation Japanese Americans and their children. They were held in "war relocation camps" until their release in 1944. Other drastic actions taken during the war include the rationing of food and materials; freezes on prices, salaries, and wages; and restrictions on the freedoms of speech. In 1944, Roosevelt successfully ran for a fourth term. Due to his declining health, however, Roosevelt died in April 1945.

Lyndon B. Johnson (1963–1969): The Vietnam War and Civil Rights

Another president who tested the limits of his power was Lyndon B. Johnson, who succeeded to the presidency in 1963 after the assassination of John F. Kennedy (1961–1963). During Kennedy's presidency, an ongoing war in Vietnam, between the Communist North (Vietcong) and the Republican South (Army of the Republic of Vietnam), escalated. Kennedy had sent 16,000 military aides to assist the South Vietnamese in an effort to contain communism.

In August 1964, an American ship called the *Maddox* exchanged gunfire with three North Vietnamese torpedo boats in the Gulf of Tonkin. Two days later, the crew of the *Maddox* claimed that the North Vietnamese had attacked the ship. Armed with this information, Johnson asked Congress for "a resolution expressing the unity and determination of the United States in supporting freedom and in protecting peace in Southeast Asia." In response, Congress passed the Gulf of Tonkin Resolution, authorizing "the President, as Commander in Chief, to take all necessary measures to repel any armed attack against the forces of the United States and to prevent further aggression." Thus, Congress granted Johnson more war powers than any president had ever had. (Years later, it was determined that Johnson had exaggerated the severity of the Gulf of Tonkin Incident in the account that he had delivered to Congress and the public.)

After Congress passed of the Tonkin Gulf Resolution, Johnson sent thousands of troops to assist South Vietnamese forces, thereby fully engaging the United States in the war. As the war continued and American casualties mounted, an antiwar movement took root and grew in the U.S. At the same time, Johnson's popularity rating plummeted, especially after North Vietnam's surprise attack on South Vietnamese and American forces (known as the Tet Offensive because it occurred during the Vietnamese holiday of Tet).

On the domestic front, Johnson worked tirelessly to implement his **Great Society** program. Two pivotal laws passed during the Johnson presidency were the Civil Rights Act of 1964 and the Voting Rights Act of 1965, passed over opposition from some of the nation's white population. The Civil Rights Act made most forms of **segregation** illegal, while the Voting Rights Act made discrimination in voting illegal. In addition, Johnson's introduced programs aimed at eliminating poverty in the United States. He successfully pushed Congress to pass the Social Security Act of 1965, which established

As the White House is both the president's home and office, it is not only a center of power in the United States but also serves as a highly recognizable symbol of the nation. (AP Images, Khue Bui)

the Medicare program to provide federal financial aid for medical costs to people over age 65. Later that year, at Johnson's insistence, Congress extended federal financial aid for medical care to welfare recipients. In addition, Johnson pushed the Head Start program, which established special education programs to schools with a high concentration of low-income children.

Ronald Reagan (1981–1989): Reaganomics and the Cold War

Upon entering the presidency in 1981, Ronald Reagan introduced his plan to boost the economy. This plan, which became known as "Reaganomics," involved cutting taxes, revising and simplifying the tax code, and reducing domestic spending while increasing defense spending. Critics of the plan said that it would increase the national debt and that it benefited the rich without regard for the poor. Reagan argued that the tax cuts would increase investment and economic growth, create more jobs, and increase wages. While many of Reagan's predictions did come true, the tax cuts led to a large increase in the national debt, raising it from $700 billion to $3 trillion.

In addition to economics did, the sold war played a major part in Reagan's presidency. Rejecting the diplomatic détente, or relaxation of tensions, used by his predecessors, Reagan took a more aggressive approach to communism, one that many people thought to be too harsh and provoking. He ordered a buildup of the military and revived or created new weapons-development programs. After Soviet Union fighter planes brought down a Korean commercial airliner, Reagan barred Soviet passenger flights from arriving in the United

States and ceased negotiations on several agreements that were being considered between the United States and the Soviet Union, thereby hurting the Soviets financially. Reagan also intimidated the Soviets in 1983 by introducing the Strategic Defense Initiative, a defense system that, as he claimed, would make a nuclear attack on the U.S. impossible.

The military buildup on both sides continued, along with American efforts to hurt the Soviet Union's economy. Then, in 1985, Mikhail Gorbachev, who had shown a willingness to engage in diplomacy to end the cold war, came to power in the Soviet Union. Gorbachev and Reagan held four "summit meetings" that resulted in the 1987 signing of the Intermediate-Range Nuclear Forces Treaty, which called for great reductions in the supply of nuclear weapons on both sides. Increasing financial pressure on the Soviet economy was a major factor leading to the fall of the Soviet Union in December 1991.

Over the years, presidents such as Abraham Lincoln and Franklin D. Roosevelt have pushed the limits of their presidential powers in order to protect and preserve the nation, thereby increasing public expectations that future presidents to do the same. It is therefore essential that American citizens put presidential power in the hands of someone who will wield it with wisdom and strength, and with the best interests of the American people at heart. This is where the citizens of the United States put their voting power to use, and, like the president, they must use it wisely.

See also: Chief Diplomat; Chief Economist; Chief Executive; Chief of State; Presidency and the Media.

Further Reading

Ferrell, Robert H. *Presidential Leadership: From Woodrow Wilson to Harry S. Truman.* Columbia, MO: University of Missouri Press, 2005.

Kernell, Samuel. *Going Public: New Strategies of Presidential Leadership,* 4th ed. Washington, DC: CQ Press, 2006.

Neustadt, Richard E. *Presidential Power and the Modern Presidents: The Politics of Leadership from Roosevelt to Reagan.* New York: Free Press, 1991.

Roberts, Jeremy. *George Washington (Presidential Leaders).* Minneapolis, MN; Lerner, 2003.

Thurber, James A. *Rivals for Power: Presidential-Congressional Relations,* 3rd ed. Lanham, MD: Rowman and Littlefield, 2005.

Waterman, Richard. *The Changing American Presidency: New Perspectives on Presidential Power.* Mason, OH: Atomic Dog, 2006.

Power Trip? How Presidents Have Increased the Power of the Office

Today, there is no doubt that the president of the United States wields great authority. However, this was not what the Founders had had in mind. In fact, of the three branches of government—legislative, executive, and judicial—it was Congress, the legislative branch, that the Founders had envisioned would exercise the greatest power.

In addition, many of the men attending the Constitutional Convention of 1787 were fearful of a powerful executive. Indeed, some Founders proposed a multiple executive to prevent a single individual from gaining too much power. How did the office of the presidency become so central to the nation's government?

The President and Legislation

Article II of the Constitution outlines the structure of the presidency but gives only the barest guidelines as to the limits of presidential powers. Whereas the Constitution establishes the presidency as separate and distinct from the other branches of the federal government, it leaves the matter of executive powers unsettled. Over the years, a major question has been whether the president is meant primarily to serve Congress in executing the laws or whether the president is meant to exert essential and independent powers.

The Framers of the Constitution designed the American system of government so that there would be a certain balance between the legislative and executive branches. At times, a struggle for power has developed between these two branches. Frequently, this struggle has emerged when presidents have tried to increase their legislative power as a means to increase their political power.

As the nation has grown and developed, and as its relative position in the world community has become increasingly important, greater demands have been made on the federal government and on the president. For example, the demands increased sharply in the 1930s during the **Great Depression,** which the Franklin D. Roosevelt administration (1933–1945) felt could only be ended by bold federal action. From that time on, the public has taken a different view of the duties of the federal government and the specific role of the president as a national leader. The public has increasingly relied upon presidents to recommend legislation to deal not only with emergencies but also with various other situations—ranging from the economy to the environment—in an ever-changing and complex society.

Since 1921, the president's role as chief legislator has grown. The Budgetary and Accounting Act passed that year gave the president **jurisdiction** over the preparation of the nation's annual budget. The act established the Bureau of the Budget (later reorganized and renamed the Office of Management and Budget [OMB]) as a part of the president's executive office. All **bills** submitted by the various government agencies must be approved by the Office of Management and Budget. The comprehensive budget that is then prepared by the OMB and submitted to Congress becomes the basis for that year's legislative program.

During the 1970s, Congress determined that it should take part in the budget-making process and take action to better control spending. To meet these needs, the Budget and Impoundment Control Act of 1974 was passed. This law provided Congress with a budget office and a staff of specialists. In addition, a budget committee in each house was to report a comprehensive budget plan for the coming year. In considering the president's budget, these committees were to work within the limits of the comprehensive budget plan. The law also restricted the president's power to **impound,** or refuse to spend, funds **appropriated** by Congress. By a simple majority, either house could overturn a presidential decision to delay or defer spending on a federal program.

The President and Foreign Policy

For most if its early history, the United States thought itself somewhat safe from European aggression. Bounded on two sides by oceans and on the other sides by friendly neighbors, Americans felt securely isolated. Today, foreign policy takes much of the president's time. To a degree, the peace and security of the entire world rests with the president.

With the spectacular economic growth of the United States in the first part of the twentieth century, as well as World War I (1914–1918), the nation was forced out of its position of isolation. As the country expanded its worldwide trade, the president's position in world affairs also expanded. The military technology that was developed during the twentieth century—including atomic submarines, jet and supersonic aircraft, and missiles—made it easier for aggressors to reach the nation's shores. These developments also made it necessary to increase the size of the nation's military forces in order to protect U.S. shores and the nation's political and economic interests abroad. Thus, the president's power as commander-in-chief of the nation's military forces grew significantly. This trend has increased since the devastating attacks of September 11, 2001.

Foreign Aid

Still another way in which the president's power has grown is through the control of foreign aid. Since the end of World War II (1939–1945), the United States has extended aid to countries all over the world. The president is responsible for recommending the amounts and kinds of aid as part of the budget process. In addition, the president administers foreign aid laws once Congress passes them.

Executive Agreements

A key way in which presidential power has increased—at the expense of congressional power—is through the use of executive agreements. An executive agreement does not require congressional approval, but can commit the nation to a particular course of action. Therefore, the president is able to involve the country is serious foreign obligations even if the majority of the Congress is opposed. President Franklin D. Roosevelt, for one, extensively used executive agreements in foreign relations. He approved the Litvinov Agreement recognizing the Soviet Union in 1933, and the 1940 destroyer bases deal with Great Britain. During World War II (1939–1945), Roosevelt and his successor, Harry S. Truman (1945–1953), made secret agreements with World War II allies during conferences at Cairo, Yalta, and Potsdam. These agreements affected much of the world after the war finally ended.

While members of Congress frequently object to the use of this presidential power, they have not been able to rally enough support to curtail it. Thus, the use of the executive agreement remains a special presidential privilege. Because it enables the president to negotiate directly with the heads of other nations, the executive agreement is one of the president's most important instruments in formulating foreign policy.

The President and Military Power

During the twentieth and twenty-first centuries, the president's power to send military forces to any area of the world has further made the president a dominant force in foreign affairs. A number of presidents have used this power. John F. Kennedy (1961–1963) used it in his quarantine of Cuba during the Soviet build-up of missiles in 1962. During the Vietnam War era (1964–1975), amid growing protests at home, both Lyndon B. Johnson (1963–1969) and Richard M. Nixon (1969–1974) used this power to send U.S. combat forces to Southeast Asia. In 1975, Gerald R. Ford (1974–1977) sent a military force to rescue an American ship—the *Mayaguez*—and its crew, captured by Cambodians.

In 1980, Jimmy Carter (1977–1981) sent specially trained American commandos into Iran in an attempt to free more than 50 American hostages held there. Ronald Reagan (1981–1989) sent American troops to the Caribbean nation of Grenada to protect American medical students on the island. In 1991, George H.W. Bush (1989–1993) put together an international coalition to counter the Iraqi invasion of the small desert nation of Kuwait. Near the end of the century, Bill Clinton (1993–2001) committed U.S. troops as a part of a larger NATO force to bring an end to the devastating wars in the former Yugoslavia. George W. Bush (2001–2009) sent American military forces—as part of a NATO force—to topple the fundamentalist Islamist Taliban regime in Afghanistan. Later, in 2003, Bush ordered American troops to Iraq to overthrow the dictatorship of Saddam Hussein; he continued to send troops into Iraq until the end of his presidency, despite overwhelming disapproval by the majority of the American people.

The use of force as a tool of foreign policy, as indicated by these actions, is, of course, a most important point. These presidents, by their actions,

Essays

established that the United States would not tolerate aggressive behavior that threatened the interests or security of the United States. The presidents also demonstrated their willingness to commit American troops to combat without a declaration of war from Congress—although this power is limited somewhat by the War Powers Resolution of 1973, which attempted to restrict the president's power to commit American forces overseas.

The Use of Presidential Power

Although the presidency has certain powers granted by the Constitution and has acquired others over the years, how these powers are used varies from president to president. Depending to a large degree on the president's view of the office, the president is often able to mold public opinion. This is because no other public official has closer communication with the people than the president. In general, whatever the president says or does is treated as important news. The president is able to call a press conference at any time and usually receives free television time to address the nation. Therefore, the president's power to influence the public through the mass media is extraordinary.

Presidential Personality—Strict Constructionists

One view of the presidency is that the president's powers should be limited to those powers specifically stated in the Constitution. The presidents who held to this "strict constructionist" interpretation of the Constitution felt their role was not so much to lead the nation as it was to respond to national opinion. These presidents believed that the nation could best be served by listening to the voice of the people as they spoke through their representatives in Congress. Furthermore, in keeping with this view, these presidents avoided establishing **precedents** that would centralize great power in the presidency.

Thomas Jefferson (1801–1809) was one of the presidents who believed in the limited powers of the presidency. Jefferson also believed in retaining the bulk of governmental power in state governments. It was on that point—state government versus federal government—that Jefferson's position differed most sharply from the ideas held by Alexander Hamilton. Hamilton advocated a strong central government led by a strong executive.

Many other presidents have accepted Jefferson's view of the president's role. After working with the aggressive Theodore Roosevelt (1901–1909), William Howard Taft (1909–1913), who served as Roosevelt's secretary of war, had reservations about the power of the presidency. Although Taft's presidential candidacy had been sponsored by Roosevelt, Taft could not accept Roosevelt's broad conception of presidential powers.

66 *President Taft noted:*

The true view of the Executive functions, is as I conceive it, that the President can exercise no power which cannot be fairly and reasonably traced to some specific grant of power, or justly implied and included within such grant of power and necessary to its exercise.

This view of the presidency is typical of the presidents who were strict constructionists.

President George W. Bush met with President-elect Barack Obama in the Oval Office shortly after Obama's historic win in November 2008. (AP Photo, The White House, Eric Draper)

Even during crises, when conditions demanded bold action and programs, certain presidents have refused to expand their presidential powers. Herbert Hoover (1929–1933), in the midst of the Great Depression, was restricted in his actions by what he saw as the limitations of the presidency. As a result, Hoover, who was opposed to an increase in presidential power even in emergencies, did not assume the powers necessary to deal with the severe economic problems facing the nation in 1931—which undoubtedly led to his defeat in the election of 1932.

In more recent times, there have been presidents who felt that their role was to be the servant, rather than the leader, of the people. Dwight D. Eisenhower (1953–1961), for example, even after a landslide victory in 1952, refused to see his victory as a mandate from the people to take a strong leadership role.

All actions of the President, either domestically or in foreign relations, must be within and pursuant to constitutional authority.

President Eisenhower noted:

Many political scientists believe that Eisenhower put more emphasis on the president's role as law enforcer than as chief legislator. Consequently, Eisenhower recommended relatively little legislation and, instead, followed the lead of Congress.

Presidential Personality—Loose Constructionists

In contrast, some presidents maintained that their presidential powers were limited only in those instances where the Constitution specifically denied them

Essays

particular powers. These presidents shared the idea that to meet the responsibilities of office, a president must assert leadership and seek to broaden the powers of the presidency. Theodore Roosevelt, as one of the loose constructionists, stated his views of the presidential office.

> ❝ *President Roosevelt wrote:*
>
> I declined to adopt the view that what was imperatively necessary for the Nation could not be done by the President unless he could find some specific authorization to do it. My belief was that it was not only his right but his duty to do anything that the Nation demanded unless such action was forbidden by the Constitution or by the law.

In addition to George Washington (1789–1797), one of the first national leaders to establish the presidency as a strong and independent position was Andrew Jackson (1829–1837). Jackson had very strong ideas as to the constitutional privileges of the presidency and often tired to dominate Congress in ways few of his predecessors had dared. During Jackson's two terms, for example, he used the **veto** more often than did all six previous presidents together. Jackson was rarely concerned about whether or not he was overstepping his constitutional authority.

Other presidents have also asserted new levels of presidential authority. For example, Franklin D. Roosevelt asserted the powers of the presidency to combat the Great Depression. Within 100 days of assuming office, Roosevelt had sent an **unprecedented** number of recommendations to Congress—all in an effort to ease the nation's economic crisis. Later, as World War II loomed, the majority of the members of Congress favored not getting involved in the war. Rather than deal with an isolationist Congress, Roosevelt used executive agreements to fight the war, believing the nation should support the world's democracies against the **tyranny** of Nazism and **fascism.**

Throughout the last half of the twentieth century and into the twenty-first century, those elected to the nation's highest office have adopted a loose constructionist view on both domestic and foreign issues. In the domestic sphere, presidents have led the nation—and the Congress—in the areas of civil rights, health care, the energy crisis, the economy, and the environment. In foreign affairs, presidents have worked to topple the Berlin Wall, end the cold war, bring peace to the Balkan Peninsula, and fight terrorism abroad.

See also: Constitutional Convention and the Presidency; Emergency Powers; Executive Agreements; Foreign Policy and the Presidency; National Security Council; Presidency and Congress; Presidency and the Media; The Treaty Power.

Further Reading

Calabresi, Steven G., and Christopher S. Yoo. *The Unitary Executive: Presidential Power from Washington to Bush.* New Haven, CT: Yale University Press, 2008.

Shapiro, Robert Y., Martha Joynt Kumar, and Lawrence R. Jacobs, eds. *Presidential Power.* New York: Columbia University Press, 2000.

Is the U.S. President the Most Powerful Leader in the World?

In recent times, the United States indeed has been called the most powerful nation in the world. Yet, this does not automatically make the president of the United States the most powerful leader of the world. Or does it? Some experts believe so.

[**B**arack Obama] will enter office as the most powerful president who ever sat in the White House.

According to Jack Balkin, a constitutional law professor: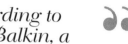

The president is still under the control of the **checks and balances** of the government and must answer to the people. On the other hand, as the leader of the most powerful country in the world, the president has great influence with many other national leaders. The president is also the commander in chief of the most powerful military in the world and can call troops into action when necessary. Yet, to really understand the power of the president, one must look at how that power has grown along with the nation, its military, and its economy.

Defining the Presidency

Between the 1800s and the 1900s, the United States grew significantly along with the responsibilities of the presidency. Starting as just thirteen states at the **ratification** of the Constitution, the new country had to go through a lot of growth in order to become the superpower that it is today. The ratification of the Constitution in 1788 was just the first step in this process. This document, in addition to specifying how the new government would be structured, defined the responsibilities of the government's officials, including those of the president. The Constitution states that the president is the head of the **executive** branch and is responsible for enforcing the laws made by Congress. Additionally, the president is the commander in chief of the United States armed forces and has the ability to grant pardons, manage foreign policy, appoint federal judges and ambassadors, and veto bills. While the president's job description has gone unchanged over the years, the level of influence the president affords as a leader has grown with the size and reputation of the country.

As the first president of the United States, George Washington (1789–1797) set many **precedent**s for both domestic and foreign policy. He established the custom of the two-term limit for presidents and initiated the formation of the cabinet. At the same time, Washington established an isolationist foreign policy that the United States would follow until the country entered World War II

★ ★

(1939–1945) in 1941. Washington encouraged the government not to get involved in "entangling alliances" with other countries. The new government also shied away from building up the armed forces, because of the heavy cost that it would entail, a national distrust of standing armies, and the strong faith that the nation had in its state militias.

The Presidency and the New Nation

During the country's early years, the United States established itself economically. At the end of the costly American Revolution (1775–1783), the new country was in substantial debt. To get a handle on the union's finances, Alexander Hamilton, the first secretary of the treasury, focused on paying off the war debt. He did this by establishing customs duties and excise taxes. He also spearheaded the chartering of the First **Bank of the United States** in 1791. This institution would help regulate the nation's finances. Hamilton's efforts to tackle the national debt helped the new government, and its president, earn the respect of many foreign nations.

In the years that followed, the executive branch and its leader, known as the chief executive, would prove their power as enforcers of the law. Hamilton's excise tax on alcoholic beverages sparked many protests , especially in the state of Pennsylvania. These protests eventually turned violent, forcing President Washington to take action. Gathering a militia, Washington ordered the containment of what came to be known as the Whiskey Rebellion. The rebellion was contained and the new central government established itself as an enforcer of the law and the president as the chief enforcer. The United States military continued to prove itself by suppressing attacks made by Native Americans and by suppressing attacks on American shipping initiated by Tripoli (in North Africa) and France.

The United States first declared war during the James Madison administration (1809–1817). Americans, once again, found themselves facing British forces in the War of 1812 (1812–1814). The war demonstrated to Americans the benefits of having an established armed forces. After the war, the United States began to build up its military, thereby increasing the responsibility of the president in the role of commander in chief.

Growth of the Nation and of Presidential Responsibility

By the beginning of the 1800s, the United States had sixteen states in the Union and was looking to expand westward. In 1803, during the Jefferson administration (1801–1809), the United States acquired the massive Louisiana Territory from France. America paid $15 million for the entire region, which doubled the size of the United States. After making the deal, French leader Napoleon Bonaparte acknowledged the power of the United States and saw the young country as a possible threat to his British enemies.

The 1840s brought the Mexican-American War (1846–1848) in which the United States fought with Mexico over the state of Texas. This took place during the James K. Polk administration (1845–1849). The war ended with the signing of the Treaty of Guadalupe Hidalgo. The treaty recognized that Texas, which extended to the Rio Grande, was under the control of the United

States. The treaty also gave the United States control over a vast region known as the Mexican Cession, an area that included present-day California, Nevada, Utah, and parts of Colorado, Arizona, New Mexico, and Wyoming. In exchange, Mexico received $15 million.

By acquiring these large tracts of land, the United States increased its size significantly; the country now stretched from the Atlantic Ocean to the Pacific Ocean. Americans set out to settle these new territories and built up towns and cities in the process. The new lands provided more space to expand both agriculture and industry, which, in turn increased productivity. With this great increase in territory, the president's **jurisdiction** and, by association, his power grew.

Prosperous Economy

The economy remained prosperous after the end of the War of 1812, but eventually took a downturn that resulted in the Panic of 1837. The Panic of 1837 caused a five-year **depression** with massive unemployment and the downfall of many businesses. Yet as the years passed, the country was able to recover. The implementation of better forms of transportation, such as railroads and steamboats, boosted the economy during the 1800s. The railroad industry was just one part of America's Industrial Revolution, which saw increased urbanization and manufacturing throughout the nineteenth century. The United States was becoming an economic power, gaining further power for its president.

America's economic success continued during the late 1800s, a time known as the Gilded Age. During this period, the U.S. economy trumped that of Great Britain. Presidents now had the most powerful economy in the world at their fingertips. This prosperity was largely due to innovations in technology, including the invention of the telephone, refrigerated railroad cars, and electric lights. Oil, coal, iron, and steel were also large moneymaking industries. In addition, new mass-production techniques were utilized to make industry more efficient. The **Progressive** Era, from about 1890 to 1920, saw the creation of many labor regulations. Around this time the federal government became more involved in the regulation of the nation's industry. Some of the laws that were passed included regulations on railroads, the banning of monopolies, and restrictions on child labor.

The Civil War and Post-Civil War Military Action

In the 1860s, the United States faced one of its darkest moments, with the split of the nation and the devastation of the Civil War (1861–1865). As the Union and the Confederacy faced off over the issues of states' rights and slavery American resources were being drained, especially in the largely agricultural South. President Abraham Lincoln (1861–1865) led the country through the war and used his power as the commander in chief to issue the Emancipation Proclamation in 1863, which abolished slavery in the Confederacy. Along with ultimately bringing an end to slavery, the Civil War, often said to be the first "modern war." saw the premiere of many of the newest innovations in combat technology, including submarines, machine guns, trench warfare, and aerial reconnaissance. The president now had a more powerful military under his command.

The United States military and its commander in chief oversaw continued growth and expansion in the years following the Civil War. The westward movement of settlers led to conflicts with Native Americans, but these were suppressed by superior U.S. military force. The United States also began to engage in conflict oversees. The first of these conflicts was the Spanish-American War (1898), in which the United States acquired control over Spanish colonies in Cuba, Puerto Rico, Guam, and the Philippines. Foreign policy was beginning to drift toward being internationalist rather than **isolationist.**

World War I

In 1917, the United States made its first major step in becoming a world military power by declaring war on Germany and involving the country in World War I (1914–1918). Before entering the war, Americans, including President Woodrow Wilson (1913–1921), made strong efforts to remain **neutral,** but the United States did help to supply and finance British and French troops. Despite the Americans' efforts, the Germans pulled them into the war by instigating submarine attacks on American ships that were sending supplies to Britain. In 1918, not long after the United States entered the war, the German government agreed to an **armistice.** After the war ended, the United States worked to reinstate its isolationist foreign policy by passing the **Neutrality** Acts in the 1930s, despite President Franklin D. Roosevelt's (1933–1945) protestations. These acts made it illegal for the United States to support any other nation in a war.

The Great Depression

The end of World War I was followed by the beginning of the Roaring Twenties, a time of great economic prosperity that led to the widespread use of the automobile. This new form of transportation, in turn, led to the growth of the oil industry, an increase in tourism, and eventually the availability of telephones and electricity in rural areas. Yet, the prosperity did not last. Instead, it came to a crashing halt with the Wall Street Crash of 1929, marking the beginning of the **Great Depression.** In response to the Depression, President Roosevelt instituted new policies and new federal organizations that were part of his recovery plan known as the New Deal. Roosevelt's used the **legislative** powers of his office to work to end the Depression by increasing the role of the government in the nation's economy. The domestic powers of the presidency grew significantly during this time.

World War II

Before entering World War II (1939–1945) in 1941, the United States once again tried to maintain its neutrality. Yet, President Roosevelt was able to find a way around the Neutrality Acts by encouraging the passing of the Lend-Lease Act, which allowed the United States to give financial and material support to the Allies. Then, in 1941, the Japanese attacked Pearl Harbor, Hawaii, forcing the Americans to declare war on the Axis powers—Japan, Germany, and Italy. With the aid of the American forces, the Allied powers were able to defeat Italy by May 1943 and Germany by May 1945. The war against Japan continued. In order to end it quickly and efficiently, President Harry S. Truman (1945–1953) ordered the dropping of atomic bombs on the

★ ★ ★ ★ ★ ★ ★ ★ ★ ★ ★ ★ ★ ★ ★ ★ ★ ★ ★ ★

Japanese cities of Hiroshima and Nagasaki. These bombs caused massive devastation and loss of life, the likes of which had not been seen before. The Japanese surrendered in August 1945.

The United States's involvement in the war led the nation to become a military superpower. The nation's position was partly because of the development of modern military weaponry. In addition, in the mid-1940s, the United States was only nation to possess the atomic bomb. Thus, the president, as commander in chief, had sole power over the world's most destructive weapon.

The Cold War

While the power of the United States increased significantly during and after World War II, it grew even more during the cold war, a period of high tension with the Soviet Union that followed. After the World War II, the Soviet Union developed its own atomic bomb, thus gaining superpower status alongside the United States. Hostility between the communist Soviet Union and the capitalist United States eventually escalated into a dangerous "arms race." Each country built more and more atomic bombs and continuously threatened each other with obliteration. The U.S. arsenal of atomic and hydrogen bombs grew quickly, giving presidents the ability to authorize massive destruction. As the United States tried to dispel the communist threat, it became involved in two significant conflicts: the Korean War and the Vietnam War. These wars were known as proxy wars because of the indirect involvement of the U.S. and the Soviet Union on either side. The United States also showed its determination in Cuba.

The Korean War

The Korean War (1950–1953), fought between communist North Korea and non-communist South Korea, was the first of the proxy wars. The United States and the United Nations (UN) joined forces to support South Korea, while North Korea was being supported by the Soviet Union and communist China. In the end, there would be no decisive victory for either side. The war ended with an armistice, and the country was left divided at the 38th parallel.

Bay of Pigs and the Cuban Missile Crisis

In the following years, the United States became involved in many conflicts around the world as part of its ongoing battle to contain communism. Several of these conflicts brought embarrassment to the American presidency and contributed to the American citizens' growing resentment of the United States military. One such conflict was the failed Bay of Pigs invasion (1961), a CIA operation that used inexperienced Cuban exiles to invade Cuba to attempt to overthrow Fidel Castro, the island's communist dictator. The exiles were quickly overwhelmed. The original plan of the mission included extra military support, which was supposed to be provided by the U.S. Marines. Yet, President John F. Kennedy (1961–1963), refused to send troops. The exiles were quickly captured, only to be released after Kennedy agreed to give Cuba $53 million in food and medical supplies. The Kennedy administration was embarrassed by this catastrophe.

In 1962, President Kennedy was informed that the Soviet Union was installing nuclear missiles, which were capable of reaching targeted cities in

the United States, in Cuba—just 90 miles south of Florida. Kennedy called on the Soviet Union to remove the missiles, and implemented a naval blockade around Cuba. The blockade was designed to prevent Soviet ships from reaching the island's ports. After several tense days of negotiations between the United States and the Soviet Union, an agreement was reached. The Soviets promised to remove the missiles from Cuba in return for a U.S. promise to not invade the island. Later, the United States removed its missiles from Turkey, which borders the Soviet Union.

The Vietnam War

Among the most troublesome wars for the American public and for the government was the Vietnam War (1964–1975). Much like Korea, Vietnam was split into a communist north and a non-communist south in 1954. Tension escalated between both sides, resulting in war. In 1964, after determining that a U.S. naval ship was supposedly attacked in the Gulf of Tonkin by North Vietnamese torpedo boats, President Lyndon B. Johnson (1963–1969) proposed the Gulf of Tonkin Resolution to Congress. This resolution would increase the president's war powers, giving Johnson the authority to use virtually unlimited military force against the North Vietnamese without an official declaration of war.

The joint resolution was quickly passed by Congress. Over the next few years, the American military presence in Vietnam increased significantly, assisting the army of the Republic of Vietnam (South Vietnam). The National Liberation Front (NLF) of North Vietnam was backed by the Soviet Union and the Chinese communists. During the course of the war, about 58,000 American lives were lost. The war became increasingly unpopular in the United States and protests erupted across the nation. Through negotiation with the North Vietnamese, the United States finally pulled out of the war in 1973, following President Richard Nixon's (1969–1974) plan of "Vietnamization." Two years later, the U.S. Embassy in Vietnam was overrun by the communists, leading to a frantic evacuation effort. Again, the American presidency found itself embarrassed by an unsuccessful military action. To limit the president's power to commit troops overseas, Congress passed the War Powers Resolution in 1973.

A Fluctuating Economy

While the reputation of the United States military was mixed during the Cold War Era, the nation's economic standing grew. Many improvements to the American economic system were made during the early 1950s by the new Council of Economic Advisors. The CEA was even able to help ease Americans through the 1953–1954 **recession** by initiating public works programs, easing credit, and reducing taxes. In 1961, President Kennedy passed the largest tax cut in history up to that time, while thousands of war bonds—dating from the World War II era—matured and the American middle class continued to grow. Inflation caused severe problems in the early 1970s, including rising unemployment and interest rates. Yet, after he won the presidency in 1980, Ronald Reagan (1981–1989) helped the country to bounce back by using fiscally expansive economic policies, dubbed "Reaganomics." These were policies that worked to

Essays

reduce government spending, government regulation of the economy, and tax rates on income, and to control the money supply. In the end, Reaganomics helped to lower income tax, inflation rates, and unemployment. Yet, the national debt was higher than ever. In the 1990s, the economy remained stable, reaching a high point later in the decade with the dot-com boom—the rapid growth of Internet businesses. However, the boom did not last for long. The economy faced a **recession** in 2001.

In 2008, the nation's economy was hit by a combination of economic difficulties, which many observers compared to the Great Depression of the 1930s. The price of gasoline and other fuels soared to new heights, hurting not only consumers but also the transportation industry. Hardest hit was the airline industry, which was still recovering from the economic aftermath of the September 11, 2001, terrorist attacks. The nation's banks tightened credit to consumers and businesses, thus curtailing new loans and investments. At the same time, the housing industry entered a deep slump, and two federally protected mortgage businesses—the Federal National Mortgage Association, nicknamed Fannie Mae, and the Federal Home Mortgage Corporation, nicknamed Freddie Mac—became insolvent, or bankrupt, and were taken over by the federal government in a $700 billion emergency bailout. The nation's stock market fluctuated wildly, and investors lost millions of dollars as stock values plunged. Despite federal intervention, including the lowering of interest rates and a government tax rebate for most taxpayers, the economy tottered on the edge of recession. As the year ended, the state of the nation's economy remained uncertain.

Persian Gulf War

In 1991, the American military won back favor with the American citizens with a decisive victory in the Persian Gulf War. This conflict started when Iraqi troops invaded the neighboring country of Kuwait in 1990. Coalition forces made up of troops from 34 nations took military action in early 1991. The coalition was able to drive the Iraqis out of Kuwait with ease. The lack of morale and good leadership in the Iraqi military led to quick and easy surrenders. This marked the first time that the American military was able to use much of its new technology, including stealth aircrafts, infrared sights, and radar-seeking missiles. The war ended quickly with negotiations and a peace agreement. President George H.W. Bush (1989–1993) did not think it appropriate to remove Iraqi dictator, Saddam Hussein (1979–2003), from power.

War on Terrorism

The "war on terrorism" began in response to the devastating terrorist attacks that took place in New York City and Washington, D.C., on September 11, 2001. These attacks were organized and carried out by members of a terrorist group called al-Qaeda and resulted in the loss of thousands of American lives. To retaliate, President Bush first dispatched American troops to Afghanistan to take down the Taliban government, which harbored and supported al-Qaeda, as well as al-Qaeda terrorist training camps. This was followed by altercations with terrorists in the Philippines and Liberia.

In late 2008, President-elect Barack Obama was invited to the White House to confer with President George W. Bush (2001–2009) and world leaders to try to solve the global financial crisis. (AP Photo, Pablo Martinez Monsivais)

In 2003, the U.S. turned its sights toward Iraq. The Iraqis were believed to have weapons of mass destruction, which would have been in violation of the ban placed by the UN on Iraqi production and possession of such weapons. A coalition force made up of troops from the United States and the United Kingdom invaded Iraq in 2003 and ousted Saddam Hussein. U.S. troops continued to occupy Iraq while they set up a new government and military these. The invasion of Iraq, however, has been controversial throughout the world and has caused some American citizens to question the president's war power, much like they did during the Vietnam War

Many have questioned the Bush Administration's justification for invading Iraq. The reason that President Bush provided for invading Iraq was that he believed Iraq was a threat to U.S. security and that the country was developing— or had already developed—weapons of mass destruction. Never before had the United States taken a pre-emptive strike against another nation. It was later discovered that the Bush administration's claims were inaccurate. Those opposed to the war have said that the invasion of Iraq went against inter-national law as well as the principles of the United Nations.

Critics of the so-called war on terrorism point out that the effort has reduced civil liberties in the United States, because under the Patriot Act, the government was able to obtain more data about its citizens. After the September 11, 2001, terrorist attacks, the Bush administration imposed several policies that are meant to help detect terrorists within the United

★ ★ ★ ★ ★ ★ ★ ★ ★ ★ ★ ★ ★ ★ ★ ★ ★ ★

States. Some of these policies have increased the power given to law enforcement officials, while others have permitted racial profiling and warrantless telephone tapping.

Several sections of the Patriot Act have been questioned in court. For example, a case was brought to court by the American Civil Liberties Union (ACLU) concerning the government's requiring companies to reveal personal information about their employees without prior court approval. In September 2004, U.S. District Judge Victor Marrero of the Southern District Court of New York ruled that this practice is unconstitutional.

> **D**emocracy abhors undue secrecy, an unlimited government warrant to conceal . . . has no place in our open society. Under the mantle of secrecy, the self-preservation that ordinarily impels our government to censorship and secrecy may potentially be turned on ourselves as a weapon of self-destruction. . . . At that point, secrecy's protective shield may serve not as much to secure a safe country as simply to save face.

Judge Victor Marrero ruled: ,,

Evidence of torture occurring in prisons that hold suspected terrorists has also been revealed. Bush administration critics have also objected to the administration's policy of imprisoning suspected terrorists without charging the suspects with a crime or allowing them to stand trial. The Bush administration has identified these prisoners as "enemy combatants" who are not under the rule of a recognized government and, therefore, do not posses the same rights as those under recognized governments. Again, the administration's critics have seen these actions as a violation of both international and United States law.

Conclusion

Clearly, the president of the United States is one of the most powerful leaders in the world, if not the most powerful. Some people may say that the president is too powerful. With the world's most powerful army, a strong economy, and large amounts of international and domestic influence at his fingertips, it would be easy to take the responsibilities of the office too far. Yet, the nation's system of checks and balances was specifically designed to prevent one branch of government from becoming too powerful. Today, the question becomes: Are these checks and balances still strong enough to reign in the president of the United States? It is a question for students, scholars, members of government, and the American people.

See also: Chief Diplomat; Chief Economist; Chief Executive; Chief of State; Commander in Chief; Emergency Powers; Executive Orders; Foreign Policy and the Presidency; Presidency and Congress.

Further Reading

Shapiro, Robert Y., Martha Joynt Kumar, and Lawrence R. Jacobs, eds. *Presidential Power.* New York: Columbia University Press, 2000.

Yoo, John. *The Powers of War and Peace: The Constitution and Foreign Affairs after 9/11.* Chicago: University of Chicago Press, 2006.

PART TWO

The Presidency A to Z

★ ★ ★ ★ **A** ★ ★ ★ ★

Adams, John, Administration of (1797–1801)

Government under the second president of the United States. Few American chief **executives** have faced a tougher set of national circumstances than John Adams (1797–1801). In addition to having the difficult task of succeeding of the popular and revered George Washington (1789–1797), Adams assumed the presidency during a time of foreign policy crisis. The Jay Treaty (1794) had averted war with Great Britain, but it greatly worsened U.S. relations with France, which, after Napoleon Bonaparte had beaten Austria in October 1797, was at the height of its power. Moreover, when France retaliated with attacks on American ships, Adams had difficulty maintaining Washington's policy of **neutrality.**

In an attempt to settle differences with France, Adams sent three U.S. representatives to Paris. In turn, the French foreign minister, Charles-Maurice de Talleyrand, dispatched three representatives of the French government (referred to in dispatches as "X, Y, and Z") to ask the American emissaries how much the United States was willing to pay in bribes to French officials and loans to the French government to secure a treaty. When the "XYZ Affair" became public early in 1798, a furor broke loose in the United States that seemed to make war with France inevitable.

Adams's efforts to come to terms with this international crisis were hindered as much by

members of his own Federalist Party as by the opposition. Although the Democratic-Republicans, led by Vice President Thomas Jefferson (1801–1809), were expected to oppose Adams's actions, "the Federalists were often as recalcitrant or bitter toward the president." His most influential Federalist critic was Alexander Hamilton, who believed that Adams was too moderate politically and unable to deal with the nation's problems.

Adams was a party man, but he intended to follow Washington's example of standing as much as possible above party. This conviction was evident in his approach to the problems with France. Unlike the so-called Arch-Federalists, led by Hamilton, Adams was willing to accept war if declared by France, but he hoped to avoid it. His primary objective was to protect U.S. **commerce,** through diplomacy and naval expansion, and to force the French Republic to respect the American flag. Hamilton and his allies in the party, however, were more interested in exploiting the conflict with France than containing it. In addition to taking strong measures that would prepare the nation for war, they wanted to suppress the Democratic-Republican opposition.

Hamilton severely tested Adams's authority in other ways. He was determined to guide governmental policy, although he was not a government official. He had retired from the treasury department at the end of January 1795, but toward the end of Washington's second term and throughout Adams's tenure, he remained at the center of the Federalist Party.

Hamilton's influence was enhanced after 1797 because of Adams's decision to retain Washington's cabinet. Three members of Washington's

JUSTICE FOR ALL

Midnight Judges

In March 1801, William Marbury was appointed by the defeated Federalist President John Adams (1797–1801) as a justice of the peace in the District of Columbia. Marbury, as well as several of Adams's other judicial appointees, became known as "Midnight Judges," because Adams supposedly made the appointments just before his term in office ended, to maintain Federalist control of the judiciary.

A judicial commission granting Marbury his position was signed and sealed but not delivered to him before the Democratic-Republicans, who had the won the 1800 elections, had taken office. President Thomas Jefferson (1801–1809), upon learning that Marbury had not yet received the commission, instructed Secretary of State James Madison not to deliver it. Marbury ultimately requested that the Supreme Court issue a **writ of mandamus**—a written order commanding a government official to perform a specific duty—to the secretary of state. Section 13 of the Judiciary Act of 1789 gave the Supreme Court **jurisdiction** to issue such writs.

In the landmark case *Marbury v. Madison* (1803), Chief Justice John Marshall attacked the constitutionality of Section 13 of the Judiciary Act of 1789. Marshall noted that the Constitution grants the court a very limited original jurisdiction and that issuing writs of mandamus is not a part of that jurisdiction. The Court determined that because Section 13 was **unconstitutional,** it did not have the authority to force Madison to deliver the commission. Thus, the Court established the principle of **judicial review.**

A–Z

cabinet, Secretary of State Timothy Pickering, Secretary of War James McHenry, and Oliver Wolcott, who succeeded Hamilton as secretary of the treasury, largely owed their government positions to Hamilton. In all-important questions they looked to him, and not Adams, to guide their actions. Only Charles Lee, the attorney general and the least powerful cabinet member, and Benjamin Stoddert, who joined the cabinet as head of the newly established Navy Department in 1798, were loyal to Adams.

The rising conflict between Adams and the Arch-Federalists culminated in 1799. Early that year, Adams prepared to send a second mission to France in an effort to avoid war. In February 1799, without previous consultation with the secretary of state or the cabinet, he nominated William Vans Murray, then minister to the Netherlands, as minister plenipotentiary to the French Republic. Murray was chosen because of his good relations with France. Adams learned through Murray of France's willingness to receive a new U.S. mission and desire to avoid war with the United States. The Senate, which was sympathetic to Hamilton's views, would have rejected the nomination, but Adams's quick and unilateral action caught the legislators by surprise. So the Senate compromised by asking for a commission of three, to which the president consented.

After countering attempts by Secretary of State Pickering to postpone the second mission—which in addition to Murray included Oliver Ellsworth and William B. Davie—Adams placed the mission on board a U.S. frigate. The mission arrived in time to take advantage of France's uncertain situation, one created by a series of

Before Massachusetts patriot John Adams (1797–1801) was elected the second president of the United States, he served in a number of important positions, including vice president, minister to Great Britain, and on the committee that wrote the Declaration of Independence. (Library of Congress)

military defeats at the hands of the British. Although Adams's bold course aggravated his problems with the cabinet and the Federalist Party, it achieved a commercial agreement with France that ended the threat of war, thus preserving the principle of neutrality toward Europe that he inherited from the Washington administration.

Although historians have praised John Adams for upholding the authority of the presidency in the face of a badly divided cabinet and party, he has been criticized for his role in the passage and enforcement of the **Alien and Sedition Acts** in 1798. The Alien Act gave the president authority to expel foreigners considered dangerous to the public peace; the Sedition Act, which caused most of the controversy in the nation, made it a crime, punishable by fine or imprisonment, to bring "false, scandalous and malicious" accusations against the president, Congress, or the government. Adams himself, however, had little sympathy for the more extreme purposes of the Alien and Sedition Acts.

See also: Jefferson, Thomas, Administration of (1801–1809); Washington, George, Administration of (1789–1797).

Further Reading

Diggins, John Patrick. *John Adams.* New York: Times Books, Henry Holt and Company, 2003.
Grant, James. *John Adams: Party of One.* New York: Farrar, Straus and Giroux, 2005.
McCullough, David. *John Adams.* New York: Simon & Schuster, 2001.

Adams, John Quincy, Administration of (1825–1829)

Government under the sixth president of the United States. In 1824, for the second time in American history (the first occurrence was in 1800), an election was determined not by the voters, but by the House of Representatives. Senator Andrew Jackson (1829–1837) of Tennessee, the hero of the Battle of New Orleans, received the most electoral votes, 99, but fell far short of the 131 necessary for a majority and election. John Quincy Adams (1825–1829), who felt that as secretary of state he was the logical heir to the presidency, came in second with 84 electoral votes. William Crawford, secretary of the treasury under James Monroe (1817–1825), was the choice of the Democratic-Republican **caucus.** Crawford finished third with 41 votes. The powerful Speaker of the House, Henry Clay of Kentucky, finished fourth with 37 votes.

According to the Twelfth **Amendment,** the House was to choose from the top three candidates. This removed Clay from contention, but he still held considerable influence over his fellow representatives. He used that influence to help secure Adams's election, and the new president rewarded Clay by naming him secretary of state.

Not surprisingly, Jackson's supporters were furious, charging that Adams and Clay had made a corrupt bargain to violate the will of the people. Although the charge of conspiracy against Adams and Clay was probably unfounded, the controversial election of 1824 ensured the demise of what had come to be called "King Caucus." It also laid the foundation for Jacksonian democracy, a movement that sought to reform election procedures and broaden citizens' participation in government.

See also: Jackson, Andrew, Administration of (1829–1837); Monroe, James, Administration of (1817–1825).

Further Reading

Remini, Robert V. *John Quincy Adams.* New York: Times Books, Henry Holt and Company, 2002.
Wheelan, Joseph. *Mr. Adams's Last Crusade.* New York: Public Affairs, 2008.

Agriculture, Department of

See Department of Agriculture (USDA).

Air Force One

Official plane of the President of the United States. When presidents first became airborne, the U.S. Army Air Corps, later known as the Air Force, became air chauffeur to the commander in chief. It has been in charge of selecting and piloting presidential planes ever since. The first official plane used by a president was an Army Air Corps Douglas C-54 Skymaster, dubbed the *Sacred Cow* by the press. Shortly before his death in 1945, Franklin D. Roosevelt (1933–1945) used the plane once. Harry S. Truman (1945–1953), who enjoyed flying, used the *Sacred Cow* often for presidential trips. In the summer of 1947, the official presidential plane was upgraded to a state-of-the-art Douglas Aircraft DC-6. Named the *Independence* after Truman's hometown in Missouri, the plane was equipped with weather radar, long-range capability, and a teletype system that allowed the president to stay in touch with Washington even when he was three thousand miles away. The *Independence* served him through-out his administration.

Dwight D. Eisenhower (1953–1961) enjoyed flying even more than Truman. Although he did not pilot the planes himself, he had a pilot's license. President Eisenhower's first official plane was a Lockheed Constellation 749. Named *Columbine II,* after the military craft he used during World War II (1939–1945) and the official flower of his wife's home state of Colorado, the model was a personal favorite. Because of rapidly advancing aviation technology, the plane was replaced in 1954 by *Columbine III* a Lockheed 1049C Super-Constellation, which remained the official plane for the remainder of Eisenhower's administration. On a whirlwind, eighteen-day tour of eleven countries in Europe, Africa, and Asia in 1959, Eisenhower chose not to use the propeller-driven *Columbine III* and became the first president to travel by jet.

The distinction of being the first president to travel regularly by jet, however, belonged to John F. Kennedy (1961–1963). In 1962, a Boeing 707 was delivered to Kennedy; it became officially known as 26000 and designated *Air Force One,* as is any plane in which the president might be flying. Previous planes had been military in appearance, but designer Raymond Loewy, along with First Lady Jacqueline Kennedy, created a new exterior that would become widely recognized around the world. Among the changes, "United States Air Force" was replaced with "United States of America" on the body of the craft. Mrs. Kennedy added amenities for which the plane became famous.

President Kennedy was not able to enjoy *Air Force One* for very long, however. On the day of his assassination, November 22, 1963, Kennedy's body was flown from Dallas to Washington in the plane he had used for just over thirteen months. Nine years later, the plane Kennedy had first used became the backup to a newer version of the Boeing 707. These two planes remained the president's planes for more than twenty-five years. By the 1980s, however, the 707s were obsolete: Their range, space, and amenities were limited; factory parts were hard to obtain; and their engines were too loud to meet many local airport noise rules.

George H.W. Bush (1989–1993) was the first president to fly on the most recent version of *Air Force One.* Two identical Boeing 747–200Bs, at a

Because it can be refueled in midair, *Air Force One*, the president's plane, can stay aloft indefinitely. (U.S. Air Force)

cost of approximately $400 million, were supposed to have been ready during the Reagan administration but were not delivered until September 1990. At a cost of $35,000 an hour to operate, the new *Air Force One* has a top speed of 640 miles per hour and can fly at least twice as far as the older 707s without refueling—more than 7,140 miles. The plane can accommodate seventy passengers and twenty-three crew members, and its galley can handle preparation of one hundred meals at the time.

Equipped with every amenity imaginable, the plane provides the president with an excellent work environment. The Boeing 747 has a conference room, a staff room, several workstations with computers, a guest area, space for members of the media and their telecommunications equipment, a facsimile machine, eighty-five telephones, and medical facilities, including an operating room for emergency surgery by the president's personal physician. Communications equipment and the crew are on the second level. The president's bedroom suite, including a dressing room and lavatory with a shower-tub, is in the nose of the aircraft. Other special touches include fresh flowers and memo pads, napkins, playing cards,

and matches embossed with the presidential seal and the words "Aboard Air Force One."

Air Force One is more than just a well-equipped mode of transportation; as much as any other trapping of the presidency it contributes to the mystique of the imperial presidency. Beyond symbolism, however, *Air Force One* is where presidents negotiate politics and make history. Perhaps the most historic flight of the new *Air Force One* occurred in November 1995 when former presidents Jimmy Carter (1977–1981) and George H.W. Bush joined President Clinton (1993–2001) in attending the funeral of Prime Minister Yitzhak Rabin of Israel. Others aboard the flight to Israel were Senate Majority Leader Robert J. Dole, House Speaker Newt Gingrich, House Minority Leader Richard A. Gephardt, Senate Minority Leader Tom Daschle, Secretary of State Warren Christopher, Secretary of Defense William J. Perry, and former secretaries of state Cyrus R. Vance and George P. Shultz.

Further Reading

Walsh, Kenneth T. *Air Force One: A History of the Presidents and Their Planes.* New York: Hyperion, 2003.

Arthur, Chester A., Administration of (1881–1885)

Government under the twenty-first president of the United States. The Republican National Convention of 1880 pitted New York senator Roscoe Conkling and his antireform party faction known as the Stalwarts against James G. Blaine and the slightly more moderate Half-Breeds. After thirty-six ballots, the convention turned to a **dark-horse candidate,** James A. Garfield of Ohio. In an effort to appease the Stalwarts and unify the party, Republican leaders offered the vice presidency to Chester A. Arthur, who had never held elective office. Garfield and Arthur defeated the Democratic ticket of Winfield Scott Hancock and William H. English by fewer than ten thousand popular votes but won in the electoral college, 214–155.

Garfield served only 199 days of his presidential term, however. On July 2, 1881, he was shot by an assassin in Washington, D.C. The gunman, Charles J. Guiteau, declared after the attack, "I am a Stalwart; now Arthur is President!" Garfield initially survived his wounds but died on September 19, after months of failed attempts by his doctors to remove the bullet.

Although Arthur had no connection to Guiteau, he was sensitive to charges that he and the Stalwarts may have been involved in Garfield's death. Therefore, once Arthur had assumed the presidency, he severed his ties to Conkling and the New York political **machine.** The new president demonstrated his independence by backing the investigations of post office scandals in which several Stalwarts were implicated.

Arthur was not, however, ready to embrace **civil service reform,** which had been a favorite cause of James Garfield. He advocated instead a continuation of the **partisan** system of dispensing **patronage.** Nevertheless, on January 16, 1883, Arthur signed the Pendleton Civil Service Reform Act. The act set up a commission to develop and administer examinations for many federal positions previously filled through patronage.

In economic policy, Arthur sought to reduce the government's continuing budget **surplus** that took money out of the economy. He proposed reducing **tariffs,** building up the navy, and reducing the federal debt with the surplus. Arthur succeeded in making moderate improvements to the navy and reducing the national debt, but Congress rejected his proposals to cut tariffs.

Upon leaving office, Arthur returned to New York City to practice law. He soon accepted the presidency of the New York Arcade Railway Company, which was trying to construct a subway in New York City.

In February 1886, Arthur retired after a medical examination revealed that he had Bright's disease, a life-threatening kidney ailment. He died later that year in New York City.

See also: Cleveland, Grover, Administrations of (1885–1889, 1893–1897); Garfield, James A., Administration of (1881).

Further Reading
Karabell, Zachary. *Chester Alan Arthur.* New York: Times Books, 2004.

Assassinations and Assassination Attempts

Half of the presidents who have died in office were felled by assassins' bullets: Abraham Lincoln in 1865, James A. Garfield in 1881, William McKinley in 1901, and John F. Kennedy in 1963. All except Kennedy (1961–1963) were killed early in their terms [Lincoln (1861–1865) and McKinley (1897–1901) in their second term and Garfield (1881) in his first term], leaving their successors to serve out nearly full terms of office. Lincoln is the only president who is known to have been killed as part of a political conspiracy.

Although William Henry Harrison (1841) was the first president to die in office and Lincoln the first president to be assassinated, Andrew Jackson (1829–1837) came close to being the first in both categories. On January 30, 1835, while Jackson was attending the funeral of South Carolina representative Warren Davis in the rotunda of the Capitol, a housepainter named Richard Lawrence tried to shoot him. Aiming from a distance of only seven feet, Lawrence fired two pistols at the president. Both guns misfired, however, and the president was spared. Lawrence was captured and later was judged to be insane.

Abraham Lincoln

The death of a president is always a shock to the nation. Lincoln's death was probably the greatest shock of all, however, for three reasons: It was the third in a twenty-five-year series of presidential deaths (Harrison had died in 1841 and Zachary Taylor in 1850, both of natural causes); it came just when the nation was beginning to see an end to the terrible bloodshed of the Civil War (1861–1865); and, especially, it was the first instance of a presidential assassination. The **unprecedented** murder of a president was shocking to a people who had come to pride themselves on their country's record of peaceful and orderly transfers of **executive** power, which had been uninterrupted even by war since the first presidential election in 1789.

Throughout his first term, Abraham Lincoln had been a controversial president. The demands of leadership during the nation's Civil War had led him to exercise expansive presidential powers, which in turn had prompted congressional and **partisan** disapproval. Lincoln's second term began well. Within a month of his March 4, 1865, inauguration, the capital of the Confederacy, Richmond, Virginia, fell to Union forces. A few days later, on April 9, General Robert E. Lee surrendered to General Ulysses S. Grant at Appomattox, Virginia. Lincoln decided to celebrate the end of the war by taking his wife, Mary Todd Lincoln, to see the play *Our American Cousin* at Ford's Theatre in Washington, D.C. They went on Good Friday, April 14.

While watching the play from a box, President Lincoln was shot by John Wilkes Booth, an actor and a Confederate sympathizer. Booth had been plotting for months to kidnap or kill the president. Once he learned that the president would be in the theater that evening, he quickly set in motion an assassination plan. Standing less than four feet behind the president, Booth fired. The single bullet struck Lincoln behind the left ear, passed through his skull and brain, and came to rest behind his right eye.

Nothing could be done for the president except to keep vigil. During the night members of the cabinet, the vice president, members of the president's family, the surgeon general, the president's pastor, and others visited, waiting for the inevitable. At 7:22 on the morning of Saturday, April 15, Lincoln breathed his last at the age of fifty-six. As a brief prayer, Secretary of War Edwin M. Stanton said, "Now he belongs to the ages."

James A. Garfield

A scholar, a soldier, and a politician, James Garfield was nominated for president as a **dark-horse** compromise candidate on the thirty-sixth ballot of the 1880 Republican national convention. The forty-eight-year-old senator-elect from Ohio had been a member of the Electoral Commission that was formed to resolve the disputed election between Rutherford B. Hayes and Samuel J. Tilden in 1876. Garfield also had served as the Republican floor leader in the House of Representatives. Chester A. Arthur, a product of the New York Republican political **machine** (the Stalwarts), was nominated as Garfield's running mate.

After the election, Garfield confronted a host of political and administrative problems related to political **patronage.** Assembling a cabinet from a Republican Party that was deeply divided between Stalwart and Half-Breed (or moderate reformist) wings was a complex task that consumed much of the president-elect's time and energy. In fact, Garfield did not succeed in completing his cabinet until March 5, 1881, the day after his inauguration. Nevertheless, this was only the first of the new president's problems with government appointments. The line of job applicants that awaited him after he took the oath of office stretched down Pennsylvania Avenue. Meanwhile, the expectations of **civil service reformers** were at odds with those of Republican activists, who felt entitled to patronage positions in return for their support during the campaign.

Wearied by patronage woes, and increasingly committed to reform, Garfield decided to undertake a two-week tour of New England, including Massachusetts, where he planned to attend commencement exercises at Williams College, his alma mater. On the morning of July 2, 1881, as the president and Secretary of State James G. Blaine walked through the Washington depot of the Baltimore and Ohio Railroad, shots rang out and Garfield fell to the floor, bleeding. He had been hit by two bullets, one grazing his arm and the other lodging in his spinal column. The assassin, who was captured immediately, was identified as Charles J. Guiteau. While being arrested, Guiteau declared: "I did it and will go to jail for it. I am a Stalwart; now Arthur is president!"

Initially, little hope was held out for Garfield's recovery. Then the president rallied for a time and the doctors became optimistic. During the first three weeks of July, Garfield seemed to make steady progress and a day of national thanksgiving was declared for July 18. August, however, was a roller coaster ride of gains and setbacks, recovery and relapse. Finally, after another rally, the president asked to be moved from the White House to a cottage on the New Jersey shore at Elberon. On September 19, less than two weeks after making the trip, Garfield complained of a sudden pain in his chest, then died.

William McKinley

William McKinley (1897–1901) was chosen as president in 1896, in an election that established the Republicans as the majority party for the next third of a century. A former member of Congress and two-term governor of Ohio, McKinley was a champion of the protective **tariff** and a **nationalist** in world affairs. During his first term as president, he worked to restore prosperity to an economically troubled nation; by the time of his second inauguration on March 4, 1901, McKinley was able to declare, "Now every avenue of production is crowded with activity, labor is well employed, and American products find good markets at home and abroad." McKinley's successful conduct of the Spanish-American War of 1898 was crowned by U.S. acquisition of the Philippine Islands, Puerto Rico, and Guam. That same year he annexed the Hawaiian Islands.

Five months after his second inauguration, President McKinley traveled to the Pan-American Exposition in Buffalo, New York. On September 5, President's Day at the exposition, McKinley delivered a speech that outlined his goals for the second term and trumpeted the historic accomplishments of the Republican Party. The next day, the president attended an afternoon public reception at the Temple of Music. Congress had officially entrusted the Secret Service with the protection of the president in 1906, and McKinley was accompanied by a contingent of Secret Service agents, as well as by four special guards and several soldiers. Nonetheless, Leon Czolgosz, an **anarchist,** fired two shots at McKinley as the president stood in the receiving line and greeted people. One bullet bounced off a coat button and the other hit the fifty-eight-year-old president in the stomach.

An operation was performed immediately on President McKinley, but the bullet could not be found. The wounds were then bathed, and the president seemed to be on the road to recovery. On September 10, Vice President Roosevelt and most of the cabinet, who had come to Buffalo, were told that the president's condition had improved so much that they could safely disperse. Roosevelt departed for a vacation with his family in the Adirondack Mountains.

During the next three days, however, gangrene set in around the path of McKinley's wounds, causing a high fever and weakening him severely. Once again, the vice president and the cabinet were summoned to Buffalo. President McKinley died in the early morning hours of Friday, September 14, 1901. Theodore Roosevelt described McKinley as "the most widely loved man in all the United States."

John F. Kennedy

When he entered office in January 1961, forty-three-year-old John F. Kennedy was the youngest person ever elected as president. Succeeding as he did the oldest (to that date) person ever to be president, Dwight D. Eisenhower (1953–1961), Kennedy and his administration seemed to inject new energy into government. Nevertheless, Kennedy had won an extremely close election in 1960, and after some initial **legislative** successes (including the creation of the Peace Corps), he was having increasing difficulty getting a **conservative** Congress to enact his programs into law. Thus, the president placed his hopes on a strong reelection victory in 1964 that would enable him to capitalize on the political and policy foundations he had laid during his first term.

In November 1963, as part of his preparations for the 1964 election, the president traveled to Dallas, Texas. Kennedy's support in the South, especially Texas, was waning, and with the help

A – Z

of Vice President Lyndon B. Johnson, a Texan, the president hoped to persuade the Texas Democratic Party's quarreling factions to put their differences aside and unite behind him in 1964.

On the morning of November 22, 1963, a motorcade was formed at Love Field outside the city to bring the presidential party through downtown Dallas. Kennedy and First Lady Jacqueline Bouvier Kennedy were in the lead car, along with Texas governor John B. Connally and his wife, Nell. Vice President Johnson, his wife, Lady Bird Johnson, and Senator Ralph W. Yarborough, a Democrat from Texas, were in the next car.

As the motorcade turned off Main Street onto Elm and rolled passed the Texas School Book Depository, a brief series of short, sharp noises startled everyone. Some thought they were firecrackers; others thought a car engine was backfiring. Hunters instantly recognized the sound of rifle fire.

Within seconds the lead car was awash in blood: the president had been shot twice, and one of the bullets that hit Kennedy had also struck Governor Connally. As Mrs. Kennedy cradled her husband's shattered head, the motorcade's lead car raced for the nearest hospital. Secret Service agents near the vice president's car pushed Johnson down in his seat and rushed him to the hospital too.

Medical efforts to save President Kennedy were futile; the wounds were too severe. At two o'clock in the afternoon, the television networks interrupted regular programming to bring word to a stunned nation that President Kennedy had died. In truth, Kennedy had been pronounced dead at 1:15, but the announcement was delayed until Johnson was safely at the Dallas airfield. In no other instance of presidential assassination, not even Lincoln's, had death come so quickly. Before many Americans knew that the president had been hurt, he was dead.

Johnson, on board *Air Force One,* now awaited the arrival of Mrs. Kennedy and the late president's casket. Meanwhile, the Dallas police had identified and apprehended the suspected assassin, Lee Harvey Oswald, a worker at the book depository who had lived in the Soviet Union and been involved in pro-communist causes. On Sunday, November 24, shortly before Kennedy's funeral procession to the Capitol was scheduled to begin,

Oswald was shot and killed in Dallas as he was being transferred from one jail to another. Jack Ruby, a local nightclub owner, had elbowed through the crowd of police and reporters. Just before he shot Oswald he shouted, "You killed the president, you rat!" The shooting was caught on national television and rebroadcast repeatedly in the days that followed. Although retribution against presidential assassins usually had been swift, never before had an assassin been killed so quickly, publicly, and illegally.

Other Assaults and Issues of Presidential Security

In addition to the four presidents who died at the hands of assassins, five other presidents have withstood assassination attempts: Andrew Jackson in 1835, Franklin D. Roosevelt in 1933, Harry S. Truman in 1950, Gerald R. Ford (twice) in 1975, and Ronald Reagan in 1981.

Threatening situations have plagued still other presidents, dating back to John Quincy Adams (1825–1829), who was accosted by a court-martialed army sergeant demanding reinstatement. President John Tyler (1841–1845) once was the target of rocks thrown by an intoxicated painter. During the Nixon administration (1969–1974) a would-be assailant tried to hijack an airplane and crash it into the White House. Gerald Ford (1974–1977), in addition to being targeted by two would-be assassins armed with guns, was the target of a man who claimed he had wired himself with explosives in hopes of ramming his car through the White House gates; another intruder scaled the White House security fence armed with what appeared to be a bomb. The intruder was fatally shot by security officers.

On March 30, 1981, twenty-five-year-old John W. Hinckley Jr. shot and wounded President Ronald Reagan (1981–1989) outside a Washington, D.C., hotel. Presidential press secretary James Brady, a Secret Service agent, and a District of Columbia police officer also were wounded. Hinckley was arrested at the scene of the shooting and, less than a month later, was indicted by a grand jury for trying to assassinate the president and on twelve additional counts related to the injuries he inflicted on the others. Hinckley, who had been under psychiatric care, claimed that he had shot the president to impress Jodie Foster, a young movie actress with whom he was infatuated. At his trial, he was found not guilty by reason of insanity and confined for an indefinite period to St. Elizabeth's Hospital in Washington, an institution for the mentally ill.

After the shooting, the seventy-year-old president was rushed to George Washington University hospital with a bullet lodged in his left lung. The operation to remove the bullet lasted two hours, and the president remained hospitalized until April 11. Reagan made his first major public appearance after the shooting on April 28, when he delivered a nationally televised speech on the economy to a **joint session** of Congress. The dramatic appearance galvanized support for his economic programs, which were passed into law that summer. Thus, Reagan became the only president in history to recover fully from injuries sustained in an attempted assassination.

President Bill Clinton (1993–2001) experienced a series of strange and threatening events during the fall of 1994. On September 12, Frank Corder, a Maryland truck driver, crashed a small Cessna plane into a large magnolia tree just outside the president's White House bedroom. Corder was killed in the crash but the president and his family, who were staying at Blair House while renovations were being made on the executive mansion, were unaffected.

On October 29, while Clinton was watching a basketball game on television in the second-floor family quarters of the White House, a Colorado hotel worker named Francisco Duran fired a spray of bullets at the mansion's north facade from Pennsylvania Avenue, only fifty yards away. A few weeks later, in the early morning hours of December 17, several bullets were fired by an unknown gunman at the south facade of the White House from the Ellipse, a large park bordering the White House. Several days later, on December 20, a knife-wielding homeless man, Marcelino Corniel, was shot to death by police on the Pennsylvania Avenue sidewalk in front of the White House.

After the late 1994 attacks on the White House, together with the massively destructive car bombing of an Oklahoma City federal building on April 19, 1995, Clinton accepted a Secret Service recommendation that the two blocks of Pennsylvania Avenue on which the White House is situated be closed to vehicles and converted to a more easily secured pedestrian mall. The new policy took effect May 21, 1995. Security on the White House perimeter was tightened again after the September 11, 2001, terrorist attacks on New York City's World Trade Center and the Pentagon in Virginia.

See also: Jackson, Andrew, Administration of (1829–1837); Kennedy, John F., Administration of (1961–1963); Lincoln, Abraham, Administration of (1861–1865); Reagan, Ronald, Administration of (1981–1989); Secret Service; Twenty-fifth Amendment (1967).

Further Reading

Rauchway, Eric. *Murdering McKinley.* New York: Hill and Wang, 2003.

Swanson, James L. *Manhunt: The 12-day Chase for Lincoln's Killer.* New York: William Morrow, 2006.

The Warren Report: The Official Report on the Assassination of President John F. Kennedy. New York: The Associated Press, 1964.

A – Z

★ ★ ★ B ★ ★ ★

Bill of Rights

See Constitution of the United States.

Buchanan, James, Administration of (1857–1861)

Government under the fifteenth president of the United States. James Buchanan (1857–1861) was just as eager as President Franklin Pierce (1853–1857) to defuse the slavery controversy. He was, however, determined to avoid the political damage that Pierce had suffered by the passing of the Kansas-Nebraska Act. In his inaugural address, Buchanan referred to an as yet undecided Supreme Court suit by a sixty-two-year-old slave, Dred Scott, who claimed that residence in free territories had made him a free man. Buchanan pledged that he would "in common with all good citizens . . . cheerfully submit" to the decision of the Supreme Court.

Buchanan's attempt to settle the agitation over slavery through the Court failed miserably. The Court's decision, *Dred Scott v. Sandford,* opened the entire West to slavery, regardless of what the people in the territories might want. This aggressive foray of the Supreme Court into the realm of controversial policy not only damaged the prestige of the Court, it also opened the floodgates to an outpouring of sectional strife that further fractured the Democratic Party and catapulted an obscure Illinois Republican, Abraham Lincoln (1861–1865), to the presidency in the election of 1860.

See also: Pierce, Franklin, Administration of (1853–1857); Lincoln, Abraham, Administration of (1861–1865).

Bush v. Gore (2000)

A controversial Supreme Court decision that ultimately determined the winner of the 2000 presidential election. Until 2000, the Court had never become involved in a presidential election. Although Vice President Al Gore received received 50,996,116 votes, 539,947 more than the 50,456,169 votes tallied by Texas governor George W. Bush, Gore ultimately lost the election. State electors cast the true votes for president, and in all but two states—Maine and Nebraska—the state's electors vote as a bloc for one candidate. The winner of the state's popular vote, even if by a mere handful of votes, receives all of the electors' votes.

Moreover, the process of counting votes is not exact. Different states and different counties, even neighboring precincts, use varying means of counting votes, and that difference determines the likelihood that a vote will be tabulated. In Florida in 2000, some precincts used paper card ballots that were punched out by the voter and counted by a tabulating machine. Others used more modern computer scanning systems. The older punch-card system does not count as high a percentage of ballots as more modern systems, and in a close election such a difference can be vital.

On election night, November 7, 2000, the television networks first called Gore, the Democratic candidate, the winner in Florida, but later changed it to Bush, the Republican standard bearer. By early the next morning, the networks gave up and said it was too close to call. That is

JUSTICE FOR ALL

The *Dred Scott* Case (1857)

Dred Scott was a slave owned by John Emerson, an army surgeon who was transferred frequently across the country. While working for Dr. Emerson, Scott lived and worked in the free state of Illinois and then in the Wisconsin Territory, a free territory. After Emerson's death, Scott and his wife, also a slave, were left to Emerson's widow. Scott tried to buy his freedom, but was refused. He then petitioned a Missouri court for freedom, based on the fact that he had resided in a free state and a free territory

After many years of court decisions and reversals, the case finally made it to the United States Supreme Court in 1856. Unfortunately for Scott, a majority of Supreme Court justices were supporters of slavery. One of those supporters, Chief Justice Roger B. Taney, read the courts seven-to-two decision in 1857. Because Scott was black he was not a citizen and, therefore, had no right to appeal to the courts, Taney stated. In regards to the assertion in the Declaration of Independence that "all men are created equal," the majority opinion indicated: "It is too clear for dispute, that the enslaved African race were not intended to be included, and formed no part of the people who framed and adopted this declaration." Along with turning down Scott's appeal, the Court declared the Missouri Compromise of 1820, the law that forbade slavery north of the 36° 30' lines of latitude, to be **unconstitutional.** Slavery became legal in all states and territories.

Northerners were greatly angered by the decision, especially the declaration of the Missouri Compromise's unconstitutionality. Many claimed that the constitutionality of the Missouri Compromise was not under trial in the *Dred Scott* case, and therefore the Court could not make this declaration in its verdict. Periodicals from the North and South battled each other in print, publishing articles that passionately argued the merits of the decision. The Northerners' anger led the Republican Party to nominate Abraham Lincoln, who opposed the spread of slavery into the territories, as their candidate for the presidency in 1860. Lincoln's election resulted in the **secession** of the South and the Civil War (1861–1865).

After his case was decided, Dred Scott was sold to the sons of his former owner, Peter Blow. The sons freed Scott and his wife, but Scott died six months later from tuberculosis.

where things stood for more than a month. Gore had won 267 electoral votes, just short of the 271 needed for victory, and Bush had won 246. Florida's twenty-five electoral votes would determine the winner. On election night, Bush had a lead of 1,784 votes in Florida, but his margin decreased to 327 votes after the mandatory machine recount. Gore and his lawyers, convinced a majority of Floridians had voted Democratic, decided to challenge the outcome in court. Bush's advisers said the Texas governor had won narrowly but fairly, and the election was over.

Gore's legal team faced an uphill fight from the start. Florida's election laws were confusing and out-of-date. Moreover, they were written to regulate the sixty-seven county election boards, not the state as a whole. Gore could not simply ask for a statewide recount under Florida law. He had to take his fight to the individual counties. Over the next month, petitions were heard by county courts and the Florida Supreme Court.

Florida's Secretary of State Katherine Harris, an elected Republican, announced two key interpretations of state law that supported Bush's argument that a recount was not called for. First, she said the "inability of voting systems to read an improperly punched punch-card ballot is not 'an error in the vote tabulation' and would not trigger the requirement" for a manual recount. Second, she said her office would enforce a one-week deadline for the counties to submit their election tallies. State law says the counties' returns must be submitted "on the seventh day following" the election and that "such returns may be ignored" if they are not filed on time.

Fearing that Harris would ignore the recounts, Gore's lawyers appealed to state circuit court judge Terry Lewis, but lost. "I give great deference to the interpretation by the Secretary of the election laws," he said, in addition to concurring that she could ignore the manual recounts if they were filed late. The Florida Supreme Court then stepped in to resolve the legal conflict between the county election boards' duty to manually recount ballots and the secretary of state's refusal to include those votes in the final tally. In the first major ruling of the developing legal dispute, the Florida Supreme Court sided 7–0 with Gore and the county officials, thus contradicting Harris. "[T]he will of the people, not a hyper-technical reliance upon statutory provisions, should be our guiding principle in election cases," the state justices said in *Palm Beach County Canvassing Board v. Harris* (2000). Getting the right result was more important than getting it done on time, they concluded. Their decision, handed down on November 21, extended the time for the counties to recount ballots for five more days, until Sunday, November 26.

The day after the Florida Supreme Court ruled, Washington attorney Theodore B. Olson, repre-

senting Bush, asked the U.S. Supreme Court to intervene. While lawyers for Gore and Bush had been fighting in the Florida state courts, Olson had taken a separate track into the federal courts, believing that the ultimate decision may well depend on the Supreme Court. On November 24, the Court announced that it would hear the Republicans' challenge to the Florida court's decision extending the deadlines. It was not clear what constitutional matters were at issue or whether the extended deadline made much difference. Two days later, on November 26, Harris's office declared Bush the winner of Florida's twenty-five electoral votes. The final tally was 2,912,790 for Bush and 2,912,253 for Gore, a difference of 537 votes.

Gore's lawyers then challenged the state's decision to certify the winner under a separate provision of state law called a Contest of Election. It indicates that candidates can contest the result in court if they can point to the "rejection of a number of legal votes sufficient to change or place in doubt the result of the election." A judge who finds merit in the challenge may "provide any relief appropriate under the circumstances." Gore's lawyers noted that more than 9,000 punch-card ballots in Miami-Dade alone had gone through the tabulating machines, but were not counted as votes. If these ballots contained legal votes, they would certainly "place in doubt" the outcome of the Florida election, the lawyers argued. On Friday, December 8, a divided Florida Supreme Court agreed. "This election should be determined by a careful examination of the votes of Florida's citizens," the state court said. "In close elections the necessity for counting all legal votes becomes critical." In a 4–3 vote, it ordered a hand recount of all the remaining untabulated ballots in Florida by December 12, beginning with the 9,000 ballots in Miami Dade. By some estimates, more than 40,000 ballots statewide needed to be tallied by hand.

The December 12 deadline was rooted in federal law. The disputed presidential election of 1876 between Republican Rutherford B. Hayes and Democrat Samuel Tilden also turned on Florida, which had submitted two slates of electors. In response to this fiasco, Congress passed the Electoral Vote Count Act of 1887 to set rules for resolving such disputes. It says a state's electors "shall meet and give their votes on the first Monday after the second Wednesday in December." In 2000, December 18 was the first Monday after the second Wednesday. Another provision of the law says the state result "shall be conclusive" if all controversy over the selection of the electors is resolved "at least six days before the time fixed for the meeting of electors." In the fight for Florida, December 12 was therefore the deadline for resolving the controversy.

The Florida Supreme Court, in its concluding sentence, instructed that the recounting teams do their best to determine what the voter intended. The Republicans had complained of the use of a "selective" recount in a few Democratic-leaning counties. Taking that criticism into account, the state judges said that all the counties should tabulate their "undervotes," referring to punch-card ballots that did not register as votes when they were put through the tabulating machine. This occurred mostly when the voter had not punched out the paper hole cleanly and instead left a "hanging **chad.**" Sometimes, the voter put only a dent in the card, failing to punch through it.

The Florida court's opinion did not specify whether an indented ballot should be counted as a legal vote. The court also did not order a count of so-called overvotes—ballots with more than one marking—because Gore had not asked for one. For example, if a voter punched out a chad next to Gore-Lieberman, and then wrote below "GORE," the ballot could not be counted because it had two markings, although the voter's intent was clear. Some of the state justices said they would have voted to tally these overvotes as well when the voter's intent was obvious.

Time, however, was short. The hurried recount started again on December 9, but at midday it was halted by a surprise order from the U.S. Supreme Court. In a 5–4 vote, the justices had granted an emergency motion filed by Olson to block the Florida court's ruling from taking effect. To obtain an emergency order that stays a lower court decision, the appealing party must show he will suffer "an irreparable harm" unless the court intervenes. Beyond that, he must assert convincingly that five justices—a majority—are likely to rule for him and reverse the lower court. For lawyers, showing an "irreparable harm" to their client is quite difficult.

In Bush's motion, Olson said the Texas governor would suffer an irreparable harm if the Floridians conducted a "standardless" recount. Five members of the Court agreed: Chief Justice William H. Rehnquist, and Justices Sandra Day O'Connor, Antonin Scalia, Anthony M. Kennedy, and Clarence Thomas. "It suffices to say that . . . a majority of the Court . . . believe that the petitioner [Bush] has a substantial probability of success," Scalia said in a statement defending the stay. "The counting of votes that are of questionable legality does in my view threaten irreparable harm to [Bush] and to the country, by casting a cloud upon what he claims to be the legitimacy of his election."

Justice John Paul Stevens spoke for the four dissenters (who also included Stephen G. Breyer, Ruth Bader Ginsburg, and David H. Souter): "Counting every legally cast vote cannot constitute irreparable harm. On the other hand, there is a danger that a stay may cause irreparable harm to the respondents [Gore and Lieberman]—and, more importantly, the public at large. . . . Preventing the recount from being completed will inevitably cast a cloud on the legitimacy of the election."

The stay order signaled the end of the fight for Florida and a final victory for George Bush. Lawyers then hastily filed new briefs on Sunday, and on Monday morning the Court heard an oral argument that was later broadcast nationwide via audiotape.

On December 12, the Court handed out copies of its decision in *Bush v. Gore* (2000). It was an unsigned opinion and labeled a "per curiam," or opinion of the court, which usually refers to a unanimous and uncontroversial ruling. This decision, however, was anything but. Attached were four separate dissents by Justices Breyer, Ginsburg, Souter, and Stevens. In addition, a concurring opinion written by Chief Justice Rehnquist was joined by Justices Scalia and Thomas. That meant, by a process of deduction, that the authors of the decisive opinion were the two unnamed members of the Court: Justices Kennedy and O'Connor. During the oral argument, Kennedy in particular spoke about the equal protection problem, and he is credited as being the opinion's primary author.

Bush's appeal had raised two questions: whether the Florida courts had violated federal

The confusion over the popular vote in Florida after the 2000 election led both Republican and Democratic citizens to voice their opinions—supporting either Bush or Gore. (Scott J. Ferrell, CQ)

election law by establishing "new standards" for resolving the disputed election and whether the "use of standardless manual recounts violates the Equal Protection and Due Process Clauses" of the Fourteenth **Amendment.** "[W]e find a violation of the Equal Protection Clause. . . . The individual citizen has no federal constitutional right to vote for electors for the President of the United States," the Court's opinion said, unless and until the state legislature chooses popular election as the means of choosing its electors. Once it has settled on elections, however, the state must give "equal weight . . . to each vote and equal dignity . . . to each voter. . . . The State may not, by later arbitrary and disparate treatment, value one person's vote over that of another." As **precedent,** the opinion cited the Warren Court rulings that abolished **poll taxes** and set the "one person, one vote" rule for drawing electoral districts.

Of course, both sides claimed they were protecting the right to vote, as the Court noted. The Democrats said the recounts were needed to assure that every voter's ballot was counted. The Republicans said a flawed recount based on hazy and subjective rules was fundamentally unfair and unreliable. The Court adopted the second argument. "The recount mechanisms . . . do not satisfy the minimum requirement for non-arbitrary treatment of voters necessary to secure the fundamental right" to vote, the opinion said. Since the case had developed quickly, the justices had only limited information on how the recounts were being conducted. Republican officials complained that some recount to "unequal evaluation of ballots."

Without question, however, the Court's ruling ensured Bush's victory. It said December 12 was indeed the deadline for recounting votes in Florida, and by handing down the opinion at 10 P.M. on December 12, the possibility for any further action in Florida was foreclosed. "That date is upon us, and there is no recount procedure in place . . . that comports with minimal constitutional standards," the Court concluded.

The Court's ruling succeeded in bringing a swift and decisive end to a seemingly endless election battle. Less than twenty-four hours after the decision, Gore conceded defeat. "While I strongly disagree with the Court's decision, I accept it," he said in a televised address. The Court had never previously decided such an intensely political case.

See also: Bush, George W., Administration of (2001–2009); Presidency and the Supreme Court; Gore, Albert (1948–)

Further Reading

Ackerman, Bruce. *Bush v. Gore: The Question of Legitimacy.* New Haven, CT: Yale University Press, 2002.

Sergis, Diana K. *Bush v. Gore: Controversial Presidential Election Case.* Berkeley Heights, NJ: Enslow, 2003.

Bush, George H.W., Administration of (1989–1993)

Government under the forty-first president of the United States. George H.W. Bush (1989–1993) attended Phillips Academy in Andover, Massachusetts, where he excelled in athletics and academics and was elected president of his senior class. He graduated in 1942 and joined the navy, becoming the youngest bomber pilot in that branch of the service.

On September 22, 1944, while flying a mission from the light aircraft carrier *San Jacinto,* Bush was shot down, but parachuted safely into the Pacific Ocean. After four hours, he was rescued by a submarine. He received the Distinguished Flying Cross. After World War II (1939–1945), Bush enrolled in Yale University, where he majored in economics and was also captain of the baseball team; he graduated in 1948. Bush then moved to Texas, where he made a small fortune in the oil business. In 1964, he unsuccessfully ran for the Senate against **incumbent** Ralph Yarborough, a Democrat.

Political Career

In 1966, when **reapportionment** gave Houston, Texas, another House of Representatives seat, Bush ran for it and won. He served on the Ways and Means Committee and became an outspoken supporter of Richard Nixon (1969–1974). Bush was reelected to the House in 1968, the year Nixon captured the presidency. Two years later, Bush followed Nixon's advice and abandoned his safe House seat to run for the Senate. He was defeated by **conservative** Democrat Lloyd Bentsen.

After the 1970 election, Nixon appointed Bush ambassador to the United Nations (UN). When Nixon was reelected in 1972, he asked Bush to leave the UN to take over as chair of the Republican National Committee. Bush served in that post during the difficult days of the Watergate scandal, in which Congress's Judiciary Committee voted in July 1974 to introduce **impeachment** articles accusing Nixon of obstruction of justice, abuse of presidential powers, and contempt of Congress. At first, Bush vigorously defended Nixon. As the evidence against Nixon mounted, however, Bush avoided public criticism of the president, but privately he expressed doubts about the president's innocence. On August 7, 1974, Bush wrote a letter asking Nixon to resign, which the president did two days later.

When Gerald R. Ford (1974–1977) succeeded to the presidency upon Nixon's resignation, Bush was a leading candidate to fill the vice-presidential vacancy. Bush wanted the job, but he was bypassed in favor of Governor Nelson A. Rockefeller of New York. Ford offered Bush the ambassadorship to Britain or France. Bush chose, however, to take the post of chief of the U.S. Liaison Office in the People's Republic of China.

In 1975, Ford called Bush back to the United States to become director of the Central Intelligence Agency (CIA). As CIA chief, Bush's primary goal was restoring the reputation of the agency, which had been damaged by revelations of its illegal and unauthorized activities during the 1970s, including assassination plots against foreign officials and spying on members of the domestic anti-war movement. Bush won **bipartisan** praise for his efforts to repair the agency's morale and integrity. After being replaced as CIA director when Democrat Jimmy Carter became president in 1977, Bush returned to Houston to become chairman of First International Bank. He stayed active in politics by campaigning for Republican candidates before the 1978 midterm election. On January 5, 1979, he declared his intention to seek the presidency. Bush campaigned full-time during 1979 and established himself as the leading challenger to Republican front-runner Ronald Reagan when he won the Iowa **caucuses** on January 21, 1980. During the primary campaign, Bush attacked Reagan as an ultraconservative and called his economic proposals—including tax cuts for the wealthiest Americans, on the theory that these savings would ultimately "trickle down" to the middle class and the poor—"voodoo economics." Reagan, however, prevailed in the primaries and secured enough delegates for the nomination before the Republican National Convention in Detroit in July 1980.

At the convention, Reagan's team, in an attempt to unify the party, asked Bush to be the vice-presidential nominee. Bush accepted, and the Republican ticket defeated President Jimmy Carter (1977–1981) and Vice President Walter F. Mondale in a landslide.

Despite Bush's differences with Reagan during the campaign, as vice president he was extremely loyal to the chief **executive.** When Reagan was wounded by an assailant in 1981, Bush, while exerting leadership over the administration as Reagan convalesced, emphasized that Reagan was still president. Bush, who was frequently called upon to make diplomatic trips overseas, visited more than seventy countries during Reagan's presidency. Reagan and Bush won a second term in 1984 by easily defeating the Democratic ticket of Walter F. Mondale and Geraldine Ferraro.

Late in Reagan's second term, Bush launched his campaign for the presidency. Despite his status as a two-term vice president, he was challenged for the nomination by Senate Minority Leader

VIEWPOINTS

ECONOMIC-POLITICAL CURRENCY

©1992 HERBLOCK

President George H.W. Bush (1989–1993) was soundly criticized for breaking his promise of "No new taxes." Bush lost the election of 1992 in part because of the nation's weak economy. (A 1992 Herblock Cartoon, copyright by *The Herb Block Foundation*)

Robert J. Dole of Kansas and several other candidates. Dole defeated Bush in the Iowa caucuses, but Bush scored a decisive victory in the New Hampshire primary and secured the nomination before the end of the primary season.

Bush faced Governor Michael S. Dukakis of Massachusetts in the general election, during which Bush attacked his opponent for **liberal** policies and promised to continue Ronald Reagan's diplomacy with the Soviet Union. Despite the presence of massive budget deficits, Bush also pledged not to raise taxes. Bush overcame speculation about his role in the Reagan administration's Iran-contra affair (a covert CIA operation in support of the contras, a guerrilla force in

Nicaragua that opposed that country's left-wing government) and criticism of Dan Quayle, his vice-presidential choice, to defeat Dukakis. Bush won the election decisively in the electoral college, 426–112.

Presidency

Bush had pledged to continue the conservative legacy of Ronald Reagan. However, he had also promised to preside over a "kinder, gentler America," implying that **partisanship** had gone too far during the Reagan period. Nevertheless, **partisan** battles with the Democratic Congress would characterize much of Bush's presidency. In November 1990, after months of negotiation and posturing, Bush signed a budget **bill** that aimed to trim about $500 billion off the deficit over five years. Congressional Democrats forced Bush to accept a tax increase as part of the deal. Many Americans saw Bush's acquiescence to the tax increase as a betrayal of his campaign pledge.

The previous August, events in the Persian Gulf region had intruded on Bush's other priorities and provided a troubling backdrop to the budget negotiations. On August 2, Iraqi forces invaded and quickly occupied the small, oil-rich nation of Kuwait. Bush responded by rallying international opposition against Iraq and sending hundreds of thousands of American troops to join the coalition assembling in the region. The administration argued that this aggression by Iraqi leader Saddam Hussein had to be reversed because it threatened the stability of world oil markets and set a dangerous **precedent** that could encourage other acts of aggression. Bush also was concerned about mounting evidence that Iraq was engaged in an ambitious nuclear weapons program.

On January 17, 1991, Bush ordered a devastating bombing campaign against Iraqi military forces. On February 24, after thirty-eight days of sustained bombing, coalition ground forces attacked the Iraqi troops, routing them from Kuwait. The ground war lasted just one hundred hours before Bush gave the cease-fire order.

The stunning success of the operation and the low casualty figures boosted the president's popularity to a high of 89 percent immediately following the war. Commentators speculated that Bush's victory in the Gulf might make his reelection in-evitable in 1992, and several prominent Democrats declined to enter the race because of Bush's standing. However, his popularity did not last. After the war, the American people turned their attention back to domestic matters. The nation had entered a **recession** in the summer of 1990. As wages stagnated and unemployment continued to rise, Bush was perceived as having no answers to domestic problems. He also was seen as spending too much time on foreign affairs, the area of policy in which he had the most expertise and success.

Bush's reelection chances were further damaged when he was challenged for the Republican nomination by conservative political commentator Pat Buchanan. Although Buchanan did not seriously threaten Bush's nomination, the challenger's attacks from the right weakened enthusiasm for Bush among conservatives and forced the president to defend himself instead of preparing for the fall election.

Democrats nominated Governor Bill Clinton of Arkansas to face Bush. Billionaire Ross Perot mounted a self-financed independent candidacy that also drew significant attention. Clinton won the election with 43 percent of the popular vote and 370 electoral votes. Bush finished second with 37 percent of the popular vote and 168 electoral votes. Perot did not win any states but finished with 19 percent of the popular vote. Clinton capitalized on Bush's inattention to domestic matters by promising to focus "like a laser beam" on the economy.

Bush left office declaring that he would spend time in retirement with his grandchildren. His son, George W. Bush, won the White House in 2000, marking the second time that a son of a president was elected to the presidency.

See also: Clinton, Bill, Administration of (1993–2001); Reagan, Ronald, Administration of (1981–1989); Watergate Scandal.

Further Reading

Bush, George H.W. *All the Best, George Bush: My Life in Letters and Other Writings*. New York: Scribner, 2000.

Naftali, Timothy. *George H.W. Bush*. New York: Times Books, 2007.

A–Z

Bush, George W., Administration of (2001–2009)

Government under the forty-third president of the United States. George W. Bush graduated from Yale University in 1968. He then held a series of jobs, including campaign chairman for his father, George H.W. Bush (1989–1993), when the elder Bush ran unsuccessfully for the U.S. Senate in 1970. George W. Bush then entered Harvard Business School. He graduated in 1974 with a master's degree in business administration and returned to Midland, Texas, to start an oil company.

Bush left the oil business in 1986. The next year he went to Washington and spent eighteen months working in his father's successful presidential campaign. He took little interest in policy questions and positions but served more as the family watchdog over the professional campaign staffers. He learned the details of running a campaign, from budgeting to scheduling.

After George Bush's victory, George W. returned to Texas. In 1989, with $600,000 he borrowed, he bought a 2 percent stake in the Texas Rangers baseball team. As the team's managing general partner, he supervised construction of a new stadium and traveled widely to promote the team. Bush and his aides gradually built the team into a contender that won the American League's Western Division title in 1994, which was Bush's last year with the Rangers. He sold his share for some $15 million.

Political Career

In 1994, two years after his father lost the presidential election to Bill Clinton (1993–2001), Bush ran for the Texas governorship. With high name recognition and admired for his work with the Texas Rangers, Bush was well placed to mount a challenge to Democratic **incumbent** Ann Richards, who had been elected in 1990. Bush campaigned on educational reform and school accountability, and he pulled out an upset win, taking 53 percent of the vote to Richards's 46 percent. Bush was easily reelected in 1998 with 68 percent of the vote, becoming the first Republican governor of Texas to be elected to a second term.

His margin of victory and high popularity ratings made Bush a leading contender for the 2000 Republican presidential nomination. Bush quickly raised a record sum of more than $60 million to finance his primary campaigns. He then had to spend most of it fending off a strong challenge from maverick Republican John McCain, Arizona's senior senator, who defeated Bush in several of the early races. Bush was never seriously challenged thereafter and was chosen the party's nominee at its Philadelphia convention in August. Bush chose Richard B. Cheney, a former representative from Wyoming and defense secretary during the George H.W. Bush administration, as his running mate.

Bush called himself a "compassionate conservative," attempting to put a kindly face on an image tarnished somewhat by the hard-line conservatives who were credited with the Republican Party's unexpected successes in the 1994, when the party gained majorities in both houses of Congress. Bush proposed a $1.3 trillion income tax cut if elected and said he wanted to reform Social Security by allowing people to create private investment accounts. On the environment, he favored voluntary cleanups instead of mandated action by the Environmental Protection Agency, a position that, ultimately, would substantially weaken that agency.

Presidency

In one of the closest presidential races in history, with the election results from Florida hotly disputed, Bush won the White House by narrowly defeating the Democratic ticket of Vice President Al Gore (1993–2001) and his running mate, Senator Joseph Lieberman of Connecticut. The outcome of the cliffhanger race was not known until five weeks after the election. Although the vote in Oregon and New Mexico was so close that absentee ballots had to be counted over several days before the winner of those states could be determined, Florida's twenty-five electoral votes were key to Bush's victory. Both campaigns raised numerous legal challenges in state and federal court on the legitimacy of Florida's final tally, especially in regards to manual recounts of

VIEWPOINTS

REX BABIN THE SACRAMENTO BEE

BLOWING SMOKE

Environmentalists and others criticized President George W. Bush (2001–2009) for his weak response to global warming and other changes in the world's atmosphere. (Sacramento Bee, North America Syndicate, MCT, Landov)

A–Z

disputed votes. The dispute was finally resolved when a deeply divided U.S. Supreme Court, in a 5–4 decision, halted a statewide recount, giving Bush the presidency.

Although Bush won the electoral vote, he lost the popular vote by half a million votes. Only three times in U.S. history had a presidential candidate lost the popular vote but won the election. The last time was in 1888 when Benjamin Harrison (1889–1893) defeated Grover Cleveland (1885–1889, 1893–1897).

The terrorist attacks on the World Trade Center and Pentagon on September 11, 2001, shaped Bush's first term into one focused on homeland security and a so-called "war on terrorism." The Bush administration quickly engaged in a war in Afghanistan, overthrowing the Taliban government and installing new leadership. In late 2002, Bush won approval from Congress and the United

Nations (UN) for the possible use of force against Iraq, and on March 19, 2003, Bush told the nation that the military operation against Iraq had begun. While the attack succeeded in rapidly toppling Iraqi dictator Saddam Hussein, the insurgency that followed proved bloody, with the war continuing through the remainder of Bush's presidency.

At home, after first opposing it, Bush agreed to the establishment of a new Department of Homeland Security, which merged security-related functions from other government agencies. The department began operations on March 1, 2003, with responsibilities over the Secret Service, the Coast Guard, and the Customs Service, among other agencies.

On the domestic side, Bush's first term was perhaps best known for its tax cuts. The administration pushed through a $1.35 trillion tax cut in its first year, and followed with three more tax cuts over the next three years. Other major pieces of legislation included a **bipartisan** education reform **bill,** signed into law in January 2002, and a Medicare reform bill, signed in December 2003. Bush campaigned hard in the 2002 midterm elections, stumping for congressional candidates around the country. In the end, the Republican Party picked up additional House seats and won control of the narrowly divided Senate, a rare midterm success for the party of an incumbent president.

Bush's Democratic opponent in the 2004 presidential election was Senator John Kerry of Massachusetts. The campaign's key issues included the war in Iraq, the economy, and both men's military service during the Vietnam War era. Although Kerry had initially supported giving Bush the authority to use force in Iraq, he attacked Bush's Iraq policy, charging that the administration did not have a plan for the war's aftermath and that Kerry could do a better job of bringing allies into the effort. In addition, Kerry tried to drive home the point that one of Bush's major justifications for invading Iraq—that Saddam Hussein possessed weapons of mass destruction—had proved unfounded. Bush responded that Kerry had no consistent position on the war and that he could not be trusted as commander in chief in an era marked by terrorism. Bush and Kerry also sparred over the state of the economy, with Bush citing improvements under his watch and Kerry pledging to roll back Bush's tax cuts somewhat by raising taxes on people earning more than $200,000 per year.

The election was expected to be close, with polls indicating a neck-and-neck race for much of the period leading to Election Day. Bush's win in Ohio helped to secure victory for him in both the electoral (286 to 251) and the popular vote (50.7 percent to 48.3 percent). Bush thus became the first president since his father's 1988 victory to win a majority of the popular vote.

Bush soon faced numerous challenges during his second term. Although he was able to secure Senate confirmation for two Supreme Court nominees, John Roberts and Samuel Alito, his first major **legislative** effort of the term, a partial privatization of Social Security, failed. Meanwhile, Bush's approval ratings in public opinion polls fell into the 30 percent range as the Iraq War dragged on. Furthermore, the Bush administration was soundly criticized for its slow reaction to Hurricane Katrina, which devastated New Orleans and much of the Gulf cost. These, along with scandals involving Republican legislators, were among the factors that resulted in the Democratic Party wresting control of both houses of Congress from the Republicans in the midterm elections of November 2006. That election, which Bush himself referred to as a "thumping," left Bush to contend with low approval ratings, an opposition Congress, and a devastating economic recession.

See also: Bush v. Gore (2000); Clinton, Bill, Administration of (1993–2001); Department of Homeland Security (DHS).

Further Reading

Campbell, Colin, and Bert A. Rockman, eds. *The George W. Bush Presidency: Appraisals and Prospects.* Washington, D.C.: CQ Press, 2003.

Kessler, Ronald. *A Matter of Character: Inside the White House of George W. Bush.* New York: Sentinel, 2004.

Bush, Laura

See First Lady.

Cabinet

The heads of each of the **executive** departments and an advisory body to the president. Although not specifically mentioned in the Constitution or provided for by law, the cabinet has become an institutionalized part of the presidency.

The secretaries of the executive departments comprise the majority of the cabinet. The president's cabinet, however, has been expanded in recent years to give cabinet-rank to other members of the president's advisory circle. President George W. Bush (2001–2009), for example, included in his cabinet not only the heads of the fifteen departments, but the vice president, the White House chief of staff, the director of the Office of Management and Budget, the U.S. trade representative, the administrator of the Environmental Protection Agency, and the director of the Office of National Drug Control Policy.

Executive departments are the largest units of the federal executive branch. Each department covers broad areas of responsibility. At the start of 2009, there were fifteen cabinet departments: Agriculture, **Commerce,** Defense, Education, Energy, Health and Human Services, Homeland Security, Housing and Urban Development, Interior, Justice, Labor, State, Transportation, Treasury, and Veterans Affairs.

Origin and Development of the Cabinet

The idea of an advisory council for the president was discussed at the Constitutional Convention during the summer of 1787. Gouverneur Morris and Charles Cotesworth Pinckney, the first delegates to use the term *cabinet* at the convention, proposed creation of a council of state, composed of the executive department heads, to advise the

Cabinet Departments		
Department	Year established	Federal civilian employees
Agriculture	1889	92,000
Commerce	1913	39,000
Defense	1947	623,000
Education	1980	4,000
Energy	1977	15,000
Health and Human Services	1980	60,000
Homeland Security	2003	149,000
Housing and Urban Development	1965	10,000
Interior	1849	66,000
Justice	1870	105,000
Labor	1913	16,000
State	1789	14,000
Transportation	1966	53,000
Treasury	1789	109,000
Veterans Affairs	1989	239,000

There are 15 cabinet departments. Their sizes, members' roles, and budgets vary greatly from department to department.

president. This proposal failed to win adoption, but advocates of a cabinet kept the idea alive throughout most of the convention.

The cabinet concept ultimately failed to win majority support among the convention's delegates.

A-Z

Most of the Founders apparently feared that the presidency might become too overburdened with unnecessary advisory councils. Consequently, when the Committee of Style finished drafting the Constitution, all that remained of the idea was the authorization that the president "require the Opinion, in writing, of the principal Officer in each of the executive Departments, upon any Subject relating to the duties of their respective Offices" (Article II, Section 2).

Seeking both administrative and advisory help in his new administration, Washington asked Congress to create three executive departments to oversee foreign affairs, military affairs, and financial concerns. For more than two months, Congress debated the establishment of these three executive departments. Primarily concerned with the relationship of each department to Congress and believing that not all departments should be alike in this relationship, most members of Congress preferred that the departments concerned with foreign affairs and war be primarily under the control of the executive.

The treasury, however, had some **legislative** purposes and thus should fall more under the control of Congress. The statutes setting up the departments reflected these preferences. On July 27, 1789, Congress established the Department of Foreign Affairs. The secretary of foreign affairs was given the responsibility of performing duties assigned by the president. (Two months later Congress changed the name to the Department of State.) Similarly, the statutory language setting up the War Department placed it squarely under the control of the president. The Treasury Department, however, was not designated by Congress as an "executive department." Instead, the secretary of the treasury was directed to report fiscal matters to Congress. Part of the rationale for this special status was the constitutional requirement that **revenue bills** originate in the House of Representatives.

President George Washington (1789–1797) meets with his first cabinet. To the president's left are Henry Knox, secretary of war; Alexander Hamilton, secretary of the treasury; Thomas Jefferson, secretary of state; and Edmund Randolph, attorney general. (Library of Congress)

Washington's use of the cabinet soon resulted in the institution that the Framers of the Constitution had declined to include. The president eventually appointed Alexander Hamilton as secretary of the treasury, Henry Knox as secretary of war, and Thomas Jefferson, who had been serving as minister to France, as secretary of state. In addition, Edmund Randolph was named attorney general, although there was no Department of Justice until 1870.

Alexander Hamilton, who became Washington's dominant adviser, used his status in the cabinet to increase the cabinet's prestige and independence. In addition to his abilities and his special relationship with Washington, Hamilton's rise was partly due to the importance of the Treasury Department in the new government.

Cabinet Members as Advisers

Some presidents intentionally avoid placing their cabinets in an advisory role; others consider such a role the ideal one for the presidential cabinet. During the administrations of Franklin Roosevelt (1933–1945), Harry S. Truman (1945–1953), John F. Kennedy (1961–1963), Lyndon B. Johnson (1963–1969), and Richard M. Nixon (1969–1974), department heads discussed issues and problems informally, primarily to exchange information. The cabinet of Dwight D. Eisenhower (1953–1961) regularly considered specific issues, using papers authored by cabinet members and circulated prior to meetings. Both the president and the cabinet were aided by agendas, concise records, and a small secretariat. Under both Eisenhower and Truman, the National Security Council provided summaries of issue papers that earlier had been subjected to a thorough interdepartmental review, with dissenters identified and alternative language proposed.

Most presidents have come to expect little from their cabinets except to manage large bureaucracies within their departments and to implement the president's agenda. At best, the cabinet may serve as a source of advice for the president, but this use of the cabinet has been rare. Even when presidents, such as Nixon and Jimmy Carter (1977–1981), emphasized the importance of their cabinets in the first months of the administration, their commitment to a strong cabinet soon diminished. As administrations mature, daily managerial issues and domestic and international crises often take increasing amounts of a president's time. Moreover, presidential programs and goals become fixed, and cabinet secretaries, as heads of their departments, may find themselves competing for scarce resources. Cabinet meetings thus become less frequent and less enthusiastic, as well as a burden for both the department secretary and the president.

See also: Department of Agriculture (USDA); Department of Commerce; Department of Defense (DOD); Department of Education; Department of Energy (DOE); Department of Health and Human Services (HHS); Department of Homeland Security (DHS); Department of Housing and Urban Development (HUD); Department of the Interior; Department of Justice; Department of Labor; Department of State; Department of Transportation (DOT); Department of the Treasury; Department of Veterans Affairs.

Camp David

See Carter, Jimmy, Administration of (1977–1981).

Campaign Finance

See Presidential Campaigns.

Carter, Jimmy, Administration of (1977–1981)

Government under the thirty-ninth president of the United States. Although born James Earl Carter, Jr., from childhood on James preferred to be called Jimmy. After high school, Carter briefly attended Georgia Southwestern College before being appointed to the U.S. Naval Academy. In 1948, he applied and was accepted for submarine duty. He spent two and a half years as a crewmember on a Pacific submarine then was selected to work in the navy's nuclear submarine program. When his father died in 1953, however, he decided to retire from the navy.

Carter returned to his home in Plains, Georgia, where he took over the family peanut farm. He gradually increased his landholdings and started several agriculture-related businesses, including a peanut-shelling plant and a farm-supply business. As Carter's wealth grew, he became involved in local politics.

In 1970, Carter ran for the governorship of Georgia. He surprised political observers by defeating former governor Carl E. Sanders in the Democratic primary, and then went on to win the general election. As governor, Carter openly denounced racial **segregation** and became a symbol of the more moderate social attitudes of the "New South." He also reorganized the state government, supported measures to protect the environment, and opened government meetings to the public.

Georgia law prohibited a governor from running for two consecutive terms, so Carter set his sights on the presidency. Carter's candidacy was a long shot. He was an inexperienced, one-term governor from a southern state who had to defeat several better-known Democrats for the nomination.

A - Z

On March 26, 1979, after days of intense negotiations, Egyptian president Anwar Sadat (left), U.S. president Jimmy Carter (1977–1981) (center), and Israeli prime minister Menachem Begin (right) completed the signing of the peace treaty between Egypt and Israel. (AP Images, Bob Daugherty)

Carter campaigned tirelessly during 1975 and 1976 and gained national attention by winning the Democratic **caucuses** in Iowa on January 19, 1976. When he won again in the New Hampshire primary on February 24, he became the front-runner. Before the June 1976 Democratic National Convention in New York, he had earned enough delegates in primaries and caucuses to lock up the nomination.

Carter emerged from the convention with a solid lead in public opinion polls over Republican **incumbent** Gerald R. Ford (1974–1977), whose candidacy suffered from several years of economic troubles and his pardon of former president Richard M. Nixon (1969–1974). This gap narrowed as the election approached, but Carter won 297–240 in the electoral college.

One of Carter's early presidential goals was to "depomp" the presidency and make it more responsive to the people. He underscored his inten-

tion by walking back to the White House from the Capitol after his inauguration. Carter also stopped the tradition of having a band play "Hail to the Chief" when he arrived at an occasion. The public liked Carter's open, informal style, but the president could not sustain his popularity.

In the late summer 1977, journalists and government investigators accused Carter's budget director, Bert Lance, of having engaged in questionable financial practices during his career as a banker before he joined the Carter administration. For several months, Carter defended Lance, but on September 21, 1977, Lance resigned under the weight of the accusations. Although Lance was ultimately exonerated—a jury acquitted him of bank fraud charges in 1981—the Lance affair appeared on the surface to contradict Carter's claim that he was holding the officials of his administration to a higher ethical standard than previous presidents had.

The state of the economy further damaged Carter's presidency. During the 1976 campaign, Carter had criticized President Ford for the high inflation and unemployment the country was suffering. Under Carter, however, the economic situation grew even worse. Prices had risen 6.5 percent the year Carter took office, but they rose 11.3 percent in 1979 and 13.5 percent in 1980. Unemployment, which stood at about 7.7 percent in 1980 during Carter's reelection campaign, was also uncomfortably high.

In foreign policy, Carter achieved notable successes. He mediated negotiations between Prime Minister Menachem Begin of Israel and President Anwar Sadat of Egypt. The talks produced the 1979 Camp David Accords, which established peace between those two countries. He also formalized relations with the People's Republic of China on January 1, 1979, and secured Senate approval in 1978 of treaties transferring control of the Panama Canal to Panama on December 31, 1999.

The last two years of Carter's term, however, brought several foreign policy failures. On June 18, 1979, Carter and Soviet leader Leonid Brezhnev signed a treaty in Vienna to limit strategic nuclear weapons, but the Senate refused to **ratify** this agreement, known as SALT II. In 1980, Carter withdrew the SALT II treaty after the Soviets invaded Afghanistan in December 1979 to prop up a procommunist government there. In response to the Soviet invasion, Carter also imposed a grain **embargo** and refused to allow the U.S. team to participate in the 1980 Olympic Games in Moscow.

On November 4, 1979, Iranian militants stormed the U.S. embassy in Tehran, the capital city, taking American diplomats and embassy personnel hostage. Carter's efforts to free the hostages, including an abortive helicopter raid in April 1980 in which eight soldiers died, proved ineffective. The hostage crisis dominated the last year of Carter's presidency; the Iranians did not release the hostages until January 20, 1981, minutes after Carter had left office.

Despite these problems, Carter fought off a challenge for the 1980 Democratic presidential nomination from Senator Edward M. Kennedy of Massachusetts. Carter's opponent in the general election was Ronald Reagan, the **conservative** former governor of California. Reagan defeated Carter 489–49 in the electoral college, with Carter winning only six states and the District of Columbia.

After leaving the presidency, Carter returned to his home in Plains. He lectured and wrote about world affairs, launched the Carter Presidential Center in Atlanta to examine public policy issues, and became involved in several voluntary service projects.

In 1994, Carter carried out a series of high-profile diplomatic missions to North Korea, Bosnia, and Haiti. The Haiti trip produced a last-minute agreement that allowed U.S. military forces, which were set to invade Haiti, to enter the country peacefully. In May 2002, Carter became the first U.S. president—sitting or former—to visit Cuba since Calvin Coolidge in January 1928. Carter gave a speech from Havana calling on the United States to end its forty-year economic embargo against Cuba. In October 2002, Carter was awarded the Nobel Peace Prize for his decades of effort to promote world peace, human rights, and economic and social development.

See also: Ford, Gerald R, Administration of (1974–1977); Reagan, Ronald, Administration of (1981–1989); Watergate Scandal.

Further Reading

Brinkley, Douglas G. *The Unfinished Presidency: Jimmy Carter's Journey Beyond the White House.* New York: Penguin, 1999.

Kaufman, Burton I., and Scott Kaufman. *The Presidency of James Earl Carter, Jr.,* 2ded. Lawrence, KS: The University of Kansas Press, 2006.

Checks and Balances

See Presidency and the Bureaucracy.

Cheney, Richard B. (1941–)

See Bush v. Gore (2000); Bush, George W., Administration of (2001–2009).

Chertoff, Michael

See Department of Homeland Security (DHS).

Chief Diplomat

The president's role as the director of U.S. foreign policy. While the Constitution makes presidents the sole head of state, it does not give them sufficient authority to make foreign policy simply on their own. The branches of the federal government share foreign policy powers, and Congress has many ways to influence the substance and execution of policies. In addition, policy must be coordinated within a complex of often competing advisers, departments, and agencies. Even under the most favorable conditions, presidents frequently struggle to maintain control of policy formulation and implementation.

Distribution of Foreign Policy Power

The Constitution gives the president fewer powers related to the making of foreign policy than Congress, and the powers of the presidency are checked in ways that seem designed to prevent the president from making independent commitments abroad. The only unshared power in this area is the president's responsibility to "receive Ambassadors and other Public ministers." Presidents may appoint ambassadors only with the "Advice and Consent of the Senate," and the Senate is meant to be involved throughout all treaty negotiations. The president's authority as commander in chief is constrained, as a policy-making power, by Congress's constitutional control over declarations of war and the raising and support of all armed forces.

Besides its influence over the use of force and the powers it shares with the president, Congress has broad foreign policy powers that are checked only by the president's **veto.** As spelled out in Article I of the Constitution, Congress controls the legal context of international affairs through its powers "to define and punish Piracies and Felonies committed on the high Seas and Offences against the Law of Nations . . . and make Rules concerning Captures on Land and Water." Most significant is Congress's authority to "regulate **Commerce** with foreign Nations." These powers are broadened by the so-called elastic clause to "make all Laws which shall be necessary and proper for carrying into Execution the foregoing Powers."

Altogether, Congress's formal constitutional authority in foreign affairs is broader and less qualified than the president's. In addition, the **legislative** branch's general power to make laws, control **appropriations,** and "provide for the common Defense and general Welfare of the United States" gives it broad authority to become involved in any foreign policy decision or action not specifically reserved for the president by the Constitution. Congress and, especially, the Senate were, it seems, to control general policy and any long-term foreign commitments.

The grants of power in the Constitution do not begin to answer all the questions about how foreign policy decisions should be made and implemented. The actual distribution of shared foreign policy powers between the president and Congress could be established only by events. The particular struggles have produced periods of interbranch stalemate and partnership, presidential subordination and domination.

Presidential Dominance of Foreign Policy

In 1948, addressing members of the Jewish War Veterans, President Harry S. Truman (1945–1953) stated: "I make foreign policy." Most historians and political scientists would agree that Truman's assessment of presidential power exaggerates only slightly the influence of modern presidents over foreign policy. At least until the end of the cold war with the Soviet Union, Congress retained an important role in foreign affairs. On many occasions, Congress was able to frustrate, delay, modify, or negate presidential foreign policy. The president, however, dominated the formulation and initiation of foreign policy, and Congress's actions were usually responses to presidential policies. Certainly, the American public and foreign governments expect the president to make decisions and to implement them. It is even common for members of Congress from both parties to criticize a president for failing to provide foreign policy leadership.

Because the constitutional division of power between the **executive** and legislative branches is vague in the area of foreign affairs, the establishment of presidential control over foreign relations cannot be attributed simply to the grants of power in the Constitution. The ambiguity of the document ensured that skills, circumstances, public opinion, customs, and **precedents** would order and reorder the distribution of influence over foreign affairs. The branch most capable of asserting its interests and demonstrating its ability to make effective foreign policy would likely emerge as the more powerful. This branch has proved to be the executive.

Yet the principle of "presidential control" seemed to be an inaccurate characterization of foreign policy making in the era that began in the early 1990s with the disintegration of the Soviet Union and the Warsaw Pact. Conflicts between President William Clinton (1993–2001) and Congress over foreign aid, U.S. participation in United Nations missions, and many other foreign policy issues suggested a return to a sharper struggle for control of foreign policy. On the other hand, President George W. Bush's (2001–2009) control of the diplomatic and military policies in response to the September 11, 2001, terrorist attacks on New York and Washington, D.C., indicates that the presidency retains its advantage in these policy arenas.

Presidential Advantages

A mix of influences has shaped the history of foreign policy-making and the eventual rise of presidential responsibility for leadership and control. These include presidential skills, public opinion, precedents, constitutional principles, and circumstances. The presidents' enduring advantages are their status as chief of state and the various constitutional powers that establish them as the principal communicator, the "sole organ of the nation in its external relations, and its sole representative with foreign nations."

Although presidents do not have the full authority to commit the nation and Congress to a foreign policy, their powers allow them to speak first in defining a policy and course of action for the nation. When coupled with the status as the only nationally elected officer (along with the vice president), these powers give an enterprising and determined president considerable advantage over policy. Insofar as any contradiction to their lead may reflect on the nation, presidents can saddle the congressional opposition with responsibility for embarrassing the nation and harming the credibility of the presidency in future negotiations.

These advantages are enhanced by the president's other positions. As commander in chief of the armed forces, head of the diplomatic corps, and head of the intelligence agencies, presidents should be in the best position to judge the capacity of the U.S. government to carry out a given foreign policy. Congress has regularly recognized the inherent advantages of the presidency's focused responsibility. Unlike Congress, with its many voices and centers of power, presidents are able to work with speed and secrecy, two capabilities that are essential in many diplomatic situations, and especially in crises that threaten the security of the nation. As the most identifiable leaders and visible symbols of the nation, presidents are the most capable of rallying national support in a crisis.

Congress retains nonetheless a substantial arsenal of constitutional counterclaims and can at any time reassert itself. The persuasiveness of presidential assertions of authority depends in part on **precedent:** claims of authority that have received the agreement of Congress, the courts, and public opinion. Successful assertions, and especially those backed by actions with favorable results, tend to strengthen the president's constitutional position and reaffirm the practical advantages of presidential control over policy.

Reaping the full potential of constitutional and practical precedents requires the cooperation of circumstances. Any crisis in foreign affairs that directly or indirectly threatens the security and well-being of U.S. citizens, the nation, or close allies will focus attention on the president as the chief of state and as the officer most able to respond flexibly and decisively in diplomatic and military matters. Congress regularly recognizes its clumsy inability to compete with these presidential qualities.

After World War II (1939–1945), however, the expansive global commitments and permanent national security crisis led to a full and enduring realization of the president's constitutional and practical potential in foreign policy leadership and control. In the post-cold war era, the frequent conflicts between Congress and President Clinton over issues such as participation in peacekeeping missions suggest that securing consistent presidential leadership in the future will be much more difficult. On the other hand, Iraq's invasion of Kuwait in 1990 and the September 11, 2001, terrorist attacks on New York City and Washington, D.C., suggest that circumstances can still enhance presidential authority and leadership.

See also: Chief Economist; Chief Executive; Commander in Chief; Executive Departments.

Further Reading

Crenson, Matthew, and Benjamin Ginsburg. *Presidential Power: Unchecked and Unbalanced.* New York: W.W. Norton, 2007.

Roleff, Tamara L. *What Limits Should Be Placed On Presidential Powers?* Farmington Hills, MI: Greenhaven, 2006.

Chief Economist

The president's role in the nation's financial affairs and the economy. The Constitution grants the president no specific economic powers. Nevertheless, the Framers expected presidents to have significant influence over the fiscal policy. They would, after all, oversee the implementation of Congress's spending and taxing decisions, suggest economic legislation in their State of the Union address and other communications to Congress, negotiate commercial treaties with foreign nations, and have the power to **veto** legislation on economic matters.

Presidential economic power, however, has developed beyond these constitutional specifications. Presidents have effectively used their visibility and prerogatives in the execution of policy to promote their economic programs. In addition, as management of the economy has grown more complex, Congress has given presidents greater economic power through statutes.

Because the American people associate the presidency—the nation's most powerful and identi-

fiable political office—with the performance of the federal government, they have come to expect presidents to produce economic prosperity for the United States, just as presidents are expected to enforce the country's laws and ensure its security.

Limitations

When unemployment, inflation, and budget deficits rise, presidents receive most of the blame. Herbert Hoover (1929–1933), Gerald R. Ford (1974–1977), Jimmy Carter (1977–1981), and George H.W. Bush (1989–1993) lost their reelection bids in part because of the poor economic conditions that prevailed during their presidencies. The president's party also may suffer in midterm congressional elections if the economy is in a **recession.**

Presidents themselves are partially responsible for high public expectations of their economic management. As candidates, future presidents usually overestimate their ability to improve the economy. To be elected, presidential aspirants must promise to produce economic growth with low inflation and balanced budgets, even if their predecessors have left them with serious economic problems that cannot be corrected quickly or easily.

This relationship between presidential popularity and the economy, however, may also work to a president's advantage. Presidents are quick to take credit for economic upturns, price stability, and low unemployment. Presidential candidate Ronald Reagan capitalized on poor economic conditions in 1980 by asking voters, "Are you better off now than you were four years ago?" Voters responded "no" and elected Reagan (1981–1989) to succeed Carter. Four years later, when the economy was in the midst of a strong expansion after the recession of 1981–1982, Reagan repeated the question, and the American people re-elected him in a landslide.

How the public deals with complex political and economic issues and information also influences presidential actions and may limit policy alternatives. Oftentimes voters mistakenly believe that a specific presidential policy—promoting free trade, for example—that is intended to affect economic activity in the nation as a whole should also affect each individual the same way. Opponents of free trade argue that import restrictions will save jobs, which may be true in the industries that are affected, such as steel manufacturing. Voters may mistakenly believe that this saving of jobs should extend to the entire economy.

Economists argue that in the entire economy, import restrictions are not likely to save jobs outside of the affected industries. This is because more efficient businesses are not allowed to beat out less efficient businesses or more efficient industries are forbidden (by policy) from replacing less efficient ones, which results in a loss in jobs in the economy as a whole as well as fewer innovative products becoming available to the public.

Even though presidents and their advisers generally understand the benefits of free trade, the politics of governing often take precedence over economic theory. A good example occurred in early 2002 when Republican president George W. Bush (2001–2009), leader of the party traditionally associated with free trade, imposed **tariffs** on steel and lumber imports. Observers noted that states that were expected to be important to Bush if he sought reelection in 2004—such as Pennsylvania and West Virginia—had troubled steel industries, including companies that faced bankruptcy. The lumber industry was also important to influential members of Congress, including Senate Minority Leader Trent Lott of Mississippi, who were in a position to help the Bush administration win free trade agreements in coming months. Lumber imports from Canada were providing increasingly tough competition to American suppliers. However, these details are often lost on the public.

Inaccurate Information

Similarly, an anti-inflation strategy based on inaccurate information can deepen a recession. That occurred at the beginning of 1980 when the inflation rate had skyrocketed to 18 percent. Economists had predicted that a recession was coming, but President Carter nevertheless imposed credit controls designed to lower inflation. Later in the year, economic statistics showed that the predicted recession was already underway when Carter acted, which contributed significantly to the sharpest decline in gross national product (GNP) in a single three-month period since World War II (1939–1945). Incomplete economic information induced Carter to take measures that worsened the economy's troubles.

Assets and Opportunities

In spite of these limitations, no person has more influence over the U.S. economy than the president. As chief executive, the president oversees the government's economic and regulatory functions and appoints cabinet and Federal Reserve Board members who make many economic decisions. As chief legislator, the president proposes federal spending, taxation, and other economy-related legislation and can use the **veto**—or the threat of the veto—to influence legislation before Congress. As commander in chief, the president oversees the Defense Department's multibillion-dollar purchases. As chief diplomat, the president negotiates with foreign governments about trade and currency issues; and as chief of state the president affects the morale, attitudes, and expectations of the American people.

One area of presidential strength is the continued improvement in economic knowledge. For example, in 2002 much agreement existed about the importance of stability in key economic areas. Of first importance is price stability, that is, preventing inflation. This consensus emerged in part from policy mistakes that in the 1970s contributed to **stagflation,** an unusual combination of inflation and economic stagnation. It is not an accident that Presidents Clinton (1993–2001), in the 1990s, and Reagan, in the 1980s, despite their large **partisan** differences, had similar stances on price stability.

Another strength may be a president's standing with the public on particular economic outcomes. Even though a policy may create economic troubles for some workers, a president with high public credibility can often overcome voter concerns because of Americans' longstanding tendency to assume the chief executive's actions are in the nation's best interests. This gives the president the ability to address some social concerns with policies that have economic risks attached to them, but that may be the most effective means to deal with a particular problem.

See also: Chief Diplomat; Chief Executive; Commander in Chief; Executive Departments.

Further Reading

Crenson, Matthew, and Benjamin Ginsburg. *Presidential Power: Unchecked and Unbalanced.* New York: W.W. Norton, 2007.

Roleff, Tamara L. *What Limits Should Be Placed on Presidential Powers?* Farmington Hills, MI: Greenhaven, 2006.

Chief Executive

The president as leader of the **executive** branch. Article II of the Constitution lists the president's powers. Section 1 of the article clearly grants executive power to the president: "the executive Power shall be vested in a President. . . . " Section 3 makes the president responsible for the execution of federal laws: the president "shall take Care that the Laws be faithfully executed. . . . "

In theory, these directives make the president responsible for carrying out—that is, executing—the laws of the federal government. In practice, however, the vagueness of this directive has increased the power of the presidency. For example, by broadly interpreting the authority to execute the law, Grover Cleveland (1885–1889, 1893–1897) used federal troops to break a labor strike in the 1890s and Dwight D. Eisenhower (1953–1961) sent troops to help integrate a public school in Little Rock, Arkansas, in 1957.

Chief Administrator

Although the Founders placed a high priority on the president's executive duties, the Constitution provides very few instructions about the president's tasks as head of the executive branch. Specific presidential administrative powers have evolved as the office of the presidency has grown over the years.

The Constitution does not make direct provisions for the vast administrative structure that the president must oversee. However, in Article II, Section 2, it authorizes the president to demand written reports from the "principal Officer in each of the executive Departments, upon any Subject, relating to the Duties of their respective Offices". This clause implies a division of labor within the executive branch and clearly establishes an administrative hierarchy with the president as chief administrative officer.

Similar to chief executives in private corporations, the chief executive in the White House tries to persuade subordinates in government to conform to presidential objectives. In other words, the chief executive tries to give direction to the administration. Presidents do not have time to follow through on every action taken by the bureaucratic departments and agencies directly under their control. After all, they sit atop a federal executive structure that has approximately three million civilian employees. They must, then, develop techniques that give them control over this vast administrative organization.

Chief of State

The country's leader who symbolizes the nation and presides over ceremonial functions. In many countries this responsibility is fulfilled by a monarch or figurehead with little governmental authority, or an official whose post was created to shelter the chief **executive** from ceremonial drudgery. In the United States, the chief executive is the chief of state.

In the United States, however, the chief of state role involves more than presiding over ceremonial functions for which presidents must smile while they put their numerous other duties—including chief executive, commander in chief, chief diplomat, chief legislator—on hold. Like a monarch, a U.S. president is the embodiment of the American people and a focal point for national unity. In times of crisis, a president's demeanor will have a profound effect on the nation's confidence. Presidents symbolize the country's history, liberty, and strength. They can delegate some ceremonial functions to their representatives, but while they are in office, they cannot escape their chief of state role.

Ceremonial Duties and Functions

As chief of state, presidents preside over functions that range in tone from the solemnity of the inauguration to the informality of a White House barbecue. They greet foreign ambassadors, dedicate monuments, pin medals on war heroes, buy Girl Scout cookies, visit schools, throw out the first ball on opening day of the baseball season, and hold state dinners for foreign heads of state. National ceremonies have much the same purpose for the country as religious rituals have for a church: the development and admiration of shared symbols and sentiments that comfort, motivate, and unify people.

Constitutional Ceremonial Duties

The Constitution obliges presidents to take an oath of office, periodically inform Congress about the state of the Union, and receive "Ambassadors and other public Ministers." Because these constitutional ceremonial duties firmly designate the president as leader of the nation, the first U.S. president, George Washington (1789–1797), and his successors could safely assume the role of chief of state. Both the oath of office ceremony and State of the Union address physically place the president in front of other government officials and focus the nation's attention on the president's opinions and recommendations.

The president's duty to receive ambassadors implies that foreign governments are to regard the president as the official representative of the United States. Because the international community sees the president as chief of state, domestic chief of state responsibilities cannot be assumed gracefully by anyone but the president.

See also: Chief Diplomat; Chief Executive; Constitution of the United States.

Further Reading

Calabresi, Steven G., and Christopher S. Yoo. *The Unitary Executive: From Washington to Bush.* New Haven, CT: Yale University Press, 2008.

Civil Service System

Federal system in which government employees are hired and retained based on merit, rather than political support. The way presidents fill positions in the federal government has been an issue throughout much of U.S. history. In the nineteenth century most federal jobs were filled through **patronage**—that is, presidents awarded jobs to their supporters. Patronage, however, was a power shared with Congress. Although it had no constitutional mandate, Congress by the end of the nineteenth century was able to exert tremendous influence on presidential appointments. Under the patronage system, widespread job turnover occurred after almost every presidential election.

Employees who were qualified for specific jobs but were not of the president's political party had trouble finding government positions. Today, however, only a small percentage of federal employees—usually top-ranking policy-makers—are replaced with each new administration. Most jobs in the federal government are filled through the competitive civil service and are awarded according to the competence of the applicant.

Early Years

The number of federal employees remained low and relatively stable until the early part of the twentieth century. The population of the United States at the time of George Washington's presidency (1789–1797) was about three and a half million, just a little more than the number of civilian federal employees in the mid-1990s. At the beginning of Washington's administration, there were only nine employees in the State Department, fewer than 100 in the War Department, and only about 350 in the entire federal government. The largest department was the Post Office, with seventy-five offices throughout the nation. By the beginning of the nineteenth century, the number of **executive** branch employees had increased to about 2,100. During the Civil War (1861–1865), the federal government employed approximately 37,000 people. By 1900, the federal civil service comprised 208,000 employees.

During and after World War I (1914–1918), however, the number of employees on the executive branch payroll began to expand more rapidly, reaching 570,000 by 1923. The years of the New Deal and the Great **Depression** pretty much overlapped during the 1930s **Great Depression** and the New Deal, Franklin D. Roosevelt's (1933–1945) program to help the nation recover from the Depression, saw tremendous growth in the number of federal employees—from 620,000 in 1933 to 1.3 million in 1939. Federal workers constituted 0.7 percent of the population of 130 million in 1939. By the end of World War II (1939–1945), the number of employees in the federal civil service had reached 3.8 million. Even after the massive war effort ended and federal

A – Z

employment declined, the number of federal workers remained high.

Government by Gentlemen, 1789–1829

When George Washington became president in 1789, he had the opportunity to build an entirely new executive structure and to appoint a fresh slate of civil servants. Not surprisingly, many people attempted to influence his selection of employees.

In setting an early standard, Washington sought to nominate individuals to office on the grounds of "fitness of character." He refused appointment even to many veterans of the Revolutionary War, arguing that past service did not outweigh the need for excellence in the job. He also did not see kinship as a reason for appointment.

Washington's idea of competence, however, did not always consist of looking for people who possessed specific qualifications for certain jobs. Instead, he was interested in the honesty and integrity of his appointees and, above all, in their loyalty to the new federal government. Technical expertise mattered much less than reputation. Washington also strove for equitable geographic representation. In the end, Washington created a civil service that came from the elite of society: the well educated, the well-to-do, and the well respected.

John Adams's administration (1797–1801) moved further toward **partisanship** in the use of presidential appointments. Although Adams's conscience and personal honesty prevented him from using his patronage powers fully, his Federalist administration increasingly manipulated political appointments to maintain its **partisan** advantage.

When Thomas Jefferson (1801–1809) came into office, many expected him to expand the base of political appointments because Jefferson, as a Democratic-Republican, had a sincere commitment to broadening the egalitarian foundation of government. Upon assuming office, he found that Federalists held nearly every government position. Jefferson believed that his presidential election victory in 1800 was a mandate for change, yet he used care in replacing employees. Although he dismissed some of the early Federalist appointees, he retained many more than he fired.

During the twenty years after Jefferson's presidency, the pattern of executive personnel appointments changed very little. Because presidents James Madison (1809–1817), James Monroe (1817–1825), and John Quincy Adams (1825–1829) were also Democratic-Republicans, they found little reason to replace existing employees. As a result, from 1803 to 1828 the makeup of the civil service changed little.

Government by the Common Man, 1829–1883

Andrew Jackson (1829–1837) pushed the civil service into a new era. Many people attribute the patronage practice known as the spoils system to Jackson, and the term "spoils system" did get its name during Jackson's administration, but not from Jackson. Senator William L. Marcy of New York popularized the term in 1832 when he remarked that politicians "see nothing wrong in the rule that to the victor belong the spoils of the enemy."

Still, Jackson's actions probably were based more on his desire to democratize the American public service than on a lack of commitment to merit. In running for the presidency in 1828, Jackson appealed to landless people who recently had won the vote when property ownership was abolished as a voting requirement. Jackson promised **civil service reform,** and stated that he would appoint "men whose diligence and talents will insure in their respective stations able and faithful cooperation." In his inaugural address, Jackson defended the practice of rotating federal employees in government jobs because, he said, the duties of public office did not require any special abilities. He argued, too, that no one had any intrinsic right to an official position.

Because Jackson felt the American people had voted for change when they elected him, he instituted a large-scale spoils system: Those who came from his own political party were awarded jobs. In this respect, Jackson's concern for competence was not as strong as his concern for loyalty. Yet Jackson's method of dispensing spoils removed only a few more people from office than had his predecessors'.

Just as Washington's system of hiring the competent elite had set a pattern for subsequent administrations to follow, Jackson's advocacy of the spoils system made it easier for later presidents to strengthen their political parties and gain congressional support for their programs. By appointing the friends and patrons of various members of Congress, presidents were able to trade patronage for congressional votes. Even though the opposing Whigs were extremely critical of the way Jackson and his successor, Martin Van Buren (1837–1841), used the appointment power, they nonetheless employed the same tactics—although not to the same degree. When William Henry Harrison (1841), a Whig, assumed office, he faced the demands of an estimated 30,000 to 40,000 office seekers.

The spoils system reached its peak during Abraham Lincoln's presidency (1861–1865). In 1861, in an effort to consolidate the federal government behind his program and the war effort, Lincoln, the first Republican to become president, did a more thorough housecleaning than any of his predecessors. In the higher levels of his administration, he replaced nearly every federal employee with Republican loyalists. Lincoln's use of patronage was not without purpose, however: through it he skillfully won cooperation and concessions from a predominantly Republican Congress in managing the Civil War.

Although Jackson's open support of the spoils system had drawn widespread public attention, the subsequent problems and misbehavior of patronage appointees in the administrations of Andrew Johnson (1865–1869) and Ulysses Grant (1869–1877) attracted even more attention to the procedure. No real evidence exists that corruption in the civil service increased during and after Jackson's presidency, but by the late 1860s, the press had certainly begun to pay more attention to corruption and to the problems of the spoils system.

By the time Ulysses Grant became president in 1869, **civil service reform** had became a popular concern among legislators and critics. Indeed, the corruption of the Grant administration did much to contribute to this public dissatisfaction. During Grant's presidency several top officials were found to be involved in kickbacks, land speculation, fraud, embezzlement, tax evasion, and other scandalous behavior. Reformers argued that all of these problems could be traced to the spoils system. True or not, this argument gave conviction and determination to the reform movement that had begun to take shape.

Calls for civil service reform were heard throughout Washington. President Rutherford B. Hayes (1877–1881), who succeeded Grant and had campaigned on a reform-in-government Republican Party platform, also tried to promote a system of merit appointment. Because of opposition from the more **conservative** elements in his own party, however, Hayes was unsuccessful. Hayes, like Grant, used civil service appointments as a means of rewarding those who had helped him reach the presidency.

The Garfield Assassination

Significant civil service reform did not occur until after the assassination of President James A. Garfield (1881). As a member of the House of Representatives, Garfield had supported civil service reform, so when he became president, reformers had high expectations that he would quickly institute meaningful changes in the system. However, Garfield did not initiate reform immediately. The new president instead spent much of his time trying to satisfy thousands of demands for federal jobs by party workers who had helped him in the election.

It is estimated that for every appointment Garfield was able to make, twenty office seekers were turned down. Among those who did not receive an appointment was Charles J. Guiteau. On July 2, 1881, Guiteau shot Garfield as he was walking through a Washington railroad station. After suffering for more than eleven weeks, Garfield died on September 19, 1881. Garfield's successor, Chester A. Arthur (1881–1885), began to support reform measures.

Civil Service Act of 1883

Meaningful civil service reform finally came on January 16, 1883, when Arthur signed the Civil Service Act of 1883, also known as the Pendleton Act, into law. Senator George H. Pendleton (D-OH) had first presented his reform bill to Congress in 1880, but it was not until after Garfield's death that it gained enough momentum to become law. The act required that government employees be chosen "from among those graded highest" in competitive examinations. It also prohibited political parties from requiring federal employees to contribute funds to help party candidates.

Government by the Good, 1883–1906

Passage of the Civil Service Act in 1883 brought about a new era in the administration of civil service jobs. It did not bring about a complete change in the way that presidential appointments were made, but it did signal a change in direction.

The Civil Service Act actually built on the tradition of egalitarianism and equal opportunity that prevailed during the earlier period of public employment. In other words, the authors of the act did not abandon the Jacksonian belief in widespread access to jobs in the federal administrative structure. Instead, they provided for "practical" entrance tests that would ensure that applicants would be able to do their jobs. The drafters of the act had no intention of filling federal positions with an "administrative class" specially educated to administer the government permanently.

The Civil Service Act, which placed the Civil Service Commission within the executive branch, allowed the president to use the commission to make rules and regulations governing the selection of personnel to fill executive positions. The president, with the advice and consent of the Senate, appointed the three-member commission. No more than two members of the commission could be from the same political party. The act did not eliminate presidential influence on appointments covered by the Civil Service Act altogether. Presidents influenced the commission itself just by their power to appoint and remove commission members. Reformers hoped, though, that the members of the commission would raise loud enough public cries to embarrass presidents who tried to bypass their efforts.

When Grover Cleveland (1885–1889, 1893–1897) became president in 1885, he attempted to change the balance of federal workers to favor Democrats by firing Republicans, but only on leaving office did he extend classification to the 10 percent of positions that had not been competitive previously. This extension not only broadened the merit system; it also ensured that Cleveland's political appointees would remain on the job for some time to come—and that their successors, unlike them, would have to take examinations.

Benjamin Harrison (1889–1893), a Republican, followed Cleveland's pattern by firing many opposition party federal workers, hiring members of his own party, and blanketing in many of his party before leaving office. He dismissed more than 35,000 employees in the first year of his administration alone, appointing replacements from the Republican Party.

In 1893, when Cleveland became president for the second time, he once again appointed mostly partisans to fill executive offices. When his presidency ended in 1897, he again blanketed in a large number of his appointees by increasing the classified civil service, this time by a full one-third.

Even though many political employees were protected in their jobs through classification, the number of positions under the merit system increased through this process. By 1897, the newly inaugurated president, William McKinley (1897–1901), had the smallest percentage of patronage jobs to offer of any previous president. Some Republicans suggested that positions placed under the merit system by Cleveland be made political appointments again. However, that became unnecessary when many new, unclassified jobs were created as the federal civil service expanded during the Spanish-American War (1898). This increase allowed McKinley to make political appointments without taking many positions out of the classified category.

Theodore Roosevelt (1901–1909) played a significant role in the growth of the merit system. Benjamin Harrison's appointment of Roosevelt as chairman of the Civil Service Commission in 1889 began a period of innovation and expansion for the merit service. Among his major changes, Roosevelt introduced a promotion system based on individual employees' efficiency records, instituted a program that systematized the hiring of workers in the navy yards, and successfully classified the Bureau of Indian Affairs, which had suffered through many patronage-related scandals.

After he became president, Roosevelt continued to advance the merit system. Between 1901 and 1909 an additional 35,000 jobs acquired civil service classification, making almost 64 percent of federal jobs merit positions. Because he was a Republican who succeeded a Republican,

Roosevelt felt no need to fire vast numbers of federal employees because of their political affiliations. Roosevelt therefore was able to make many civil service improvements without the pressure and demands of patronage.

Government by the Efficient, 1906–1937

The principle of the separation of politics from personnel administration continued to be of primary importance during this period. In addition, a desire for efficiency also developed, mainly from developments in business administration advanced by the scientific management school. The main value of scientific management was efficiency, or doing the job without wasting time, money, and effort. Specifically, during this stage in the development of the federal merit system the Civil Service Commission concentrated on classifying jobs that had a logical relationship to one another and on developing job descriptions for each position. In 1923, Congress passed the Classification Act, which guaranteed the principle of equal pay for equal work. This act allowed jobs to be defined by the responsibilities and qualifications necessary to carry them out. Also, the classification of positions made it possible for examinations to measure objectively the qualifications for a particular position.

When Woodrow Wilson (1913–1921), a Democrat, took office after sixteen years of Republican control, he faced tremendous pressure to "clean house." The Democratic Party pushed for opportunities for patronage, and Wilson's supporters descended on Washington much as other job seekers had in previous years. Wilson acceded to some of the demands and exempted 8,000 internal revenue deputy collectorships from the classified service. However, he opposed other attempts to increase patronage and actually contributed to the growth of the merit system.

Wilson also introduced several measures to make the civil service more impartial. Perhaps his greatest contribution to reform was withstanding pressure from his party to take partisan advantage of World War I (1914–1918). As the war began to occupy more of the federal government's resources and energy, new agencies developed and the number of federal employees increased. Resisting pressure to make these patronage positions, Wilson placed most of the new positions in the competitive service.

Warren G. Harding (1921–1923), a Republican, confronted many of the same pressures Wilson had faced in succeeding a president of the opposing party. The Republicans were as hungry for patronage after eight years of Democratic control of the White House as the Democrats had been after the Republicans' sixteen years in power. Harding, however, was in a much more difficult position than Wilson. As the war machinery demobilized and the need for as large a federal civil service diminished, it became extremely difficult to satisfy Republican office seekers. As a result, Harding reversed some of the earlier reforms, exercising a small measure of patronage by dismissing some employees.

Presidents Calvin Coolidge (1923–1929) and Herbert Hoover (1929–1933) treated the merit system more favorably. Together, they classified about 13,000 positions during their time in office. More significantly, they were both committed to the concept of a competent and efficiently run government, and thus did not allow the reduction of the federal workforce caused by the end of World War I to be accompanied by a reduction of the classified civil service. As a result, the percentage of classified jobs in relation to the entire number of federal jobs amounted to about 80 percent by 1924.

When Franklin D. Roosevelt (1933–1945) became president, Democrats were eager for patronage jobs after twelve years of Republican control of the White House. This time, however, the **Great Depression,** which had begun in 1929, during Hoover's presidency, compounded the pressure for political appointments. With the unusual lack of private sector jobs, the prospect of public employment was especially appealing to Democratic Party loyalists. The security of jobs in the merit system, and what were regarded as outstanding benefits such as sick leave, retirement pensions, and paid vacations, made the civil service especially attractive to those seeking employment of any kind. In the face of this challenge, the future of the merit system seemed uncertain.

Government by Administrators, 1937–1955

As the government grew larger in its efforts to solve the social and economic problems caused by the depression, the need for a stronger, more active administration emerged. In assuming this more active role, public administrators (that is, civil servants) found themselves increasingly involved in establishing policy.

With the public relying more and more on New Deal programs from 1937 to 1945, it became apparent to Roosevelt that the success of these programs depended on their efficient administration. He therefore began to push for civil service reform.

Roosevelt's extension of merit had a twofold purpose. Not only did he attempt to increase the efficiency of New Deal programs by putting a large number of positions in the protected category, he also blanketed in thousands of Democrats who had been placed in their jobs through patronage. Roosevelt's moves befuddled Republicans. If they opposed him, they would open themselves to the charge of opposing the merit system itself. Their only option was to wait for a Republican administration and face the problem then.

As more Roosevelt Democrats were blanketed in, many reformers became concerned that the principle of political **neutrality** would be violated. Because most federal employees owed their jobs to FDR and the Democratic Party, it seemed normal for them to campaign for the Democrats.

In the election of 1938, however, a coalition of Republicans and **conservative** Democrats won control of Congress, and in 1939 they passed the Act to Prevent Pernicious Political Activities, known as the Hatch Act. The original Hatch Act prohibited federal workers from taking an active role in the political management of campaigns. Federal workers could vote, attend political rallies, and talk privately about politics. However, they were prohibited from participating in partisan voter registration drives, endorsing candidates, or working for or against a candidate. In addition, the Hatch Act prohibited the use of rank to force federal employees to support certain candidates or to make political contributions.

When Harry S. Truman (1945–1953) became president, he faced very little demand for patronage jobs. The Democrats had been in control of the executive branch since 1933. Between 1946 and 1951, Truman blanketed in another 35,000 jobs, bringing the percentage of executive branch jobs in the classified service to 87 percent.

Not surprisingly, Republican president Dwight Eisenhower (1953–1961) faced patronage problems when he took office because Democrats had controlled the presidency since 1933. No president since McKinley had as few patronage positions to distribute as Eisenhower did, because so many workers from the opposition party been locked into their jobs. Eisenhower ultimately resorted to a technique used by many of his predecessors: He unclassified jobs that originally had been filled on a noncompetitive basis and then put under merit protection.

Because previous Democratic administrations had blanketed in so many positions that only about 15,000 employees could be dismissed for political purposes, the Eisenhower administration felt justified in unclassifying some positions. On March 31, 1953, Eisenhower canceled civil service removal protection for 134,000 full-time positions. Half of this number, however, retained removal protection through the Veterans Preference Act of 1944, and 68,000 were overseas positions not usually subject to patronage. Although he did not engage in a wholesale housecleaning, Eisenhower's unclassifications marked a setback for the merit system.

Further confusing matters for Republicans, Democrats held many of the important policy positions, and they were protected from dismissal by civil service regulations. Thus in making the transition to power, Eisenhower had to determine how to make a largely Democratic federal bureaucracy responsive to the policies of a Republican administration. Conflicts existed between political appointees and career employees, or those whose activities the new political appointees would oversee.

Government by Professionals, 1955 to the Present

In 1955, the civil service began requiring applicants to take the Federal Service Entrance Exam (FSEE). This exam had several important objectives. First, it served as a single point of entry to the civil service system. Applicants could take a standard examination that agencies could uses to make personnel decisions. Second, the common entrance examination made it easier to move employees from one agency to another. When each agency had its own entrance qualifications

Civil Service Reforms

With the passage of the Civil Service Act of 1883 (Pendleton Act), the executive branch experienced its most dramatic restructuring since George Washington first set up the federal bureaucracy. Known as the Magna Carta of civil service reform, the act:

- Created a **bipartisan** Civil Service Commission of three members appointed by the president with the consent of the Senate; members were subject to removal by the president at any time.
- Gave the Civil Service Commission a mandate to prepare rules for the management of the competitive civil service, consisting of those federal employees who were under the rules and regulations of the commission.
- Allowed the president to issue executive orders bringing positions into the competitive service that had previously been outside. It also allowed the president to remove any positions at any time from the competitive service.
- Based entrance into the merit system on competitive examination.
- Provided that examinations should test the practical skills required to do the job.
- Allowed applicants, regardless of age, to enter into the competitive civil service at any rank or grade for which they were qualified.
- Provided that competitive civil service employees could not be removed for refusing to contribute money or services to a political party.

In 1978 Congress passed the Civil Service Reform Act, the major civil service reform effort of the twentieth century. The act became effective January 1, 1979, and incorporated a wide variety of provisions. The reform act:

- Created the Office of Personnel Management and the Merit Systems Protection Board, replacing the Civil Service Commission.
- Delegated personnel management authority to agencies themselves.
- Streamlined the process used to dismiss employees.
- Strengthened procedures to protect whistle-blowers.
- Established a comprehensive statutory framework for conducting labor-management relations.
- Authorized a merit pay system for midlevel supervisors based on performance rather than longevity.
- Established a Senior Executive Service (SES) for top-level career decision-makers.
- Required that objective and job-related performance standards be developed for members of the SES.
- Enacted both a set of explicit merit principles and a statement of prohibited personnel practices.

Source: George J. Gordon, Public Administration in America (New York: St. Martin's, 1992), 284.

Government reformers had long called for a civil service system for the hiring of federal employees. The Civil Service Act of 1883 was the first meaningful law to require some government employees to be hired based on merit rather than on the "spoils system."

and examinations, it was difficult to foster an environment in which broad professional skills were encouraged. Third, the FSEE made recruiting more efficient. Recruiters from the Civil Service Commission could visit colleges and universities and offer potential applicants a standardized examination.

By placing a premium on professional skills, the FSEE marked another change in emphasis in the federal civil service: the elevation of professionalism, and therefore effectiveness and efficiency, in the federal government to match that of the business community. Consequently, since 1955 the federal government has hired more professionally trained personnel than ever before, including military officers who have entered the civil service, those who have trained to become Foreign Service officers, civil engineers, physicians, educators, lawyers, foresters, and scientists from almost all disciplines.

Civil Service Reform Act of 1978

The conflicting functions of the Civil Service Commission, as both manager and watchdog of civil servants, led many reformers to demand that some of the commission's duties be assigned to another agency. President Jimmy Carter (1977–1981) oversaw the most sweeping reform of the civil service since 1883. The Civil Service Reform Act of 1978 (CSRA), primarily the work of Alan K. Campbell, head of the Civil Service Commission during the Carter administration, abolished the 95-year-old commission. In its place, the act set up the Office of Personnel Management and the Merit Systems Protection Board. The CSRA recognized the conflict between the dual functions of personnel management and protection of employees against merit violations by setting up new administrative machinery to perform these roles. One of the main goals of the CSRA was to increase presidential control of the bureaucracy by increasing the political responsiveness of top career civil servants. Civil service restructuring became effective on January 1, 1979.

See also: Cabinet; Government Agencies and Corporations.

Further Reading

Pfiffner, James P., and Douglas A. Brook (eds.). *The Future of Merit: Twenty Years After the Civil Service Reform Act.* Baltimore, MD: Johns Hopkins University Press, 2000.

Schultz, David A., and Robert Moranto. *The Politics of Civil Service Reform.* New York: Peter Lang Publishers, 1998.

Cleveland, Grover, Administrations of (1885–1889, 1893–1897)

Government under the twenty-second and twenty-fourth president of the United States. Grover Cleveland is the only president to serve two non-

consecutive terms. In 1881, Cleveland was elected mayor of Buffalo, New York, and immediately took action to reform the city's government. His well-deserved reputation as a reformer earned him the Democratic nomination for governor of New York in 1882. He easily won the election and assumed office on January 3, 1883. As governor, Cleveland combated corruption and the spoils system with his **veto** power.

Cleveland's successes and reform principles made him an attractive presidential candidate in 1884. He was nominated on the second ballot at the Democratic Convention in Chicago. The Republicans nominated James G. Blaine, a senator from Maine, who had been linked to several scandals.

Cleveland's election hopes were damaged, however, when a newspaper report disclosed that he had fathered an out-of-wedlock child, whom he continued to support. Cleveland admitted his paternity and instructed his campaign workers to

An 1893 banner celebrates the return of Grover Cleveland (1885–1889, 1893–1897) and his wife, Frances, to the White House in March of that year. Cleveland is the only president to serve two non-consecutive terms. (Library of Congress)

"tell the truth." Cleveland also was attacked for not serving in the Civil War (1861–1865), although Blaine had avoided service as well. In the end, Cleveland received just 60,000 more votes than Blaine and defeated him 219–182 in the electoral college.

Cleveland's First Term

During his first term, Cleveland attempted to bring to the presidency the same reform principles that he had followed as governor of New York. For example, he implemented the Pendleton Civil Service Act, signed into law by Chester A. Arthur (1881–1885), which shifted thousands of government jobs from **patronage** to a **merit system** of hiring. He also vetoed numerous private pension **bills** for Civil War veterans. Cleveland was unsuccessful, however, in lowering the **tariff,** which he considered to be unfair to farmers and workers and unnecessary given the large federal budget **surplus.**

In 1888, Cleveland ran for reelection against Indiana Republican Benjamin Harrison. Although Cleveland garnered 100,000 more popular votes than Harrison, he lost to Harrison in the electoral college, 233–168. Had Cleveland won his home state of New York's 36 electoral votes, as he did in 1884, he would have won the election.

After leaving office, Cleveland moved to New York City, where he practiced law. Four years later, his party again nominated him for president. The 1892 election was a rematch between Cleveland and President Benjamin Harrison. Cleveland easily defeated Harrison in the electoral college, 277–145, but received only 46.3 percent of the popular vote because the **third-party** candidacy of James B. Weaver of the People's Party drew more than one million votes.

Cleveland's Second Term

Soon after Cleveland took office for the second time, the Panic of 1893 sparked a deep economic depression. More than 500 banks failed, and unemployment rose sharply as businesses went bankrupt. Cleveland believed **inflation** and a decline of business confidence had caused the depression. Thus, with the support of many congressional Republicans, he convinced Congress in 1893 to repeal the mildly inflationary Sherman Silver Purchase Act. He also authorized the purchase of several million ounces of gold from private holders to replenish the government's shrinking gold reserves.

The depression lingered, however, and in 1894 the economic situation worsened when a strike at the Pullman Palace Car Company near Chicago led to a railroad strike throughout the Midwest. After violence erupted in Chicago, Cleveland sent federal troops there to break the strike, despite the protests of Illinois governor John P. Altgeld. Cleveland's action earned him support from the business community but the anger of labor organizations.

Although the depression had greeted Cleveland as he entered office, he received much of the blame for the nation's economic troubles. After Republicans gained congressional seats in the 1894 midterm elections, Cleveland had difficulty exerting much control over Congress or even his

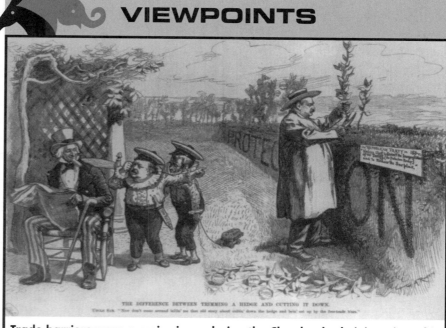

VIEWPOINTS

THE DIFFERENCE BETWEEN TRIMMING A HEDGE AND CUTTING IT DOWN.

Trade barriers were a major issue during the Cleveland administration. This 1888 cartoon shows President Cleveland (1885–1889, 1893–1897) trimming the "barrier hedge" while legislators complain to Uncle Sam. (Library of Congress)

A–Z

party. The 1896 Democratic convention nominated William Jennings Bryan of Nebraska for president, and many Democratic candidates distanced themselves from Cleveland.

Regarding foreign affairs, in March 1893 Cleveland withdrew a treaty negotiated in the closing months of the Harrison administration that would have **annexed** Hawaii. He considered the treaty unfair and blocked any further attempt to **annex** the islands. He also resisted the temptation to yield to public pressure and go to war with Spain over their suppression of a rebellion in Cuba that began in 1895.

Upon leaving office for the second time, Cleveland settled in Princeton, New Jersey. He devoted his time to fishing, delivering lectures, and writing books and articles. In 1901, he was appointed to the board of trustees of Princeton University, and in 1904 he became the president of that board while future president Woodrow Wilson (1913–1921) served as president of the university. During his last years, Cleveland's heart and kidneys weakened. He died of a heart attack in Princeton, New Jersey, in 1908.

See also: Arthur, Chester A., Administration of (1881–1885); Electoral College; Harrison, Benjamin, Administration of (1889–1893); McKinley, William, Administration of (1897–1901).

Further Reading

Graff, Henry F. *Grover Cleveland.* New York: Times Books, 2002.

Jeffers, H.P. *An Honest President: The Life and Presidencies of Grover Cleveland.* New York: Harper Perennial, 2002.

Clinton, Bill, Administration of (1993–2001)

Government under the forty-second president of the United States. Bill Clinton was born William Jefferson Blythe IV, in Hope, Arkansas, two months after his father was killed in a car accident. Four years later he was adopted by his mother's second husband, Roger Clinton. The future president grew up in Hot Springs, Arkansas, where he excelled in school and played saxophone in the band. In 1968, he graduated from Georgetown University in Washington, D.C., with a degree in international affairs. He earned a Rhodes Scholarship and attended Oxford University in England for two years. He returned to the United States in 1970 and entered Yale University Law School, earning his law degree in 1973.

Political Career

Politics has been Clinton's lifelong passion. In 1972, he managed the Texas campaign of Democratic presidential nominee George McGovern. After a brief time as a staff member of the House Judiciary Committee, he began teaching law at the University of Arkansas in 1973. The next year, he ran unsuccessfully for a House seat. Although he lost, his strong showing established his position in Arkansas politics.

In 1976, Clinton was elected attorney general of Arkansas. Then in 1978, the thirty-two-year-old Clinton defeated a crowded field of Democratic contenders for the gubernatorial nomination and easily won the general election. Two years later, however, Clinton lost his bid for reelection.

After his defeat, Clinton went to work for the Little Rock law firm Wright, Lindsay, and Jennings, but spent much of his time preparing to retake the governorship. During his 1982 campaign, he declared that the tax increases of his first term had been a mistake. He won and was reelected to a two-year term in 1984 and to four-year terms in 1986 and 1990.

During the late 1980s and early 1990s, Clinton achieved national prominence as a reform governor and was often mentioned as a future presidential candidate. He served two terms as chair of the National Governors Association. In 1990 and 1991, he also headed the Democratic Leadership Council, a national organization of Democrats who favored the party's realignment to more moderate positions. On October 3, 1991, Clinton announced he would seek his party's presidential nomination.

In the general election, Clinton faced **incumbent** George H.W. Bush (1989–1993) and billionaire Ross Perot, who ran as an independent. Bush's support had been weakened by a stagnant economy and a widespread belief that he had little interest in domestic policy. Clinton promised to make economic policy and the middle class his top priorities, promoting himself as a fiscally conscientious agent of change who would reform the country's health care, welfare, and education systems. He chose Senator Al Gore of Tennessee as his running mate. The two young southern Democrats (both then in their mid-forties) projected a youthful energy that appealed to many voters, including younger voters. Clinton won the election with 43 percent of the popular vote and 370 electoral votes. Bush finished second with 37 percent and only 168 electoral votes. Perot garnered nearly twenty million votes, almost half of Bush's total.

Presidency

In 1993, Clinton scored three major victories. His aggressive lobbying led to the passage of a budget plan that was projected to reduce the anticipated deficit by about $500 billion over five years. The House, voting along strict party lines, passed the budget 218–216 on August 5; the next day the Senate passed it 51–50, with Vice President Gore casting the tie-breaking vote. Later in the year, Clinton scored major **legislative** successes with the North American Free Trade Agreement (NAFTA), primarily on the strength of Republican votes, and the Brady **bill,** named after the presidential press secretary who was gravely wounded when a gunman attempted to assassinate President Ronald Reagan in 1981. The bill, which mandated a five-day waiting period for the purchase of a handgun, was the first major gun-control legislation to pass Congress since 1968.

In 1994, however, Clinton was less successful. With First Lady Hillary Clinton serving as the head of Clinton's task force on health care, the administration attempted to advance a major reform plan. Republicans attacked it as overly complex, expensive, and bureaucratic. By early fall, lacking sufficient congressional, industry, or public support, the bill was withdrawn without coming to a vote in either house.

The 1994 congressional elections stunningly realigned the politics of Washington, D.C. With many Republican candidates campaigning against Clinton's policies, Republicans gained control of both houses of Congress for the first time in four

decades. Clinton suddenly faced an aggressive, **conservative,** Republican-controlled Congress intent on rolling back years of Democratic legislation. Congress also reinvigorated an ethics investigation arising from investments the Clintons had made in a failed Arkansas land development project known as "Whitewater" during his time as governor, establishing a charged political climate in Washington.

During 1995, Clinton blocked many Republican priorities with adept use of the **veto,** a weapon he did not use during his first two years in office. Most notably, Clinton vetoed Republican legislation to balance the budget in seven years, terming the proposed cuts in health care, education, environment, and welfare as too severe. With the polls showing strong support for his position, Clinton was able to keep a firm hand in the budget negotiations. His stubborn style proved successful, and the final 1996 fiscal spending bill reflected his priorities, not the deeper cuts sought by the congressional Republicans.

As he had promised during his campaign, Clinton deemphasized foreign policy to focus on domestic problems, but world events soon altered this approach. Clinton actively promoted a broadening of the accord signed earlier between Israel and the Palestine Liberation Organization (PLO) on achieving peace in the Middle East, and he advanced negotiations between warring factions in Ireland. Clinton also expanded the humanitarian mission in Somalia that had been launched during the Bush administration. However, when U.S. military units began experiencing casualties, Clinton withdrew American troops. In 1994, Clinton sent American forces to Haiti to reestablish the deposed government of Jean-Bertrand Aristide.

Clinton's largest foreign policy endeavor during his first term was in the Balkans. In 1995, he sent twenty thousand U.S. troops to a NATO peacekeeping mission in war-torn Bosnia. The deployment followed the signing of a complex U.S.-brokered peace agreement in Dayton, Ohio. Critics charged that the United States had no vital interests in Bosnia, that the troops would be targets, and that the factions would resume fighting when the NATO force eventually withdrew. However, Clinton followed through with his commitment to deploy American peacekeepers if a peace agreement was signed.

During the second half of 1996, Clinton moved to the political center in preparation for his November reelection bid. He signed, despite opposition from **liberal** Democrats, a landmark welfare reform bill pushed by the Republican Congress. The Republicans might have gone further than Clinton wanted, but "ending welfare as we know it" was part of his campaign platform. Clinton also signed Republican bills to phase out most farm subsidies and establish a presidential line-item veto (later found **unconstitutional** by the Supreme Court), and Democratic bills to increase the minimum wage and provide for health insurance portability.

Clinton faced former Senate majority leader Robert J. (Bob) Dole in the 1996 presidential election. Despite several embarrassing White House ethics questions and the ongoing inquiries into the Whitewater affair, Clinton overwhelmingly led Dole in the polls throughout the campaign. He benefited from having led the country during a strong economy, low inflation and unemployment, and the perception of many voters that congressional Republicans had been exceedingly harsh in pursuit of their own agenda. In fact, President Clinton received 49 percent of the popular vote and defeated Dole 379–159 in the electoral college.

In 1997, Clinton and the Republican majority in Congress struck a historic agreement to balance the federal budget within five years. However, with a strong economy boosting federal tax receipts, a $70 billion **surplus**—the first government surplus in twenty-nine years—was attained just one year later. The debate in Washington quickly turned from how to balance the budget to how to spend the surplus.

Despite his popularity and many successes in office, on December 19, 1998, Clinton was **impeached** by the House of Representatives. The **impeachment** grew out of an investigation by Independent Counsel Kenneth Starr into reports that Clinton had lied to cover up a sexual relationship with a White House intern, Monica Lewinsky. The relationship had come to light because of a sexual harassment suit brought against Clinton by a former Arkansas state employee, Paula Corbin Jones, and Clinton's efforts to conceal his relationship with Lewinsky from Jones's attorneys.

President Bill Clinton (1993–2001) successfully mobilized public support to win passage of the North American Free Trade Agreement (NAFTA) in 1993. (Michael Jenkins, CQ)

Clinton acknowledged "an inappropriate relationship" with Lewinsky in a televised address on August 17, 1998, and Starr, on September 9, turned over to the House what he termed was "substantial and credible information that may constitute grounds" for impeaching the president.

Despite his televised admission, Clinton's standing in public opinion polls held strong. Through the last two months of 1998, the House Judiciary Committee heard testimony and then voted virtually on party lines to **impeach** Clinton on four counts. On December 19, the full House, again almost on strict party lines, voted for two articles of impeachment (charging Clinton with giving false and misleading testimony and obstructing justice). Clinton thus became the second president in U.S. history—Andrew Johnson (1865–1869) was the first—to be impeached.

Beginning on January 7, 1999, Chief Justice William H. Rehnquist presided over Clinton's trial in the Senate. Senate leaders set ground rules in which no witnesses were called, but House managers and White House lawyers were allowed to assert their cases. The trial's outcome, however, was never in doubt as the Republicans held only fifty-five seats, and a two-thirds vote of Senate members (or sixty-seven votes) was needed for conviction. On February 12, the Senate found the president not guilty on both counts. Not a single Democrat voted against the president on either count; in fact, five Republicans broke ranks to vote against the obstruction of justice charge.

In foreign policy during his second term, Clinton increased U.S. involvement in the turbulent Balkans after reports of widespread atrocities in Serbia's **ethnic cleansing** campaign against ethnic Albanians, many of whom were Muslims, in the Serbian province of Kosovo. After the failure of negotiations with Serbian president Slobodan Milosevic in 1999, NATO nations led by U.S. warplanes began an extensive bombing campaign against Milosevic's Yugoslavia, flying more than thirty-five thousand **sorties** and inflicting devastating damage on that nation's infrastructure. After eleven weeks of bombing, Milosevic finally pulled out of Kosovo, allowing NATO peacekeepers in and giving Clinton a foreign policy triumph.

Clinton spent part of his last year in office trying to broker a historic peace agreement between Israel and the Palestinians. Despite encouraging progress, disagreement over the status of Jerusalem and the eruption of violence in the Middle East in September 2000 brought the talks to a halt.

Clinton remained embroiled in scandal through his last days in office. Just hours before leaving the White House Clinton pardoned more than 130 people. These included his brother Roger, publishing heiress Patricia Hearst, and billionaire financier Marc Rich; the Rich pardon was particularly controversial as he had been indicted for tax evasion and had been a fugitive in Switzerland for twenty years.

Clinton has spent his time out of office traveling the globe and giving speeches. He also vigorously campaigned for Hillary Clinton during her quest for the 2008 Democratic presidential nomination.

See also: Bush, George H.W., Administration of (1989–1993); Bush, George W., Administration of (2001–2009); Impeachment, Presidential.

Further Reading

Clinton, Bill. *My Life.* New York: Knopf, 2004.
Harris, John F. *The Survivor: Bill Clinton in the White House.* New York: Random House, 2006.

Commander in Chief

The power of the United States president as commander of the nation's armed forces. The Framers of the Constitution distrusted both **executive** and military power, and believed the possibility for **tyranny** was great when the two were combined. Among the colonial grievances cited in the Declaration of Independence were the charges that the British monarch had "kept among us, in times of peace, Standing Armies without the Consent of our legislatures" and "affected to render the Military independent of and superior to the Civil Power."

The Framers therefore rejected a proposal to grant the president the authority to declare war. Instead, they divided the war-making power between the executive and Congress, and placed a strict time limit on military **appropriations.** Although many war powers, including the decision to go to war, could be safely placed in the hands of Congress, command of U.S. forces during a conflict required the unified and flexible leadership that only a single person could provide. As Alexander Hamilton noted: "Of all the cares or concerns of government, the direction of war most peculiarly demands those qualities which distinguish the exercise of power by a single hand."

The Framers therefore assigned the commander-in-chief power to the presidency. Few presidents, however, have been as well suited, in skills and integrity, for the role as the first commander in chief, George Washington. Some presidents have mismanaged military affairs, a few have misused their military power, and there have been many confrontations between the executive and **legislative** branches over the scope and use of the war powers, with charges of abuse of power often being leveled at the president. Nevertheless, contrary to the experiences of many other nations, no president has used the forces at his command to interfere with the ordinary course of electoral accountability or the powers and functions of the other branches.

Because conflicts over the executive's use of the war power typically arise during military engagements, efforts to check the president often falter in the face of ongoing events. During the Civil War (1861–1865), World War I (1914–1918), and World War II (1939–1945), presidents boldly and firmly interpreted the commander-in-chief power broadly. In each case, American success stopped any attempts to limit presidential power.

The aftermath of the Vietnam War (1964–1973) marked the first time that Congress aimed systematically to constrain the president's ability to send troops into combat. After the terrorist attacks of September 11, 2001, the American public and Congress followed the traditional pattern of "rallying 'round the flag" to support the president's foreign and military policies. Nevertheless, as the global war on terrorism declared by George W. Bush (2001–2009) continued, particularly with difficulties occurring in the war Bush pushed for in Iraq, attempts to restrict presidential power in military affairs have begun to develop.

Distribution of War-Making Power

The Framers of the Constitution made the highest civilian officer also the commander in chief of the nation's military forces. Article II, Section 2 of the Constitution states: "The President shall be Commander in Chief of the Army and Navy of the United States, and of the Militia of the several States, when called into the actual Service of the United States." This statement is all the Constitution says about the president's war-making power.

The Framers did not regard war-making as an inherently executive function. Indeed, they originally gave the federal official to provide for decisive action in emergencies, the balance of constitutional powers still favored Congress. Textual ambiguities have, nevertheless, allowed presidents to argue that they possess the power or duty traditionally associated with the office of supreme military commander. Consequently, wide-ranging actions and powers have been justified under a broad interpretation of the commander-in-chief clause. In addition, foreign policy and chief executive powers give presidents responsibilities in the area of national security that are used in conjunction with the commander-in-chief authority to expand the president's war powers.

Power to Declare War

Congress's power to raise armies and fund wars, and the president's command of the military in times of war, are unquestioned. The authority to decide when and where to employ military force, however, has been a source of conflict between the executive and legislative branches. The Framers could have given the president the power to declare war with the "advice and consent of the Senate," as they had with the treaty power. Instead, the Constitution grants Congress the sole authority to take the country from a state of peace into a state of war. By giving Congress the power to declare war, the Framers sought to contain executive ambition. They also sought to ensure that these important decisions would be made by the deliberative branch and especially by the representatives of the people who would be called on to shoulder the cost in lives and treasure.

The Framers recognized that speed and secrecy, which only a single decision-maker could provide, were essential to the safety of the nation. By separating the power to declare war from the power to conduct it, the Framers left the power to repel sudden attacks in the hands of the president. Congress, in short, decides when to go to war unless the hostile actions of another nation thrust the United States into a state of war. In *The Federalist Papers,* Hamilton, one of the Constitutional Convention's foremost advocates of a strong chief executive, interpreted the commander-in-chief power narrowly: The president is to be commander-in-chief of the army and navy of the United States.

Fearing that a legislature, cumbersome in itself and frequently out of session, might inhibit action in an emergency, the delegates separated the power to declare war from the power to command or direct the military forces. The latter was given to the president. This division of responsibility left the president free to repel invasions and respond to other acts of war. The Framers were careful, though, to prevent the president

Major U.S. Military Interventions, 1961–2008

The following are major instances of U.S. military intervention since 1961 (not including participation in multinational peacekeeping forces, such as those deployed in Lebanon in the 1980s and Somalia and Bosnia in the 1990s):

November 1961. Navy ships and planes arrive off the Dominican Republic as show of force to discourage members of the Trujillo family from attempting to retake the government they lost when dictator Rafael Trujillo was assassinated the previous May.

May–July 1962. A marine expeditionary unit of five thousand lands in Thailand to support the government against threat of outside communist pressure. Marines depart nine weeks later.

October–December 1962. Challenging a Soviet introduction of missiles into Cuba, President Kennedy orders 180 U.S. Navy ships and a B-52 bomber force carrying atomic bombs into the Caribbean to effect a quarantine. Troop carrier squadrons of the U.S. Air Force Reserve are recalled to active duty when Soviet premier Nikita Khrushchev agrees to withdraw the missiles.

May 1963. A U.S. Marine battalion is positioned off the coast of Haiti in the wake of domestic protest against the Duvalier regime and a threat of intervention by the neighboring Dominican Republic.

November 1964. U.S. transport aircraft in the Congo carry Belgian paratroopers in an operation to rescue civilians, among them sixty Americans held hostage by antigovernment rebels near Stanleyville.

May 1964–January 1973. Beginning as retaliation for the downing of American reconnaissance planes flying over Laos, U.S. Navy jets attack Pathet Lao communist strongholds. Air attacks on Laos continue into the 1970s.

April 1965. After a communist-leaning revolt in the Dominican Republic, President Lyndon B. Johnson dispatches 21,500 U.S. troops to protect Americans and to offer supplies and military assistance to locals. By fall, constitutional government is restored.

June 1967. During the Arab-Israeli War, President Johnson sends the U.S. Sixth Fleet within fifty miles of the Syrian coast as a warning to the Soviet Union against entering the conflict.

July–December 1967. Responding to an appeal from Congolese president Joseph-Désiré Mobutu, President Johnson sends three C-130 transport planes with crews to aid government forces battling white mercenaries and Katangese rebels.

April–June 1970. U.S. ground troops attack communist sanctuaries in Cambodia.

May 1975. President Gerald R. Ford sends combined force of navy, marine, and air force to rescue thirty-nine crew members of the U.S. merchant ship *Mayaguez*, which had been captured by Cambodian communists.

April 1980. Ninety-man U.S. commando team in Iran aborts effort to rescue American hostages held in the U.S. embassy in Tehran. Eight die in collision between transport plane and helicopter.

October 1983. U.S. Marines and troops from neighboring eastern Caribbean nations invade the island of Grenada.

April 1986. President Ronald Reagan orders air strikes from the Gulf of Sidra against Libyan military installations in response to terrorist attacks.

(continued on next page)

A – Z

A - Z

Major U.S. Military Interventions, 1961–2008, *continued*

1986–1988. American ships patrol the Persian Gulf during Iran-Iraq war. Thirty-seven American sailors are killed in attack on U.S. vessel in 1987.

December 1989. After fatal attack on an American serviceman in Panama, President George H. W. Bush sends 27,000 American troops into Panama, overthrowing dictator Manuel Noriega.

January–February 1991. After Iraq invades and occupies Kuwait in August 1990, Bush begins massive American military buildup in the Mideast (to about 500,000 U.S. soldiers). In January 1991 Congress invokes War Powers Resolution for the second time and authorizes use of military force. From January 16 to February 23, United States and its allies fly almost 100,000 air missions against Iraqi positions. After brief pause, a land invasion is launched. Iraqi troops are routed in one hundred hours of fighting; seventy-two U.S. soldiers are killed.

December 1994. President Bill Clinton sends troops to Haiti to peacefully restore the regime of Bertrand Aristide.

February 1995; August–September 1995. President Clinton orders air strikes in Bosnia-Herzegovnia to thwart Serbian aggression.

August 1998. Clinton orders missile strikes against sites in Afghanistan and Sudan in order to destroy centers of terrorist activity. Osama bin Laden, thought to be behind the 1998 terrorist bombings of American embassies in Kenya and Tanzania, was said to be at the Afghanistan site, but he avoided injury.

1999. Clinton orders a massive air campaign against Serbian targets in the Federal Republic of Yugoslavia to alleviate Serbian ethnic cleansing of ethnic Albanians. The Serbs are successfully driven out.

2001–2002. In the aftermath of the September 11, 2001, terrorist attacks against the World Trade Center in New York City and the Pentagon, President George W. Bush orders the deployment of several thousand American ground troops to Afghanistan and extensive air action against the country's controlling Taliban regime, as well as the capture or death of Al Qaeda terrorist leader and September 11 mastermind Osama bin Laden. The objective is to disrupt and destroy terrorist training facilities and bases. The Taliban is driven from power with the help of Afghan allies, but bin Laden escapes. The action is dubbed Operation Enduring Freedom.

2003–present. President Bush receives authorization from Congress in October 2002 to invade Iraq if the Saddam Hussein regime fails to comply with United Nations directives and American demands to verify that it does not possess weapons of mass destruction. In March 2003, an American-dominated force invades Iraq, quickly overrunning the country and toppling the Hussein regime. In May, Bush declares "mission accomplished," but an insurgency rapidly develops, and soon the 130,000 American troops are battling for control of the country. Terrorist bombings, killings, and kidnappings escalate, and sectarian violence among Iraq's three main ethnic groups—Shiites, Sunnis, and Kurds—increases. Bush comes under increasingly heavy criticism that his administration deceived the American people regarding the justification and evidence for the invasion, that it failed to plan for regime stabilization after the initial invasion, and that the size of the American force was inadequate to secure the country. By the end of 2008, with the war becoming increasingly unpopular in the United States, more than 2,500 American soldiers had died. In late 2008, the Iraqi and American governments reached an agreement to withdraw all American troops by the end of 2011.

Sources: Congressional Quarterly Weekly Report, October 29, 1983, 2222; CQ Weekly, various issues.

Since the end of World War II (1939–1941), the United States has exercised its military strength across the globe to protect American citizens and American property.

from initiating a war on his own authority, and Congress was given most war-related powers.

As Congress's enumerated war powers indicate, the Framers intended Congress to have full control over the size and character of any national armed forces. A president seeking to become a military dictator would be hindered by Congress's exclusive authority to raise, equip, and organize the armed forces. This includes the authority to eliminate all or any part of the standing forces. Presidents might wish to act, but without Congress's support they would lack the necessary tools to do so.

The exact authority of the commander in chief was left undefined. Nothing is said directly about the president's authority to initiate military actions short of war in the absence of an invasion or attack. Similarly, the Constitution says nothing directly about the power of Congress to control the scope of conflict once war has been declared.

In sum, the consensus of the founding generation was, as President Washington argued, that the Constitution "vests the power of declaring war with Congress; therefore no offensive expedition of importance can be undertaken until they have deliberated upon the subject, and authorized such a measure." Although some ambiguity remains about what an expedition "of importance" would be, the general thrust is clear.

The historical record, however, is far more complicated. Congress has declared war only five times—the War of 1812 (1812–1814), the Mexican War (1846–1848), the Spanish-American War (1898), World War I, and World War II—and yet the United States has been involved in more than one hundred violent military conflicts. Only some of these have been explicitly authorized by Congress, and some of the unauthorized actions were quite large in scale and arose from radically expansive interpretations of the commander-in-chief power.

This historical record suggests that presidents, having direct command of military forces and being responsible for defending the nation, have been in a better position than Congress to exploit the constitutional ambiguity. When presidents have believed a war or military action to be necessary, they usually have found ways to maneuver the nation into a conflict. Particularly after a

direct attack on the United States, such as Pearl Harbor in 1941 or the terrorist attacks of September 11, 2001, presidents have directed military action with full support from Congress and the public. Even if military action extends beyond the immediate response to the attack, as was the case with the Iraq war in 2003, Congress usually defers to presidential leadership and direction in military affairs.

See also: Constitutional Convention and the Presidency; Chief Diplomat; Chief Economist; Chief Executive; Chief of State.

Further Reading

Fisher, Louis. *Presidential War Power.* Lawrence, KS: University Press of Kansas, 2004.

Yoo, John. *The Powers of War and Peace: The Constitution and Foreign Affairs after 9/11.* Chicago: University of Chicago Press, 2006.

Commerce, Department of

See Department of Commerce.

Constitution of the United States

The governing document of the United States since 1788. The Constitution not only defines the basic form of national government, but also the political relationship between the federal government and the states. The Constitution established the three branches of the government—**executive, legislative,** and judicial—as well as a **bicameral,** or two-house, Congress.

Prior to **ratification,** or approval, of the Constitution by the states, the country operated under the Articles of Confederation. The Articles created a weak central government that had little power to compel the states to follow its orders. Many early leaders such as George Washington (1789–1797) and Thomas Jefferson (1801–1809) feared that the country could not survive without a stronger central authority. As a result, in 1787, national leaders met in Philadelphia to revise the Articles. The delegates to that meeting, known as the Constitutional Convention, ended up abandoning the Articles and creating an entirely new governmental structure as set forth in the Constitution. The states finally **ratified** the Constitution in 1789.

An important power divided between the two houses of Congress is the power to **impeach** federal officials, or charge them with crimes or misconduct while in office. The Constitution gives the House the power to begin **impeachment** proceedings. Trials for impeached officials are held in the Senate, however, which ultimately decides whether the accused is guilty or innocent.

See also: Constitutional Convention and the Presidency; Impeachment, Presidential.

Further Reading

Stewart, David O. *The Summer of 1787: The Men Who Invented the Constitution.* New York: Simon & Schuster, 2007.

Constitutional Convention and the Presidency

The office of the president as created by the delegates to the Constitutional Convention held in Philadelphia in 1787. During the course of the Constitutional Convention, the presidency developed along two major lines. First, the rather loosely designed **executive** of the Virginia Plan took on greater clarity and specificity. Second, the weak executive, subordinate to the legislature, which most of the delegates initially seem to have favored, was made stronger. These two developments manifested themselves in a variety of specific issues of executive design. The issues included whether there would be one or several executives, the method of executive selection, the length and character of the executive's term in office, the means of removal in extraordinary circumstances, the institutional separation of executive and legislature, and the powers of the executive.

An Overview of the Creation of the Presidency

The design of the executive was one of the most troublesome problems of the Constitutional Convention, and its solution was the convention's most creative act. Other issues were more controversial, but they typically lent themselves to compromise solutions, such as when the small states split the difference with the large states and provided for a **bicameral** legislature, and when northern and southern delegates worked out the three-fifths rule for counting slaves (each slave would be counted as three-fifths of a person for the purpose of determining state population). When it came to the nature and powers of the executive, however, the delegates labored in a realm of such intellectual and political uncertainty that the politics of compromise was largely irrelevant. The result, although long in coming, was that "the presidency emerged not from the clash of wills to gain a long-contested point, but from a series of ingenious efforts to design a new institution that would be suitably energetic but safely **republican**."

One problem the delegates encountered was that their experience offered several models of what they did not want in an executive but few models that they found attractive. The British monarch and the royal colonial governors had been, in their eyes, tramplers of liberty. The state constitutions that were written after independence provided for governors who were unthreatening but also weak. The national government of the Articles of Confederation had no chief executive at all. The proposals for an executive that various delegates offered during the convention are more a mark of their uncertainty than of any strongly held desires:

- Three executives, each from a different part of the country.
- An executive joined with a council.
- A single executive, with a life term.
- A president, without a life term, chosen by the people.
- A single executive, chosen by the Congress and eligible for reelection.
- A single executive, chosen by the Congress and ineligible for reelection.

- An executive chosen by the governors of the states.
- A president chosen by members of the Congress, to be drawn by lot, or chosen by the Congress the first time and by electors the second time, or chosen by electors (selected by state legislators, or selected by voters) all the time.

A second problem that confounded the delegates came from their general uncertainty about executive authority. They wanted an executive branch that was strong enough to check a runaway legislature, but not so strong as to become **despotic.** This mixed feeling was shared by the American people, whose hatred of monarchy existed side by side with their longing to make George Washington (1789–1797) king.

In reality, the public's longing for Washington was just that: a longing for Washington, not for a monarchy. Some historians have noted that Washington's wide-ranging responsibilities as commander in chief during the revolutionary war meant that "he had in a certain sense been acting as President of the United States since 1775." Delegates and citizens alike knew that Washington would wield power responsibly and give it up voluntarily—he had already done so once. Would others? "The first man at the helm will be a good one," Benjamin Franklin told the convention. "No body knows what sort may come afterwards."

Despite the delegates' difficulties, the presidency slowly took shape as the convention wore on. For all their intellectual uncertainty, the delegates moved steadily in the direction of a clearly designed executive.

Strength
For all the uncertainty of its beginning, the national executive of the Virginia Plan generally accorded with what most delegates at the start of the Constitutional Convention seem to have been looking for—namely, an agent of restraint in a basically **legislative** government. The executive in James Madison's (1809–1817) proposed government was weak (it was bound by a council and devoid of enumerated powers), but it certainly was stronger than in the government of the Articles of Confederation. The executive also was subordinate to the legislature, which was empowered to elect it. Never-

theless, it was not subservient, as demonstrated by its fixed term, the **veto** power, and the ban on legislative reductions of the executive's salary.

Dissatisfied with the convention's early consensus on a subordinate executive, a group of committed and talented delegates worked diligently and effectively to strengthen the office's constitutional power. They were led by James Wilson, who envisioned the executive as "the man of the people," and by Gouverneur Morris, who regarded a properly constituted executive as "the great protector of the Mass of people."

During the course of the convention, the pro-executive delegates won victory after victory:

- The executive was defined as a unitary, not a committee-style, office and was left unshackled by a council.
- The executive, instead of being chosen by the legislature for a single term, was given its own electoral base and the right to run for reelection. Indispensable to this victory was Wilson's conversion of Madison, who declared on July 19 that "it is essential then that the appointment of the Executive should either be drawn from some source, or held by some tenure, that will give him a free agency with regard to the Legislature. This could not be if he was appointable from time to time by the Legislature."
- The Committee of Detail spelled out an extensive list of executive powers, including those of military command, involvement in the legislative process, pardon, and the execution of the laws.
- After the Connecticut Compromise transformed the Senate into the small states' bastion in Congress, large-state delegates joined with pro-executive delegates to transfer some of the Senate's powers to the executive, notably those of appointment and treaty making.

Number of the Executive
The number of the executive was the first issue to rouse the delegates. The debate on this issue took two forms. First, should the executive be unitary or plural—that is, a single-person or a committee-style office? Second, should the executive be forced to consult with a council before exercising some or all of its powers?

Unitary or Plural?

The Virginia Plan said nothing about the number of the executive, perhaps because Madison had no clear opinion on the matter or perhaps because, like Roger Sherman of Connecticut, Madison felt that the legislature should be free to define the executive number as it saw fit.

On June 1, the convention, meeting as the Committee of the Whole, heard a motion from James Wilson that the executive be a single person. According to Madison's notes, "a considerable pause ensu[ed]" as the usually talkative delegates lapsed into silence, discomforted by the prospect of discussing the issue in the presence of George Washington, whom everyone assumed would be the leader of whatever executive branch was created. After Franklin reminded his colleagues that they were obliged to speak freely, however, the debate was joined, and the issue became an early test for the pro-executive forces at the convention.

Wilson defended his motion shrewdly. To be sure, he argued, a single executive would be a source of "energy" and "dispatch"—that is, of leadership and action—in the new government. However, Wilson also urged that a single executive was indispensable to control executive power; how could responsibility for incompetence or for abuses of power be assigned to a committee? These arguments were persuasive to most delegates. They feared monarchy, but realized how much the national government had suffered under the Articles of Confederation from the lack of executive responsibility.

Selection and Succession

James Wilson was as much opposed to the part of the Virginia Plan that provided for the executive "to be chosen by the National Legislature," as he was in favor of a unitary executive. Legislative selection would make the executive a creature of (and thus subservient to) the legislature, Wilson believed. On June 1, he proposed instead that the executive be elected by the people. Wilson noted that he could think of no better way to keep the executive and legislative branches "as independent as possible of each other, as well as of the states."

The delegates virtually ignored Wilson's proposal for popular election. In principle, the idea was too democratic. (They thought of democracy as suited only for small communities.) In addition, by requiring voters to pass judgment on candidates about whom they might knew little or nothing, popular election seemed impractical. Mason stated both of these objections cogently: "It would be as unnatural to refer the choice of a proper character for chief Magistrate to the people, as it would to refer a trial of colours to a blind man." On behalf of the southern delegates, Madison added a more overtly political point: in direct elections, candidates from the more populous north almost always would win.

Undiscouraged, Wilson returned to the convention on June 2 with a proposal for an electoral college to select the executive. For purposes of election, each state would be divided into a few districts; the voters in these would choose electors, who in turn would gather at a central location to select an executive. A plan similar to the one Wilson proposed was accepted on July 19 and ultimately adopted in September, but at this stage of the convention it still seemed too novel. The delegates voted instead to affirm the legislative selection provision of the Virginia Plan.

The delegates remained unhappy with the decision for legislative selection, although it was reaffirmed in several votes taken in July and August. The source of their unhappiness was that, in the delegates' minds, a legislatively selected executive could not be allowed to stand for reelection, lest executive power and **patronage** be used for the purpose of, in effect, bribing legislators for their support. Yet the delegates also believed that eligibility for reelection was a valuable incentive to good performance in office and regretted that legislative selection of the executive ruled reelection out. The result was an ongoing search for a selection process that was desirable in its own right and that allowed the executive to run again. This was no easy task.

The search for an alternative to legislative selection became more urgent after August 24. Until that day, no consideration had been given to how the legislature was to choose the president. Now, by a vote of seven states to four, the convention approved a motion that Congress would elect the president by a "joint ballot" of all the members of the House of Representatives and Senate, following the practice most states used to elect their governors. This decision, by giving the large states a clear majority in the presidential selection process (there would be many more representatives than senators), threatened to reignite the large–state/small-state controversy that already had split the convention once. To avert this catastrophe, Roger Sherman, the author of the Connecticut Compromise between the large and small states on legislative apportionment, moved on August 31 to refer the whole issue of presidential selection to the Committee on Postponed Matters.

On September 4, the committee proposed the electoral college as a method to elect the president, with no restrictions on the president's right to seek reelection. The president would be selected by a majority vote of the electors, who would be chosen by the states using whatever methods they individually adopted. (The delegates expected that most states would entrust the selection of electors to the people.) Each state would receive a number of electoral votes equal to its representation in Congress. If no presidential candidate received votes from a majority of electors, the Senate would elect the president from among the five highest electoral vote recipients. Finally, to ensure that the electors would not simply support a variety of home-state favorites, each was required to vote for two candidates for president from two different states (an idea first proposed by Gouverneur Morris on July 25), with the runner-up in the presidential election filling the newly created office of vice president.

The proposal for an electoral college was generally well received by the delegates. Only one aspect of the proposed electoral college was controversial among the delegates: Senate selection of the president in the absence of an electoral college majority. Large-state delegates objected because the Senate underrepresented them in favor of the small states. Moreover, not foreseeing the development of a two-party system, some delegates believed that after Washington (the obvious choice as the first president) left office, majorities seldom would form in the electoral college and the Senate would choose most presidents.

Once again, Sherman proposed an acceptable compromise: let the House of Representatives elect the president if the electoral college failed to produce a majority, but assign each state delegation a single vote. The Senate still would choose the

vice president. Quickly, on September 6, the convention agreed.

One issue that the creation of the vice presidency resolved, at least partially, was: What happens if the president dies, resigns, becomes disabled, or is **impeached** and convicted? The Committee of Detail was the first to address the matter. It recommended that the president of the Senate be designated "to discharge the powers and duties of [the Presidency] . . . until another President of the United States be chosen, or until the disability of the President be ended." When Madison and other delegates objected to this proposal because it might give the Senate an incentive to remove a president in favor of one of its members, the issue was referred to the Committee on Postponed Matters.

The committee proposed that the vice president, not a senator, be president of the Senate; it also designated the vice president as the person to step in if a vacancy occurs in the presidency. The convention agreed, but only after passing an additional motion that seemed to call for a special presidential election before the expiration of the departed president's term. Somehow, this intention was lost when the Committee of Style wrote its final draft of the Constitution. No one caught the error. As a result, the convention left the Constitution vague on two important matters. First, in the event of the president's death, resignation, disability, or removal, was the vice president to become president or merely to assume the powers and duties of the presidency? Second, was the vice president to serve out the unexpired balance of the president's term or only fill in temporarily until a special election could be held to pick a new president?

Term of Office

Questions about length of term, eligibility for reelection, and selection were so interwoven in the minds of the delegates that they could not resolve any of them independently of the others. The Virginia Plan left the length of the executive's term of office blank—literally. ("Resolved, that a National Executive be . . . chosen by the National Legislature for a term of _____ years.") The plan also stipulated that the executive was "to be ineligible a second time." When these provisions came before the Committee of the Whole on June 1, several alternatives were proposed, including a three-year term with no limit on reeligibility, a three-year term with two reelections allowed, and a seven-year term with no reeligibility. Although the delegates approved the single seven-year term, the vote was narrow, five states to four.

Underlying the delegates' uncertainty was a basic choice between two alternatives concerning the executive that they regarded as incompatible—eligibility for reelection and legislative selection. George Mason forcefully stated the reason that, in his view, one could not have both: if the legislature could reelect the executive, there would be a constant "temptation on the side of the Executive to intrigue with the Legislature for a re-appointment," using political patronage and illegitimate favors in effect to buy votes.

On July 17, the convention voted for both legislative selection and reeligibility, but when James McClurg of Virginia pointed out the contradiction between these two decisions, ineligibility for reelection was reinstated. McClurg, supported by Gouverneur Morris and by Jacob Broom of Delaware, offered a different way out of the dilemma: election of the executive by the legislature for a life term. However, this proposal smacked too much of a king to suit the other delegates.

On July 24 and 26, the convention voted again to have the legislature select the executive for a single seven-year term. Nevertheless, the advantages the delegates saw in reeligibility were so powerful that the issue remained alive. Reeligibility, in addition to allowing the nation to keeping a good executive in office, also would give the executive what Morris called "the great motive to good behavior, the hope of being rewarded with a re-appointment."

To complicate their task, the delegates' decision between legislative selection and reeligibility implied a related decision between a short term for the executive and a longer term. If the executive were to be chosen by the legislature for a single term only, the delegates believed, the term should be long. If the executive were eligible for reelection, a shorter term was preferable.

In late August, the convention changed course for the last time. Effectively deciding against legislative selection of the president, the delegates created the Committee on Postponed Matters to propose an alternative. The committee's recommendation, adopted by the convention, was that an electoral college choose the president for a four-year term, with no limit on reeligibility.

See also: Constitution of the United States; Elections, Presidential; Electoral College; Presidential Succession; Separation of Powers; Vice Presidency.

Further Reading

Ellis, Richard J., and Michael Nelson (eds.). *Debating the Presidency: Conflicting Perspectives on the American Executive.* Washington, DC: CQ Press, 2006.

Milkis, Sidney M., and Michael Nelson. *The American Presidency: Origins and Development, 1776–2007,* 5th ed. Washington, DC: CQ Press, 2007.

Conventions, Presidential Nominating

Meeting of political party loyalists who come together every four years to nominate their presidential and vice-presidential candidates. The first national party nominating convention was held by the Anti-Masons, a short-lived **third party,** in Baltimore, Maryland, in September 1831. With 116 delegates attending from thirteen states, the convention nominated William Wirt for president and Amos Ellmaker for vice president. During the next eight months, the two major parties followed suit. In December, the National Republicans held a convention and nominated Henry Clay and John Sergeant, and in May 1832, the Democrats convened to nominate Andrew Jackson (1829–1837) and Martin Van Buren. With the 1832 election, the convention system was born and has remained in place ever since.

Convention Sites

Baltimore proved to be a popular spot for the earliest conventions, partly because of the city's central location. From 1831 to 1852, ten conventions (including the Democratic Party's first six) were held there. Most other popular convention cities of this era (such as Harrisburg, Philadelphia, and Pittsburgh, all in Pennsylvania) met that criterion as well, although Buffalo, New York, hosted the northern-based Liberty Party in 1843 and Free Soil Party in 1848.

The choice of convention sites after 1856 reflected the country's expansion westward. For the past century and a half, Chicago has been the most popular choice: it had hosted twenty-five major party conventions by 2000. Cincinnati and St. Louis were popular sites in the latter 1800s.

Until recently, few conventions were held in the South. In 1860, the Democrats met in Charleston, South Carolina, for a tumultuous convention in that ultimately deadlocked, forcing a second convention to be held in Baltimore. The Democrats did not hold another southern convention until 1928, when Houston, Texas, was chosen to appease southerners who, party leaders knew, would be unhappy with the nomination of Al Smith, a Catholic from New York. The Republicans did not hold their first southern convention until 1968, when the party convened in Miami Beach, Florida. In 1988, however, both parties held their conventions in the South—the Democrats in Atlanta and the Republicans in New Orleans. In 2008, the Republicans met in Minneapolis, Minnesota, and the Democrats held their convention in Denver, Colorado.

At some point, the desire for a central location gave way to a more pressing need: money. For a time, the major consideration in choosing a convention site was the amount of money that cities offered to the national party committee in cash and services. By 1968, contributions from cities were approaching $1 million. Local economies get a significant boost from the influx of thousands of conventioneers and journalists into their cities. Illinois officials estimated that the 1996 Democratic convention in Chicago would provide a $100 million boost to the local economy. Chicago won the right to host the event by offering Democrats a package worth $32 million.

Convention Financing

Campaign finance legislation passed in the wake of the Nixon administration's (1969–1974) Watergate scandal prohibited corporate funding of conventions and provided for each national party to receive $2.2 million from the government to finance its convention. Although that amount has increased to reflect inflation ($13.5 million for each major party in 2000, as well as $2.5 million

for the Reform Party, based on its share of the popular vote in the 1996 election), it is still far less than is needed to fund a convention. As a result, the Federal Election Commission (FEC) has loosened its restrictions by (1) allowing private businesses to offer services, such as free hotel accommodations, as long as the other party receives comparable benefits; and (2) permitting state and local governments to offer a number of services free of charge, including security and the use of a convention hall.

The choice of a convention city also depends on the facilities that are available. Conventions require 20,000 or more hotel and motel rooms to house delegates, party officials, journalists, television crews, and the candidates' staffs. The city also needs a convention hall large enough to seat delegates and accommodate the media, including space for overhead booths for the television networks.

Security considerations play a major role in the choice of a convention site. New York hosted Democratic conventions in 1976, 1980, and 1992 only after state and city officials offered to provide extraordinary security measures. President Nixon approved Miami Beach for the Republican convention in 1972 when he was assured that antiwar protesters would be kept at bay.

The choice of a site often serves as a gesture to a particular part of the country or reflects the personal preference of an **incumbent** president running for reelection. Ronald Reagan, for example, wanted to have Dallas selected as the site of the 1984 Republican convention because of the support he had received from Texas **conservatives** in 1976 and 1980.

A city usually is chosen more than a year before the convention by a committee of a dozen or so party members appointed by the national chair. The national party committee officially announces the convention's dates and site, and then appoints its officers and committees. An unwritten rule holds that when the race for the party nomination is wide open, states with candidates cannot host the convention.

Delegates

Setting the number of votes that each state delegation will have at the national convention is one of the most important parts of the formal call to the convention. This apportionment of votes originally coincided with the number of votes each state had in the electoral college, which in turn was determined by the size of the state's congressional delegation. From the beginning, however, states often sent more delegates to the convention than the number of their electoral votes allowed.

In 1848, the Democrats tried without success to limit the actual voting power of each state delegation to its electoral college vote, regardless of the number of delegates sent by the state. In an effort to deal with the problem of extra delegates, the Democrats passed a rule in 1852 giving every state twice as many delegates as it had electoral votes, with each delegate receiving a half vote. To do away with fractional votes, the number of votes was doubled in 1872, giving each delegate a whole vote.

From its first convention in 1856, the Republican Party also followed a system of apportionment that roughly corresponded to the electoral college. The GOP gave each state six at-large delegates, plus three delegates for each congressional district. This was changed in 1860 to four at-large delegates, plus two delegates for each congressional district.

Both parties, then, followed a system that allocated convention delegates mainly according to population rather than their voting strength in each state. That system of apportionment came under attack after the Civil War (1861–1865) with the rise of one-party states. In such states, a minority party, such as the Republicans in the post-**Reconstruction** South, would be overrepresented at the GOP convention.

Since 1972, the Republicans have followed a complicated formula. It gives each state six at-large delegates, three delegates for each congressional district, a number of delegates equal to 60 percent of the state's electoral vote total (rounded up), four-and-a-half bonus delegates if the Republican ticket carried the state in the last presidential election, one bonus delegate for each Republican senator, one bonus delegate for a House delegation that is at least one-half Republican, and one bonus delegate for states with a Republican governor. In addition, the party awards fourteen delegates to the District of Columbia, eight to Puerto Rico, and four each to Guam and the Virgin Is-

lands. The GOP rule also ensures states that they will receive at least as many convention votes as they had in the previous election.

The Democrats did not institute a bonus system until 1944. For that year's convention, they simply awarded two bonus delegates to each state that the party had carried in the last presidential election. The number of bonus delegates was increased to four in 1948. Since then, the Democrats have used a variety of delegate allocation formulas. Beginning in 1972, they used a formula that based nearly half of a state's voting strength on its Democratic vote in the last three presidential elections. The other measure of voting strength was based on the state's electoral votes.

The number of delegates attending national conventions has increased dramatically. The first convention, held by the Anti-Masons in 1831, boasted 116 delegates. The Democratic convention the next year had 283. In 1856, 567 delegates attended the first Republican convention. By the early 1900s, both major party conventions had approximately 1,000 delegates. That number remained fairly stable until the 1950s, when the Democratic Party began to increase participation in its national convention.

In 1956, the Democrats allowed states to send delegates on a "half-vote" basis. Under that system, states could send twice as many delegates to cast the same number of votes. Between 1952 and 1956, the number of Democratic delegates increased from 1,642 to 2,477. At the same time, the number of delegate votes began increasing as well. This increase initially reflected the use of bonus delegates, but later was spurred by the Democrats' greater democratization of their conventions in the aftermath of the party's post-1968 reforms. Thus, the number of delegate votes at Democratic conventions increased to 3,331 in 1980. In 2008, 4,223 regular delegates and 824.5 superdelegates—a total of 5,074.5—cast votes at the Democratic convention.

The size of Republican conventions has not increased quite so dramatically. Nevertheless, party reforms in the early 1970s provided for a 60 percent increase in delegate strength. As a result, the number of delegates at the Republican convention rose from 1,348 in 1972 to 2,259 in 1976. By 2008, the number of Republican delegates had reached 2,380.

Preconvention Committees

Three major committees carry out the preparatory work of the national convention: credentials, rules, and platform. These committees traditionally meet before the start of the national convention, usually during the week before it begins. More recently, the Democrats have begun holding committee sessions several weeks before the convention.

Credentials Committee

The Credentials Committee reviews all disputes concerning the credentials of convention delegates. Before the convention begins, the committee receives a list of the delegates from each state. It then holds hearings on any challenges to those delegates (usually based on the procedures by which they were chosen) and offers its recommendations about which delegates should be seated to the convention, which makes the final decision on the matter. Such disputes usually involve rival delegations for the same seats. If a challenge is found valid, the committee may recommend seating the competing delegation.

When a close presidential nominating contest is close, the Credentials Committee can influence which candidate is nominated. A notable instance was the 1912 Republican convention when President William Howard Taft (1909–1913) was locked in a bitter nomination battle with former president Theodore Roosevelt (1901–1909). Roosevelt forces contested 254 pro-Taft delegates, but the Credentials Committee recommended that all but nineteen of them be seated. The convention upheld that recommendation, virtually guaranteeing Taft's renomination.

The credentials challenge with the greatest long-term consequences occurred at the 1964 Democratic convention in Atlantic City. The Mississippi Freedom Democratic Party (MFDP), a new and racially integrated organization formed at a time when African Americans were not allowed to vote in the state's presidential primary, demanded to be seated at the convention. MFDP's delegates had been selected in a state convention that was open to all Mississippians. Civil rights leaders Martin Luther King Jr. and James Farmer, among others, testified for the insurgents in nationally televised hearings of the Credentials Committee. After nervous negotiations, convention officials agreed to give the MFDP two "at-large" seats and require that Mississippi send integrated convention delegations in the future. The MFDP contingent rejected the compromise and went home. The drama, which enlivened an otherwise calm convention, attracted national attention to the growing voting rights movement. By the 1968 convention, the party had opened its delegations to African Americans.

Rules Committee

The Rules Committee is responsible for proposing the operating rules of the convention. Until 1972, the Democratic Party did not have a formal set of rules that it retained from convention to convention. Instead, the party's rules evolved in an ad hoc fashion, although many rules from the previous convention invariably were readopted. In contrast, Republican rules were strictly codified.

Among the most controversial rules used by the Democrats were the "two-thirds" rule and the "unit" rule. The two-thirds rule required that any nominee for president or vice president receive a two-thirds majority of the convention vote. Because the two-thirds rule made it harder to win the nomination, protracted balloting was commonplace. The Republican Party, which has always nominated by simple majority, has had just one convention in its entire history that required more than 10 ballots (36 in 1880). In contrast, the Democratic Party had seven such conventions during the life of the two-thirds rule: 49 ballots in 1852, 17 in 1856, 59 (spread over two conventions) in 1860, 22 in 1868, 46 in 1912, 43 in 1920, and 103 in 1924.

Proposals were introduced to abolish the two-thirds rule in the wake of the 103-ballot 1924 marathon convention and again in 1932 by supporters of Franklin D. Roosevelt (1933–1945), who feared that he might not be able to gather all the votes necessary to win the nomination. At Roosevelt's urging, and despite considerable opposition, the Democrats finally eliminated the two-thirds rule at their 1936 convention. The South, in particular, objected to the change because the two-thirds rule had given that region a virtual **veto** over any nominee. To make up for that loss, southern state delegations were granted more votes at later conventions.

The unit rule allowed the majority of a delegation at the Democratic convention to cast all of the votes of that delegation for the candidate or position supported by a majority of the state's delegation. (This rule was never used by the Republicans.) Proponents of the unit rule argued that it muted conflict within the party by overriding dissident minorities, and therefore strengthened state party organizations. Opponents argued that the rule was undemocratic. Conceivably, a candidate with a minority of the delegates could win the nomination by controlling the votes of a narrow majority of the dozen or so largest state delegations. In 1968, the Democratic Rules Committee recommended that the unit rule be repealed and the convention adopted its recommendation.

Actions by the Rules Committee can influence the outcome of a convention. In 1976, Ronald Reagan (1981–1989) announced his intention to nominate Pennsylvania senator Richard Schweiker as his running mate if he won the Republican presidential nomination, then proposed a rules change to force his opponent, Gerald R. Ford (1974–1977), to offer his own nominee. Reagan, who entered the convention trailing Ford slightly, hoped he might be able to win enough delegates alienated by Ford's choice for vice president to secure the nomination. However, Ford's supporters voted down the rules change, and Ford went on to become the Republican nominee.

The so-called "bound delegate" rule required delegates to vote according to their pledge at the time they were selected. The rule was the subject of a major fight at the 1980 Democratic convention. President Jimmy Carter (1977–1981) supported the rule because it bound the majority of delegates who had been chosen to support him. Carter's rival, Senator Edward Kennedy, fought to overturn the rule in the hope that some of those delegates would transfer their support to him if they could. The Carter forces won the rules fight and the nomination.

Platform Committee

The Platform Committee is responsible for presenting a proposed platform, or statement of party principles and promises, to the convention for its approval. Because party leaders want to mute conflict within the party and appeal to as wide a range of voters as possible, platforms seldom have much punch. Wendell Willkie, the Republican nominee in 1940, called them "fusions of ambiguity."

Nevertheless, platforms sometimes cause bitter fights. The addition of a strong civil rights plank to the 1948 Democratic platform provoked opposition from southern states and prompted the Mississippi delegation and thirteen members of the Alabama delegation to walk out. Some of the disgruntled southerners then formed their own party—the States' Rights Democratic Party, or the Dixiecrats—who held their own convention in Birmingham, Alabama, and nominated South Carolina governor J. Strom Thurmond for president and Mississippi governor Fielding L. Wright for vice president.

Party platforms offer interest groups a welcome opportunity to influence the parties. Dozens of groups typically appear before each party's platform committee. Most groups appeal to the party that offers them greater access and a friendlier ear. They direct their appeals to the party's likely nominee, except in circumstances when working with the underdog candidate enables them to make a splash at the convention. About one-fifth of all interest groups who testify before platform committees take the "even money" approach and appeal to both parties.

Convention Officers

A national party convention is called to order by the party's national committee chair, who presides until a temporary convention chair is appointed. The temporary chair then wields the gavel until the convention approves the recommended slate of candidates for permanent officers. During the first half of the twentieth century, the temporary chair served as the keynote speaker at the convention. It also was traditional for the temporary chair to be a senator. Since 1952, when General Douglas MacArthur delivered the keynote address at the Republican convention, the keynote speaker usually has been someone other than the temporary chair. In recent years, the tradition of appointing a senator to be temporary chair has been less frequently observed.

The permanent chair usually is appointed on the second day of the convention, but the national committee's choice for the post is announced before the convention begins. He or she invariably is approved by the convention with no contest. The permanent chair presides while the platform is adopted and during the actual nominating process. Thus the permanent chair may be in a position to make strategic rulings that can help or hinder particular candidates. Indeed, the permanent chair is often described as the convention's most important officer.

In the late 1800s and early 1900s, prominent state and local political leaders usually filled the post of permanent chair. Beginning in the 1930s, however, it became customary for the party's leader in the House of Representatives to serve as permanent chair. In 1972, the Democrats undermined that custom by requiring that the position alternate every four years between men and women.

Presidential Nomination

For some time national conventions have been mere ratifying assemblies; since 1952, all the nominees of the two major parties have been chosen on the first ballot. Candidates now use the conventions as a form of extended advertising, a way to introduce themselves and their themes to the millions watching the proceedings on television.

Several factors account for the decline of conventions as deliberative assemblies. The **abolition** of the unit rule and the two-thirds rule by the Democrats helped to reduce the protracted balloting that was common in that party. Even more important was the changing nature of the political landscape: the rise of primaries (which bind delegates to candidates before the convention), the increased cost of campaigning (which quickly narrows of the field of potential nominees, because losers in early primaries find themselves without financial resources), and the televising of conventions (in which appearing unified is the party's main concern).

The democratization of the selection process makes an old-style brokered convention, at which party **bosses** choose the nominee behind closed doors, all but impossible. To corral votes at the convention, campaign managers keep in close contact with state delegations. Candidates have floor leaders to direct their supporters' voting and to deal with any problems that may arise among the delegations. In addition, "floaters" wander around the convention floor in search of trouble. All of these people have access to virtually instant communication with their candidate's command post via walkie-talkies, cell phones, and handheld computers. Floor leaders and floaters often wear specially colored clothing or baseball caps so they can be spotted easily. Candidates go to these lengths because they are eager to please the delegates and to ensure their enthusiastic support, not just at the convention but afterward. In 1976, Carter met and shook hands with each of the more than 1,800 delegates pledged to him.

Nominating speeches mark the beginning of the formal selection process. The convention of the National Republican Party (which met in Baltimore in December 1831, three months after the Anti-Masons held the first national party convention) is said to have had the first nominating speech. In the early years, such speeches were short. In 1860, Abraham Lincoln's (1861–1865) name was placed into nomination with only twenty-seven words. The name of his chief rival for the nomination, William H. Seward of New York, was put forward with only twenty-six. Over the years, the length of nominating speeches increased. It also became customary to schedule a series of shorter seconding speeches after the nominating speech. The seconding speeches were interspersed with floor demonstrations in support of the nominee.

Television has reshaped nominating and seconding speeches, just as it has reshaped the rest of the activity at national conventions. Eager for coverage of their event to be streamlined so that viewers do not lose interrerst, convention managers have encouraged a return to shorter nominating speeches and fewer seconding speeches.

Once the nominating and seconding speeches are over, the roll call of the states begins. When the name of each state is called, the chair of the state's delegation rises to announce the vote of that delegation. At early conventions, the order of the roll call was determined partly by geographical location and partly by the order in which states had entered the Union. Since the late 1800s, however, both parties have called the roll of states in alphabetical order, with one exception. In 1972, the Democrats determined the order of the roll call by lottery, thereby giving each state, including those that came early in the alphabet, the chance to have the honor of pushing the nominee over the top. By luck of the draw, the roll call in 1972 started with California and ended with Oklahoma. Despite these good intentions, the

JUSTICE FOR ALL

Geraldine Ferraro (1935–)

Geraldine Ferraro was a teacher and a lawyer in Queens, New York, before she got involved in politics. While she was an Assistant District Attorney, she was on the Advisory Council for the Housing Court of the City of New York and she served as the president of the Queens County Women's Bar Association. In 1978, she decided to run for a seat in the United States House of Representatives, which she won after a very expensive campaign. During her six years as a representative, Ferraro served as the Secretary of the House Democratic **caucus.** As a Democrat, she supported **liberal** issues while also trying to meet the demands of her **conservative** constituency.

In 1984, after holding extensive interviews with many contenders, former vice president Walter Mondale, the Democrat's presidential candidate, chose Ferraro to be his running mate. Ferraro thus became the first woman to run for vice president on a major party ticket. As the campaign progressed, however, many people began to question Ferraro's qualifications for the job, noting that after only six years in the political arena she was not experienced enough for the vice presidency. In addition, Ferraro's finances came under question along with those of her husband, John Zaccaro. Both Ferraro and her husband were accused of illegal financial dealings and Ferraro was called in front of the House Ethics Committee. Ferraro refused to hand over her husband's tax returns, which hurt the Democrats' campaign. Mondale and Ferraro lost in a landslide to **incumbent** President Ronald Reagan (1981–1989).

After her vice presidential campaign, Ferraro made two attempts to win a seat in Congress, but the scandals of the past hurt her efforts. When Bill Clinton (1993–2001) became president, however, he appointed her as the U.S. Ambassador to the United Nations Commission on Human Rights. She later supported Hillary Rodham Clinton in her campaign for the 2008 Democratic presidential nomination.

change was a disaster because delegation chairs were not familiar with the new order and seldom were ready to announce their delegations' votes when they were called on.

Choosing the Vice-Presidential Nominee

After nominating the presidential candidate, the convention chooses a vice-presidential candidate. Until the mid-twentieth century, presidential candidates had little role in selecting their running mate. The 1920 Republican convention ignored Warren Harding's recommendation of Senator Irvine L. Lenroot of Wisconsin and chose Massachusetts governor Calvin Coolidge instead. The choice was the prerogative of the party leaders.

This practice changed in 1940 when Franklin Roosevelt threatened not to run unless the convention accepted his vice-presidential choice: Secretary of Agriculture Henry A. Wallace. The convention reluctantly gave in, but Wallace was prevailed on not to deliver an acceptance speech.

The method of nominating the vice-presidential candidates mirrors the procedure for presidential nominations: nominating and seconding speeches, floor demonstrations, and balloting. In recent years, likely nominees have selected their running mates before the convention begins.

The choice of the vice-presidential candidate sometimes is motivated by geographical considerations in an effort to "balance" the ticket. For years, a balanced ticket was one that boasted an easterner and a midwesterner. More recently, the balance usually has been between a northerner and a southerner. Ideological considerations sometimes play a part in ticket balancing. Thus, a **liberal** presidential candidate may pair himself with a more **conservative** running mate in hopes of attracting a broader base of votes. The choice of the vice-presidential candidate also may be used to appease factions within the party that are unhappy with the presidential candidate.

Because an increasing number of vice presidents go on to be president, greater public attention is now given to the abilities of the person who is chosen as running mate. Hopefuls seldom campaign openly for the vice-presidential nomination, but Jesse Jackson made it clear in the days before the 1988 Democratic convention that he wanted to be offered the number-two spot. The presidential nominee, Michael Dukakis, ultimately chose conservative Texas senator Lloyd Bentsen as his running mate in an effort to forge a Democratic ticket with a balance of ideology, experience, and geography.

In 1992, Bill Clinton (1993–2001) selected Al Gore for vice president after a quiet search conducted by Vernon Jordan, a corporate lawyer and former head of the National Urban League. The pick was considered unconventional because Clinton and Gore were from the neighboring states of Arkansas and Tennessee. Nevertheless, Gore helped Clinton to compensate for his lack of Washington and foreign policy experience, avoidance of military service during the Vietnam War, questionable personal morality, and suspect status with environmental groups.

Acceptance Speeches

The acceptance speeches of the candidates for president and vice president are now the conventions' capstone events. Acceptance speeches became a part of conventions in 1932, when Franklin Roosevelt broke **precedent.** Eager to show that his physical disability would not keep him from acting vigorously, Roosevelt made a

dramatic flight from Albany to Chicago to address the Democratic convention that had nominated him for president. Noting that he was the first candidate ever to deliver an acceptance speech to a national convention, Roosevelt said: "I am here to thank you for the honor [of nominating me]. Let it be symbolic that in so doing, I broke traditions. Let it be from now on the task of our party to break foolish traditions." In 1944, New York governor Thomas Dewey became the first Republican nominee to deliver an acceptance speech.

The drafting of acceptance speeches is a major undertaking, often involving the work of many writers. Strategic lines are inserted to satisfy specific voting blocs and interest groups, and the overall structure and delivery of the speech are designed to capture the interest of the millions of television viewers. Candidates rehearse their acceptance speeches extensively. They realize that the speech marks not just the end of the nominating process, but also the beginning of the general election campaign.

Television and Other Press Coverage

Modern national party conventions are media events. They offer a flamboyant setting with cheering crowds, passionate speakers, poignant appearances by party elders, and limitless opportunities for on-the-spot interviews and human-interest stories. The convention system originated before the telegraph or telephone, in an age when newspapers were highly **partisan** mouthpieces of political parties. Communication and transportation were slow, so conventions took place in relative isolation. Today, all that has changed. Thousands of reporters and camera operators attend conventions, making millions of Americans privy to the action.

The 1924 conventions were the first to be broadcast on the radio. The 1940 Republican convention was televised on an experimental basis, but it was seen by only a tiny audience. The televised 1948 Democratic convention reached about 400,000 viewers along the eastern seaboard. The Democrats also used closed-circuit television that year so that an overflow crowd of 6,000 could watch the proceedings in an auditorium adjacent to the convention hall.

A–Z

The advent of the television age had a tremendous effect on national party conventions. Television brought the 1952 conventions—the first to be nationally televised—into the living rooms of several million Americans.

Conventions are now almost completely choreographed for television. Convention planners are careful to prevent boring lulls in the action, to keep potentially divisive rules or platform fights out of prime-time viewing hours, and to orchestrate "spontaneous" demonstrations and telegenic events such as the release of thousands of colorful balloons from the ceiling down to the convention floor. Consultants coach speakers on makeup, wardrobe, and how to read the TelePrompTer.

News organizations that cover the convention also are concerned with image. Officials of each television network are anxious to win higher ratings than their competitors, and they assign their best-known reporters to cover the event. Indeed, many Americans are more familiar with the reporters than with the politicians. Anchors and analysts cover the convention from overhead booths, while scores of reporters roam the floor in search of fast-breaking stories. The networks also hire spotters to scan the floor for possibly interesting interviews.

See also: Presidential Campaigns; Vice Presidency.

Further Reading

CQ Press. *National Party Conventions, 1831–2004.* Washington, DC: CQ Press, 2005.

Panagopoulos, Costas. *Rewiring Politics: Presidential Nominating Conventions in the Media Age.* Baton Rouge, LA: Louisiana State University Press, 2007.

Coolidge, Calvin, Administration of (1923–1929)

Government under the thirtieth president of the United States. Born in Vermont, Calvin Coolidge moved to nearby Northampton, Massachusetts, after graduating from Amherst College. There he got a job as a law clerk. He was admitted to the

bar in 1897, started his own law practice, and became involved in Northampton politics as a Republican. He served as a member of the city council, city solicitor, and chairman of the county Republican committee. He suffered his only political defeat in 1905 when he was beaten for a seat on the Northampton school board. In 1906, however, he was elected to the Massachusetts House of Representatives. After two terms, he returned to Northampton in 1909 and was elected mayor the following year.

In 1911, Coolidge won a seat in the state senate. After four one-year terms he was elected lieutenant governor in 1915. He served three one-year terms in this office before being elected governor by a slim margin in 1918.

In September 1919, the Boston police staged a strike that opened the way for a criminal rampage. After two days, Governor Coolidge called out the state militia to keep order in Boston. When Samuel Gompers, head of the American Federation of Labor, accused Coolidge of acting unfairly, Coolidge sent him a wire declaring, "There is no right to strike against the public safety by anybody, anywhere, any time." The statement made Coolidge famous across the country.

Although Coolidge was one of many Republicans whose name was placed in nomination for the presidency at the 1920 Republican National Convention in Chicago, he was not a leading candidate for the nomination. The convention was deadlocked between several candidates during the early balloting but eventually turned to Senator Warren G. Harding of Ohio as a compromise candidate. Harding had been chosen by party leaders who expected their choice for vice president, Wisconsin senator Irvine Lenroot, to be similarly **ratified** by the convention. When Coolidge's name was put into nomination for vice president after Lenroot's, however, the convention unexpectedly threw its support behind the popular governor. Coolidge received 674 votes to Lenroot's 146 and was chosen on the first ballot.

During the 1920 campaign, Harding and Coolidge promised to raise **tariffs** to protect U.S. industry and to keep the country out of war and entangling alliances. They won more than 60 percent of the popular vote on their way to a 404–127 victory in the electoral college over Democrats James M. Cox and Franklin D. Roosevelt.

In 1923, Vice President Coolidge was spending the summer in Vermont when a telegraph messenger arrived at his home after midnight on August 3 with the news that President Harding (1921–1923) had unexpectedly died in San Francisco. Coolidge's father, who was a notary public, administered the oath of office. The next day Coolidge left for Washington, D.C.

Coolidge retained Harding's cabinet, but when the scandals that pervaded the Harding administration were revealed, he asked for the resignations of those involved, including Secretary of the Navy Edwin Denby and Attorney General Harry Daugherty. Coolidge dutifully prosecuted the former Harding administration officials who had committed crimes.

As president, Coolidge quickly became a symbol of simple, practical leadership. Coolidge was fondly called "Silent Cal" by the public because of his quiet ways. He was an honest and successful administrator who made the national government more efficient and economical.

Coolidge ran in 1924 against Democrat John W. Davis. Despite the scandals of the Harding administration, Coolidge's personal honesty, his small-town image, and national prosperity carried him to victory. He defeated Davis in the electoral college, 382–136.

During his second term, Coolidge was successful in decreasing the national debt and cutting income taxes. These policies put more money into the hands of consumers and helped stimulate investment. Coolidge's hands-off policies toward business activities, however, deferred needed reforms of the financial industry and encouraged overspeculation that contributed to the stock market crash of 1929 and the subsequent **Great Depression.**

In foreign relations, Coolidge reestablished diplomatic relations with Mexico, which had been severed under Woodrow Wilson (1913–1921), and improved relations with other Latin American nations. Although Coolidge opposed U.S. entry into the League of Nations, he backed the multilateral Kellogg-Briand Pact of 1928, which outlawed war between nations.

After leaving office, Coolidge retired to Northampton, Massachusetts, where he bought Beeches, a nine-acre estate. During his short retirement, Coolidge wrote newspaper columns and served on the board of directors of the New York Life Insurance Company. In January 1933, less than four years after leaving the White House, Coolidge died of a heart attack.

See also: Harding, Warren, Administration of (1921–1923); Hoover, Herbert, Administration of (1929–1933).

Further Reading

Greenberg, David. *Calvin Coolidge.* New York: Times Books, 2006.

Sobel, Robert. *Coolidge.* Washington, DC: Regnery, 2000.

Corruption and Graft

See Grant, Ulysses S., Administration of (1869–1877); Harding, Warren, Administration of (1921–1923); Nixon, Richard M., Administration of (1969–1974).

A–Z

Davis, Jefferson

See Lincoln, Abraham, Administration of (1861–1865).

Defense, Department of

See Department of Defense (DOD).

Democratic Party (1828–)

The oldest political organization in the United States. Indeed, a history of the Democratic Party is in some ways a political history of the nation. In the first few years of the Republic, political parties did not exist, although factions tied to issues and the ambitions of political leaders influenced elections and policies. The Democratic Party traces its roots to this **factionalism,** beginning with opposition to the Federalist policies of Alexander Hamilton during George Washington's (1789–1787) first term.

Origins of the Democratic Party

Opposition to Federalist policies, organized by Representative James Madison (1809–1817) and Secretary of State Thomas Jefferson (1801–1809), first formed around Hamilton's proposal for a national bank, which Congress passed and Washington signed, over the strong objections of Jefferson and Madison. The two Virginians were more successful, however, in preventing the adoption of Hamilton's plan for federal support of

American industrial development. The Federalists, led by Hamilton and John Adams (1797–1801), favored a strong central government and a flexible interpretation of the Constitution. Key to their program was a national bank, which would facilitate economic growth and strengthen national and international **commerce.**

Jefferson's Democratic-Republicans advocated a less flexible, **strict constructionist** interpretation of the Constitution and opposed a national bank. Moreover, they favored friendly relations with France, while the Federalists sought to forge friendly diplomatic and commercial relations with Great Britain. Both parties had supporters throughout the country, but the Democratic-Republicans were strongest in the South and among slaveholders, and the Federalists were strongest in New England and among leaders with commercial and manufacturing interests. From the 1790s until the late 1820s various terms—Democratic-Republicans, Jeffersonian Republicans, Jeffersonian Democrats, and National Republicans—were applied to the people and leaders who, opposed to the Federalists, gradually became known as Democrats.

The Democratic-Republicans grew stronger as the Federalists began to fade during the presidency of John Adams. An alliance of southerners and urban northerners helped Jefferson defeat Adams in 1800 and win reelection in 1804. After Jefferson, the presidency went to his friends and allies, James Madison and James Monroe (1817–1825). By 1820, the Federalist Party had all but disappeared, and James Monroe won reelection with no opposition.

The inherent instability of one-party politics became clear in 1824, as four candidates—Andrew Jackson (1829–1837), John Quincy Adams (1825–1829), William Crawford, and Henry Clay, all claiming to represent the Jeffersonian tradition—ran for president. No candidate received a majority of popular or electoral votes, and the House of

Representatives chose Adams, although Jackson had received more popular votes and more electoral votes.

The Jackson Legacy

War of 1812 hero Andrew Jackson defeated John Quincy Adams in 1828 and became the first president to represent the "Democratic Party." The party has maintained that name ever since. Jackson, nominated in 1828 by the Tennessee legislature, led the Democrats into adopting a nominating convention as the method for choosing the party's future candidates. The Democrats held their first national convention in Baltimore, Maryland, in 1832, eight months after the Anti-Masons held the first such convention, also in Baltimore.

From Jackson's election in 1828 until the end of James Buchanan's (1857–1861) presidency, the Democrats dominated national politics. In this period the Democrats opposed a national bank, high **tariffs**, and internal improvements. High points of Jackson's presidency include his **vetoes** of **bills** to support internal improvements and to extend the charter of the Second **Bank of the United States.** Jackson and other Democrats in this period vigorously supported territorial expansion through Indian removal, the **annexation** of Texas, and ultimately the Mexican-American War (1846–1848). Their support for territorial gains followed Jefferson's expansionist policies that led to the purchase of Louisiana from France in 1803.

Between 1828 and 1861, most Democrats supported the demands of the South on issues regarding slavery. Meanwhile, Jackson's opponents—led by Henry Clay, Daniel Webster, and William Henry Harrison (1841)—formed the Whig Party. The Whigs—who favored higher tariffs, a national bank, federally funded internal improvements, and a weak presidency—provided the main opposition to the Democrats until the emergence of the Republican Party in 1854.

Jackson's election ushered in an era known as "Jacksonian emocracy," which stressed political equality—for white men. Jacksonians discriminated relentlessly against free black voters, taking away their voting rights in Pennsylvania, New Jersey, Tennessee, and North Carolina and opposing their voting rights elsewhere. Jackson himself led the movement to force Native Americans out of the states east of the Mississippi River.

Jefferson, considered the father of the Democratic Party, had been the first president to remove officeholders and replace them with his supporters. Jackson renewed this policy through the spoils system, a term that stemmed from the phrase "to the victors go the spoils." As the party in power during most of the period from 1829 to 1861, the Democrats controlled the growing bureaucracy and rewarded many supporters with **patronage** jobs.

Jackson's legacy was a Democratic Party that has endured into the twenty-first century. Dominating national politics during the first half of the nineteenth century, the Democrats lost the presidential election only twice between 1800 and 1856—in 1840 and 1848.

Despite their long-term success, the Democrats barely survived their severest test—over slavery and **secession.** In 1846, northern Democrats supported the Wilmot Proviso, introduced in the House by Pennsylvania Democrat David Wilmot. The proviso would have prohibited slavery in any territory acquired during the Mexican-American War. Southern Democrats opposed the proviso. In 1848, many antislavery Democrats from New York, Pennsylvania, and New England voted for former president Martin Van Buren (1837–1841), who was running on the Free Soil Party ticket. These defections led to the election of the Whig candidate, Zachary Taylor (1849–1850).

The Democrats regained the presidency in 1852, but slavery soon splintered the party. In 1856, Democrat Franklin Pierce (1853–1857) became the first elected president denied renomination by his own party. He had alienated fellow northerners by signing legislation that allowed slavery into Kansas Territory, which in turn led it to become a battleground between pro- and antislavery forces. Another northerner, James Buchanan, won the nomination but also became a one-term president. By 1860, many northern Democrats, among them Senators Salmon P. Chase of Ohio and Hannibal Hamlin of Maine, had joined the new Republican Party.

At the 1860 convention in Charleston, South Carolina, northern and southern Democrats were divided. Northerners, backing Stephen A. Douglas of Illinois, favored opening all territories to slavery under a system of **popular sovereignty,** in which settlers would decide for themselves whether to permit slavery. Most of the southerners bolted after the convention failed to call for a federal slave code for the territories and for federal guarantees of slaveholders' rights to take their human property into the territories. The northern delegates nominated Douglas for president and the southern Democrats nominated John C. Breckinridge of Kentucky. Even had the Democrats remained united, it is doubtful they could have prevented the Republican candidate, Abraham Lincoln (1861–1865), from winning an electoral majority, as he swept every free state but New Jersey, which he split with Douglas.

Decline and Resurgence

During the Civil War (1861–1865), northern Democrats remained divided. War Democrats generally supported the war effort and Lincoln's initial goal of bringing the South back into the Union. They objected, however, to Lincoln's emancipation policies, and after 1863, were less enthusiastic about the war or its goals. By contrast, the Copperhead faction opposed the war and sought peace negotiations with the Confederacy.

Democrats came back together after the Civil War, but their commitment to white supremacy continued. During **Reconstruction,** Democrats opposed civil rights laws and the Fourteenth and Fifteenth **Amendments,** which were designed to establish blacks' citizenship, recognize blacks' civil rights, and guarantee blacks' voting rights. As late as the 1880s, the Democrats were termed the party of "rum, romanism, and rebellion," because of the party's opposition to **temperance laws,** its support among Irish Catholics, and the fact that much of its support came from former Confederates.

In 1876, the Democratic governor of New York, Samuel J. Tilden, won the popular vote against Republican Rutherford B. Hayes (1877–1881), but Tilden lost the election when a congressional compromise awarded Hayes all the disputed electoral votes of three southern states. Election fraud, intimidation, and outright violence by white southern Democrats prevented thousands of blacks from voting. Had the election been run fairly, Hayes probably would have won outright. As part of the compromise that brought Hayes to the White House, the new president promised to re-move federal troops from the South, ending Reconstruction. The troops' removal led to a gradual loss of blacks' voting rights in the South, which became reliably Democratic and would remain known as the "Solid South" until the 1964 presidential election. Despite a virtual lock on all southern electoral votes, the Democrats captured the presidency only twice between 1860 and 1912: Grover Cleveland (1885–1889, 1893–1897) won in 1884 and 1892.

By the late nineteenth century, the Democratic Party's policies had changed somewhat from the antebellum period. Still a "white man's party," it was hostile to African Americans' civil rights and to Chinese immigration. With slavery ended, however, the party no longer favored expansionism. Cleveland refused to **annex** Hawaii, and some Democrats opposed the Spanish-American War in 1898. Democrats remained hostile to high tariffs, but they split on the issue of an expansive monetary policy; western Democrats favored the free coinage of silver, and eastern Democrats, including Cleveland, opposed it.

The Republican Party continued to dominate presidential politics for during the first dozen years of the twentieth century. In 1912, former president Theodore Roosevelt (1901–1909) failed in his attempt to gain his party's nomination over the **incumbent,** William Howard Taft (1909–1913). Roosevelt ran anyway, on the **Progressive**—or Bull Moose—ticket, winning six states and 4.1 million votes. Roosevelt came in second, and Taft a distant third, but Taft and Roosevelt combined for 1.3 million more popular votes than did the Democrat, Woodrow Wilson (1913–1921). Had the Republicans been united, their candidate undoubtedly would have won. Divided, they enabled Wilson to carry forty states and the election.

Wilson, demonstrating the Democrats' hostility to civil rights and racial equality, ordered the **segregation** of all federal facilities in Washington, D.C. He was, however, a progressive reformer on many issues, and favored such innovations as the Federal Reserve System. Wilson also led the Democrats away from their historic position on foreign policy. In 1917, Wilson successfully asked Congress for a declaration of war, and he continued his policies after the end of World War I (1914–1918), as he worked to bring the United States into the League of Nations. For the next half-century, the Democratic Party stood for intervention and international responsibility, while the Republicans retreated into **isolationism.**

After World War I, the Republicans took back the White House in 1920, kept it in 1924, and won again with Herbert Hoover's 1928 victory over Democrat Alfred E. (Al) Smith, the first Roman Catholic presidential nominee. After the stock market crashed in 1929, however, the **Great Depression** paved the way for a new Democratic dominance in the White House and an even longer one in Congress.

New Deal to Great Society

The 1932 election of Franklin D. Roosevelt (1933–1945) signaled a dramatic and lasting change in American politics. Democrats sang "Happy Days Are Here Again" as they became the majority party and rallied behind FDR's bold New Deal programs. Democrats, long the party of states' rights, became identified with national initiatives on economic and social issues. Once a party opposed to regulation, the Democrats helped create a massive bureaucracy to regulate the economy. Social programs, most notably Social Security, set the stage for the modern nation that provides a social safety net for vulnerable citizens.

During the Roosevelt years and after, for the first time in its history, the Democratic Party welcomed African American support and even supported some civil rights legislation. President Roosevelt and his successor, Harry S. Truman (1945–1953), issued **executive** orders to combat some types of racial **segregation** and discrimination. The New Deal coalition—northern blacks, southern whites, farmers, labor unionists, intellectuals, and ethnic urban voters—kept Roosevelt and Truman in office for twenty consecutive years, ending in 1953.

As Europe moved toward war in the 1930s, Roosevelt pushed an international agenda, building on Wilson's legacy. Opposition came from Republican **isolationists** but, unlike Wilson, FDR was able to bring the nation along with him, and the United States took the lead in establishing the United Nations (UN). Truman continued this internationalist policy, first with the Marshall Plan to help Europe recover from World War II (1939–1945) and then with the development of NATO and other international defense pacts. In

1950, Truman pushed for UN intervention when North Korea attacked South Korea, and soon the United States was heavily involved in another war in Asia.

In domestic politics, Truman pushed an activist agenda that he called the Fair Deal and called for expanded enforcement of African Americans' civil rights. Running for another term in 1948, he confronted splits within his party from two quarters: the South and the left. Displeased with Truman's civil rights stand, **conservative** southerners bolted the Democratic Party in 1948 and ran J. Strom Thurmond of South Carolina as the States' Rights Democratic, or Dixiecrat, nominee. Under the Progressive Party banner, Henry A. Wallace also challenged Truman. Thurmond won four states; Wallace took none. Despite the split, Truman defeated Republican Thomas E. Dewey.

After Truman left office in 1953, a Republican, Dwight D. Eisenhower (1953–1961), served the next two terms, but then the Democrats took back the White House in 1960, as John F. Kennedy (1961–1963), the first Roman Catholic president, narrowly defeated Eisenhower's vice president, Richard M. Nixon. Kennedy's slogan, the New Frontier, mirrored traditional Democratic slogans, such as Wilson's New Freedom, FDR's New Deal, and Truman's Fair Deal. Kennedy continued the Democratic agenda of internationalism, with the Peace Corps and aid to the pro-Western regime in South Vietnam, and of federal support for domestic improvements, with a massive tax cut and federal programs in housing. Kennedy made tentative moves in civil rights, but he went cautiously because of the power of southern whites within his party.

After Kennedy's assassination in 1963, President Lyndon B. Johnson (1963–1969) completed much of Kennedy's New Frontier agenda and called for additional programs in pursuit of the **Great Society,** including a civil rights program that was termed by some a "second Reconstruction." Applying all the skills he had learned as Senate majority leader, Johnson pushed through the Civil Rights Act of 1964. Johnson's support for civil rights ended the Solid South as a Democratic stronghold. In 1964, Johnson won in a landslide. Carrying all but five states, he took 61.1 percent of the popular vote, the largest popular victory of any presidential election in U.S. history.

A - Z

The South, however, supported Republican Barry Goldwater, who had opposed the Civil Rights Act of 1964. Johnson's mandate enabled him to win passage of the Voting Rights Act of 1965, further solidifying Democratic support among African Americans while further undermining Democratic power among white southerners.

Johnson expanded U.S. involvement in the unpopular war in Vietnam, thereby splitting the party and prompting his decision not to run for reelection in 1968. Vice President Hubert H. Humphrey, nominated without entering any primaries, faced competition in November from the American Independent candidacy of George C. Wallace, former Democratic governor of Alabama. These divisive factors contributed to Humphrey's narrow defeat by Republican Richard Nixon (1969–1974).

The Democratic Party Since 1968

In the 1970s, the Democrats drastically reformed their delegate-selection and nominating rules, encouraging minority representation, dividing delegations equally between men and women, and awarding delegates to candidates in proportion to their primary votes. The changes enhanced the role of primary elections in the nominating process, leading to more primaries and fewer state **caucuses.**

The 1972 election was the last privately financed presidential election. Nixon raised $61.4 million versus McGovern's $21.2 million. McGovern, running as a peace candidate with a commitment to massive domestic spending, lost to Nixon in a landslide. The election-related Watergate scandal, however, drove Nixon from office two years later and brought Vice President Gerald R. Ford (1974–1977) to the presidency.

Skillful use of the primaries, as well as Ford's unpopular full pardon of Nixon for his criminal activities in the Watergate cover-up, helped the relatively unknown Jimmy Carter (1977–1981) of Georgia defeat **incumbent** Ford in 1976. Carter's primary strategy also served him in 1980, when he survived a renomination challenge from Senator Edward M. Kennedy, brother of the late president. Nevertheless, Carter's inability to curb inflation or obtain the release of American hostages held in Iran for 444 days doomed him to defeat at the hands of Republican Ronald Reagan (1981–1989).

Although the popular Reagan handily won reelection in 1984, his vice president and successor, George Herbert Walker Bush (1989–1993), fell victim in 1992 to Bill Clinton (1993–2001) of Arkansas, as Democrats returned to the White House after twelve Republican years. During his campaign, Clinton addressed economic worries. His advisers reminded campaign workers, "It's the economy, stupid," and the strategy worked. He was the first Democrat to win without taking Texas and, with Al Gore of Tennessee as his running mate, the first president elected on an all-South ticket since Andrew Jackson and John C. Calhoun won in 1828.

Clinton won as a moderate, declaring, "The era of big government is over." His support came from a modified New Deal coalition that included "Reagan Democrats," union members, women, African Americans, Hispanics, Jews, a majority of Roman Catholics, public sector employees, and intellectuals. Peace and an improved economy soon had the Democratic administration basking in high approval ratings in public opinion polls. Nevertheless, the voters in 1994 broke the Democratic lock on Congress, turning both chambers over to Republican control.

Two years later the electorate opted to continue a divided government, giving Clinton another four-year term while leaving Congress in Republican hands. Although he was the first Democrat elected to a second full term since Franklin D. Roosevelt, Clinton again won with less than a majority of the popular vote.

Democrats made history several times from 1960 through the end of the century. In 1960, the party ran the nation's first successful Catholic presidential candidate, John F. Kennedy. In 1968, New York voters elected Democrat Shirley Chisholm as the first black woman member of the House of Representatives, and in 1992, another Democrat, Carol Moseley-Braun of Illinois, became the first black woman senator. When former vice president Walter F. Mondale chose Geraldine A. Ferraro as his running mate against Reagan in 1984, she became the first woman in American history to run on a major-party ticket. In 1989, L. Douglas Wilder of Virginia became the first African American to be elected state governor. In

2000, the Democratic nominee for president, Vice President Al Gore, chose Senator Joseph Lieberman of Connecticut as his running mate. This was the first time a Jew was on a national ticket. Also in 2000, Hillary Rodham Clinton became the first presidential wife to seek a major elective office, winning a Senate seat from New York.

Nevertheless, the 2000 elections were a major disappointment for Democrats. Gore lost a disputed election to Republican George W. Bush (2001–2009), son of the former president. Moreover, the Republicans retained control of both houses of Congress, although by the narrowest of margins.

The 2000 and 2004 presidential elections reasserted trends of recent years. In the South, the Republicans again showed their strength. The Democrats' strength was on the west and east coasts, north of Virginia, and in the industrial heartland of the upper Midwest. The Republicans dominated everywhere else—a giant "L"-shaped area from the South through the Plains states and Southwest and into the Mountain states. However, in the 2008 election, Democrats captured the usually Republican-leaning states of Indiana, Virginia, and North Carolina, as well as the swing states of Ohio and Florida.

See also: Bush v. Gore (2000); Republican Party (1854–); Whig Party (1834–1856).

Further Reading

Wagner, Heather Lehr. *The History of the Democratic Party.* New York: Chelsea House Publications, 2007.

Witcover, Jules. *Party of the People: A History of the Democrats.* New York: Random House, 2003.

Department of Agriculture (USDA)

Department that assists the nation's farmers through a variety of programs, including subsidies (money grants), credit, and rural development. USDA also oversees the nation's food quality and provides nutrition education programs. USDA's research facilities conduct experiments to find ways to improve agriculture. Moreover, the depart-

ment supports environmental protection through its resource conservation programs. Other responsibilities of the department include administering food distribution programs; managing the nation's national forests and grasslands; and helping developing nations improve food production.

From Small Beginnings

The idea of establishing an agricultural agency in the federal government first surfaced in 1776, but the USDA was not created until 1862. It was made a part of the cabinet in 1889. The law that defined the responsibilities of the department instructed it

> to acquire and to diffuse . . . useful information on subjects connected with agriculture in the most general and comprehensive sense of the word.

In carrying out this mandate, the commissioner of agriculture was to conduct experiments, collect statistics, and

> procure, propagate, and distribute among the people new and valuable seeds and plants.

Expansion of Functions

The Forest Service was established in 1905 as oversight of the national forests was transferred from the Department of the Interior to USDA. USDA was given additional regulatory authority as well, including the responsibility for administering the 1906 Meat Inspection and Food and Drug Acts (the latter was transferred to the Food and Drug Administration in 1940).

In 1914, the passage of the Smith-Lever Agricultural Extension Act allowed the department and land grant colleges, under formal cooperative agreements, to carry the information that was learned from research directly to farmers. In 1916, the department also became active in establishing standards and grades for agricultural products.

The USDA's responsibilities continued to grow during the **Great Depression.** To help farmers meet market needs, the Bureau of Agricultural Economics was established in 1922 to foster statistical and economic research. During the depression Congress responded to the farmers' plight by

A–Z

passing a number of significant laws, among them the 1933 Agricultural Adjustment Act (AAA), which provided for production adjustment to be achieved principally through direct USDA payments to farmers. The Farm Credit Act, passed the same year, consolidated all farm credit programs under the Farm Credit Administration. The Soil Conservation Service was established in 1935, as were the Resettlement Administration (which later became the Farm Security Administration and Farmers Home Administration) and the Rural Electrification Administration. In 1936 the Supreme Court declared the AAA **unconstitutional;** Congress responded by passing the Soil Conservation and Domestic Allotment Act.

Postwar Farm Policy

Responding to overseas food needs following World War II (1939–1945), USDA urged U.S. farmers to expand their productive capacity. By the end of the Korean War (1950–1953), however, the policy of emphasizing maximum production had resulted in **surpluses** and falling farm prices. Faced with that problem, Secretary of Agriculture Ezra Taft Benson chose to institute programs to expand markets rather than establish price supports. Nevertheless, a Soil Bank Program was put into place whereby farmers were paid to take farmland out of cultivation.

Years later, the Reagan administration (1981–1989) launched a drive to end many depression-era farm programs and eliminate the assumption that the federal government is directly responsible for farmers' well-being. In 2002, a 1996 farm law that deregulated agriculture expired. As **commodity prices** continued to slump because of oversupply, Congress faced the prospect of again having to bail out farmers with tens of billions of dollars in emergency aid. Bush advocated temporary emergency assistance during the transition to deregulation, but some farm groups urged a permanent system of aid during times of low prices.

Department of Commerce

Department of the cabinet that is responsible for foreign and domestic **commerce;** mining, manu-facturing, shipping, and fishery industries; labor interests; and transportation. It was created on March 4, 1913, after a law separated the Department of Commerce and Labor.

Expansion of the Department

During Herbert Hoover's seven-year tenure as secretary during the 1920s, the Department of Commerce acquired several organizations, and their respective responsibilities, from other departments. These organizations included a Building and Housing Division (1922), the Bureau of Mines and the Patent Office(1925), an Aeronautics Division (1926), and a Radio Division (1927). Until the Department of Transportation was established in 1967, Commerce was also the principal overseer of national transportation programs. The Department of Commerce now shares responsibilities in international economics with special presidential advisers, the Department of the Treasury, and the Office of the U.S. Trade Representative.

Functions

The Department of Commerce is organized according to the following functions.

Trade

The International Trade Administration (ITA) helps formulate foreign trade and economic policies, works with the U.S. Trade Representative and other agencies, and administers legislation to counter unfair foreign trade practices. Also included in the function of trade is the Bureau of Export Administration. This bureau formulates U.S. policy for the control of high-technology exports and monitors such exports.

In the category of tourism, there is the U.S. Travel and Tourism Administration (USTTA) that replaced the U.S. Travel Service in accordance with the National Tourism Policy Act of 1981. The U.S. Travel Service was originally established in 1961 to address a $1.2 billion balance-of-payments deficit in tourism.

Science and Technology

The Commerce Department's science and technology organizations are expected to use, or promote the development of, science and technology in order to improve Americans' quality of life. These organizations include the National Oceanic and Atmospheric Administration (NOAA), which monitors and predicts the weather, charts the seas and the skies, protects ocean resources, and collects data on the oceans, atmosphere, space, and sun. The Office of Technology Administration helps U.S. businesses become more competitive overseas by fostering government and private partnerships to encourage the development and spread of innovative technologies.

The National Institute of Standards and Technology is charged with custody, comparison, and, establishment of standards. The agency also has a growing role in the development of advanced technology, such as factories that produce corn-based plastic and stem cells that can repair diseased hearts.

Finally, The National Telecommunications and Information Administration's mandate is to develop policies on the advancement and use of new technologies in common carrier, telephone, broadcast, and satellite communications systems. Another part of the Department of Commerce, the Patent Office, began registering trademarks in

1870. In 1975, the agency's name was changed to the Patent and Trademark Office.

See also: Department of Labor.

Department of Defense (DOD)

Department that provides the umbrella for the army, navy, Marine Corps, air force, and reserves. As Professor Richard A. Stubbing wrote, the secretary of defense is responsible for taking account of the various defense interests that affect the country, and for deciding if and how to address these interests. The secretary must also form a military program that best suits the overall goals of himself and his administration. Considering the vast amount of defense interests that are associated with the United States, these tasks may often seem overwhelming or even impossible.

A - Z

Defense Secretary Robert Gates testified on Capitol Hill in April 2008, calling for more air support in the wars in Iraq and Afghanistan. (AP Images, Susan Walsh)

SPOTLIGHT

Department of War and Department of the Navy

The Department of War was established by Congress in 1789 with the purpose of overseeing the armed forces. A secretary of war, who served as a member of the president's cabinet, headed the department. The navy, formed in 1775, was under the authority of the new department until 1798, when Congress established a separate Department of the Navy.

The Department of War remained in control of the army and, eventually, gained several additional functions. These new responsibilities included non-combative tasks such as managing Indian affairs and the **reconstruction** of the South after the Civil War (1861–1865). Later, the Department of War took control of the National Guard and the officers' reserve corps that were created under the National Defense Act of 1916.

From 1941 to 1945, many attempts were made to combine the branches of the military under one department. Finally, Congress passed the National Security Act of 1947. This piece of legislation grouped the army, navy, and air force under one National Security Establishment headed by a secretary of defense. The Department of War became the Department of the Army under the umbrella of the National Security Establishment. This reorganization led to the loss of the Department of War's cabinet status along with some of the department's functions. Yet, under the National Security Establishment, each branch of the military remained self-governing, answering only to the secretary of defense. The heads of each branch still had the authority to speak directly to the president.

A 1949 **amendment** to the National Security Act of 1947 resulted in the National Security Establishment becoming the Department of Defense. The amendment gave the secretary of defense more authority, and required that each branch of the military to be led by a secretary who reported directly to the secretary of defense.

Creation of the National Military Establishment

Congress passed the National Security Act of 1947 on July 25. The law created a national military establishment, to be headed by the secretary of defense and to consist of the Departments of the Army, Navy, and Air Force. The secretary was designated "the principal assistant to the President in all matters relating to the national security." At the same time, the three service departments were to be "administered as individual **executive** departments by their respective Secretaries." These secretaries retained the right to present "to the President or to the Director of the Budget . . . any report or recommendations relating to his department which he may deem necessary." The Joint Chiefs of Staff (JCS) were given authority as the principal military advisers to the president and the secretary of defense. They have the authority to prepare strategic plans, establish **unified commands,** and review the military forces' major material and personnel requirements. President Harry S. Truman (1945–1953) signed the law on July 26, 1947.

1949 Amendments

The National Security Act amendments of 1949 converted the national military establishment into a cabinet-level Department of Defense. The amended act incorporated the military departments of the three services and stated that each was to be separately administered by a secretary under the direction, authority, and control of the secretary of defense. The secretary was forbidden, however, from acting to transfer, abolish, or consolidate any of the services' combatant functions.

The law also provided for a deputy secretary of defense, three assistant secretaries, and a nonvoting chairman of the Joint Chiefs of Staff (to replace the chief of staff to the president), who was to rank first in the JCS but hold no command.

After the Korean War (1950–1953) revealed more organizational shortcomings of the military complex, President Dwight D. Eisenhower (1953–1961) asked a group of prominent citizens to propose changes in the Defense Department. Their recommendations were embodied in a reorganization plan that the president submitted to Congress. The plan was adopted, providing for six additional assistant secretary positions. It also gave the secretary the power to select the director of the joint staff of the Joint Chiefs of Staff.

Department of Education

Department that oversees the nation's educational systems. Congress passed legislation creating the Department of Education in 1979.

Predecessors of the Department

The first Department of Education was downgraded quickly to the status of a bureau in the Interior Department. For the next seventy years, it limped along as a small recordkeeping office, collecting information on the modest federal education efforts. In 1939, the renamed Office of Education was transferred to the Federal Security Agency, which became the Department of Health, Education, and Welfare (HEW) in 1953.

With the tremendous expansion of federal education programs after World War II (1939–1945), arguments for a separate department grew more persuasive. In 1972, Congress established within HEW an Education Division, headed by an assistant secretary for education. It included the existing Office of Education.

Controversy Over Its Creation

One of the main arguments for a separate education department was the confusing and contradictory structure of the existing federal educational administration. In 1978, the hundreds of federal educational programs were located in more than forty different agencies. Grouping all these programs in one department, however, proved to be very difficult politically. For every program going into the department, some other department would have to lose power and money.

In 1979, after over a year of struggling, the proposal's supporters effectively lobbied Congress, attaining the margin needed to create the department. Some 152 federal education-related programs were consolidated in the new agency.

Yet, the new department was inhibited in its authority by the long-standing tradition in the United States that education is primarily a state and local function. Congress restated the commitment to decentralized control in the act that was passed to create the department. In accordance with this act, the Department of Education distributes most of its program funds directly to the states as formula grants. The amounts are based on the number of students in various special categories, and the states then distribute the money to local districts under department-approved plans.

See also: Department of Health and Human Services (HHS).

A - Z

Department of Energy (DOE)

Department that assumed the powers and functions of Federal Energy Administration (FEA), Energy Research and Development Administration (ERDA), Federal Power Commission (FPC), and the four regional power commissions. DOE also absorbed energy-related programs formerly administered by the Interstate Commerce Commission and the Departments of the Interior, Defense, Commerce, and Housing and Urban Development. The department assumed as well the role of consultant to the Department of Transportation and the Rural Electrification Administration on energy-related matters.

Response to the Energy Crisis

President Richard M. Nixon (1969–1974) was the first president to suggest that the federal agencies dealing with energy be reorganized and consolidated. Nixon's proposal was denied twice by Congress, but as the energy crisis became a fact of life, Congress responded in 1974 to Nixon's requests to create FEA and ERDA. A few years later, President Gerald R. Ford (1974–1977) submitted a plan to Congress for reorganizing the federal energy programs into a Department of Energy. President Jimmy Carter (1977–1981) offered a similar proposal a few months later.

The **bill** that finally reached Carter's desk for his signature on August 4, 1977, differed in only one major respect from his original proposal. Carter and Congress disagreed over who in the new energy structure should have the power to set prices for natural gas, oil, and electricity. Carter would have given this power to the secretary of energy, but majorities in both chambers of Congress were opposed on the ground that it was unwise to give such power to a single person who served at the pleasure of the president. Instead, in the DOE legislation Congress included language that created an independent Federal Energy Regulatory Commission (FERC) that would set energy prices. If the president found that a national emergency required quick action on such matters, however, the secretary could take responsibility for setting oil prices.

Department of Health and Human Services (HHS)

Department that oversees federal programs that promote human health and welfare. It was established in 1979 as the successor to the Department of Health, Education and Welfare (HEW).

Product of Reorganization

HEW evolved in a series of presidential reorganization plans and laws that became effective between 1939 and 1953. These reorganization plans saw to the creation of the Federal Security Agency (FSA). They also saw to the transfer of several offices and responsibilities from their respective departments to the FSA. These departments and responsibilities included the Public Health Service (PHS), the Office of Education, the Food and Drug Administration, the Children's Bureau, the Office of Vital Statistics, the Office of Employment Security, and the management of the Federal Credit Union Act of 1934. Other changes due to presidential reorganization included the replacement of the Social Security Board with the Social Security Administration (SSA), and the creation of an office of vocational rehabilitation in FSA.

On March 12, 1953, President Dwight D. Eisenhower (1953–1961) submitted to Congress a reorganization plan that transformed FSA into a cabinet-level Department of Health, Education and Welfare. The plan, which took effect on April 11, did not vest all departmental powers directly in the new secretary; instead, it left the functions of the PHS and Office of Education as the responsibility of those two agencies. They would be subordinate units of the new department operating under the secretary's general supervision.

The plan also provided for the creation of a new post of special assistant to the secretary for health and medical affairs. The special assistant, to be appointed by the president, was to be a person of wide nongovernmental experience in that field, but not necessarily a physician. The plan also provided for the presidential appointment, subject to Senate confirmation, of a commissioner of Social Security.

Expansion of Responsibilities

During the next few years, the responsibilities of HEW increased significantly. In 1954, far-reaching changes were made in the Old Age and Survivors Insurance (OASI) program, greatly extending coverage. In 1956, OASI was changed to OASDI to include disability insurance. Also that year, Congress authorized the PHS to create a National Library of Medicine.

The department's responsibilities continued to grow as the administration of Lyndon B. Johnson (1963–1969) initiated various social programs under the banner of the **Great Society.** The most dramatic development was the establishment of the Medicare program in 1965 to provide hospital insurance for seniors, financed through the Social Security system. Also in 1965, a Medicaid—a program that pays for medical care for the poor—was enacted. Jimmy Carter's (1977–1981) first HEW secretary, Joseph A. Califano Jr., would eventually consolidate administration of the Medicare and Medicaid programs in a new Health Care Financing Administration (HCFA).

Existing programs were also broadened to include community mental health and retardation as well as aid to education for doctors, nurses, and other health specialists. Social Security was revised, with retirement benefits raised and eligibility requirements eased.

A more dramatic reorganization occurred in 1979 when Congress voted to consolidate the education functions of HEW and several other cabinet departments in a separate Department of Education. The remaining HEW responsibilities were given to the renamed Department of Health and Human Services.

Another change occurred in 1994 when both houses of Congress passed and President Bill Clinton (1993–2001) signed legislation making the Social Security Administration independent as of March 31, 1995. The SSA became self-governing, administered by a commissioner and deputy commissioner. The commissioner and deputy commissioner are appointed by the president to six-year terms, subject to Senate confirmation. They are advised by a seven-member board, to which the president appoints three members and Congress

appoints four. The department has four operating divisions.

Administration on Aging

The Administration on Aging is the principal office for carrying out the orders of the 1965 Older Americans Act. It advises the secretary and other federal departments on the characteristics and needs of older people and develops programs designed to promote their welfare.

Public Health Service

The Public Health Service (PHS) had its origin in a July 16, 1798, act that authorized a Marine Hospital Service for the care of American merchant sailors. Subsequent legislation vastly broadened the scope of its activities. Organizations currently working under PHS include the Agency for Health Care Policy and Research, the Centers for Disease Control (CDC), the Agency for Toxic Substances and Disease Registry, the Food and Drug Administration, the Health Resources and Service Administration, the Indian Health Service, the National Institutes of Health (NIH), the Substance Abuse and Mental Health Services Administration, and the surgeon general. PHS also administers grants to promote health services, research, education, and planning.

Administration for Children and Families

The Administration for Children and Families (ACF) is responsible for federal programs that promote the economic and social well-being of families, children, individuals, and communities. It recommends actions and strategies designed to improve coordination of family support programs among HHS, other federal agencies, state and local governments, and private-sector organizations.

See also: Department of Education.

Department of Homeland Security (DHS)

Department that is responsible for helping to protect against and respond to acts of terrorism within the United States. Following the terrorist attacks of September 11, 2001, on the World Trade Center and the Pentagon, Congress acted to create a federal agency to oversee homeland security. On November 25, 2002, President George W. Bush (2001–2009) signed into law the Homeland Security Act of 2002, creating the Department of Homeland Security (DHS). Creation of DHS, the newest of the federal government's fifteen cabinet-level departments, did not emerge automatically after the terrorist attacks. On October 8, 2001, President Bush signed an **executive** order creating the White House Office of Homeland Security and the Homeland Security Council, whose purpose was to

> **d**evelop and consolidate the implementation of a national strategy to secure the U.S. from terrorist threats or attacks.

The decision to move swiftly to focus the federal government on terrorism received **bipartisan** support in Congress, but how the federal government should handle the process was heavily debated. Senators Arlen Specter (R-PA) and Joseph Lieberman (D-CT) sought a different solution to coordinating homeland security. In October 2001, they proposed that a Department of Homeland Security be created that would have its own budget and whose secretary would be accountable to and could be called to testify before Congress.

Throughout the following months, President Bush and members of Congress were at odds over where the coordinating body for homeland security would be lodged: within the White House, or as a cabinet-level department? As Brookings Institution scholars Ivo H. Daalder and James M. Lindsey noted,

> **B**ush resisted the proposal for months, insisting that his decision to create an office of Homeland Security in the White House was sufficient. "Creating a cabinet post," argued White House spokesman Ari Fleischer in March 2002, "didn't solve anything."

Under growing pressure to create a cabinet-level department, President Bush relented in June 2002 and six months later Congress passed the

Homeland Security Act, establishing the new department.

DHS spent its first three years developing a manageable organizational structure to integrate the different agencies that were pulled together into the department. In addition, the department was tasked, by its initiating legislation, with creating the national homeland security strategy. The most visible part of the strategy was the published "threat assessment level" that gave daily updates on potential terrorist threats by way of a color-coded scale.

A major test of the department came in 2005, when the Federal Emergency Management Agency (FEMA) was criticized for mishandling the federal response to the devastation along the Gulf Coast and in New Orleans following Hurricane Katrina. (FEMA had been absorbed into DHS as part of the overall mandate for homeland security). The department faced other challenges in 2005, including charges that the borders had not been adequately secured from terrorists and that a foreign company from Dubai should not have been allowed to win a bid for managing key ports. After protests from both Democratic and Republican members of Congress, the department terminated the tentative agreement with the Dubai ports-management company. In 2006, as President Bush pushed an immigration **bill** in Congress, the department was again criticized for failing to secure the Mexican border from an influx of undocumented aliens. Because the Customs and Border Protection agency within DHS did not have the workforce to secure the border, President Bush sent in National Guard troops to patrol the U.S.-Mexican border.

Organization

The Department of Homeland Security is organized into four major directorates: Border and Transportation Security, Emergency Preparedness and Response, Science and Technology, and Information Analysis and Infrastructure Protection. The Border and Transportation Security directorate includes the U.S. Customs Service, the Immigration and Naturalization Service, the Federal Protective Service, the Transportation Security Administration, the Federal Law Enforcement Training Center, the Animal and Plant Health

DECISION MAKERS

Michael Chertoff (1953–)

Michael Chertoff was sworn in as the second secretary of homeland security on February 15, 2005. Before his appointment, Chertoff was a United States circuit judge for the Third Circuit Court of Appeals. As a graduate from Harvard Law School, Chertoff began his career as a federal prosecutor, holding jobs as a U.S. attorney for the district of New Jersey, a first assistant U.S. attorney for the district of New Jersey, and an assistant U.S. attorney for the southern district of New York. Through these positions, Chertoff became known as an extremely aggressive prosecutor. This aggression was clearly shown when he prosecuted the leaders of the La Cosa Nostra for directing the criminal activities of the American Mafia, leading to their conviction and sentencing to one hundred years in prison.

Chertoff went on to become the assistant attorney general for the criminal division in the Department of Justice in 2001. While he held this position, Chertoff became a key leader in the George W. Bush (2001–2009) administration's war on terrorism. He oversaw the investigation of the September 11, 2001, terrorist attacks, leading to the prosecution of Zacarias Moussaoui, the only person to be charged for the attacks.

After claiming the office of the secretary of the Department of Homeland Security, Chertoff continued to be a controversial figure. In January 2008, he established new rules for drivers' licenses that made them more secure from identity fraud. Many opponents of the new regulations argued that they were too costly, and that carrying them out would result in privacy violations. Chertoff was also criticized for ignoring many environmental laws in order to rush construction of a fence along the Mexican border that would keep undocumented immigrants out of the United States.

Inspection Service, and the Office of Domestic Preparedness.

The Emergency Preparedness and Response directorate includes the Federal Emergency Management Agency (FEMA), Strategic National Stockpile and National Disaster Medical System, Nuclear Incident Response Team, Domestic Emergency Support Teams, and National Domestic Preparedness Office. The Science and Technology directorate includes CBRN Countermeasures Programs, the Environmental Measurements Laboratory, the National BW Defense Analysis Center, and the Plum Island Animal Disease Center. Finally, the Information Analysis and Infrastructure Protection directorate includes the Federal Computer Incident Response Center, the National Communications System, the National Infrastructure Protection Center, and the Energy Security and Assurance Program.

The department is organized with a deputy secretary, an undersecretary for management, an undersecretary for science and technology, and an undersecretary for the directorate for preparedness. In addition, the department has seven assistant secretaries, six agency directors, and the commandant of the U.S. Coast Guard.

A - Z

Department of Housing and Urban Development (HUD)

Department responsible for federal housing and programs that affect the development and preservation of urban communities and the enforcement of equal housing opportunities. These responsibilities include administering Federal Housing Administration (FHA) mortgage insurance programs that help families become homeowners and facilitate the construction and rehabilitation of rental units. HUD also provides rental assistance programs for lower-income families, as well as programs to combat housing discrimination and promote fair housing. Other programs of the department promote community and neighborhood development and preservation, protect home-buyers in the marketplace, and provide temporary and transitional housing for homeless people. Finally, HUD administers the Government National Mortgage Association (GNMA, or Ginnie Mae), mortgage-backed securities that help ensure an adequate supply of mortgage credit.

HUD was established by one of two major housing **bills** that became law in 1965. The first bill authorized rent supplements for poor persons unable to pay for decent housing. The bill establishing HUD. Accompanying legislation, passed between 1965 and 1968, gave the department additional, and controversial, responsibilities: administering rent supplements to help the poor who could not afford decent housing, a model cities program intended to pump extra federal funds into needy cities, and a program to promote home ownership by poor people.

Creation of HUD

The idea of establishing a department of housing was first proposed by John F. Kennedy (1961–1963) in 1961, but was rejected by Congress. On March 2, 1965, in his Message on the Cities, Lyndon B. Johnson (1963–1969) made a similar attempt, calling for a department of housing and urban development. The president's proposal ran into difficulties in Congress, yet it still passed the House on June 16 by a 217–184 vote. The Senate concurred on August 11.

As signed by Johnson on September 9, 1965, the HUD bill upgraded the existing House and Home Finance Agency (HHFA) to cabinet-level status. The HHFA then consisted of the Office of the Administrator and five operating units: the Federal Housing Administration, the Public Housing Administration, the Federal National Mortgage Association, the Community Facilities Administration, and the Urban Renewal Administration.

The new department was not given authority to administer all federal programs related to cities and urban problems. One section of the bill, however, required a study of the functions of other agencies to determine if any should be transferred to HUD. The bill did not attempt to define an urban area or to limit the size of communities that could benefit from a HUD program.

Development of HUD's Programs

By the late 1970s, the federal government was providing a wide range of housing assistance, including direct mortgage and rent subsidies; direct government-insured mortgages; loans; secondary market programs; and programs designed to help special-risk homeowners and renters. In addition to HUD, the Veterans Administration and the Department of Agriculture's Farmers Home Administration participated in these programs.

In 1977, the administration introduced a new urban development program called Urban Development Action Grants (UDAG). Aimed at urban areas with the most severe problems, UDAG used federal funds to spur private investment.

Organization and Functions

The HUD secretary is assisted by a deputy secretary; both are advised by two assistants, one for field management and the other for labor relations. The office of the secretary also contains four staff offices with department-wide responsibility in specialized areas: Indian and Alaskan native programs, small and disadvantaged business utilization, administrative and judicial proceedings, and contract appeals.

Two external organizations complement the

DECISION MAKERS

Alphonso Jackson (1945–)

Alphonso Jackson was confirmed as the thirteenth secretary of the U.S. Department of Housing and Urban Development (HUD) on March 31, 2004. Before becoming secretary, Jackson was the deputy secretary and chief operating officer of HUD; he and became acting secretary when Mel Martinez left the post in November 2004.

Jackson's tenure as secretary was characterized by crisis and scandal. In August 2005, Hurricane Katrina slammed into the Gulf Coast, causing massive amounts of damage and many deaths. Jackson and HUD were key contributors to the redevelopment of the destroyed neighborhoods. The growing mortgage crisis was another problem HUD faced at this time. During this crisis, people had a much harder time selling their homes, while others found it difficult to acquire loans in order to buy homes. While dealing with this issue, Jackson faced many accusations of ethics violations, including charges that he selected contractors based on politics. For example, Jackson reportedly revoked a contract from a contractor who publicly stated that he did not like President George W. Bush. Jackson was also accused of having a conflict of interest when he awarded $127 million to Columbia Residential, a builder of residential communities, to be used to help redevelop New Orleans. It was discovered that Columbia Residential had financial ties with Jackson. Jackson also reportedly punished the director of the Philadelphia Housing Authority (PHA) when he refused to turn over property to a company associated with Jackson's friend, Kenny Gamble.

In March 2008, Senators Christopher Dodd (D-CT) and Patty Murray (D-WA) called for Jackson's resignation, stating that he was too distracted by accusations of ethics violations to give the appropriate attention to the mortgage crisis. Jackson resigned on March 31, 2008, claiming personal reasons. President Bush stated after the resignation was announced that Jackson had "made significant progress in transforming public housing, revitalizing and modernizing the Federal Housing Administration, increasing affordable housing, rebuilding the Gulf Coast, decreasing homelessness, and increasing minority home ownership."

department's responsibilities. The Interagency Council on the Homeless, which receives administrative support from HUD, is responsible for reviewing and coordinating the programs and activities of seventeen federal agencies designed to help the homeless. The Federal Housing Finance Board, established as an independent agency within the **executive** branch, oversees the Federal Home Loan Banks.

See also: Department of Agriculture (USDA); Department of Veterans Affairs.

Department of Justice

Department that investigates violations of federal law (ranging from income tax evasion to criminal syndicates), supervises the custody of those accused or convicted of federal crimes, oversees legal and illegal aliens, and directs U.S. domestic security against threats of foreign or internal subversion. Justice polices narcotics trafficking; helps state and local governments expand and improve police departments, courts, and correctional institutions (through federal aid); advises the president and other government agencies on legal matters; and drafts legislation. The Justice Department also conducts all suits in the Supreme Court to which the U.S. government is a party. The attorney general supervises and directs these activities, as well as those of the U.S. attorneys and U.S. marshals in the nation's various judicial districts.

The U.S. attorney general was one of the first positions to be established, with cabinet rank, in the federal government. The Judiciary Act of September 24, 1789, made the attorney general the chief legal officer of the federal government. The Department of Justice itself was established in 1870, with the attorney general as its head.

Evolution of the Department in the 1960s

Before the 1960s the department's mission was perceived as primarily one of prosecuting violations of the Internal Revenue Code, instituting antitrust suits, and keeping watch over subversives and **public enemies.** In the 1960s, however, Justice became intimately involved with major domestic issues, including racial violence, mass demonstrations, riots, draft resistance to the Vietnam War (1959–1975), and rising crime rates. To cope with its increased responsibilities the department created a number of new divisions, and by 1970, it had 208 units.

Organization and Functions

The attorney general provides overall policy and program direction for the offices, divisions, bureaus, and boards of the department and represents the United States in legal matters generally. The attorney general also makes recommendations to the president about appointments to federal judicial positions. The attorney

Senator John F. Kennedy (right) confers with his brother, Robert F. Kennedy, at the 1957 Rackets Committee hearings in Congress. After Senator Kennedy was inaugurated as president in 1961, Robert Kennedy served as his attorney general and a trusted adviser. (John F. Kennedy Presidential Library and Museum)

JUSTICE FOR ALL

John Mitchell (1913–1988)

Before he became Richard Nixon's (1969–1974) attorney general, John Mitchell was a successful municipal bond lawyer in New York. In 1967, Mitchell met Nixon in 1967, when his law firm merged with the law firm of Nixon Mudge Rose Guthrie and Alexander. Mitchell put his law career on hold in 1968 to become Nixon's presidential campaign manager. After Nixon won the election, he made Mitchell his attorney general. Mitchell held the post from 1969 until 1972, when he left to head Nixon's Committee to Re-elect the President (CRP).

That year, G. Gordon Liddy approached Mitchell with the "Gemstone" plan, a $1 million scheme to steal political secrets from the Democratic Party. Mitchell convinced Liddy to do a cheaper version of the plan that involved breaking into the Democratic National Committee headquarters at the Watergate Hotel and bugging the telephone of the Democratic Party chairman. The police arrested the five men who attempted the break-in.

After the plot was discovered and revealed by *Washington Post* reporters Carl Bernstein and Bob Woodward, Mitchell helped Nixon to cover up the White House's involvement. Evidence showed that Mitchell had met with Nixon on three different occasions to discuss the cover-up. Mitchell admitted later that he knew about the cover-up, but claimed to have kept this information from Nixon so as not to distract him from his reelection campaign. Mitchell also resigned from his position on the Committee to Re-elect the President in order to distance himself from the situation. He explained his resignation by saying that he wanted to spend more time with his wife and daughter. It was later revealed by the *Washington Post* that, during his term as attorney general, Mitchell had control over a secret fund that was being used to gather intelligence that could be used against Democrats. The Watergate break-in was financed by this fund.

Mitchell was brought before a federal grand jury in May 1973 and convicted of obstructing justice, perjury, and conspiracy to obstruct justice. He was sentenced to two and a half to eight years in prison, which was later reduced to one to four years. After only nineteen months, Mitchell was released on parole for medical reasons. He returned to Washington, D.C., where he died on November 9, 1988, from a heart attack. He insisted, until the day he died, that Nixon was not involved in the Watergate plot.

general is assisted by a deputy attorney general and associate attorney general, who are responsible for managing the department.

The office of the solicitor general supervises and conducts government litigation in the Supreme Court. The solicitor general, often called the tenth justice of the Court, determines which cases the government will seek to have the Supreme Court review, as well as the position the government will take on each case. Another function of the office is to decide which cases, of those lost before the lower courts, the United States should appeal.

In addition to its divisions and bureaus, the department consists of various offices. These include the Office of Legal Counsel, that assists the attorney general as legal adviser to the president and all the **executive** branches, and the Office of **Legislative** Affairs, which acts as a liaison between the department and Congress. There is also the Justice Management Division, which assists senior management officials with matters related to basic department policy, and the Community Relations Service (CRS) that helps to resolves disputes through its field staff of mediators and conciliators. The Office of the Pardon Attorney receives and reviews all petitions for executive clemency, initiates the necessary investigations, and recommends to the president which form of executive clemency—pardon, commutation of sentence, remission of fine, or reprieve—it finds appropriate in certain cases.

Other Department of Justice divisions include the Office of Professional Responsibility, which investigates allegations of misconduct by department employees, and the Inspector General's office, which enforces fraud, waste, abuse, and integrity laws and regulations within the department. The Office of Policy and Communications consists of an Office of Policy Development and an Office of Public Affairs. These offices are responsible for developing and coordinating department policy and communicating with the media, the law enforcement community, and the public. The Executive Office for United States Attorneys provides U.S. attorneys with executive assistance, and the Office of Intelligence Policy and Review advises the attorney general on matters of national security. Finally, there are the U.S. trustees, which ensure compliance with federal bankruptcy laws, and the Office of Special Counsel for Immigration Related Unfair Employment Practices.

Department of Labor

Department whose job it is to foster, promote, and develop the welfare of the wage earners of the United States, to improve their working conditions, and to advance their opportunities for profitable employment. The department deals with wide-ranging and significant areas of workers' well-being, including unemployment insurance and workers' compensation, minimum wages and overtime pay, occupational health and safety, discrimination in employment, protection of pension rights, job training, and the right to free collective bargaining. The department compiles statistics on prices, employment, and other appropriate subjects, and works to improve the employment opportunities of minorities, youth, older workers, women, and people with disabilities.

Advocacy for a Labor Department

In 1884, Congress passed and President Chester A. Arthur (1881–1885) signed a **bill** that established a Bureau of Labor in the Interior Department. The bureau was to gather information pertaining to workers and devise a means of promoting their material, social, intellectual, and moral prosperity. President Grover Cleveland (1885–1889, 1893–1897) pressed for enlarging the bureau and empowering it to investigate and judge labor disputes. The Knights of Labor lobbied for creation of a cabinet-level department and succeeded in having a bill introduced in 1888. The legislation was watered down, however. The bill that emerged from Congress established an independent Department of Labor, but without cabinet status. Cleveland signed the legislation on March 21. During the next few years, the department gained in stature as the most important federal statistics-gathering agency and as author of significant reports on such subjects as labor legislation, compulsory insurance, housing, railroad labor, and the status of women in the workforce.

Merger, Then Independence

On becoming president, Theodore Roosevelt (1901–1909) suggested appointing a secretary of commerce and industries, with cabinet status. "It should be his province to deal with **commerce** in its broadest sense, including among many other things whatever concerns labor and all matters affecting the great business corporations," Roosevelt said. Legislation creating the new department, its name changed to the Department of Commerce and Labor, was signed into law in February 1903. Representative William Sulzer (D-NY) introduced a bill for a separate Department of Labor in 1912; it cleared both chambers and was signed into law on March 4, 1913.

See also: Department of Commerce.

Department of State

Department that advises the president on foreign affairs. The State Department is the senior **executive** department of the U.S. government. Americans employed by the department are members of either the civil service or the foreign service. Those in the civil service generally do not serve overseas, while foreign service personnel spend approximately 60 percent of their years of service in foreign countries.

History of the Department
The present-day Department of State had its beginnings in 1781 when Congress established a Department of Foreign Affairs, which was redesignated as the Department of State in September 1789. The department was reorganized by Secretary Louis McLane (1833–1834) into bureaus dealing with diplomatic, consular, internal, and servicing functions. That arrangement continued until 1870, when Secretary Hamilton Fish (1869–1877) split the diplomatic and consular bureaus into two geographically oriented units. In the early 1900s, Secretaries Elihu Root (1905–1909) and Philander C. Knox (1909–1913) reorganized the department into regional divisions, which is the basis of today's structure. The 1924 Rogers Act combined the diplomatic and consular services in a single foreign service.

Responding to the expansion of State's activities during World War II (1939–1945), Secretary Cordell Hull (1933–1944) grouped related functions under individual assistant secretaries and established eleven coordinating offices. In 1949, Secretary of State Dean Acheson (1949–1953) rearranged the existing eighteen offices into five bureaus (four geographic and a Bureau of United Nations Affairs), as well as units dealing with economic, intelligence, public, and press affairs. Eventually, there were six substantive and eight functional agencies.

Condoleezza Rice first served as President George W. Bush's (2001–2009) national security adviser. In 2005, the president appointed her secretary of state. (AP Images, Dita Alangkara)

Secretary's Position
The secretary of state is generally considered a member of the president's inner cabinet, among the chief **executive's** closest advisers. However, the influence of the department has varied according to personalities and circumstances. President Harry S. Truman (1945–1953), for example, relied heavily on the advice of Secretary George C. Marshall in the **reconstruction** of Europe after World War II (1947–1949). In the following years of mounting international tension, presidents continued to look to their secretaries for principal foreign policy leadership.

Organization and Functions
The secretary of state is responsible for the overall direction, coordination, and supervision of U.S. foreign relations and for the interdepartmental

A–Z

DECISION MAKERS

Thomas Jefferson (1743–1826)

Thomas Jefferson was appointed as the first secretary of state by President George Washington (1789–1797) on September 29, 1789. Before his appointment, Jefferson served as the American minister to France, a position that he was reluctant to leave. He was known to be a supporter of the French Revolution, yet, as secretary of state, he maintained the policy of U.S. **neutrality** in regards to European conflicts. During his term, Jefferson began the practice of requiring periodic reports from all U.S. diplomatic and consular posts. Jefferson also defined the difference between diplomatic and consular posts, saying that diplomatic posts are more politically oriented, while consular posts are more commercially oriented.

While he was the secretary of state, the pro-French Jefferson often clashed with the pro-British secretary of the treasury, Alexander Hamilton. Jefferson believed that Hamilton's use of government finances was unwise and **unconstitutional.** He accused Hamilton of trying to establish monarchist principles within the American government. The conflict between these two men led to the formation of the first two major political parties: the Federalists and the Democratic-Republicans. The Federalists were a party formed by Hamilton that supported his financial policies and desired a financially sound and **nationalistic** government. Jefferson created the Democratic-Republican Party to combat the Federalists, who Jefferson equated with "royalists". As President Washington began siding more and more with Hamilton, Jefferson became frustrated and resigned from the position of secretary of state on December 31, 1793. During his tenure, Jefferson had laid the groundwork for the resolution of foreign policy issues such as the protection of American territorial integrity from Great Britain and Spain and the right to navigate the Mississippi River.

activities of the U.S. government overseas. The secretary is the highest ranking member of the cabinet and a member of the National Security Council.

The secretary is assisted by a deputy secretary and five undersecretaries (arms control and international security affairs; global affairs; political affairs; economic, business, and agricultural affairs; and management). Also attached to the secretary's office are the U.S. ambassador to the United Nations, several ambassadors-at-large (who undertake special missions), the chief of protocol, and the Policy Planning Staff.

Regional Bureaus

Primary substantive responsibility in the department rests with the six regional bureaus (European and Canadian Affairs, African Affairs, East Asian and Pacific Affairs, Inter-American Affairs, Near Eastern Affairs, and South Asian Affairs), which are headed by assistant secretaries. These bureaus advise the secretary on the formulation of U.S. policies toward countries within their regional **jurisdiction** and guide the operations of the U.S. diplomatic establishments in those countries.

The Bureau of International Organization Affairs manages U.S. participation in the United

Nations and its system of programs and agencies. The bureau also deals with international problems such as food production, air traffic safety, communications, health, human rights, education, and the environment. In addition, the bureau is responsible for U.S. participation in international conferences, some hosted by the United States.

Functional Bureaus

The remaining bureaus are organized by function. These include the Bureau of Economic and Business Affairs; the Political-Military Affairs Bureau; the Bureau of Democracy, Human Rights, and Labor; and the Bureau of International Narcotics and Law Enforcement Affairs. Other functional bureaus include the Bureau of Oceans and International Environmental and Scientific Affairs; the Bureau of Population, Refugees, and Migration; the Bureau of Administration; the Bureau of Consular Affairs; the Bureau of Diplomatic Security; and the Bureau of Finance and Management Policy. Finally, there is the Office of Foreign Missions; the legal adviser; the Bureau of Intelligence and Research; the Bureau of Public Affairs; the Bureau of **Legislative** Affairs; and the Bureau of International Communications and Information Policy.

Some of these programs are carried out in cooperation with other federal agencies, including the Agency for International Development, the Immigration and Naturalization Service in the Department of Justice, and the Office of Refugee Resettlement in the Department of Health and Human Services.

Foreign Service

The United States has diplomatic relations with 160 countries. In some smaller countries where the United States does not maintain a mission, official contacts are made through embassies in neighboring countries or the United Nations. Ambassadors, or chiefs of mission, are the personal representatives of the president as well as representatives of the Department of State and all other federal agencies. They have full responsibility for the implementation of U.S. foreign policy by all U.S. government personnel within their country of assignment, except those under military commands.

See also: Department of Defense (DOD).

Department of the Interior

Department responsible for almost 600 million acres of public lands, or about 30 percent of the total U.S. land area. The Department of Agriculture, however, oversees the nation's forests.

Proposals to establish a home office were made as early as 1789, but it was not until the 1840s that need for a Department of the Interior became absolutely necessary. This need came from the fact that the Department of the Treasury was burdened by the vast amount of newly acquired land from the Louisiana Purchase (1803), the Mexican War (1846–1848), and the 1848 treaty with Great Britain by which the United States acquired the Oregon Territory.

Congressional Struggle Over Interior

On February 12, 1849, the House Ways and Means Committee reported out a **bill** to establish a Department of the Interior. The House passed the bill three days later with only minimal debate. The Senate Finance Committee reported out the bill on March 3, the last day of the Thirtieth Congress. That night, in a dramatic session, the full Senate approved the measure by a margin of only six votes, 31–25.

Congress transferred to the new Interior Department the General Land Office from the Treasury Department, the Patent Office from the State Department, and the Bureau of Indian Affairs and Pension Office from the War Department. Other responsibilities assigned to the department included supervising the commissioner of public buildings, the Board of Inspectors, the Warden of the Penitentiary of the District of Columbia, and the Census of the United States. It also was responsible for supervising the accounts of marshals and other officers of the U.S. courts and the accounts of lead and other kinds of mines in the United States.

Evolution of the Department's Policy

For a long time, the Department of the Interior's policy mirrored the more general public sentiment

A – Z

JUSTICE FOR ALL

Albert Fall (1861–1944)

Albert Fall was appointed by President Warren G. Harding (1921–1923) as the twenty-eighth secretary of the interior on March 5, 1921. Prior to accepting the office, Fall had been a lawyer and a senator representing New Mexico, and had held various offices in New Mexico when it was still a territory.

Fall's term as secretary of the interior is best known for the Teapot Dome scandal. Not long after his appointment, Fall convinced Secretary of the Navy Edwin Denby that the Department of the Interior should take responsibility for U.S. Navy oil Reserves at Elk Hills, California; Buena Vista, California; and Teapot Dome, Wyoming. Fall secretly leased parts of these reserves to his friends, Harry F. Sinclair and Edward L. Doheny. In return, Doheny offered Fall a bribe of $385,000, which Fall accepted. The three men tried to cover up the act, but suspicions began to rise when Fall began spending large amounts of money on land.

On April 14, 1922, the *Wall Street Journal* reported that Fall had leased Teapot Dome to Sinclair. President Harding claimed that he had given Fall permission to lease the land. A Senate investigation of the incident began on October 15, 1923, led by Thomas J. Walsh (DMT). After hearing the testimonies of many witnesses and Doheny's admission that he had "loaned" Fall $100,000, the Senate ruled that the leases for the naval reserves "were executed under circumstances indicating fraud and corruption". Fall and Denby were forced to resign from their cabinet seats. Fall was also convicted of accepting a bribe and was sentenced to one year in prison and fined $100,000. Fall died in El Paso, Texas, on November 30, 1944.

that natural resources were the limitless foundation on which a powerful nation could be built. As a result, public policy on their exploitation was extremely permissive.

Gradually, however, Americans realized that their natural resources were not inexhaustible. Some of the former secretaries' efforts to protect the environment include a Jimmy Carter (1977–1981) appointee, Cecil D. Andrus, who worked to protect the Alaskan wilderness. Years later, a Bill Clinton (1993–2001) appointee, Bruce Babbitt, also made efforts to protect the wilderness, this time in the California desert and the Florida Everglades.

See also: Department of Agriculture (USDA).

Department of the Treasury

Department whose primary function is the management of the monetary resources of the United States. Among other responsibilities, it regulates national banks, assesses and collects income taxes and customs duties, manufactures coins and **bills,** advises the president on international economic policy, reports the federal government's financial transactions, conducts international and domestic economic research, enforces tax and **tariff** laws, directs anti-counterfeiting operations, and provides protection for **executive** branch officials.

One of the oldest cabinet departments, Treasury was established by the first session of Congress on September 2, 1789. Alexander Hamilton, Treasury's first secretary, established a tradition for the position's power in advising the president, as well as the controversy surrounding many of the position's holders. The department is not only influential; its leaders have numbered among the presidents' closest advisers.

Evolution of the Department

Treasury's authority expanded considerably during the Civil War (1861–1865). The loss of customs income from the seceded southern states necessitated the establishment of the Bureau of Internal Revenue, as well as the printing of paper currency and the establishment of a national banking system. The growth of international trade following World Wars I (1914–1918) and World War II (1939–1945) resulted in a central role for Treasury in the 1944 Bretton Woods Conference, which established the International Monetary Fund (IMF) and the postwar monetary system.

Organization and Functions

The Department of the Treasury is divided into two major components: the office of the secretary and the operating bureaus. The secretary, who is officially the second-ranking cabinet officer, has primary responsibility for formulating and

DECISION MAKERS

Alexander Hamilton (1757–1804)

Alexander Hamilton became secretary of the treasury in 1789 after being appointed by President George Washington (1789–1797). As the department's first secretary, Hamilton was able to structure the department and set the standard for its secretary's strong influence as the president's top adviser. Hamilton began by tackling the debt acquired by the United States during the American Revolution (1775–1783). By acquiring money through customs duties and excise taxes, Hamilton was able to sizably reduce the war debt. This helped the United States to gain the respect and confidence of foreign nations. Hamilton also established the First **Bank of the United States** in 1791, to manage the federal government's finances. In order to keep the department on track, Hamilton often sent reports to Congress on the public credit and on the national bank.

During his time as treasury secretary, Hamilton often clashed with Thomas Jefferson, who disagreed with Hamilton's belief that the United States should have a strong central government. Eventually, Hamilton and his followers formed the Federalist Party, which supported his political views. In response, Jefferson and his followers formed the Democratic-Republican Party.

Hamilton was forced to resign from his position as secretary of the treasury in 1795, due to personal financial pressure. He continued to advise his successor, Oliver Wolcott, and remained in close contact with President Washington. After his resignation, Hamilton worked as a lawyer in New York. He died in 1804 as a result of a gunshot wound he had received in a duel with Vice President Aaron Burr, which had been sparked by a political dispute.

recommending domestic and international financial, economic, and tax policy; participating in the preparation of broad financial policies that have general significance for the economy; and managing the public debt. As chief financial officer of the government, the secretary serves as chair pro tempore (temporary chair) of the Economic Policy Council. The secretary also serves as U.S. governor of the International Monetary Fund, International Bank for Reconstruction and Development, Inter-American Development Bank, Asian Development Bank, and African Development Bank. The Treasury secretary is required by law to submit periodic reports to Congress on the government's financial operations, including an annual report.

The secretary is assisted by a deputy secretary, two undersecretaries (domestic finance and international affairs), a general counsel, and an inspector general. Nine assistant secretaries are responsible for different areas, such as economic policy, international affairs, financial affairs, and financial institutions. There are also assistant secretaries responsible for **legislative** affairs, management, tax policy, public affairs and public liaison, and enforcement.

The Office of the Treasurer of the United States was established on September 6, 1777. Initially, the treasurer was responsible for the receipt and custody of government funds. Over the years, however, these duties have been dispersed throughout various Treasury bureaus. In 1981, the treasurer was assigned oversight of the Bureau of Engraving and Printing, which prints paper currency and postage stamps, and the U.S. Mint, which produces coins and medals.

Other organizations that work under the Department of the Treasury include the Office of the Comptroller of the Currency, which oversees the laws related to nationally chartered banks and sets rules and regulations governing their operation. It also administers the U.S. Customs Service, which collects revenue from imports and enforces customs and related laws. The Bureau of Alcohol, Tobacco and Firearms (ATF) enforces federal laws that require excise taxes on alcoholic substances, control of firearms and explosives, and regulation of the tobacco industry. There is also the Internal Revenue Service (IRS), which collects income taxes, and the Bureau of the Pub-

lic Debt, which is responsible for managing the national debt.

The Treasury secretary traditionally has been one of the most important of the cabinet positions because the department is looked to, along with the Federal Reserve, by business leaders and Wall Street for policies that will promote economic stability and growth. The stature of the secretary with this sector of the nation has always been an important consideration when presidents decide who to select for the job.

See also: Department of State.

Department of Transportation (DOT)

Department that oversees federal transportation policies and programs. Development of a coordinated national transportation policy did not exist in the in the early 1960s. President John F. Kennedy's (1961–1963) successor, Lyndon B. Johnson, (1963–1969) nonetheless pursued the idea of establishing a transportation department, and Congress approved his plan in 1966.

The **bill** creating DOT established a National Transportation Safety Board, independent of the secretary and other units. This board would oversee major accident investigations, determine the cause of such accidents, and review appeals of licenses and certificates issued by the Department of Transportation. The existing separation of aviation safety functions was continued by transferring the Federal Aviation Agency's (FAA) safety duties to the new federal aviation administrator, whose decisions would be final. The Civil Aeronautics Board's responsibilities, which included accident investigations, probable cause determination, and review of appeals, were given to the safety board.

The First Two Decades

Upon its establishment, DOT assumed responsibility for administering the High Speed Ground Transportation Program that was transferred to DOT from the Department of Commerce. In July 1967, the Urban Mass Transportation Administration was shifted from the Department of Housing and Urban Development (HUD) to DOT. During

1967, DOT issued the first thirteen national highway safety standards under the Highway Safety Act. The first set of federal motor vehicle standards also went into effect that year.

During the administration of Jimmy Carter (1977–1981), Congress enacted legislation to deregulate the airline, railroad, and trucking industries. The new laws, for which DOT was the major overseer, whittled away years of federal regulations that threatened the health of the industries and, in many cases, resulted in higher consumer costs. Deregulation continued under the Ronald Reagan (1981–1989), George H.W. Bush (1989–1993), and Bill Clinton (1993–2001) administrations.

Transportation Under Recent Presidents

In early 1995, Frederico F. Peña, who served as secretary under Bill Clinton, announced a DOT reorganization plan that would consolidate the department into three agencies based on transportation over land, sea, and air. A new Aviation Administration would control all FAA functions except air-traffic control, which would be under a separate government corporation. The Intermodal Transportation Administration would incorporate highway, mass transit, railroad, maritime and other agencies, but the U.S. Coast Guard would remain intact. The Coast Guard, however, is now part of the Department of Homeland Security.

See also: Department of Homeland Security (DHS).

Department of Veterans Affairs

Department that oversees federal programs that aid American war veterans. American veterans have been receiving financial, medical, and various other types of aide from the government since the American Revolution (1775–1783). Congress greatly expanded veterans' benefits after the United States entered World War I (1914–1918) in 1917, establishing disability compensation, insurance for service personnel and veterans, and vocational rehabilitation for disabled personnel. Congress also established a family allotment program for

service personal. This program allows military personal to have a part of their paycheck automatically placed into a savings account or to pay a loan. With the exception of the vocational rehabilitation program, all were administered by the Bureau of War Risk Insurance, which had been created in 1914. At the same time, another agency, the Public Health Service, provided medical and hospital care.

Consolidation of Veterans' Programs

The division of responsibilities for veterans among various departments and agencies proved awkward. Responding to the recommendations of a presidential study commission to consolidate functions in a single agency, Congress established the United States Veterans' Bureau in 1921. Nonetheless, two other agencies also continued to administer veterans' benefits: the Bureau of Pensions in the Interior Department and the National Homes for Disabled Volunteer Soldiers.

In 1930, Congress authorized the president to further combine and coordinate government activities affecting war veterans. The three existing agencies became bureaus within the new Veterans Administration (VA). To deal with the drastic increase in the number of veterans served by the VA after World War II, VA facilities were substantially enlarged, and significant new programs, such as those created by the GI **bill** (signed into law June 22, 1944), were established.

Establishing the Department

Bills to elevate the Veterans Administration to cabinet-level status had been introduced in at least seventeen successive Congresses without success. Nonetheless, only a week after President Ronald Reagan (1981–1989) announced his support for a cabinet-level VA, the House of Representatives, on November 17, 1987, overwhelmingly passed its version of a law creating the VA, and the Senate followed suit in July 1988.

Legislation establishing the VA as the Department of Veterans Affairs (it retained the acronym VA) was signed into law by President Reagan on October 25, 1988. The VA Department came into being on March 15, 1989, making it the fourteenth **executive** department and the fifth to be created since 1953.

A - Z

Education, Department of

See Department of Education.

Eisenhower, Dwight D., Administration of (1953–1961)

Government under the thirty-fourth president of the United States. Dwight David Eisenhower lacked the money to attend college, so he worked in a creamery after graduating from high school. After a year, he applied for admission to both the Naval Academy at Annapolis and the Military Academy at West Point. He was rejected by Annapolis because he was too old, but he was nominated to West Point. He played football and was an above-average student, graduating sixty-fifth in his class of 164 in 1915.

Military Career

When the United States entered World War I (1914–1918) in 1917, Eisenhower served as a troop instructor at several U.S. bases. He rose through the ranks, and by 1940, he was a lieutenant colonel. During the next three years he would be promoted above hundreds of senior officers on his way to becoming a full general. When the United States entered World War II (1939–1945) in 1941, Eisenhower was a brigadier general serving as chief of staff of the Third Army in San Antonio, Texas. In February 1942, he was called to Washington, D.C., where he took command of the War Plans Division of the War Department's general staff.

In November 1942, Eisenhower directed the successful Allied invasion of North Africa. In 1943, he attained the rank of full general and commanded the Allied invasions of Sicily and Italy. In December 1943, President Franklin D. Roosevelt (1933–1945) named Eisenhower supreme commander of all Allied forces in Europe and instructed him to develop a plan for an invasion of France. On June 6, 1944, the forces under Eisenhower's command landed in Normandy, France, in the largest **amphibious** invasion ever

A 1956 political cartoon comments on President Dwight D. Eisenhower's (1953–1961) first inaugural address, in which he emphasized civil rights and preserving freedom at home and overseas. (A 1956 Herblock Cartoon, copyright by *The Herb Block Foundation*)

undertaken. The troops gained a beachhead and began driving toward Germany. Eisenhower accepted the surrender of the German army on May 7, 1945.

In 1950, President Truman asked Eisenhower to return to active service to become supreme commander of the North Atlantic Treaty Organization (NATO) forces in Europe. During his time in Europe, both major political parties again courted Eisenhower. Finally, in January 1952, he announced that he would accept the Republican nomination for president if it were offered. He resigned his NATO command in May and was nominated by the Republicans on the first ballot at their national convention in Chicago in July.

Eisenhower's opponent was Governor Adlai E. Stevenson II of Illinois. Eisenhower avoided detailed discussions of his political positions and relied primarily on his outgoing personality and his popularity as a war hero to win votes. He won a landslide popular vote victory and defeated Stevenson 442–89 in the electoral college.

Presidency

When Eisenhower became president in 1953, a Korean War (1950–1953) settlement was within reach. In December 1952, after the election, he had fulfilled a campaign promise to go to Korea to survey the situation. On July 27, 1953, an **armistice** was signed ending the war.

Although superpower tensions eased somewhat with the death of Soviet leader Joseph Stalin in March 1953 and the Korean War settlement, the cold war continued. Eisenhower endorsed Harry Truman's policy of containing communist expansion, but sought to avoid conflict when possible. In 1954, he refused to aid the French garrison surrounded at Dien Bien Phu, Vietnam, by Vietnamese **nationalists,** who eventually drove the French out of Indochina, and he protested the attack on Egypt by Great Britain, France, and Israel in 1956 over Egypt's nationalization of the Suez Canal. Following this Suez crisis, Eisenhower announced the Eisenhower Doctrine, a commitment by the United States to use force to stop international communist aggression in the Middle East. In accordance with this doctrine, he sent U.S. troops to Lebanon in 1958 when the Lebanese government requested assistance fighting insurgents.

As supreme commander of Allied forces in Europe during World War II (1939–1945), Dwight D. Eisenhower walks with British prime minister Winston Churchill. Probably the most celebrated military officer of the war, Eisenhower went on to win the presidential election of 1952. (Library of Congress)

On September 24, 1955, Eisenhower suffered a heart attack that limited his activity for several months. The following June he underwent an operation for an attack of ileitis, an inflammation of the small intestine. Eisenhower's illnesses raised questions about his fitness for a second term. In November 1956, however, the voters reelected him over Adlai Stevenson by an even larger margin than he had enjoyed in 1952. President Eisenhower was confined to bed a third time in 1957 after suffering a stroke. His periods of disability fueled efforts to develop a procedure for transferring power to the vice president when the president was incapacitated by illness. The Twenty-fifth **Amendment, ratified** in 1967, established such a procedure.

A – Z

In domestic policy, Eisenhower favored anti-inflation policies over measures to stimulate economic growth. He produced budget **surpluses** in three of the eight years of his presidency. He also warned of the dangers of the development of a **military-industrial complex** and sought to limit defense spending. He signed **bills** that compensated farmers for taking land out of production and that initiated the national interstate highway system. In 1957, he sent federal troops to Little Rock, Arkansas, when local citizens and state officials tried to block integration of public schools.

Eisenhower held several summits with Soviet leaders in attempting to improve U.S.-Soviet relations. He met with Soviet premier Nikolai Bulganin and Allied leaders in 1955 at Geneva, and with Soviet first secretary Nikita Khrushchev in 1959 at Camp David, Maryland. Eisenhower's plans for a 1960 summit, however, soured when the Soviets shot down an American U2 reconnaissance plane over the Soviet Union on May 1 of that year. Khrushchev protested the U2 overflights and refused to attend a summit in Paris with Allied leaders later that month. Eisenhower took full responsibility for the missions and defended them as vital to the security of the United States.

Eisenhower left office at the age of seventy, the oldest person to serve as president up to that time. He retired to his 230-acre farm near Gettysburg, Pennsylvania, where he enjoyed a quiet retirement. He died in March 1969 from a heart attack, two months after his former vice president, Richard Nixon (1969–1974), was elected president.

See also: Kennedy, John F., Administration of (1961–1963); Truman, Harry S., Administration of (1945–1953).

Further Reading

Korda, Michael. *Ike: An American Hero.* New York: Harper Perennial, 2008.

Wicker, Tom. *Dwight D. Eisenhower.* New York: Times Books, 2002.

Election of 2008

A hotly contested, landmark election, which had been preceded by one of the longest campaigns in United States history, giving the nation its first African American president. Not since the election of 1952 had the presidential race been so wide open, as neither an **incumbent** president nor vice president was seeking the nation's highest office. In addition, candidates from both the Republican and Democratic parties announced their candidacies earlier than ever.

The Democrats

On February 10, 2007, Senator Barack Obama announced his candidacy in front of the Old State Capitol building in Springfield, Illinois. The choice of the site was symbolic, particularly for the man who would become the first African American president, because it was where Abraham Lincoln delivered his "House Divided" speech in 1858. Obama was quickly joined by several Democratic hopefuls, including New York senator Hillary Rodham Clinton, former North Carolina senator and 2004 vice-presidential nominee John Edwards, and several others. Throughout 2007 and 2008, the candidates engaged in more than twenty-five debates and ran in more than fifty state caucuses or primary elections. By March 2008, the leading candidates were Senator Obama and Senator Clinton. After the June 3 primaries, however, when it became clear that Obama had clinched the nomination, Senator Clinton suspended her campaign and gave her full support to Senator Obama. On August 27, at the Democratic convention, Senator Clinton interrupted the roll-call vote and asked that Senator Obama be officially nominated by acclamation. Thus, Obama became the first African American to head a major party ticket. The nominee selected Senator Joe Biden of Delaware as his vice-presidential running mate.

The Republicans

Several Republicans sought the nomination of their party. Arizona Senator John McCain informally announced his candidacy on the David Letterman show on February 28, 2007 and a formal announcement on April 25, 2007. Other candidates included former New York City mayor Rudy Giuliani, former Massachusetts governor Mitt Romney, and former Arkansas governor Mike Huckabee. At the beginning of the campaign, McCain did poorly, and no candidate emerged as the front-runner. By the end of December 2007, however, McCain clearly led the other candidates. In March 2008, McCain clinched the nomination by sweeping the state primaries. He chose Alaska governor Sarah Palin as his vice-presidential running mate, making Palin the first woman on the party's top ticket.

The Campaign and the Election

The Democratic and Republican candidates crisscrossed the nation making appearances and giving speeches. For the first time, each of the candidates set up homepages on YouTube, the Internet video-sharing website, in a concerted effort to reach younger voters. Throughout the campaign the candidates traded barbs and accusations and aired negative campaign ads. Both candidates claimed to be the leader who, as president, would bring about the changes needed in the nation.

As Election Day approached, record numbers of voters cast absentee ballots or chose to vote early—a relatively new opportunity for many voters with lines lasting for four or five hours. Political experts predicated an unprecedented turnout on November 4. On election night, Senator Obama won an overwhelming victory, winning more than 50 percent of the popular vote and 365 electoral votes to John McCain's 173. Whereas in 2004 the margin of victory between Republican President Bush and John Kerry had been only 3 million popular votes, Obama beat McCain by 8.5 million votes.

In Grant Park in Chicago, more than 125,000 people gathered to witness president-elect Obama's historic acceptance speech: "If there is anyone. . . . who still wonders if the dream of our fathers is alive in our time. . . , tonight is your answer."

See also: Bush, George W., Administration of (2001-2009); Elections, Presidential; Electoral College.

Further Reading

Obama, Barack. *Dreams from My Father: A Story of Race and Inheritance.* New York: Three Rivers Press, 2004.
——. *The Audacity of Hope: Thoughts on Reclaiming the American Dream.* New York: Vintage Books (reprint edition), 2008.

Elections, Presidential

Process that occurs every four years in which American voters elect the president of the United States. The original electoral system aspired to be a republic, in which sovereign power resided in the people and was exercised by their elected representatives. Democracy, in the sense of direct popular rule, was considered a negative term. The Founders premised their insulated system on the ability of an "electoral college" of the nation's most virtuous and learned men to rise above petty factions and select leaders with national vision.

Since the election of the first president, George Washington (1789–1797), the **franchise,** or right to vote, in American presidential elections has expanded by class, race, sex, and age. Only property-owning men could participate in the nation's early elections. By 1971 virtually every adult citizen eighteen years or older was eligible to vote.

The process for electing the president not only has shifted political power from the few to the many but also has become longer, more complex, and more subject to the unintended consequences of reform and the changing technologies of business and everyday life. In fact, overall, a vast array of interlocking elements now makes up the campaign to elect one person as president. The people involved in a campaign include the candidate and his or her family, a vice-presidential running mate, political allies, campaign strategists, lawyers and accountants, television producers and consultants, schedulers and advance people, advertising experts, issues experts, fund-raisers, pollsters, computer analysts, website designers, and sometimes the **incumbent** president. The organizations that affect the campaign include corporations, labor unions, interest groups, political action committees, the national party, state parties, and third parties. Constitutional requirements for candidates and complex national and state campaign laws establish rules that the campaign must follow. The campaign must direct itself toward state primaries and **caucuses,** conventions, televised debates, and the vote of the electoral college (and possibly Congress, and, as in 2000, the Supreme Court). Not least among these diverse elements are the substantive and symbolic issues of the day.

Presidential elections are perhaps the most important events in national politics, giving shape to dominant issues, the makeup of national parties and interest groups, regional economic and political alignments, and the way citizens understand and talk about society.

Campaigns for the White House have shaped American politics over the years. For example, as the franchise has expanded, presidential politics has become more concerned about the way government can address the needs and demands of countless groups. Historically, presidential elections have been at the center of political controversies involving federalism, banking, **tariffs** and other taxes, economic change, corporate power, unions, international affairs, social welfare programs, moral values, consumer issues, and disputes among the branches of government. Presidential elections have expressed the changing moods of the nation since the first election.

See also: Electoral College; Presidential Campaigns.

Further Reading

CQ Press. *Presidential Elections 1789–2004.* Washington, DC: CQ Press, 2005.

Hopkins, David A. *Presidential Elections: Strategies and Structures of American Politics.* Lanham, MD: Roman and Littlefield, 2007.

Electoral College

As specified by the United States Constitution, the method by which the president is chosen. How the president was to be elected proved to be one of many vexing problems for the fifty-five men who assembled in Philadelphia in May 1787 to draft the Constitution. The Articles of Confederation, which the Constitution would replace, were riddled with weaknesses. Adopted in 1781, the Articles established an impotent federal government consisting of a weak Congress and no **executive** branch.

From the start of the convention, it was clear that the federal government would be strength-

ened and that there would be some sort of executive branch. The convention was split, however, between those who wanted a strong executive (the "presidentialists") and those who were wary of executive authority and wanted instead to increase the power of the national legislature (the "congressionalists").

There also was the question of whether the national executive should consist of several persons or just one. Congressionalists wanted a plural executive with minimal power. Presidentialists wanted a strong executive with power vested in the hands of a single individual.

As it became clear that the executive power would be vested in one person, the tension between the two camps shifted to the question of presidential selection. Congressionalists, intent on having the executive remain subordinate to the legislature, wanted the president to be elected by Congress. Presidentialists, however, wanted the president to be chosen independently.

The Compromise

The issue remained unresolved for most of the summer. By the end of August 1787, there still was no consensus on how to select the president. Therefore, that issue—along with other "questions not settled"—was sent to the convention's Committee on Postponed Matters for resolution. Because the committee was dominated by presidentialists, it pushed for a proposal that would avoid **legislative** appointment. The result was a compromise that was reported to the convention on September 4, 1787, and that served, with little alteration, as the basis for the actual constitutional provision.

The compromise, as finally approved, provided for election of the president by what soon would be known as the electoral college. This system allowed each state to appoint, in the manner directed by its legislature, the same number of electors as it had senators and representatives in Congress. Virginia, for example, had two senators and ten representatives in Congress and so could choose twelve electors. Those electors would then meet in their respective states and vote by ballot for two persons, at least one of whom must be from a state other than the elector's own state. When the ballots of all the electors from all the states were tallied, the candidate with

The Electoral College 1900–2008

Year	Winner (Party)	Electoral Votes	Loser (Party)	Electoral Votes	Electoral Votes Cast for Others
1900	McKinley (R)	292	Bryan (D)	155	0
1904	T. Roosevelt (R)	336	Parker (D)	140	0
1908	Taft (R)	321	Bryan (D)	162	0
1912	Wilson (D)	435	T. Roosevelt (P)	88	8
1916	Wilson (D)	277	Hughes (R)	254	0
1920	Harding (R)	404	Cox (D)	127	0
1924	Coolidge (R)	382	Davis (D)	136	13
1928	Hoover (R)	444	Smith (D)	87	0
1932	F.D. Roosevelt (D)	472	Hoover (R)	59	0
1936	F.D. Roosevelt (D)	523	Landon (R)	8	0
1940	F.D. Roosevelt (D)	449	Willkie (R)	82	0
1944	F.D. Roosevelt (D)	432	Dewey (R)	99	0
1948	Truman (D)	303	Dewey (R)	189	39
1952	Eisenhower (R)	442	Stevenson (D)	89	0
1956	Eisenhower (R)	457	Stevenson (D)	73	1
1960	Kennedy (D)	303	Nixon (R)	219	15
1964	L.B. Johnson (D)	486	Goldwater (R)	52	0
1968	Nixon (R)	301	Humphrey (D)	191	46
1972	Nixon (R)	520	McGovern (D)	17	1
1976	Carter (D)	297	Ford (R)	240	1
1980	Reagan (R)	489	Carter (D)	49	0
1984	Reagan (R)	525	Mondale (D)	13	0
1988	G. Bush (R)	426	Dukakis (D)	111	1
1992	Clinton (D)	370	G. Bush (R)	168	0
1996	Clinton (D)	379	Dole (R)	159	0
2000	G.W. Bush (R)	271	Gore (D)	266	0
2004	G.W. Bush (R)	286	Kerry (D)	251	1
2008	Obama (D)	365	McCain (R)	173	0

(D) = Democratic Party; (R) = Republican Party; (P) = Progressive Party

According to the United States Constitution, the presidential candidate who wins the electoral college vote, not the popular vote, is elected to the presidency. In most elections, the popular vote winner is the same as the electoral vote winner. However, in four presidential elections—1824, 1876, 1888, and 2000—the popular vote winner lost the electoral college vote.

A – Z

A–Z

the greatest number of votes would become president (assuming it was a majority), and the second-place candidate would become vice president. In case of a tie, or if no candidate received a majority, the House of Representatives would choose the president from among the top five electoral vote recipients.

The compromise won the support of the convention because it appeased all parties. First, the provision that the president be selected by electors satisfied the presidentialists, who were opposed to appointment by Congress. It also satisfied those who were wary of direct election by the people. Electors, it was thought, would infuse an element of judgment into the selection process, thereby stabilizing the whims of mass opinion.

Second, individual state legislatures were allowed to determine how electors would be chosen in their respective states. As a result, the convention did not have to agree on one method of appointing electors for all the states.

Third, if no candidate received a majority, the outcome of the election would be determined by the House of Representatives. Because it was widely assumed that few candidates after George Washington (1789–1797) would receive a majority of electoral votes, many thought that selection by the House would become the norm. Thus, congressionalists could argue that they had lost the battle but won the war. From their perspective, electors usually would nominate candidates, and the House would select the winner.

Finally, because each elector voted for two persons for president—one of whom could not be from the elector's own state—**favorite-son** candidates would tend to cancel one another out. This helped to dispel the fear that all presidents would hail from large states. However, because the number of electors from each state would equal the state's total number of senators and representatives in Congress, the relative weight of the more populous states would not be discounted.

Constitutional Changes

Despite the Framers' good intentions, numerous flaws emerged in the electoral system in the nation's early years. A constitutional crisis developed in 1800, for example, when the Democratic-Republican Party's presidential and vice-presidential candidates both claimed to have

won the presidency. The Twelfth **Amendment** (1804), which required that electors vote separately for president and vice president, was adopted to prevent a repeat of that crisis.

However flawed the early electoral system was, it met the needs of the moment and its basic form has endured for more than two centuries. The electoral college was an acceptable compromise among the diverse positions within the Constitutional Convention.

See also: Constitution of the United States; Elections, Presidential.

Further Reading

Ross, Tara. *Enlightened Democracy: The Case for the Electoral College.* Dallas, TX: Colonial Press, 2005.

Schumaker, Paul D., and Burdett A. Loomis, eds. *Choosing a President: The Electoral College and Beyond.* Washington, DC: CQ Press, 2002.

Emergency Powers

Presidential powers during times of crisis. In times of crisis, presidents frequently assert claims to extraordinary unilateral power to preserve the nation, promote the general welfare, or provide for the common good of the people. However, the Constitution does not grant express "emergency" powers either to the president or to Congress. Instead, such powers are judged to reside purely in the fundamental need for a nation to protect its **sovereignty** and to preserve domestic order. To many constitutional scholars the "great silences" in the Constitution imply the existence of an array of residual powers for each branch to draw upon in times of crisis.

The doctrine of emergency powers is a variation of what the Framers knew as the Lockean Prerogative. John Locke, the early-eighteenth-century English philosopher, believed strongly in a government of laws. Nevertheless, he also argued that, in dire emergencies, "the laws themselves . . . give way to the **executive** power, or rather to this fundamental law of nature and government . . . [namely] that, as much as may be, all the members of society are to be preserved." Limited government was the ideal at all other times, but in emergencies, responsible leaders might have to resort to extraordinary actions simply because legislatures usually are slow to move and the imperative for national self-preservation is superior to legal niceties. Of equal importance, wrote Locke, is "the people's permitting their rulers to do several things of their own free choice, where the law is silent, and sometimes, too, against the direct letter of the law, for the public good, and their acquiescing in it when so done."

The Framers of the Constitution were well versed in the writings of philosophers such as Locke, but nowhere in the Constitution did they indicate explicitly that the national government, much less the president, could exercise unspecified emergency powers. In fact, the only possible such authority granted to the president was the ability to grant reprieves and pardons (Article II, Section 2), which the Framers believed might be useful in resolving domestic insurrections such as Shays's Rebellion of 1786 (which in many ways had prompted the Constitutional Convention in the first place). The Constitution also provided for suspending writs of **habeas corpus** in cases of rebellion or invasion, which would allow for arrest without due cause, but this power was enumerated to Congress in Article I, Section 9.

Even so, the notion that government can wield emergency powers is arguably implied in the document. For example, Article II mandates that the president shall "preserve, protect and defend" the Constitution and uphold its provisions. This duty could require the president to bring to bear the commander-in-chief and chief executive powers from which many implied powers arise.

The debate over emergency powers is a highly practical one. The structure of the U.S. system of government is designed to fragment political power in the name of safeguarding the rights of the states and the people. It is therefore prone to tremendous inertia, even stalemate, because no branch of the national government can easily or quickly overpower the others. These structural constraints might be maddening to participants in "normal" times, but they could be fatal to the Republic when crisis or war intrudes, particularly in a world of intercontinental ballistic missiles and a highly integrated economy. That the president might have to act quickly and with flexibility

when the situation demands was a reality that the Framers apparently acknowledged when they created the single executive and endowed it with powers as chief executive and, particularly, as commander in chief.

Thus in times of crisis the question is not who should lead; rather, it is how to preserve the nation and the Constitution when the Republic is threatened. Abraham Lincoln (1861–1865), in defending his remarkable usurpation of power during the early months of the Civil War (1861–1865), asked simply, "Is there in all republics this inherent and fatal weakness? Must a government of necessity be too strong for the liberties of its people, or too weak to maintain its own existence?" Or, as Lincoln later asked, "Was it possible to lose the nation and yet preserve the Union?"

Powers in Wartime

The United States has entered into five declared wars, one civil war, and numerous undeclared hostilities in its history. In each instance, presidents invariably have asserted claims to some type of emergency powers to deal with the threat.

Lincoln and Inherent War Powers

Faced with **secession** by the states of the Confederacy, Abraham Lincoln claimed such an extensive array of emergency war powers to preserve the Union that he became, in the words of presidential scholar Clinton Rossiter, a "constitutional dictator." Yet Lincoln did run for reelection in 1864. However one characterizes Lincoln, there is little doubt that he used extraordinary and often **unconstitutional** means to quell the rebellion.

Congress was not in session when Fort Sumter fell in April 1861. With the onset of hostilities, Lincoln unilaterally proclaimed a blockade of Southern ports, mobilized state militias, increased the size of the army and navy, sent weapons to Unionists in Virginia who established the state of West Virginia, authorized the construction of ships for the navy, and **appropriated** funds for purchases of war materiel.

Lincoln also conveniently failed to call Congress into session for eleven weeks, and when he did, he claimed his actions were justified by the inherent powers of the presidency, especially as commander in chief. Congress ultimately gave

Lincoln retroactive authority for his actions, even though some (such as expanding the army and spending unappropriated funds) clearly were unconstitutional. Legal nuances paled before the emergency at hand, however, and Lincoln continued to assume and exercise independent war powers even with Congress in session.

The Union also faced insurrection behind its own lines. The situation was particularly troublesome around Washington, D.C., with secessionist Virginia on one side and Maryland filled with rebel sympathizers on the other. The mayor of Baltimore was decidedly pro-Confederate; mobs attacked federal troops; bridges were sabotaged; and the Maryland legislature was about to convene with the real possibility of voting to secede. Lincoln responded by declaring martial law and suspending writs of **habeas corpus** behind the Northern lines, thus allowing military authorities to arrest without warrants members of the Maryland legislature and other rebel sympathizers. Lincoln also suppressed opposition newspapers and ordered censorship of postal and telegraph communications. Some of these actions provoked clashes with the judiciary. In *Ex parte Merryman* (1861), Chief Justice Roger B. Taney, sitting as a circuit court judge, ruled that Lincoln had taken the sole power of Congress to suspend writs of habeas corpus during an emergency. Lincoln ignored Taney, whose majority opinion in the controversial Dred Scott decision four years earlier was widely reviled in the North. Congress later affirmed Lincoln's actions in the Habeas Corpus Act of 1863.

Lincoln's continued reliance on preemptive arrests and the use of military courts to try civilians set in motion another confrontation. In *Ex parte Milligan* (1866), the Supreme Court ruled that Lincoln lacked the constitutional authority to use military courts behind Northern lines so long as the civil judicial system remained intact. The Constitution worked "equally in war and in peace," said the justices, and national preservation was not cause enough to violate its principles.

However, Lincoln was already dead and the Civil War over by the time the Court ruled. *Milligan* thus joined the judicial decisions that over time would create doubts about whether the Court would challenge a sitting president during national crises. These doubts reemerged during

World War II (1941–1945) when Franklin D. Roosevelt (1933–1945) ordered some 112,000 Japanese Americans from their homes on the West Coast to internment camps in the southwestern desert. The forced relocation was challenged in the courts, but with no great effect on Roosevelt's actions.

World War and Delegated Powers

Unlike Lincoln, both Woodrow Wilson (1913–1921) and Franklin Roosevelt (1933–1945) fought wars on foreign soil based largely on powers at least broadly delegated to them by Congress. By the twentieth century, the nature of war itself had changed. Both World War I (1914–1918) and World War II (1939–1945) were "total wars," in which the lines between combatants and civilians were blurred; struggles involved not only armies but also the entire social, economic, and industrial capacities of nations; and control over national populations was key to success. Total war thus required swift, massive, and sustained national organization and mobilization, the capacities for which lay mostly in the executive branch.

For both world wars, Congress recognized these realities and delegated broad powers to the presidency to carry out military functions and to regulate the domestic economy. In 1917, Congress passed several laws granting Wilson a range of war-related powers. The Lever Food and Fuel Control Act empowered the president to seize defense-related facilities, to regulate food production, manufacturing, and mining, and to fix prices on commodities. The Selective Service Act enabled the president to raise an army. The Espionage Act gave Wilson the power to restrict exports; and the Trading with the Enemy Act authorized the president to regulate and censor external communications. Wilson also was granted broad authority to monitor actions by resident aliens, to regulate or operate transportation and communications facilities, and to reorganize executive branch agencies where necessary. In effect, Wilson was granted almost free rein to conduct the war and to maintain the domestic economy. This pattern of congressional delegation was repeated a little more than two decades later for Franklin Roosevelt.

Even with the generous congressional delegation of emergency powers, neither Wilson nor Roosevelt shied away from asserting inherent privileges as commander in chief. Both claimed the right to go beyond the scope of congressional authorization and to create wartime agencies, to enforce "voluntary" press censorship, and to coordinate private industry. Roosevelt in particular claimed emergency powers to sidestep congressional declarations of **neutrality** as Europe fell into war. In 1939, he declared a "limited" state of emergency, which allowed him to invoke existing statutes (many of which had been enacted in Wilson's day) to prepare the nation militarily. In early 1941, he declared an "unlimited" state of emergency under which he reorganized the executive branch and prepared to deal with the domestic economy once the United States entered into hostilities. In neither instance did Roosevelt seek prior congressional authorization for his actions, although he usually tried to cloak his actions in existing statutory powers.

Once Congress declared war, however, Roosevelt dropped even the pretense of delegated powers. His seizure of defense plants immediately after the Japanese bombed the U.S. naval base at Pearl Harbor, for example, was based on claims of authority given to him by the Constitution and "the laws," although he never made clear which ones. His most intriguing claim came in 1942, when he asked Congress to repeal legislation regulating farm prices. If Congress did not do so, Roosevelt warned, he would repeal the provisions himself because "the president has the powers, under the Constitution and under congressional acts, to take measures necessary to avert a disaster which would interfere with the winning of the war." Congress quickly gave in, so whether Roosevelt would have acted on his threat was never tested.

Truman and the Limits of Emergency Powers

Neither Wilson nor Roosevelt made sweeping claims to *inherent* emergency powers during either world war. Both made at least an effort to base their actions on broad statutory authority. Later presidents operated differently, however, as the United States in the late 1940s began a period of prolonged confrontation with the Soviet Union. Conventional war gave way to ongoing friction, with the potential for catastrophic thermonuclear

war at one extreme and localized wars of containment at the other.

The cold war-era debate over inherent powers first emerged in 1952. Harry S. Truman (1945–1953) had put the nation on a war footing in 1950 after the invasion of South Korea by North Korea, and in late 1951 he ordered the seizure of strike-threatened steel mills to avoid shortages. Truman based his action not on his statutory authority to resolve labor disputes but "on the authority vested in me by the Constitution and laws of the United States, and as President of the United States and Commander in Chief of the armed forces of the United States." When challenged on this rationale Truman argued simply, "The President has very great inherent powers to meet national emergencies."

The Supreme Court, in *Youngstown Sheet and Tube Co. v. Sawyer* (1952), declared the seizure of the steel mills unconstitutional because Congress in passing the 1947 Taft-Hartley Labor Act had not given presidents any right to take over industrial facilities shut down by strikes. Truman's greatest problem in the steel seizure case probably came from overstating the gravity of the situation. If Congress and the people had backed Truman—as they had backed Roosevelt in the internment of Japanese Americans—it is doubtful that the Court would have challenged his claims. Indeed, the cold war period raised concerns that the nation's strategic commitments and ongoing readiness for war created conditions ripe for unregulated claims to inherent presidential war powers.

War on Terrorism

Such concerns were placed on the back burner when terrorists attacked the United States in 2001. There was little debate about whether the president should have broad authority to act against a real threat to the country. Indeed, President George W. Bush (2001–2009) acted to expand the authority of the executive branch to fight the war on terrorism. Bush created the Office of Homeland Security by executive order and gave that office authority to coordinate antiterrorism efforts. Congress quickly approved $20 billion for domestic security.

The military phase of the antiterrorism campaign, Operation Enduring Freedom, began on

Categories and Examples of Emergency Powers

When emergencies are declared, or during times of crisis, the president has at hand a broad array of potential powers. These emergency powers can be grouped into three categories of actions the president may take:

Powers over Individuals

Confine individuals seen to be threats to national security.

Restrict travel of Americans to other nations (such as Cuba) or travel of some foreigners to the United States.

Restrict movement of citizens within the United States.

Require persons, because of their backgrounds, associations with certain groups, or ownership of particular articles (such as weapons), to register with government officials.

Restrict certain persons from working in industries critical to national security.

Remove federal employees regarded as threats to national security.

Suspend writs of habeas corpus.

Declare martial law.

Assign armed forces to conflicts in foreign nations.

Powers over Property

Order stockpiling of strategic materials (such as uranium).

Impose restrictions on exports (such as computer equipment).

Allocate materials in ways necessary to aid national defense.

Require industries to give priority to government contracts and seize industries failing to comply with such orders.

Fix wages and prices.

Powers over Communications

Withhold information from Congress and the public deemed potentially sensitive to national security.

Monitor and censor communications between the United States and other nations.

Require foreign representatives to register with the U.S. government.

Sources: **U.S. Congress, House of Representatives, Committee on the Judiciary, Subcommittee on Administrative Law and Governmental Relations, *Hearings on H.R. 3884, National Emergencies Act,* 94th Congress, 1st session, March 6–April 9, 1975, pp. 22–23; DiClerico, Robert E. *The American President.* Englewood Cliffs, NJ: Prentice-Hall, 1979, chap. 8.**

Presidents of the United States have a wide array of emergency powers at their command.

October 7, 2001. For months, the U.S. military attacked terrorist training camps in Afghanistan and seized suspected terrorists. In November 2001, the president issued an executive order that set forth procedures for detaining and then trying, in military tribunals, noncitizens suspected of terrorist activities. The order called for secret proceedings and prohibited any form of **judicial review.**

Powers in Economic Crises

Presidents also exert emergency powers during periods of serious economic instability outside of actual wartime. During such times, presidential power appears to emanate exclusively from statutes, although presidents have shown ingenuity in stretching the boundaries of that authority. For example, the Trading with the Enemy Act of 1917 gave the president the authority to impose an array of economic measures in times of war or national emergency. This law was intended as a wartime measure, but it was not repealed at war's end. Later presidents discovered the apparent legal justification for emergency actions to manage a faltering economy.

The best lesson on how to rely on "old" statutory authority came in 1933, when the newly inaugurated Franklin Roosevelt faced the imminent collapse of the nation's financial system. The day after his inauguration, Roosevelt declared a national state of emergency and closed the banks, basing his actions on the Trading with the Enemy Act. Roosevelt's interpretation of an old wartime statute was hotly debated, but it nonetheless reflected his desire to cloak his action in legal authority. Congress sanctioned his move three days later when it passed the Emergency Banking Act, and in the months that followed it granted Roosevelt a wide range of new powers to address the economic emergency. In fact, the single greatest outpouring of major legislation in peacetime U.S. history took place between March 9 and June 16, 1933, known to history as the First Hundred Days.

Powers during Domestic Unrest

Presidential emergency powers also include the authority to call out federal troops or to take control of state national guards (descendants of the state militias) to quell domestic unrest or to deter violence. Such authority has been used in the United States to put down illegal labor strikes, ensure delivery of the mail, impose order during natural disasters and urban riots, and prevent volatile situations from exploding.

Before the 1940s, and particularly during the late nineteenth century, presidents became involved in domestic disorders most frequently during labor strikes. Until passage of the Wagner Act of 1935, which ensured the right to collective bargaining and which established procedures for labor negotiations, strikes usually were considered illegal and often resulted in dramatic outbreaks of violence between strikers and company security forces. This was true particularly in the coal mining, steel, railroad, and, later, automobile industries—sectors in which relations between companies and workers were adversarial in the best of times. President Grover Cleveland's (1885–1889, 1893–1897) use of troops to break the 1894 Pullman strike in Chicago was but one famous example of a practice that had virtually ended by the 1950s.

In the 1950s and 1960s, presidents relied on federal troops or state national guards to ensure calm during efforts to enforce racial desegregation. The first and perhaps most notable instance was in 1957 when Dwight Eisenhower (1953–1961) sent troops into Little Rock, Arkansas, to enforce desegregation of the public schools in the face of resistance from state officials and angry mobs. In 1962, John Kennedy (1961–1963) "federalized" the Mississippi National Guard to ensure the peaceful integration of the University of Mississippi, and in 1963 he confronted Alabama governor George Wallace when he sent federal troops to enforce the integration of the University of Alabama. Kennedy, and Lyndon Johnson (1963–1969) after him, also on occasion used troops to protect civil rights marchers.

During the late 1960s, troops were used frequently to quell urban riots or to maintain order during demonstrations against U.S. involvement in Vietnam (1964–1975). For example, the April 1968 assassination of civil rights leader Martin Luther King Jr. sparked widespread rioting throughout more than 100 cities and forced Lyndon Johnson and various governors to call out some 55,000 troops. In May 1970, President Richard Nixon (1969–1974) called out troops to maintain order on some college campuses after the deaths of students at Kent State University in Ohio and at Jackson State University in Mississippi during protests against the U.S. incursion into Cambodia.

Nixon also figured in a different kind of military mobilization. In March 1970, he responded to a postal strike in New York, which threatened to cripple postal service nationally, by declaring a state of emergency and calling out federal troops to take over the postal system and keep mail deliveries flowing. Nixon's use of troops to sort and deliver the mail was unusual, but it showed how presidents can react to potential disturbances.

Powers during Natural Disasters

Presidents rely on legal authority to declare a state of emergency in areas of the country hit by hurricanes, floods, earthquakes, or other natural disasters. By declaring a place a "natural disaster area," the president sets in motion the government machinery that can provide immediate aid, such as food, shelter, and police protection, not to mention longer-term assistance such as federally guaranteed, low-interest home and business loans. In doing so, the federal government ensures that the economic effects of the disaster will be softened somewhat.

See also: Commander in Chief; Constitution of the United States.

Further Reading

Freeman, Michael. *Freedom or Security: The Consequences for Democracies Using Emergency Powers to Fight Terror.* Westport: CT: Praeger, 2003.

Gross, Oren, and Fionnuala Ní Aoláin. *Law in Times of Crisis: Emergency Powers in Theory and Practice.* New York: Cambridge University Press, 2006.

Energy, Department of

See Department of Energy (DOE).

Executive Agreements

Pacts other than treaties made by presidents or their representatives with foreign leaders or governments. The **executive** agreement is a powerful foreign policy tool. Presidents have asserted that their powers to execute laws, command the armed forces, and function as the sole organ of foreign policy give them the full legal authority to make these pacts without congressional approval. Unlike treaties, executive agreements do not supersede U.S. laws with which they conflict, but in every other respect they are binding.

Although the vast majority of international pacts are executive agreements, most executive agreements either are routine extensions of existing treaties or are based on broad **legislative** directives. Agreements made by the president to carry out legislation or treaty obligations are often called "congressional-executive international agreements." Other executive agreements have been supported by joint **resolutions.** Occasionally, presidents seek the approval of a majority of both houses of Congress for executive agreements when they do not have the support of two-thirds of the Senate but they want, or need, some type of specific congressional consent. This practice has, at times, elicited strong objections from senators, but it is generally supported by **partisan** majorities and by the House of Representatives, which is, through this procedure, given a much larger voice in foreign policy. Congressional authorization and joint approval have been used frequently in areas, such as **tariffs,** where congressional, or House, authority is definitive.

The very small percentage of agreements—about 3 percent—that do not fall under these categories are the "pure" executive agreements, which are negotiated and implemented without congressional approval. The president's authority to make such agreements is usually not disputed, especially when presidents are otherwise acting within their sphere of authority and when the practical advantages of a flexible power of agreement are great. For example, the commander in chief must frequently make and alter agreements with allies during the course of a war. However, the proper scope of the president's authority to commit the nation has often been disputed. As the scope of executive agreements has broadened, these have become the most important and controversial pacts.

The use of executive agreements grew dramatically in the twentieth century. Today, executive agreements are used to conduct business once reserved for treaties. Indeed, contemporary presidents can accomplish through an executive agreement almost anything that can be accomplished through a treaty.

Constitutional Dilemma

The Constitution does not prohibit executive agreements, and the Supreme Court in *United States v. Curtiss-Wright* (1936) explicitly affirmed the power of the national government to make international agreements other than treaties. However, the Founders' careful division of the treaty power in the Constitution must be interpreted as an attempt to ensure that Congress has a direct voice in making international commitments. The use of executive agreements by presidents and their representatives to avoid congressional interference has been widely regarded by constitutional scholars and members of Congress as a serious deterioration of constitutional **checks and balances** in the area of foreign policy.

The development of the United States into a world power with security commitments and economic interests in every corner of the world has made some degree of executive flexibility in making executive agreements desirable. Like President Thomas Jefferson (1801–1809), who was confronted with the irresistible opportunity to buy the Louisiana Territory in 1803, contemporary presidents are sometimes faced with an international situation that calls for making commitments with speed and secrecy. In addition, executive agreements often provide a simpler method of transacting the less important international business that would overload the already tight legislative schedule if treaties were used.

The root of the problem is that some important international agreements should receive some sort of congressional approval, yet there are no concrete guidelines to indicate which pacts need Senate consent, which need approval by both houses, and which can be handled simply by the president. Presidents may, therefore, use their discretion in deciding how to make a particular agreement. Numerous presidents, faced with the prospect of fighting for two-thirds approval in the Senate, have used executive agreements to skirt the treaty requirements imposed by the Constitution rather than abandon a diplomatic initiative. Treaties, therefore, have become an exception to the rule, which is presidential policy making.

Landmark Executive Agreements

The first major executive agreement concluded between a president and a foreign power was the Rush-Bagot agreement with Great Britain. The pact, which imposed limitations on naval forces on the Great Lakes, was concluded under the supervision of President James Monroe (1817–1825) in 1817. A year after the agreement was put into operation, Monroe sent it to the House and Senate and asked the legislators if they thought it required Senate consent. The Senate endorsed the "arrangement" with a two-thirds vote but stipulated that its action did not constitute an approval of a treaty, and the United States and Great Britain never exchanged instruments of **ratification.**

Although Monroe's executive agreement was significant in establishing a **precedent,** President John Tyler's (1841–1845) **annexation** of Texas by executive agreement in 1845 was even more important, because it was the first time a president had used an executive agreement to circumvent the treaty process. Tyler wished to bring Texas into the Union to keep it out of foreign hands and to serve southern slave interests, but he didn't have the necessary two-thirds support in the Senate to conclude a treaty of annexation. With sufficient public support for annexation, he called on Congress for a joint resolution to bring Texas into the nation. The resolution passed the House by a 120–98 vote and the Senate by a spare two-vote margin. With this annexation agreement in hand, Tyler invited Texas to become a state. In 1898, William McKinley (1897–1901) used the same method to annex Hawaii to the United States as a territory.

Theodore Roosevelt (1901–1909) was not timid about using executive agreements to accomplish foreign policy objectives that would have been delayed or undermined by the treaty process. When Santo Domingo (now the Dominican Republic) fell into heavy debt to European creditors in 1905, Roosevelt oversaw negotiations of a treaty that extended U.S. protection to Santo Domingo and put the United States in control of collecting the country's customs in order to satisfy the creditors. Roosevelt hoped the Senate would consent to the draft treaty, but when it did not, he continued the arrangement under an executive agreement.

During World War II (1939–1945), Franklin D. Roosevelt (1933–1945) used an executive agreement to avoid the treaty process in 1940. At the time, the United States was still officially **neutral** and a predominantly **isolationist** Senate would not have approved a treaty that provided Britain with ships to defend against German submarines. Roosevelt therefore used an executive agreement to trade old U.S. destroyers for the right to lease several British naval bases in the Western Hemisphere. Because the deal violated two **neutrality** laws and altered the **neutral** status of the United States, it clearly should have been accompanied by some sort of congressional approval.

Yet Congress regularly authorizes the president to avoid the treaty clause, even for major international agreements. In 1993 and 1994 the North American Free Trade Agreement (NAFTA) and a new General Agreement on Tariffs and Trade (GATT), which comprehensively revised the nation's trade policy, were validated only by authorizing legislation passed in the House and Senate. It has been standard practice for more than a century for Congress to authorize the president to make tariff adjustments through executive agreements, and the House would have had a well-founded complaint if significant changes in tariff laws had been submitted only to the Senate. GATT, however, went beyond the adjustment of tariffs and committed the nation's trade practices to a regime of oversight and sanction by an international body, the World Trade Organization. Even so, the loudest objections were to the agreement itself and not to the mode of approval.

Attempts to Limit Executive Agreements

Since the end of World War II in 1945, Congress has made two major attempts to control the president's power to make international agreements and secret commitments. The more intrusive one was a constitutional **amendment** proposed by Senator John W. Bricker (R-OH) in 1953 that would have placed restraints on the president's power to make executive agreements and decreased the effect of the agreements on domestic law. The second occurred in the early 1970s and resulted in the Case Act of 1972, which was intended to compel the executive branch to report all executive agreements to Congress or to selected congressional committees. Except for a clarification of the Case Act passed in 1977, subsequent efforts by Congress to make the executive branch more accountable for its agreements with other nations have been unsuccessful.

Bricker Amendment

Senator Bricker, a **conservative** Republican, chaired the Senate Interstate and Foreign **Commerce** Committee for two years beginning in 1953. In the postwar era, when the United States was expanding its defense commitments and its participation in international organizations, Bricker and his followers argued that the president's broad power to make international agreements that supersede the constitutions and laws of states threatened the constitutionally guaranteed rights of the states and the American people. Moreover, many senators were alarmed by the growing tendency of presidents to use executive agreements to implement military pacts and UN programs.

In January 1953, Bricker and sixty-three cosponsors introduced an amendment aimed at establishing congressional review of executive agreements and making treaties unenforceable as domestic law without accompanying legislation. Two provisions of the amendment would have radically altered the way the United States entered into agreements with foreign governments. Every treaty and executive agreement would have required implementing legislation to make it enforceable as domestic law, and any executive agreement made by a president would have been subject to regulation by Congress. The ability of presidents to make foreign policy through executive agreements and to negotiate treaties without involving Congress would have been severely curtailed. The amendment did not, however, come to a vote by the time Congress adjourned in August 1953. In 1954, a milder version of the Bricker amendment came within one vote of passing the Senate with a two-thirds majority. Thereafter, support for the amendment ebbed, in part because President Dwight D. Eisenhower (1953–1961) strongly opposed it.

See also: Foreign Policy and the Presidency; Presidency and Congress.

Further Reading

Genovese, Michael A. *The Power of the American Presidency: 1789–2000.* New York: Oxford University Press, 2000.

Moss, Kenneth B. *Undeclared War and the Future of U.S. Foreign Policy.* Baltimore, MD: Johns Hopkins University Press, 2008.

Executive Departments

The various departments, offices, and bureaus that make up the **executive** branch. Often the term *bureaucracy* is considered negative, because to many it suggests red tape, inflexibility, and confusion. Opposition to "big government" has become almost synonymous with opposition to bureaucracy. Political candidates from both major political parties usually decry the evils of the growing U.S. bureaucracy. They denounce it for removing Americans from the decision-making process of their federal government.

Those who work in the federal bureaucratic structure—"bureaucrats"—are often criticized for being unproductive and obstinate. *Bureaucracy,* however, has a technical meaning. The German sociologist Max Weber saw the bureaucratic model of organization as one distinguished by its large size, its formulation of rules and procedures, the presence of a clear hierarchy, the systematic main-tenance of records, and the employment of full-time personnel who perform specific duties using technical knowledge.

By this definition, a large corporation or university is a bureaucracy, and so is the federal government. The departments, agencies, bureaus, commissions, and offices of the executive branch make up most of the federal bureaucracy. Although not as large and usually not as visible as the executive branch, Congress and the courts have their own bureaucracies.

Despite the negative connotations of the term, a bureaucrat is simply an administrator who carries out the policies of elected government officials. The structure of the federal bureaucracy under the president's control can be broken down into the Executive Office of the President, the cabinet departments, the executive agencies, and the regulatory commissions.

Executive Office of the President

In 1939, Executive Order 8248 created the Executive Office of the President (EOP) to advise the president and to help manage the growing bureaucracy. The EOP includes the White House Office, the Council of Economic Advisers, the National Security Council (NSC), and the Office of Management and Budget (OMB)—agencies conceived to help the president control the expanding executive branch.

Since then the EOP has grown tremendously, employing almost seventeen hundred people in 2000. Its most important components are the White House Office, the NSC, and OMB.

The White House Office consists of the president's closest assistants. Their actual titles vary from one administration to another, but under each new president it is the people in this group who oversee the political and policy interests of the administration. Serving as a direct extension of the president, they do not require Senate confirmation. The creation of the White House Office has allowed the president to centralize executive power within the White House, often at the expense of the cabinet secretaries. For example, Henry A. Kissinger, Richard Nixon's (1969–1974) assistant for national security affairs, forged such a strong power base in foreign affairs that his authority eclipsed that of the secretary of state.

In 1947, early in the cold war, Congress passed the National Security Act, which created the NSC to help harmonize military and foreign policies. Responsible for coordinating activities between the State Department and the Defense Depart-ment, the NSC has four statutory members: the president, the vice president (added in 1949), the secretary of state, and the secretary of defense. The act further names the chairman of the Joint Chiefs of Staff and the director of the Central Intelligence Agency (CIA) as advisers to the NSC.

The NSC staff, made up of foreign policy advisers and headed by the national security adviser, has evolved into an apparatus used by many presidents to implement their own foreign policy goals. Because the role of the National Security Council and its staff is purely advisory, presidents have used the NSC to varying degrees. President John F. Kennedy (1961–1963), prefer-ring his own close advisers, used it infrequently. President Nixon, however, gave the NSC formal authority in formulating and executing foreign policy.

In 1970, Nixon created the Office of Manage-ment and Budget to replace the Bureau of the Budget, established in 1921. OMB is the largest of the EOP agencies—in 2000, it operated with about 510 employees. Its staff members help presidents achieve their policy objectives by formulating and administering the federal budget. Departments and agencies of the executive branch must submit annual budget requests to OMB.

A - Z

President Bill Clinton (1993–2001) meets with key presidential adviser George Stephanopoulos and with Howard Paster, the director of the White House Office of Legislative Affairs. (AP Images)

Besides preparing the budget, OMB serves as an important managerial tool of the president by reviewing the organizational structure and management procedures of the executive branch, assessing program objectives, and developing reform proposals. OMB has tremendous power within the federal government. In the early 1980s, President Ronald Reagan (1981–1989) relied heavily on OMB director David Stockman for the technical expertise necessary to implement his political objective of cutting the budget.

Cabinet Departments

The cabinet is made up of the heads—or "secretaries"—of the major government departments. Originally, there were only three cabinet departments—State, War, and Treasury. By 2002, the number had grown to fifteen. The newest cabinet-level department, the Office of Homeland Security, was created by President George W. Bush (2001–2009) in late 2001, in response to the terrorist attacks on the United States on September 11, 2001.

Lacking any constitutional or statutory base, the cabinet is primarily an advisory group. Although presidents may work closely with individual cabinet officers, they rarely use the collective cabinet for advice. President Abraham Lincoln (1861–1865), opposed by his entire cabinet on an issue, famously remarked, "Seven nays, one aye; the ayes have it." President Eisenhower (1953–1961), who held regular cabinet meetings and listened to opinions of others, came closer than any other modern president to making the cabinet a truly deliberative body.

Each cabinet secretary is appointed to head a specific department with a specific constituency. Although presidents make their own appointments, with Senate confirmation, the power they have over a specific department is limited. One reason is that the president can appoint only a limited number of a department's employees. When

Civilian Employees, Executive Branch, 1816–2006

Year	Number of employees[a]
1816	4,837
1821	6,914
1831	11,491
1841	18,038
1851	26,274
1861	36,672
1871	51,020
1881	100,020
1891	157,442
1901	239,476
1911	395,905
1921	561,142
1931	609,746
1941	1,437,682
1951	2,482,666
1961	2,435,804
1971	2,862,894
1981	2,947,428
1991	3,138,180
2001	2,719,529
2006	2,718,917

[a]Excludes employees of the Central Intelligence Agency and National Security Agency.
Source: Stanley, Howard W., and Richard G. Niemi. *Vital Statistics on American Politics, 2007–2008.* Washington, DC: CQ Press, 2008, table 6–12, pp. 272–273.

The number of federal civilian employees has soared since the nation's founding.

President Bill Clinton (1993–2001) came into office, for example, he could appoint only about one hundred people to positions in the Department of Transportation—less than 1 percent of its employees.

Executive Agencies

Executive agencies are agencies or commissions that are not considered a part of the cabinet and that often have quasi-independent status by law. Examples of these executive agencies include the National Aeronautics and Space Administration (NASA) and the Peace Corps.

The difference between a "presidential" agency and an "independent" agency often is vague. Generally, heads of presidential agencies and commissioners serve at the discretion of, and may be removed by, the president. Independent agency heads and commissioners are appointed for fixed terms of office and have some independence from the president in their operations.

Government corporations, such as the Tennessee Valley Authority (TVA), also fall in the category of executive agencies. Similar to private corporations, these organizations perform business activities such as operating a transportation system (Amtrak) or selling electricity (TVA). Government corporations are generally controlled by boards of directors and are run like businesses. Because the president appoints these boards and their chairs, they have come increasingly under the control of the presidency.

Regulatory Commissions

Regulatory commissions are responsible for regulating certain segments of the economy. Many of them, such as the Food and Drug Administration (FDA) and the Occupational Safety and Health Administration (OSHA), are located within cabinet departments. FDA is a part of the Department of Health and Human Services, and OSHA is in the Labor Department. Other regulatory agencies, such as the Consumer Product Safety Commission and the Federal Trade Commission, are independent in their relationship to the executive branch and so are insulated from regular presidential control and policy direction.

By statutory law each independent regulatory agency is governed by a **bipartisan** board of commissioners, who serve overlapping terms of five years or more. Although presidents have the power to appoint board members, they do not have the power to remove these appointees from office unless they can prove incompetence. Presidents cannot fire commission members simply because they do not like the policy direction of

A - Z

A – Z

the agency, nor can they **veto** agency actions. This ensures the commissioners a certain amount of independence from executive control.

Executive Office of the President (EOP)

See Executive Departments.

Executive Orders

Directives issued by the president, which may have the force of law. Article II of the Constitution assigns to the president the "**executive** power," one of the document's least specific but potentially most far-reaching grants of power. Before 1787, state legislatures generally defined executive power for their respective governors. However, the drafters of the Constitution, learning from their experiences with the state legislatures as well as with the Articles of Confederation, shied away from having Congress dictate the limits of presidential action. Instead, they left the range of executive powers undefined, open-ended, and ripe for reinterpretation.

This silence proved critical. When paired with the Article II provision requiring presidents to "take Care that the Laws be faithfully executed," the executive power clause provides for a range of "implied" powers whose extent and clout have grown beyond anything the Founders could have foreseen. The Constitution gives the president a limited array of "express" powers, leaving the clear impression that Congress is dominant on almost all other matters. However, the powers implied in the Constitution and given substance by years of continuous reinterpretation are the sources of the president's ability to act alone, often without specific congressional statute. Much of U.S. history has involved a struggle between presidents claiming the power to act without clear constitutional mandates and their critics arguing to the contrary.

On its face, the "take care" clause directs the president to administer statutes in a manner faithful to **legislative** language and intent. Like so many constitutional provisions, however, the clause is vague in meaning and elastic in potential ramifications. In an 1890 case, for example, the Supreme Court ruled that the clause pertained not only to statutes enacted by Congress but also to any "rights, duties, and obligations growing out of the Constitution itself, our international relations, and all the protection implied by the nature of the government under the Constitution."

This decision seemed to suggest that the president possessed a range of discretionary power broader than any expressed specifically in the Constitution. These powers were derived from the president's dual roles as chief executive and commander in chief. By this reasoning, presidents theoretically can undertake any action deemed necessary to carry out their constitutional duties, to provide for the nation's defense or to protect the common good. To make matters murkier, the Constitution is mute on what the "common good" entails—one of those "great silences" that makes the potential of implied powers so controversial.

An offspring of the implied powers doctrine is the executive order. This instrument of presidential power is defined nowhere in the Constitution but generally is construed as a presidential directive that is intended to carry out other executive powers. As such, an executive order's legal authority derives either from existing statutes or from the president's other constitutional responsibilities, not from any specific congressional approval. Executive orders usually pertain directly to government agencies and officials. They are used most frequently by presidents to establish executive branch agencies, modify bureaucratic rules or actions, change decision-making procedures, or give substance and force to laws. However, their effects often extend to average citizens. For example, one of the first actions by President Bill Clinton (1993–2001) was to sign an executive order on January 22, 1993, ending a "gag rule" that had, under the administrations of Ronald Reagan (1981–1989) and George H.W. Bush (1989–1993), prohibited abortion counseling and referrals at family planning clinics that received federal funding.

The Constitution does not specify procedures for issuing executive orders; during the nation's first hundred or so years, they were issued without any system of publication or recording. The

Executive Orders, By President, 1789–2008

President	Years in office	Number of orders	Average per year
Washington	8.00	8	1.00
J. Adams	4.00	1	0.25
Jefferson	8.00	4	0.50
Madison	8.00	1	0.13
Monroe	8.00	1	0.13
J.Q. Adams	4.00	4	1.00
Jackson	8.00	11	1.38
Van Buren	4.00	10	2.50
W.H. Harrison	0.08[a]	0	—
Tyler	4.00	17	4.25
Polk	4.00	19	4.75
Taylor	1.25	4	3.20
Fillmore	2.75	13	4.73
Pierce	4.00	35	8.75
Buchanan	4.00	15	3.75
Lincoln	4.00	48	12.00
A. Johnson	4.00	79	19.75
Grant	8.00	223	27.88
Hayes	4.00	92	23.00
Garfield	0.50	9	—[b]
Arthur	3.25	100	30.77
Cleveland (1st term)	4.00	113	28.25
B. Harrison	4.00	135	33.75
Cleveland (2d term)	4.00	142	35.50
McKinley	4.75	178	37.47
T. Roosevelt	7.25	1139	157.10
Taft	4.00	752	188.00
Wilson	8.00	1841	230.13
Harding	2.60	487	187.31

(continued on next page)

A - Z

Executive Orders, By President, 1789–2008, *continued*

President	Years in office	Number of orders	Average per year
Coolidge	5.40	1259	233.15
Hoover	4.00	1011	252.75
F. Roosevelt	12.33	3728	302.35
Truman	7.67	896	116.82
Eisenhower	8.00	486	60.75
Kennedy	2.92	214	73.29
L. Johnson	5.08	324	63.78
Nixon	5.60	346	61.79
Ford	2.40	169	70.42
Carter	4.00	320	80.00
Reagan	8.00	381	51.13
G.H.W. Bush	4.00	166	41.50
Clinton	8.00	364	45.50
G.W. Bush	8.00[c]	285	35.63

Notes: Includes both numbered and unnumbered executive orders.
[a]W.H. Harrison died after only one month in office.
[b]Garfield was assassinated after six months in office, during which he issued nine executive orders. At that rate his average would have been eighteen per year.
[c]Through 2008.
Sources: Ragsdale, Lyn. *Vital Statistics on the Presidency*, Third Edition. Washington, D.C.: CQ Press, 2009, pp. 447–454.
The Federal Register (www.archives.gov/federal-register/executive-orders/.)

As governing has grown more complex, presidents have turned to executive orders to ensure that their policies are carried out. Not surprisingly, Franklin D. Roosevelt (1933–1945) issued the most executive orders during his slightly more than twelve years in office.

numbering of executive orders began only in 1907, with numbers assigned retroactively to the time of Abraham Lincoln (1861–1865). About 13,600 executive orders were officially recorded through 2008, though haphazard record keeping throughout much of history, even after 1907, leads scholars to estimate that between 15,000 and 50,000 directives never were recorded. To respond to growing concerns that these lax conditions undermined democratic accountability, Congress in the Administrative Procedures Act of 1946 mandated that the number and text of all executive orders, executive branch announcements, proposals, and regulations must be published in the *Federal Reg-ister,* the official U.S. government record. Exceptions to this rule are the "classified" executive orders pertaining directly to sensitive national security matters, which are entered into the *Federal Register* by number only.

See also: Executive Agreements.

Executive Powers

See Chief Diplomat; Chief Economist; Chief Executive; Chief of State; Commander in Chief; Presidential Pardons; Veto Power.

Fall, Albert

See Department of the Interior.

Federalism

System of government in which power is shared between a central government and individual state or provincial governments. The United States is a federal republic, consisting of a national government and fifty separate state governments. Under the U.S. Constitution, states have authority over matters within their borders, but they are bound to uphold all laws passed by the national government.

The Constitution grants specific powers to Congress, known as expressed powers. It also imposes limitations on the powers of Congress, such as forbidding it from passing certain types of taxes, granting titles of nobility, or suspending **habeas corpus.** In addition, it **cedes** to the states any powers not specifically granted to the national government. This gives the states great leeway to act within their own boundaries.

Article VI of the Constitution, however, provides that the laws and treaties of the United States "shall be the supreme law of the land . . . and that the Judges of the several States shall be bound thereby in their decisions, anything in the respective Constitutions or laws of the individual States to the contrary notwithstanding." This so-called supremacy clause means that state judges and officials are bound to uphold the Constitution over any local or state laws. The supremacy clause was reinforced by a provision stating that all members of Congress and the state legislatures, as well as all **executive** and judicial officers of the national and state governments, "shall be

bound by Oath or Affirmation to support this Constitution."

The supremacy clause was designed to prevent the states from passing laws contrary to the Constitution. To eliminate any doubt of their intention to put an end to irresponsible acts of the individual states, the delegates specified what the states could *not* do as well as what the states were required to do. Acts prohibited to the states were placed in Section 10 of Article I, while those required of them were placed in Sections 1 and 2 of Article IV.

Most of these provisions were uncontroversial. For example, states were required to use gold or silver as legal tender unless Congress agreed to another form of currency. Article IV also required that each state give "full faith and credit" to the acts of other states, respect "all Privileges and Immunities" of every citizen, and deliver up fugitives from justice. As with the rest of the Constitution, the supremacy clause assigned the enforcement of these provisions to the courts.

See also: Constitution of the United States; Presidency and Congress.

Federalist, The

See Presidency and the Media.

Federalist Party (1792–1816)

One of the first political parties. The Federalist Party favored a strong federal government and dominated national politics in the 1790s. The Federalist Party emerged from those leaders, also

Alexander Hamilton served as the first secretary of the treasury. His far-sighted economic plans, including the assumption of state and federal debts and the creation of the Bank of the United States, helped the young nation gain a sound financial footing. (Library of Congress)

known as federalists, who favored **ratifying** the Constitution. Among this group were George Washington (1789–1797), John Adams (1797–1801), Alexander Hamilton, and James Madison (1809–1817).

The men were not identical, however. Madison, after successfully working for the adoption of the new Constitution, led a political opposition that emerged in 1792. He, along with fellow Virginian Thomas Jefferson (1801–1809), argued for **strict construction**—limiting the powers of the national government to those specified in the Constitution. They organized a rival political party, the Democratic- (or Jeffersonian) Republicans, which came to power with Jefferson's election in 1800.

The Federalist Party, led by Hamilton as President George Washington's (1789–1797) secretary of the treasury, dominated national politics during the administrations of Washington and John Adams. The Federalists wanted to make the national government stronger by assuming state

debts, chartering a national bank, and supporting manufacturing interests. In foreign affairs, they pursued policies that would protect commercial and political friendship with Britain, goals that led to **ratification** of Jay's Treaty in 1795. Under the treaty, Britain withdrew the last of its troops from American outposts and the United States agreed to honor debts owed to British merchants.

Though committed to a **republican** form of government, Federalists believed that politics was best left to the "natural aristocracy" of wealthy and talented men. Consequently, Federalists generally sought to limit **suffrage,** tighten naturalization policy, and silence critics.

Federalists drew their support primarily from the Northeast, where their commercial and manufacturing policies attracted merchants and business leaders. Although they had some southern strongholds in parts of Virginia and the Carolinas, especially Charleston, Federalists had less success in attracting the support of western farmers and southern planters because the Federalists were generally opposed to slavery and strongly favored the growing manufacturers of the Northeast.

Several factors contributed to the end of the Federalist Party. Its passage of the highly unpopular **Alien and Sedition Acts of 1798** served as a rallying cry for Jeffersonian Republicans. Another factor was the Federalists' sharp division in the 1800 elections over Adams's foreign policies. Many Federalists opposed the War of 1812. In 1814, several extreme Federalists convened the **Hartford Convention,** which considered **secession** from the Union. Thus, the Federalist name became associated with disloyalty. Federalists, however, continued to play a limited role in state and local politics into the early 1820s.

Federalist leadership during the nation's critical early years contributed greatly to preserving the American experiment. In large part, Federalists were responsible for laying the foundation for a national economy, a national foreign policy agenda, and creating a strong national judicial system. The last of these was perhaps the Federalists' most enduring legacy, as John Marshall used his position as the Supreme Court's chief justice (1801–1835) to incorporate Federalist principles into constitutional law.

Ferraro, Geraldine

See Conventions, Presidential Nominating.

Fillmore, Millard, Administration of (1850–1853)

Government under the thirteenth president of the United States. President Zachary Taylor (1849–1850) died before the crisis created by the 1850 debate over slavery was settled. His successor, Vice President Millard Fillmore (1850–1853) of New York, repeated Whig assurances in favor of restraint over **executive** power, yet proved no more willing than Taylor to leave critical domestic matters to Congress. Fillmore, however, was as determined to see the Compromise of 1850 passed

---

Key Provisions of the Compromise of 1850

- California would enter the Union as a free state.

- The settlers of the New Mexico and Utah territories could decide for themselves whether to allow slavery or not.

- Texas would give up the lands that it claimed in present-day New Mexico, for which it would receive $10 million in compensation.

- The slave trade, but not slavery, would be abolished in the District of Columbia.

- The Fugitive Slave Law made it possible for any escaped slave to be returned to slavery and imposed fines for federal officials who did not arrest runaway slaves.

Rather than settle the slavery issue, the Compromise of 1850 only delayed the inevitable confrontation for ten years.

---

as his predecessor was committed to preventing its enactment. His support was politically important. One member of the House reported that before Taylor's death between twenty and thirty representatives opposed the provisions of the compromise legislation that would allow for an expansion of slavery into the territories acquired in the Mexican War. They did a dramatic turnabout, however, in the face of Fillmore's support of the slavery compromise.

Having seen the Compromise of 1850 through to enactment, Fillmore was determined to enforce the new and stringent Fugitive Slave Act vigorously. When Massachusetts refused to cooperate in the prosecution of its citizens who violated the act, Fillmore declared that his administration would admit "no right of **nullification** North or South." In practice, however, the president was never able to find a reliable means of securing compliance in those areas of the country where fugitive slaves were protected.

Fireside Chats

See Roosevelt, Franklin D., Administration of (1933–1945).

First Lady

Wife of the president of the United States. Many first ladies are not well known, but others have achieved fame on their own. Particularly since 1900, the First Lady has been increasingly active politically and visible to the public. She is now among the best-known figures in American politics, often better known than members of Congress and cabinet secretaries, and even the vice president.

The term *FirstLlady* was not applied to the president's wife until after the Civil War (1861–1865). In its early days the Republic, uncertain of how much respect was due its leader's wife, tried several titles without success. Among them were Lady Washington, Mrs. President, presidentress, and **republican** or democratic queen. Sometimes

A - Z

no title was used at all. Julia Grant (1869–1877) was the first presidential spouse to be called the First Lady, in 1870, but the title did not gain wide acceptance until Lucy Hayes held the position from 1877 to 1881.

The modern First Lady has a varied, demanding role. She acts as the manager of the White House as well as the hostess at receptions, parties, and formal dinners. She also is expected to play a political role and participate in social causes on behalf of her husband's administration—all while continuing to fulfill her family responsibilities. Yet the First Lady holds no official position—the Constitution does not mention the president's spouse—and earns no salary. Instead, the First Lady's modern importance stems from history and changing customs.

The First Lady as Hostess

The public has long held that the primary responsibility of the First Lady is to organize and to act as hostess at social events. Presidents, too, are concerned with such events; they view the social calendar as a political tool. George Washington (1789–1797) used the social season to serve his political aims just as, more than a century and a half later, Lyndon B. Johnson (1963–1969) used White House functions as occasions to persuade people to adopt his point of view.

Although the First Lady has both a personal staff and the White House domestic staff to assist her, the basic responsibility for arranging presidential teas, receptions, banquets, coffees, and state dinners is still hers, even on those occasions when she does not have to act as hostess. Most first ladies have carefully selected the menus, entertainment, decorations, and even chairs for social events. For example, Mamie Eisenhower (1953–1961) replaced all the banquet chairs in the **executive** mansion after she decided the old ones were too small.

Not all first ladies, however, have been willing to accept the social role generally expected of them. Some, such as Dolley Madison (1809–1817) and Julia Tyler (1844–1845), enjoyed company and loved to entertain at the White House. For others, such as Helen Taft (1909–1913), Eleanor Roosevelt (1933–1945), and Hillary Rodham Clinton (1993–2001), entertaining was largely a necessary formality. Still others avoided it altogether.

One of the most active First Ladies was Eleanor Roosevelt, the wife of Franklin D. Roosevelt (1933–1945). She traveled across much of the country and reported her findings to the president. She was an avid supporter of workers' rights and favored the passage of the Social Security Act, among other things. (Library of Congress)

For example, Letitia Tyler (1841–1842), Margaret Taylor (1849–1850), and Abigail Fillmore (1850–1853) made few, if any, social appearances, leaving relatives to act as hostess.

In her social role, the First Lady frequently can use parties and other social events to soothe ruffled feathers and charm the uncommitted, thereby helping the president. Perhaps the best First Lady at this was Dolley Madison, famous for her glorious parties. Dolley Madison's charm and ability to put people at ease won numerous friends for her aloof husband, James Madison (1809–1817), who was described by American writer Washington Irving as a "withered little applejohn." In truth, social occasions have political consequence, a fact openly acknowledged when the Bill Clinton administration (1993–2001) designated the White

SPOTLIGHT

Martha Washington and Laura Bush

Fascinatingly, the position of First Lady has never been officially defined. The woman who holds the position is not paid and does not have an official job description, yet she has an assumed responsibility as the hostess of the White House. This tradition was started during the first presidency by Martha Washington, who held formal dinners and public receptions in various presidential houses. Along with establishing the First Lady's role as the hostess of the White House, Martha Washington started the tradition of the First Lady's involvement in charity work. As the wife of the leader of the Congressional Army, Martha Washington was very sympathetic toward soldiers and veterans. She worked to support them, sometimes financially, leading her to become much beloved by military personnel. Her support of the troops included her involvement in recruiting women volunteers to provide support for the Congressional Army. As the first person to assume the role of First Lady, Martha Washington also set the **precedent,** probably unintentional, for the First Lady's status as a public figure. The press often followed her on outings with her grandchildren, and she was doted on by the public. Yet, unlike modern First Ladies, Martha Washington had no formal education and no occupation other than helping to run the Washingtons' plantation. She also remained uninvolved in the politics of her husband's presidency, although she was said to have supported his ideals.

In the more than 200 years since Martha Washington's tenure as First Lady, the position has been remolded again and again as First Ladies deal with the public's expectations, their own desires to make a difference, and the public's fear of their influence over the president. Laura Bush, the wife of George W. Bush (2001–2009) is a prime example of a modern First Lady. She holds a degree in education from Southern Methodist University and has worked as a librarian. Much like Martha Washington, she acts as White House hostess by holding events for various causes and purposes. She is also heavily involved in charity work, supporting causes that promote education, literacy, and the preservation of American history.

Laura Bush has maintained the tradition of the First Lady being a public figure, yet she does so to a much greater extent than Martha Washington. In today's world, the First Lady is considered a celebrity with her constant presence in the media and her roles as spokesperson for different causes. Unlike Martha Washington, Laura Bush is involved in the political arena. Some of her political activities have included testifying before the Senate Education Committee; meeting with the oppressed women of Afghanistan and bringing attention to their suffering; and becoming honorary ambassador for the United Nations Educational, Scientific, and Cultural Organization's Decade of Literacy.

House social secretary as an assistant to the president.

The First Lady as Manager

Besides organizing parties, the First Lady is expected to be a traditional homemaker. However, when one's home is the White House, that may be a challenging duty. The First Lady acts as the general supervisor of the White House, much like the mistress of a large estate. She oversees food selection, decorations, furnishings, cleaning, and other household duties. Again, some first ladies have been much more concerned with these duties than others. Eleanor Roosevelt had little or no interest in how well the White House was kept up. One visitor to the White House, after soiling her gloves on the banisters, wrote that Eleanor Roosevelt should spend less time traveling and more time cleaning the house.

In contrast, her successor, Bess Truman (1945–1953), was quite concerned with the cleanliness of the mansion and had a running battle with the housekeepers to improve their cleaning in general and their dusting in particular. Mamie Eisenhower, who succeeded Bess Truman and was also a demanding mistress, was particularly fussy about the carpets, insisting that they be vacuumed several times each day so as not to show footprints. Mamie Eisenhower ran a tight ship; one of her first demands was that she alone approve all menus.

The First Lady as Public Figure

Because receptions and dinners have long been part of Washington life, the First Lady has always had a social role to play;. Similarly, the duties of household manager are not new. The letters of First Lady Abigail Adams, wife of John Adams (1797–1801), reveal her continual concern with her budget and her home, and subsequent first ladies have had the same worries in managing the White House.

Early first ladies were not expected to play any political role at all. Social custom dictated that men and women move in separate spheres: men in the public and political arena, women in the private and domestic. Being the gracious hostess at social functions was the norm, and any activities beyond that were frowned on. The established model for women was that of passive purity; they were thought to be both above and unsuited for the dirty world of politics. A woman had her place, and the First Lady, like any other woman, was expected to remain there.

The modern First Lady, however, undertakes a wide range of public activities. Indeed, rarely have first ladies been as visible as they are today, and the public expectations of the First Lady are higher than ever before. It is no longer enough for the First Lady to be a good hostess and to manage the White House well. Now she must be publicly engaged in some social cause that benefits the nation. If she is not so engaged, she is open to serious criticism. At the same time, certain areas remain off limits; if she ventures into them, she is criticized for exercising too much power or behaving inappropriately. In general, "social" issues are the proper sphere for a First Lady; "political" ones are not. Thus, first ladies are expected to be prominently involved in efforts to combat drug abuse or reduce illiteracy, whereas efforts to represent the president to foreign leaders or to spearhead major policy reform are open to criticism.

Further Reading

Boller, Paul F., Jr., *Presidential Wives: An Anecdotal History*. New York: Oxford University Press, 1988.

Roberts, John B., II, *Rating the First Ladies*. New York: Citadel Press, 2003.

Truman, Margaret. *First Ladies: An Intimate Group Portrait of White House Wives*. New York: Random House, 1995.

Ford, Gerald R., Administration of (1974–1977)

Government under the thirty-eighth president of the United States. Ford graduated from the University of Michigan in 1935. In 1938, he was admitted to Yale Law School and earned his law degree in 1941.

Ford practiced law in Grand Rapids, Michigan, for less than a year before joining the navy early in 1942. Ford returned to his Grand Rapids law practice in late 1945. He became involved in local politics and decided to run for the U.S. House of Representatives in 1948. Ford eventually won thirteen consecutive terms in the House, always with at least 60 percent of the vote. He turned down an opportunity to run for the U.S. Senate in 1952 because wanted to continue building seniority in the House. Ford rose gradually to leadership positions among House Republicans. In 1963, he became chairman of the House Republican Conference, and in 1964, President Lyndon B. Johnson (1963–1968) appointed him to the Warren Commission, which was investigating the assassination of John F. Kennedy (1961–1963). Ford was elected House minority leader on January 4, 1965. He remained minority leader for nine years.

In 1973, Vice President Spiro T. Agnew resigned after being accused of income tax evasion and accepting bribes. When the vice presidency is vacant, under terms of the Twenty-fifth **Amendment** (1967), the president nominates a new vice president who then must be confirmed by both houses of Congress. Because the credibility of the administration had been seriously damaged by Agnew and the unfolding Watergate scandal, President Richard Nixon (1969–1974) wanted a vice president of unquestioned integrity. He chose Ford, who had developed a reputation for honesty during his years in the House. Nixon announced the appointment of Ford on October 12, 1973, in the East Room of the White House. After two months of inquiry by Congress, Ford's nomination was approved 92–3 by the Senate and 387–35 by the House. He was sworn in as vice president on December 6.

The Watergate scandal forced President Nixon to resign on August 9, 1974. Later that day, Ford became the first president to gain that office without being elected either president or vice president. He nominated former New York governor Nelson A. Rockefeller to be vice president. After a congressional inquiry into Rockefeller's finances, he was confirmed and sworn into office on December 19, 1974.

After taking the oath of office, Ford declared, "our long national nightmare is over." Ford's un-questioned character, his friendly relations with Congress, and the public's desire for a return to normalcy led to an honeymoon with the American public. Seventy-one percent of respondents to a Gallup poll expressed their approval of the new president, while just 3 percent disapproved.

Ford's honeymoon, however, did not last long. On Sunday morning September 8, he announced to a small group of reporters that he was granting Richard Nixon an unconditional pardon. Ford was sensitive to speculation that he had promised to pardon Nixon in return for his nomination as vice president, so he took the **unprecedented** action of voluntarily going before a House Judiciary subcommittee to explain the pardon. Ford justified the highly unpopular action by saying it was needed to heal the political and social divisions caused by the Watergate scandal. Although no evidence of a secret bargain with Nixon surfaced, the pardon severely damaged Ford's standing.

The most pressing domestic problems facing Ford during his term were **inflation** and a sluggish economy. The president initially attempted to fight inflation by **vetoing** spending **bills** and encouraging the Federal Reserve to limit the growth of the money supply. In 1975, however, unemployment had become the more serious problem, and Ford compromised with Congress on a tax cut and a spending plan designed to stimulate the economy. Although inflation and unemployment remained at historically high levels, the economy recovered during late 1975 and 1976.

In foreign affairs, Ford attempted to build on President Nixon's expansion of relations with the Soviet Union and China. Congressional restrictions on U.S. military involvement in Southeast Asia prevented Ford from providing military assistance to South Vietnam, which North Vietnam conquered in 1975. When the U.S. merchant ship *Mayaguez* was seized by Cambodia that year, however, he ordered marines to rescue the crew. The operation freed the crew, but forty-one of the rescuers were killed.

In September 1975, Ford was the target of two assassination attempts. Lynette "squeaky" Fromme, a follower of mass murderer Charles Manson, pointed a loaded pistol at the president on September 5 as he moved through a crowd in Sacramento. A Secret Service agent disarmed her before she could fire. Fromme was convicted of attempted assassination and sentenced to life imprisonment. Two weeks later, on September 22, political activist Sara Jane Moore fired a handgun at Ford as he was leaving a hotel in San Francisco. The bullet struck and slightly wounded a taxi driver. Moore was apprehended by a bystander and two police officers before she could fire a second shot. She, too, was convicted of attempted assassination and sentenced to life in prison.

In early 1976, Ford appeared unlikely to retain the presidency. Even his party's nomination was in doubt, as **conservative** former California governor Ronald Reagan (1981–1989) made a strong bid for the nomination. Neither Ford nor Reagan collected enough delegates in the primaries. However, Ford went on to win enough delegates to narrowly defeat Reagan at the party's convention. In late 1975, Ford had asked Rockefeller to remove himself from consideration for the vice-presidential nomination in 1976. The president chose Senator Robert J. Dole of Kansas as his running mate.

Jimmy Carter (1977–1981), the Democratic presidential candidate, was heavily favored to defeat Ford in the general election, but Ford made up ground during the fall campaign. Carter narrowly defeated the president in the electoral college, 297–240.

After leaving the presidency, Ford retired to Palm Springs, California. In 1979, he published his autobiography, *A Time to Heal*. Ronald Reagan approached Ford about becoming his vice-presidential running mate in 1980, but Ford turned him down. Ford died on December 26, 2006, at age 93.

See also: Carter, Jimmy, Administration of (1977–1981); Nixon, Richard M., Administration of (1969–1974); 📖 Gerald R. Ford's Pardon of Richard Nixon, 1974, in the **Primary Source Library;** Watergate Scandal.

Further Reading

Brinkley, Douglas. *Gerald R. Ford.* New York: Times Books, 2007.

Kennerly, David Hume. *Extraordinary Circumstances: The Presidency of Gerald R. Ford.* Austin, TX: The Center for American History, the University of Texas at Austin, 2007.

Foreign Policy and the Presidency

The president's power to deal with foreign nations and international incidents. In the nineteenth century, when U.S. foreign interests were limited primarily to trade and western expansion, presidents were able to concentrate largely on domestic policy. Today, the wide array of U.S. economic, political, and military commitments abroad ensures that presidents will spend at least half of their time on foreign affairs. Nevertheless, as economic life becomes more globalized, the distinction between domestic and foreign policy is blurring.

The Constitution makes the president the formal head of state. As the "sole representative with foreign nations," the president speaks for the nation as a whole and is often the focus of national hopes and fears, pride and shame. In the role of chief negotiator and national spokesperson, the president has great advantage in any competition with Congress for control of the nation's foreign policies. The president has made important decisions on foreign affairs often after consultations with only a few trusted advisers. The desire of political friends and foes alike to present a united front has frequently produced initial support for and general deference to the president's lead.

Circumstances such as wars or threats of armed conflict enhance this advantage. They have allowed presidents to dominate the formulation and implementation of foreign policy. Even during periods of relative international calm, foreign affairs issues usually have offered presidents the greatest freedom to exercise their power and the best opportunity to affect policy personally.

In contrast, domestic policy decisions commonly involve many officials and interest groups, require less secrecy, and entail the full participation of Congress and its committees. Consequently, presidents may choose to retreat to the refuge of foreign affairs where they can exercise their powers most freely as leader of the nation.

Indeed, foreign affairs often afford the president the opportunity to gain an enduring

President Bill Clinton (1993–2001) and Vice President Al Gore strived to keep the Mideast peace process moving by meeting with leaders of the region. In 1996, they met with PLO leader Yassir Arafat (far left), King Hussein of Jordan, and Israeli prime minister Benjamin Netanyahu. (AP Images, Dita Alangkara)

place in history. Steadfast wartime leadership, the prevention or resolution of dangerous crises, bold policy and diplomatic initiatives, and historic summit meetings with important foreign leaders can create presidential legends:

- Thomas Jefferson's (1801–1809) Louisiana Purchase (1803)
- James Monroe's (1817–1825) Monroe Doctrine (1823)
- James K. Polk's (1845–1849) national expansion (1845–1848)
- Theodore Roosevelt's (1901–1909) Panama Canal (1904)
- Harry S. Truman's (1945–1953) Marshall Plan (1948)
- Richard Nixon's (1969–1974) trip to China (1972)

Following the lead of Theodore Roosevelt, whose successful management of negotiations to end the Russo-Japanese War (1904–1905) earned

him a Nobel Peace Prize in 1906, presidents have used their stature and skills to resolve conflicts less directly related to U.S. interests. Jimmy Carter's (1977–1981) Camp David summit in 1978 led to a peace agreement between Egypt and Israel, and Bill Clinton's (1993–2001) participation in the Dayton, Ohio, negotiations helped to move the civil war in Bosnia toward a resolution. On the other hand, Clinton's repeated efforts to resolve the conflicts in Northern Ireland and between Israel and the Palestinians were, at best, partial and temporary successes.

The foreign policy records of few administrations are completely triumphant. Although George Washington's administration (1789–1797) was honored for a balanced policy of **neutrality,** the Jay Treaty (1794) with Great Britain provoked virulent **partisan** attacks. Thomas Jefferson's purchase of the Louisiana territory must be paired with the miserable failure of his **embargo** against Great Britain. Woodrow Wilson (1913–1921), the victorious World War I (1914–1918) leader, was humiliated by the defeat of the Treaty of Versailles in 1920 and his internationalist foreign policy. Jimmy Carter's triumph in facilitating an Israeli-Egyptian peace accord at Camp David was followed by his inability to resolve the hostage crisis with Iran. Moreover, while Ronald Reagan's (1981–1989) hard-line anticommunist policies were bearing some fruit, his administration was mired in the Iran-contra scandal.

Recent presidents who entered office possessing greater expertise and interest in domestic policy have been distracted, seduced, or overwhelmed by foreign affairs. Lyndon B. Johnson's (1963–1969) **Great Society** plans were undercut by the resource demands of the Vietnam War (1964–1975) and the divisions the war created in the American public. Carter, a former governor with little foreign policy experience, became personally absorbed with foreign policy issues such as recognition of the People's Republic of China, arms control, and the Camp David peace process between Egypt and Israel. Events in Somalia, North Korea, Haiti, and Bosnia taught Bill Clinton that even in the post–cold war era no president can avoid the dangerous complications of foreign affairs. Similarly, the terrorist attacks on New York City and Washington, D.C., in September 2001 immediately turned President George W. Bush's (2001–2009) agenda from domestic policy to engaging in diplomacy and waging war.

Sharing Powers

While the Constitution makes presidents the sole head of state, it does not give them sufficient authority to make foreign policy on their own. The branches of the federal government share foreign policy powers, and Congress has many means of influence over the substance and execution of general and specific policies. In addition, policy must be coordinated within a complex of often competing advisers, departments, and agencies. Even under the most favorable conditions, presidents frequently struggle to maintain control of policy formulation and implementation. In the current era, which lacks the ideological clarity of the cold war and the unifying fears of nuclear confrontation between two superpowers, achieving presidential leadership and control of foreign policy has become more difficult and complicated.

See also: Chief Diplomat; Presidency and Congress.

Further Reading

Hook, Stephen W. *U.S. Foreign Policy: The Paradox of World Power,* 2nd ed. Washington, DC: CQ Press, 2007.

Nolan, Cathal, and Carl Hodge. *U.S. Presidents and Foreign Policy: From 1789 to the Present.* Santa Barbara, CA: ABC-CLIO, 2006.

Garfield, James A., Administration of (1881)

Government under the twentieth president of the United States. At the 1880 Republican National Convention the party was sharply divided over whom to nominate for president. President Rutherford B. Hayes (1877–1881) had declined to run for reelection. The radical Stalwart faction of the Republican Party, headed by New York senator Roscoe Conkling, a powerful political **boss,** supported former president Ulysses S. Grant (1869–1877). The less radical Half-breed faction backed Senator James G. Blaine (R-ME). Garfield, who had been elected to the Senate earlier in the year but had not yet taken his seat, had promoted the compromise candidacy of John Sherman of Ohio. The convention, however, nominated Garfield himself on the thirty-sixth ballot. In a gesture to the Stalwarts the convention nominated Chester A. Arthur (1881–1885), a Conkling associate, for vice president.

On July 2, 1881, as Garfield was in the Baltimore and Potomac railroad station in Washington, D.C., on his way to deliver the commencement address at his alma mater, Williams College, he was shot by Charles J. Guiteau. Guiteau shot the president once in the back and fired another bullet that grazed his arm. Garfield was taken to the White House, where he remained for two months while doctors unsuccessfully probed for the bullet that was lodged near his spine. On September 6, the president asked to be moved to Elberon, New Jersey, in the hope that the sea air would help him recover. He died in Elberon on September 19, 1881. Ironically, Garfield probably would have survived if his doctors had left the bullet undisturbed rather than searching for it with unsterile instruments, which spread infection.

Guiteau had been captured at the time of the shooting and was put on trial in Washington, D.C., two months after the president's death. At the time of the attack the assassin had shouted, "I am a Stalwart; now Arthur is president!" Guiteau, however, was not associated with Roscoe Conkling and the Stalwarts. The assassin believed his distribution of pro-Republican Party literature during the 1880 presidential campaign entitled him to a diplomatic appointment. Repeated rejections by the White House angered him, and he claimed to have received a divine vision instructing him to kill the president. The assassin's lawyers argued that their client was insane and should be acquitted, but the jury found him guilty and sentenced him to death. Guiteau was hanged in Washington, D.C., on June 30, 1882.

See also: Assassinations and Assassination Attempts; Hayes, Rutherford B., Administration of (1877–1881); Arthur, Chester A., Administration of (1881–1885).

Further Reading

Ackerman, Kenneth D. *Dark Horse: The Surprise Election and Political Murder of President James A. Garfield.* Jackson, TN: Da Capo Press, 2004.

Rutkow, Ira. *James A. Garfield.* New York: Times Books, 2006.

Gore, Albert (1948–)

The forty-fifth vice president of the United States. In 1969, Albert Arnold Gore Jr. graduated from Harvard University with a degree in government. Gore opposed the Vietnam War (1965–1975), but he enlisted in the army and served for six months as a military journalist in Vietnam without seeing combat. From 1971 to 1976, Gore worked as a reporter for the *Tennessean,* a Nashville newspaper, writing investigative pieces and covering local politics.

In 1976, at the age of twenty-eight, Gore won his father's former seat in the House of Representatives and was easily reelected in the heavily Democratic district in 1978, 1980, and 1982. In the House, Gore led a campaign to televising its floor proceedings. When that campaign succeeded, he delivered the chamber's first televised speech on C-SPAN in March 1979. Gore successfully jumped to the Senate in 1984, winning with 61 percent of the vote.

Reelected to his Senate seat in 1990, Gore was one of only ten Democrats in the Senate to vote to authorize of the use of military force against Iraq in January 1991. Gore's vote upset some Democratic Party loyalists, but he repaired the damage by vigorously defending Democrats who had voted against the measure from charges that they were unpatriotic.

In 1992, Bill Clinton (1993–2001) of Arkansas surprised many commentators by picking Gore as his vice-presidential running mate. Presidential candidates usually try to balance the ticket with a running mate who is from another region and who has a somewhat different political ideology. In contrast to this norm, Gore shared Clinton's moderate southern Democrat outlook and was from a state that borders Arkansas. Moreover, they were only a year and a half apart in age. Nevertheless, Clinton and Gore used these similarities to project an image of unity and youthful energy. Gore's service in Vietnam also aided Clinton, who had avoided military service. Clinton and Gore defeated **incumbents** George H.W. Bush (1989–1993) and Dan Quayle by an electoral vote of 370–168.

Gore, with his extensive experience in Washington, became one of President Clinton's closest advisers. Gore took on many critical assignments, serving as the head of the president's effort to "reinvent government," a long-term project to reduce the size of and reengineer the federal government to achieve efficiency and cost savings. Gore also functioned as the administration's point man on congressional relations, environmental protection, defense, and high technology.

During the summer of 1993, after much **partisan** debate in Congress over Clinton's budget plan, Vice President Gore, presiding over the Senate, cast the deciding vote for the plan. Another celebrated moment for Gore came on November 9, 1993, when he debated the merits of the North American Free Trade Agreement (NAFTA) with billionaire H. Ross Perot on the "Larry King Live" talk show. Polls showed after the debate that Gore and the pro-NAFTA position had won decisively, giving proponents a big psychological boost. The outcome induced many wavering members of Congress to support the agreement, which passed both houses.

In 1996, Gore and Clinton faced Republicans Bob Dole and Jack Kemp in the general election. Gore proved to be an effective defender of Clinton administration positions during the vice-presidential debate with Kemp, handily winning it, according to most political observers. The Clinton-Gore ticket defeated Dole and Kemp by an electoral vote margin of 379 to 159.

Gore dominated the 2000 Democratic primaries, despite increasingly pointed charges by his opponent, former senator Bill Bradley of New Jersey, about Gore's truthfulness and changes of position on gun control and abortion rights. Gore chose Joseph Lieberman, a respected senator from Connecticut, as his running mate, making Lieberman the first Jewish person to run for vice president. This decision was based partly on Lieberman's role as the first Democratic senator to publicly criticize Clinton's behavior.

In one of the closest presidential races in history, with the election results from Florida hotly disputed, Gore lost his White House bid to George W. Bush (2001–2009) of Texas. The outcome of the contest was not known until five weeks after the election. Although Gore won several states by razor-thin margins, he needed Florida's twenty-five electoral votes for victory. Both campaigns raised numerous legal challenges in state and federal court on the legitimacy of the state's final tally. Stepping in to end the dispute, the Supreme Court ruled in favor of Bush in a 5–4 decision. Although Gore lost the electoral vote 266 to 271, he garnered half a million more popular votes than Bush, marking the third time in U.S. history that the winner of the popular vote did not advance to the presidency.

After the election, Gore took a teaching position at Columbia University's Graduate School of Journalism. He and his wife, Tipper, published two books in 2002 on the subject of families, titled *Joined at the Heart* and *The Spirit of Family*. As the next presidential race drew closer, many expected Gore to run again. Although he would have been the automatic front-runner, the former vice president announced in December 2002 that he would not seek his party's 2004 nomination. In December 2003, Gore endorsed former Vermont governor Howard Dean, passing over Lieberman, who also was running for president; both men eventually lost the nomination to Senator John Kerry of Massachusetts.

Gore reentered the public eye in 2006 with the release of his environmental documentary *An Inconvenient Truth,* which garnered a great deal of media attention, and for which Gore received the Nobel Peace Prize for his environmental activism and two Oscars at the film industry's 2007 Academy Awards.

See also: Bush v. Gore (2000); Clinton, Bill, Administration of (1993–2001).

Further Reading

Maraniss, David, and Ellen Nakashima. *The Prince of Tennessee: The Rise of Al Gore.* New York: Simon & Schuster, 2000.
Turque, Bill. *Inventing Al Gore: A Biography.* Boston: Houghton Mifflin, 2000.

Government Agencies and Corporations

Various agencies and organizations that are a part of the **executive** branch. Some of these agencies are independent of any cabinet department, whereas others are part of the cabinet hierarchy but have the power to operate largely as separate entities. No matter what kind of organizational relationship these agencies have to the rest of the executive branch, however, the president has direct legal responsibility for them and often exerts considerable control over them.

These independent and semi-independent agencies have different objectives, powers, methods of determining their members, and organizational structures. Any similarity derives from their existence largely outside the traditional lines of authority of the executive departments. Their independent or semi-independent status results either from the desire of Congress to remove their operations from the control of the cabinet hierarchy or from presidential attempts to show concern for specific problems that could best be solved in an environment lacking political pressure. These agencies can be divided into three general categories: regulatory agencies, independent **executive** agencies, and government corporations.

Regulatory Agencies

Regulatory agencies and commissions regulate aspects of the economy and, more recently, consumer affairs. The **commerce** clause of the Constitution (Article I, Section 8) gives the federal government authority "to regulate Commerce with foreign Nations, and among the several States." Although there is no universally accepted definition, in 1977 the Senate Government Operations Committee (later renamed the Governmental Affairs Committee) defined a federal regulatory agency as "one which (1) has decision-making authority, (2) establishes standards or guidelines conferring benefits and imposing restrictions on business conduct, (3) operates principally in the sphere of domestic business activity, (4) has its head and/or members appointed by the president

. . . and (5) has its legal procedures generally governed by the Administrative Procedure Act."

Regulatory agencies are organizationally either independent of the cabinet hierarchy or part of an existing executive department. Independent regulatory agencies are governed by **bipartisan** commissions of five or more members. These commissioners usually serve lengthy, fixed terms, and they cannot be removed by the president. Among the major independent regulatory agencies are the Federal Reserve Board (FRB), National Labor Relations Board (NLRB), Federal Communications Commission (FCC), Federal Trade Commission (FTC), and Securities and Exchange Commission (SEC).

Semi-independent regulatory agencies—agencies within an executive branch department—serve under the authority of the department in which they are located. The heads of these agencies are subject to appointment and dismissal by the president or the department secretary. Regulatory agencies within executive branch departments include the Food and Drug Administration (FDA), in the Department of Health and Human Services, and the Occupational Safety and Health Administration (OSHA), in the Department of Labor.

Although independent regulatory agencies oversee a variety of activities, they share certain jurisdictional and organizational characteristics. Sometimes called quasi-agencies because they are legally empowered to perform quasi-legislative, quasi-executive, and quasi-judicial functions, independent regulatory agencies can issue rules that govern certain sectors of the economy, oversee implementation of those rules, and adjudicate disputes over interpretation of the rules.

In creating these agencies, Congress has attempted to protect their independence. For example, commissioners, who are appointed by the president and confirmed by the Senate, serve overlapping fixed terms, usually of four to seven years. Even though they are political appointees, presidents cannot simply fire them. In a further attempt to ensure political independence from the president, Congress made these commissions bipartisan and placed limits on the number of appointees from any single political party. Generally, neither political party may have a majority of more than one. This organizational design makes

A – Z

these agencies and commissions independent of other executive organizations and places responsibility for the execution of their policies with the commissioners rather than the president.

Presumably, appointees to regulatory commissions should not only be experts in the policy area but also objective parties who would not unfairly favor one side over another in a policy dispute. In practice, however, regulatory agencies tend to develop reciprocal relationships with the interests they are supposed to regulate. Political scientist Samuel Huntington has suggested that regulatory agencies inevitably are "captured" by the interest groups they are supposed to be regulating. Thus, the FDA would look out for the interests of drug manufacturers, and the Nuclear Regulatory Commission (NRC) for the interests of the nuclear industry.

Whereas the original regulatory activity of the federal government was primarily economic regulation, modern agencies undertake regulation that goes beyond the traditional economic spheres, moving more and more into social concerns. Although these social concerns usually are related to economic activities, their scope is different in that they touch upon issues important to individual consumers. For this reason, regulatory activity can be divided into economic regulation and social regulation.

Economic Regulation

In 1887, the federal government undertook its first major regulation of a private sector of the economy when Congress, exercising its constitutional right to regulate interstate commerce, created the Interstate Commerce Commission (ICC). The ICC became the first target in the wave of deregulation that occurred in the last decade of the twentieth century and was abolished by an act of Congress in 1995. Many of its functions were transferred to a newly created surface transportation board in the Department of Transportation.

Ironically, Congress did not intend to make the Interstate Commerce Commission independent of presidential control. During congressional debate on creation of the ICC, matters of independence and presidential control were never considered. Congress first placed the ICC in the Interior Department, which subjected its budget,

staff, and internal management to control by an executive department. Two years later Congress gave the ICC control over its own affairs.

It was several years after achieving independence from Interior that the ICC gained any real power. At first the ICC lacked the power to do anything more than issue cease-and-desist orders to stop railroads from violating provisions of the Interstate Commerce Act of 1887. It had neither the authority to set or adjust railroad shipping rates nor any coercive power to enforce its rulings. Moreover, in the early years the courts closely reviewed ICC orders, often substituting their own judgments favoring railroads for those of the commission. The railroads quickly learned that they could circumvent the ICC by appealing judgments to the courts.

Gradually the ICC became powerful. In 1906, Congress passed the Hepburn Act, which gave the commission the authority to adjust rates that it deemed unreasonable or unfair. In 1910, with passage of the Mann-Elkins Act, Congress strengthened the commission's enforcement ability by authorizing it to suspend and investigate new rate proposals and to set original rates.

Abandoning the idea that the ICC might be able to handle the regulation of all commerce, Congress created a network of new regulatory agencies patterned after the ICC. In 1913, the Federal Reserve System began to regulate banking and the supply of money. The following year the Federal Trade Commission began to regulate business practices and control monopolistic behavior. Between 1915 and 1933, the beginning of Franklin Roosevelt's administration (1933–1945), Congress set up seven other regulatory agencies, including the **Tariff** Commission (1916), Commodities Exchange Authority (1922), Customs Service (1927), and Federal Power Commission (1930).

After the onset of the **Great Depression** and beginning with Franklin D. Roosevelt's New Deal, an extraordinary flood of regulatory programs passed Congress. Between 1932 and 1938, eight major regulatory agencies were set up to handle problems created by the economic crisis of the depression. These included several agencies that have become mainstays in the United States. For example, the Federal Deposit Insurance Corporation (FDIC), created by the Banking Act of 1933, continues more than seven decades later to regulate state-chartered, insured banks that are not members of the Federal Reserve System and to provide federally guaranteed insurance for bank deposits. The Securities and Exchange Commission, founded in 1934 to protect the public against fraud and deception in securities and financial markets, carries out the same mandate today. Finally, the Wagner Act of 1935 created the National Labor Relations Board, which continues to prevent "unfair labor practices" and to protect the right of collective bargaining.

Social Regulation

The New Deal was the true beginning of large-scale federal regulation of the economy, but it also provided the foundation for the many social regulatory agencies that arose in the 1960s and 1970s. As New Deal programs expanded the scope of the federal government, the American people came to accept the government's role in solving the nation's economic and social problems. By the mid-1960s, the federal government was providing medical care, educational aid, nutritional help, urban renewal, and job training, among other services. By the mid-1970s social activism had grown to such an extent that many consumer and environmental groups were calling for a new wave of regulation to achieve social goals such as clean air and consumer protection. These social regulatory agencies can be divided into four areas of concern: consumer protection, environmental protection, workplace safety, and energy regulation.

By the early 1970s, the consumer movement had begun to make its mark on American life. Consumers demanded protection against false advertising and faulty products. Organized groups pressed for safer and better products and lower prices for food, fuel, and medical care. Earlier, in 1965, Ralph Nader had almost single-handedly launched consumerism as a political movement with the publication of his book *Unsafe at Any Speed,* which attacked the automobile industry's poor safety record.

Through Nader's efforts and those of other consumer advocates interested in automobile safety, the National Highway Traffic Safety Administration (NHTSA) was created within the Department of Transportation in 1970. With its authority to set automobile safety and fuel efficiency standards, the agency represents one of the early efforts at consumer legislation. In contrast to the semi-independent NHTSA, the Consumer Product Safety Commission was created as a wholly independent consumer protection agency. With passage of the Consumer Product Safety Act in 1972, Congress gave the commission the task of protecting consumers against unreasonable risks of injury from hazardous products.

Advocates of a cleaner environment were also part of the consumer movement. The creation of the Environmental Protection Agency (EPA) in 1970 stemmed directly from their efforts. Set up as an independent executive agency, EPA was charged with supervising and protecting the nation's environment, including its air, water, and land, and with reducing noise pollution. EPA has become one of the most controversial of all federal agencies, largely because of its wide-ranging responsibilities and the costs of the programs that it implements to clean up the environment.

Workplace safety was another concern of the consumer movement. Consumers wanted to minimize hazards in the workplace by establishing guidelines for safety and health on the job. The Occupational Safety and Health Administration, established as an agency within the Labor Department in 1970, was charged with promulgating and enforcing worker safety and health standards. It is authorized to conduct unannounced on-site inspections and to require employers to keep detailed records on worker injuries and illnesses. OSHA thus has considerable regulatory power that it can wield in carrying out its quasi-legislative, quasi-executive, and quasi-judicial functions.

In the 1970s, the United States faced the dual problems of a dwindling energy supply and rising energy costs. In an attempt to insulate consumers from these problems, Congress created several agencies. In 1973, it established the Federal Energy Administration (FEA) to alleviate short-term fuel shortages, and in 1974 it created the Energy Research and Development Administration (ERDA) to develop nuclear power and new energy sources. Also in 1974, Congress created the Nuclear Regulatory Commission (NRC) to regulate nuclear safety. All of these agencies, except the NRC, were abolished in 1977 when their functions

A - Z

were moved to the newly created Department of Energy.

Independent Executive Agencies

Independent executive agencies are similar to independent regulatory agencies in that they are not part of a cabinet department. However, they are normally considered to be part of the presidential hierarchy and report to the president. The most important of these agencies are the National Aeronautics and Space Administration (NASA) and the General Services Administration (GSA).

Many of these agencies were created in an effort to overcome bureaucratic inertia, which often resulted in the failure of existing departments to accomplish their objectives. In 1964, for example, the Lyndon B. Johnson (1963–1969) administration created the Office of Economic Opportunity (OEO) to help implement its **Great Society** programs. By locating OEO in the Executive Office of the President and not in a specific department, the White House was able to exert more control over its operation and ensure that the administration's antipoverty functions were carried out. Similarly, NASA was located outside the control of a specific department to help expedite its formation and operation, free from the traditional demands of departmental control. In addition, it was set up apart from the Department of Defense to ensure that the U.S. space program would be controlled by civilians rather than the military.

Often agencies are made independent in response to vested interests. Members of Congress and interest groups want to guarantee that these agencies are responsive to their wishes. In addition, presidents and Congress often want these agencies free from the traditional constraints and methods of old-line departments. For example, in an effort to directly challenge actions detrimental to the environment, Congress made the EPA independent of old-line departments that might have had traditional environmental interests.

Since they have some degree of autonomy from hierarchical executive control, independent executive agencies can maneuver more openly than departmental agencies in ways that will maximize their objectives. This kind of freedom, however, often means that independent agencies will have few allies in the executive branch, possibly diminishing their overall influence on the formulation of executive policy. Some agencies—the Civil Rights Commission (CRC), for example—have been successful at developing coalitions with groups not traditionally represented by executive departments. Established in 1957 as a bipartisan, six-member independent agency, the CRC used its autonomous organizational status to become a constructive critic of federal civil rights policies. Between 1959 and 1970, by forging coalitions outside the executive branch, the commission was able to get more than two-thirds of its recommendations either enacted into law or included in executive orders.

Executive independence can result, however, in overlapping **jurisdictions** and conflicts between the independent agencies and other executive organizations. Until the Civil Service Commission was replaced by the Office of Personnel Management in 1978, its independence made it an easy target for groups seeking to influence federal personnel policy. The attempt to remove politics from the federal personnel selection process resulted in just the opposite; politics became a primary factor in determining federal job selection.

Government Corporations

A third type of agency, which operates either independently or semi-independently of the regular departmental structure, is the government corporation. Even though investors in government corporations cannot buy stock and collect dividends, these organizations operate much like a private corporation that sells a service. Government corporations usually provide a service that the private sector has found too expensive or unprofitable to offer.

Three of the best-known government corporations are the Tennessee Valley Authority (TVA), created in 1933 to develop electric power and navigation in the Tennessee Valley region; the National Railroad Passenger Corporation, or Amtrak, the nation's passenger train service; and the U.S. Postal Service. Several successful government corporations have been based on the TVA model, including Comsat, which sold time-sharing on NASA satellites until it was absorbed by Lockheed-Martin Corporation as part of a privatization effort in 1999.

The Postal Service became a government corporation only in 1970. Originally created in 1775 by the Continental Congress with Benjamin Franklin as its postmaster general, this longtime cabinet department assumed its corporate status during the administration of Richard Nixon (1969–1974). In urging reorganization of the Postal Service, Nixon argued that it would operate more efficiently if freed from the direct control of the president and Congress and the resulting bipartisan pressure.

By incorporating these organizations, Congress has given them greater latitude in their day-to-day operations than that given to other agencies. As corporations, federal agencies can acquire, develop, and sell real estate and other kinds of property, acting in the name of the corporation rather than the federal government. They have the power as well to bring lawsuits on behalf of the corporation, and they can be sued. Also like private corporations, these agencies are headed by a board of directors or board of commissioners. Some corporations, such as the Postal Service, have a single head who is assisted by a board. Corporation heads and members are appointed by the president and confirmed by the Senate. They serve long, staggered terms to prevent any one president from controlling the corporation.

See also: Cabinet.

Grant, Ulysses S., Administration of (1869–1877)

Government under the eighteenth president of the United States. In 1843, Ulysses S. Grant graduated twenty-first in his class of thirty-nine at West Point, the military academy. Later, during the Mexican-American War (1846–1848), he was recognized for his bravery and promoted to first lieutenant after the capture of Mexico City in September 1847. In July 1848, Grant returned to the United States and was stationed at several posts around the country. In 1854, he resigned his military commission.

After the Civil War (1861–1865), General Ulysses S. Grant was popular and easily won the presidency in 1868. He was reelected in 1872. (Library of Congress)

Civil War

In April 1861, President Abraham Lincoln (1861–1865) called for volunteers to put down the insurrection in the South. Because of his military experience, Grant was appointed colonel of an Illinois regiment in June. He impressed his superiors and in August was promoted to brigadier general. In March 1864, after a string of victories during the Civil War (1861–1865), Lincoln promoted Grant to lieutenant general and appointed him general in chief of the army. After a year of heavy fighting, the Confederate general Robert E. Lee surrendered to Grant at Appomattox Court House in Virginia on April 9, 1865.

Presidency

In 1868, the Republicans nominated Grant as their candidate for president. Grant, whose Civil War record had made him the most idolized person in America, received 52.7 percent of the popular vote and defeated Democrat Horatio Seymour 214–80 in the electoral college.

When Grant took office, **Reconstruction** of the South was the primary issue confronting his administration. Grant supported the Reconstruction laws enacted during Andrew Johnson's administration (1865–1869) and the **ratification** of the Fifteenth **Amendment** in 1870 giving African Americans the right to vote. Although Grant opposed blanketing the South with troops to guarantee the rights of blacks and to oversee other aspects of Reconstruction, he did respond forcibly to violations of the law. As Grant's term progressed, however, many northerners came to believe that federal attempts to keep southern whites from controlling state governments could not go on forever and were causing southern whites to use intimidation and terror to achieve their ends. Grant, therefore, was less willing and able to rally support for an activist Reconstruction policy.

In foreign affairs, Grant and Hamilton Fish, his capable secretary of state, successfully negotiated the Treaty of Washington with Great Britain. The treaty, signed in May 1871, provided for the settlement of U.S. claims against Great Britain for destruction caused during the Civil War by the *Alabama* and other ships built in Britain for the Confederacy. Grant was unsuccessful, however, in his attempts to **annex** Santo Domingo. His personal secretary, Orville Babcock, negotiated an annexation treaty, but it was rejected by the Senate.

Grant retained his popularity during his first term and in 1872 won an overwhelming victory over Horace Greeley, editor of the *New York Tribune*. Grant defeated Greeley, 286 electoral votes to 66. Greeley died less than a month after the election.

Although Grant himself was honest, many of his appointees and associates were not. Grant's administration, particularly his second term, is notable for its scandals. Before Grant's second inauguration, the Crédit Mobilier scandal was revealed. Grant's outgoing vice president Schuyler Colfax and incoming vice president Henry Wilson both were implicated in the bribery scheme, which involved skimming profits made from the construction of the transcontinental railroad. In 1875, a Treasury Department investigation revealed that several prominent Republicans were involved in the Whiskey Ring, a group that had used bribery

VIEWPOINTS

African American men were guaranteed the right to vote after the ratification of the Fifteenth Amendment in 1870. President Ulysses S. Grant (1869–1877) strongly supported the passage of this amendment. (Library of Congress)

to avoid taxes on liquor. In 1876 Grant's secretary of war, William Belknap, resigned just before being impeached by the House of Representatives for accepting bribes. In his last annual message to Congress in 1876, Grant acknowledged that he had made mistakes during his presidency but assured the legislators that "failures have been errors of judgment, not of intent."

In August 1884, Grant was diagnosed with cancer. He began writing his memoirs in an attempt to give his family financial security before his death. Although suffering extreme pain, Grant lived longer than his doctors had predicted and finished his memoirs on July 19, 1885, four days before he died. The two-volume *Memoirs of U.S. Grant* sold 300,000 copies and earned Grant's widow nearly a half million dollars in royalties.

See also: Hayes, Rutherford B., Administration of (1877–1881); Johnson, Andrew, Administration of (1865–1869).

Further Reading

Bunting, Josiah III. *Ulysses S. Grant.* New York: Times Books, 2004.

Grant, Ulysses S. *The Personal Memoirs of Ulysses S. Grant.* New York: Cosimo Classics, 2007.

Hamilton, Alexander

See Department of the Treasury.

Harding, Warren, Administration of (1921–1923)

Government under the twenty-ninth president of the United States. After Warren Harding graduated from Ohio Central College in 1882, he taught in a country school for one term, before giving up the profession and moving to Marion, Ohio. In 1884 he and two friends bought the *Marion Star,* a bankrupt, four-page newspaper. Harding bought out his friends in 1886 when they lost interest in the enterprise. Gradually, he made the paper a financial success and a political force in Ohio.

Early Political Career

In 1892, Harding ran for county auditor but was defeated badly by his Democratic opponent. He remained active in state politics, however, frequently making campaign speeches for Republican candidates. In 1899, he ran for the state senate and was victorious. He won a second term in 1901 and was elected lieutenant governor in 1903. Two years later, however, he refused to be renominated for lieutenant governor in favor of returning to manage his paper in Marion.

In 1909, Harding ran for governor of Ohio but was defeated. He gained national prominence in June 1912 when he delivered the speech nominating William Howard Taft (1909–1913) for president at the Republican National Convention in Chicago. Two years later, he ran for the U.S. Senate. After winning the Republican Party's first direct primary for senator in Ohio, Harding was elected.

Harding took his undistinguished record to the 1920 Republican National Convention in Chicago. His was one of many names entered into nomination for president, but he was not among the favorites in the early balloting. After four ballots, none of the front-runners could muster a majority of support. Fearing a deadlock that would threaten party unity, Republican leaders retired to a proverbial smoke-filled room at the Blackstone Hotel. At the urging of Harding's close friend and political mentor, Harry Daugherty, they decided to give the nomination to Harding, who possessed good looks, an amiable personality, and a willingness to be led by the party.

During a "front porch" campaign reminiscent of William McKinley's 1896 effort, Harding promised a "return to normalcy" after the Woodrow Wilson years (1913–1921). This promise appealed to American voters, who had lived through a difficult period during World War I (1914–1918) and were skeptical of Wilson's internationalist idealism. In the first presidential election in which women could vote, Harding defeated James M. Cox in a landslide, receiving over sixteen million votes to his opponent's nine million. Harding received 404 electoral votes, while Cox managed

A-Z

to win just eleven states, all in the South, for a total of 127 electoral votes.

Presidency

During Woodrow Wilson's term, the Senate had rejected the Treaty of Versailles ending World War I because a majority of senators objected to U.S. membership in the League of Nations. Consequently, a separate agreement was needed to formally end the war. In 1921, the Harding administration concluded treaties with Germany, Austria, and Hungary, officially making peace with those nations. In 1921, Harding also called the Washington Disarmament Conference. This meeting, masterminded by Secretary of State Charles Evans Hughes, succeeded in producing a treaty that reduced the navies of the United States, Great Britain, France, Germany, Japan, and Italy.

In domestic policy, Harding cut taxes on high incomes and signed the Fordney-McCumber Act, which raised **tariff** rates that had been lowered during the Wilson administration. A lasting contribution to U.S. government left by Harding was the Bureau of the Budget (now the Office of Management and Budget), which was created by the Budget Act of 1921.

Harding's administration is best known, however, for the scandals that were revealed after his death. Harding appointed to high government posts many friends and cronies who used their position for personal enrichment. Harding is not known to have participated in the crimes committed by his associates and advisers, but he did little to prevent the corruption within his administration. One of the most famous scandals involved Secretary of the Interior Albert Fall who, in return for a substantial amount of money, leased government oil reserves at Teapot Dome, Wyoming, and Elk Hills, California, to private interests. Fall was later fined and imprisoned for his actions. Secretary of the Navy Edwin Denby, Attorney General Harry Daugherty, and Charles Forbes, head of the Veterans Bureau, also were found to have participated in the scandals.

When the Republicans lost seats in both houses of Congress in the 1922 midterm election, Harding decided to go on a speaking tour in early 1923 to boost his party's and his own popularity. It is also probable that Harding wished to leave Washington to escape the developing rumors about the corruption within his administration.

After visiting Alaska and then moving on to Seattle, Harding was stricken with pains that were diagnosed as indigestion but may have been a heart attack. Harding improved, but then died suddenly in San Francisco. His doctors suspected a blood clot in the brain may have killed him, but his wife refused to permit an autopsy. The absence of conclusive evidence about his death and the later scandals led to public speculation that he may have committed suicide or been poisoned, but no evidence of an unnatural death exists. The news of Harding's death brought an outpouring of public grief. As details of the scandals of his administration became known in 1923 and 1924, however, Harding's public reputation declined.

See also: Coolidge, Calvin, Administration of (1923–1929); Wilson, Woodrow, Administration of (1913–1921).

Further Reading

Dean, John W. *Warren Harding.* New York: Times Books, 2004.

McCartney, Laton. *The Teapot Dome Scandal: How Big Oil Bought the Harding White House and Tried to Steal the Country.* New York: Random House, 2008.

Harrison, Benjamin, Administration of (1889–1893)

Government under the twenty-third president of the United States. Born and schooled in Ohio, Benjamin Harrison moved to Indianapolis, Indiana, in 1854 to establish a law practice. Soon after moving to Indianapolis, Harrison became active in the Republican Party. In 1857, he was elected Indianapolis city attorney. The following year he served as secretary of the Indiana Republican central committee, and in 1860, he was elected reporter of the Indiana Supreme Court.

In 1876, Harrison received the Republican nomination for governor but lost by five thousand votes to Democrat James D. Williams. Harrison, however, had not sought the nomination and was happy to return to his law practice. He presided over the Indiana Republican convention in 1878 and was chair of his state's delegation to the Republican National Convention in 1880.

In 1881, Harrison was elected to the U.S. Senate, where he chaired the committee on territories. In this capacity, he defended the interests of homesteaders and Native Americans against the railroads. Harrison also was a strong advocate of Civil War veterans and worked to protect and expand their pensions. Harrison ran for reelection in 1886, but the Democrats had gained control of the Indiana legislature two years before and voted him out of office.

At the 1888 Republican National Convention in Chicago, Harrison was nominated on the eighth ballot to run for president against **incumbent** Grover Cleveland (1885–1889, 1893–1897). The primary issue of the campaign was the **tariff,** which Harrison promised to raise if elected. Harrison lost the popular vote but won in the electoral college, 233–168, with the help of a narrow victory in New York that gave him that state's thirty-six electoral votes.

During Harrison's term, the Republicans controlled both houses of Congress. As a result, he was able to implement much of his economic program. In July 1890, he signed the Sherman Antitrust Act and the Sherman Silver Purchase Act. The Sherman Antitrust Act outlawed trusts and business combines that restrained trade. The Sherman Silver Purchase required the Treasury to purchase large quantities of silver with notes that could be redeemed in gold. Later in 1890, Harrison signed the McKinley Tariff Act, which was sponsored by House member and future president William McKinley (1897–1901). The act sharply raised tariffs as Harrison had promised, providing protection to some U.S. industries, but is also meant higher prices for many consumer goods.

In foreign policy, the Harrison administration enjoyed several successes. Harrison's secretary of state, James G. Blaine, presided over the Inter-American Conference in Washington, D.C., in 1889 and 1890, out of which came the Pan American Union. Blaine also secured an agreement in 1889 with Britain and Germany to preserve the independence of the Samoa Islands under a protectorate. In 1892, Harrison demanded and re-

VIEWPOINTS

THE RAVEN.

An 1890 cartoon shows President Benjamin Harrison (1889–1893) unable to fill the "big hat" of his grandfather, William Henry Harrison (1841), the ninth president. (Library of Congress)

A–Z

ceived an apology and reparations from Chile for an attack by its citizens on U.S. sailors who were on shore leave in Valparaiso, Chile. He failed, however, in his attempt to **annex** Hawaii late in his term. An 1893 coup, in which Americans participated, had led to the overthrow of the Hawaiian queen. The U.S. minister in Hawaii hastily concluded a treaty of **ratification** with the new provisional government, but Senate Democrats blocked the treaty until Harrison's term expired. Incoming president Grover Cleveland (1885–1889, 1893–1897) withdrew the treaty.

At the end of his term, Harrison attended the inauguration of Grover Cleveland, who four years before had accompanied Harrison to the Capitol as the outgoing president. Harrison then returned to Indianapolis, where he resumed his lucrative law practice. From 1897 to 1899, he represented Venezuela in a boundary dispute with Great Britain that was to be decided by an international **arbitration** tribunal. After he traveled to Paris in 1899 to present his case, the tribunal upheld most of Venezuela's claims. He died in Indianapolis in 1901 from pneumonia.

See also: Cleveland, Grover, Administrations of (1885–1889, 1893–1897).

Further Reading

Calhoun, Charles W. *Benjamin Harrison.* New York: Times Books, 2005.

Moore, Anne Chieko. *Benjamin Harrison: Centennial President.* Hauppauge, NY: Nova, 2008.

Harrison, William Henry, Administration of (1841)

Short-term government under the ninth president of the United States, who died one month after his inauguration. The triumph of the Whig candidate William Henry Harrison (1841) in the election of 1840 posed a challenge not only to the Jacksonians' domestic program but also to their institutional achievements. The triumphant Whig Party was united above all else by its opposition to the expansion of **executive** power that had taken place during Andrew Jackson's administration (1829–1837). Accordingly, Whig leaders, such as Henry Clay and Daniel Webster, saw the Panic of 1837 as an opportunity to reassert the powers of Congress.

Clay had been the obvious candidate to head the Whig ticket in 1840. He was both the architect of the anti-Jackson program and a founder of the Whig Party. Believing Harrison to be more electable than Clay, however, the Whigs nominated the aged (he was sixty-seven years old at the time of his election) hero of the War of 1812's Battle of Tippecanoe. Perhaps it consoled Clay

and his allies that the general had proclaimed his support for the Whig assault on the executive in 1838, dedicating himself to a program that would limit the executive to one term, free the Treasury from presidential control, and confine the exercise of the **veto** to legislation that the president deemed **unconstitutional.** Although the 1840 campaign was not distinguished by its attention to serious discussion of issues, Harrison continued his attack on the power of the presidency, even pledging to step down after one term.

Harrison's inaugural address, which Webster and Clay helped write, provided further reason to believe that the Whig victory in 1840 would undo Andrew Jackson's reconstruction of the presidency. When Harrison deemed "preposterous" the idea that the president could "better understand the wants and wishes of the people than their representatives," Jacksonians suspected that designing Whig leaders may have persuaded the politically inexperienced president to accept the status of figurehead, delegating the powers of the executive to Congress.

Yet the Jacksonian presidency survived the Whig challenge. The importance of the presidency was so firmly established in the popular mind by 1840 that the executive no longer could be restored to the weak position it maintained during the latter stages of the Jeffersonian period.

The Whigs contributed to the permanent transformation of the presidency by how they conducted the 1840 campaign. Jackson's political enemies had looked with disfavor on the popular campaign tactics that the Democratic Party had employed during the three previous presidential campaigns. Having been the victims of the effective Democratic efforts on behalf of Jackson and Martin Van Buren (1837–1841), however, the Whigs did everything in their power to "go to the people" in 1840. They bought up newspapers for party propaganda, held great mass rallies, used popular party spokesmen for speech-making tours, and concentrated on mobilizing the largest possible number of voters.

As a result, the 1840 contest stimulated tremendous interest and enthusiasm in the country, resulting in a substantial increase in turnout. The 2.4 million voters who cast their ballots represented 80.2 percent of the eligible voters in the country, a percentage that has been surpassed only twice (in 1860 and 1876) in presidential elections. By accepting and expanding on the successful campaign techniques of the Democrats, the Whigs in effect **ratified** the Jacksonian concept of the president as a popular leader. The Whig anti-executive doctrine notwithstanding, the presidency could not be restored to its late Jeffersonian status, however inept a particular president might be.

See also: Tyler, John, Administration of (1841–1845); Van Buren, Martin, Administration of (1837–1841); Whig Party.

Hayes, Rutherford B., Administration of (1877–1881)

Government under the nineteenth president of the United States. In March 1876, Ohio governor Rutherford B. Hayes was put forward as a **favorite son** presidential candidate by his home state delegation at the Republican nominating convention. James G. Blaine of Maine, the preconvention favorite, received the most votes on the first ballot but fell short of the number required for nomination. Blaine's opponents recognized they had to rally behind a single candidate and chose Hayes because he was uncontroversial and free of scandal. Despite trailing four other candidates on the first ballot, Hayes was nominated on the seventh.

When the votes had been counted, it appeared that Democrat Samuel J. Tilden had beaten Hayes by about 260,000 votes in the popular election and 203–166 in the electoral college. Republican leaders, however, were determined to retain the presidency and challenged the results in Florida, Louisiana, and South Carolina. Republican leaders claimed that blacks had been intimidated from going to the polls. If the electoral votes of these three states were given to Hayes he would triumph, 185–184. Southern Republican election officials from the three disputed states disqualified votes from Democratic precincts and declared Hayes the winner.

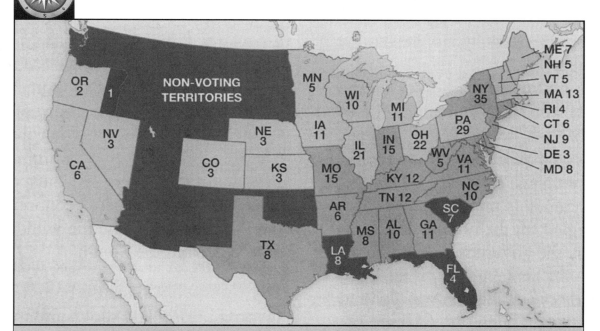

DISPUTED ELECTION OF 1876

The presidential election of 1876 was one of the most contentious in the nation's history. Because of widespread voter fraud and the intimidation of African American voters, three states sent in two sets of electoral votes. Finally, a special Electoral Commission awarded the disputed electoral votes—and the presidency—to Ohio Republican Rutherford B. Hayes (1877–1881).

Democratic leaders from these states accused the Republicans of corruption and sent rival sets of electoral votes to Congress, which was left to deal with the mess. With no way to determine who really deserved the electoral votes, members of Congress struck a deal. Democratic members agreed to the formation of an election commission that favored the Republicans in return for secret assurances that federal troops would be withdrawn from the South. The commission voted 8–7 in favor of Hayes.

When Hayes became president, he honored the agreement made with the Democrats to withdraw federal troops from the South. This move ended the **Reconstruction** era and enabled white Democrats to reestablish their political control over the southern states.

Hayes was well-intentioned, but the stigma of the deal that had made him president, his quarrels with **conservatives** in his party, and Democratic control of the House from 1877 to 1879 and the Senate from 1879 to 1881 limited his ability to push legislation through Congress. When Congress tried to stimulate the economy by coining overvalued silver coins, Hayes, an advocate of sound money, **vetoed** the inflationary measure. Congress, however, passed the **bill** over Hayes's veto. The president's calls for **civil service reform** also had little effect, as Congress refused to act on his proposals. In 1877, however, Hayes demonstrated his ability to take decisive action when he dispatched federal troops to stop riots that had broken out in several cities because of a nationwide railroad strike.

When his term expired, Hayes retired to Fremont, Ohio, where he managed several farms he had bought. He also promoted humanitarian causes, including prison reform and education opportunities for southern black youth. While returning to Fremont from a business trip, Hayes had a heart attack aboard a train on January 14, 1893. He died three days later.

See also: Grant, Ulysses S., Administration of (1869–1877); Garfield, James A., Administration of (1881).

Further Reading

Levy, Debbie. *Rutherford B. Hayes*. Minneapolis, MN: Lerner Books, 2006.

Trefousse, Hans. *Rutherford B. Hayes*. New York: Times Books, 2002.

Health and Human Services, Department of

See Department of Health and Human Services (HHS).

Homeland Security, Department of

See Department of Homeland Security (DHS).

Hoover, Herbert, Administration of (1929–1933)

Government under the thirty-first president of the United States. Herbert Hoover attended Stanford University in California. After graduating in 1895, he was hired as an engineering assistant for a mining company. During the next seventeen years, Hoover managed mines in Africa, Asia, Europe, Australia, and the United States. Before the age of forty, he was one of the world's most successful mining engineers and worth several million dollars.

Public Servant

When World War I (1914–1918) began, Hoover was living in London. He served as chairman of a committee of Americans who helped U.S. tourists stranded in Europe to secure passage home. He then became chairman of the Commission for Relief in Belgium, a private charity group. In this role, he raised funds to aid the people of that war-torn country and made arrangements with the warring nations to distribute the aid.

When the U.S. Congress declared war on Germany in 1917, Hoover returned to the United

States, where President Woodrow Wilson (1913–1921) appointed him U.S. food administrator. In this post, Hoover was responsible for stimulating food production and distributing and conserving food supplies. In 1918, Hoover was appointed chairman of the Allied Food Council, which distributed food to millions of Europeans left impoverished by the war. After the war, Hoover attended the Versailles Peace Conference as an economic adviser to President Wilson.

Hoover's relief activities made him one of the most famous and admired Americans of his day and a prospective candidate for public office. However, his political affiliation was unclear because he had supported Republican Theodore Roosevelt's third-party candidacy in 1912 and had worked closely with President Wilson, a Democrat. In 1920, however, Hoover declared that he was a Republican and received some support for the party's presidential nomination, which eventually went to Warren G. Harding (1921–1923).

When Harding was elected president, he appointed Hoover secretary of **commerce.** Hoover remained in this post for eight years. He reorganized the department and helped solidify the progress toward an eight-hour workday and a prohibition against child labor. He was an economic adviser to both President Harding and Vice President Calvin Coolidge, but he remained free of the scandals that plagued the Harding administration.

Presidency

Hoover was the popular choice of Republicans for the party's presidential nomination in 1928. Despite the opposition of some **conservative** party leaders, Hoover was nominated at the Kansas City Republican National Convention on the first ballot. He then won the general election over Democrat Al Smith of New York. Hoover received more than twenty-one million popular votes to Smith's fifteen million. Hoover even captured several traditionally Democratic southern states on his way to a 444–87 electoral vote victory.

Hoover had run on a Republican platform that took credit for the prosperity achieved during the 1920s. Ironically, seven months after Hoover's inauguration the October 1929 stock market crash began the economic **depression** that left about a quarter of the workforce unemployed. After the crash, Hoover tried to assure the nation that the economy was sound and that business activity would soon recover, but the **Great Depression** grew worse during his term. Although he had not created the conditions that caused the Depression, many Americans blamed him for it.

Hoover tried to fight the growing Depression through limited public works projects, increased government loans to banks and businesses, reductions in the already low income tax, and personal appeals to industry to maintain wages and production levels. However, these measures did little to ease the country's economic problems.

Hoover's preoccupation with balancing the federal budget and his belief that federal relief violated the American principle of self-reliance prevented him from taking more sweeping actions. He therefore opposed federal benefit programs to help the poor and unemployed and deficit spending that would have created jobs. He reluctantly signed the Smoot-Hawley Act of 1930, which dramatically raised **tariff** rates to protect U.S. industries, thereby initiating a trade war that hurt the American and world economies.

The Republicans nominated Hoover for a second term, but the nation, desperate for relief from the Depression, turned against him. His Democratic opponent, Franklin D. Roosevelt (1933–1945), won in a landslide.

Later Years

In 1946, President Harry S. Truman (1945–1953) tapped Hoover's famine relief experience by appointing him chairman of the Famine Emergency Commission, which was charged with preventing starvation after World War II (1939–1945) ended in Europe.

In 1947, Truman appointed Hoover chairman of the Commission on Organization of the **Executive** Branch of the Government. The "Hoover Commission" recommended hundreds of organizational changes, many of which were adopted, to make the executive branch more efficient. The commission submitted its final report in 1949, but in 1953 President Dwight D. Eisenhower (1953–1961) appointed Hoover to chair a second commission on government organization. The second Hoover Commission functioned until 1955. Hoover retired

A–Z

from government service after 1955, but continued to write on politics and speak at Republican conventions. He died in New York City in 1964 at the age of ninety.

See also: Coolidge, Calvin, Administration of (1923–1929); Roosevelt, Franklin D., Administration of (1933–1945).

Further Reading

Burner, David. *Herbert Hoover: A Public Life.* Newtown, CT: American Political Biography Press, 2005.

Leuchtenburg, William E. *Herbert Hoover.* New York: Times Books, 2009.

Housing and Urban Development, Department of

See Department of Housing and Urban Development (HUD).

Impeachment, Presidential

Congressional authority to charge the president with crimes or misconduct while in office. Most **impeachment** proceedings, however, have been directed against federal judges, who cannot be removed by any other method.

Constitutional Basis

The provisions on impeachment are scattered through the first three articles of the Constitution. Impeachments may be brought against "the President, Vice President and all civil officers of the United States" for "treason, bribery or other high crimes or misdemeanors." The House of Representatives has the power to bring charges against an official. If a majority of the members agree to impeachment, the accused official is tried by the Senate. Convicted officials are removed from office and may be barred from holding further public office.

There is no appeal of a conviction. The Constitution states that the presidential power to grant reprieves and pardons does not include cases of impeachment. Officials convicted and removed from office remain subject to prosecution in the regular courts.

Treason and bribery are fairly straightforward charges, but "high crimes or misdemeanors" can be almost anything that the prosecution wants to make them. In 1970, Representative Gerald R. Ford of Michigan declared, "An impeachable offense is whatever a majority of the House of Representatives considers it to be at a given moment in history." Ironically, Ford ascended to the presidency four years later when Richard Nixon (1969–1974) resigned to avoid impeachment proceedings.

House Proceedings

The House has no standing rules dealing with its role in the impeachment process. Impeachment proceedings have started in a variety of ways. The eight cases to reach the Senate between 1900 and 1991 were based initially on Judiciary Committee **resolutions.** When President Bill Clinton (1993–2001) was **impeached** in 1998, a court-appointed independent counsel initiated impeachment proceedings.

After bringing charges against an official, the House creates a committee to investigate the matter. The committee decides whether the subject of the inquiry has the right to be present at committee proceedings, to be represented by an attorney, and to present and question witnesses. If the investigation seems to support the charges, the committee issues an impeachment resolution.

If a majority of the House votes to adopt a resolution of impeachment, the case goes to the Senate for a trial. House members are selected to present the case, acting as prosecutors in the Senate trial. An odd number—from five to eleven—traditionally has been selected, including members from both parties who voted in favor of impeachment.

Senate Trial

An impeachment trial is conducted in a fashion similar to a criminal trial. Both sides may present witnesses and evidence, and the defendant is allowed counsel, the right to testify, and the right of cross-examination. If the president or the vice president is on trial, the Constitution requires the Chief Justice of the United States to preside. The Constitution does not specify a presiding officer for lesser defendants. By Senate custom, the vice president or the president pro tempore of the Senate presides.

The presiding officer can compel witnesses to appear and enforce obedience to Senate orders. He or she makes final rules on all questions of evidence, although senators may request a vote on such matters. The presiding officer questions witnesses and asks questions submitted in writing by senators, who do not directly question witnesses themselves.

If the defendant faces several articles or charges, the Senate votes separately on each article. A two-thirds vote is required for conviction. If no article is approved by two-thirds of the senators present, the impeached official is acquitted. If any article receives two-thirds approval, the person is convicted. The Senate may vote separately to remove the person from office, but this is not required.

The Senate also may vote to disqualify the person from holding future federal office. Disqualification is not mandatory. Only two of the seven officials convicted in an impeachment trial have been disqualified. Disqualification requires only a majority vote instead of the two-thirds needed for conviction.

History

Through 2008, the House has impeached two presidents—Andrew Johnson (1865–1896) in 1868 and Bill Clinton in 1998. In 1974, the House was considering impeachment articles against Richard Nixon, but the president resigned in the face of almost certain conviction by the Senate.

Andrew Johnson

The first presidential impeachment occurred in 1868, when Andrew Johnson was charged with violating a federal statute, the Tenure of Office Act. The impeachment, however, was part of a larger political struggle dealing with questions such as control of the Republican Party and the chaos in the South following the Civil War (1861–1865).

Johnson, the only member of the U.S. Senate from a seceding southern state (Tennessee) to remain loyal to the Union in 1861, was chosen to be Abraham Lincoln's running mate in 1864. Although Johnson was a lifelong Democrat, he and Lincoln (1861–1865) ran on the Union Ticket in an attempt to bridge the divisions within the war-torn nation. When Lincoln was assassinated in 1865, Johnson succeeded to the presidency. His ideas on rebuilding and readmitting the southern states to the Union clashed with those of Congress, which was overwhelmingly controlled by the Republicans.

In March 1867, Congress passed the Tenure of Office Act, overriding Johnson's attempt to **veto,** or reject, the **bill.** The act forbade the president from removing civil officers without the approval of the Senate. In December, however, Johnson suspended Secretary of War Edwin Stanton without consulting the Senate. The Senate refused to accept this action and returned Stanton to his post. On February 21, 1868, citing the power and authority vested in him by the Constitution, Johnson fired Stanton.

This action enraged Congress, who impeached Johnson three days later. There were eleven articles of impeachment, the main one directed at Johnson's removal of Stanton in violation of the Tenure of Office Act. The Senate, however, fell one vote shy of convicting Johnson on any of the articles.

Bill Clinton

When impeachment proceedings began against President Bill Clinton in 1998, he had been under

A - Z

scrutiny in two legal investigations for four years. One focused on his involvement in a failed Arkansas land deal involving a company called the Whitewater Development Corporation. Clinton also was the defendant in a sexual harassment suit brought against him in February 1994 by Paula Corbin Jones, a former Arkansas state employee.

Jones's attorneys hoped to show that Clinton's alleged misconduct with Jones was part of a broader pattern of sexual harassment. They compiled a list of women whose names had been linked with Clinton's. The list included Monica S. Lewinsky, a Pentagon employee who had been a White House intern. Lewinsky argued that she had no information relevant to the Jones case and filed a sworn statement in which she denied ever having sexual relations with Clinton. However, Linda R. Tripp, one of Lewinsky's friends, taped conversations in which Lewinsky described her intimate relationship with Clinton and said that Clinton had urged her to lie about it.

Clinton told Jones's attorneys that he had never had sexual relations with Lewinsky. However, Lewinsky admitted to a grand jury that she and Clinton had had an affair but insisted that he never told her to lie about it. Ultimately, confronted with DNA evidence, President Clinton admitted to an "inappropriate" relationship with Lewinsky and to making "misleading" statements under oath, but he denied that he had done anything illegal. On September 9, special prosecutor Kenneth Starr delivered a report to the House charging that Clinton had committed impeachable offenses. The House approved two articles of impeachment against Clinton. The first accused him of lying in his grand jury testimony about Lewinsky. The second charged Clinton with obstruction of justice for "using the powers of his high office" to "delay, impede, cover up and conceal" his involvement with Lewinsky.

On February 12, 1999, the article accusing Clinton of committing perjury before a federal grand jury, was defeated, 45–55, with ten Republicans joining all 45 Democrats. Article II, which charged the president with obstructing justice, was also defeated 50–50.

In the aftermath of the trial, bitterness over the impeachment remained in Congress. Republicans blamed it on the president himself, saying that his character flaws brought about the national ordeal. Democrats, with some admitting that the president had committed moral misdeeds, saw the whole affair as a **partisan** witch-hunt intent only embarrassing Clinton.

See also: Presidency and Congress; Watergate Scandal.

Further Reading

Aaseng, Nathan. *Famous Trials–The Impeachment of Bill Clinton.* Farmington Hills, MI: Lucent, 1999.

Benedict, Michael Les. *The Impeachment and Trial of Andrew Johnson.* New York: W.W. Norton, 1999.

Nichols, John. *The Genius of Impeachment: The Founders' Cure for Royalism.* New York: New Press, 2006.

Impoundment Powers

The power of the president to not spend money **appropriated** by Congress. Until 1974, the most powerful presidential tool in overcoming the congressional funding prerogative was the power of impoundment—the president's refusal to spend funds that Congress had appropriated for a particular purpose. Historically, presidents have claimed both constitutional and statutory authority to **impound** funds either by treating the funding as optional, rather than mandatory, and then controlling spending authority, or by deferring spending to future years. The impoundment power is similar to the **veto** power in that both are attempts to block or thwart congressional actions.

One of the most famous early examples of a president's use of the impoundment power was Thomas Jefferson's (1801–1809) refusal in 1803 to spend a $50,000 **appropriation** for gunboats on the Mississippi River to protect the western frontier. Jefferson told Congress that the money should be used for the purchase of more advanced boats the next year. Similarly, President Ulysses S. Grant (1869–1877) refused to spend funds that Congress had appropriated for public works projects, arguing that they could be completed for less money than had been appropriated. In both cases,

Congress accepted the president's power to refuse to spend congressionally appropriated money.

Congress eventually gave impoundment authority a statutory basis by passing the Anti-Deficiency Acts of 1905 and 1906. These laws allowed presidents to withhold funds for a period of time to prevent deficiencies or overspending in an agency. In 1921, the Bureau of the Budget established impoundment authority when its director, Charles G. Dawes, announced that "the president does not assume . . . that the minimum of government expenditures is the amount fixed by Congress in its **appropriations.**"

Under the New Deal, President Franklin D. Roosevelt (1933–1945) occasionally used impoundments for budgetary or policy purposes. In some cases, the president acted with at least the implied consent of Congress. During the **Great Depression,** for example, spending **bills** were sometimes treated as ceilings, allowing Roosevelt to refuse to spend money that he believed to be unnecessary. During World War II (1939–1945), Roosevelt argued that his war powers gave him the authority to cut spending that was not essential to national security. Presidents Harry S. Truman (1945–1953), Dwight D. Eisenhower (1953–1961), and John F. Kennedy (1961–1963) all used impoundments to cut military spending.

President Lynton B. Johnson (1963–1969), however, used impoundments to curtail domestic spending during the Vietnam War (1964–1975). As the war progressed and inflation rose, Johnson impounded funds designated for agriculture, conservation, education, housing, and transportation. These impoundments were usually temporary, and the funds eventually were released. Although Johnson did not use the power of impoundment to cripple congressionally appropriated programs, his actions did set an example of impoundment power being used to combat inflation—a power later adopted and expanded by Richard M. Nixon (1969–1974).

Both Johnson and Nixon used impoundment to control spending, but Nixon's use was **unprecedented** in its scope and effects. Whereas Johnson relied on temporary deferrals rather than permanent cuts and worked personally with Congress to soothe tempers, the Nixon administration's impoundments seemed designed to eliminate or to curtail particular programs favored by the Demo-

cratic Congress. Between 1969 and 1974, the administration made a determined effort to redistribute funding for government services. When Congress overrode Nixon's veto of the Federal Water Pollution Control Act Amendments of 1972, for example, the Nixon administration impounded half of the $18 billion that had been allotted for fiscal years 1973–1975, thereby handicapping the program. In addition, the Nixon administration undertook major impoundment reductions in low-rent housing construction, mass transit, food stamps, and medical research programs.

By 1973, Nixon had impounded more than $20 billion, and his budget for fiscal 1974 contained a list of 109 reductions he wanted to make, 101 of which he said would require no congressional approval. Eventually, more than thirty lower-court cases overturned Nixon impoundments. The Supreme Court then tackled Nixon's impoundment of funds for water pollution control. In *Train v. City of New York,* the Court ruled that once water pollution control funds had been appropriated by an act of Congress, funds could not be withheld at a later stage by impoundment.

Eventually, public pressure began to build for Congress to do something about Nixon's use of the impoundment power. At first, individual members attempted to intervene personally with the president in an effort to restore funds to certain projects. By 1972, many subcommittees had become concerned about the impoundment pattern that was beginning to emerge—a pattern that threatened their control of the policy-making process. In 1973, the House and Senate Appropriations committees began holding hearings on the impoundment of funds for low-income housing, and Congress began inserting mandatory language in certain spending bills to eliminate the discretionary authority that had allowed presidential impoundment.

In 1974, Congress adopted the Congressional Budget and Impoundment Control Act. Besides setting up the Congressional Budget Office to improve congressional monitoring of the budget, the act also sought to control presidential impoundment. It stipulated two new procedures—rescissions and deferrals—by which presidents could temporarily override or delay congressional appropriations decisions. If presidents wish to rescind (that is, cancel) all or part of the appropriated funds, they must inform Congress. Unless Congress passes a rescission bill within forty-five days permitting the cancellation of funding, presidents must spend the funds. As the Congressional Budget and Impoundment Control Act was originally written, either house of Congress could block a deferral (that is, a delay) of spending. But in 1983, the Supreme Court, in *Immigration and Naturalization Service v. Chadha,* ruled the one-house **legislative** veto **unconstitutional.** The effect of *Chadha* was to require a resolution by a majority vote of both houses directing that appropriated funds be spent immediately.

Because Nixon resigned in 1974, a few months before the implementation of the impoundment control provisions of the budget act, he never felt the force of the act. The first administration to be confronted with these statutory impoundment limitations was the Ford administration (1974– 1977). Of the $9 billion in rescissions requested by President Ford during his term in office, 86 percent of his requests were denied by Congress. Only 24 percent of his deferral requests were rejected, however. This pattern has been followed fairly consistently since the Ford administration. Congress usually grants deferrals; in most years, it allows 90 percent of them. However, rescissions are a different matter. Congressional approvals have ranged from 80 percent in 1979 to none in 1990. Usually, Congress approves fewer than half of presidential rescissions.

Both the Ronald Reagan (1981–1989) and George H.W. Bush (1989–1993) administrations called for increased rescission authority in their efforts to reduce the deficit. In March 1996, the Republican-controlled Congress ended months of negotiation to grant to the president "enhanced rescission" authority—a type of line-item veto. President Bill Clinton (1993–2001) signed the bill on April 9, 1996. The law gave the president, beginning in 1997, the power to "cancel" individual items in spending and tax bills unless overturned by a two-thirds vote of both houses of Congress. The president did not possess this authority for long; the Supreme Court struck down the line-item veto as an unconstitutional violation of separation of powers in *Clinton v. City of New York* (1998).

See also: Nixon, Richard M., Administration of (1969–1974); Office of Management and Budget.

Inaugural Address

The first official speech of a newly inaugurated president after taking the oath of office. George Washington (1789–1789) established the tradition that presidents should deliver an inaugural address after taking the oath. Most presidents have used this speech to restate their political and moral philosophies, invoke the traditions of the Founders, establish a mood of optimism, challenge the nation to pursue ambitious goals, and appeal for unity.

Unity is an important and common theme of inaugural addresses, because presidential elections tend to divide the nation along party lines. After the divisive election of 1800, which led outgoing president John Adams (1797–1801) to snub Thomas Jefferson's inauguration, Jefferson (1801–1809) declared, "We have called by different names brethren of the same principles. We are all Republicans. We are all Federalists." John F. Kennedy (1961–1963) called for unity after his close election victory over Richard Nixon (1969– 1974): "We observe today not a victory of party, but a celebration of freedom." Jimmy Carter (1977–1981) opened his inaugural address by praising his 1976 election opponent, President Gerald R. Ford (1974–1977): "For myself and for our nation, I want to thank my predecessor for all he has done to heal our land."

In the second paragraph of George W. Bush's (2001–2009) first inaugural address, he thanked both the outgoing president, Bill Clinton (1993– 2001), as well as the person he had defeated in the bitterly contested election in November 2000, Vice President Al Gore. Appealing for unity at a time when many Americans questioned the legitimacy of his victory, the new president said:

Sometimes our differences run so deep, it seems we share a continent, but not a country. We do not accept this, and we will not allow it. Our unity, our union, is the serious work of leaders and citizens in every generation. And this is my solemn pledge: I will work to build a single nation of justice and opportunity.

In his moving inaugural address on January 20, 1961, President John F. Kennedy (1961–1963) challenged his fellow American citizens, "Ask not what your country can do for you—ask what you can do for your country." (AP Images)

The inauguration and the parades and parties that usually follow it also provide the first glimpse of the new chief of state's ceremonial style. After the stiff formality and royal pomp observed during the Washington and Adams administrations, Jefferson wanted his inaugural to symbolize the democratic spirit he intended to bring to the presidency. He therefore eschewed a carriage in favor of walking unceremoniously from his boardinghouse to the Capitol to take the oath of office.

Andrew Jackson's (1829–1837) election was regarded as a triumph for common people. Thousands of enthusiastic supporters descended on the White House, destroying furniture, china, glassware, and other household items.

More than a century later, John Kennedy's inaugural was a formal affair that reflected the intellectual and cultural sophistication he would bring to his presidency. Kennedy sent 155 special inaugural invitations to noted writers, artists, and scholars; he had Robert Frost read a poem at the inaugural ceremony; and he decreed that male participants in the ceremony should wear top hats.

Jimmy Carter, like Jefferson, used his inaugural to project a simpler presidential image. He wore a business suit instead of formal dress and chose to walk in his inaugural parade rather than ride in a limousine.

Pomp came back into style with the election of Ronald Reagan (1981–1989). His 1981 inaugural festivities—the most expensive up to that time—included a parade with eight thousand marchers, eight $100-a-ticket balls, and a nationally televised inaugural "gala" that featured many Hollywood celebrities. The cost of the festivities was estimated at $16 million, compared with $3.5 million spent for the Carter inaugural in 1977.

George H.W. Bush (1989–1993), Bill Clinton, and George W. Bush followed Reagan's lead in choosing to host elaborate inaugural celebrations. George H.W. Bush's 1989 inaugural cost $30 million and included a parade with 214 marching bands. Clinton's 1993 inaugural cost about $25 million and featured eleven inaugural balls. George W. Bush's 2001 inaugural committee raised nearly $40 million to pay for elaborate celebrations that drew tens of thousands of Bush supporters to Washington, D.C. A record number of supporters attended Barack Obama's historic inauguration in January 2009, with the costs reaching into the millions of dollars.

See also: Chief of State.

Further Reading

Boller, Paul F. *Presidential Inaugurations*. Orlando, FL: Harcourt, 2001.

Incumbency

See Presidency and the Media; Presidential Campaigns.

Interest Groups

See PACs (Political Action Committees).

Interior, Department of the

See Department of the Interior.

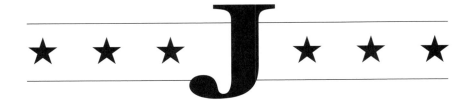

★ ★ ★ **J** ★ ★ ★

Jackson, Alphonso

See Department of Housing and Urban Development (HUD).

Jackson, Andrew, Administration of (1829–1837)

Government under the seventh president of the United States. Jackson was the first "outsider" to become president of the United States. His predecessors had undergone extensive apprenticeships in national politics and diplomacy. The hero of the battle of New Orleans (January 1815) had less formal education than any of the country's first six presidents. Moreover, he had little experience in Congress and none in public administration. He was a self-made man, a powerful symbol of his times, who had risen from a small cabin in the pine woods of South Carolina, to a plantation near Nashville, Tennessee, to the White House in Washington. Jackson's principles and presence were to hold sway over the country for nearly three decades. This period in U.S. history is often called the "Age of Jackson."

Jacksonian Democracy

The most important political theme of the Age of Jackson was the widespread desire for equality of opportunity, the belief that no one should have special privileges at the expense of anyone else. Jackson followed Thomas Jefferson (1801–1809) in believing that to eliminate privilege, political leaders must strictly limit the role of the national government. The rapid expansion of the country was accompanied by a dynamic society and economy that seemed to foster unlimited opportunity. Within that expansive environment, Jacksonians believed that the best approach to government was to confine power as much as possible to the state governments. Yet, Jacksonian democracy did not extend to Native Americans or African Americans. Jackson himself was a slaveholder, and he strongly supported the removal of the Cherokee nation to west of the Mississippi River. Their trek west became known as the Trail of Tears.

Jackson's View of the Presidency

The Age of Jackson had its conflicting aspects when it came to the authority of the national government. The Jacksonians regarded the president as the tribune of the people, a view that invested the **executive** with tremendous influence. During the Jeffersonian era, the presidency began to develop a closer relationship with the people. Jackson tried to establish a direct relationship between the executive and the people, thus challenging Congress's status as the national government's main representative institution. The strengthened presidency, especially during Jackson's two terms, "gave voice in a new age to the rising spirit of democratic **nationalism**," one that sustained and strengthened the Union in the face of serious sectional conflict over the **tariff** and slavery.

Jackson, although a states' rights supporter, also personified and defended the **sovereignty** of the nation during his presidency, never more so than in the **nullification** crisis that arose near the end of his first term. Seeking to compel the federal government to accede to its demands for a lower tariff, South Carolina's legislature summoned a convention on November 24, 1832, that declared the 1832 tariff law "null and void." South Carolina cited the "nullification doctrine" advanced by John C. Calhoun, a South Carolinian and Jackson's first vice president, which held that a state could declare a federal law null and void within its boundaries whenever it deemed such a law **unconstitutional.**

In the face of this threat to the Union, Jackson issued a proclamation that vigorously rejected South Carolina's right to disobey a federal statute. The power to annul a law of the United States, assumed by one state, he argued, was

> incompatible with the existence of the Union, contradicted expressly by the letter of the Constitution, unauthorized by its spirit, inconsistent with every principle on which it was founded, and destructive of the great object for which it was formed.

Jackson rested the defense of the Union squarely upon the shoulders of the president. It was the people, acting through the state ratifying conventions, who had formed the Union, and the president—not Congress or the states—embodied the will of the people. The idea that the president is the direct representative of the people was grounded in ongoing political changes that were associated with Jacksonian democracy. Jackson's election as president coincided with changes in election laws in the states. These modifications ended the dominance of state legislatures over the choice of electors, thus making popular election

the major means of their selection. In the first three presidential elections, most electors were chosen by the state legislatures. Electors were selected by popular vote in all but six states in 1824; by 1832, in all states except South Carolina, which retained **legislative** selection until the Civil War. Jackson was arguably the first popularly elected president of the United States, thus strengthening his conviction that his mandate came directly from the "sovereign" people.

The president's claim to be the direct representative of the people also was advanced by the expansion of the electorate. Jacksonian democracy advocated the extension of voting rights, resulting in the elimination of almost all property qualifications for voting and the establishment of almost universal white manhood **suffrage** by 1832.

This development brought into the electorate farmers, mechanics, laborers—those Jackson, popularly known as Old Hickory, referred to as "the humble members of society"—who regarded the executive office under Jackson as a rallying point. Their support rescued the executive office from the congressional dominance that characterized presidential administrations from James Madison (1809–1817) to John Quincy Adams (1825–1829). With the collapse of the congressional **caucus** in 1824, Jackson became the first president since George Washington (1789–1797) not to be chosen in an election involving the national legislature. Taking office in 1829, Jackson therefore found himself in the position to revitalize the presidency with a new independence and energy.

Party Conventions

The advent of the Jackson presidency was associated with important developments in the party system. The decline of "King Caucus" as a nominating device in presidential campaigns left a vacuum that was filled by the national convention. The party convention did not exist when Jackson became president but was employed by the Democrats in 1832 and accepted by the Whigs in the campaign of 1836.

Jackson's Struggle with Congress

The transformation of the presidency from a congressional to a popularly based office did not take place without a tremendous struggle. The

Whig Party, although winning only two presidential elections between 1828 and 1856, offered vigorous opposition to the Democrats.

Proclaiming the ideas of Kentucky statesman Henry Clay and John Quincy Adams, the Whigs took a national approach to the country's problems, advocating a program, known as the American plan, to recharter the Second **Bank of the United States,** enact a protective tariff, and foster internal improvements. This program, which rested on a broad interpretation of the Constitution, contradicted the states' rights policies of the Democrats. Yet the Whigs, who formed as a party of opposition to Jackson, resisted the expansion of executive power and defended the legislature as the principal instrument of representative democracy. Jackson and the Democratic Party firmly controlled the House. The Senate, however, led by such forceful Whig statesmen as Clay and Daniel Webster, was in a position to challenge Jackson's policies.

Veto of the Bank Bill

The conflict between the president and the Whigs came to a head in July 1832, when Jackson **vetoed** the **bill** to recharter the national bank four years before the expiration of its charter. Jackson's veto of the bank bill and the defense of this action in his message to Congress of July 10, 1832, was, according to historian Robert Remini, "the most important veto ever issued by a president."

The veto established a **precedent** that notably strengthened the presidency. Beginning with Washington, Federalist and Democratic-Republican presidents alike had agreed that a veto should be cast only when the president believed that a piece of legislation was unconstitutional. In forty years under the Constitution, only nine acts of Congress had been struck down by the chief executive, and only three of those dealt with what could be considered important issues. Yet Jackson successfully vetoed twelve bills in eight years, even putting the pocket veto to use for the first time. He believed, and so stated in the message to Congress that accompanied the bank veto, that a presidents should reject any bill that they felt would injure the nation. For Jackson, a veto was justified if the president had a policy disagreement with Congress. In demanding the right to be involved in the development of legislation, Jackson "essentially altered the relationship between the executive and legislative branches of government."

Two other aspects of Jackson's famous veto message were significant. First, it contained Jackson's view—one that Thomas Jefferson first articulated—that the president, as well as Congress, possessed coordinate power with the courts to determine questions of constitutionality. Jackson articulated such a view in maintaining that the national bank was an illegitimate exercise of congressional authority. His Whig opponents considered this claim outrageous, given Chief Justice John Marshall's decision in *McCulloch v. Maryland* (1819) that it was not unconstitutional for Congress to charter a bank.

Jackson insisted, however, that in matters of constitutional interpretation the executive was no more bound by judicial rulings than by acts of Congress. Congress, the executive, and the Supreme Court, he asserted, "must each for itself be guided by its opinion of the Constitution." Thus Jackson's veto message dramatically reopened the question, seemingly settled by *Marbury v. Madison,* of the appropriate authority to be allowed the federal courts. His claim in support of the president and Congress, the popularly elected branches of government, to interpret the Constitution was yet another example of his determination to forge a stronger connection between the people and their government.

Concerned about the political effects of the bank war, Congress failed to override the president's veto. Jackson's overwhelming defeat of Clay in the 1832 election, which was fought in large measure over the bank issue, convinced even his political opponents, as the weekly *Niles' Register* reluctantly reported after the election, that the president "had cast himself upon the support of the people against the acts of both houses of Congress" and had been sustained. Jackson's victory confirmed his conviction that the president, not Congress, was the immediate and direct representative of the American public.

Aftermath of the Veto

The Jacksonian revolution was extended after the bank veto. Regarding his reelection in 1832 as a vindication of his action, Jackson decided to kill off the bank once and for all by withdrawing its public deposits and placing these monies in selected state banks. Because Congress refused Jackson's request for authority to remove the bank's funds, the authority to do so remained with the secretary of the treasury, who had been granted this right in the law chartering the second bank. When Secretary of the Treasury Louis McLane opposed removal of deposits, he was transferred to the State Department and replaced by William J. Duane. Duane also resisted the president's efforts to kill the bank and was dismissed within four months of taking the oath of office. His replacement, Roger B. Taney, formerly the attorney general, gave Jackson the cooperation he was looking for, which provoked the Senate to pass a **censure resolution** that accused the president of assuming "authority and power not conferred by the Constitution and laws."

Taken together, Duane's dismissal, Taney's removal of public deposits from the national bank, and the Senate's censure of Jackson raised a fundamental constitutional question: Can the president, using the constitutionally implied dismissal power, dictate how a discretionary power that Congress has vested exclusively in the head of a department shall be exercised?

The Senate censure controversy—one battle in the long-standing war between the president and Congress for control of executive administration—was won decisively by Jackson. Because Jackson's "protest" to the Senate's resolution of censure became the leading issue in the next round of Senate elections, Jackson's Democratic allies took control of the upper house in 1837. Thus before Jackson left office, he had the satisfaction of seeing the resolution of censure formally expunged on January 16, 1837. The Senate's decision to recant not only signified a personal and political triumph for Jackson, but it also confirmed his broad interpretation of the present's power to control the executive branch.

The Limits of the Jacksonian Presidency

According to the Whigs, the main legacy of Jackson's presidency was a dangerous expansion of presidential prerogatives. The bank controversy demonstrated, they argued, that the chief executive now possessed powers that dwarfed the influence of Congress as well as the judiciary, thus undermining the separation of powers.

The legacy of Jackson's two terms in office, however, was less certain than his political opponents believed. The extension of executive powers during his presidency did not simply extension of executive power depended on the emergence of the president as popular leader, a role that was mediated in critical ways by the party organizations. For example, Jackson's "appeal to the people" in his war on the national

VIEWPOINTS

GENERAL JACKSON SLAYING THE MANY HEADED MONSTER.

President Andrew Jackson opposed the Second Bank of the United States and called it a "many headed monster." He believed that the Bank favored eastern business interests at the expense of the common people. (Library of Congress)

bank was not entirely direct; instead, the bank battles were fought mainly through the party.

Patronage

Jackson also started a system of rotation in government personnel, using the president's power of appointment and removal to replace federal employees for purely **partisan** reasons. Until Jackson became president, the prevailing belief was that the government workforce should be stable and politically **neutral.** Beginning in 1829, however, Jackson and every one of his successors during the nineteenth century rejected this principle and removed or sanctioned the removal of hundreds, even thousands, of federal workers for partisan reasons. The credo of the new **patronage** system was, as New York senator William L. Marcy put it, "to the victor belong the spoils of the enemy."

The powers of the presidency ushered in by the Jacksonian era were not only limited by the party system but also by the doctrine of the Democratic Party that was organized to advance Jacksonian principles. This doctrine, as evidenced by Jackson's veto of the bank bill, was dedicated to limiting the role of the national government. Jackson defended the principle of Union against the extreme states' rights claim of South Carolina in the nullification controversy. Generally, however, he was a strong advocate of the rights of the state governments and opposed expanding the responsibilities of the national government and executive.

See also: Adams, John Quincy, Administration of (1825–1829); Van Buren, Martin, Administration of (1837–1841).

Further Reading

Schlesinger, Arthur. M., Jr. *The Age of Jackson.* Old Saybrook, CT: Konecky and Konecky, 1971.
Wilentz, Sean. *Andrew Jackson.* New York: Times Books, Henry Holt and Company, 2005.

Jefferson, Thomas, Administration of (1801–1809)

Government under the third president of the United States. Jefferson's triumph in the 1800 election marked a critical realignment of political forces in U.S. politics, resulting in the dominance of the Democratic-Republican Party from 1801 to 1824. During the last decade of his life, in a letter to the legal scholar Spencer Roane, Jefferson spoke of the "revolution of 1800," saying that although effected peacefully in the course of a popular election, it was "as real a revolution in the principles of our government as that of 1776 was in its form."

Jefferson's concern with ensuring the integrity of majority decisions motivated his ongoing disagreements with the federal judiciary. In an attempt to maintain a foothold on the national government, the Federalists tried to "pack" the courts before leaving office. The Judiciary Act of 1801 increased the number of federal judgeships, and these positions were hurriedly filled by the "midnight" appointments of the John Adams (1797–1801) administration. To the Jeffersonians the judiciary constituted "the final barrier to be assaulted in the advance of popular government and political liberty." To the Federalists the courts represented "the last bastion of moderation and sanity arresting the progress of mob rule and anarchy."

More was at stake than power relationships, however. The Democratic-Republicans opposed the courts being vested with a broad grant of authority that would enable them to override the actions of elected representatives. The Federalists, to the contrary, supported the judiciary possessing a power of **judicial review** that would make it the ultimate authority on constitutional issues. Although Jefferson and his followers did not challenge the right of the courts to decide matters of constitutionality, they insisted that each branch of government, and the state governments as well, shared that right equally.

These issues of power and principle came to a head in the case of *Marbury v. Madison* (1803). Chief Justice John Marshall decided in favor of Jefferson, but on grounds that claimed powers for the judiciary that Jefferson denied it had. In effect, Marshall gave Jefferson a free hand to dismiss Federalist appointees (while he scolded Jefferson for wishing to do so), but only on condition that the president accept the Court's power to pass upon the constitutionality of acts of Congress. Jefferson was unwilling to accept such a condition, but, because of Marshall's clever ruling, he was unable to deal with the chief justice and the judiciary as he had hoped. Soon after the *Marbury* case, when he failed to remove Supreme Court Justice Samuel Chase by **impeachment,** Jefferson ended his confrontation with the judiciary.

The Democratic-Republican Party Program

The Democratic-Republicans sought to repeal Federalist policies that Jeffersonians believed had undermined the Constitution. Jefferson and Congress, which the Democratic-Republicans also captured in the 1800 election, acted to remove all traces of the Sedition Act. The act had expired the day before Jefferson took office. Wanting to underscore his fierce opposition to it, the president pardoned everyone (mostly Democratic-Republican newspaper publishers) convicted under the act. Moreover, at Jefferson's request, Congress voted to repay with interest all the fines that were levied as part of their sentences. During Jefferson's first term, Congress also abolished most of the internal taxes, including the unpopular excise and direct property taxes, that the Federalists enacted in 1798 to prepare for a possible war with France. Finally, Congress reduced the size of the already small military establishment, severely cutting army and naval **appropriations.**

Jefferson stressed the need to restrain the role of the national government. His main concern was to make the government more responsive to the will of the people. "His faith in the people," as one scholar remarked, "gave to his views on power a flexibility that permitted the use of power in positive ways to emphasize the freedom from government." In those areas where the national government's responsibility was properly exercised—that is, in matters pertaining to external affairs and the regulation of relations between the states—Jefferson believed that the powers of the central government should be exercised with energy and efficiency.

Given certain conditions, Jefferson was willing to tolerate government action that seemed to contradict his stated principles. Thus in 1803, he consented to the purchase of Louisiana, which doubled the territory of the United States. However, as he noted in a letter to Kentucky senator John Breckinridge, he did not feel the Constitu-

tion provided "for our holding foreign territory, still less for incorporating foreign nations into our union." Seeking to maintain the long-standing U.S. commitment to **neutrality** in struggles between Britain and France, Jefferson also was willing to pronounce and enforce an **embargo** on all foreign **commerce** in 1804.

In important respects, then, the revolution of 1800 brought no sweeping alterations in the government's institutional arrangements. Hamilton was among those who recognized that Jefferson was not opposed to the firm exercise of **executive** power and assured his colleagues in 1801 that "it is not true, as alleged, that he [Jefferson] is for confounding all the powers in the House of Representatives." Hamilton's observations predicted accurately how Jefferson was to act as president.

Nevertheless, Jefferson's presidency marked an important change in the executive's relationship to the people. Jefferson's predecessors, George Washington (1789–1797) and John Adams, believed that presidential power derived from the Constitutional. Jefferson, while not rejecting this view out of hand, maintained that the strength of the presidency depended upon the "affections of the people." Jefferson clearly implied in his first inaugural address that the program of the Democratic-Republican Party should be enacted because of its endorsement by a majority of the people in the 1800 election.

Washington and Adams viewed their task as one of maintaining some distance from the people and serving as a moderating force in the clash of parties and interests in Congress. But Jefferson believed that the most effective and responsible way to lead the government was through the institutions that were rooted most firmly in a popular base—the House and, to a lesser extent, the Senate. Instead of standing apart from developments occurring in the legislature, he sought to direct them. Thus in contrast to Hamilton's concept of a strong presidency, which emphasized the need for independent executive initiatives, Jefferson assumed the mantle of party leader in an effort to direct the separate branches of government.

The Jefferson administration produced other important institutional changes to forge a closer relationship between the president and the people. One such change was to reduce the ceremonial trappings of the executive office. Jefferson stripped away much of the pomp and ceremony to which Washington and Adams had adhered, regarding excessive formality in the conduct of the presidency as incompatible with a popularly based government. Unlike Washington, Jefferson rode around the capital not in a coach, but on his own horse, with only one servant in attendance. His clothing stressed republican simplicity, to the point of offending some who regarded his appearance as unsuitable for a head of state.

Jefferson's interest in removing the "monocratic" features from the executive office also brought about efforts to simplify the president's relationship with Congress. His decision to submit his first annual message to Congress in writing instead of delivering it in person was "a calculated political act, designed to reduce the 'relics' left by the Federalists and to underline the return to sound republican simplicity." Jefferson thus inaugurated what turned out to be the century-long practice of presidents' sending their State of the Union messages to Congress to be read aloud by the clerk of the House.

The move of the capital from Philadelphia to Washington, D.C., in 1800 left members of Congress, executive branch officials, and diplomats, who had been accustomed to the well-developed culture and comforts of Philadelphia, "stranded" on the banks of the Potomac. One historian described Washington in the early 1800s as "a village pretending to be a capital, a place with a few bad houses, extensive swamps, hanging on the skirts of a too thinly peopled, weak and barren country." Yet Jefferson, who was never fully comfortable in cities, appreciated the change in setting. His informal style was compatible not just with his view of the executive office but also with Washington's rustic surroundings.

The Limits of Popular Leadership

Popular presidential leadership had its limits during the Jeffersonian era. Neither Jefferson nor his Democratic-Republican successors—James Madison (1809–1817), James Monroe (1817–1825), and John Quincy Adams (1825–1829)—tried to enhance their power by bartering **patronage** or other sorts of favors in return for legislation in Congress. Until 1829, presidents seldom used the spoils of federal appointments to enhance party

unity or to obtain legislation. Nor was it considered respectable during the Jeffersonian era for the president to appeal directly to the public. Until the twentieth century, presidents usually exercised popular leadership indirectly, through their influence on the party mechanisms in Congress and the state governments.

For example, Jefferson was able to get an embargo enacted by using his popularity to exert influence indirectly on Democratic-Republican leaders in Congress. Notwithstanding the controversy over the embargo, Jefferson never took the issue to the people. To have done otherwise would have violated the custom that prohibited presidents from trying to influence public opinion directly.

After fourteen months of existence, the embargo was repealed by a rebellious Congress. The defeat of Jefferson's embargo policy marked the first striking example of the limits of presidential power. It also marked the beginning of a long decline in the influence of the presidency that affected the administrations of Jefferson's three Democratic-Republican successors. A combination of personal factors and institutional developments caused the presidency after Jefferson to shrink to its limited constitutional role as prescribed by the mainstream Democratic-Republican doctrine.

See also: Adams, John, Administration of (1797–1801); Madison, James, Administration of (1809–1817).

Further Reading

Appleby, Joyce. *Thomas Jefferson*. New York: Times Books, Henry Holt and Company, 2003.

Dunn, Susan. *Jefferson's Second Revolution: The Election Crisis of 1800 and the Triumph of Republicanism*. Boston: Houghton Mifflin, 2004.

Ferling, John. *Adams vs. Jefferson: The Tumultuous Election of 1800*. New York: Oxford University Press, 2004.

Johnson, Andrew, Administration of (1865–1869)

Government under the seventeenth president of the United States. In 1835, Johnson was elected as a Democrat to the Tennessee legislature. He espoused the ideals of Andrew Jackson (1829–1837), became an advocate of the common farmer and small business owner, and earned a reputation as a powerful orator. In 1837, he was defeated for a second term in the Tennessee legislature, but he won reelection in 1839. Two years later he was elected to the state senate, and in 1843 his congressional district sent him to the U.S. House of Representatives.

In Washington, Johnson supported the Mexican War (1846–1848) and the Compromise of 1850. He served four terms in the House, but an 1853 Whig redistricting plan made his reelection impossible. Consequently, Johnson ran for governor of Tennessee and won two terms before the Tennessee legislature sent him to the U.S. Senate in 1857.

In 1860, Johnson was proposed as a presidential candidate, but he withdrew his name from nomination and supported John Breckinridge. When Abraham Lincoln (1861–1865) was elected, Johnson surprised many of his fellow southerners by declaring his loyalty to the Union. He campaigned against the **secession** of Tennessee, and when his state did secede in June 1861, he was the only southern senator to remain in the Senate. In 1862, after Union forces had captured most of Tennessee, Lincoln appointed Johnson military governor of his state. With Johnson's urging, Tennessee became the only seceding state to outlaw slavery before the 1863 Emancipation Proclamation.

Johnson's loyalty to the Union was rewarded with a vice-presidential nomination in 1864. Lincoln's first-term vice president, Hannibal Hamlin, wanted to be renominated, but Lincoln refused to back his candidacy. Delegates to the National Union convention in Baltimore (the Republican nominating convention expanded to include Democrats loyal to the Union) hoped that having a southern Democrat on the ticket would attract support from northern Democrats and voters in border areas.

Lincoln and Johnson defeated Democrats George McClellan and George Pendleton in the electoral college, 212–21. Johnson served as vice president only six weeks before President Lincoln died on April 15 from a gunshot wound inflicted by assassin John Wilkes Booth. The new president thus faced the immense problem of reconstructing a broken South, which had surrendered six days before.

Johnson tried to implement the lenient **Reconstruction** program envisioned by Lincoln, but he was blocked by **radical Republicans** in Congress who were intent upon punishing the region and limiting the influence of white southerners in national politics. Johnson successfully **vetoed** several harsh Reconstruction **bills** early in his presidency, but in the 1866 congressional elections the radical Republicans gained overwhelming control of Congress and were in a position to override the president's vetoes.

On March 2, 1867, Congress passed the first Reconstruction Act over Johnson's veto. It established martial law in the South, granted universal **suffrage** to blacks, and limited the voting rights of Southern whites. The same day Congress overrode Johnson's veto of the Tenure of Office Act, which prohibited the president from removing without Senate approval any appointee who had been confirmed by the Senate. Johnson's defiance of this act forced a showdown between the president and Congress. On August 12, 1867, while Congress was in recess, Johnson replaced Secretary of War Edwin Stanton with General Ulysses S. Grant (1869–1877) without the Senate's approval.

On January 13, 1868, the Senate declared the president's action illegal and reinstated Stanton. Grant complied with the Senate's order, but Johnson again dismissed Stanton and ordered Major General Lorenzo Thomas to take Stanton's place. Three days later, on February 24, 1868, the House voted 126–47 to **impeach** the president. Radical Republicans had been searching for an excuse to impeach Johnson since early 1867.

The president's fate was then in the hands of the Senate, which could remove him from office with a two-thirds vote. On March 13, Johnson's trial began in the Senate chambers with Chief Justice Salmon P. Chase presiding. The Senate voted 35–19 for the impeachment articles, one vote short of the necessary two-thirds needed for conviction. Although Johnson's radical Republican opponents controlled the Senate, seven believed that the charges against Johnson did not warrant his removal and voted against conviction despite the consequences for their political careers. The decisive vote belonged to freshman Senator

Edmund G. Ross (R-KS), whose "not guilty" acquitted Johnson.

Although Johnson's presidency was dominated by Reconstruction and his battles with Congress, he and his secretary of state, William H. Seward, achieved a notable foreign policy success in 1867 when they negotiated the purchase of Alaska from Russia for only $7.2 million.

When Johnson's term expired in 1869 he returned to Tennessee. In 1874, the Tennessee legislature elected him to the Senate. He returned to Washington, where he resumed his fight for more lenient Reconstruction policies. Johnson only served five months of his Senate term before he died of a stroke in 1875 while visiting his daughter at Carter's Station, Tennessee.

See also: Lincoln, Abraham, Administration of (1861–1865); Grant, Ulysses S., Administration of (1869–1877).

Further Reading

Havelin, Kate. *Andrew Johnson.* Minneapolis, MN: Lerner Publications, 2004.

Means, Howard. *The Avenger Takes His Place: Andrew Johnson and the 45 Days That Changed the Nation.* Orlando, FL: Harcourt, 2006.

Johnson, Lyndon B., Administration of (1963–1969)

Government under the thirty-sixth president of the United States. In 1937, Johnson was given the opportunity to run for Congress when James P. Buchanan, the House member from Johnson's Texas district, died suddenly. Johnson entered the special election held to fill his seat and beat several candidates.

Johnson won reelection to the House in 1938 and 1940, but was narrowly defeated when he ran for a Senate seat in 1941. After the Japanese attacked Pearl Harbor that December, Johnson was the first House member to volunteer for active duty in the armed forces. He was commissioned as a lieutenant commander in the navy and sent to the South Pacific, where he undertook

a fact-finding mission of the Australian combat zone. Johnson's service was short, however. In July 1942, President Franklin D. Roosevelt (1933–1945) ordered all members of Congress to leave the military and return to Washington, D.C.

Johnson served in the House until January 1949, when he took the Senate seat he had won the previous November. After just four years, his Democratic colleagues elected him minority leader. In January 1955, he was elected majority leader when the Democrats took control of the Senate. During his six years as majority leader, Johnson became known as one of the most skilled **legislative** leaders in congressional history. His ability to use flattery, coercion, and compromise to get legislation passed was a valuable asset when he became president.

Johnson ran for president in 1960, but he was defeated for the Democratic nomination by Senator John F. Kennedy of Massachusetts. Kennedy offered the vice presidency to Johnson, however, and the majority leader accepted. Kennedy and Johnson defeated Republicans Richard Nixon and Henry Cabot Lodge in a close election. Many political observers believed Kennedy might not have won without Johnson on the ticket. Johnson's presence was valuable in helping Kennedy win five southern states, including Texas.

Although Johnson was not an insider in the Kennedy administration (1961–1963), he undertook many diplomatic missions, and the president frequently sought his advice, especially on legislative matters. When Kennedy was shot while he rode in a motorcade through Dallas, Texas, Johnson was riding in a car behind the president. He followed the president's car to a hospital, where Kennedy was pronounced dead. Johnson then proceeded to the Dallas airport and boarded *Air Force One,* the official plane of the president of the United States. He decided to take the oath of office immediately, rather than wait until he returned to Washington. While the plane sat on the runway, federal judge Sarah T. Hughes administered the oath of office to Johnson, who became the thirty-sixth president.

In the days following the assassination, Johnson declared his intention to carry out Kennedy's programs and asked Kennedy's cabinet to remain. Johnson, recognizing that public sentiment for the slain president improved his chances of enacting

Kennedy's legislative program, vigorously lobbied Congress to pass a civil rights bill and a tax cut. Congress passed both bills in 1964. The tax cut succeeded in stimulating the economy, and the Civil Rights Act of 1964 established the Equal Employment Opportunity Commission and forbade discrimination because of race or sex by employers, places of public accommodation, and labor unions.

In 1964, Johnson ran for a presidential term of his own against Republican Senator Barry Goldwater of Arizona. Many Americans were worried that Goldwater's **conservative** positions were too extreme. Johnson outpolled Goldwater by more than 15 million votes and defeated him 486–52 in the electoral college.

Johnson regarded his landslide victory as a directive to enact the **Great Society** social programs that he had outlined in his campaign. Johnson's Great Society was a plan designed to fight poverty, ignorance, disease, and other social problems. During his second term, he guided numerous bills through Congress establishing federal programs that provided expanded aid for medical care, housing, welfare, education, and urban renewal.

Although Johnson had hoped that his administration would be able to concentrate on his Great Society programs, the involvement of the United States in Southeast Asia soon came to dominate his presidency. The government in North Vietnam and guerrillas in South Vietnam were attempting to unify the country under communist rule by defeating the South Vietnamese regime militarily. Since Vietnam had been split into North and South Vietnam in 1954, the United States had supported the South with weapons, U.S. military advisers, and economic aid. In 1965, Johnson increased the U.S. commitment by sending American combat troops to South Vietnam.

Johnson continued to escalate U.S. involvement in the war in response to communist provocations and the inability of the South Vietnamese government to defend its country. The growing war diverted attention and dollars away from Johnson's domestic programs. Although many citizens supported the war, by 1966 college campuses had erupted in protest against it. Johnson hoped that

each increase in U.S. troop strength and expansion of bombing targets would produce a breakthrough on the battlefield that would lead to a negotiated settlement preserving the independence and security of South Vietnam, but the communists refused to give up their goal of reunification.

By early 1968, public opinion had swung decisively against the war and Johnson. He recognized that there was a good chance that his party might not renominate him for president. Senators Eugene J. McCarthy of Minnesota and Robert F. Kennedy of New York, the late president's brother, were running for the Democratic presidential nomination on antiwar platforms and were receiving substantial support. On March 31, 1968, Johnson delivered a television address in which he announced a partial halt to U.S. air attacks on North Vietnam to emphasize the U.S. desire for peace. He then stunned the nation by saying that he would not seek or accept the Democratic nomination for president.

After leaving Washington in 1969, Johnson retired to his ranch near Johnson City, Texas. He wrote a book about his presidential years, *The Vantage Point,* which was published in 1971. On January 22, 1973, Johnson, who had a history of heart problems, was suffered a heart attack at his ranch and was pronounced dead on arrival at Brooke Army Medical Center in San Antonio.

See also: Kennedy, John F., Administration of (1961–1963); Nixon, Richard M., Administration of (1969–1974).

Further Reading

Dallek, Robert. *Lyndon Johnson: Portrait of a President.* New York: Oxford University Press, 2005.

Schulman, Bruce J. *Lyndon Johnson and American Liberalism: A Brief Biography with Documents,* 2nd ed. New York: Palgrave Macmillan, 2006.

Justice, Department of

See Department of Justice.

Kitchen Cabinet

See Cabinet.

Kennedy John F., Administration of (1961-1963)

Government under the thirty-fifth president of the United States. In 1936, John F. Kennedy entered Harvard University, where he studied economics and political science. Kennedy was an average student, but his grades improved dramatically at the end of his college career, and he graduated with honors in 1940. *Why England Slept,* his senior thesis published in book form, was an examination of British **appeasement** of **fascism** before World War II (1939–1945).

Early Career
In 1941, Kennedy joined the navy and he received a commission as an **ensign** in October of that year. After attending PT (patrol torpedo) boat training, he was given command of a PT boat in the South Pacific in April 1943. On August 2, 1943, his boat, PT109, was rammed and sunk by a Japanese destroyer. Eleven of his thirteen crewmembers survived, and he led them on a four-hour swim to a nearby island. During the swim, he towed an injured crewmember by clenching the man's life preserver strap between his teeth. Kennedy and his crew were rescued and Kennedy was sent back to the United States, where he was hospitalized for malaria.

After his recovery, Kennedy worked briefly as a reporter for the International News Service, then decided to run for Congress from his Massa-

chusetts district. He was elected in 1946 and served three terms before being elected to the Senate in 1952. In 1954 and 1955, he underwent two more operations for his chronic back condition. While convalescing, Kennedy published *Profiles in Courage,* a book about U.S. senators who had demonstrated courage during their careers. The book became a best-seller and earned Kennedy the 1957 Pulitzer Prize for biography.

In 1956, Kennedy tried to secure the Democratic vice-presidential nomination on the ticket with Adlai Stevenson. After leading on the second ballot at the Democratic National Convention in Chicago, Kennedy lost the nomination to Senator Estes Kefauver of Tennessee. Despite this defeat, Kennedy's political reputation continued to grow. In 1957, he was assigned to the Senate Foreign Relations Committee, where he gained foreign policy experience. In 1958, he won reelection to the Senate by a record margin in Massachusetts.

By 1960, Kennedy was the leading candidate for the Democratic presidential nomination. His rivals for the nomination were Senate Majority Leader Lyndon Johnson of Texas, Senator Stuart Symington of Missouri, Senator Hubert H. Humphrey of Minnesota, and former Democratic presidential candidate Adlai Stevenson. Kennedy prevailed on the first ballot at the Democratic National Convention in Los Angeles in July 1960 and convinced Lyndon Johnson, who had finished second, to be his running mate.

Kennedy's opponent was Republican Vice President Richard Nixon. Kennedy and Nixon engaged in a series of four televised debates, the first in presidential election history. Out of almost 69 million votes cast, Kennedy received only 120,000 more than Nixon. Kennedy won in the electoral college, 303–219.

Presidency
Kennedy was the youngest person ever to be elected president, although Theodore Roosevelt

The Berlin Wall, 1961 and 1989

After World War II (1939–1945), Germany, as well as its capital of Berlin, had been divided among four Allied nations—the United States, Great Britain, France, and the Soviet Union. The divided city of Berlin lay deep inside the Soviet zone, which later became the Communist nation of East Germany. In 1961, tensions between the capitalist west and the Communist Soviet Union were rising—especially between East Berlin and West Berlin. To prevent East Berliners from crossing into the west, the Soviet Union built a wall through the city—completely cutting off the east from the west. East Berliners who attempted to reach West Berlin were shot on sight. In 1963, President John F. Kennedy (1961–1963) went to Berlin and demonstrated U.S. support for the city when, speaking in front of the Berlin Wall, he declared, "Today in the world of freedom, the proudest boast is, "Ich bin ein Berliner!" [I am a Berliner.] . . . All free men, wherever they may live, are citizens of Berlin. And therefore, as a free man, I take pride in the words "Ich bin ein Berliner!"

In 1987, President Ronald Reagan (1981–1989) also traveled to West Berlin. There, speaking in front of the Berlin Wall, he challenged the Soviet Leader Mikhail Gorbachev, "If you seek peace, if you seek prosperity for the Soviet Union and Eastern Europe, if you seek liberalization: Come here to this gate! Mr. Gorbachev, open this gate! Mr. Gorbachev, tear down this wall!"

East-West tensions slowly eased, especially after Gorbachev instituted his policies of *glasnost* (openness) and *perestroika* (economic restructuring), which led to new freedoms. By August 1989, Communist Hungary opened its borders with Austria. Soon, other barriers fell. November 9, 1989, is recognized as the day on which the Berlin Wall officially fell.

(1901–1909) was younger than Kennedy when he succeeded to the presidency after the death of William McKinley in 1901. Kennedy's youth, idealism, and attractive family would make him one of the most popular presidents of the twentieth century.

Soon after entering office, Kennedy endorsed a CIA plan developed during the Eisenhower presidency (1953–1961) to arm, train, and land 1,400 Cuban exiles in Cuba in an attempt to overthrow the communist regime of Fidel Castro. The April 17, 1961, operation, which came to be known as the Bay of Pigs invasion, was a complete failure as twelve hundred of the Cuban exiles were captured. The president accepted full responsibility for the blunder.

The following year, in October 1962, Kennedy was informed that **aerial reconnaissance photography** proved that the Soviet Union was building offensive missile bases in Cuba. Kennedy believed Soviet missiles in Cuba, which was just ninety miles from Florida, would seriously diminish U.S. national security and increase the chances that the Soviets would try to force the United States into concessions in other parts of the world. The president demanded that the bases be dismantled, but he rejected the option of an air strike against the sites in favor of a naval blockade of Cuba. The confrontation brought the United States and Soviet Union to the brink of nuclear war, but the Soviets ultimately backed down and agreed to remove the missiles.

Tensions decreased following the Cuban Missile Crisis, but the incident caused the Soviets to undertake a military buildup that enabled them to achieve nuclear equality with the United States by the late 1960s. In 1963, Kennedy concluded an important arms control treaty with Great Britain, France, and the Soviet Union that banned nuclear tests in the atmosphere, in outer space, and under water.

Kennedy also increased U.S. involvement in the developing world. In 1961, he established the Peace Corps, an agency that sent skilled volunteers overseas to assist people of underdeveloped countries. He also initiated the Alliance for Progress, an aid program aimed at developing the resources of Latin America.

In domestic policy, Kennedy made substantial progress in furthering the cause of civil rights. He advocated school desegregation, established a program to encourage registration of African American voters, issued rules against discrimination in public housing built with federal funds, and appointed a record number of blacks to public office. Kennedy used federal troops several times to maintain order and enforce the law in the South during the civil rights movement. He sent federal troops and officials to oversee the integration of the University of Mississippi in 1962 and the University of Alabama in 1963. He proposed sweeping civil rights legislation in 1963, but the measure did not come to a vote during his lifetime.

After the president's advisers convinced him that a tax cut would stimulate the economy and bring growth without large budget deficits or inflation, Kennedy tried—unsuccessfully—to persuade Congress to cut taxes.. After Kennedy's death, President Lyndon Johnson (1963–1969) was able to secure passage of the Kennedy tax cut and civil rights legislation.

During fall 1963, Kennedy made several trips around the country to build political support for his reelection bid the following year. In late November, he scheduled a trip to Texas. While riding through Dallas in an open car on November 22, Kennedy was shot once in the head and once in the neck. He was pronounced dead at a nearby hospital. Vice President Lyndon Johnson was sworn in as president that afternoon.

Police quickly apprehended the alleged assassin, Lee Harvey Oswald, a former marine who had once renounced his U.S. citizenship and lived in the Soviet Union. Initial investigations concluded that Oswald had shot Kennedy with a rifle from a sixth-story window of the Texas School Book Depository building. Three days after the shooting, Oswald was murdered in front of millions of television viewers by Jack Ruby, owner of a Dallas nightclub. The Warren Commission, a seven-member panel appointed by President Johnson to investigate the assassination, determined that Oswald acted alone. However, several questions surrounding the assassination—including Oswald's violent death, his unknown motivation, and the difficulty of a single marksman firing several accurate shots so quickly—have fostered speculation that Oswald may have been part of a conspiracy.

See also: Assassinations and Assassination Attempts; Eisenhower, Dwight D., Administration of (1953–1961); Johnson, Lyndon B., Administration of (1963–1969).

Further Reading

Dallek, Robert. *An Unfinished Life: John F. Kennedy, 1917–1963.* Boston: Back Bay Books, 2004.

O'Brien, Michael. *John F. Kennedy: A Biography.* New York: St. Martin's Griffin, 2006.

Kissinger, Henry

See National Security Council.

Labor, Department of

See Department of Labor.

Legislative Leader

The power of the president to recommend legislation to Congress and the power to **veto bills** passed by Congress. The U.S. Constitution "blends" power among the three branches of government. Yet, despite the popular notion that the branches were created equal, the **legislative** branch alone has the constitutional authority to make laws. The Framers believed that only Congress could reflect the diversity of opinions bound to exist in a free society.

By contrast, the Framers limited the president's ability to influence legislation to two enumerated or "express" powers: the power to recommend to Congress measures deemed "necessary and expedient" (Article II, Section 3) and the power to veto bills passed by Congress (Article I, Section 7). Presidents have the sole legal authority to negotiate treaties with other nations, but treaties gain the force of law only when "two-thirds of the Senators present concur" (Article II, Section 2). Presidents also have the authority to convene "emergency" sessions of Congress (Article II, Section 3), but these are extraordinary events.

Even today, the presidency's relationship with Congress remains fluid and indefinite. Much of what presidents desire or need, especially in the domestic sphere, still demands congressional cooperation, whether to enact new laws, **appropriate** funds, or, in the case of the Senate, approve treaties and **executive** and judicial branch appointments. In short, every president needs

Congress. The legislature, for its part, often proves so divided, independent, or uncooperative that residents of the White House rarely can take its support for granted, even when Congress is controlled by the president's own political party. Presidents may have considerable potential advantage with Congress, but they usually have to earn their victories.

The Veto

The veto is the primary formal tool used by presidents to influence congressional lawmaking. All other means of influencing the shape and direction of legislation must be understood with reference to this formal power, because only the president's legal capacity to stop legislation gives the other instruments for shaping public policy their teeth.

The president's authority to block acts passed by Congress has its origins in the 1787 debate over the Constitution, in particular the Framers' efforts to prevent any single branch—and, by extension, any individual or group—from gaining tyrannical political power. These concerns go back to the very roots of the colonial rebellion against England.

Anyone who has studied the Declaration of Independence and the events surrounding it is well aware of the colonists' complaints against England's King George III and their eventual fear of a powerful national executive. Yet often overlooked is their equal dread of unchecked legislative power. Thomas Jefferson's (1801–1809) second villain in the Declaration of Independence was the English Parliament, a legislature unobstructed by written constitutional limits and loathed widely in the colonies for its apparent disregard for due process of law.

These general fears about an overly strong national government were reflected in the Articles of Confederation, the Republic's first constitution. The Articles, which went into effect in 1781, essentially created a league of friendship among the thirteen newly independent states that made the national government a creation of the states and dependent on them for its powers and funds.

Ultimately, however, the national government under the Articles proved unable to promote either national unity or effective government. One problem, at least for those who called for major changes in the Articles, was the absence of any independent national executive authority to administer the laws and resist legislative **tyranny.** Not only had Congress under the Articles proven unable to govern by itself, but the political and fiscal excesses of state legislatures during the 1780s led to the perception that such bodies were as dangerous to liberty as an unrestrained monarch. Jefferson, reflecting on his experiences as governor of Virginia, wrote, "All the powers of government . . . result to the legislative body. The concentrating of these in the same hands is precisely the definition of **despotic** government." These sentiments were shared by many of the delegates to the Constitutional Convention, even those who otherwise feared an overly strong national government.

The concept of a *veto* (Latin for "I forbid") was well known to the Framers. Indeed, in ancient Rome the veto was used by the plebeians to protect the common people from the excesses of a senate dominated by aristocrats. It later surfaced in medieval Europe as a royal check on newly developing legislatures. In England before the seventeenth century, the monarch had the *absolute* power to deny acts by Parliament, a weapon that Queen Elizabeth I, who reigned from 1558 to 1603, used quite frequently. Closer to home, by 1787 a few state constitutions, such as that of Massachusetts, contained a form of executive veto.

Not surprisingly, then, virtually every plan put forth for revisions in the Articles included some form of an executive check on laws passed by Congress. The Virginia Plan called for a "council of revision" of members from both the executive and the judicial branches. Critics of this idea argued that such a "plural" veto would be too weak, because disputes within the council would undermine decisive executive action. Other delegates expressed discomfort with having judges act on bills before they came up as legal cases. So the convention eventually granted the veto to the president alone.

Some proponents of a strong executive initially supported an absolute veto, giving Congress no opportunity to respond, but this idea found no support among delegates who were concerned about unresponsive and unpredictable executives. After some debate, the Framers gave the new executive a "partial negative." The president could reject bills or joint **resolutions** passed by Congress, but Congress in response could "override" a veto by extraordinary majorities of two-thirds of the members present in each chamber. Presidents could not veto constitutional **amendments,** concurrent resolutions, or resolutions passed by only one chamber.

Opponents of the veto, even those worried about unrestrained legislative power, argued that Congress alone represented the people. The veto might undermine democratic values by allowing the president to block "good" laws or simply to thwart majority rule. However, Hamilton retorted that unrestrained majorities are just as dangerous as an unchecked elite, and "the injury which might possibly be done by defeating a few good laws will be amply compensated by the advantage of preventing a number of bad ones." Moreover, allowing the executive to threaten a veto might induce legislative moderation, making actual use of the veto unnecessary.

The President's Program

The president's second express constitutional duty in the legislative process is to "from time to time give to the Congress Information of the State of the Union, and recommend to their Consideration such Measures as he shall judge necessary and expedient" (Article II, Section 3). This authority to "recommend . . . Measures" seems rather minor, but over time, it has become the primary mechanism used by presidents in seeking to shape the nation's political agenda, particularly when the nation is not in crisis.

Presidents naturally would love to have complete control over the agenda of government, especially at the very start of their terms in office. In reality, however, a president's control over the agenda is shaky. At times, it is overwhelmed by natural disasters, war, or sudden shifts in the economy. When a crisis occurs, the existing agenda is thrown aside, and a president's "success" is judged solely by the pace and suitability of the response. Franklin Roosevelt's (1933–1945) reaction to the virtual collapse of the banking system on the eve of his inauguration in 1933 often is cited as an example of strong presidential leadership. Within days of taking office, Roosevelt led Congress in reorganizing the entire federal banking system. Even more important, he went on national radio to persuade citizens to return their savings to the banks, instilling renewed faith in the financial system and taking the first steps toward economic recovery.

Ronald Reagan (1981–1989), by contrast, was criticized roundly in October 1987 for his late and passive response to a sudden plunge in the stock market. Financial analysts argued that the downturn reflected investors' unease with the deadlock between Reagan and Congress over resolving the federal budget deficit. Whether the "crisis" over the budget caused the market crash or whether Reagan responded inadequately is hard to say, yet common perceptions that he had not dealt forcefully with the situation eroded confidence in his leadership. In similar ways, fairly or not, the presidency of George W. Bush (2001–2009) may well be defined by the ways in which he and his administration dealt with the terrorist attacks of September 11, 2001, and their aftermath.

Crises aside, the presidency has a singularly unique *institutional* capacity to shape the nation's agenda of debate and action. No other government institution can subject Congress to so much pressure in so organized a manner, and no other political figure regularly commands so much attention from the public regardless of the issue. The presidency always has been a focal point of American politics because it (and the vice presidency) is the only political office in the United States filled through a national election. Yet its psychological and political importance also mushroomed in the second half of the twentieth century. The growth in the scope and influence of the federal government, the emergence of the United States as a superpower—which amplifies the president's role as commander in chief—and the emergence of modern telecommunications have all converged to place the presidency

squarely in the public eye, both at home and abroad.

See also: Emergency Powers; Line-Item Veto; Pocket Veto.

Lincoln, Abraham, Administration of (1861–1865)

Government under the sixteenth president of the United States. In 1846, Lincoln was elected to the U.S. House of Representatives. Despite the popularity of the Mexican War (1846–1848) in his district, he joined fellow Whigs in denouncing the war as unjust. Lincoln also opposed the extension of slavery into the territories, but did not advocate abolishing slavery where it already existed. Lincoln had promised Illinois Whig Party leaders that he would serve only one term, so when his term expired he returned to his home in Springfield, Illinois. He spent the next several years developing his successful law practice.

In 1854, Lincoln ran for the Senate but backed out of the race when his candidacy threatened to split the antislavery vote. Two years later, Lincoln joined the new Republican Party, which had formed in 1854. He campaigned for the party's 1856 presidential candidate, John C. Fremont, who lost to Democrat James Buchanan (1857–1861).

The Illinois Republican Party nominated Lincoln for senator in 1858. He faced **incumbent** Democrat Stephen A. Douglas, author of the Kansas-Nebraska Act of 1854, which was favored by many proslavery Democrats. The act gave the people in the territories of Kansas and Nebraska the option to permit slavery.

Lincoln challenged Douglas to a series of seven debates focusing on slavery. During the debates, which attracted huge crowds, Lincoln questioned the morality of slavery and argued against its expansion into territories where it did not exist already. The state legislature elected Douglas over Lincoln 54–46, but the debates made Lincoln famous throughout the country and a likely candidate for the Republican presidential

Jefferson Davis

On February 18, 1861, Jefferson Davis became the first and only president of the Confederate States of America. He was inaugurated in Montgomery, Alabama.

Davis was born in Christian (now Todd) County, Kentucky, on June 3, 1808, to Samuel and Jane Davis. He attended private schools and Transylvania University in Lexington, Kentucky, before his brother, Joseph, secured his appointment to West Point in 1824.

After graduating from West Point, Davis was stationed in Wisconsin under Colonel Zachary Taylor (1849–1850). There he saw action in the Black Hawk War during the early 1830s and fell in love with Taylor's daughter, Sarah Knox. In 1835, he left the army, married Sarah, and settled on a plantation in Mississippi. Tragically, Sarah died from malaria three months after the wedding. For the several years, Davis devoted himself to developing his land and wealth.

In 1845, Davis married Varina Howell, a member of the Mississippi aristocracy, and was elected to the U.S. House of Representatives. He served in Washington less than a year before the Mexican War (1846–1848) began. He gave up his seat to accept a commission as a colonel, and became a national hero when his company made a stand at the Battle of Buena Vista.

In 1847, he left the army and was elected to the Senate. He served there until 1851, when he ran unsuccessfully for governor of Mississippi. He returned to Washington in 1853 after being appointed as secretary of war by President Franklin Pierce (1853–1857). Davis was credited with strengthening the armed forces during his time in office. He also was influential in bringing about the Gadsden Purchase from

nomination in 1860. During the next two years, he made several highly publicized speaking tours, including one to the East in early 1860. His name was placed in nomination at the Republican National Convention in Chicago in 1860, but he trailed New York senator William Seward on the first and second ballots. On the third ballot, however, Lincoln secured the nomination.

The Democratic Party, meanwhile, split into two factions. Stephen A. Douglas was nominated by northern Democrats, and Vice President John C. Breckinridge of Kentucky was nominated by southern Democrats. The remnants of the Whig and Know-Nothing Parties further complicated the election by joining to nominate John Bell as the candidate of their new Constitutional Union Party. Lincoln won the four-candidate race with less than 40 percent of the popular vote. He captured eighteen northern states with 180 of the total 303 electoral votes. Breckinridge and Bell followed with 72 and 39, respectively. Douglas, who finished second to Lincoln in the popular vote, won only Missouri's 12 electoral votes.

Presidency

Lincoln's election caused the **secession** crisis that the nation had feared for several decades. In December 1860, South Carolina left the Union, followed by six more states early in 1861. The rebelling states formed the Confederate states of America and elected Jefferson Davis as their president.

Lincoln tried to ease southern fears that he intended to abolish slavery. He declared in his first inaugural address that he had no intention or authority to "interfere with the institution of slavery where it already exists." However, he warned the southern states that he did not recognize their

SPOTLIGHT

Mexico in 1853, which added southern areas of present-day Arizona and New Mexico to the United States.

In 1857, Davis was reelected to the Senate. Although he became a leading spokesperson for the South, he did not advocate secession until 1860 when it had become inevitable. Davis hoped to be appointed commanding general of the South's army, but instead he was chosen as president by a convention of the seceding states.

Davis believed his first priority as president was to preserve Southern independence. He tried to secure French and British assistance for the Confederacy, but he was largely unsuccessful. Like President Abraham Lincoln (1861–1865), he helped develop military strategy and on occasion interfered with the plans of his generals. In managing the war effort, Davis was hampered by his paradoxical position. The South could fight most effectively as a unified nation run by the central government in Richmond, Virginia, but the Southern states had seceded in part to preserve their rights as independent states. Davis took actions, including the suspension of **habeas corpus** and the establishment of conscription, that were regarded as tyrannical by many Southerners.

When the Union's victory appeared imminent in early 1865, Davis fled south from Richmond, but was captured by federal troops in Georgia. He was indicted for treason and imprisoned for two years, but he never stood trial. He lived in Canada and Europe for several years before retiring to Mississippi. There he wrote his *Rise and Fall of the Confederate Government*, which was published in 1881. He died in New Orleans on December 6, 1889.

secession and would enforce federal law and defend the Union. He declared, "In your hands, my dissatisfied fellow-countrymen, and not in mine, is the momentous issue of civil war." War came when rebels attacked and captured Fort Sumter in Charleston, South Carolina, in April 1861. The attack on the federal fort signaled the South's unwillingness to return to the Union. On April 15, Lincoln called for seventy-five thousand volunteers to put down the rebellion. Soon after, four more Southern states seceded, raising the number of states in the Confederacy to eleven.

During the next three months, Lincoln refused to call Congress into session, while he took extraordinary actions to prepare for war, many of which violated the Constitution. He blockaded the South, doubled the size of the armed forces, suspended the writ of **habeas corpus** in some areas, and spent Treasury funds, all without congressional approval. Finally, on July 4, he convened Congress, which **ratified** most of his war measures.

Lincoln and the North hoped that the rebellion could be put down quickly, but the war turned into a protracted and bloody conflict. The Union won victories in the West under General Ulysses S. Grant. In the East, Union generals were repeatedly outmaneuvered by Robert E. Lee and other Confederate generals. On January 1, 1863, Lincoln issued the Emancipation Proclamation, which declared that the slaves in the rebellious states were free. So that the proclamation would have greater credibility, he had waited to make this move until after the Union won a victory, which came at the Battle of Antietam near Sharpsburg, Maryland, in September 1862.

In July 1863, the Union victory at Gettysburg, Pennsylvania, put the Confederacy on the defensive. Lincoln traveled to Gettysburg on November 19,

A – Z

U.S. During the Civil War

Legend:
- Free states
- Slave states remaining in the Union
- Slave states of the Confederacy
- Separated from Virginia, 1861: admitted to the Union, 1863

At the beginning of the Civil War (1861–1865), eleven southern states attempted to secede, or leave the Union, and form the Confederate States of America. In 1863, the western counties of Virginia chose to remain loyal to the Union and organized the state of West Virginia.

where he delivered his famous Gettysburg Address during a ceremony to dedicate the battlefield's cemetery.

In 1864, Lincoln took an important step toward winning the war when he ordered Grant east to take command of all Union armies. That year Lincoln ran for reelection against Democratic candidate George B. McClellan, one of his former generals. Lincoln had relieved McClellan of his command of the Union army in 1862 because the general was overcautious and ineffective. During the spring of 1864, Lincoln's reelection had been in doubt as Grant's army fought a series of indecisive and costly battles in Virginia at the Wilderness, Spotsylvania, and Cold Harbor. Nevertheless, by September, Union general William T. Sherman had captured Atlanta, and Grant had besieged Petersburg, Virginia. Voters sensed that the Union was close to victory and reelected the president. Lincoln won all but three states and defeated McClellan 212–21 in the electoral college.

During the final year of the war, Grant fought a battle of attrition against Lee's forces in Virginia, while Sherman's army drove though Georgia and North and South Carolina, destroying Southern crops and industries. Finally, on April 9, 1865, Lee surrendered to Grant at Appomattox Court House in Virginia, ending the war.

In his second inaugural address, delivered on March 4, 1865, Lincoln had proposed a magnanimous peace, saying "with malice toward none, with charity for all, with firmness in the right as God gives us to see the right, let us strive on to finish the work we are in, to bind up the nation's wounds."

Assassination

Lincoln, however, did not have the opportunity to implement his generous **Reconstruction** plans. On April 14, 1865, while watching a production of the play *Our American Cousin* at Ford's Theater in Washington, D.C., he was shot in the back of the head at close range by actor John Wilkes Booth. After shooting Lincoln, Booth jumped from the presidential box to the stage, fled the theater, and rode south. On April 26, federal troops surrounded and killed him at a farm in Virginia. Booth, who had sympathized with the Confederacy, was part of a conspiracy to kill several government officials, including Vice President Andrew Johnson. With the exception of Secretary of State William Seward, who received a nonfatal stab wound at his home, the other assassination targets escaped harm.

Lincoln was treated by a doctor at the theater, and then carried across the street to a house where he died the next morning, April 15, without regaining consciousness. Johnson (1865–1869) took the oath of office later that day. Lincoln's body lay in state in the Capitol and White House before being carried back to Illinois on a train viewed by millions of mourners.

See also: Assassinations and Assassination Attempts; Buchanan, James, Administration of (1857–1861); Johnson, Andrew, Administration of (1865–1869).

Further Reading

Carwardine, Richard. *Lincoln: A Life of Purpose and Power.* New York: Knopf, 2006.

Donald, David Herbert. *Lincoln.* New York: Simon & Schuster, 1995.

Harris, William C. *Lincoln's Rise to the Presidency.* Lawrence, KS: University of Kansas Press, 2007.

Line-Item Veto

The power of a chief **executive** to reject parts of an approved **bill** without rejecting the entire bill. The **veto** is a blunt tool for executive influence because it is an all or nothing matter. A president is not able to pull out items deemed wasteful within an otherwise acceptable spending bill. Those who have supported greater presidential control over federal spending have considered this a major flaw in the veto process, particularly during the era of large federal budget deficits in the late 1980s and early 1990s. Thus, proposals to give presidents the capacity to pick and choose among specific **appropriations,** called a *line-item veto* have emerged periodically throughout history. However, the effort has been thwarted by legislators fearful of even greater executive advantage within their constitutionally prescribed domain.

The Framers appear to have given no attention to a line-item veto during the drafting or **ratification** of the Constitution. Moreover, the Framers showed their bias by granting to Congress full power over appropriations and revenues. However, the idea that the president should be able to excise parts of spending bills has enjoyed some popularity throughout American history.

Efforts to pass a constitutional **amendment** granting such executive power have popped up since the 1870s, but without success. Yet by the 1990s, governors in forty-three states had some form of line-item veto. Most of these provisions pertain primarily to spending bills, but others also allow governors to modify substantive laws. At least ten states allow their governors to actually **amend** spending bills and send them back to the legislature for reconsideration.

Some mid-twentieth-century presidents expressed strong support for a line-item veto, most notably Franklin D. Roosevelt (1933–1945) and Dwight D. Eisenhower (1953–1961). Roosevelt came closest to realizing his wish when the House of Representatives voted in 1938 to give the president that power; the effort died in the Senate, however.

The issue was set aside through the 1970s, but arose again in the 1980s as the federal budget deficit became a major problem. Like the budget, however, the line-item veto quickly became enmeshed in **partisan** politics, with Republican presidents Ronald Reagan (1981–1989) and George H.W. Bush (1989–1993) in favor and congressional Democrats generally opposed. Supporters argued that the line-item veto would give presidents greater control over federal spending, especially on programs and projects for which Congress may lack the political will to make cuts. Opponents expressed fears that a line-item veto would give the president excessive power over an area in which Congress traditionally—and constitutionally—took the lead.

This clash of partisan and institutional perspectives prevented proposals for the line-item veto from getting very far during the 1980s. In 1985, Reagan and congressional Republicans pushed for a two-year trial run, but the proposal was rejected both then and a year later. Even if the Senate had approved the line-item veto in 1986, it was unlikely that the House, which jealously guards its constitutional power of the purse, would have gone along. President George H.W. Bush also pushed publicly for a line-item veto, but he too had little success.

By the mid-1990s, however, the political dynamics surrounding the line-item veto had changed dramatically. President Bill Clinton (1993–2001), who had possessed a line-item veto as governor of Arkansas, openly supported one for the president. Yet key congressional Democrats continued to fight any action that might infringe on Congress's control over the budget. As it turned out, Clinton found an ally on this issue in congressional Republicans, who in 1994 gained control of both chambers of Congress for the first time since 1952. The line-item veto was a key part of the Republicans' "Contract with America," and thus the prospects for passing some kind of line-item veto improved dramatically. However, efforts to pass a constitutional amendment creating a line-item veto soon fell victim to resistance in the Senate, where even some Republicans opposed it, so proponents took another tack. After months of negotiations, a **bipartisan** majority voted to grant to the president "enhanced rescission" authority, that is, the power to "cancel" automatically individual items in spending and tax bills unless overturned by a two-thirds vote of both houses of Congress. President Clinton signed this bill into law on April 9, 1996.

Clinton used this new statutory authority for the first—and only—time in 1997, when he cut items in eleven spending bills. Members of Congress who supported the new authority suddenly were faced with actual cuts in pet projects, and Clinton suffered one of his only two veto overrides when Congress restored funding he had struck out in a military construction-spending bill. Officials of both parties in New York, upset over some of Clinton's cuts, supported a lawsuit against the president over the new authority. The Supreme Court, in *City of New York v. Clinton* (1998), struck down the Line Item Veto Act as **unconstitutional.**

See also: Pocket Veto.

Madison, James, Administration of (1809–1817)

Government under the fourth president of the United States. The decline of presidential influence was especially evident during James Madison's two terms in office. While he was president, major developments transferred power from the **executive** to the **legislative** branch. One such development was the advent of the congressional nominating **caucus** as an independent source of power.

The nomination of Thomas Jefferson (1801–1809) in 1800 and 1804 was a foregone conclusion, but the Democratic-Republican caucus of 1808 had a real decision to make. Secretary of State Madison generally was regarded as Jefferson's heir apparent, but the leader of the anti-Jefferson faction in the Democratic-Republican Party, Representative John Randolph of Virginia, tried to secure the nomination for James Monroe (1817–1825). Although Madison was nominated and elected, the promises he made to win support from his party members in Congress suggested that subsequent presidential nominations might become occasions "to make explicit executive subordination to congressional president-makers." Some scholars believe that Madison's renomination by the Democratic-Republican Party in 1812 was delayed until he assured **war hawks** in the congressional caucus that he supported their desire for war with Great Britain.

The emergence of Henry Clay of Kentucky as an important leader in Congress, and his extraordinary use of the his authority as Speaker of the House during the Madison administration, further reduced executive power in relation to Congress. Until Clay's election as Speaker in 1811, party leadership in the House usually was shared among several designated floor leaders, with the Speaker acting mainly as a moderator.

Clay sought the role of Speaker with the intention of doing what Madison had been unable to do: persuade Congress to declare war against Great Britain. Clay succeeded in this purpose, and until the last day of Madison's administration the initiative in public affairs remained with Clay and his associates in the House of Representatives.

Under Clay's direction, the House strengthened its capacity to meet its broader legislative obligations by expanding the number and influence of its standing committees, which enabled each representative to specialize in an area of interest. Because the committees' activities were coordinated by the party leaders, the House became an effective legislative instrument. From 1811 to 1825, Clay was arguably the most powerful man in the nation.

The decline of the presidency was demonstrated most dramatically during the War of 1812 (1812–1814). Madison's message of June 1, 1812, which urged Congress to declare war against Great Britain, was the first war message by an American president. Congress declared war on June 18, 1812. Later historical developments were to establish formidable wartime powers for the president, but Madison's command of the nation's military effort was undistinguished. He was handicapped not only by his inability to exert influence over Congress but also by personal qualities that were poorly suited for the tasks at hand. Madison's figure was slight, his manner was quiet (even somber), his speaking voice was weak, and the force of his personality was, at best, moderate. As Gaillard Hunt, a generally sympathetic Madison biographer, has written of the president's war leadership:

The hour had come but the man was wanting. Not a scholar in governments ancient and modern, not an unimpassioned writer of careful messages, but a robust leader to rally the people and unite them to fight was what the time needed, and what it did not find in Madison.

From a military standpoint, the War of 1812 was the most unsuccessful in American history. The low point in the war occurred in August 1814, when President Madison had to evacuate the capital for three days as a British force of fewer than five thousand men moved unchecked up the Chesapeake Bay and marched with little resistance into the heart of Washington, burning the Capitol, the White House, the Navy Yard, and most other public buildings in Washington.

The nation eventually was saved from disaster by Britain's decision not to prosecute the war on a massive scale. Morale was boosted belatedly by General Andrew Jackson's (1829–1837) victory at New Orleans on January 8, 1815, even though it had no effect on the outcome of the war. (A peace treaty had been signed two weeks earlier.) In the wake of Jackson's triumph, the American people greeted the end of the war joyfully, which allowed Madison to retire as president in 1817 with some measure of honor. New Orleans also rendered a fatal political wound to the pro-British Federalists, many of whom opposed the war from the beginning. At best, the War of 1812 was a stalemate.

In important respects, Madison's failures transcended his limitations: they were attributable in part to the legacies he inherited from the Jefferson administration and from the Democratic-Republican tradition of which he had been one of the major architects. He and Jefferson had preached economy and had taken measures to undo the military preparations undertaken during the administration of John Adams (1797–1801) administration; indeed, they opposed the creation of even a minimal standing army. They were thus completely dependent on solving the country's foreign policy problems with France and Britain through diplomatic channels. Failing this, the Democratic-Republicans were forced to rely on the 1807 **embargo**—an impractical policy of peaceful coercion that proved disastrous for the U.S. economy, without stopping either Britain or France from interfering with American ships. The collapse of his own embargo, enacted in 1812, left Madison no alternative but war when British provocations continued, even though he knew the country was neither prepared nor united for battle.

Years later, Madison recounted that he had hoped to overcome the nation's unpreparedness by "throw[ing] forward the flag of the country, sure that the people would press onward and defend it." Yet the rapid decline in the status of the presidency left Madison in a poor position to rally Congress and nation. Contrary to his expectations, the traditional Democratic-Republican doctrine of hostility to centralized power was not abandoned during wartime. Congress was willing to declare war but not to provide the revenue required to carry it out. Moreover, the Madison administration's plan to use the state militia was scuttled by the state governments' lack of cooperation. The governors of Massachusetts and Connecticut, for example, refused to release their militias for fighting the war, while the president, a strong advocate of states' rights, "offered no suggestion for stopping so grave a defiance of federal authority."

Madison began to face the limitations of Democratic-Republican principles in his seventh annual message to Congress in December 1815, in which he recommended a number of policies to solidify the national resolve, including the chartering of the Second **Bank of the United States.** (The Democratic-Republicans had allowed the first bank charter to expire in 1811.) With no national bank in operation during the War of 1812, the federal government lacked a convenient and stable source of currency, exacerbating a financial crisis that saw the national debt grow from $45 million in 1811 to $127 million by the end of 1815. Believing that a national bank was a necessary evil, Madison signed the bank **bill** into law in 1816. The severe economic disruptions of the war and the hope of achieving a stable currency persuaded Madison and the Democratic-Republicans to embrace "the ghostly presence of [Alexander] Hamilton's national bank, with all its potential for corrupting the republic."

Madison never ceased to express profound concerns, however, about the potential abuses of executive power that he believed Hamilton had encouraged and committed during the 1790s. In every one of his critical relationships and decisions—in bringing the nation to war, dealing with Congress, arranging his cabinet, overseeing the executive branch, and enduring near treasonable dissent—Madison sought to uphold Democratic-Republican principles of executive leadership. In the final analysis, these principles were not congenial to dynamic presidential leadership.

See also: Jefferson, Thomas, Administration of (1801–1809); Monroe, James, Administration of (1817–1825).

Further Reading

Wills, Gary. *James Madison.* New York: Times Books, Henry Holt and Company, 2002.

McCain, John

See Election of 2008.

McKinley, William, Administration of (1897–1901)

Government under the twenty-fifth president of the United States. After studying law in Youngstown, Ohio, and Albany, New York, in 1867 William McKinley opened a law practice in Canton, Ohio. He ran for prosecuting attorney of Stark County, Ohio, as a Republican in 1869 and won despite the county's traditional Democratic voting record. Two years later, however, he was narrowly defeated for reelection.

In 1876, McKinley won a seat in the U.S. House of Representatives. He served seven consecutive terms in the House until 1891. As a member of Congress, McKinley supported **civil service reform,** voting rights for African Americans, and government coinage of silver. He was best known, however, for his support of high **tariffs** to protect U.S. industries. While serving as the chair of the House Ways and Means Committee, he sponsored the McKinley Tariff Act of 1890, which raised tariff rates to new highs. The tariff resulted in higher prices for consumers and contributed to voter disaffection with the Republican Party. McKinley was voted out of office along with many other Republican members of Congress in 1890.

McKinley returned to Ohio, where he ran successfully for governor. He served two two-year terms, during which he was increasingly promoted as a presidential candidate. In 1892, he served as the chair of the Republican National Convention in Chicago. President Benjamin Harrison (1889–1893) was nominated on the first ballot, but McKinley came in second in the balloting.

In 1896, with McKinley's approval, Ohio party **boss** Mark Hanna and other leading Republicans actively promoted McKinley's candidacy in the months leading up to the nominating convention. His nomination was almost ensured when the convention met in St. Louis, Missouri, in June 1896. The delegates nominated him on the first ballot.

McKinley waged his campaign from his front porch, speaking to crowds that came to Canton by railroad. In contrast, the Democratic candidate, William Jennings Bryan, traveled more than eighteen thousand miles and delivered hundreds of speeches during his campaign. The Republican nominee received the strong support of business and financial leaders who feared that a Bryan presidency would bring inflation. They helped raise great amounts of campaign money for McKinley, who won in the electoral college 271–176.

McKinley's top priority upon entering office was the economy, which had been stalled in a **depression** during much of Cleveland's second term. Congress quickly passed the Dingley Tariff Act of 1897 in response to McKinley's requests. Thereafter, the economy began to grow. Although the tariff bill may not have been the cause of the recovery, McKinley took credit for the economic improvement.

McKinley's first term was dominated by the Spanish-American War (1898) and its aftermath. Americans were disturbed by numerous press accounts of atrocities committed by Spanish colonialists upon the Cuban people. McKinley responded to public pressure for war by sending a war message to Congress on April 11, 1898. Congress declared war two weeks later on April 25. Although the United States was not prepared for the war, victory came easily. Spanish control of Cuba was broken, and the U.S. Asiatic fleet under Commodore George Dewey destroyed the Spanish Pacific fleet in the Battle of Manila Bay. The fighting was over by August. On December 10, 1898, Spain signed a treaty freeing Cuba and ceding the Philippines, Puerto Rico, and Guam to the United States.

McKinley agonized over how to deal with the Philippines, but decided to take possession of them rather than grant them their independence. McKinley took several important steps in other parts of Asia and the Pacific. He oversaw the **annexation** of Hawaii in 1898. Secretary of State John Hay negotiated an agreement with European nations in 1900 that established an "Open Door" policy toward China, under which all nations doing business with China would enjoy equal trading rights.

McKinley was renominated without opposition in 1900. His close friend and first-term vice president, Garret Hobart, had died in 1899, however, and the Republican National Convention chose Theodore Roosevelt (1901–1909) as his running mate. The Democrats again ran William Jennings Bryan, but the nation's economic recovery since McKinley took office gave the Republicans a strong election issue. McKinley improved upon the popular and electoral vote margins of victory he had enjoyed in 1896, defeating Bryan in the electoral college 292–155.

After Roosevelt's nomination, Mark Hanna, who regarded the vice-presidential candidate as an unpredictable reformer, wrote McKinley saying, "Your duty to the country is to live for four years from next March." Six months after his inauguration, however, McKinley traveled to Buffalo, New York, to deliver an address at the Pan-American Exposition, a fair celebrating friendship in the Western Hemisphere. The following day the president greeted thousands of people who waited in line to shake his hand at a public reception. Leon Czolgosz, an **anarchist,** waited in line until it was his turn to shake McKinley's hand. Czolgosz then pulled out a gun and fired two shots that struck McKinley in the chest and stomach.

Doctors initially thought the president would recover. Vice President Roosevelt, who had cut his vacation short and rushed to Buffalo upon hearing that the president had been shot, even resumed his holiday when he was informed of the doctors' prognosis. After a week, however, gangrene set in and McKinley's condition deteriorated. He died early in the morning on September 14.

See also: Assassinations and Assassination Attempts; Cleveland, Grover, Administrations of (1885–1889, 1893–1897); Roosevelt, Theodore, Administration of (1901–1909).

Further Reading

Morgan, H. Wayne. *William McKinley and His America.* Kent, OH: Kent State University Press, 2004.

Phillips, Kevin. *William McKinley.* New York: Times Books, 2003.

Mitchell, John

See Department of Justice.

Monroe, James, Administration of (1817–1825)

Government under the fifth president of the United States. James Madison's Democratic-Republican successors, James Monroe (1817–1825) and John Quincy Adams (1825–1829), were unable to restore the strength of the presidency that had dissipated after Thomas Jefferson (1801–1809) retired. Monroe, although a forceful statesman and a stronger personality than his predecessor, was stiff and formal in his personal dealings. This made it difficult for him to lead the party effectively. Like George Washington (1789–1797) and John Adams (1797–1801), he was more suited to the task of presiding than directing.

Monroe also was hindered by a growing split within his party between "old" Democratic-Republicans, who favored a **strict construction** of the Constitution, and "new" Democratic-Republicans, or National Republicans, who were more **nationalist** in outlook. Monroe was identified with the first group.

One of the major domestic issues of the day, internal improvements, turned on whether it was constitutional for the national government to construct roads and canals. Monroe informed Con-

gress of his belief that an **amendment** to the Constitution would be required for the national government to undertake such a responsibility. Nevertheless, Congress, under the strong direction of Henry Clay, defied Monroe and passed a **bill** to repair the main east-west highway, known as the Cumberland Road. The president's **veto** of this bill signaled a breakdown within the ranks of the Democratic-Republicans that was to plague Monroe throughout his two terms.

This split in the Democratic-Republican ranks reinforced the transfer of power from the **executive** to the **legislative** branch. In his battle with Clay and Congress, Monroe, adhering to the prevailing custom, rarely used the veto power. Following the practice begun under Washington, Monroe vetoed only legislation he deemed **unconstitutional,** such as the Cumberland Road measure.

Monroe's deference to the legislature went beyond custom. More than any of his predecessors, Monroe believed in legislative supremacy. Hence, he abstained almost completely from involvement in the greatest issue of the day: the admission of Missouri as a state, which for the first time forced Congress to debate the status of slavery in the Louisiana Territory. Now a private citizen, Jefferson observed the bitter debate about Missouri with great concern. Writing to Representative John Holmes of Maine, he said: "This momentous question, like a fire-bell in the night, awakened and filled me with terror. I considered it at once the knell of the Union." The Missouri Compromise of 1820 settled the slavery controversy for a time, but President Monroe had virtually no hand in resolving this crisis, except for signing the final bill hammered out in Congress.

The passive character of the Monroe administration prompted Supreme Court Justice Joseph Story to remark in 1818 that "the Executive has no longer a commanding influence. The House of Representatives has absorbed all the popular feeling and all the effective power of the country."

Justice Story's lament was not as pertinent to foreign affairs as to domestic matters, however. Monroe reinforced the right of presidents to take the initiative in foreign affairs by issuing the Monroe Doctrine, which became one of the pillars of U.S. foreign policy. The Monroe Doctrine resulted from the president's attempt to respond to the revolt of Spanish colonies in Latin America that nearly liquidated the Spanish empire. The Monroe administration was alarmed at reports that European powers, France in particular, had designs on several Latin American nations. Simultaneously, Czar Alexander I of Russia reportedly was interested in staking out claims to the territory on the northwest coast of the Oregon region. Because Russia maintained a trading station at Fort Ross, near San Francisco, the czar issued a decree claiming exclusive trading rights to the area north of the fifty-first parallel. In response, the president included in his State of the Union address to Congress on December 2, 1823, a sweeping statement that denounced colonization in the Western Hemisphere and proclaimed the independence of the American nations from interference by the European powers.

The Monroe Doctrine provided an important example, at a time of general executive weakness, that the president was paramount in making foreign policy. Monroe's expression of hemispheric independence committed the United States to new diplomatic and military responsibilities, most of which would fall upon the chief executive. For a time, this commitment had little effect, but its importance to the nation's foreign policy was realized by the end of the nineteenth century.

The end of the Monroe presidency in 1825 also marked the end of a political dynasty. Monroe was the last member of the Virginia **triumvirate**—Jefferson, Madison, and Monroe—to serve as president. Each of these men played important roles in the formation and early history of the Republic; each was a founder of the Democratic-Republican opposition to the Federalists and a leader during its rise as a governing party. Monroe was the last of the revolutionary presidents, the generation that had won the War of Independence. The Democratic-Republicans no longer were led by national figures whose stature could hold the party together.

Ironically, political unity became all the more difficult to achieve because of the extraordinary electoral success of the Democratic-Republican Party. Mobilizing popular support for a governing party requires a believable opponent. Yet during Monroe's first term as president, the Federalist Party disappeared as a national organization. Monroe was unopposed for reelection in 1820. The Era of Good Feelings followed the second war with England, between 1815 and 1824, when Democratic-Republican dominance over the nation was unquestionable.

With the Federalists vanquished, the 1824 presidential election became a contest of individuals, not issues. Rival and sectional leaders, each supported by his own personal organization and following, contested for the presidency in one of the most bitter and fragmented elections ever staged. The results of this contest caused a storm of controversy and led to a revolt against party procedures that had prevailed for a quarter century. Moreover, John Quincy Adams, the eventual winner, inherited an impossible governing situation, one that ended the Democratic-Republican era amidst bitter conflicts that endured for a generation.

See also: Adams, John Quincy, Administration of (1825–1829); Madison, James, Administration of (1809–1817).

Further Reading

Hart, Gary. *James Monroe*. New York: Times Books, Henry Holt and Company, 2005.

A–Z

National Security Council

Organization within the Executive Office of the President (EOP) that supports the president in diplomatic and foreign affairs. In the decades following World War II (1939–1945), the EOP assumed an increasingly important role in all aspects of the management of foreign and defense policy. A key vehicle used by most presidents to expand their authority in these areas has been the National Security Council (NSC).

Formally, the NSC is composed of the president, the vice president, and the secretaries of state and defense, with the director of central intelligence and the chairman of the Joint Chiefs of Staff serving as advisers. It is the highest-level advisory body to the president on military and diplomatic issues.

The National Security Council was established in 1947 to help the president coordinate the actions of government agencies into a single cohesive policy for dealing with other nations. Many members of Congress saw the new panel also as another institutional check on President Harry S. Truman's (1945–1953) power in the areas of foreign affairs and defense. The council has acted as a true decision-making body on only a few important occasions. In 1956, for example, members of the NSC helped formulate President Dwight D. Eisenhower's (1953–1961) response to the Soviet invasion of Hungary.

Instead, the prime significance of the NSC has stemmed from its development into an apparatus used by presidents to implement their personal visions of U.S. foreign policy. The NSC staff is composed of policy experts who analyze foreign policy issues and make recommendations to the president. Presidents have turned to the NSC because it is subject to little effective control from Congress and is without the independent institutional loyalties frequently evident in the State, Defense, and other departments.

The role of the NSC has varied greatly over the years, usually depending on the personal influence of the president's national security adviser, who heads the NSC staff. When the national security adviser has been a relatively weak figure within the government, the NSC staff has been merely a bureaucratic shell with little power. At other times, however, it has been the dominant institutional force in setting foreign policy. This was the case under President Richard M. Nixon's (1969–1974) national security adviser, Henry A. Kissinger.

Since Kissinger's term as national security adviser, a debate has raged about how much independent authority the NSC staff should exercise. Many experts in the area of foreign policy argue that the NSC staff should be limited to managing the flow of information and policy options from the departments to the president. However, some former national security advisers argue that the NSC and its staff should have considerable authority to help the president define overall policy and to control the departments to ensure that this policy is carried out.

Origins and Development of NSC

Formation of the NSC represented the first institutional attempt in U.S. history to foster coordination and cooperation among the organizations contributing to U.S. national security policy. Before the NSC's formation, the president was essentially the only person able to impose harmony on the often opposing positions and actions of the State and War Departments and other agencies.

The conflicts and lack of coordination among the military services and civilian agencies during

World War II convinced many government officials that a fundamental reorganization of the national security structure was needed. This realization led in 1947 to passage of the National Security Act, landmark legislation that created the Defense Department out of the old War and Navy Departments. The act also established the Central Intelligence Agency (CIA).

Passage of the National Security Act was marked by bitter debate in Congress and in the services about the creation of a single military command system. Nevertheless, the law's provisions establishing the NSC as a permanent agency for policy coordination enjoyed broad support. According to the act, the purpose of the NSC was to "advise the president with respect to the integration of domestic, foreign, and military policies relating to the national security."

In its early years under President Truman, the NSC was not a major factor in the formulation of foreign and defense policy. Truman viewed the council as only an advisory body and rarely attended its meetings. President Eisenhower, by contrast, carried out a major expansion and institutionalization of the NSC. Perhaps most important, he appointed an assistant to the president for national security affairs—a position not mentioned in the 1947 act—to head the council staff. He frequently attended NSC meetings, moreover, and relied on the council's advice during times of international crisis.

Eisenhower's heavy reliance on the NSC led to complaints from the Senate Government Operations Committee and others that the council had become "overinstitutionalized." President John F. Kennedy (1961–1963) came into office determined to rely more on a small group of personal advisers than on the NSC bureaucracy. Although Kennedy worked closely with his national security adviser, McGeorge Bundy, he ordered a substantial reduction in the NSC's staff and responsibilities. President Lyndon B. Johnson (1963–1969) followed a pattern similar to Kennedy's. Although the NSC system as a whole was not a major factor in determining policy, Walt W. Rostow, who became national security adviser in 1966, played an important role in encouraging Johnson to order a major escalation of the Vietnam War (1964–1975).

The role of the NSC underwent a radical change under Nixon and his national security adviser, Kissinger. The NSC staff tripled in size, to about fifty high-level professional experts, and it wielded **unprecedented** power within the Washington bureaucracy. Kissinger himself became the coarchitect of Nixon's key foreign policy moves, including the negotiated end to the Vietnam War, the opening to the People's Republic of China, and the onset of détente with the Soviet Union.

Kissinger enlarged the power of his office in two major ways. One was by shifting from the strictly advisory role played by his predecessors to an active involvement in diplomatic negotiations. Beginning in 1969, for example, he engaged in secret diplomacy with the North Vietnamese, holding private talks with enemy leaders in Paris that eventually led to a peace settlement. Even more dramatic was his secret trip to China in 1971. At that point, Nixon and Kissinger were ready to end the decades-old hostility of the United States toward the Communist Chinese regime, but they were unwilling to reveal their intentions to the world. On a trip to Pakistan, Kissinger eluded the press and observers and flew unnoticed to Peking, where he met with Communist leaders. After Kissinger returned to the West, Nixon made an announcement that shook world power diplomacy: the potential alliance of the United States and China against the Soviet Union.

Kissinger also succeeded in completely overshadowing Nixon's secretary of state, William P. Rogers. He worked to exclude Rogers from key information and negotiations, resulting in a strong personal and institutional antagonism that affected relations between subsequent national security advisers and secretaries of state.

The conflict between the national security adviser and the secretary of state ended for a time when, in 1973, Kissinger assumed the latter post while retaining the former. Tensions resumed at a relatively low level when Gerald R. Ford (1974–1977) became president following Nixon's resignation in 1974. In November 1975, Kissinger relinquished his position as Ford's national security adviser to Lieutenant General Brent Scowcroft. Scowcroft viewed his responsibilities primarily in terms of coordinating and overseeing foreign policy actions. He did not attempt to challenge Kissinger's dominance in determining foreign policy.

A-Z

DECISION MAKERS

Henry Kissinger (1923–)

Henry Kissinger became President Richard Nixon's (1969–1974) national security advisor in 1968 after having been a foreign policy consultant for the John F. Kennedy (1961–1963) and Lyndon B. Johnson (1963–1969) administrations and a Harvard professor. During his term as national security advisor, Kissinger was involved in many negotiations with China, Vietnam, and other nations. Before Nixon made his visit to China in 1972, Kissinger met twice with Premier Zhou Enlai, who was in charge of Chinese foreign policy. These meetings paved the way for the 1972 visit, which led to the formation of an alliance and diplomatic relations between the United States and China.

When Nixon was elected president in 1968, the Vietnam War was a major issue. In order to assist Nixon with keeping his campaign promise of "peace with honor", Kissinger helped him to put his new policy of "Vietnamization" into effect. This policy involved slowly taking troops out of Vietnam and allowing the Army of the Republic of Vietnam to take over the fight.

When Nixon appointed Kissinger secretary of state in 1973, Kissinger kept his position as national security advisor. In his new role, Kissinger continued to oversee influential negotiations, such as those between Israel, Egypt, and Syria that ended the Yom Kippur War (1973).

Throughout his tenure as both national security advisor and secretary of state, Kissinger promoted a policy called détente, especially when it came to relations between the United States and the Soviet Union. This type of foreign policy involved the decreasing of tension between two powers by the use of diplomacy. By using détente, Kissinger was able to negotiate many agreements and treaties that promoted peace between the rival powers.

After Gerald R. Ford (1974–1977) assumed the presidency, much of the public began to dislike the détente policy, claiming that the United States was becoming too friendly with countries that violated Americans' concept of basic human rights. Kissinger became very unpopular when he encouraged the U.S. government to remain friendly with anti-Communist dictatorships in Latin America. In the end, détente failed, bringing about the reversal of many of Kissinger's peace agreements. He left his position as secretary of state in 1977 and returned to teaching.

President Jimmy Carter (1977–1981) came into office proclaiming his intention to place more responsibility in the departments and agencies while reducing the policy-making role of the NSC. Almost from the start, however, sharp conflicts arose between National Security Adviser Zbigniew Brzezinski and Secretary of State Cyrus R. Vance. Not content with being a mere facilitator of the policy views of others, Brzezinski was determined to assert his views, which centered on a policy of hard-line confrontation with the Soviet Union. Carter did not indicate whether he agreed with Brzezinski or with Vance, who stressed mutual co-operation and arms control agreements with the Soviets. As a result, the American public and foreign governments frequently were left in confusion about which man truly reflected U.S. foreign policy. Finally, however, Vance resigned in protest against the unsuccessful 1980 attempt to conduct a military rescue of American hostages held in Iran, leaving Brzezinski with more influence over foreign policy during the last year of Carter's presidency.

Ronald Reagan (1981–1989) assumed the presidency affirming cabinet government as his model. Although Reagan was somewhat more willing than his immediate predecessors to hold formal NSC meetings with the vice president and secretaries of state and defense, he de-emphasized the role of the NSC staff and dismantled much of the elaborate system of NSC staff committees that analyzed and formulated policy. He did not move to establish a formal NSC structure until 1982. At the same time, he designated the secretary of state as his principal foreign policy adviser.

During his first six years in office, Reagan had four national security advisers, who were viewed in Washington as relatively weak figures, lacking either strong foreign policy experience or close ties to the president. In late 1986, Reagan appointed Frank C. Carlucci as national security adviser, who moved to scale back the power of the NSC staff. Colin L. Powell then served as national security adviser from 1987 until the end of Reagan's presidency.

President George H.W. Bush's (1989–1993) choice for national security adviser, Scowcroft, reflected the characteristics common to all of Bush's foreign policy appointees, whom one writer termed a "mix of professionals and buddies." Scowcroft, a retired lieutenant general, had served as Ford's national security adviser following Kissinger's resignation and had chaired the Scowcroft Commission on arms control in the early 1980s. He was also a trusted associate of the president, dating back to the Ford administration, when Bush served first as U.S. liaison to China and then as director of the CIA.

Unlike Reagan, Bush was actively involved in the formulation and management of national security policy, and he had a collegial and trusting relationship with Scowcroft throughout his term. Scowcroft, like Secretary of State James Baker III and Secretary of Defense Richard B. Cheney, was a powerful player both behind-the-scenes and publicly in an administration whose greatest accomplishments were in foreign policy, particularly in the mobilization of a multinational coalition against Iraq during the 1991 Persian Gulf War. Although Scowcroft restored an image of purpose and accountability to the NSC, major national security decisions, such as the invasion of Panama, continued to be made behind closed doors by Bush's collective foreign policy team. Formal NSC meetings were infrequent.

President Bill Clinton's (1993–2001) first national security adviser, Anthony Lake, had been a special assistant to Kissinger in the Nixon White House, resigning in 1970 to protest the secret U.S. invasion of Cambodia. During the Carter Administration, Lake was the director of policy planning at the State Department, and he became one of Clinton's foreign policy advisers during the 1992 campaign. A professor of international relations, Lake was viewed as bringing intellectual depth to the administration's national security strategy, which had taken up little space on candidate Clinton's campaign platform.

Immediately after Clinton took office, his foreign policy team was faced with challenges throughout the world, especially in the Balkans, Somalia, Haiti, Korea, and Iraq. Almost from the outset, the Clinton administration was criticized by the press and members of both parties in Congress for its inconsistent stance on such crises as the escalating violence in Bosnia and the insecure role of U.S. forces in UN peacekeeping operations in Somalia. In contrast to the implementation of foreign policy under the first President Bush, the Clinton team presented a fractured front. Lake had entered the NSC pledging to serve the president as an "honest broker," and although he was respected as a behind-the-scenes policy coordinator, the administration's early foreign policy performance was widely seen as uneven.

Early in Clinton's first term, the NSC deliberative system was restructured to stress the primacy of the economic dimensions of Clinton's post–cold war national security policy and to formalize the interagency decision-making process. The secretary of the treasury and the director of

A – Z

the new National Economic Council (NEC) met with NSC members on high-priority issues before the issues were brought up in formal NSC meetings. Less immediate concerns were covered in meetings of a "deputies committee," headed by the deputy assistant for national security and attended by the deputy chiefs of staff for key agencies. In addition, "working groups" convened over medium-term matters.

In Clinton's second term, Lake was replaced by his deputy, Samuel R. "Sandy" Berger, an old friend of Clinton's. Although involved in policy matters, Berger sought to coordinate rather than compete with Secretary of State Madeleine Albright and Secretary of Defense William Cohen, holding weekly "ABC" luncheons and other regular meetings with them. Berger and Albright spoke as often as thirty times a day and coordinated their public appearances.

Unlike his father, George W. Bush (2001–2009) entered the White House with little background in foreign policy. He selected as head of NSC a trusted friend and professor at Stanford University, Condoleezza Rice—the first woman to hold the national security adviser post. Known for her **conservative** views and her focus on unilateral rather than multilateral foreign policy actions, Rice, who had served as a Russia specialist on George H.W. Bush's NSC staff, also had been the younger Bush's foreign policy adviser during the 2000 presidential race. Because of her close ties to Bush, Rice held her own in the foreign affairs arena with Secretary of State Colin Powell and Secretary of Defense Donald Rumsfeld. Rice saw synthesizing the information flow to the president as her main responsibility. Despite Bush's initial disinclination to focus on world events, the terrorist attacks of September 2001 turned him into a foreign policy president, and Rice became a key player in the country's subsequent war against terrorism.

See also: Commander in Chief; Foreign Policy and the Presidency.

Further Reading

Ditchfield, Christin. *Condoleezza Rice: National Security Advisor.* New York: Franklin Watts, 2003.

Hogan, Michael J. *A Cross of Iron: Harry S. Truman and the Origins of the National Security State, 1945–1954.* New York: Cambridge University Press, 2000.

Inderfurth, Karl F., and Loch K. Johnson, eds. *Fateful Decisions: Inside the National Security Council.* New York: Oxford University Press, 2004.

Wagner, Heather Lehr. *Henry Kissinger.* New York: Chelsea House, 2006.

Nixon, Richard M., Administration of (1969–1974)

Government under the thirty-seventh president of the United States. In 1945, Nixon was persuaded by a California Republican committee to run for Congress. He faced Democratic House member Jerry Voorhis, who had represented his California district for ten years. In a series of debates, Nixon put Voorhis on the defensive by accusing him of being a socialist. Nixon won the election and was reelected in 1948.

Nixon won a Senate seat in 1950. Democrats accused him of employing dirty campaign tactics, but his aggressive campaigning and his huge margin of victory impressed many Republican leaders. He became an early supporter of General Dwight D. Eisenhower (1952–1961) for the 1952 Republican presidential nomination and was chosen as the party's vice-presidential candidate when Eisenhower was nominated.

In September 1952, however, Nixon's vice-presidential candidacy was jeopardized by a *New York Post* story that accused him of using secret funds provided by California business interests for personal expenses. Eisenhower refused to dismiss his running mate but said that Nixon would have to prove that he was "as clean as a hound's tooth." In an emotional televised speech on September 23 viewed by 60 million people, Nixon denied any wrongdoing and said he and his family lived simple lives without the benefit of many luxuries. The address became known as the

"Checkers Speech" because, after admitting that he had accepted the gift of a dog his daughter had named Checkers, he asserted that he would not give it back. The address brought an outpouring of support from the American people and saved Nixon's candidacy.

Dwight Eisenhower's status as a war hero and his pledge to find a settlement to the Korean War (1950–1953) brought victory to the Republican ticket. Four years later Nixon was renominated for vice president, and he and Eisenhower were reelected. As vice president, Nixon was more visible than many of his predecessors. He chaired several domestic policy committees and made numerous trips overseas, including a 1958 good-will tour of Latin America and a 1959 diplomatic visit to Moscow, where he engaged in a famous spontaneous debate with Soviet premier Nikita Khrushchev on the merits of capitalism and communism.

Nixon ran for president in 1960 and received the Republican nomination. He and his Democratic opponent, Senator John F. Kennedy of Massachusetts, engaged in the first televised presidential debates in history. Nixon is considered to have lost the important first debate to Kennedy because he appeared pale and tired on camera. Kennedy (1961–1963) defeated Nixon by a slim 120,000-vote margin and won 303–219 in the electoral college.

After the defeat, Nixon returned to California to practice law. In 1962, he ran for governor but lost to Edmund G. Brown. Following the election, he told reporters that they would not "have Richard Nixon to kick around anymore."

In 1963, he moved to New York City, where he joined a law firm. Nixon's political ambitions remained alive, however, and he continued to give speeches on foreign policy. He campaigned for Republican candidates in 1966 and maneuvered for the 1968 Republican presidential nomination. At the Republican National Convention in Miami in 1968, he was nominated for president on the first ballot. Nixon promised to end the war in Vietnam (1964–1975) and combat rising inflation. In an election that was almost as close as his 1960 loss, Nixon defeated his Democratic opponent, Vice President Hubert H. Humphrey, 301–191 in the electoral college.

President Richard M. Nixon (1969–1974) waves from the steps of the *Spirit of '76* on August 9, 1974, the day after he announced his resignation. He became the first president in the nation's history to resign. (AP Images)

Presidency

Nixon's first priority as president was achieving "peace with honor" in Vietnam. He proposed a plan to "Vietnamize" the war by providing the South Vietnamese military with upgraded training and weaponry, while slowly withdrawing U.S. troops from Indochina. Nixon believed that the South Vietnamese armed forces could be built into a force capable of defending their country from North Vietnamese aggression. While this slow withdrawal was taking place, Nixon ordered several controversial military operations, including an invasion of Cambodia in 1970 that increased domestic protests against the war. Nevertheless, the majority of Americans supported Nixon's slow withdrawal. During this period, Nixon's national security adviser, Henry Kissinger, conducted negotiations with the North Vietnamese on ending the war. In January 1973, the Nixon administration finally concluded an agreement that ended direct U.S. participation in the Vietnam War and provided for an exchange of prisoners. Nixon had secretly promised South Vietnamese president Nguyen Van Thieu that the United States would not allow his regime to be overthrown by the communists. These commitments, however, would not be met. The communists conquered the South in 1975 after Nixon had left office and Congress had placed strict limitations on U.S. military activities in Southeast Asia.

The most notable successes of the Nixon administration came in relations with China and the Soviet Union. In 1972, he became the first American president to travel to the People's Republic of China. His summit meeting with Chinese leaders signaled a new beginning for U.S.-Chinese relations, which had been hostile since the communists came to power in 1949. In 1972, Nixon also became the first sitting president to travel to Moscow. His summit with Soviet leader Leonid Brezhnev was the result of a relaxation of tensions between the superpowers known as détente. Brezhnev and Nixon signed agreements limiting nuclear weapons and antiballistic-missile systems at the Moscow summit. The Soviet leader returned Nixon's visit in June 1973, when he came to Washington, D.C., for a summit meeting.

On of Nixon's most significant domestic policy actions was his imposition of **wage and price controls** on August 15, 1971. Nixon took this drastic measure to combat rising inflation that he thought might threaten his reelection chances in 1972. The controls initially slowed inflation, but their removal late in Nixon's presidency, combined with a jump in the price of oil caused by an Arab oil **embargo,** led to sharp increases in **inflation.** Prices rose 6.2 percent in 1973 and 11.0 percent in 1974.

The 1971 wage and price controls allowed Nixon to stimulate the economy in 1972 without fear that inflation would skyrocket. With unemployment falling, peace at hand in Vietnam, and the memory of Nixon's dramatic 1972 trips to China and the Soviet Union fresh in the minds of voters, the president was reelected in a landslide. Democratic challenger Senator George McGovern of South Dakota won only Massachusetts and the District of Columbia.

Despite Nixon's overwhelming election victory, his second term soon became consumed by the Watergate scandal. On June 17, 1972, during the presidential campaign, five men with ties to the Committee for the Reelection of the President (dubbed "CREEP" by Nixon's opponents) were arrested while breaking into the Democratic National Committee headquarters in the Watergate Hotel complex in Washington, D.C. Investigations of the burglary and the White House's attempt to cover up its connections to the burglars led to disclosure of numerous crimes and improprieties committed by members of the Nixon administration. Nixon claimed he was innocent of any wrongdoing, but evidence showed that he had participated in the cover up of illegal administration activities. In July 1974, the House Judiciary Committee recommended to the full House that Nixon be impeached for obstruction of justice, abuse of presidential powers, and contempt of Congress.

On August 9, 1974, Richard Nixon became the first president ever to resign from office. Vice President Gerald R. Ford became president. Nixon had chosen Ford to replace his first vice president, Spiro T. Agnew, who had resigned in 1973 because of a scandal unrelated to Watergate. Nixon did not have to face criminal proceedings, however, because on September 8, President Ford (1974–1977) granted him a "full, free, and absolute pardon."

After leaving the presidency, Nixon wrote extensively about his time in office and world affairs. Although he remained tainted by the Watergate scandal, he came to be regarded as an elder statesman by many Americans because of his successes in foreign policy. Presidents of both parties and other officials often asked his advice on dealing with the Soviets and other matters. Nixon died April 22, 1994, at age eighty-one.

See also: Ford, Gerald R., Administration of (1974–1977); Johnson, Lyndon B., Administration of (1963–1969); Gerald R. Ford's Pardon of Richard Nixon, 1974, in the **Primary Source Library;** Watergate Scandal.

Further Reading

Black, Conrad. *Richard Nixon: A Life in Full.* New York: PublicAffairs Books, 2007.

Drew, Elizabeth. *Richard M. Nixon.* New York: Times Books, 2007.

Oath of Office

The Presidential oath of office, as stated in Article II, Section 1, of the Constitution is:

> **B**efore he enter on the Execution of his Office, he shall take the following Oath or Affirmation:—"I do solemnly swear (or affirm) that I will faithfully execute the Office of President of the United States, and will to the best of my Ability, preserve, protect and defend the Constitution of the United States."

The oath is taken by the president-elect on inauguration day, January 20 of the year after the election. The oath is also taken when a sitting vice president assumes the presidency should that office become vacant due to death, disability, or resignation.

Virtually no debate or discussion accompanied the writing of the president's oath by the Constitutional Convention. The first half of the oath was proposed by the Committee of Detail on August 6: "I solemnly swear (or affirm) that I will faithfully execute the office of President of the United States of America." On August 27, George Mason and James Madison (1809–1817), both from Virginia, moved that the phrase "and will to the best of my judgment and power, preserve, protect and defend the Constitution of the United States" be added to the oath. James Wilson of Pennsylvania objected that a special presidential oath was unnecessary,

but Mason and Madison's motion passed handily. On September 15, the delegates substituted "abilities" for "judgment and power," but no discussion is recorded that explains this change.

Departing from the practice that prevailed in most of the states, the convention barred the imposition of religious oaths on the president and other officials of the national government. At that time, some state constitutions required an adherence to Christianity as a condition for serving as governor, others to Protestant Christianity. North Carolina, for example, insisted that its governor affirm the existence of God and the truth of Protestantism and hold no religious beliefs that were opposed to the "peace and safety" of the state. On August 30, Charles Pinckney of South Carolina moved that "no religious test shall ever be required as a qualification to any office or public trust under the authority of the U. States." Roger Sherman of Connecticut said he thought the proposal was "unnecessary, the prevailing liberality being a sufficient security agst. [against] such tests." Nonetheless, Pinckney's motion was approved. The oath of office has remained unchanged since the founding of the nation.

Obama, Barack, Administration of (2009–)

See Election of 2008.

A–Z

O'Connor, Sandra Day

See Bush v. Gore (2000).

Office of Management and Budget

The **executive** office that assists the president with developing and managing the federal budget. In 1970, President Richard M. Nixon (1969–1974) changed the name and modified the function of the Bureau of the Budget (BOB). Emphasizing the management roles of the budget agency, Nixon renamed it the Office of Management and Budget (OMB). As the word *management* implies, new emphasis was placed on providing departments with advice on ways to improve their efficiency to reduce the costs of their operations.

Nixon specifically assigned four major roles to OMB. First, it was to continue many of BOB's functions, especially writing the federal budget. Second, it was to serve as a clearinghouse for new programs and legislation. Third, Nixon wanted some part of the Executive Office of the President to have the ability to track legislation as it moved through Congress. OMB was vested with this capacity. Fourth, OMB was given the specific authority to provide management advice to the various departments and agencies. Since its inception, OMB has served as the centerpiece of presidential budgeting.

Although the president's budget is not submitted to Congress until the February before the first day of the new fiscal year (October 1), the presidential budget process begins at least nineteen months before submission of the finished budget proposal. The budget cycle begins in early spring with OMB informing the departments of the fiscal outlook and the spending priorities of the president. During the summer, the OMB director issues specific revenue projections and imposes specific guidelines for departmental spending. On September 1, agencies submit their initial budget requests to OMB. OMB then holds formal hearings on these requests at which departmental offi-cials justify their proposed budgets before OMB examiners.

OMB's director examines the entire budget from November 1 to December 1. Often the director will invite the National Security Council, the Council of Economic Advisers, and several White House aides to participate in the review. The OMB director makes final decisions subject to the economic forecast for the coming fiscal year and communicates these decisions to the departments. The departments may appeal the decisions directly to the president. Usually, however, each department will revise its formal budget to coincide with the budget director's wishes, for presidents rarely reverse their budget directors' decisions.

Congress receives the first official hint of what the president wants in the State of the Union address at the end of January, and specifics are then spelled out in the president's budget message in February. Pending approval by Congress, the budget goes into effect with the new fiscal year, October 1.

Current Services Budget

Under the provisions of the 1974 Congressional Budget and Impoundment Control Act (PL 93–344), presidents must submit two budget proposals. When they submit their budget for the upcoming fiscal year, they must also submit, through the supervision of OMB, a *current services budget.* The current services budget provides Congress with an indication of the cost of existing budget obligations and a guide for evaluating additional budget proposals. Specifically, the current services budget includes the "proposed budget authority and estimated outlays that would be included in the budget for the ensuing fiscal year . . . if all programs were carried on at the same level as the fiscal year in progress . . . without policy changes."

Uncontrollable Spending

In any given year, much of OMB's current service estimates can be classified as *uncontrollable spending*—that is, expenditures mandated by current law or some previous obligation. Any changes to the spending on these mandated programs require congressional action. By 1995, 64 percent of the federal budget could be classified as uncontrollable spending. These expenditures can be broken down into three major categories.

The first category, fixed costs, consists of legal commitments made by the federal government in previous years. These commitments require the government to spend whatever is necessary to meet these expenses. The largest and most important component of this category is interest on the national debt. Another fixed-cost expenditure is public housing loans. Fixed costs are "uncontrollable" because they can be eliminated only by extreme measures such as default.

The second category is large-scale government projects that require long-term financing. These multiyear contracts and obligations include the building of dams, weapons systems, aircraft, and the space shuttle. Many of these projects are reviewed annually, and expenditure levels are occasionally modified. For example, in 1994 funding was reduced for the space program. Historically, however, most are not.

The third category of expenditures officially designated as uncontrollable is the largest. These programs, called "entitlements," commit the federal government to pay benefits to all eligible individuals. Any attempt to control these expenditures would require changing the laws that created them. Entitlements include Social Security, Medicare, Medicaid, Supplemental Security Income, food stamps, public assistance, and federal retirement pensions. In some cases, the federal government pays individuals directly; in other cases, the states determine eligibility and administer the programs. Most of these programs have no limit on the amount of spending they may entail. As more people become eligible for benefits, expenditures increase.

As uncontrollable spending has pushed federal budget deficits higher, presidents have tried to reduce such expenditures. Richard Nixon and Gerald R. Ford (1974–1977), for example, attempted to decrease entitlement expenditures by restricting eligibility and establishing a limit on benefit increases for several programs. In his first full

budget year, Ronald Reagan (1981–1989) proposed an entitlement cut of $11.7 billion. His budget proposal reflected the frustration that many presidents have felt in attempting to deal with uncontrollable expenditures. It said in part, "The explosion of entitlement expenditures has forced a careful reexamination of the entitlement or automatic spending programs. . . . When one looks behind the good intentions of these programs, one finds tremendous problems of fraud, waste, and mismanagement. Worse than this, the truly needy have not been well served."

Controllable Spending

The president does have some control over several categories of expenditures. Expenditures that can be classified as controllable are used for salaries and fringe benefits for both civilian and military personnel. Although these expenses technically fit the category of controllable expenditures, the practical problems surrounding spending on salaries and fringe benefits make it difficult for a president to control them completely. Seniority and civil service rules protect so many federal employees that it is futile to attempt meaningful cutbacks in expenditures going to salaries.

A second category of controllable federal expenditures is the general operating expenses of the various departments and agencies. Although conservation measures can be applied to such things as heating, cooling, electricity, transportation, and supplies, expenses will always continue if operations continue. In addition, operating expenses usually increase as inflation increases.

The third category of controllable expenditures is research and development. Medical research, weapons research, and grants to state and local governments make up a large proportion of controllable expenditures. Again, budget cuts can be made in this category, but only within limits. As a result, even the controllable categories of the federal budget give the president little latitude in budget decisions.

See also: Chief Executive; Impoundment Powers.

A–Z

PACs (Political Action Committees)

Committees created to raise and distribute money for political purposes. Political action committees, popularly known as PACs, have been controversial in recent years because of their explosive growth, negative campaign tactics, special-interest messages, and limited accountability. Potential presidential candidates often form their own "leadership" PACs to make political contacts and explore the possibility of running. For the most part, however, PAC influence is limited to congressional and state campaigns. PACs account for a tiny fraction of all spending in presidential elections.

Many PACs are affiliated with corporations, trade and professional associations, or labor unions. Others are based on a political cause or issue. Between 1974 and 1988, the number of PACs grew from 608 to 4,268. Since then the number has never varied by more then a few hundred organizations from year to year, with 4,184 registered in 2004. PAC contributions to or independent spending for federal candidates have continued to grow—from $77.4 million in 1978 to $842.9 million in 2004, with a substantial percentage going to congressional campaigns.

The PAC that provided the most money to federal candidates in 2004 was the National Association of Realtors Political Action Committee. Other leading donors were PACs for the National Automobile Dealers Association, the International Brotherhood of Electrical Workers, and the National Beer Wholesalers Association.

Leadership PACs

Much more important than PAC spending on presidential campaigns are the leadership PACs that would-be candidates create before the election year. These PACs supposedly are designed to promote a wide range of congressional and state campaigns across the country; by law, a PAC must contribute to at least five federal candidates. In reality, however, most of these PAC dollars are used to support the presidential aspirations of the PACs' founders. Because PACs do not have the legal status of campaign organizations, they escape many of the spending and reporting requirements of formal campaign structures.

Among the advantages of leadership PACs over presidential campaign organizations, donors may contribute $5,000 annually to a multi-candidate PAC, but only $2,000 to a presidential campaign. In addition, PACs are not subject to the campaign spending ceilings and other regulations that formal campaign organizations must heed. As recently as 1976, none of the prospective candidates set up their own PACs. Before the 1980 election, however, four of the ten candidates established PACs. Five of nine did so before the 1984 election. By the start of the 1988 election, nine of fourteen candidates had set up PACs, and three others had set up similar organizations. Political scientist Anthony Corrado argues that the preelection-year PAC "fosters inequities" by favoring well-known potential candidates with an ability to raise money early in the election cycle. In this way, candidates with sophisticated fund-raising operations can become favorites for the nomination, leaving behind long-shot candidates.

Pierce, Franklin, Administration of (1853–1857)

Government under the fourteenth president of the United States. The presidency of Millard Fillmore (1850–1853) demonstrated that the Jacksonian

KANSAS-NEBRASKA ACT

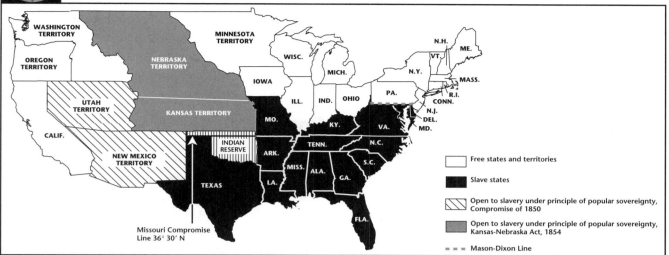

The 1854 Kansas-Nebraska Act, an attempt to solve the country's slavery issue, repealed the Compromise of 1820 and allowed slavery into the western territories. The Act brought the North and the South closer to civil war.

era had irrevocably transformed the presidency. Yet even the strengthened **executive** was no match for the crisis engendered by the slavery question. The final two presidents of this era, Franklin Pierce (1853–1857) of New Hampshire and James Buchanan (1857–1861) of Pennsylvania, were weak leaders who sought vainly to hold the northern and southern factions of the Democratic Party together. Each tried to diffuse, rather than come to terms with, slavery as a political issue. The nation's polarization over slavery was only aggravated by the efforts of Pierce and Buchanan to put the issue aside.

The Kansas-Nebraska Act of 1854 was the most telling failure of Pierce's attempt to calm sectional conflict. This legislation, the brainchild of influential Illinois senator Stephen Douglas, was an effort to bury the slavery question by resting the determination of slavery's status in a new territory on the principle of **popular sovereignty.** According to this principle, the people of the new territory would decide whether or not they would have slavery as soon as they obtained a territorial legislature. Because the Kansas-Nebraska Act would apply popular sovereignty to the Great Plains territory of Kansas and Nebraska, the central part of the 1820 Missouri Compromise, which prohibited slavery north of Missouri's southern boundary, latitude 36° 30',

would be repealed. The debate over this **bill** dragged on for three months, and Pierce made every effort to employ the power of his office, including **patronage,** to ensure its passage. Party discipline prevailed.

On May 25, 1854, the Kansas-Nebraska bill passed the Senate by a comfortable margin and was signed into law by Pierce. Within six months, however, it became apparent that the repeal of the Missouri Compromise had aggravated, not quelled, the slavery controversy and had divided the Democratic Party. Ironically, Pierce's forceful leadership of his party hastened its demise as a governing institution. A new political alignment emerged in the election of 1856. The collapse of the Whigs after 1852 and the northern crusade against slavery in Kansas (that Nebraska would become a free territory was never in doubt) led to the emergence of a new party dedicated to saving the West from slavery. Offering a platform that stood squarely against any further expansion of slavery, the newly formed Republican Party nominated John C. Fremont for president in 1856. The Republicans made a good showing, but they received no support in the South and were not yet sufficiently organized in the North to overcome this handicap. Winning his home state of Pennsylvania, as well as Indiana, New Jersey, California, Illinois, and all 112 of the southern electoral votes, the Democratic candidate, James Buchanan, was elected president.

Pocket Veto

The authority of the president to ignore **bills** passed by Congress after the legislature has **adjourned.** The Constitution specifically mentions the **veto,** as well as the method to be used for congressional override. However, like much of the Framers' handiwork, minor provisions have evolved over time into major constitutional battles between Congress and the presidency. One of the most heated of these battles has been over what is now known as the pocket veto.

Constitutional Provision

The Constitution gives the president ten **legislative** days (excluding Sundays) to sign a bill into law or return it to Congress with a veto message. A bill not approved or vetoed by the president becomes law after ten days "unless the Congress by their Adjournment prevent its Return, in which Case it shall not be a Law" (Article I, Section 7). This provision apparently was meant to make it possible to ward off last-minute actions by Congress that might prove dangerous or foolhardy. The president cannot possibly veto and return bills to Congress as prescribed in the Constitution if Congress already has left for home after adjournment, so the Framers determined that under such circumstances it was better that any bill left unapproved at adjournment simply die.

A pocket veto results from executive inaction, not anything the president does actively, and the term reflects the notion that the president "pocketed" a bill rather than acted on it. A president technically cannot "issue" a pocket veto: the entire situation occurs simply because Congress has adjourned and the bill cannot be returned with a regular veto message. Even so, many presidents have asserted a right to use the pocket veto as if it were an active power of the office.

The first president to rely on a pocket veto was James Madison (1809–1817), in 1812, and only twice more before 1830 did a president pocket a bill. The incidence of pocket vetoes increased thereafter, especially against the many private

pension bills passed by Congress in the second half of the nineteenth century. The champion of the pocket veto in absolute numbers is Franklin Roosevelt (1933–1945), who pocketed 264 bills, but Grover Cleveland (1885–1889) used the device more frequently (averaging thirty a year in office, compared with Roosevelt's twenty two), largely against the private pension bills for Civil War veterans.

Constitutional Issues

The pocket veto is controversial because Congress and the president often disagree over what constitutes congressional adjournment. The Constitution, as so often is the case, is not clear on this point except for adjournment *sine die* (Latin for "without a day," meaning "without a day being set for meeting again"). Adjournment *sine die* marks the end of a two-year Congress, which itself runs the course of the two-year term of the House of Representatives.

That the pocket veto is constitutional upon adjournment *sine die* is undisputed; the controversy concerns whether its use is constitutional with other types of recesses or adjournments. Any interpretation narrowing its use to adjournment *sine die* alone tends to benefit Congress. A more expansive definition magnifies executive power over legislation, because presidents might be able to defeat bills through inaction whenever Congress takes a recess, such as between sessions of the same Congress or during holidays occurring within any single session.

This question was not an issue during the nineteenth century, because Congress sat in session, on average, only half a year, and calling members back to Washington to override vetoes could take weeks. However, as Congress began to stay in session almost full time and as new technology made communications to and recall of Congress far easier than the Framers ever envisioned, the issue of when the president can legally use the pocket veto grew in importance.

The first real shot in this battle came with the 1929 *Pocket Veto Case,* in which the Supreme Court ruled that President Calvin Coolidge (1923–1929) could pocket-veto an Indian claims bill passed just before a four-month congressional recess. The justices ruled that the term *adjournment* applied to any break in the congressional calendar that prevented the return of a bill within the required ten-day period, in this case adjournment between sessions. The ruling was based in part on the idea that, if Congress was in adjournment, no officer or agent was authorized to receive on behalf of Congress a bill rejected by the president. To close this apparent loophole, both chambers began to appoint "agents"—usually the clerk of the House and secretary of the Senate—to receive presidential veto messages while members were away, thus theoretically negating a president's rationale for a pocket veto. After all, once Congress returned it could deliberate and perhaps override a presidential veto at any time before adjournment *sine die.*

Franklin D. Roosevelt (1933–1945) asserted that this strategy was **unconstitutional** when he declared a pocket veto of a bill passed before Congress went on a three-day recess. However, the Supreme Court ruled in 1938 that pocket vetoes could not occur during such brief recesses if the appropriate agents had been so named by Congress. Regular veto procedures, the justices argued, gave the president enough time to consider a bill *and* gave Congress the opportunity to respond, so the use of agents to receive veto messages was deemed constitutional. Congress, not surprisingly, made this practice commonplace thereafter.

The issue lay dormant until the early 1970s, when Richard Nixon's (1969–1974) application of the pocket veto again sparked controversy about what kind of congressional adjournment "prevents" regular veto procedures. Despite the 1938 ruling, Nixon declared in 1970 that he would use a six-day holiday recess to pocket the Family Practice of Medicine Act, which provided funds for medical training. Congress had passed the bill unanimously, had appointed agents to receive presidential messages, and arguably would have overridden a regular veto, but Nixon did not give Congress the chance to respond.

Nixon created a furor when he asserted that the short recess was analogous to adjournment *sine die.* Members of Congress countered that the bill had indeed become law because Nixon could not pocket a bill during the recess, and Senator Edward M. Kennedy (D-MA) subsequently brought suit against the administration. Kennedy's case was upheld by a U.S. court of appeals, which es-

sentially reaffirmed the 1938 Supreme Court decision. The Nixon administration chose not to make appeal ruling to the Supreme Court.

Senator Kennedy figured in a similar lawsuit after President Gerald Ford (1974–1977) declared a pocket veto against a bill passed just before the intersession break of the Ninety-third Congress. Once again, a federal court of appeals overturned a lower court decision and ruled that the pocket veto cannot be used except after adjournment *sine die* so long as both chambers appoint agents. The Ford administration announced that it would abide by the ruling.

Despite these **precedents,** in 1983 Ronald Reagan (1981–1989) reasserted a more expansive view when he declared a pocket veto of a bill barring U.S. aid to El Salvador. The legislation had been passed just before the end of the first session of the Ninety-eighth Congress. Like Nixon and Ford, Reagan administration officials argued that the pocket veto applied to any congressional recess longer than three days. And, just as before, many in Congress declared that the device applied only to adjournment *sine die.* Thirty-three House Democrats sued the administration, and a U.S. court of appeals in 1984 again reversed a lower-court decision and reaffirmed the standard set in 1938. The administration appealed the decision to the Supreme Court, which in January 1987 declared the particulars of the case moot (since the dispute over aid to El Salvador had long passed) and upheld the decision of the court of appeals. Both sides voiced disappointment that the high court had not settled the matter conclusively.

President George H.W. Bush (1989–1993) confused the issue further. In August 1989, with Congress out on a summer recess, Bush declared a pocket veto of a minor bill that would have expedited the signing of legislation to bail out the nation's failing savings and loan industry. In doing so, Bush became the first president since Nixon to pocket a bill during a **legislative** session. In November 1989, Bush declared a pocket veto of a bill to allow dissident Chinese students to remain in the United States, but nonetheless returned the bill with a "memorandum of disapproval" outlining his objections. The Senate failed to override this "veto."

The Bush administration defended its actions on the basis of the *Pocket Veto Case* of 1929, which had upheld the use of the pocket veto during short congressional recesses. However, many in Congress—especially Democrats—looked instead to the series of more recent federal appeals court cases that had limited the pocket veto to adjournment *sine die,* and in 1990 they responded to Bush's actions with legislation that would codify these rulings. This bill was approved along party-line votes by the House Judiciary Committee and the House Rules Committee, but the legislation failed to get to the floor of either chamber.

What constitutes constitutional application of the pocket veto thus remains a point of contention between a Congress eager to protect legislative privileges and presidents equally keen to find ways to kill unwanted legislation. Thus, the issue of the pocket veto may not be settled until the Supreme Court acts.

See also: Line-Item Veto; Presidency and Congress.

Political Parties and the President

Presidents and their role as party leader. The presidential role of party leader emerged outside of the Constitution established in 1787. National political parties were not a part of the political order. Moreover, the Founders were generally antagonistic toward them. George Washington (1787–1789), the first president, stood second to no one in upholding this position.

Emergence of Political Parties

Nevertheless, almost immediately after the new government took effect, political parties appeared on the national scene. At least in part, the origins of political parties could be found in the division within the newly formed cabinet convened by President Washington. This division pitted the secretary of the treasury, Alexander Hamilton, against the secretary of state, Thomas Jefferson (1801–1809).

Their conflict had roots in ambition, interest, and ideology. Each saw himself as heir to President Washington. Moreover, each realized that the new constitutional order provided a skeletal framework for development that would inevitably need to be fleshed out, and their respective visions of what the new nation should become were at odds.

Hamilton favored the urban areas and their resident merchants and financiers; Jefferson idealized the rural setting and saw the real America embodied in the hard-working farmer. Hamilton perceived the need for strong, dynamic national government; Jefferson thought a weak central government more appropriate. During the early years of the Washington administration, conflict between these two principals rocked the cabinet. Among the issues in dispute: assumption of state debts, establishment of a **Bank of the United States,** and the protective **tariff.** The foreign policy differences that arose later only intensified the cleavage.

In the framework created by the Constitution, with its decentralized separation of powers, these disputes could not be contained within the **executive** branch. Inevitably, they extended into Congress and the states. Consequently, the respective Hamiltonian and Jeffersonian interests organized themselves. The Hamiltonians became the Federalists, a name previously used by those who favored **ratification** of the Constitution. Jefferson's followers were called Republicans or Democratic-Republicans.

In contrast to Hamilton, Jefferson was not especially visible in the early stages of this process. Rather, his long-standing ally James Madison (1809–1817), a member of the House of Representatives, propelled their common cause and opposed Hamilton's measures in Congress.

Early Presidents' Attitudes Toward Parties

President Washington viewed these developments with alarm, in keeping with his strong opposition to political parties. He implored Hamilton and Jefferson to resolve their differences, while holding himself above the emerging **partisan** battles dividing the government. The president could not remain unaware, however, to the disputes over policy. Indeed, his office forced him to take a stand. Regularly, he opted for Hamilton's recommendation, even as he denied the legitimacy of partisan conflict. Washington's legacy to presidential party leadership was to reject emphatically its propriety while tentatively embracing its inevitability.

Washington's successor as president, John Adams (1797–1801), found himself in an exceedingly awkward position in the ongoing party conflict. During the Washington administration, Vice President Adams generally had supported Hamilton's public policies. Personally, however, he was far closer to Jefferson than to Hamilton. Adams's vice presidency made him the logical successor when Washington chose to retire after two terms, and the Federalists readily embraced his candidacy in 1796. Nevertheless, he had not played any significant role within the Federalist Party—this was Hamilton's area. Meanwhile, Jefferson was put forward as a candidate by Madison and other Democratic-Republican Party members. Adams won a narrow electoral-vote victory in the first presidential election conducted along party lines.

The third president, Jefferson, is truly the father of presidential party leadership. By the time Jefferson won the presidency in 1800, partisan institutions had begun to take shape. Within the executive branch, appointments to federal positions were being made with party affiliation in mind. Inside the legislature, assemblies or **caucuses** of like-minded members were meeting, not only to plot legislative strategy but also to nominate party candidates for president. Finally, at the state and local level, electoral organizations had formed to secure the selection of candidates to public offices.

The Democratic-Republicans looked clearly to Jefferson for leadership. While sharing many of his predecessors' cautions about presidential party leadership, he nevertheless exercised it in a way that established high expectations of his successors.

Effects of Parties on the Presidency

Before the presidential election of 1804, Congress proposed and the state legislatures **ratified** the Twelfth **Amendment.** The change separated the ballots for president and vice president, allowing presidential electors effectively to vote for party tickets. This amendment fundamentally altered the status of the electors. They quickly lost the independent agent status envisioned by the Framers. Instead, they became instruments of political party will.

In addition, the parties' monopoly over presidential selection had the result of adding a presidential eligibility requirement beyond those enumerated in the Constitution—a party nomination. The expectations and requirements for presidential candidates, which until then had been public service and esteem, came to include not only party affiliation but also party nomination.

In turn, the presence of a party's candidate for president at the head of the party ticket for elective public offices conferred on that individual the status of party leader. Once elected, that person could presume to be something more than the head of the executive branch. Indeed, there was now a basis for claiming government chieftainship, with the idea and organization of party unifying separated national institutions under the leadership of the president.

The emergence of political parties had a profound effect on the executive office. The constitutional principle of separation of powers envisioned a clearly divided governmental structure with three distinct branches: executive, legislative, and judicial. **Checks and balances,** while blurring these divisions, nevertheless were intended to inhibit cooperation by encouraging rivalries among the branches. The appearance of national political parties altered this setting. They provided a foundation and an opportunity for coordination, cooperation, and unity in government.

Modern Presidents and Parties

Political scientist Daniel Klinghard credits two late-nineteenth-century presidents, Grover Cleveland (1885–1889, 1893–1897) and William McKinley (1897–1901), with reviving presidential party leadership. After the turn of the twentieth century, the balance of power continued to shift in favor of the president. Strong, assertive occupants of the White House such as Theodore Roosevelt (1901–1909) and Woodrow Wilson (1913–1921) invigorated the presidency with their personality. An increasing world role for the United States enhanced the visibility and power of the presidential office, and advancing communications technology placed the president increasingly in the spotlight. In keeping with these developments, the president's party leadership position became more commanding.

Franklin D. Roosevelt (1933–1945) ushered in the modern era in president-party relations with his long presidential tenure. In responding to the **Great Depression** and World War II

A - Z

(1939–1945), Roosevelt presided over a dramatic increase in the size and scope of the federal executive. This expansion had important implications for party relations, because Roosevelt came to rely on executive branch personnel to perform many of the political and social service roles that had traditionally been the province of the political party.

Since then, further advancements in communications technology, especially television, have served to connect the president even more directly with the public, thereby weakening the party's traditional position as intermediary between the two. In addition, and partly in response, party identification in the electorate has declined, and party reforms have reduced the power of the party organization in the nomination of the president.

The Presidency and Two-Party Competition

The emergence of parties transformed American political contention. At first, such conflict mainly divided states. Later, these rivalries quickly were supplanted by competition between parties. Moreover, contests pitted two major parties against each other. This promoted consensus by reducing the potential for fragmentation from among thirteen states to between two parties.

The enduringly dualistic character of party competition in the United States is in contrast to the multiparty competition prevalent in many European countries and the absence of party competition in the few remaining communist countries and in many of the nation-states of the developing world. In seeking to explain the two-party phenomenon, scholars have pointed to diverse factors such as tradition, culture, and electoral arrangements.

Early on, the political conflicts in America divided the participants into opposing pairs: patriots versus loyalists, Federalists versus anti-Federalists, Federalists versus Democratic-Republicans. The resulting tradition of two-party competition hindered the emergence of alternatives. The American political culture contributes to the two-party system because it is supportive of accommodation and compromise. The culture encourages diverse interests to ally under a party banner despite significant differences. Absent this spirit of concession, the various groups would likely form their own, separate political

organizations, and a multiparty system would prevail.

Finally, electoral arrangements are critical to understanding the persistence of the two-party system. American elections are for the most part organized on the principle of the single-member district, winner take all. Electoral units designate a single individual—the one who receives the most votes—to occupy a public office. The winner-take-all provision works against minor parties that may win sizable numerical minorities but cannot triumph in an absolute majority over the two entrenched major parties.

See also: Democratic Party (1828–); Federalist Party (1792–1816); Republican Party (1854–); Whig Party (1834–1856).

Further Reading

Adkins, Randall E., ed. *The Evolution of Political Parties, Campaigns, and Elections: Landmark Documents, 1787–2008*. Washington, DC: CQ Press, 2008.

Polk, James, Administration of (1845–1849)

Government under the eleventh president of the United States. The outstanding achievements of James K. Polk's (1845–1849) administration did not come easily. He faced activist Whig minorities in both houses of Congress, and he was elected as the head of a Democratic Party that had begun to reveal the first serious signs of breaking apart as a result of the slavery issue. The conflict over slavery, especially its role in the expanding U.S. territories, was the issue that led to Polk's surprising election to the presidency.

Winning the Nomination

Former President Martin Van Buren (1837–1841) was widely expected to receive the 1844 Democratic nomination, but then the issue of Texas and its **annexation** to the United States, intervened. Just before the nominating conventions of the Whigs and the Democrats, John C. Calhoun,

Tyler's secretary of state, concluded a treaty with the Republic of Texas for its annexation. As a result, the two principal contestants for president, Van Buren and Henry Clay, the leading Whig contender, were forced to announce their views on annexation, an issue that aroused serious disagreements over the desirability of expanding the cotton-growing and slave-holding territory of the United States.

Clay's opposition to annexation caused little controversy, but when Van Buren took the same position, a firestorm erupted in the Democratic Party. The Democrats, and their hero, Andrew Jackson (1829–1837), had long supported territorial expansion, an issue sacred to the emerging frontier interests in the South and the West. To defeat the Whigs, the Democrats needed strong support in the South, where states' rights advocates looked westward to expand slavery. Yet Van Buren, best known as a pragmatic politician, chose to follow what he called "the path of duty" and resist the extension of slavery. His decision cost him his chance to return to the White House. With Van Buren's candidacy seriously wounded, Governor James K. Polk of Tennessee emerged at the deadlocked Democratic convention as a compromise choice between North and South, the first **dark-horse candidate** in the history of American presidential elections.

Reasserting Presidential Power

By a combination of shrewd political maneuvering and forceful statesmanship, Polk was able to overcome successfully the forces that were beginning to dominate U.S. politics during the late 1840s. After winning the Democratic nomination, he stole one of the Whigs' main issues by disclaiming any intention of seeking a second term. Yet during his four years in office, Polk asserted vigorously and effectively **executive** functions that reinforced, even expanded, the Jacksonian conception of presidential power. Most significant, he was the first president to exercise close, day-to-day supervision over the executive departments.

Until Polk, routine and consistent executive influence had been specially absent from the president's relations with the Treasury Department. Presidents never had been granted legal responsibility to oversee the various departmental budget-

ary estimates that were submitted annually to Congress. Instead, in the Treasury Act of 1789 Congress had assigned to the secretary of the treasury the duty to prepare and report estimates of expenditures to the legislature.

George Washington's treasury secretary, Alexander Hamilton, did not even consult the president in this matter. Hamilton was typical, as was Albert Gallatin, who served in the Jefferson and Madison administrations, in taking the initiative in budgetary policymaking. Their successors as treasury secretary only gathered together the departmental estimates and submitted them to Congress in one package. In 1839, for example, Van Buren's secretary of the treasury, Levi Woodbury, denied any responsibility for a composite budget or for a review of budget items submitted to him by other departments.

One of Polk's major achievements was to begin to coordinate the formulation of budgetary policy. For the first time in the history of the presidency, there was an executive budget. Not only did Polk review the budget requests, but he also insisted that the department heads revise their estimates downward. Polk faced the need for tight fiscal control after the Mexican War began in 1846, especially because he was operating under the reduced **tariff** rates of the Walker Act, which he considered one of the major accomplishments of his administration.

Like his fellow Tennessean Andrew Jackson, Polk displayed a strong commitment to limiting government expenditures and a hatred of public debt. Intent upon establishing a record of sound fiscal economy for his administration and determined to assert aggressively the prerogatives of the chief executive, Polk effectively functioned as the director of the budget. That Polk was successful in his efforts to control the budget was demonstrated by the tight rein he imposed on fiscal matters after the end of the Mexican War, directing his secretary of war, William Marcy, to force his bureau chiefs to accept a return to the prewar level of expenditures.

The **precedents** Polk established were not followed by any of his nineteenth-century successors, with the exception of Abraham Lincoln (1861–1865). Polk's assertions of the president's right and duty to control the departmental activities of the executive branch implanted the Jacksonian concept of the presidency more deeply in the American constitutional order.

Polk was only the second president to wield power as commander in chief in wartime, and James Madison, who during the War of 1812 (1812–1814) became the first to assume this role, had done little to reveal the potential of this grant of constitutional authority. Polk did not push the power of commander in chief to its furthest limits; this task was accomplished by Abraham Lincoln during the Civil War (1861–1865). Unlike Madison during the War of 1812, however, Polk did establish the precedent that a president without previous military experience could control his generals. Polk insisted on being the final authority in all military matters.

Polk's efforts as commander in chief were not without **partisan** motivation or serious blunders. A loyal Democrat, he was disconcerted that the war was making a hero of General Zachary Taylor (1849–1850), who was a Whig and potentially a formidable opponent for the Democrats in 1848. In a mean and petty partisan action, Polk refused to sign an order requiring the troops to fire a salute in honor of Taylor's victory in Buena Vista.

The president's relations with the army's top commander, General Winfield Scott, also a Whig, were similarly governed by **partisanship.** Polk attempted, for example, to create a post of lieutenant general for Democratic senator Thomas Hart Benton of Missouri, so that the senator could supersede General Scott as the commanding officer in the field. Benton's military experience was so limited that the Democratic Senate narrowly rejected the president's recommendation.

Polk's problems with his generals could be traced in part to the close relationship between the Jacksonian presidency and the newly institutionalized party system. Partisan practices had become so embedded in presidential politics during the 1830s and 1840s that these practices could not easily be put aside even in wartime.

Notwithstanding the limitations of partisan practices and doctrine, Polk's command of the Mexican War was, on the whole, very able. The general strategy he personally devised and commanded realized a decisive victory by 1848, resulting in the acquisition of New Mexico and California. Thus, Polk obtained the major objective of the war and became, except for Jefferson, the president who brought the most territory under the domain of the United States. By demonstrating that the president as commander in chief could plan and oversee the execution of war strategy, Polk effectively asserted the principle that the president is responsible for the military operations of the United States.

See also: Taylor, Zachary, Administration of (1849–1850); Tyler, John, Administration of (1841–1845).

Further Reading

Seigenthaler, John. *James K. Polk.* New York: Times Books, Henry Holt and Company, 2004.

Popular Sovereignty

See Pierce, Franklin, Administration of (1853–1857); Lincoln, Abraham, Administration of (1861–1865).

Presidency and Congress

The chief officer of the United States and the relationship of the **executive** branch with Congress. The Constitution established a government composed of three separate branches and gave each branch distinct powers and responsibilities. However, it also divided some powers among the **legislative** and executive branches, which has led to continuing struggles between the president and Congress.

Separation of Powers

Article I of the Constitution lays out the specific, or expressed, powers granted to Congress. These include the power to raise and spend money, to declare war, to regulate **commerce,** and to "make all Laws which shall be necessary and proper for carrying into Execution the foregoing Powers." This gives the Congress wide scope for action.

Article II outlines the expressed powers of the executive branch, which are much narrower than those of Congress. The president has the power to appoint a large number of important government officials, including the heads of cabinet departments, ambassadors, and Supreme Court justices. The president may make treaties with foreign powers and is commander in chief of the armed forces. In that role, the president has the power to commission military officers. He or she also has the power to grant pardons for crimes, except in cases where a government official is **impeached,** or charged with crimes or misconduct while in office.

The president can perform many of these functions only with "the Advice and Consent" of Congress. That is, the president must seek approval from the legislature to carry out many of the duties of office. The Senate must approve all presidential nominees for federal offices, except those that Congress grants the president authority to appoint without consent. The Senate must also **ratify** all treaties signed by the president. In each of these cases, **ratification** requires the support of two-thirds of the senators present and voting.

The president also exercises a check over Congress with the power to **veto,** or reject, any bill passed by Congress. The Congress can override a presidential veto if two-thirds of the members of both chambers vote to do so. In this case, the bill becomes law even though the president refused to sign it. The president has ten days after receiving a bill to veto it; otherwise it automatically becomes law. However, if that ten-day period expires after Congress **adjourns,** or suspends its activities, the bill is automatically vetoed. This type of veto, called a pocket veto, cannot be overridden by Congress.

Appointments and Treaties

Virtually every president has faced difficult confirmation battles with the Senate. Presidents with solid political support have generally fared better than those who had to contend with a hostile Senate. Even strong chief executives sometimes have been subjected to embarrassing defeats of their nominees. While such battles dominate the news, they are the exception.

Appointments

In the vast majority of cases, the Senate's power over appointments is little more than a bureau-

cratic formality. In 1993, the first year of Bill Clinton's (1993–2001) presidency, the Senate received more than 42,000 nominations. Over 39,000 of those were routine military commissions and promotions; only about 700 involved high-level positions that might require Senate scrutiny. Some appointments, however, generate considerable controversy and friction between Congress and the president.

In the past few decades, much of this controversy has centered on appointments to the U.S. Supreme Court. President Ronald Reagan (1981–1989) had the opportunity to fill three vacancies on the Court during his two terms of office. His most divisive nominee was Robert Bork, whom Reagan named to replace retiring Associate Justice Lewis Powell in 1987. Civil rights groups strongly opposed Bork, who was critical of major civil rights legislation that Powell had championed while on the Court. In the end, the Senate rejected the nomination. Reagan's successor, George H.W. Bush (1989–1993), also ran into stiff opposition to his nomination of Clarence Thomas to the Court. After a bitter confirmation hearing, the Senate narrowly approved Bush's choice.

Treaties

The clause that clearly gives the president the power to make treaties is unclear on some points. For example, the Constitution never spelled out the Senate procedure for advising the president, nor did it specify at what stage in the treaty-making process the Senate was to advise the president.

In the early years of the nation, the executive branch sought to incorporate Senate advice into the treaty process. It held presidential meetings with senators, allowed the Senate to confirm negotiators, and sent the chamber special presidential messages about treaties. As international relations became more complicated, however, presidents abandoned these various devices to obtain the Senate's advice.

The Senate responded by attaching drastic **amendments,** or formal changes to some treaties, and rejecting others outright. The classic display of senatorial dissatisfaction came in 1919 and 1920. After prolonged debate, the Senate ultimately rejected the Treaty of Versailles, which ended World War I (1914–1918). The treaty also

A – Z

Presidential Appearances Before Congress, 1789–2008

President	Number of appearances	Occasions
Washington	10	8 annual messages (1789–1796); 2 inaugural addresses (1789, 1793; second inaugural before Senate only)
J. Adams	6	4 annual messages (1797–1800); inaugural address (1797); relations with France (1797)
Wilson	26	6 annual messages (1913–1918); tariff reform, bank reform, relations with Mexico (1913); antitrust laws; Panama Canal tolls; relations with Mexico; new tax revenue (1914); impending rail strike (1916); "Peace without Victory" (Senate only); breaking relations with Germany; arming of merchant ships; request for war declaration against Germany (1917); federal takeover of railroads; "14 points" for peace; peace outlook; need for new revenue; request for ratification of women's suffrage amendment (Senate only); armistice (1918); request for approval of Versailles treaty (Senate only); high cost of living (1919)
Harding	7	2 annual messages (1921–1922); federal problems (1921); 2 on the Merchant Marine (1922); coal and railroads (1922); debt (1923)
Coolidge	2	1 annual message (1923); George Washington's birthday (1927)
F. Roosevelt	16	10 annual messages (1934–1943); 100th anniversary of Lafayette's death (1934); 150th anniversary of First Congress (1939); neutrality address (1939); national defense (1940); declaration of war (1941); Yalta conference report (1945)
Truman	17	6 State of the Union messages (1947–1952); prosecution of the war (1945); submission of UN charter (Senate only, 1945); Congressional Medal of Honor ceremony (1945); universal military training (1945); railroad strike (1946); Greek-Turkish aid policy (1947); aid to Europe (1947); national security and conditions in Europe (1948); fiftieth anniversary of the liberation of Cuba (1948); inflation, housing, and civil rights (1948); steel industry dispute (1952)
Eisenhower	7	6 State of the Union messages (1953–1954; 1957–1960); Middle East (1957)
Kennedy	3	3 State of the Union messages (1961–1963)
L. Johnson	8	6 State of the Union messages (1964–1969); assumption of office (1963); Voting Rights Act (1965)
Nixon	7	4 State of the Union messages (1970–1972, 1974); Vietnam policy (1969—separate addresses to House and Senate); economic policy (1971); Soviet Union trip (1972)

Presidential Appearances Before Congress, 1789–2008, *continued*

President	Number of appearances	Occasions
Ford[a]	6	3 State of the Union messages (1975–1977); assumption of office (1974); inflation (1974); state of the world (1975)
Carter	6	3 State of the Union messages (1978–1980); energy program (1977); Middle East talks at Camp David (1978); SALT II arms control treaty (1979)
Reagan	11	7 State of the Union messages (1982–1988); 2 budget addresses (1981); Central America (1983); U.S.-Soviet summit (1985)
G. Bush	5	3 State of the Union messages (1990–1992); budget address (1989); Persian Gulf crisis (1991)
Clinton	9	7 State of the Union messages (1994–2000); budget address (1993); health policy reform (1993)
G.W. Bush[b]	9	7 State of the Union messages (2002–2008); budget address; September 11 terrorist attacks (2001)

Source: Guide to Congress, 6th ed. Washington, D.C.: CQ Press, 2007; CQ Weekly, various issues; John Woolley and Gerhard Peters, The American Presidency Project (online) (presidency.ucsb.edu/ws/?pid=29643), accessed February 2, 2007.
Notes: a. On October 17, 1974, President Gerald R. Ford testified before the Subcommittee on Criminal Justice of the House Judiciary Committee on his pardon of former president Richard Nixon for crimes possibly committed during the Watergate affair. b. Through 2008. Note also that incoming presidents now give a "budget speech" to Congress within weeks of the inauguration. This speech, while not technically a State of the Union address, serves to outline the new president's overall legislative agenda.

Presidents George Washington (1789–1797) and John Adams (1797–1801) gave annual addresses to the members of Congress. The third president, Thomas Jefferson (1801–1809), thought the practice was too similar to the king of Great Britain's addressing Parliament. Rather than appearing in person, Jefferson sent written addresses to Congress. In 1913, President Woodrow Wilson (1913–1921) once again began the custom of appearing before Congress to give the annual State of the Union address.

created the League of Nations, an international body that was the predecessor to today's United Nations (UN). Many senators were opposed to the structure of the proposed League of Nations. They tried to **amend** the treaty to alter the League's structure, but, dooming the treaty to Senate rejection, President Woodrow Wilson (1913–1921) refused to accept their changes.

War Powers

The wording of the Constitution also makes it unclear which branch has the final authority to commit U.S. forces to combat. Article I gives Congress the power "to declare war," while Article II makes the president commander in chief of the armed forces. This distinction has produced a number of conflicts between the branches, and called into question the relevance of Congress's power to declare war.

Congress has declared war only five times in more than 200 years. The last congressional declaration of war occurred shortly after the Japanese attack on Pearl Harbor in December 1941 that brought the U.S. into World War II (1939–1945). Since that time, the U.S. has fought two major wars and dozens of smaller conflicts and multinational military operations. In almost every instance, the president cited national security interests to commit U.S. troops without prior congressional approval. In each case, Congress has—often reluctantly—agreed to support the president's action.

In 1973, Congress passed the War Powers Resolution to try to reclaim its role in the

A – Z

deployment of U.S. troops. The **resolution** required the president to notify Congress before sending troops into battle and to seek congressional approval within forty-eight hours of doing so. It also prevented the president from committing troops for more than ninety days without congressional approval. In practice, the resolution has done little to limit the president's power to deploy the nations' armed forces.

Impeachment

The last section in Article II states simply, "The President, Vice President and all civil Officers of the United States, shall be removed from Office on Impeachment for, and Conviction of, Treason, Bribery, or other high Crimes and Misdemeanors." Article I gives Congress the power both to start **impeachment** proceedings and to determine the guilt or innocence of the accused. Congress has exercised its impeachment power only rarely against the president, but each time it has been accused of using the power for purely political purposes.

One source of controversy concerning the impeachment power is the meaning of the term "high crimes and misdemeanors." The phrase is so vague that it could include any number of charges. When the House impeached President Andrew Johnson (1865–1869) in 1868, the stated reason was Johnson's refusal to follow the Tenure of Office Act. The act prohibited the president from dismissing certain appointed officials without congressional approval. Most historians, however, agree that Johnson's unpopularity with members of his own party in Congress was the driving force behind his impeachment.

Bill Clinton (1993–2001) was also the subject of what many observers considered a politically motivated impeachment attempt. This time, however, it was members of the opposing party who launched the effort. House Republicans impeached Clinton in 1998 after the president lied under oath about a sexual relationship with a White House intern. As with Johnson, the Senate failed to convict Clinton. Unlike Johnson, Clinton remained popular with the American public despite the impeachment attempt.

Divided Government

Tensions between the legislative and executive branches tend to flourish in times of divided government, when one party controls Congress and the other holds the presidency. The impeachment of President Clinton, for example, was the climax of a long and bitter **partisan** battle between the Republican-controlled Congress and the Democratic Clinton administration.

In the first half of the twentieth century, divided government was rare. From 1900 to 1955, there were only eight years in which the same party failed to hold the presidency and both chambers of Congress simultaneously. Since that time, however, divided government has been the rule rather than the exception. Between 1956 and 2009, the same party has controlled the executive and legislature just one-third of the time. It has been during this time that most of the struggles over war powers and many of the most contentious appointment battles have been waged.

However, single party dominance of both the executive and **legislative** branch is no guarantee of friendly relations between the two. Such conflicts have often come at times of strong presidential leadership. Abraham Lincoln (1861–1865), Woodrow Wilson, Theodore Roosevelt (1901–1909), and Franklin D. Roosevelt (1933–1945) had difficulties with their parties' congressional leaders, although all four men were largely successful in enacting their legislative programs.

Congress has also clashed with less aggressive presidents of their own party, usually when attempting to force through its own legislative program. One of the earliest examples came when House Speaker Henry Clay used his political influence to pressure President James Madison (1809–1817) to pass a series of anti-British measures. The move led to war with Britain, a development that Clay favored and Madison opposed.

See also: Impeachment, Presidential; Separation of Powers; The Treaty Power; Veto Power; War Powers Resolution; Watergate Scandal.

Further Reading

Sollenberger, Mitchel A. *The President Shall Nominate: How Congress Trumps Executive Power.* Lawrence: University of Kansas Press, 2008.

Thurber, James A. *Divided Democracy: Cooperation and Conflict Between the President and Congress.* Washington, DC: CQ Press, 1991.

Wright, Jim. *Balance of Power: Presidents and Congress from the Era of McCarthy to the Age of Gingrich.* Nashville, TN: Turner, 1996.

Presidency and the Bureaucracy

The units of the executive branch of the U.S. national government—staffed mainly by unelected public officials—that carry out public policy. The term *bureaucracy* does not appear in the U.S. Constitution, yet the bureaucracy has become one of the most powerful elements of modern American government. In fact, it often is called the "fourth branch" of government because of its prominence in contemporary politics. From their vantage point in the White House, presidents quickly discover that they can accomplish little without help from the bureaucracy. Thus, their relationship with it is one of the most important aspects of any administration.

For many people, the term *bureaucracy* conjures up images of red tape, impersonality, and rigidity, and applies wherever those characteristics are found—from government to universities to large corporations. The Founders probably would be startled by the scope and complexity of today's federal bureaucracy. It did not, however, take its present shape suddenly; the bureaucracy has been evolving for more than two hundred years.

Constitutional Foundations

Although the Constitution barely mentions the **executive** branch and says nothing at all about a bureaucracy, the document is nevertheless crucial to the bureaucracy. The evolution of the bureaucracy has been shaped by what the Founders thought about the executive branch and by what the Constitution says==and does not say—about it. Subsequent constitutional interpretations also have played a role.

The Founders issued relatively explicit guidelines for the presidency, the Congress, and, to a lesser extent, the judicial system, but they said little about how the government's decisions were to be executed or about how the executive branch should be organized. Some delegates to the Con- stitutional Convention suggested, to no avail, that the details of the executive branch be fleshed out. The clauses that were inserted into the Constitution, though brief, did at least set the boundaries for the development of the modern bureaucracy.

The position of the executive branch in the Constitution's overall scheme of government is ambiguous. Article II, section 1, states that "the executive Power shall be vested in a President of the United States of America," but it does not spell out exactly what that power includes. The next section provides only some help by specifying two powers. First, the president "may require the Opinion, in writing, of the principal Officer in each of the executive Departments, upon any Subject relating to Duties of their respective Offices." Second, the president "shall nominate, and by and with the Advice and Consent of the Senate, shall appoint Ambassadors, other public Ministers and Consuls, Judges of the Supreme Court, and all other Officers of the United States, whose Appointments are not herein otherwise provided for, and which shall be established by Law." The second power comes with a condition, however: "The Congress may by Law vest the Appointment of such inferior Officers, as they think proper, in the President alone, in the Courts of Law, or in the Heads of Departments." These few provisions are all that the Constitution says specifically about the executive branch.

Organization of Executive Power

The Founders' relative lack of attention to executive power does not mean that they thought it was unimportant. To the contrary, the short yet turbulent history of the American colonies clearly indicated the critical role of administration. The colonists had suffered "a long train of abuses" at the hands of British administrators and thus had developed an intense distrust of, but a grudging respect for, strong executive power.

America's own attempts at administration also had taught some lessons. The Continental Congress, intent on avoiding the dangers of executive power, had tackled the immense executive task of running the Revolutionary War without outside administrative help. Instead, committees composed of members of Congress had been formed to deal with even the most minor executive issues. Congress quickly

VIEWPOINTS

WEEDING 'EM OUT.

An 1893 cartoon shows President Grover Cleveland (1885–1889, 1893–1897), Secretary of Agriculture Julius Morton, and other members of the administration weeding out the government bureaucracy. (The Granger Collection, New York)

discovered that this system was unwieldy and ineffective, but administration by committees of amateurs serving part-time continued throughout the war and under the government established by the Articles of Confederation.

When they met to construct a new form of government, the Founders were determined to correct the executive situation. Aware of the problems created by administrative committees, they agreed that executive functions should be grouped in a limited number of executive departments, each with a single head. Although the Constitution does not mandate this specific structure, references to "the principal Officer in each of the executive Departments" and "Heads of Departments" support this interpretation. The major disagreement at the Constitutional Con-

vention concerned how heads of departments would be selected and to whom they would be responsible. The delegates decided that the president, with the advice and consent of the Senate, would choose department heads, but they left the question of responsibility unanswered.

Another question left unanswered was the removal of officials appointed by the president with Senate approval: Did the president alone have the power to dismiss such officials? The First Congress (1789–1791) debated this issue at length before narrowly deciding that presidents can remove appointees from office on their own authority. Although that decision makes executive branch officials technically subordinate to the president, Congress still holds tremendous influence.

One major source of influence is the considerable freedom that the Constitution gives Congress in deciding how to organize the executive branch. Congress has the right to create and abolish departments and agencies, to arrange them as it sees fit, and to decide how many employees they have and how those employees are selected. Congress also exerts control over the bureaucracy by **appropriating** money and conducting investigations.

The Constitution grants the president "executive power" to "take Care that the Laws be faithfully executed," but it is ambiguous about what that power and responsibility entail. Congress settled one issue by deciding that the president has the authority to remove appointed officials from office, but much of the relationship between the president and the executive branch hinges on the attitudes and strategies of individual presidents. In this context, the words "executive power," applied to the president by Article II, have been called a "term of uncertain content," the meaning of which can be supplied only by a particular president.

See also: Executive Departments.

Presidency and the Media

The relationship between U.S. presidents and the news media. Through the decades, new forms of media have changed the ways in which people receive information. Beginning in the late seventeenth century, newspapers played an active part in the political debate that surrounded the founding of the United States. The first colonial newspaper, *Publick Occurrences Both Forreign and Domestic,* was published in Boston on September 25, 1690, and its first issue happened to be its last. The *Boston News-Letter,* which followed in 1704, was the first continually published newspaper in colonial America.

While the Constitution was being drafted in the late eighteenth century, the citizens of major cities were able to read in more than one newspaper timely, solid political discussions of the emerging document. In New York, for example, newspapers were available four days a week, and

political information, either by subscription or through quick perusal in taverns or coffeehouses, was plentiful. Indeed, essays by Alexander Hamilton, John Jay, and James Madison in support of the Constitution initially appeared as letters published in New York's *Independent Journal;* they then were reprinted in newspapers around the country. The documents collectively became *The Federalist.*

Executive Use of the Press

All presidents have valued the press. They may have not necessarily liked the people who report or who publish or air the news, but they have understood that the media are an important vehicle for reaching the public. When the first president, George Washington (1789–1797), needed to explain to the public his rationale for leaving his presidency, he did so through the press. His farewell address was not spoken directly to Congress nor was it even presented as a speech. Instead, at President Washington's request it was published as a communication to the people in Pennsylvania's *Daily American Advertiser* on September 19, 1796. Philadelphia was the nation's capital at that time, so Washington chose a local newspaper as his venue. His choice for such an important statement confirmed his high regard for the press as a presidential resource. His successors also have recognized the value of news organizations. When President Ronald Reagan (1981–1989) addressed the American public at the end of his eight years in office, he delivered a televised farewell speech from the Oval Office. He, too, chose the media as the vehicle to deliver his message to the people collectively.

The Modern Presidential News Conference

The most important of the direct exchanges of information between the president and the press is the presidential news (or press) conference. Although each side has complained about the conduct and performance of the other in these exchanges, the news conference has proved to be a durable institution. Woodrow Wilson (1913–1921) convened the first news conference on March 15, 1913, and since then every president has held conferences using a question-and-answer format: reporters ask the questions and presidents respond. The exchange itself has evolved from the "just-between-us" basis in the Wilson administration to the public nature of today's conference, and the evolution from an off-the-record session to an official event has brought with it variations in the way presidents use press conferences.

Many presidents have not been enthusiastic about press conferences and have tried to use them to suit their own purposes. Presidents from Harry S. Truman (1945–1953) through Lyndon B. Johnson (1963–1969) held approximately two news conferences a month. Since President Johnson, there has been little stability either in the numbers or in the location of press conferences; the only presidents to hold at least two conferences a month have been George H.W. Bush (1989–1993) and Bill Clinton (1993–2001). In the administrations of Richard Nixon (1969–1974) and Ronald Reagan (1981–1989), news conferences were reduced to the lowest numbers the presidents and their staffs could manage. As for George W. Bush (2001–2009), it is difficult to compare the frequency of his news conferences and those of previous presidents. Although Bush often answered reporters' questions, especially in joint appearances with foreign leaders, he held no so-called formal news conferences, and the White House halted the practice of numbering presidential news conferences.

Presidential press conferences have endured because presidents and reporters alike have found them to be useful. For the president, the primary distinction of the press conference is its usefulness in advancing policy and electoral goals; it is an opportunity to explain policies and seek support for them. Moreover, conferences can be timed to coincide with **legislative** initiatives or foreign policy events.

The press conference is the closest the president gets to having a conversation with the nation. In response to a reporter's question at one of the gatherings, President Eisenhower (1953–1961) spoke of the importance of the press conference as a communication device:

> The presidency is not merely an institution. In the minds of the American public, the President is also a personality. They are interested in his thinking. . . . At the same time, they believe the President, who is the one official with the Vice President that is elected by the whole country, should be able to speak to the whole country in some way. . . . I believe [what] they want to see is the President, probably, capable of going through the whole range of subjects that can be fired at him and giving to the average citizen some concept of what he is thinking about the whole works. . . . [T]he press conference is a very fine latter-day American institution.

Other than the press conference, there is no established forum where a president regularly submits to questions. Advisers and cabinet officers cannot be expected to engage in the rigorous questioning of the president that reporters favor in press conferences. The president is, however, in a vulnerable position when appearing before correspondents. Reporters and the public may find this an attractive feature of the press conference, but it represents an element of concern for the president and the White House staff. For that reason, as the event has become increasingly public, presidents and their staffs have had to invest a considerable amount of time in preparations for the conference. The presidential briefing books that appeared in the Truman administration have been maintained ever since. Staff members also pose questions to the president in preparatory sessions. Both of these practices reduce the risks the president faces when appearing before reporters. It is fairly easy to predict almost all the questions that will be raised.

Until the George H.W. Bush administration, presidents could reasonably expect their press conferences to be televised, but conferences held in the early afternoon attract much smaller audiences than those held in the evening. Neither Bush nor Clinton favored the evening East Room event, preferring less formal settings. Bush held only two conferences at eight o'clock in the evening, and the second one was not televised by the regular networks because it was too close to the election and network executives believed that "equal time" questions could be raised. With cable television in so many homes today, the networks are no longer willing to commit evening time to a presidential press conference. If people want to watch a press conference, the networks contend, they can tune in to CNN (Cable News Network) or C-SPAN (Cable-Satellite Public Affairs Television).

Reporters also find press conferences useful. The gatherings give them an opportunity to take the president's measure—that is, they learn a great deal about a president as a person when the president must respond publicly and extemporaneously to their questions. The absence of other forums in which the president must respond to questions posed by people outside the administration increases the significance of the presidential news conference. In addition, reporters become part of a presidential event in a news conference. In televised conferences, their colleagues in the press corps, back at the office, and at corporate headquarters can watch them at work.

The Media after 9/11

The president's relationship with the media changed profoundly with the terrorist attacks on America of September 11, 2001. It is not likely to change back any time soon.

The attacks, which took nearly three thousand lives, and the war on terrorism that followed presented new challenges to President George W. Bush and his successors and their need to communicate through the media with the nation and the world. Unlike other wartime presidents, Bush faced a shadowy, suicidal, hate-driven enemy. More even than the Vietnam War (1964–1975), the war on terrorism was a battle for the hearts and minds of people not in a single country but in many lands where American ideals of religious freedom were little understood and even less appreciated.

President Bush recognized that the war on terrorism was more like a third world war than a regional overseas conflict, and he repeatedly warned Americans that they were in for a long siege. At a news conference on March 13, 2002, he told reporters: "I believe this war is more akin to World War II than it is to Vietnam. This is a war in which we fight for the liberties and freedom of our country."

Barely seven months before the September 11 attacks, Bush had seemed unprepared for such a monumental challenge. Besides his tendency to mangle the English language and lack of foreign policy experience, he had lost the 2000 popular vote to Democrat Al Gore by more than a half-million votes. He owed his electoral college victory to a 5–4 Supreme Court decision halting the disputed Florida recount, prompting humorist Mark Russell to quip, "The people have spoken—all five of them."

As commander in chief of the armed forces and as leader of the sole remaining world power, President Bush needed the media's help in overcoming the public's low expectations of his ability to cope with the terrorist threat. By most accounts he succeeded. He assembled a 174-nation coalition to support the U.S. war on terrorism, and within days of the attacks, American troops were in Afghanistan, helping to dismantle the extremist Taliban government and pursue Osama bin Laden, mastermind of the September attacks, and his terrorist al Qaeda network. At home, Bush's public approval ratings soared. For a time, it seemed almost unpatriotic to criticize the president, even on matters unrelated to the war, and administration supporters tried not very subtly to squelch dissent on that basis.

Just as President Bush relied on the media to help rally the nation and its allies behind his war on terrorism, reporters needed his administration's cooperation to cover the war thoroughly without divulging secrets to the enemy or endangering themselves needlessly. Despite the precautions, several journalists were killed covering the war and at least one, Daniel Pearl of the *Wall Street Journal,* was kidnapped and murdered in Pakistan. On the whole, relations between the U.S.-led military and the press were cooperative. Defense secretary Donald H. Rumsfeld won praise for his accessibility and his frequent on-the-record news briefings.

This kind of working relationship was essential in fighting a war of words, ideas, and images. One of the most respected observers of the Middle East, *New York Times* columnist Thomas L. Friedman, returned from that area warning of "a much larger war of civilizations. You can smell it in the incredibly foul wind blowing through the Arab-Muslim world these days." Young Arabs, he pointed out, frustrated "with their own lack of freedom and jobs . . . express themselves in the most heated anti-Israel and anti-American sentiments that I've ever felt."

A–Z

Wars and similar crises underscore the importance of the news media in the U.S. system of government; they are a president's lifeline to the citizenry. Television and radio networks, wire services, newspapers, Internet news sources, and periodicals disseminate presidential statements, chronicle administration actions, and analyze administration programs and progress. They also serve as vehicles for opposing views. Although the mix among statements, facts, analyses, and opinions has varied through the years, the president's need for the news media has remained unchanged.

See also: Commander in Chief.

Further Reading

Cohen, Jeffrey E. *The Presidency in the Era of 24-Hour News.* Princeton, NJ: Princeton University Press, 2008.

Ponder, Stephen. *Managing the Press: Origins of the Media Presidency, 1897–1933.* New York: Palgrave Macmillan, 2000.

Presidency and the Supreme Court

The relationship between the **executive** and judicial braches of government. Judicial decisions usually uphold executive power, just as presidents usually enforce judicial decisions. When conflicts between the president and the judiciary occur, however, they can be dramatic. Accounts of conflicts therefore often dominate discussions of the president and the Court.

Jefferson's Conflicts with the Court

Presidents George Washington (1789–1797) and John Adams (1797–1801) had the opportunity to appoint members of the judiciary who were compatible with their judicial philosophies. When Thomas Jefferson (1801–1809) arrived in office, however, he faced a judiciary that had been stacked against him by the Federalists, who consistently opposed many of his political ideas. Jefferson favored states' rights, but the Marshall Court was attempting to consolidate national powers.

Conflict between Jefferson and the courts developed in at least three areas. The act that resulted in the Supreme Court decision in *Marbury v. Madison* (1803) was Jefferson's order to his secretary of state to withhold a commission from William Marbury. The outgoing Adams administration had appointed Marbury as a justice of the peace, but the commission was not delivered, and Marbury sued. Marshall used his opinion to lecture Jefferson and assert the authority of the judiciary to void acts of legislation that the Court believed to be in conflict with the Constitution. However, Marshall's decision declaring that a **writ of mandamus** could not issue from his Court meant that he made no command that Jefferson might refuse to obey.

The **impeachment** of Justice Samuel Chase was the second occasion for conflict. The Democratic-Republicans moved against Justice Chase in 1803. While riding circuit, Chase had made **partisan** and injudicious remarks criticizing the Democratic-Republicans and their philosophy. As president, Jefferson directed the attention of members of Congress to Chase's behavior. He asked one of them, "Ought this seditious and official attack on the principles of our Constitution and on the proceedings of a State, go unpunished?" Jefferson personally stayed out of the fray, however, proclaiming, "For myself, it is better that I should not interfere."

However justified the Democratic-Republicans must have felt, their action threatened to convert a constitutional provision designed to punish gross malfeasance into a tool to punish officeholders for mere expressions of opinion. Ultimately, Maryland's Luther Martin and other Chase defenders who stood firmly on the Constitution's narrow grounds for impeachable offenses prevailed over Virginia's John Randolph and others who argued for impeachment on broader political grounds. Chase's opponents could muster only nineteen of the twenty-three votes needed for a two-thirds majority, and he was acquitted. Had the trial turned out differently, the Democratic-Republicans might have gone after other justices. This would have seriously threatened the independence of the judiciary as a coequal branch of government.

Two years after the Chase trial, Jefferson battled once again with Marshall. As part of his circuit-riding duties, Marshall presided at the trial in Richmond of Aaron Burr, whose conviction Jefferson favored. Burr was charged with treason—a charge that stemmed from a trip down the Mississippi River that he may have made for the purpose of separating the Southwest from the rest of the country. The evidence against him was sketchy, however, and Marshall insisted on a strict interpretation of the constitutional provision on treason. This insistence resulted in Burr's acquittal. Scholars justly credit Marshall's actions with putting "the American law of treason beyond the easy grasp of political expediency."

Jackson and Constitutional Interpretation

Like Jefferson, Andrew Jackson (1829–1837) was a strong president who left a permanent imprint on the executive branch. Jackson made his most important contribution to the ongoing debate between the presidency and the Court in his message vetoing the renewal of the national bank. John Marshall had clearly affirmed the constitutionality of the bank in *McCulloch v. Maryland* (1819), one of his most nationalistic opinions, which not only upheld the constitutionality of the bank but also struck down state powers to tax it. Arguing that the national government "though limited in its powers, is supreme within its sphere of action," Marshall had advanced the theory of broad constitutional construction that Alexander Hamilton had used to convince President Washington that the bank was proper. However, Jackson and his attorney general, Roger Taney, a future chief justice, negatively associated the bank with Eastern moneyed interests. In one of his most notable public papers, Jackson denied that judicial precedent settled the matter. Like Jefferson, Jackson asserted that each branch of government was independently responsible for interpreting the Constitution. Jackson's view clearly set the stage for future conflicts in cases where executive and judicial views of the Constitution differed.

Lincoln and Constitutional Interpretation

The Supreme Court generally supported President Abraham Lincoln's (1861–1865) wartime endeavors, but he had a number of run-ins with judges and justices, including the chief justice. Taney questioned Lincoln's power to suspend the **writ of habeas corpus,** used to determine whether a person is being legally held in custody, and to try civilians in military courts. Lincoln in turn reaffirmed and refined Jefferson and Jackson's views that Supreme Court decisions were not necessarily the final word on the constitutionality of a law.

One of the defining issues in the presidential contest of 1860 was the legitimacy of Taney's 1857 decision in *Scott v. Sandford.* Dred Scott was a slave whose master, an army surgeon, took him to a free territory and then back to a slave state. Scott later sued for his freedom. Taney denied that Scott's contention that his residence in a free territory had made him free. Instead, Taney declared that, because blacks were not and could not be U.S. citizens, Scott could not bring suit in federal court. He further declared that Congress could not exclude slavery, as the Missouri Compromise had sought to do, from the territories.

In his famous debates with Lincoln during their contest for a Senate seat from Illinois in 1858, Stephen A. Douglas argued that this case settled the constitutional issue. Lincoln did not deny that the case settled the matter for Scott, but Lincoln was concerned about slavery spreading to the territories. Accordingly, both in the debates and in his first inaugural address Lincoln denied that the Court's word was necessarily final. He went on to say that

> if the policy of the Government upon vital questions affecting the whole people is to be irrevocably fixed by decisions of the Supreme Court, the instant they are made in ordinary litigation between parties in personal actions the people will have ceased to be their own rulers, having to that extent practically resigned their Government into the hands of that eminent tribunal.

On several occasions, Lincoln asserted his own views of constitutional interpretation over those of the courts. Ultimately, the Thirteenth and Fourteenth **Amendments** overturned the position that Taney espoused in *Scott.*

A–Z

Roosevelt and the Court-Packing Plan

Of all the conflicts between the president and the judiciary, probably none is more controversial or pivotal than that over President Franklin D. Roosevelt's (1933–1945) attempt to "pack" the Supreme Court. Elected to office in the throes of the **Great Depression,** Roosevelt in his first one hundred days in office demonstrated the power implicit in the president's ability to formulate legislation. The New Deal Roosevelt launched was the most ambitious **legislative** program in American history. Many New Deal programs called for expansive readings of constitutional powers under the **commerce** clause and other grants of power to Congress.

At first, the justices appeared to back some of Roosevelt's initiatives. In the three *Gold Clause Cases* (1935), the Court upheld a controversial law that Congress had adopted providing for the payment of contracts in currency rather than in gold. The year before, in *Home Building and Loan Association v. Blaisdell* (1934) the Court upheld a Minnesota law that extended the payment time for mortgages. Although *Blaisdell* dealt specifically with state powers, the Court's comments must have been comforting to the president. Noting that "Emergency does not create power," Chief Justice Charles Evans Hughes went on to say that it "may furnish the occasion for the exercise of power."

Despite these initial causes for hope, on May 27, 1935, a day often referred to as Black Monday, the Court issued three unanimous decisions that threatened the future of the New Deal. Biding his time until after his reelection in 1936, Roosevelt surprised the nation when, in February 1937, he proposed that Congress reorganize the judiciary. The plan called for adding one Supreme Court justice (up to a total of fifteen) for every justice over age seventy who did not resign. Roosevelt justified this bill as a response to the Court's workload and to the ages of the justices, who were often referred to as the "nine old men." By March 1937, Roosevelt was more forthright about his intentions. In a "fireside chat," he likened the three branches of the federal government to three horses, one of which was pulling in the wrong direction.

While the proposed law was within the constitutional powers of Congress, **conservatives** and even many **liberals** viewed Roosevelt's plan as a blatant attempt to exert direct political influence on the Court and undermine judicial independence.

Some believe the Court had begun to chart a new direction even before Roosevelt's Court-packing plan. However, to observers in FDR's day at least, it appeared that although he lost the battle, he won the war. The Court issued its opinion in *West Coast Hotel Co. v. Parrish* just two months after the Court-packing plan was proposed. Chief Justice Hughes wrote the 5–4 decision in which the Court upheld a minimum-wage law for women and children in the state of Washington, overturning a 1923 precedent. Referring to earlier decisions in which the Court had affirmed the sanctity of liberty of contract, Hughes now noted that such liberty was not absolute.

About two weeks later, the Court issued another 5–4 decision in *National Labor Relations Board v. Jones and Laughlin Steel Corporation,* which Hughes also wrote. Here the Court upheld the congressional ban on unfair labor practices. Earlier decisions had limited federal powers under the Tenth Amendment, which reserves powers to the states. These decisions also had distinguished between the unwarranted regulation of production and the permissible regulation of subsequent commerce, as well as between activities that had an indirect rather than a direct effect on commerce.

In both cases, Justice Owen Roberts, who had often sided with the four conservative justices, provided the swing vote. Court observers began to refer to "the switch in time that saved nine," because the Court's new stance relieved what pressure remained to adopt the Court-packing plan.

Truman and the Steel Seizure Case

Like FDR, Harry S. Truman (1945–1953) found himself on the losing side of an important Supreme Court decision involving one of the most controversial actions of his administration. During America's military involvement in Korea, technically described as a "police action," Truman faced the imminent threat of a strike in the U.S. steel industry. He feared that a strike would interfere with production of materials needed for the conflict. When neither labor nor management would budge, Truman ordered his secretary of commerce, Charles Sawyer, to seize the steel mills until the crisis was over. The president's seizure triggered an immediate appeal and a great deal of criticism.

In *Youngstown Sheet and Tube Co. v. Sawyer* (1952), also known as the *Steel Seizure Case,* the Supreme Court ruled against Truman, 6–3. It decided that Truman's actions could not be justified either by his inherent powers or by any congressional legislation. The president had weakened his claim by failing to invoke the eighty-day cooling-off period that the Taft-Hartley law called for. Although Truman was surprised by the decision and believed that it represented a mistaken constitutional judgment, he quickly complied with it and averted a constitutional crisis.

Eisenhower and Little Rock

Few presidents could have desired a constitutional crisis any less than Truman's successor in office. Although President Dwight D. Eisenhower (1953–1961) faced a Court bent on recasting past judicial decisions about civil rights, he never welcomed them and only weakly supported them. In Little Rock, Arkansas, however, a governor's opposition to federal power ultimately prompted Eisenhower to take strong executive action.

Responding to the Supreme Court's historic desegregation decision in *Brown v. Board of Education* (1954), the Little Rock school board drew up a plan to begin desegregating Central High School in September 1957. Governor Orval Faubus, a fervent **segregationist,** called out the Arkansas National Guard to prevent black students from entering the school. He later responded to a U.S. district court order by withdrawing the guard and permitting chaos and mob violence to ensue. Faced with defiance of federal authority, Eisenhower federalized the Arkansas National Guard and sent in units of the U.S. Army's 101st Airborne Division to restore order and to escort African American students to their classes.

Rarely has a president acted more reluctantly. Against the advice of those who understood the situation, Eisenhower had met with Faubus and thought the two had struck a satisfactory deal. Moreover, Eisenhower was fearful that the use of troops would encourage violence. Therefore after

deploying them, he insisted that they were there "*not* to enforce integration but to prevent opposition by violence to orders of a court."

In an unusual opinion signed by each justice, the Supreme Court refused in *Cooper v. Aaron* (1958) to permit further delay in the implementation of desegregation in Little Rock. The Court's assertion of its power was as forceful a statement of the doctrine of judicial supremacy as it has ever made. The Court said that *Marbury v. Madison* (1803) had established

> the basic principle that the federal judiciary is supreme in the exposition of the law of the Constitution, and that principle has ever since been respected by this Court and the Country as a permanent and indispensable feature of our constitutional system. It follows that the interpretation of the Fourteenth Amendment enunciated by this Court in the *Brown* Case is the supreme law of the land, and Art. VI of the Constitution makes it of binding effect on the States "any Thing in the Constitution or Laws of any State to the Contrary notwithstanding."

Nixon and Executive Privilege

Richard Nixon (1969–1974) entered office determined to use the power of appointment to reverse liberal trends in judicial decision-making. He became better known for testing the limits in areas such as impoundment of congressional funds, injunctions against pending publications, unauthorized wiretapping, and presidential war-making. His most controversial claim, raised in connection with the Watergate incident, concerned executive privilege. Nixon's defeat on this issue ultimately led to his resignation.

Nixon's difficulties began during his first term in office with a series of illegal acts committed by his subordinates. The most notorious of these was the botched break-in during the 1972 presidential campaign at the Democratic National Headquarters, then housed in the Watergate complex in Washington, D.C. His attempts to cover up executive branch participation in this illegal action led him into deeper trouble. Eventually, televised hearings by the Senate Select Committee on

A – Z

Presidential Campaign Activities, chaired by Sam Ervin (D-NC), revealed in 1973 that the president had recorded all conversations made in the Oval Office.

In the meantime, public pressure had led Nixon to appoint a special prosecutor, Archibald Cox, to look into executive wrongdoing. In the "Saturday night massacre," so-called because it occurred on Saturday, October 20 Attorney General Elliot Richardson and Deputy Attorney General William Ruckelshaus resigned rather than accede to Nixon's demand that they fire Cox, who was attempting to get documents from the president. Solicitor General Robert Bork ultimately carried out Nixon's wishes. The action generated a considerable public outcry.

Nixon appointed Leon Jaworski as the new special prosecutor, and Jaworski continued the quest for tapes of White House conversations. He believed they were necessary for determining the president's role in the Watergate affair (Nixon had been named by a Washington, D.C., grand jury as an "unindicted co-conspirator") and for the prosecution of important presidential advisers John D. Ehrlichman and H.R. Haldeman and Attorney General John Mitchell. Nixon, in turn, asserted that the separation of powers doctrine prevented the special prosecutor from seeking this information and that "executive privilege" permitted him to withhold it. Perhaps more important, the president kept the nation in the dark as to whether he would obey the decision.

The Court ruled against Nixon, 8–0. Three of the four justices Nixon had appointed voted against him, and William Rehnquist, a former Justice Department employee in the president's administration, recused himself. Rejecting the separation of powers argument, the Court pointed to the unique situation that had prompted the appointment of a special prosecutor. Quoting from *Marbury v. Madison,* the Court also reasserted its authority " 'to say what the law is' with respect to the claim of privilege presented in this case." Although the Court recognized a need for presidential privacy and confidentiality, especially in foreign affairs, it decided that, in this case, the need for grand juries to have access to the best evidence outweighed the president's generalized claim of executive privilege.

Nixon reluctantly complied with the Court's order. Release of the tapes provided evidence of Nixon's active participation in the Watergate cover-up and led to his resignation on August 9, 1974.

Reagan and Constitutional Interpretation

Like Nixon, Ronald Reagan (1981–1989) assumed office intending to appoint justices who would reverse certain Supreme Court decisions and bring the judicial branch closer to his conservative leanings. Reagan also favored greater state control over matters such as criminal justice. Over the years, the Court had undermined state control by its "incorporation" of most of the guarantees of the Bill of Rights—which had initially applied only to the national government—into the due process clause of the Fourteenth Amendment, where they now applied to states as well. Other conservative presidents had been largely content to work around the edges of constitutional interpretation. Reagan decided to challenge the precedents directly. Accordingly, he chose a highly political attorney general, Edwin Meese III, who was also a close friend and adviser, and further politicized the solicitor general's office.

The administration's most direct clash with the judicial branch came not in court but in a July 1985 speech by Meese to the American Bar Association in which he declared his support for "a jurisprudence of original intention." In retrospect, the attorney general's speech, while hardly presenting the final word on constitutional interpretation, was not all that extraordinary. Arguing that the justification for **judicial review** centered on an interpretable written constitution, Meese said,

Where the language of the Constitution is specific, it must be obeyed. Where there is a demonstrable consensus among the framers and ratifiers as to a principle stated or implied by the Constitution, it should be followed as well. Where there is ambiguity as to the precise meaning or reach of a constitutional provision, it should be interpreted and applied in a manner so as to at least not contradict the text of the Constitution itself.

Because of Meese's position in the administration, however, many, including some members of the Supreme Court, viewed his words as an attack on the liberal jurisprudence that the Warren Court had initiated. Three months later, Justice William Brennan, who was considered one of the most liberal members of the Court, delivered a sharp counterattack in a symposium at Georgetown University. Arguing that the Constitution "embodies the aspiration to social justice, brotherhood and human dignity," Brennan referred to the "amended Constitution" as "the lodestar for our aspirations." He went on to declare, "The phrasing is broad and the limitations of its provisions are clearly marked. Its majestic generalities and ennobling pronouncements are both luminous and obscure." Lest there be any doubt as to Brennan's target, he specifically contrasted his view with a somewhat simplified version of the view Meese had advanced.

> There are those who find legitimacy in fidelity to what they call "the intentions of the Framers." In its most doctrinaire incarnation, this view demands that Justices discern exactly what the Framers thought about the question under consideration and simply follow that intention in resolving the case before them. It is a view that feigns self-effacing deference to the specific judgments of those who forged our original social compact. But in truth it is little more than arrogance cloaked as humility.

Brennan's speech may have been one of the factors that led many opponents of Robert Bork, whose views on constitutional interpretation were similar to Meese's, to perceive that he was vulnerable when Reagan nominated him to the Supreme Court in 1987. The resulting controversy was so bitter that a new expression was coined to describe it: to "Bork," meaning to sink, a particular nominee. Bork was a former Yale University Law School professor and a federal appeals judge who

was a prolific writer and a strong defender of original intent. The Senate eventually rejected his nomination by a 58–42 vote after extensive hearings and **unprecedented** lobbying by outside interest groups.

Bork's rejection created intense partisan rancor that bubbled up again in 1991 when George H.W. Bush's (1989–1993) nominee, Clarence Thomas, appeared before the Senate Judiciary Committee in 1991. Neither of Bill Clinton's (1993–2001) nominees, Ruth Bader Ginsburg and Stephen Breyer, proved to be as controversial. Both had fairly extensive tenures on federal appeals courts, and both were perceived as judicial moderates.

The Presidential Election of 2000: A Special Case

Although cases in which presidents clash with the Court are dramatic, far more frequently the two cooperate. Moreover, the Court is sometimes able to resolve situations surrounding the presidency that might otherwise prove to be nearly intractable. Perhaps there is no better example than the presidential election of 2000. The Court's role in the election of 2000 remains unique and controversial.

Although Democrat Al Gore carried the popular vote in the presidential election held on Tuesday, November 7, 2000, the electoral college vote, which constitutionally decides such elections, ultimately came down to determining which candidate, Gore or Republican George W. Bush (2001–2009), carried the state of Florida. The situation was extremely confusing. In the early morning hours of Wednesday, November 8, the television networks reported that Bush was leading Gore in Florida by almost 50,000 votes. This lead quickly eroded, however, and the initial official count showed Bush ahead by a mere 1,784 votes. This vote was so close that it triggered an automatic machine recount. On Tuesday, November 14, the Florida secretary of state, Republican Katherine Harris, announced that the recount had further reduced Bush's lead to 300 votes.

Meanwhile, concerns emerged about the design of certain ballots and the reliability of some voting machines in recording votes, especially those that used punch cards whose **chads** were not always completely punched through. Responding to those concerns and pressure by Gore supporters who hoped to pick up additional votes, several Florida counties began hand recounts, which Bush forces unsuccessfully challenged in a federal appeals court. Secretary of State Harris hoped to certify Bush's election after the counting of absentee ballots, most from military personnel, raised Bush's lead on November 18 to 930 votes, but, based on language in the state constitution stressing the importance of ascertaining the intent of the voters, the Democrat-dominated Florida Supreme Court ruled on November 21 that additional hand counts would have to be accepted until November 26. Some counties, believing that this deadline provided insufficient time to complete the recounts, then stopped the process. Because the recounts that were made netted Gore additional but insufficient votes to give him the lead, on Sunday, November 26, Harris certified Bush as the winner of Florida by 537 votes.

Yet Gore continued to push for hand counting of disputed ballots in Miami-Dade and Palm Beach Counties. His petition to do so, however, was rejected by Leon County judge N. Sander Sauls on Saturday, December 4. In an omen that was arguably little understood at the time, on the same day the U.S. Supreme Court vacated the November 21 decision of the Florida Supreme Court to extend the recount deadline for hand counts and asked it to clarify its decision. On Wednesday, December 6, the Eleventh U.S. Circuit Court of Appeals refused to void the manual recounts that had been completed, and two days later, over a strong dissent filed by the chief justice, the Florida Supreme Court voted 4–3 to overturn Judge Sauls's decision, which had disqualified hand-counted ballots. The Florida Supreme Court also ordered that 383 votes tabulated for Gore be added to the official state results, reducing Bush's lead to 154.

Recounts began on Friday, December 8, but, apparently concerned that there might not be any uniform standards by which votes were being validated, the U.S. Supreme Court enjoined them by a 5–4 vote the next day. Meanwhile, the Republican-controlled state legislature prepared to name its own slate of electors, and the Florida Supreme Court rejected another suit that would have disqualified 25,000 ballots that Democrats had challenged in Seminole and Martin Counties. Then, on the evening of Tuesday, December 12, the U.S. Supreme Court invalidated the Florida Supreme Court decision, effectively enjoining further manual recounts. The next day Gore conceded the election and Bush claimed victory.

Gore supporters were disappointed by the U.S. Supreme Court decision in *Bush v. Gore* (2000), but Gore accepted the decision as the law of the land. Members of the public and legal scholars, however, continue to debate the merits of this and other decisions surrounding the election. The Supreme Court has long been involved in voting rights cases, but this was the first time it became directly involved in a presidential election. After its initial intervention—trying to convince the Florida Supreme Court to suspend vote counting by vacating that court's first decision—failed, the Supreme Court majority accepted arguments from Bush's legal team that recounts violated Fourteenth Amendment standards of equal protection. The Court based this equal protection argument and the accompanying decision on the fact that there was no uniform standard within or between counties for how to ascertain voter intent. In ascertaining such intent, overseers had to decide whether to count ballots with "hanging" or "dimpled" chads and what to do with apparent undervotes (when voters cast ballots for other candidates but not for president) or overvotes (when voters marked ballots for more than one presidential candidate).

Although seven justices agreed that there were violations of equal protection, a bare five ruled that there was insufficient time to establish such a standard and manually recount the votes before Florida had to certify its electoral votes to Congress in time to be presumptively valid under federal law (known as the "safe harbor" provision). Dissenting justices argued that the Court should allow the Florida Supreme Court to interpret the state's electoral laws and decide whether there was adequate time for a recount.

Critics of the Supreme Court decision noted that it was largely split along ideological, if not strictly partisan, lines—dissenters included Justices John Paul Stevens and David Souter, both of whom had been appointed by Republican presidents. They also pointed out that the Court's intervention into the mechanism that states used to count their votes seemed inconsistent with other recent decisions stressing the virtues of federalism. Defenders of the U.S. Supreme Court argued that intervention by an activist Florida Supreme Court, whose own partisan rulings had rewritten electoral rules in the middle of, if not after, the game, effectively necessitated the U.S. Supreme Court's intervention.

Even without this decision, it appears likely that the Republican state legislature would have appointed Republican electors. Moreover, as disquieting as judicial intervention proved to be, equally unappealing was the thought of electoral votes being certified by a governor (Jeb Bush) who was the brother of the Republican candidate, or the prospect that Vice President Al Gore might be called on to resolve a possible Senate deadlock on the winner.

However else it may have been flawed, the U.S. Supreme Court decision ended the process in time for the electors to meet as scheduled under federal law and in time for the incoming candidate to make an appropriate transition into office. Arguably risking charges of **partisanship** and trading on the capital of its own authority, the Court shut down continued voting, if not partisan controversy. The idea that the one unelected branch of government ultimately made a decision that settled who would be the next president was at once an awesome tribute to its power and an unsettling reminder of how precarious democratic institutions can be.

See also: Bush v. Gore (2000); Constitution of the United States; Watergate Scandal.

Further Reading

Rosen, Jeffrey. *The Supreme Court: The Personalities and Rivalries That Defined America.* New York: Holt, 2007.

Whittington, Keith E. *Political Foundations of Judicial Supremacy: The Presidency, the Supreme Court, and Constitutional Leadership in U.S. History.* Princeton, NJ: Princeton University Press, 2007.

Presidency, Qualifications for

The qualifications for the presidency, as stated in Article II, Section 1, of the Constitution are:

No person except a natural born Citizen, or a Citizen of the United States, at the time of the Adoption of this Constitution, shall be eligible to the Office of President; neither shall any Person be eligible to the Office who shall not have attained to the Age of thirty five Years, and been fourteen Years a Resident within the United States.

No statement of qualifications for president was included in the Constitution until September 7, 1787, when the Constitutional Convention, unanimously and without debate, approved the recommendation of the Committee on Postponed Matters. The committee proposed that the president be thirty-five years or older, a natural-born citizen (or a citizen at the time of the Constitution's adoption), and a resident of the United States for at least fourteen years.

In all likelihood, the lateness of the convention's actions on presidential qualifications was the result of deliberation, not neglect. Throughout their proceedings, the delegates seem to have operated on the principle that qualifications for an office needed to be established only if qualifications for those who choose the person to fill the office were not. Thus as early as the Virginia Plan, qualifications, which were not stated for voters, were included for members of the national legislature. (Ultimately, it was decided that members of the House of Representatives must be at least twenty-five years old, seven years a citizen, and an inhabitant of the state they represented; senators must be at least thirty years old, nine years a citizen, and an inhabitant of the state.) Qualifications for judges and other appointed offices never were included in the Constitution because these officers were to be selected by other government officials for whom qualifications were stated.

Governors Who Became President

When George W. Bush was elected president in 2000, he continued the recent trend of governors advancing to the White House. Between 1976 and 2004, former or sitting governors won seven out of eight presidential elections. In all, seventeen presidents have served previously as state governors.

Following is a list of these presidents and the states they served as governor. Two additional presidents served as governors of territories: Andrew Jackson was the territorial governor of Florida and William Henry Harrison was the territorial governor of Indiana.

President	State
Thomas Jefferson	Virginia
James Monroe	Virginia
Martin Van Buren	New York
John Tyler	Virginia
James K. Polk	Tennessee
Andrew Johnson	Tennessee
Rutherford B. Hayes	Ohio
Grover Cleveland	New York
William McKinley	Ohio
Theodore Roosevelt	New York
Woodrow Wilson	New Jersey
Calvin Coolidge	Massachusetts
Franklin D. Roosevelt	New York
Jimmy Carter	Georgia
Ronald Reagan	California
Bill Clinton	Arkansas
George W. Bush	Texas

Sources: American Political Leaders 1789–2005. Washington, DC: CQ Press, 2005; America Votes 26. Washington, DC: CQ Press, 2006.

Because of their executive experience at the state level, many governors sought and won the presidency.

On August 20, Elbridge Gerry of Massachusetts moved that the Committee of Detail be revived for the purpose of proposing a list of qualifications for president. Two days later, the committee did so: the president was to be at least thirty-five years old, a citizen, and an inhabitant of the United States for at least twenty-one years. On September 4, the Committee on Postponed Matters submitted a revised statement of qualifications: thirty-five, a natural born citizen (or a citizen at the time of the Constitution's adoption), and fourteen years a resident. The delegates approved the revised recommendation on September 7.

Each element of the presidential qualifications clause was grounded in its own rationale. The age requirement had two justifications. First, the delegates presumed that age would foster maturity. Second, the passage of years left a record for the voters to assess. According to John Jay, the author of *Federalist* No. 64,

By excluding men under 35 from the first office [president], and those under 30 from the second [senator], it confines the electors to men of whom the people have had time to form a judgment, and with respect to whom they will not be liable to be deceived by those brilliant appearances of genius and patriotism which, like transient meteors, sometimes mislead as well as dazzle.

The residency and citizenship requirements for president were grounded less in principles of good government than in the politics of the moment. The stipulation that the president must be at least fourteen years a resident of the United States was designed to eliminate from consideration both British sympathizers who had fled to England during the Revolutionary War and popular foreign military leaders, notably Baron Frederick von Steuben of Prussia, who had emigrated to the United States to fight in the Revolution. As to the length of the residency requirement, the Committee of Detail's recommendation of twenty-one years probably was reduced to fourteen because the longer requirement—but not the shorter—might have been interpreted as barring three of the convention's delegates from

Members of Congress Who Became President

Twenty-five presidents have served previously in the House of Representatives, the Senate, or both.

Following is a list of these presidents and the houses in which they served. In addition, three presidents—George Washington, John Adams, and Thomas Jefferson—served in the Continental Congress, as did James Madison and James Monroe. James A. Garfield was elected to the Senate in January 1880 for a term beginning March 4, 1881, but declined to accept in December 1880 because he had been elected president. John Quincy Adams served in the House for seventeen years after his term as president, and Andrew Johnson returned to the Senate five months before he died.

House Only	Senate Only	Both House and Senate
James Madison	James Monroe	Andrew Jackson
James K. Polk	John Quincy Adams	William Henry Harrison
Millard Fillmore	Martin Van Buren	John Tyler
Abraham Lincoln	Benjamin Harrison	Franklin Pierce
Rutherford B. Hayes	Warren G. Harding	James Buchanan
James A. Garfield	Harry S. Truman	Andrew Johnson
William McKinley	Lyndon B. Johnson	John F. Kennedy
Gerald R. Ford	Richard M. Nixon	
George H.W. Bush	Barack Obama	

Sources: *Biographical Directory of the United States Congress, 1774–1989*. Washington, D.C.: Government Printing Office, 1989; *American Political Leaders 1789–2005*. Washington, DC: CQ Press, 2005).

Serving in the United States House of Representatives or the United States Senate, or both, has often been a stepping-stone to the presidency.

the presidency: Alexander Hamilton, Pierce Butler, and James McHenry.

The reason for requiring that the president be a natural born citizen was similarly tied to contemporary politics. Rumors had spread while the convention was meeting that the delegates were plotting to invite a European monarch to rule the United States. Prince Henry of Prussia and Frederick, Duke of York, who was King George III's second son, were the most frequently mentioned names. The practice of importing foreign rulers was not unknown among the European monarchies of the day and would not have seemed preposterous to Americans who heard the rumor. The delegates, aware that the mere mention of an independent executive in the Constitution was going to provoke attacks from opponents who suspected that the presidency was a type of monarchy, seem to have believed that they could squelch at least the foreign king rumor by requiring that the president be a natural-born citizen of the United States.

Constitutional Requirements for the President

He or she must be:
- a citizen of the United States,
- at least thirty-five years age,
- a resident within the United States for fourteen years

The United States Constitution provides only three specific qualifications for the office of the president.

Presidential Appearances and Public Appeals

The presidency and the relationship of the office with the American public. Presidents always work at a distance from the American public. Through public opinion polls, interest groups, the media, and relations with Congress and the bureaucracy, presidents gain indirect access to their constituents. Although speaking directly to people helps presidents to create at least the illusion of a direct relationship, it does not help them to develop the relationships they need to assemble coalitions and to govern. To build coalitions, presidents must appeal to many separate groups, or separate publics, as much as to the public at large. Presidents' frequent public appeals have made presidential governance an extension of electoral campaigns.

The President as Public Figure

The president occupies the most prominent position in American politics largely because, with the exception of the vice president, the United States has no other nationally elected leader. A related reason for the president's prominence is the availability of what Theodore Roosevelt (1901–1909) called the "bully pulpit." The president's unique ability to promote a national vision and to influence actors in both the public and private spheres has been crucial in disproving the predictions of some observers of early America that the presidency would play a minor role in national government.

In the twentieth century, the president's prominence in American politics increased not only with the growing involvement of the White House in domestic policy and the rise of the United States to international leadership, but also with the expansion of the president's role as the starring preacher in the "bully pulpit" of American politics. Using words and images as well as the actions of the administration, the modern president plays a major role in setting the terms of debate for the entire political system.

Public speaking is one of the most important ties between the president and the public. Since the end of World War II (1939–1945), public speeches by presidents have increased by over 500 percent. A 1972 report estimated that "a half million words annually flow out of the White House in a torrent of paper and ink." Not only presidents' words but also their physical appearances are important in communicating with the public. Academic studies conclude that nonverbal signs have four to ten times the effect of verbiage on "impression formation."

The development of the vocally active presidency stems from changes in the U.S. political system as well as from advances in communications and transportation technologies. The president no longer can depend on traditional bases of support such as Congress, party organizations, the print media, or the bureaucracy. Without those mediators of public policy, presidents increasingly must rely on their own ability to move people with words.

The connection between presidential speeches and the absence of institutional bases was underscored by Richard Nixon's (1969–1974) handling of the Watergate scandal in the early 1970s. As the president lost support in Congress, in public opinion polls, and among interest groups, he depended increasingly on his rhetorical powers. Nixon's last year in office was dominated by behind-the-scenes strategy sessions on how to respond to charges of lawbreaking and by the carefully crafted release of information and public statements.

Communicating complex policies to the American public is one of the most important—and difficult—tasks of the president. Issues such as interest rates, budget deficits, health care, and trade policy can be numbingly difficult to impart taken alone. When discussed as part of a comprehensive, long-term program, they become even more complicated. Jimmy Carter (1977–1981) suffered when he could not explain his complex energy proposals. Carter also addressed so many issues—energy, deregulation, taxes, the Middle East, détente with the Soviet Union, reorganization of the bureaucracy, the environment, urban development—that he could not stay focused in his efforts to sell his policies to the public. Ronald

Reagan (1981–1989), in contrast, provided a simple and coherent worldview.

President Bill Clinton (1993–2001) faced some of the same problems as Carter. Democratic constituencies pressed the new president to address concerns that had been suppressed during the previous twelve years of Republican rule. Nevertheless, Clinton's ambitious agenda often got lost in the minutiae of political battles and policy calculations. At an early meeting of the Clinton cabinet at Camp David, the Maryland presidential retreat, Clinton's communications advisers and his wife, Hillary Rodham Clinton, tried to get the president's communication with the public back on track. Hillary Clinton told the group that Clinton's success as governor of Arkansas had hinged on his ability to describe his policy initiatives as a "story" with a beginning, middle, and end, so that the people could follow complex policy initiatives. Clinton had to do the same as president, his wife declared. The story would depict the long journey that the people would travel together via the president's policy initiatives, and it would include tangible signs of progress at regular intervals. Without a coherent story line, the president would confuse the people who supported him.

Clinton used the strategy successfully in his campaigns for a deficit-reduction bill and the North American Free Trade Agreement (NAFTA). During the last six years of his presidency, when the Republicans controlled both houses of Congress, Clinton effectively presented himself as a check on ideological extremism. Using the power of words, he positioned himself in the ideological center, between the congressional Republicans on his right and the congressional Democrats on his left.

Following in Clinton's centrist footsteps, George W. Bush (2001–2009) identified himself as a compassionate **conservative.** He sought to maintain his conservative base by embracing the language of limited government, while reaching across the ideological divide to **liberals** by signaling his understanding of the need for—and his commitment to—a social and economic safety net.

Presidents apply public speaking to politics in a variety of ways. They meet regularly with reporters and other media representatives, give speeches on television and radio, address large crowds, hold informal meetings with leaders of interest groups, travel abroad to meet foreign leaders, meet and speak by telephone with members of Congress and other elected officials, and attend events that feature celebrities. Every president also commands large research and public relations operations in the White House and federal agencies. Finally, presidential appointees promote the administration's policies.

What presidents say is often less important than how they say it. In other words, the potency of presidential remarks lies not in their content but in the ceremonial way they are delivered. Deference to the president is the norm.

Presidents bask in the regal splendor of the presidency whenever they make a public appearance. The podium usually features the presidential seal, and flags often hang within the audience's frame of vision. Standing alongside the president will likely be a line of dignitaries who look on with respect and even reverence. The distance between the president and the audience increases the sense of the president's "untouchable" status.

When presidents give their annual State of the Union address, they face a rare assemblage of both houses of Congress, the Supreme Court, and the cabinet; the vice president and Speaker of the House are seated behind the president, and a huge flag hangs in the background. The address provides a backdrop for national unity—however brief. When presidents visit military officials, the backdrop might include an assemblage of officers and troops in full dress uniforms, an impressive-looking navy ship, or a military band. When they visit a foreign country, presidents are welcomed by dignitaries and bands and feted at formal dinners and presentations. When they welcome the winners of the World Series or Super Bowl, they are surrounded by the team's banners and other trappings of the sport.

Even in the most unceremonial situations, the president can use a particular setting to evoke strong national sentiment. After President John F. Kennedy (1961–1963) was assassinated in 1963, Lyndon B. Johnson (1963–1969) took the oath of office on *Air Force One,* the presidential airplane, to emphasize the suddenness of the tragedy and the swift assumption of power. Soon after the truck bombing of marine barracks in Lebanon in

1983, President Reagan stood in the drizzling rain with his wife and somberly read a statement of tribute to the murdered marines and a warning to the forces responsible for the attack. George W. Bush made one of his most effective responses to the 2001 terrorist attack on New York City during his initial visit to "Ground Zero," where the World Trade Center towers no longer stood. Speaking to relief workers without the benefit of a public address system, he was informed that his words were not being heard. Using a bullhorn, his arm draped around the shoulders of a New York fire chief, he observed that the terrorists would soon be hearing from America.

Although the major television networks occasionally refuse to broadcast an address, presidents almost always gain a wide electronic audience for their speeches and informal discussions. Radio stations generally broadcast short speeches and special events, such as Jimmy Carter's call-in show. The importance of televised speeches has increased since the 1960s as the number of press conferences has declined. Compared with the give-and-take of press conferences, the more formal talks give the president greater control over an appearance's agenda and tempo.

The Age of Presidential Leadership

During the **Great Depression,** which began in 1929, the nation turned to Franklin D. Roosevelt (1933–1945) for presidential leadership. Roosevelt was tireless in his efforts to expand the government's involvement in domestic and international politics.

Both Roosevelt's programs and his language emphasized the need for strong central direction that only a president could provide. For the first time, the government in Washington moved from its traditional role as **patronage** state to welfare state. As the government became involved in all aspects of everyday life, the need for strong **executive** direction increased. In the meantime, sophisticated systems of communication tightened the bond between the president and the public. From Franklin Roosevelt to George W. Bush almost sixty years later, the president became more a symbolic leader on a wide range of issues than an executive who dealt with a limited set of fundamentally national concerns.

By the time FDR took office, millions of American homes were tied together by the airwaves of radio broadcasting. Politics moved from the crowds to the smaller units of a radio-listening audience. Political speeches, once bombastic, became more conversational and intimate. Roosevelt was the perfect president to begin the new communication style. Over the radio, he delivered a series of "Fireside Chats" to the nation that identified him with everyday concerns.

Since the end of World War II (1939–1945), presidents have spoken in public more than ten thousand times—an average of one speech every working day. Harry S. Truman (1945–1953) used rhetoric as a tool in his relations with Congress, but the verbiage always was directed toward specific policy aims. Truman relied on rhetoric to promote his policies on European redevelopment, relations with the Soviet Union, aid to Greece and Turkey, and civil rights. Truman's 1948 election campaign was a marathon of public speaking—a whistle-stop excoriation of Congress and a call for public support. Perhaps the Truman administration's most important legacy was its rhetoric about the Soviet Union. During the Greece-Turkey crisis of 1947, Truman acknowledged overstating the Soviet threat to arouse the public after a congressional leader had advised him to "scare the hell out of the country." Harsh anti-Soviet rhetoric starting with the Truman administration may have contributed to the bitterness of U.S.-Soviet relations and the costly nuclear arms race.

Because of improved air transportation, modern presidents have traveled regularly both nationally and internationally. Presidents through Dwight D. Eisenhower (1953–1961) felt obliged to justify their trips abroad, but world travel has become a regular, expected, and even desired part of the office.

In addition to advanced systems of transportation and communication, the president's expanded role in national politics has stemmed from the decline of political party strength, the development of popular nominating systems, the rise of political consultants, the fragmentation of Congress, and the "nationalization" of politics and policy.

Modern Presidential Appearances and Speeches

Presidential rhetoric in the postwar years shifted fundamentally with the ascension of John

Kennedy to the White House. Harry Truman and Dwight Eisenhower used public speech almost solely in pursuit of a specific policy initiative, but later presidents spoke out regularly on a wide range of matters. Indeed, speech became a daily fact of life for modern presidents, who appeared willing and even compelled to talk about every possible aspect of political and social issues—even those about which they were ignorant. Presidents also began to speak before a greater variety of groups.

Whereas earlier presidents spoke formally about issues of national importance, modern presidents talk in a conversational, intimate way. Presidents even feel compelled to discuss their emotions and deeply personal experiences. Jimmy Carter talked openly about being a sinning Christian Baptist. Ronald Reagan described his alcoholic father and "Huck Finn" childhood. George H.W. Bush discussed the childhood death of his daughter Robin. Bill Clinton was arguably the most intimate of all, speaking emotionally about his fatherless childhood and proudly about his commitment to carry out his duties of office in the face of scathing personal attacks. George W. Bush frequently referred to his deep religious faith and his mediocre academic record.

See also: Presidency and the Media; Public Opinion and the Presidency.

Further Reading

Cohen, Jeffrey E. *Presidential Responsiveness and Public Policy-Making: The Publics and the Policies that Presidents Choose.* Ann Arbor, MI: University of Michigan Press, 1999.

Kernell, Samuel. *Going Public: New Strategies of Presidential Leadership,* 4th ed. Washington, DC: CQ Press, 2006.

Presidential Campaigns

The lengthy and complex process presidential candidates follow to win the general election. Once they have their party's nomination, presidential candidates focus on winning the general election. They must choose the strategy they think will propel them to victory and then pursue it in a complex political environment that includes the news media, the opposition party, and interest groups. Not least among their problems are those of organizing their own staffs—pollsters, media consultants, strategists, and other senior advisers—and coordinating their campaigns with their party's state and national organizations.

Types of Strategy

Presidential elections are fought state by state, with each candidate trying to win a combination of states that has enough electoral votes to constitute the majority required for victory. Thus, most strategies begin with geographic considerations. Democratic candidates usually are strongest in the Northeast, upper Midwest, and along the Pacific Coast. Until the 1950s, the South was a Democratic stronghold, but the white **conservative** voters who dominate southern politics increasingly have been attracted to Republican candidates in presidential elections. In 2004, Democrat John Kerry lost every southern state to **incumbent** George W. Bush (2001–2009). The Republicans also dominate the Rocky Mountain West and the Plains states.

To appeal to a large geographic constituency, most tickets consist of presidential and vice-presidential candidates from different parts of the country. When Minnesotan Walter Mondale chose Geraldine Ferraro of New York as his running mate in 1984, Ronald Reagan's (1981–1989) strategist, Lee Atwater, was elated. He predicted that the Democrats' choice of a "North-North" ticket would give the South to the Republicans and guarantee victory for Reagan. In 1992, Bill Clinton (1993–2001) of Arkansas formed a "South-South" ticket by choosing Al Gore of Tennessee as his running mate. It became the first successful all-southern ticket since Andrew Jackson (1829–1837) of Tennessee ran with John C. Calhoun of South Carolina in 1828.

Regional strength does not tell all, however. Because states do not count equally in the electoral college, candidates often concentrate their efforts on states with large electoral vote counts. As determined by the 2000 census, the electoral votes of just eleven states—California, New York, Texas, Florida, Pennsylvania, Illinois, Ohio, Michigan, New Jersey, North Carolina, and Georgia—are enough to secure victory in the general election.

A – Z

For a candidate to devote time and money to all fifty states is a waste of scarce campaign resources. Richard Nixon (1969–1974) promised to campaign in every state when he ran for president in 1960, but he regretted that pledge when he was forced to waste valuable time visiting states with few electoral votes while his rival, John Kennedy (1961–1963), was targeting the large states. This point was forcefully driven home on the last weekend before the election. As Nixon flew to Alaska to fulfill his promise, Kennedy campaigned in New York, New Jersey, and Massachusetts. When Nixon ran again in 1968 he was careful to target particular states. For example, he did not visit small and heavily Republican Kansas that year.

Since the New Deal, the Democrats consistently have had more registered voters than the Republicans, although by a steadily decreasing margin in recent years. As a result, it usually has been more advantageous for Democrats to follow an overtly **partisan** campaign than it is for Republicans. It also benefits the Democrats to encourage a large voter turnout, either by stressing the civic obligation to vote or through more tangible efforts, such as telephone reminders or even providing baby sitters and transportation to the polls. Both kinds of efforts appear to have secured Kennedy's victory in 1960.

Republican presidential candidates can be hurt by a large voter turnout or by running an intensely partisan campaign. While maintaining their base of support, Republicans also must reach out to independents and Democrats with weak party ties. To do this, Republican candidates sometimes deemphasize their party label. In 1976, Gerald Ford's (1974–1977) official campaign poster featured his picture but gave no indication that he was a Republican. Likewise, Nixon's campaign organization in 1972—the Committee to Re-elect the President—intentionally bypassed the Republican Party.

Unlike partisan campaigns, which stress party loyalty, ideological campaigns stress the candidate's devotion to a particular political ideology. In doing so, these campaigns excite and energize the candidate's core supporters. However, they can alienate moderate voters, including members of the candidate's own party.

Yet another strategy is a consensual campaign, which makes broad appeals outside the confines of either **partisanship** or ideology. When Republican Barry Goldwater in 1964 and Democrat George McGovern in 1972 ran strongly ideological campaigns, their opponents, Lyndon B. Johnson (1963–1969) and Nixon, respectively, responded successfully with consensual campaigns. George H.W. Bush's (1989–1993) failed 1992 reelection bid suffered when the Republican convention in Houston struck many observers as ideologically extreme, particularly in its strident attacks on **liberals** by speakers from the **religious right.** In contrast, Bush's son, George W. Bush, offered "compassionate conservatism" and an array of minority, female, and gay speakers at the 2000 Republican convention.

Bill Clinton's 1992 campaign stressed themes designed to appeal to moderate Republicans as well as traditional Democrats. His self-designation as a "new Democrat" was calculated to distance him from the more ideologically liberal Democratic candidates of the past. Clinton insisted that the Democratic platform state, "We reject both the do-nothing government of the last twelve years and the big government theory that says we can hamstring business and tax and spend our way to prosperity." The Clinton-approved platform offered a "third way" that combined economic growth, family vitality, personal responsibility, and law and order—all of them themes usually espoused by Republican candidates.

In 1984, Democrat Walter Mondale tried to appear honest and straightforward by taking specific stands on controversial issues. He promised, for example, to raise taxes. He also lost. Most candidates—Democrat and Republican alike—are cautious and repetitive. They strive for short sound bites that can be lifted from their speeches and included in ten- or fifteen-second segments on the evening news.

Role of the Campaign Staff

Presidential campaigns in the media age are elaborate, multimillion-dollar operations. Within these operations, important strategic decisions are made by the professional campaign consultants who form the core of a candidate's campaign organization. Consultants usually are engaged for highly specialized tasks such as public opinion sampling, data processing, policy formulation, fund-raising, accounting, website design, and the production of television commercials. The rise of professional campaign consultants is, in part, an attempt to provide the expertise needed to compete in increasingly complex modern elections. Such consultants also help to fill the void left by the now weakened party organizations that used to coordinate campaigns.

Pollsters

Candidates always have relied on advisers to guide them through the campaign. However, technological advances, especially in telecommunications and information management, have spawned a new breed of consultants. Among them, pollsters have risen to the higher echelons of presidential campaigns because they are able to gather and decipher strategic information.

Polls tell the candidates where their bases of support lie, what the voters think of them, which issues are important to the electorate, and which words and phrases most effectively convey the candidates' ideas. Thus polls can be used by candidates to decide whether or not to run, to improve their image, to target the opposition's weaknesses, to formulate mass media advertising, and to allocate scarce campaign resources with maximum efficiency. Candidates also find polls helpful in deciding how to use the media to appeal to specific blocs of voters.

Pollster Louis Harris maintains that polls can shift the outcome of an election by as much as 4 percentage points if one candidate uses polling data to target resources more efficiently than the other. Since 1960, when John F. Kennedy hired Harris, every presidential candidate has made extensive use of polls. Presidents also keep close tabs on survey data once they are in office. For example, Jimmy Carter's (1977–1981) close association with pollster Patrick Caddell strongly influenced his decisions both on the campaign trail and in the White House.

Polling played a central role in Bill Clinton's winning 1992 campaign. Pollster Stanley B. Greenberg conducted surveys that helped Clinton develop almost instantaneous responses to charges made by his opponents, Republican George H.W. Bush and Independent Party candidate Ross Perot. Polls were especially important—and volatile—in 1992 because of the presence of a strong third-party candidate. The two major parties struggled to navigate political waters roiled by the maverick Perot, who was cutting into President Bush's conservative and suburban constituencies while also challenging Clinton for the anti-incumbent vote.

Polls, however, are not infallible. There is room for error both in the polls themselves and in their interpretation. The most famous example is from 1948, when virtually every pollster predicted that Republican Thomas Dewey would defeat the Democratic incumbent, Harry Truman (1945–1953). For a variety of reasons, including poor sampling techniques and mistaken assumptions about how the undecided would vote, the pollsters were wrong. Most pollsters also substantially underestimated the size of Ronald Reagan's victory in 1980.

"Panel surveys" are used to refine strategy further by reinterviewing previous respondents to see what the campaign is doing well and what it needs to work on. These surveys are supplemented by continual tracking polls, which measure fluctuations in general voter support for the candidate on a frequent basis.

Media and Other Consultants

Image building has become especially important since the development of television. In 1976, urging Carter to take symbolic actions that would play well on television, pollster Caddell warned the candidate that "too many good people have been beaten because they tried to substitute substance for style." He encouraged Carter to hold folksy town meetings and carry his own luggage. Increasingly, candidates rely on media consultants to help them cultivate an appealing style.

Media savvy was a vital part of Clinton's successful 1992 campaign. Political strategists James Carville and Mandy Grunwald, among others, helped the Arkansas governor to keep his campaign focused. The famed "War Room"—a crisis-control center at Clinton's headquarters in Little Rock—coordinated rapid responses to media criticisms and to charges from the Bush campaign. Bus tours of small towns helped foster an appealing image for Clinton, vice-presidential nominee Gore, and their wives.

Dwight Eisenhower (1953–1961) was the first presidential candidate to make extensive use of television commercials and an advertising agency when he ran as the Republican nominee in 1952. Nixon shunned the use of an advertising agency and most modern media techniques in the 1960 campaign. Nixon's performance in the first televised debate with Kennedy was marred by his poor makeup, haggard appearance, and lack of attention to his wardrobe. Nixon lost the election. His next campaign for president (he won in 1968) was a pure case of campaigning as marketing. Since then, media consultants have become an integral part of presidential contests, coordinating everything from the personal appearance of the candidates to the color of their bumper stickers.

Media consultants also have fine-tuned their production and distribution of television advertisements. For example, Nixon's commercials stressed his foreign policy experience in 1968 after polls showed that viewers thought such experience was important. In the aftermath of Vietnam and Watergate, Carter's commercials displayed him as an honest, folksy candidate. Even the color of his campaign posters (green) stressed how Carter was different from mainstream politicians, most of whom used red, white, and blue.

Technological advances also have led to the use of direct mail. Using computers, campaign organizations send "personalized" mailings to targeted individuals whose names are culled from lists of contributors to the candidate's party, the mailing lists of conservative (Republican) or liberal (Democratic) magazines, and membership lists of various organizations.

Direct mail often is used as a fund-raising device. It was first employed in 1952 by Eisenhower, who compiled a donor list with the aid of *Reader's Digest* publisher DeWitt Wallace. However, it was not until the 1970s that vigorous use of direct mail was spurred by campaign finance legislation that limited individual contributions to $1,000 (now $2,300) per candidate. Under the new rules, direct mail served as a grassroots approach to reaching a wide base of small contributors. With a well-coordinated program that contacts both potential contributors ("prospective mailings") and those who have given money in the past ("in-house" or "contributor mailings"), a relatively small investment can reap a tremendous return.

In addition to direct mail, candidates use telephone banks and e-mail to recruit volunteers and to target potential voters. Contacting house-holds by phone or e-mail offers a means of reaching more voters with less effort than door-to door canvassing. Campaigns also use telephones and computers in their fund-raising drives. In an effort to generate contributions, some media ads encourage voters to call a toll-free number or access a website where they can make a donation by credit cards.

Recognizing that presidential campaigns are increasingly shaped by the mass media, political strategists work hard to develop memorable appeals. A large proportion of political advertising is negative. Cognitive studies have shown that voters absorb negative information more deeply than positive information. Jill Buckley, a Democratic consultant, has observed, "People say they hate negative advertising, but it works. They hate it and remember it at the same time. . . . With negative [advertising], the poll numbers will move in three or four days."

The effect of media consultants on the outcome of political campaigns is debatable, especially because both candidates in a general election are able to hire experienced and talented professionals. Their effect on the process itself, however, is clear. Professionals drive up the costs of competing, weaken the link between candidates and parties, and elevate the importance of style and image.

See also: Elections, Presidential; Presidential Debates; Presidential Primaries.

Further Reading

Boller, Paul F. *Presidential Campaigns: From George Washington to George W. Bush.* New York: Oxford University Press, 2004.

Campbell, James E. *The American Campaign: U.S. Presidential Campaigns and the National Vote.* College Station, TX: Texas A&M University Press, 2008.

Presidential Commissions

Committees or panels put together by the president to study a particular issue. Since the birth of the United States, presidents have been appointing commissions to probe subjects that normally are beyond the daily scope of presidential advisory organizations. Presidents rely on commissions to gather information and to focus public attention on specific problems.

Although commissions can be created either by the president or by Congress, they are usually placed within the **executive** office. In recent years, the number and variety of presidential commissions have increased tremendously. In truth, not all presidential commissions have worked well; some, however, have proven valuable and important.

Presidents have no specific constitutional grant of authority to appoint commissions. They usually justify such a step, however, by pointing to the general grant of authority in the Constitution to "take care that the laws be faithfully executed" and "from time to time give to the Congress information on the State of the Union, and recommend to their consideration such measures as he shall judge necessary and expedient" (Article II, Section 3). President John Tyler (1841–1845), in naming a presidential commission to investigate corruption in the New York City customhouse, was the first president to cite his constitutional authority to do so. Tyler asserted that the information collected by the commission was for his use as president, but that it probably would find its way to Congress in the form of proposed legislation. He argued,

The expediency, if not the necessity, of inquiries into the transactions of our customs houses, especially in cases where abuses and malpractices are alleged, must be obvious to Congress.

His constitutional justification of presidential commissions has stood up over the years.

Although it is generally recognized that presidents have the power to establish commissions, they often seek congressional approval anyway. One reason for requesting congressional authorization to form a commission is that the funds required to operate and staff the commission are then specifically **appropriated** by Congress. Some presidential commissions, however, are created by an executive order of the president and are financed by emergency, executive, or special projects funds, which are appropriated by Congress to be spent at the president's discretion. President Herbert C. Hoover (1929–1933), who significantly expanded the use of presidential commissions by appointing 62 during his first sixteen months in office, reportedly raised at least $2 million in private funds to finance them.

Presidential commissions date back to the administration of George Washington (1789–1797), who appointed a commission to investigate the Whiskey Rebellion. In this incident, a group of liquor distillers in western Pennsylvania threatened civil disorder over the federal liquor tax. Washington, perplexed over a situation potentially divisive to the young nation, took the problem to a group of distinguished citizens in whose findings he had confidence. In his sixth annual address to Congress, Washington flatly stated, "The report of the commissioners marks their firmness and abilities, and must unite all virtuous men."

Most nineteenth-century presidents used commissions to meet the specific needs of their administrations. President Martin Van Buren (1837–1841), for example, appointed a commission to examine the European postal systems. Strong presidents have used commissions freely. Andrew Jackson (1829–1837) appointed two commissions just to check up on the actions of the navy. The use of presidential commissions increased markedly in the twentieth century. The first serious study of commissions found that some 100 had been appointed up to 1940. A 1970 study found that another 44 had been appointed since 1945. In the early years of the twenty-first century, the General Service Administration (GSA) listed 57 commissions or committees directly advising the president.

Not all executive branch commissions, however, are "presidential" commissions. Presidential commissions are a part of a larger number of federal advisory bodies that provide advice on a broad range of topics to various departments and agencies of the executive branch. By the beginning of the twenty-first century, an average of almost 1,000 advisory committees with more than 40,000 members were advising the president and the executive branch on various issues. These included diverse topics such as the disposal of high-level nuclear waste, the depletion of atmospheric ozone, and efforts to rid the nation of illegal drugs and to improve schools, highways, and housing.

Over the years, presidential commissions have played significant roles in many policy areas. Recent commissions have investigated business regulation, **tariffs,** government waste, defense spending, the space program, Social Security, the Iran-contra affair, government reorganization, gambling, and health care. Theodore Roosevelt (1901–1909) introduced the use of commissions for substantive policy advice to the president. Inspired by the royal commissions used extensively in Great Britain to investigate policy questions, Roosevelt appointed various commissions during his administration, including the Aldrich Commission, whose recommendations led to establishment of the Federal Reserve System. Herbert Hoover, after his retirement from the presidency, headed two important commissions on government reorganization appointed by Presidents Harry S. Truman (1945–1953) and Dwight D. Eisenhower (1953–1961), respectively. Presidential commissions also have been sent overseas to supervise national elections and investigate the stability of foreign governments. In 1917, for example, after the overthrow of the Russian Czar Nicholas II, President Woodrow Wilson (1913–1921) sent a special commission to Russia to find out how democratic the regime of Aleksandr Fyodorovich Kerensky would be.

Although the objectives of presidential commissions have varied, most have been important to presidential decision making, and many have contributed significantly to the development of government policy. For example, Franklin D. Roosevelt's (1933–1945) most notable commission, the President's Committee on Administrative Management, known as the Brownlow Committee, developed the blueprint for the Executive Office of the President.

See also: Executive Orders.

Presidential Debates

Debates between presidential candidates. Presidential debates are a relatively recent occurrence. Until the second half of the twentieth century, White House nominees did not debate. Richard

Nixon (1969–1974) and John F. Kennedy (1961–1963) began the debate tradition on September 26, 1960, with the first of four televised meetings. When Abraham Lincoln (1861–1865) and Stephen Douglas held their famed debates in 1858, they were Senate candidates; they did not debate as presidential candidates two years later.

There were no debates from 1960 until 1976, when President Gerald R. Ford (1974–1977), running behind in the polls, agreed to debate the Democratic nominee, former Georgia governor Jimmy Carter. The relatively unknown Carter gained stature in the exchange when Ford made a gaffe by insisting that East European nations were not under Soviet Union control. Since 1976, all major party nominees have debated on live television. Independent candidate Perot was included in the presidential debates in 1992, but he was excluded as the Reform Party nominee in 1996. In 2000, Republican George W. Bush and Democrat Al Gore debated three times. In 2004, **incumbent** George W. Bush (2001–2009) and Democratic challenger John Kerry held three debates. Similarly, in the 2008 campaign, Republican John McCain and Democrat Barack Obama debated three times.

Unlike formal, academic debates, the presidential confrontations have been loosely structured, at first with a panel of journalists or audience members asking the questions. In most debates since 1992 journalist moderators have questioned the candidates, with the audience sometimes allowed to participate. Throughout, there have been no judges to award points and therefore no way to determine who "won" or "lost" except by public opinion polling. Media commentators make immediate assessments of winners and losers, however, and their judgments undoubtedly influence the public's opinion about which candidate did best.

With one exception, vice-presidential nominees have debated since 1976 when Ford's running mate Robert J. Dole faced Democrat Walter F. Mondale. There was no debate in 1980 between Vice President Mondale and the Republican vice presidential nominee, George H.W. Bush. The nominees in 2000, Republican Richard Cheney and Democrat Joseph I. Lieberman, debated once. In the 2004 contest, Republican Richard Cheney and Democrat John Edwards also debated once.

President Jimmy Carter (1977–1981) and Republican candidate Ronald Reagan shake hands before their presidential debate on October 28, 1980. Reagan (1981–1989) handily defeated Carter in the November election. (AP Images)

A-Z

Similarly, in 2008 Republican nominee Sarah Palin and Democrat Joseph R. Biden squared off in one debate.

Early in the presidential debate era, the television networks or the League of Women Voters sponsored the debates. Since 1988, they have been sponsored by the **bipartisan** Commission on Presidential Debates.

See also: Elections, Presidential.

Further Reading

Minow, Newton N., and Craig L. LaMay. *Inside the Presidential Debates: Their Improbable Past and Promising Future.* Chicago: University of Chicago Press, 2008.

Schroeder, Alan. *The Presidential Debates: Fifty Years of High Risk TV.* New York: Columbia University Press, 2008.

Presidential Disability

A situation in which a president is incapacitated and cannot perform the duties of the office. Presidential **impeachment** and presidential death are relatively straightforward matters compared with presidential disability. One knows when a president is dead or has been impeached and convicted, but questions of disability are inherently subjective. Yet disabilities do occur. According to one scholar's calculations, periods of presidential disability, taken together, have left the country without a functioning president for nearly a full year. Others argue that Woodrow Wilson (1913–1921) alone was disabled during the final year and a half of his presidency.

POINT/COUNTERPOINT

SHOULD THIRD PARTY CANDIDATES PARTICIPATE IN PRESIDENTIAL DEBATES?

The non-partisan Committee on Presidential Debates (CPD) claims it set forth unbiased criteria for the presidential debates that are held before every presidential election. However, a nationwide organization, Open Debates, maintains that the CPD deliberately favors the candidates of the two major parties and works to excluded third-party candidates.

The Committee on Presidential Debates

The goal of the CPD's debates is to afford the members of the public an opportunity to sharpen their views, in a focused debate format, of those candidates from among whom the next President and Vice President will be selected. In each of the last five elections, there were scores of declared candidates for the Presidency, excluding those seeking the nomination of one of the major parties. During the course of the campaign, the candidates are afforded many opportunities in a great variety of forums to advance their candidacies. In order to most fully and fairly achieve the educational purposes of its debates, the CPD developed nonpartisan, objective criteria regarding selection of the candidates to participate in its 2008 debates. The purpose of the criteria is to identify those candidates who have achieved a level of electoral support such that they realistically are considered to be among the principal rivals for the Presidency.

In connection with the 2008 general election, the CPD applied three criteria to each declared candidate to determine whether that candidate qualified for inclusion in one or more of the CPD's debates. The criteria are (1) constitutional eligibility, (2) ballot access, and (3) electoral support. All three criteria must be satisfied before a candidate is invited to debate.

1. **Evidence of Constitutional Eligibility**
   The CPD's first criterion requires satisfaction of the eligibility requirements of Article II, Section 1, of the Constitution. The requirements are satisfied if the candidate:
   a. is at least 35 years of age;
   b. is a Natural Born Citizen of the United States and a resident of the United States for fourteen years; and
   c. is otherwise eligible under the Constitution.

2. **Evidence of Ballot Access**
   The CPD's second criterion requires that the candidate qualify to have his/her name appear on enough state ballots to have at least a mathematical chance of securing an Electoral College majority in the 2008 general election.

3. Indicators of Electoral Support

The CPD's third criterion requires that the candidate have a level of support of at least 15% (fifteen percent) of the national electorate as determined by five selected national public opinion polling organizations, using the average of those organizations' most recent publicly-reported results at the time of the determination.

Open Debates

The CPD demonstrates its subservience to the two major parties during the debate negotiation process. Every four years, the CPD publicly proposes a debate schedule and publishes candidate selection criteria. Questions concerning third-party participation and debate formats, however, are ultimately resolved behind closed-doors, where Republican and Democratic negotiators draft secret debate contracts. The CPD, posing as an independent sponsor, implements the dictates of the contracts, shielding the major party candidates from public criticism and lawsuits. . . . In fact, the CPD replaced the League of Women Voters as sponsor by implementing the 1988 Memorandum of Understanding that the League had so vociferously rejected.

In 1996, for example, Bob Dole and Bill Clinton hatched a deal that ruined the presidential debates before they even started. During debate negotiations, Dole demanded the exclusion of Reform Party nominee Ross Perot, even though Perot had received $29 million in taxpayers' funds for his campaign and over three-quarters of eligible voters wanted him included. President Clinton, meanwhile, desired the smallest possible audience for the debates . . . because he was comfortably leading in the polls. As a result of their agreement, Perot was excluded, follow-up questions were prohibited, one debate was canceled, and the remaining two debates were deliberately scheduled opposite the World Series, producing the smallest audience in presidential debate history.

The CPD allows the two major-party campaigns to exercise absolute control over the selection of format, thereby eliminating spontaneity from the debates. Candidates handpick compliant panelists and moderators, prohibit candidate-to-candidate questioning, require the screening of town-hall questions, severely limit response times, and limit or ban follow-up questions. The result is a series of glorified news conferences, with the candidates' superficially glazing over the issues while reciting memorized sound-bites to fit 90-second response slots. "It's too much show business and too much prompting, too much artificiality, and not really debates," said former President George Bush. "They're rehearsed appearances."

DOCUMENT-BASED QUESTION

What criteria does the Committee on Presidential Debates (CPD) establish for the debates? Why does Open Debates believe that the CPD is influenced by the two major parties?

For most of the nation's history the issue of disability was covered entirely by a provision of Article II of the Constitution:

> In Case of . . . Inability to discharge the Powers and Duties of the said Office, the Same shall devolve on the Vice President, and the Congress may by Law provide for the case of . . . Inability, both of the President and Vice President, declaring what Officer shall then act as President, and such Officer shall act accordingly, until the Disability be removed, or a President shall be elected.

What does *disability* mean, and does it include both mental and physical impairments? What about other disabling situations, such as a presidential kidnapping? Who is authorized to declare that the president is disabled: Congress, the vice president, the cabinet, some combination of the three, or only the president? To what does the vice president succeed in the case of a presidential disability—to the "Powers and Duties of the said Office" or to the presidency itself? Is the succession temporary or permanent? During the country's first century under the Constitution, these questions seemed remote. President James Garfield's (1881) lengthy disability in 1881 made them real.

The First Lengthy Presidential Disability

The bullet that pierced President Garfield's spinal column left him incapacitated and generally unable to fulfill the powers and duties of his office during the eighty-day period between his shooting on July 2, 1881, and his death on September 19, 1881. During those months, the problem of presidential disability was discussed widely.

According to one opinion that was offered at the time, the term *disability* applied only to permanent mental incapacity. As former senator William W. Eaton (D-CT) maintained, "There could be no disability that the President can be conscious of." Others took the more general position that a disability could be mental or physical and either temporary or permanent in duration. Still others adopted a more situational approach. Former senator Lyman Trumbull (R-Il), for example, argued that a presidential disability should be declared only when an incapacity that was generally known was joined to an urgent need for executive action.

The consequences of the vice president assuming presidential authority in the event of a presidential disability also were debated. The principal view was that the vice president would act as president only temporarily, until the disabled president had recovered. Some believed, however, that once the duties of the presidency "devolved," the vice president became the president for the remainder of the term, thereby dispossessing the disabled president of the office to which he had been elected.

Opinion about who could declare a president disabled was similarly divided, in this case between those who thought it was a **legislative** function and those who thought it was up to the vice president. At one point, Garfield's cabinet decided unanimously that Vice President Chester Arthur (1881–1885) should assume presidential responsibilities. However, when they proposed this course of action to Arthur, he adamantly refused. To assume power while Garfield was alive and without Garfield's blessing, the vice president believed, would be politically reckless and constitutionally uncertain.

After Arthur became president, he repeatedly expressed concern about the ambiguities of the succession provision of the Constitution, especially the proper response to a presidential disability. Arthur's concern did not stem solely from his experience during the Garfield disability. During the summer of 1882, Arthur learned that he was suffering from an incurable kidney disease. He thus faced the possibility that his own disability or death might occur at a time when the nation lacked a vice president. A year later the illness forced President Arthur cut his schedule in half, and the work of the government slowed noticeably. Nonetheless, for political reasons Arthur did not disclose the full extent of his illness, nor did he succeed in persuading Congress to address the succession and disability issue.

The Secret Disability

Shortly after Grover Cleveland (1885–1889, 1893–1897) became president for the second time a financial panic struck the country. Major industries went bankrupt, banks closed their doors, businesses shut down, and millions of people were out of work. President Cleveland believed that a primary cause of the **depression** was the Sherman Silver Purchase Act of 1890. On June 30, 1893, he called Congress into special session to consider repealing the act.

The night Cleveland called the special session, he boarded the yacht *Oneida* in New York City and embarked on a five-day cruise of Long Island Sound. For the next month, the president alternated between visits to his summer home at Buzzards Bay in Massachusetts and cruises on the yacht. On August 5, he returned to Washington, where two days later he addressed the special session of Congress.

Unknown to the public and virtually all members of the government, including Vice President Adlai E. Stevenson, Cleveland had undergone a surgery during the initial five-day cruise and had spent the subsequent weeks recuperating. A surgeon had removed a cancerous growth from the roof of Cleveland's mouth as well as a major portion of his upper jaw. The entire operation, which had taken place while the unconscious president was strapped to a chair propped against the yacht's mast, had taken less than ninety minutes. Later, at his summer home, Cleveland was fitted with an artificial jaw so that he could speak intelligibly. In late July, during another cruise, the president underwent a second operation to remove suspicious tissue that had been noticed during the first operation.

On August 7, 1893, Cleveland was sufficiently recovered to address the special session of Congress with his customary vigor and coherence. At the end of the summer the *Philadelphia Press* published an account of the operations that was officially denounced as a hoax. Others put out a story that the president had simply suffered a toothache that required the extraction of some teeth. Because Cleveland seemed to be in fine health, with no noticeable changes in his facial structure or speech, the story faded.

Not until twenty-four years later, with the publication in 1917 of a story in the *Saturday Evening Post* by one of Cleveland's doctors, were the facts revealed. Cleveland, who died in 1908, had insisted on complete secrecy because he did not want to risk further unsettling a public that was already in the throes of a financial panic.

The Wilson Disability

On September 25, 1919, in the midst of a speaking tour of the country to rouse support for the League of Nations, President Woodrow Wilson fell ill. The public was told that the president had suffered a complete nervous breakdown brought on by overwork and the effects of an earlier attack of influenza. The rest of the tour was canceled, and Wilson returned to Washington. On October 2, he suffered a stroke that paralyzed the left side of his body.

After Wilson's stroke, the White House was turned into a nursing ward under the direction of Cary Grayson, the president's close friend and physician, and Edith Galt Wilson, the president's wife. They were assisted by presidential secretary Joseph P. Tumulty. Vague and ambiguous health bulletins sparked wild rumors about Wilson's condition. Nevertheless, Edith Wilson's first concern was to save her husband, and if that meant shielding him from the responsibilities and burdens of the presidency, she was determined to do so.

For more than six months after his stroke, President Wilson was bedridden and saw few people. Meanwhile, the country was in the midst of a difficult transition from war to peace, with the attendant challenges of shifting the economy to a peacetime footing, demobilizing the armed forces, and considering the Versailles peace treaty with its controversial provision for a League of Nations.

Clearly, presidential leadership was necessary in such circumstances. The First Lady and Tumulty did what they could to marshal and focus the president's meager energies for occasional demonstrations of competency and for official tasks such as approving papers and dictating instructions for the treaty fight. Secretary of State Robert Lansing, however, was concerned about the potential drift in government affairs. The day after Wilson's stroke, Lansing spoke to Tumulty about the possibility of asking Vice President Thomas R. Marshall to act as president. At that meeting, Lansing read the succession and disability provision of the Constitution to Tumulty, who replied that he needed no tutoring on the subject. Tumulty then declared, "You may rest assured that while Woodrow Wilson is lying in the White House on the broad of his back I will not be a party to ousting him." At a cabinet meeting on October 6, 1919, called at Lansing's initiative, a discussion of presidential disability ended abruptly when Tumulty and Grayson arrived. They informed the assembled heads of the departments that they, the president's secretary and physician, would repudiate any effort to declare Wilson disabled.

As months passed, repeated calls were made for Vice President Marshall to step in as acting president. However, in the face of ambiguous constitutional guidelines, an absence of historical **precedents,** a hostile White House, and a reluctant vice president, the affairs of state continued to drift. Marshall carefully avoided any appearance of attempting to usurp presidential authority, and he certainly was loath to incur the wrath of Edith Wilson. The vice president reportedly said, "I am not going to get myself entangled with Mrs. Wilson. No politician ever exposes himself to the hatred of a woman, particularly if she's the wife of the President of the United States."

As the senior member of the cabinet, Secretary of State Lansing continued to try to coordinate government affairs by convening informal cabinet meetings. Between October 1919 and February 1920, he called more than twenty such meetings. But because the United States has never had a system of cabinet government, many matters arose that the cabinet simply could not handle. For example, it could not respond to legislation; nearly thirty **bills** became law when they were neither signed nor **vetoed** by the president during this period. Because the cabinet could not make presidential appointments, many vacancies in government went unfilled. Needless to say, the cabinet also could not manage the League of Nations controversy in the Senate or accept the credentials of foreign ambassadors.

Perhaps it was a sign of Wilson's partial recovery that in February 1920 he wrote to Lansing to voice his objections to the secretary's initiative in convening the cabinet. In replying to the president's letter, Lansing declared that his actions betrayed no intention to assume or exercise presidential powers. Wilson responded with the blunt suggestion that Lansing resign as secretary of state, which he did on February 12, 1920. Wilson

reportedly told Tumulty, "It is never the wrong time to spike disloyalty. When Lansing sought to oust me, I was upon my back. I am on my feet now and I will not have disloyalty about me."

In the aftermath of Lansing's dismissal, two disability proposals were considered by Congress. One plan sought to empower the Supreme Court to declare a president disabled in response to a congressional **resolution** authorizing it to do so. The other plan would have allowed the cabinet to certify a presidential disability by majority vote. Hearings were held on these proposals, but no action was taken. On April 13, 1920, President Wilson held his first cabinet meeting in six months. Although he never fully recovered from his illness, the president became a bit more active and finished out the remaining months of his second term.

The Eisenhower Disabilities

The presidency of Dwight Eisenhower (1953–1961) brought the disability issue into vivid and recurring focus. Between 1955 and 1957, President Eisenhower suffered three illnesses that each left him disabled for several days or weeks. This series of illnesses prompted Eisenhower to create a set of informal precedents and procedures for dealing with presidential disabilities.

Eisenhower's first disability, a heart attack that required complete rest for about a month, occurred while he was vacationing in Colorado in September 1955. Fortunately, the illness struck when the press of public business was light—the situation abroad was calm and Congress not in session. In addition, as president Eisenhower had made extensive use of the National Security Council and the cabinet, which meant that Vice President Richard Nixon, who was a council and cabinet member, was well versed in the domestic and international issues that the administration was facing. Moreover, because Eisenhower had put in place an extensive staff structure in the White House, the conduct of the presidency did not depend on him alone.

Finally, Eisenhower and Secretary of State John Foster Dulles were fully aware of the problems presented by the Wilson disability (they had both been young men at the time) and were determined to avoid similar problems. Eisenhower remembered how the vague official reports about

Lyndon B. Johnson (1963–1969) takes the presidential oath of office on November 22, 1963, aboard the presidential plane, *Air Force One*, soon after the assassination of President John F. Kennedy (1961–1963). Johnson's wife, Lady Bird, and the former First Lady, Jacqueline Kennedy, watch as Judge Sarah T. Hughes administers the oath. (Cecil Stoughton, LBJ Library)

Wilson's condition had led to rampant speculation, so he was determined to keep the press and public fully informed about his condition and progress.

As a result, Eisenhower's first illness was handled relatively smoothly. By the end of the president's first week in the hospital both the National Security Council and the cabinet had met at their usual time, with Vice President Nixon presiding. At its meeting, the cabinet agreed on a set of administrative operating principles, including the assignment of presidential assistant and de facto chief of staff Sherman Adams to act as the primary liaison with the president. A rough and workable division of labor emerged: Adams oversaw the day-to-day business of the executive branch, and Nixon carried on the established public functions of the presidency.

The president's recuperation progressed well. He began receiving visitors after the second week and was discharged from the hospital in six weeks. Eisenhower met with the cabinet in late November and returned to the White House, completely recovered, in mid-January 1956. Indeed, the president's rapid and full recovery not only defused the disability issue, but also put to rest speculation about his ability to run for reelection in November.

Less than nine months after his heart attack, however, Eisenhower was struck by ileitis, an inflammation of part of the small intestine. The president underwent successful exploratory surgery on June 9, 1956. Within two days, he was ambulatory and able to meet with staff. Although Eisenhower needed to rest, he was quite capable of performing official acts. On July 21, for example, he embarked on a trip to Panama to attend a meeting with South American presidents. Despite his rapid recovery, Eisenhower was disturbed that in the nuclear age the country had been without a functioning president while he was on the operating table.

The president's third illness, a mild stroke, occurred a year and a half later, on November 25, 1957, a time of considerable international tension. The United States was still reeling from the Soviet launch in October of the space ship *Sputnik* I, the first man-made object to orbit the Earth. At the same time, warning signs were emerging of what would turn out to be the severe economic **recession** of 1958, and a meeting of heads of state organized by the North Atlantic Treaty Organization (NATO) was just three weeks off. Fortunately, the president's stroke caused him only some brief difficulty in speaking, and by December 2 he was back to his normal routine.

In the aftermath of his third illness, Eisenhower asked the Justice Department to recommend a procedure for dealing with presidential disabilities. The department proposed a constitutional **amendment** that would describe how to declare and terminate a disability. When, once again, Congress seemed uninterested in acting, Eisenhower and Nixon worked out their own informal arrangement through a letter of agreement that was made public on March 3, 1958. The arrangement was simple: Either the president or, if the president were unable, the vice president could decide when the vice president should step in to act as president until such time as the president declared himself restored. In the absence of a constitutional amendment, this agreement also was adopted by President John Kennedy (1961–1963) and Vice President Lyndon Johnson in August 1961, by President Johnson (1963–1969) and House Speaker John McCormack in December 1963, and by President Johnson and Vice President Hubert H. Humphrey in January 1965. The **ratification** of the Twenty-fifth Amendment in 1967 imposed a formal, constitutional procedure to deal with presidential disabilities and succession.

See also: Twenty-fifth Amendment (1967).

Further Reading
Gilbert, Robert. *Managing Crisis: Presidential Disability and the Twenty-Fifth Amendment.* New York: Fordham University Press, 2000.

Presidential Pardons

The authority of the president to forgive various offenses and to commute punishments. Article II, Section 2, of the Constitution delegates to the president the "[p]ower to grant Reprieves and Pardons for Offenses against the United States, except in Cases of **Impeachment.**" In other words, it gives the president the ability to be merciful as well as vengeful.

The pardon power was first used in 1792 when President George Washington (1789–1797) "most earnestly admonish[ed] and exhort[ed]" the whiskey manufacturers of western Pennsylvania to cease their disobedience and obstruction of the law. They were, the president's proclamation continued, not only refusing to pay taxes on the whiskey produced, but also resisting enforcement of the tax law with violence. Washington tried issuing demands to end the "Whiskey Rebellion," and he tried applying force. Law and order in the western counties of Pennsylvania, however, were not restored until the president promised and granted the offenders a full and absolute pardon.

A reprieve reduces a sentence already imposed by a tribunal. A person sentenced to death by a U.S. district court or military court martial, for example, may have his or her sentence reduced to a long term of imprisonment by presidential reprieve. The guilt is not wiped out, but the severity of the punishment inflicted on the guilty person is reduced.

Presidential pardons wipe out both guilt and punishment. They restore the person pardoned to his or her full civil rights, as if the offense had never been committed. President Gerald Ford (1974–1977), for example, granted a full and unconditional pardon to his predecessor, Richard Nixon (1969–1974), and relieved the former president of the possibility of being prosecuted for any involvement he may have had in the crimes associated with the Watergate scandal. In late December 1992, President George H.W. Bush (1989–1993) issued controversial pardons to several key figures who had been implicated in the Iran-contra scandal during the Reagan (1981–1989) administration.

Reprieves and pardons may be granted to individuals or to classes of people in the form of "amnesties." For example, Presidents Abraham Lincoln (1861–1865) and Andrew Johnson (1865–1869) signed amnesties for Confederate soldiers and political leaders, as did Presidents Gerald Ford and Jimmy Carter (1977–1981) for people who violated the Selective Service Act by evading the draft during the Vietnam War (1964–1975).

The president may attach conditions to either form of clemency. President Nixon, for example, pardoned labor leader Jimmy Hoffa on the condition that Hoffa never again become involved in union activities.

The clemency authority of the president is extensive. It applies to any federal process or offender except, by express constitutional language, those persons tried (or being tried) and convicted through congressional impeachment. Moreover, it is one of the few constitutional powers of the president that does not require **legislative** agreement. Congress, in fact, may not interfere with presidential clemency authority in any manner.

The pardon process today is handled by the Office of the Pardon Attorney, created by Congress in 1891. The pardon attorney reviews petitions for clemency and makes a recommendation to the attorney general, who then considers the petition and advises the president. Many presidents have not been reluctant to use this authority. Harry S. Truman (1945–1953) pardoned more than 1,500 people who had violated the Selective Service Act during World War II (1939–1945); Gerald Ford issued 409 pardons in just under two and a half years in office; Jimmy Carter issued 566 pardons and commutations in four years; and Ronald Reagan issued 406 pardons during his two terms in office. George H.W. Bush issued only 77 pardons in his one term, but his postelection defeat pardons of six Iran-contra scandal figures were very controversial. Finally, Bill Clinton (1993–2001) issued 450 pardons over his two terms in office.

Perhaps the most controversial gestures of clemency in the modern era were some of the 140 pardons and 36 commutations that Bill Clinton issued on January 20, 2001, his last day in office. Among those, none was more questionable than the pardon of fugitive financier Marc Rich, whose former wife had made appeals for the pardon after she contributed generously to the Democratic Party, the Clinton reelection campaign, and the Clinton presidential library. That Clinton ignored the normal pardon process in the Office of Pardon Attorney in the Department of Justice angered many critics who believed that the president had acted improperly. The unusual timing of the pardon, in the last moments of Clinton's presidency, added to the sense of suspicion about Clinton's motives. Calls for a congressional inquiry and legal challenge to the pardon were heard, but Clinton had the right under the presidential pardon power to do what he did, and his critics had no recourse other than to complain.

As of late 2008, President George W. Bush (2001–2009) issued 171 pardons and commuted the sentences of eight people. None, however, were deemed controversial.

See also: Constitution of the United States.

Presidential Powers and Roles

See Chief Diplomat; Chief Economist; Chief Executive; Chief of State; Commander in Chief; Constitution of the United States; Emergency Powers; Executive Orders; The Treaty Power.

Presidential Primaries

Elections in which the voters directly choose convention delegates. A revolutionary new mechanism for delegate selection that emerged in Florida at the turn of the twentieth century, the presidential primary was used in thirteen states by 1912. In his first annual message to Congress the following year, President Woodrow Wilson (1913–1921) advocated the establishment of a national primary to select presidential candidates:

> I feel confident that I do not misinterpret the wishes or the expectations of the country when I urge the prompt enactment of legislation which will provide for primary elections throughout the country at which the voters of several parties may choose their nominees for the presidency without the intervention of nominating conventions.

Wilson went on to suggest the retention of conventions for the purpose of declaring the results of the primaries and formulating the parties' platforms.

Before any action was taken on Wilson's proposal, the **progressive** spirit that prompted the growth of presidential primaries died out. Not until the late 1960s and early 1970s, when widespread pressures for change touched both parties, but especially the Democrats, was there a rapid growth in presidential primaries. In the mid-1980s, some states reverted to the **caucus,** but the revival of this method of delegate selection quickly ended.

Participation in the presidential primary usually is restricted to voters belonging to the party holding the primary. In some states, however, participation by voters outside the party is allowed by state-mandated open primaries, usually with the caveat, that the party in which voters cast a primary ballot is publicly recorded.

Rules in the 1980s and 1990s

In June 1982, the Democratic National Committee (DNC) adopted several changes in the presidential nominating process recommended by the party's Commission on Presidential Nominations, chaired by Governor James B. Hunt Jr. of North Carolina. The Hunt Commission, as it came to be known, suggested revisions to increase the power of party regulars and give the convention more freedom to act on its own. It was the fourth time in twelve years that the Democrats, struggling to repair their nominating process without repudiating earlier reforms, had rewritten their party rules.

One major change in the Democrats' rules was the creation of "superdelegates"—party and elected officials who would go to the 1984 convention uncommitted and cast about 14 percent of the ballots. The DNC also adopted a Hunt Commission proposal to weaken the rule obligating delegates to vote for their original presidential preference on the first convention ballot. The new rule also allowed a presidential candidate to replace any disloyal delegate with a more faithful one.

Among the most significant revisions was the Democrats' decision to relax proportional representation at the convention. Proportional representation is the distribution of delegates among candidates to reflect their share of the primary or caucus vote, both statewide and in congressional districts. Mandated by party rules in 1980, it was blamed by some Democrats for the protracted primary fight between President Jimmy Carter (1977–1981) and Senator Edward M. Kennedy of Massachusetts. Because candidates needed only about 20 percent of the vote in most places to qualify for a share of the delegates, Kennedy was able to remain in contention. While the system kept the Kennedy campaign going, it did nothing to help his chances of winning the nomination.

Although the Democrats' 1984 rules permitted states to retain proportional representation, they also allowed states to take advantage of two options that could help a front-running candidate build the momentum to wrap up the nomination early in the year.

One was a winner-take-more system. States could elect to keep proportional representation but adopt a winner bonus plan that would award the top vote-getter in each district one extra delegate.

The other option was a return to the **loophole primary,** which party rules outlawed in 1980—with exceptions allowing Illinois and West Virginia to retain their loophole voting systems. In the loophole states, voters ballot directly for delegates, with each delegate candidate identified by presidential preference. Several presidential contenders might win at least a fraction of the delegates in a given district, but the most common result is a sweep by the presidential front-runner, even if that candidate has less than an absolute majority. Loophole primaries aid the building of a consensus behind the front-runner, while still giving other candidates a chance to inject themselves back into the race by winning a major loophole state decisively.

The Democratic National Committee (DNC) retained the delegate-selection season adopted in 1978: a three-month period stretching from the second Tuesday in March to the second Tuesday in June. In an effort to reduce the growing influence of early states in the nominating process, however, the Democrats required Iowa and New Hampshire to move their highly publicized elections to late winter. Party rules maintained the privileged status of Iowa and New Hampshire before other states, but mandated that their initial nominating rounds be held only eight days apart in 1984. Five weeks had intervened between the Iowa caucuses and New Hampshire primary in 1980.

The DNC also retained rules requiring primary states to set candidate filing deadlines thirty to ninety days before the election and limiting participation in the delegate selection process to Democrats only. This last rule eliminated crossover primaries where voters could participate in the Democratic primary without designating their party affiliation. African Americans and Hispanics won continued endorsement of affirmative action in the new party rules. Women gained renewed support for the equal-division rule, which required state delegations at the national convention to be divided equally between men and women.

The Democratic Party's 1988 presidential nominating process remained basically the same as that used in 1984. The rules adopted by the national committee included only minor modifications suggested by the party's rules review panel, the Fairness Commission.

The bloc of uncommitted party and elected officials, or superdelegates, was expanded slightly to 16 percent and rearranged to reserve more convention seats for members of Congress, governors, and DNC members. The rules restricting participation in Democratic primaries and caucuses to Democrats only was relaxed so the open primaries in Wisconsin and Montana could be conducted with the approval of the national party. In addition, the share of the vote a candidate needed to win in a primary or caucus—and thus qualify for delegates—was lowered from the 20 percent level used in most places in 1984 to 15 percent.

Only the rule regarding the 15 percent "threshold" spawned much debate during the rules-writing process, and though the discussion of the issue seldom was harsh, it did reveal a gap in the party on what the proper role of the national convention should be.

Most party leaders, including DNC Chairman Paul G. Kirk Jr., wanted a threshold of at least 15 percent because they thought it would help steadily shrink the field of presidential candidates during the primary and caucus season and ensure that the convention would be a "ratifying" body that confirmed the choice of the party's voters.

Civil rights leader and presidential candidate Jesse L. Jackson, however, saw it differently, as did several other **liberal** activists. They wanted a convention that was more "deliberative," and they complained that getting one was virtually impossible under the system as it existed because the rules discriminated against long-shot candidates and produced an artificial consensus behind one candidate.

Most Democratic leaders were satisfied with the way the nominating process operated in 1984, and they felt it would be a disaster for the party to go through a free-wheeling, multiballot convention. Not since 1952, at the beginning of the television age, has a national party taken more than one ballot to nominate its presidential candidate.

At the DNC meeting where the new rules were approved, some African American committee members joined with a few white liberal activists in proposing to eliminate the 15 percent threshold. The proposal was rejected by voice vote. A proposal to lower the threshold to 10 percent was defeated 92 to 178.

The Democrats required all states, beginning in 1992, to divide their publicly elected delegates proportionally among candidates who drew at least 15 percent of the primary or caucus vote. The number of superdelegates, which the party continued to increase, reached 1,260 for the 2004 convention.

Between 1972 to 1996, the Republican Party made few changes in its nominating rules. While the Democratic rules were revised somewhat for each presidential cycle, the GOP rules remained stable. With the 2000election approaching, the Republicans, having changed their minds on the desirability of deciding the nomination contest by

March or April, provided a bonus for those states that choose their delegates to the 2000 GOP convention after March 15.

Before the 2000 convention was even held, though, Republicans were considering even more controversial solutions to spread out the primary calendar, which had become congested with events in February and March. The so-called Delaware Plan would have put the smallest states at the beginning of the nominating season in 2004, the largest states at the end. After winning the approval of the Republican National Committee (RNC) at its preconvention meeting, the proposal was killed by the convention rules committee at the behest of the party's standardbearer, Governor George W. Bush of Texas, who wanted to remove any semblance of controversy.

Republicans, though, did make several changes in delegate-selection rules for 2004, including elimination of the bonus delegates and creation of automatic superdelegate seats for members of the RNC.

Credentials Disputes

Before the opening of a convention, the national committee compiles a temporary roll of delegates. The roll is referred to the convention's credentials committee, which holds hearings on the challenges and makes recommendations to the convention, the final arbiter of all disputes.

Some of the most bitter convention battles have concerned the seating of contested delegations. In the twentieth century, most of the heated credentials fights have concerned delegations from the South. In the Republican Party the challenges focused on the power of the Republican state organizations to dictate the selection of delegates.

The issue was hottest in 1912 and 1952, when the party throughout most of the South was a skeletal structure whose power was restricted largely to selection of convention delegates. Within the Democratic Party the question of southern delegate credentials emerged after World War II (1939–1945) on the volatile issues of civil rights and party loyalty. Important credentials challenges on these issues occurred at the 1948, 1952, 1964, and 1968 Democratic conventions.

There were numerous credentials challenges at the 1972 Democratic convention, but these challenges involved delegations from across the nation and focused on violations of the party's new guidelines.

After their 1952 credentials battle, the Republicans established a contest committee within the national committee to review credentials challenges before the convention. After their divisive 1968 convention, the Democrats also created a formal credentials procedure to review all challenges before the opening of the convention.

Convention Rules

Equally important to the settlement of credentials challenges are the rules under which the convention operates. The Republican Party adopts a new set of rules at every convention. Although large portions of the existing rules are reenacted each time, general revision is always possible.

After its 1968 convention the Democratic Party set out to reform itself and the convention system. The Commission on Rules and the Commission on Party Structure and Delegate Selection, both created by the 1968 convention, proposed many changes that were accepted by the national committee. As a result, a formal set of rules was adopted for the first time at the party's 1972 convention.

Controversial Rules

Although it did not have a formal set of rules before 1972, the Democratic Party had long operated with two controversial rules never used by the Republicans: the unit rule and the two-thirds nominating rule. The unit rule enabled the majority of a delegation, if authorized by its state party, to cast the entire vote of the delegation for one candidate or position. In use since the earliest Democratic conventions, the unit rule was abolished by the 1968 convention.

From their first convention in 1832 until the 1936 convention, the Democrats employed the two-thirds nominating rule, which required any candidate for president or vice president to win not simply a majority, but a two-thirds majority. Viewed as a boon to the South, since it allowed that region a virtual **veto** power over any possible nominee, the rule was abolished with the stipulation that the South would receive an increased vote allocation at later conventions.

In its century of use the two-thirds rule frequently produced protracted, multiballot conven-

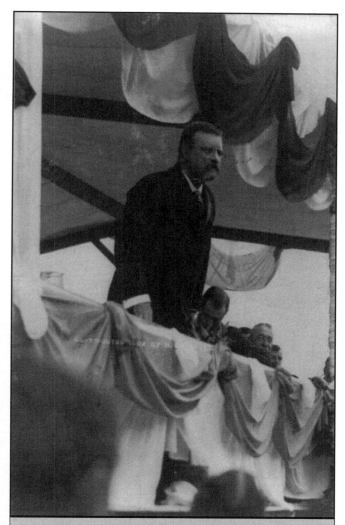

Theodore Roosevelt (1901–1909) campaigned vigorously for the presidency during the Election of 1904. (Library of Congress)

tions, often giving the Democrats a degree of turbulence the Republicans, requiring only a simple majority, did not have. Between 1832 and 1932, seven Democratic conventions took more than ten ballots to select a presidential candidate. In contrast, in their entire convention history, the Republicans have had just one convention that required more than ten ballots to select a presidential candidate.

One controversy that surfaced during the 1980 Democratic Party convention concerned a rule that bound delegates to vote on the first ballot for the candidates under whose banner they had been elected. Supporters of Senator Kennedy had devoted their energy to prying the nomination from **incumbent** President Carter by defeating that

rule. Nevertheless, the final tally showed 1,936.42 delegates favoring the binding rule and 1,390.58 opposing it. Passage of the binding rule ensured Carter's renomination, and shortly after the vote Kennedy announced that his name would not be placed in nomination.

Convention Officers

Credentials, rules, and platform are three of the major convention committees. Within the Republican Party, though, the committee on permanent organization **ratifies** the slate of convention officials. In the Democratic Party, this function is performed by the rules committee.

In both the Democratic and Republican parties, the permanent chairman presides over most of the convention. Oftentimes, since the end of World War II, the position of chairman had gone to the party's leader in the House of Representatives, particularly at the GOP convention. However, this loose **precedent** was broken in the Democratic Party by a rule adopted at the 1972 convention requiring that the presiding officer position alternate every four years between the sexes.

See also: Democratic Party (1828–); Republican Party (1854–).

Further Reading

Bartels, Larry M. *Presidential Primaries and the Dynamics of Public Choice.* Princeton, NJ: Princeton University Press, 1988.

Cook, Rhodes. *United States Presidential Primary Elections 2000–2004: A Handbook of Election Statistics.* Washington, DC: CQ Press, 2006.

Presidential Salaries and Benefits

The president's salary is determined by Congress. According to Article II, Section 1, of the Constitution: "The President shall, at stated Times, receive for his Services, a Compensation, which shall neither be increased nor diminished during the period for which he shall have been elected, and he shall not receive within that Period any other Emolument from the United States, or any

A-Z

of them." On September 24, 1789, the First Congress set the salary for the president of the United States at $25,000 a year.

The issue of paying the president had caused some controversy at the Constitutional Convention. The delegates were concerned that their president not become their king, and there was some discussion about making the office of the president one with no or little pay. Benjamin Franklin suggested that the chief **executive** of the new nation not be paid any salary at all. Franklin argued that the love of money was the root of much political evil, and he proposed to allow the president to receive "no salary, stipend, fee or reward" above what was necessary to defray the expenses of office.

Franklin's proposal was postponed and conveniently forgotten, but his goal of making the presidency largely an office of honor and not of profit was achieved when George Washington (1789–1797) declined any share of personal compensation to which he was constitutionally entitled.

With changing times and with the increased importance of the office of the presidency, the president's salary has gradually been adjusted upward. Not until after the Civil War (1861–1865), when Ulysses S. Grant (1869–1877) became president, did Congress pass the first increase in the president's salary, however. From the beginning, the salaries of all public officials in the United States were low when compared with those of other nations. In 1873, in an effort to keep top public officials from having to draw on their private resources, Congress voted to increase the salaries of some of the major federal government positions, including those of members Congress, the president, and other executive branch officials. At this time, the president's salary was doubled to $50,000 a year. Even though most of the country viewed these increases in pay as justifiable, when Congress decided to vote its own pay raises retroactive to 1871, this "salary grab" aroused great resentment among Americans and Congress eventually repealed the retroactive pay. Public indignation continued to be so great, however, that the members of Congress finally reduced their own salaries back to their former levels but left the president's raise untouched. Because Congress had approved the increase on March 3, 1873, a day before Grant's second term began,

Grant served his first term at half of what he was paid for his second term.

Since 1873, presidential pay increases have not come frequently because of political pressure against raising the salaries of public officials. Congress voted for a second pay raise for the president in 1909, increasing the annual salary to $75,000. President William Howard Taft (1909–1913) was the first to benefit from this increase in salary.

In 1949, Congress raised the salary of the president to $100,000 a year. It also decided that the president henceforth would be paid monthly rather than the customary quarterly. In addition, Congress for the first time recognized the need to assist the president in defraying the expenses of official presidential duties. President Harry S. Truman (1945–1953) was the first president to receive the $100,000 yearly salary and a $50,000 yearly tax-free expense account. In the Revenue Act of 1951, however, Congress reversed itself and subjected the president's expense account, as well as the expense accounts of members of Congress, to income taxes.

Acting upon a recommendation by President Lyndon B. Johnson (1963–1969), Congress voted to double the president's salary, to $200,000, as of January 20, 1969, inauguration day for Richard Nixon (1969–1974). Congress also voted to give the president a $100,000 travel allowance and a $12,000 entertainment allowance, both tax-free.

Although the 1989 Commission on Executive, **Legislative,** and Judicial Salaries recommended that the president's salary be raised to $350,000, it was over a decade before Congress took any action to boost the president's pay. The increase to $400,000 a year was approved in the final days of the 106th Congress as part of the Treasury and General Government **Appropriations** Act of 2000. Therefore, in 2001 President George W. Bush (2001–2009) received the first salary increase granted by Congress since 1969. During that same period of time, congressional pay increased twelve times.

Some presidents have been wealthy in their own right. Of the recent presidents, John F. Kennedy (1961–1963), Johnson, Nixon, Jimmy Carter (1977–1981), Ronald Reagan (1981–1989), George H.W. Bush, (1989–1993) and George W. Bush were all millionaires. Only one president besides Washington ever indicated that he would be willing to forego a salary: President Kennedy returned his entire salary to the U.S. Treasury.

Presidential pay does not tell the whole story, however. In addition to the $400,000 annual salary and expense, travel, and entertainment accounts, presidents receive many more tangible benefits from being in office, such as the top consideration in air traffic given *Air Force One* and the priority the president's car takes over other traffic—benefits that would seem invaluable to most air travelers and commuters. Perquisites make the job worth a great deal more than the annual salary of the officeholder.

Perquisites of Office

Concerned about the prospects for a monarchy in the new American nation, Patrick Henry warned, "Your president may easily become king." *The Federalist Papers,* written to ease the concerns of citizens in New York about the coming constitution, tried to allay the fears that the presidency would become too powerful and would resemble the British monarchy. Alexander Hamilton, in defending the constitutional provisions for the presidency, argued that no similarities existed between the new American presidency and the British monarchy.

The presidency has not become a monarchy in the sense of the eighteenth-century British monarchy. Yet over the years, the presidency has developed not only a regal style but a lavish splendor. Much of the pomp and circumstance that Hamilton refused to believe would accompany the growth of the presidency now exists.

Early Benefits and Privileges

Washington, Jefferson, and the other early presidents did not enjoy the large expense accounts of modern presidents. Until the presidency of Calvin Coolidge, presidents had to pay for all the food consumed in the White House, including food at state dinners. During his eight years in office, Jefferson recorded that he spent $10,855.90 on wine alone. With these types of expenses, and a salary of only $25,000 a year, Jefferson left office $20,000 in debt. Presidents still pay for all the food they and their families consume privately at the White House, but in the 1920s, U.S. taxpayers began paying for most of the expenses of state dinners.

Some of the nation's first presidents actually endured physical hardships while in office. John Adams (1797–1801), the first president to live in the White House, found life there not very comfortable. First Lady Abigail Adams said that the unfinished mansion did not offer many of the "luxuries" of her old home. She dried her washing in the partially finished audience hall (now the East Room) and suffered the indignity of an outdoor bathroom. On the night Franklin Pierce (1853–1857) moved into the White House in 1853, the mansion had little furniture and no lights. Pierce could find only a single candle to illuminate his way to a mattress on the floor of his bedroom. Congress subsequently allocated $25,000 for Pierce to refurbish the White House—at that time the largest sum ever set aside for improvements to the president's home. Pierce installed the White House's first furnace and had the presidential residence painted inside and out. Yet Congress balked at providing funding for someone to tend the new furnace.

Some presidents brought their own furniture to the White House and took it with them when they left. Others, such as James Monroe (1817–1825), left their furniture for future occupants.

Transportation was usually furnished by private individuals or companies to the presidents and their families. Occasionally, someone gave the president a horse or carriage to use, and the railroads allowed the president and the first family to travel free on their lines. Until the presidency of William Howard Taft, however, no funds were available for official travel expenses.

Retirement from office brought little in the way of financial rewards to the first chief executives. Most found themselves without pensions and with few benefits. Thomas Jefferson (1801–1809) retired to Monticello at the age of sixty-five. Even though he was a prolific writer, a creative inventor, and an expert architect, musician, and lawyer, he found himself in a financial crisis. Heavily in debt from his days in the presidency, Jefferson had to accept a gift of $16,500 to save himself from bankruptcy. When James Monroe left office at sixty-six, he was forced to sell one of his two Virginia estates, Ash Lawn, to help pay his debts. He later sold his Oak Hill estate and moved to New York City. At his death, seven years after his retirement, he left an estate drained of funds. In 1880, after Ulysses Grant (1869–1877) tried unsuccessfully for a third term in the White House, he set up an investment firm in New York that eventually went bankrupt. As his financial situation worsened, Grant had to sell his swords and presidential souvenirs. Before his death of throat cancer, however, he published a two-volume personal memoir that earned his family nearly $500,000.

Modern-Day Privileges

Presidential lifestyles gradually became easier and more enjoyable. The White House switched from animal transportation to the automobile during Theodore Roosevelt's (1901–1909) administration, and Congress established a travel allowance for the president; Taft was the first to receive it. Woodrow Wilson (1913–1921) was the first to travel in a yacht; Franklin D. Roosevelt (1933–1945) was the first to use airplanes; and Dwight D. Eisenhower (1953–1961) added the first helicopter squadron to the president's means of transportation. In the 1920s, Congress allocated an entertainment allowance for the president's official functions, and during President Truman's administration, it put meals for servants under the federal budget.

To a large extent the perquisites a president enjoys stems from the president's style. Thus, the rewards of office vary from time to time and from administration to administration. In an effort to back away from the image of the imperial presidency of Richard M. Nixon, President Jimmy Carter took many symbolic measures to deflate the image of excessive White House perquisites. Within a few weeks of his inauguration, Carter sold off two presidential yachts and reduced the White House motor pool by 40 percent. In addition, he removed three hundred television sets and two hundred radios from the White House and the Old Executive Office Building. Even with these reductions in presidential perquisites, however, few would argue that the quality of life was bad at the White House during the Carter years.

President Ronald Reagan restored many of the ceremonial touches that Carter had removed. Carter had ended the practice of a marine band playing "Ruffles and Flourishes" and "Hail to the Chief" at major social events. Reagan reinstated both and stationed a marine in full dress uniform at the entrance of the West Lobby of the White House just to salute and open the door. Military aides escorted each member of the official guest party at state dinners, and a color guard preceded the Reagans and their guests of honor. Fringe benefits for the presidential staff also improved under Reagan. Among other things, Reagan expanded the White House motor pool to allow senior staff members to use limousines for their business around town. No matter how Americans may feel about the perquisites of the presidency, whether because of necessity or personal style, they are considerable.

Residences

One of the luxuries that presidents and their families enjoy is the rent-free White House mansion. The full-time staff of about one hundred includes butlers, cooks, stewards, gardeners, plumbers, electricians, maids, and other assistants. Almost every imaginable convenience is available to the president within the White House complex, including a theater, a swimming pool, a gymnasium, tennis courts, a bowling alley, a putting green, a jogging track, and a library regularly supplied by the publishing industry. With all these amenities at the personal disposal of the president, the operating cost of the White House has risen considerably. The annual cost of $13,800 to run and maintain the mansion a century ago seems meager compared with today's costs of more than $16.4 million a year.

Within the West Wing, the president enjoys the advantages of the Oval Office, one of the best-equipped office complexes in the world. Total operating expenses for the White House Office exceed $50 million a year.

Almost every new chief executive wants to refurbish the White House. Some of the remodeling has been at public expense. President Kennedy, however, concerned about the public's perception of his wealthy background, refused to use public money to pay for redecorating. When Kennedy's father commissioned a mural to brighten up the White House swimming pool area, an overzealous aide ordered the General Services Administration to install better lighting to highlight the mural. When the president found out about it, he insisted that he be billed for the $56,000 expense. First Lady Jacqueline Kennedy began the practice of making souvenir books available for purchase by White House tourists to help offset the costs of remodeling. More recent presidents have tended to rely on donated funds to cover refurbishing expenses. When Gerald R. Ford (1974–1977) became president, the government made plans to build a $500,000 pool and fitness center to replace the pool that Nixon had covered over to make a pressroom. Later, however, these plans were modified, and privately donated funds were used to build a $55,000 outdoor pool. President Carter did very little redecorating, but President Reagan raised more than $1 million in private donations to refurbish the family living quarters of the mansion. President Clinton refurbished both the private living quarters and the Oval Office area, including the Treaty Room, attempting to restore them to the style of the Lincoln era. The $337,000 cost was covered by private funds.

Transportation

Perhaps the most misleading presidential expense account is the $100,000 annual travel allowance. This sum does not begin to cover even the annual salary of the crew of *Air Force One*, a cost actually borne by the Department of Defense and not charged against the president's travel allowance. In 1992, Congress considered a **bill** that would have raised the president's travel budget to $185 million, which was an estimate of what was actually being spent on White House travel. The bill would have required the White House to reimburse from that sum all federal agencies that pay for any transportation costs incurred by the president, vice president, and White House staffers. Although the bill did not pass Congress, its consideration brought to light the total costs of transporting the president and the president's family and staff.

Presidents' use of automobiles has increased tremendously since President Taft used the first official limousine provided at public expense. Today, the presidential motor pool consists of thirty-five automobiles. A dozen limousines are available for the president's use. The newest addition to the president's fleet is a Cadillac DeVille, officially put in service January 20, 2001, at the inauguration of George W. Bush. Complete with a foldaway desktop and reclining rear seats with massaging, adaptive cushions, the limousine barely resembles

the DeVilles at a Cadillac dealership. With five-inch armor, windows that are actually transparent armor, and an environmentally sealed interior designed to protect occupants from chemical and airborne germ terrorism, the automobile resembles a rolling fortress. The Secret Service provides drivers for the presidents' automobiles and additional automobiles for others in the presidential party.

Only recently have presidents engaged routinely in long-distance travel. Before World War II, only two presidents traveled outside the country while in office. Theodore Roosevelt made a quick boat trip to Panama, and Woodrow Wilson ventured to Europe at the end of World War I to attend the Paris Peace Conference. By the next world war, however, long-distance presidential travel had become a necessity. In January 1943, Franklin D. Roosevelt became the first president to fly overseas when he went to Casablanca, Morocco, to meet with British prime minister Winston Churchill and Allied commanders to plan the D-Day invasion. (Only after the trip did the rest of the world learn of the historic flight.) Roosevelt made the trip in a commercial airplane that had been pressed into wartime service. Compared with contemporary presidential air travel, Roosevelt's trip was difficult.

By the end of the twentieth century, presidential air travel overseas was commonplace. As presidents became increasingly involved in face-to-face diplomacy, they made frequent trips overseas to meet with foreign heads of state. President Reagan made twenty-five trips abroad for a total of 118 days during his two terms in office. President George H.W. Bush (1989–1993), who was in office only one term, spent 102 days overseas on twenty-five trips. The National Taxpayers Union labeled President William Clinton (1993–2001) "America's Best Traveled President." During his eight years in office, he made 133 visits to foreign countries for a total of 229 days. Clinton's trips were estimated to cost more than a half-billion dollars.

Today, the best and certainly the most expensive travel benefit for the president is the air fleet maintained by the military for the president's official use. At the president's disposal are a half-dozen Air Force jets, each outfitted with a bedroom and an office, and several soundproof Marine Corps helicopters for short trips. The president also has access to several Lockheed Jet Stars stationed at Andrews Air Force Base, which serve as courier planes to transport mail and staff when the president is out of Washington. Although the presidential air fleet was created primarily for the use of the president and the vice president, presidents have recently made the jets available to members of their immediate families for personal trips. They have felt justified in doing so for security reasons, because threats of violence against presidents and their families have multiplied.

Presidential trips to foreign countries often result in very difficult and expensive preparations. On any presidential trip at least two large jets— a backup plane and a communications plane— accompany *Air Force One.* Sometimes a large cargo plane carrying the chief executive's bullet-proof limousine will precede the presidential entourage. Overseas travel requires even more advance preparation and additional security precautions. In March 2000, President Clinton undertook a logistically difficult eleven-day trip to India, Bangladesh, Pakistan, Oman, and Switzerland. The number of stops and the various security issues that event planners faced in these countries required 146 military cargo flights ferrying everything from the presidential limousine to communication equipment to additional Secret Service agents. These transportation expenses added up to $46.5 million.

Entertainment

Like many of the other perquisites of the presidential office, the amount of money and staff resources expended on entertainment depends significantly on the person holding the office. Even though protocol requires all presidents to do some entertaining of foreign heads of state and foreign and U.S. notables, the social pace at the White House largely depends on the inclination of the president. The Trumans, for example, seldom entertained, but other presidents and their families have taken advantage of the many entertainment opportunities the White House affords. The Kennedys, Johnsons, Fords, Nixons, and both Bushes all enjoyed busy social calendars. The Carters cut back on White House social events, but the Reagans stepped up the presidential social pace, delighting in state dinners, con-

gressional breakfasts, political teas, luncheons, barbecues, receptions, and various command performances. In 1984, the magazine *U.S. News and World Report* found that President Reagan had entertained 222,758 persons during his first three years in office.

Even though the president receives an annual entertainment allowance of $12,000, most entertainment expenses are not paid out of the White House budget. The State Department pays for all state banquets and functions. Periodically, various entertainers are asked to come to the White House and perform for the president and White House guests. The distinction of performing at a White House function is so great that celebrities do so without charge. In fact, many will even cancel previously scheduled appearances to accommodate the president. At most White House affairs, the army, navy, air force, or marine bands play continuously for the pleasure of the president and White House guests. Smaller groups, such as the Army Chorus, the Air Force Strolling Strings, and the Navy Sea Chanters, also may perform. Because these are military groups, the Defense Department bears the costs of their performances. Some White House functions are paid for by the organizations that benefit from them. During the Reagan, Bush, and Clinton administrations, the national political party committees picked up the tab for several presidential **partisan** parties.

In addition to entertaining at the White House, presidents sometimes entertain dignitaries while abroad. Several presidents have gone to extremes to carry the pageantry and glamour of a White House dinner to other countries. Johnson and Nixon, for example, often took with them White House china and crystal for entertaining government officials in the countries they visited. In 1981, President and Mrs. Reagan hosted six hundred Chinese and American guests in the banquet facilities of Beijing's Great Wall Hotel—one of the largest state dinners ever held outside the United States. The Reagans treated their guests to a "typical American meal" of turkey and dressing. To accommodate the large crowd with the best possible meal, White House staff flew in forty frozen turkeys from California.

For four decades presidents had the use of a 105-foot, 100-ton, teak-paneled yacht, the *Sequoia,* for entertaining friends and dignitaries. Although

Herbert C. Hoover (1929–1933) was the first president to use the *Sequoia,* the yacht was made famous by Presidents Kennedy, Johnson, Nixon, and Ford. The yacht served as host to Kennedy's last birthday party, Johnson's lobbying for civil rights legislation, Nixon's negotiations for the first arms control treaty with the Soviet Union's Leonid Brezhnev, and Ford's meetings with various world leaders. In 1976, however, President Carter sold it for $286,000, a symbolic sacrifice in the interest of cutting back on presidential pomp.

Believing the *Sequoia* had served a useful purpose in the past by providing the president with a more intimate environment for official entertaining and lobbying, the Reagan administration tried to replace the yacht. The cost proved prohibitive, however. The *Sequoia,* restored at a cost of about $4 million, is now owned by the Sequoia Presidential Yacht Association and may be rented for $10,000 a day. Both Bill Clinton and George W. Bush have used the yacht for fund-raising and political events.

Protection

Most presidents have viewed the Secret Service as a mixed blessing. Probably the most necessary and important presidential perquisite, it is also the most annoying. The assassination of President Kennedy; the failed but close attempts on presidents Ford and Reagan; and the terrorist attacks on New York City and Washington, D.C., in September 2001, all dictated an immediate increase in Secret Service protection and a decrease in chief executives' personal freedoms.

During the Clinton administration, several attempts were made to breach White House security measures. In fact, during a one-week period in May 1995, two intruders climbed over the White House fence. Both were intercepted by White House guards and posed no real threat to the president. A few months earlier, in late October 1994, the White House had been sprayed with bullets by a disgruntled Colorado Springs upholsterer. In February 2001, the Secret Service shot and wounded a man waving a gun outside the southwest gate of the White House. These breaches of security, together with the terrorist events of September 11, have resulted in even tighter security around the executive mansion and in presidential travel.

The September 11 attacks on Washington and New York City raised security issues at the White House to a new level. As a result of the attacks, the Bush administration decided to invoke protocols developed during the cold war and revised during the Reagan administration that placed senior federal officials, including Vice President Richard B. Cheney, at secure and undisclosed locations outside Washington.

No longer can a president take a casual stroll through the streets of Washington, as Truman frequently did. Nor can they elude their Secret Service agents, as Kennedy did to visit friends in Georgetown. They cannot even take a walk around the grounds of the White House without Secret Service protection, a pleasure that Johnson enjoyed. Reagan became a virtual prisoner of the White House after he was wounded in an assassination attempt in 1981. Before the shooting, the Reagans occasionally went to church. After the attempt on the president's life, however, the Reagans decided to stop attending services so that church members would not have to be subjected to security checks. Both the Bushes and the Clintons regularly attended church services, however, which required the mobilization of dozens of police officers, White House personnel and support staff, and Secret Service agents.

Both the George H.W. Bushes and Clintons enjoyed getting out of the White House and going to Washington restaurants, but, again, such forays prompted elaborate security measures. Security agents would visit and search the restaurants before the presidential party arrived and would subject restaurant guests to metal detectors and explosives-sniffing dogs.

Although President Clinton had a jogging track built around the White House in order to avoid disrupting early morning traffic with his runs, he continued to jog outside the gates of the executive mansion to escape what he called the "splendid prison" of the White House. Doing so required that a dozen Secret Service vehicles follow him through downtown traffic.

Amid speculation that the White House may have been the target of one of the planes involved in the September 11, 2001, terrorist attacks, concerns about air attacks against the executive mansion have escalated. In the Dwight D.

Eisenhower Executive Office Building, next door to the White House, a command and control center closely monitors all aircraft using Ronald Reagan Washington National Airport, a mere three miles from the White House. Even after the September 11 attacks, at least a dozen small planes accidentally violated the airspace around the White House. On June 19, 2002, the Secret Service had to evacuate the White House when a small Cessna 182 flew into restricted airspace. The evacuation was ordered by the Secret Service when authorities could not reach the pilot on his emergency frequency.

When the president makes a public appearance such as a speech outside Washington, the Secret Service works with local law enforcement officials to make sure any risk is minimal. Security officers carefully check the motorcade route to the president's destination for any possible points of attack; they look for potential sniper posts and inspect utility holes and bridges for bombs. In case of an emergency, the Secret Service selects alternate routes and designates certain hospitals to have on hand a supply of the president's blood type. Moreover, in every city or town where a public appearance is scheduled, agents search local police and FBI files to identify anyone in the area who could pose a threat to the president. Any person considered suspicious is interrogated and put under constant surveillance.

See also: Air Force One.

Presidential Succession

The sequence of leaders who assume the office of the presidency should that office become vacant. Fifty-two years elapsed between the **ratification** of the Constitution in 1789 and the first vacancy in the presidency in 1841, when William Henry Harrison died shortly after his inauguration. Since 1841, the nation has never gone that long without the presidency becoming prematurely vacant. Because the language of the Constitution was vague, the official and unofficial records of the Constitutional Convention had not yet been published, and no delegates to the convention

were still alive, it was impossible to say authoritatively what was supposed to happen next.

Initially, Harrison's cabinet and some others seemed to think that the president's death made Vice President John Tyler only the acting president. Tyler (1841–1845) believed differently. He quickly took the oath of office as president, delivered a sort of inaugural address, declared his intention to serve out the remainder of Harrison's term, and moved into the White House. Tyler's decisiveness prevailed in a constitutionally and politically uncertain situation. An effort in Congress to address Tyler officially in correspondence as "Vice President, on whom, by the death of the late President, the powers and duties of the office of President have devolved" was defeated overwhelmingly.

Tyler's action set a **precedent** that Millard Fillmore (1850–1853) and future vice presidents were able to follow without controversy. Not until the Twenty-fifth **Amendment** was enacted in 1967, however, did the Constitution explicitly codify the vice president's right, when the presidency becomes prematurely vacant, to succeed to the office and serve for the balance of the unexpired term. Section 1 of the amendment states: "In case of the removal of the President from office or of his death or resignation, the Vice President shall become President."

Other Officials in the Line of Succession

Article II, Section 2, Clause 6, of the Constitution did not delineate a line of succession extending past the vice president. Instead, it charged Congress to provide by law for situations in which the vice presidency was vacant when a successor to the president was needed.

The Second Congress passed the Succession Act of 1792. The act stipulated that a double vacancy in the presidency and vice presidency would be remedied by a special election to a full four-year term the following November unless the vacancy occurred during the last six months of the departed president's term. During that period, the president pro tempore of the Senate or, if there were none, the Speaker of the House of Representatives would "act as President." James Madison (1809–1817), then a representative from Virginia, objected to this provision of the act,

Line of Succession

On March 30, 1981, President Ronald Reagan was shot by would-be assassin John Hinckley outside a Washington, D.C., hotel and rushed to a nearby hospital for surgery. Vice President George H.W. Bush was on a plane returning to Washington from Texas. Meanwhile, presidential aides and cabinet members gathered at the White House, where questions arose among them and in the press corps about who was "in charge."[1] Secretary of State Alexander M. Haig Jr. rushed to the press briefing room and, before an audience of reporters and live television cameras, said, "As of now, I am in control here in the White House, pending the return of the vice president. . . . Constitutionally, gentlemen, you have the president, the vice president, and the secretary of state."

Haig was, as many critics later pointed out, wrong. The Constitution says nothing about who follows the vice president in the line of succession. The Succession Act of 1947 (later modified to reflect the creation of new departments) establishes first the congressional leaders and then the heads of the departments, in the order the departments were created, in the line of succession that follows the vice president.

The line of succession is:

vice president
speaker of the house of representatives
president pro tempore of the Senate
secretary of state
secretary of the treasury
secretary of defense
attorney general
secretary of the interior
secretary of agriculture
secretary of commerce
secretary of labor
secretary of health and human services
secretary of housing and urban development
secretary of transportation
secretary of energy
secretary of education
secretary of veterans affairs
secretary of homeland security

The full import of the succession act becomes apparent to the American people every year when one department secretary does not attend the president's nationally televised State of the Union address before Congress so that the secretary will be available to succeed to the presidency if the president, vice president, and the other members of the line of succession are assassinated simultaneously. Of note, the Constitution stipulates that the president must be a natural-born citizen of the United States. Thus, this provision made Richard Nixon's (1969–1974) German-born secretary of state, Henry Kissinger, ineligible to assume the presidency.

Note: 1. "Confusion Over Who Was in Charge Arose Following Reagan Shooting," *Wall Street Journal*, April 1, 1981.

The line of succession to the presidency was established by Congress. The ratification of the Twenty-fifth Amendment in 1967, however, provides that the president nominate—and Congress approve—a vice president, should that office become vacant.

A – Z

POINT/COUNTERPOINT

SHOULD PRESIDENTIAL VACANCIES BE FILLED BY SPECIAL ELECTION?

The constitutional process of selection by succession is sometimes criticized, most often by those who regard it as inadequate to the task of ensuring effective leadership. They would prefer that vacancies in the presidency be filled by special election. Proponents of a special election argue that vice presidents are not likely to be of presidential caliber. As former Democratic representative James G. O'Hara of Michigan put it, presidential candidates will not choose running mates "to succeed them. They will choose them to succeed." Nor, special election proponents add, is the experience of being vice president helpful preparation for the presidency.

Arguments for Special Election

The critics of vice-presidential succession are as convinced of the virtues of special election as they are of the weaknesses of the vice presidency. One line of argument is idealistic: American practice should conform to the original constitutional intent that the president "be elected," an ideal later enshrined, at least in part, in the 1792 Succession Act, which provided for a special election in the event of a double vacancy in the presidency and vice presidency. The other main argument for a special election, practical in nature, draws attention to the experience of the French Fifth Republic. The constitution of France—which, like that of the United States, established a presidential system—provides that in the event of a vacancy in the presidency, the president of the Senate shall serve as the government's caretaker until a special election is held within five weeks to choose a new president for a full term of office.

Some political scientists have suggested variations on the French practice. Because any designated caretaker from Congress could well be a leader of a party different from the late president's, the acting president should be a member of the administration, preferably the secretary of state. Because American political parties are large and decentralized, the special election should not take place until ninety days after the vacancy, with the parties' national committees choosing the candidates. Finally, to allow the usual presidential selection process to run its course, no special election should be held if a vacancy occurs during the final year of a president's term. Instead, the caretaker should serve out the term.

What of the vice presidency in this new scheme? To be sure, the office need not be abolished in the course of instituting special elections. The vice president still would be the Senate president and the vital figure in situations of presidential disability. However, the office would best be eliminated under the special election proposal. It would be difficult to attract competent people to the vice presidency if its successor role were stripped from it, in which case even the office's limited powers would be exercised poorly. Also, after the special election brought in a new president, the vice presidency might well be occupied by a member of the opposition party, a problem best headed off by abolishing it.

Arguments Against Special Election

The special election idea has attracted a variety of critics. Some identify problems in the proposal itself. Unlike France, the United States is a superpower. It cannot afford the uncertainty that would attend caretaker leadership, especially in view of the frequency with which presidential vacancies have occurred during the past two centuries.

Also unlike in France, presidential selection in the United States is an inherently lengthy undertaking. The nominating process is diffuse, the pool from which presidents are drawn is broad, and a considerable amount of time is required for voters and political activists to sort through all the alternatives. Staffing a new president's administration and developing its policies also are time-consuming. In practice, the proposed ninety-day interregnum, itself long, might actually last thirty to sixty days longer, with the added time serving as a de facto transition period for the new president.

Other criticisms of the special election proposal concern its operation. For example, would the caretaker president be allowed to run in the special election? If not, the nation would be guaranteed a lack of continuity in leadership and, perhaps, deprived of an able president. If so, how would the caretaker's candidacy influence the conduct of the temporary "administration"? In addition, how would the selection of people to fill the office that provides the caretaker be affected? The qualifications of a good acting president and those of, say, a good secretary of state may be quite different. Still other questions come to mind. Could the parties' national committees do an adequate job of nominating the presidential candidates, an assignment to which they would bring little experience? Would presidential and congressional elections remain forever unsynchronized? Would the caretaker be granted the full range of presidential powers and duties?

In addition to attacking the special election idea, some critics have defended the virtues of vice-presidential succession. Above all, they argue, the traditional procedure of instant, certain, and full succession by the vice president is a source of stability in the political system. Presidential deaths are, in a literal sense, traumatic events for many citizens, triggering feelings not only of personal grief but also of fear for the Republic. In this uncertain and emotional setting, Americans historically have accepted the vice president's succession as legitimate. Indeed, survey data for the last three successions show the public rallying to support each new president to an extent unrivaled by even the most popular newly elected president. Legitimacy and stability are qualities of the historic system of vice-presidential succession.

Beyond the virtues of vice-presidential succession as a procedure in its own right, some argue that the system also works well in practice, providing able presidents when needed. In the twentieth century, voters elected four of the five successors to full terms while rejecting the reelection bids of four of the ten elected presidents who ran for reelection.

DOCUMENT-BASED QUESTION

What are the advantages of a special presidential election?
What are some disadvantages?

mostly because he thought that the presence of legislators in the line of succession violated the principle of separation of powers, and partly because the line bypassed the leader of his party, Secretary of State Thomas Jefferson (1801–1809).

Although the double vacancy provided for in the 1792 Succession Act never has occurred, the nation has frequently been at risk. Sixteen of the first thirty-six presidents—George Washington (1789–1797) to Lyndon Johnson (1963–1969)—served without a vice president for part of their terms. A particular problem arose in 1881. President James A. Garfield (1881) was assassinated at a time when there was neither a Senate president pro tempore nor a House Speaker. If anything had happened to Vice President Chester A. Arthur (1881–1885), Garfield's successor, the nation would have been without a president. Congress did nothing to correct this problem, and it arose again in 1885, when President Grover Cleveland (1885–1889, 1893–1897), a Democrat, was president. Republicans controlled the Senate that year, which drew attention to another problem with the 1792 act: a successor drawn from Congress might be of a different political party than the president.

Responding at last to the double vacancy problem, Congress passed the Succession Act of 1886. The new law located the line of succession in the president's cabinet in the order the departments were created, beginning with the secretary of state. Some members of Congress—including a future president, Representative William McKinley (1897–1901) of Ohio—opposed the measure on the grounds that it violated democratic principles by allowing president to appoint their successors. Moreover, the statute was unclear about whether succession would be temporary (pending a special election) or permanent in the event of a double vacancy.

The issue of selection by succession was reopened by President Harry S. Truman (1945–1953), who succeeded to the presidency when President Franklin D. Roosevelt (1933–1945) died near the beginning of his fourth term in 1945. Rejecting the idea that, in the absence of a vice president, the secretary of state should be next in line to the presidency, Truman said, "It now lies within my power to nominate the person who would be my immediate successor in the event of my own death or inability to act. I do not believe

that in a democracy this power should rest with the Chief Executive." In 1945 Truman called for a return to the 1792 act, but with the Speaker of the House first in the line of succession and the president pro tempore of the Senate (now largely an honorific office awarded to the most senior senator of the majority party) second.

After the 1946 midterm elections, in which the Republicans regained control of both **legislative** houses, Congress mostly accepted Truman's recommendation by passing the Succession Act of 1947. Although Congress rejected special elections for fear that they would produce an excessive discontinuity of leadership within a four-year term, it did rearrange the line of succession as follows: Speaker of the House, president pro tempore of the Senate, then cabinet members in the order of their departments were created. In the absence of a vice president, this placed Republican Speaker Joseph Martin, not Secretary of State George C. Marshall, next in line to the presidency until after the 1948 election.

The Twenty-fifth Amendment did not repeal the 1947 Succession Act. However, by providing for the filling of a vacant vice presidency, the amendment reduced the possibility that a lengthy double vacancy would occur.

See also: Twenty-fifth Amendment (1967); Vice Presidency; Vice Presidential Vacancies.

Principles of U.S. Government and Presidential Elections

See Elections, Presidential; Electoral College.

Public Opinion and the Presidency

Citizens' views on how well presidents are doing their job. Presidents and other political figures have used surveys since the early nineteenth century, but only since the development of sophisticated systems of communications and analysis have surveys and polls become a major part of White House efforts to measure and shape public opinion. Polling data are often sketchy and contradictory, but they at least reduce the uncertainty under which the president operates.

Early Polls

With the rise of mass-circulation newspapers in the 1880s, polls became regular features. A 1936 survey of *Literary Digest* readers, which predicted that Alfred Landon would defeat Franklin D. Roosevelt (1933–1945) for the presidency, both damaged polling's credibility and helped to pave the way for more sophisticated surveys. The *Digest*'s huge mistake—Roosevelt won by a landslide—was attributed to the built-in bias of the polling sample, which consisted of the magazine's predominantly Republican, well-to-do readers.

The founder of modern polling was George Gallup. Gallup wrote his doctoral thesis on sampling techniques; in 1935, with Elmo Roper and Archibald Crossley, he founded the independent Gallup poll, which was the leader in scientific polling for decades. Gallup was a key figure in giving polling its scientific credentials by using large, representative sample sizes and carefully worded questions.

Franklin D. Roosevelt (1933–1945) was the first president to use polling data regularly to interpret the public's reactions to the political and policy actions of the administration. As U.S. involvement in World War II (1939–1945) became more likely in the late 1930s, Roosevelt received advice from Gallup on how to frame his rhetoric on possible U.S. entry.

Harry S. Truman (1945–1953) in 1948 and Dwight Eisenhower (1953–1961) in 1952 used polls to develop campaign appeals. With the availability of regular information about voter attitudes, elections and governing became more and more intertwined. John F. Kennedy (1961–1963) hired pollster Louis Harris two years before his successful 1960 presidential campaign to gauge support and develop strategy. After that, polls gradually developed into a daily part of government action and the flow of news and academic analysis.

Lyndon B. Johnson (1963–1969) was the first president to hire a pollster for the White House staff. Throughout his term, Johnson kept a steady stream of polling data flowing into the White House from every state. When faced with growing opposition to the Vietnam War (1964–1975), Johnson frequently referred to polls that suggested that a majority of Americans favored the administration's war policies. Johnson rejected arguments that most of the nation was uninformed and that those who were knowledgeable about the war opposed it. When polls showed a majority of Americans opposing the war effort, Johnson moved toward a decision against seeking a second full term in office.

Richard Nixon's (1969–1974) public relations campaigns were based on the notion of the "silent majority." These Americans, the president claimed, backed his administration's policies on Vietnam, civil rights, crime, regulation, social programs and budget priorities, and the Watergate affair. The lack of widespread opposition to his policies, Nixon argued, could be interpreted as approval. Nixon's argument, in effect, gave as much weight to people with no strong feelings or knowledge as to those with well-informed, strong views.

Nixon regularly used polls to help formulate policy statements and to plan strategies for dealing with Congress and interest groups. When polls showed that he was personally popular with blue-collar workers, Nixon decided to ignore the opposition of labor union leadership on issues such as **wage and price controls.**

Public Opinion Efforts

Polls became widely used in U.S. politics in the 1970s. Today, dozens of newspapers and magazines, television and radio stations, government agencies, business firms, universities, private organizations, and Internet sites commission surveys of political and social attitudes and habits. Polling also has become a daily part of White House operations. This practice began with the presidency of Jimmy Carter (1977–1981).

Carter's Use of Polls

Jimmy Carter became president with no Washington experience and an uncertain ideology; he therefore did not have a strong sense of his role in the government. His campaign was successful partly because of the work of Patrick Caddell, a pollster who was one of the top architects of

Carter's campaign agenda. Once in the White House, Carter regularly sought advice from Caddell, and polling data assumed a prominent role in presidential decision making.

Perhaps the most significant moment of Carter's presidency was the nationally televised speech he delivered about the country's moral laziness. During a gas shortage in the summer of 1979, Carter planned to deliver a speech to promote a variety of energy conservation and development initiatives. While working on the address, however, he decided that it would fail to move a public that already had heard four such presidential speeches. Caddell gave Carter polling data and a memorandum recommending a shift in emphasis from energy conservation to calling out Americans on their lack of faith in the government. Carter's decision to act on the data was one of his presidency's fateful moments.

Carter's speech—which analyzed the American public's "crisis of confidence" in its government—originally was well received. Then a series of cabinet firings, which Carter acknowledged handling "very poorly," created an atmosphere of crisis, not so much in the nation as in the administration. The "malaise" speech, as it came to be known, became a source of ridicule rather than national unity.

Reagan's Use of Polls

Despite widespread criticism of Carter's reliance on polls, Ronald Reagan (1981–1989) brought campaign pollster Richard B. Wirthlin with him to the White House in 1981. While consistently articulating the basic themes of small government and international power, Reagan developed his rhetoric and policy proposals based on data supplied by polls and focus groups. In order to supply Reagan with this information, Wirthlin conducted one of the most extensive and expensive polls ever undertaken on behalf of a president.

Wirthlin's surveys and regular "tracking" polls—in which changes in a sample of opinion were followed daily—affected administration policy in several areas. Reagan's "honeymoon" poll results encouraged the president to seek dramatic tax and budget legislation in early 1981. Later data, as well as an outcry from **legislative** leaders and interest groups, persuaded Reagan to drop plans for wholesale changes in Social Security.

Polling data also guided administration actions on the nomination of Sandra Day O'Connor to the Supreme Court, U.S. involvement in the Lebanese civil war, Reagan's visit to the Bitburg cemetery in West Germany, and tax reform.

Wirthlin's most extensive polling took place in early 1987, when the administration struggled to control the effects of disclosures that the White House had secretly sold arms to Iran in exchange for help in releasing American hostages in Lebanon, and that profits from the sales went to help rebels, called contras, fight the government of Nicaragua. During the first six or seven weeks of the year, Wirthlin conducted rounds of interviews with 25,000 people—more people than most pollsters interview in an entire year.

The Reagan administration, attentive daily to poll results, orchestrated dramatic events that provided surges of support. Foreign summits, Oval Office speeches, military attacks on Libya and Grenada, emotional public appearances after tragedies such as the space shuttle *Challenger* explosion, and strongly worded statements after terrorist attacks and the Soviet attack on the Korean Air Lines plane—all provided "rally points" for Reagan.

Wirthlin's polling measured not only the public's attitudes toward issues, but also the public's emotional response to the president and his program. Wirthlin asked voters about how they felt toward President Reagan and his political rivals. When voters expressed doubts about the president's empathy and stability in international affairs, Wirthlin scripted public events and television advertisements that depicted Reagan as a person concerned about ordinary people's lives. The spots helped to strengthen the public's trust in and emotional attachment to Reagan.

Presidents typically do not use polls to determine major policy stances. Yet polls do give presidents information about what issues to highlight and downplay. Polls might not determine presidential policy and strategy, but they help to guide it. In a period of tumult, such guidance can be critical.

Polling during the George H.W. Bush Presidency

George H.W. Bush (1989–1993) lacked Reagan's strong ideology, and he could not claim that his election was a mandate for particular policies. He therefore had to rely increasingly on survey data over the course of his term to help him formulate his policy pronouncements and to demonstrate to Congress that these policies had public support. Because of his risky mandate, Bush needed concrete evidence of public support as an extra political resource. With high approval ratings, the president could tell Congress and other parts of the political establishment that "the people" supported White House initiatives.

After the Persian Gulf War (1991), President Bush may have paid too much attention to the polls, which showed his public approval ratings hovering near 90 percent. Bush and his advisers concluded that the American public was solidly behind the president, when in fact the polls represented a temporary surge of support. Because the president is the symbol of the nation as a whole, Bush benefited from the inclination of Americans to "rally 'round the flag" in a national emergency. Soon the nation turned its attention to other concerns, such as a slack economic recovery and a crisis in the health-care system.

Bush's inability to develop a coherent domestic policy agenda has been attributed to his overreliance on polls. Bush reacted to public opinion on such things as the budget deficit, economic **recession,** civil rights, and the Los Angeles riots of 1992. His overreaction to some opinion surveys prompted him to expend valuable time and resources advocating constitutional **amendments** mandating a balanced budget and banning flag burning as a form of protest. The president, however, did not have an overall policy framework. Thus, the public viewed his disconnected initiatives skeptically. Bush's reliance on survey data in his unsuccessful reelection campaign of 1992 reveals one of the main pitfalls of polling. Surveys underscored the importance of shoring up the **conservative** movement within the Republican Party, and Bush attempted to do just that during the party convention and fall campaign. Yet in the process, he alienated his broader pool of potential voters.

Clinton: The Perils and Profits of a Poll-Driven Presidency

Bill Clinton (1993–2001) devoted **unprecedented** presidential attention to the enterprise of polling. Far more than his predecessors, he understood and appreciated how to develop and interpret public opinion surveys.

Clinton won the presidency in 1992 with only 43 percent of the popular vote. Sensitive to the need to attract a broader base, Clinton used polls to figure out how to appeal to the independents who had voted for Texas billionaire Ross Perot. Yet Clinton's desire to appeal to the broad electorate undermined his focus and resulted in the image of a waffling politician.

All recent presidents have arranged for their national party organizations to pay for polling that assists the White House. Thus, the Democratic National Committee paid pollster Stanley Greenberg almost $2 million for polling in Clinton's first year in the White House. Greenberg conducted several polls and focus groups each week for Clinton.

To many critics, Clinton's use of polls was far too obvious. The critics decried his apparent reluctance to confront controversial domestic issues, such as reform of Social Security and Medicare, that might threaten his popularity. Clinton's aides denied that the president used polling data to guide basic decisions, pointing out his success in supporting unpopular initiatives such as the North American Free Trade Agreement (NAFTA). Yet, Clinton's aides did admit that polling was used to help package and sell the president's proposals. In 1993, Clinton used polling data to package his budget deficit reduction proposal. Clinton described his plan as "5–3–1" at a press conference— $5 in budget cuts for every $3 in additional taxes on the wealthy and $1 in additional taxes on the middle class—after surveys showed that the formulation resonated with voters.

Reliance on polling data, however, can provide a false sense of support. When they first announced their intention to overhaul the nation's health care system in 1993, President Clinton and First Lady Hillary Rodham Clinton appeared to enjoy the broad support of the public. However, support for reform was "soft." When the blueprint for reform was delayed for months, Republican opponents and interest groups mounted a long-term campaign to cast the plan as dangerous "social engineering." By the time congressional allies had scheduled a vote, public support had dropped precipitously.

After the 1994 midterm elections, in which the Democrats lost control of both houses of Congress, Clinton increased his reliance on polling. He instituted a White House-based polling operation directed by his longtime political adviser Dick Morris. Poll data and analysis played a prominent role in successful Clinton White House efforts to counter Republican congressional initiatives and to position the president for his reelection effort. Morris left during the 1996 presidential campaign, but the polling infrastructure remained intact, and Clinton's poll ratings remained strong for the rest of his presidency.

In Clinton's second term, polling data were crucial in framing the president's response to the allegations that he had engaged in improper behavior with a White House intern, Monica Lewinsky. Although this scandal humiliated the president and ultimately resulted in his **impeachment,** he was fortified throughout by his strong, stable public support. This support helped to save his presidency.

George W. Bush

In his campaign for the presidency, and in office, George W. Bush (2001–2009) presented himself as the antithesis of Clinton in the use of polling. He professed disdain for leaders who appeared to test the winds of public opinion prior to taking positions and making decisions. Still, his aides and advisers enjoyed constant access to public opinion polls commissioned by the campaign, the Republican Party, and later the White House. Certainly, Bush was much more disengaged than Clinton from the polling operation, but polling has become an institution in the contemporary presidency.

Overall Presidential Approval Ratings, 1953–2008 (percent)

	Average	High	Low
Kennedy (1961–1963)	70	83	56
Eisenhower (1953–1961)	65	79	48
G.H.W. Bush (1989–1993)	61	89	29
Clinton (1993–2001)	55	73	37
L. Johnson (1963–1969)	55	79	35
Reagan (1981–1989)	53	65	35
G.W. Bush (2001–2005)	49	90	25
Nixon (1969–1974)	49	67	24
Ford (1974–1977)	47	71	37
Carter (1977–1981)	45	74	28

Source: Gallup Organization, "Poll Topics and Trends, Presidential Ratings—Job Approval" (www.gallup.com).

The public approval ratings of presidents often vary greatly during their time in office. How a president responds to international and domestic issues plays a huge role in the public's overall opinions.

Factors in Presidential Popularity

Presidential popularity tends to decline throughout the four-year term in office, with short-term increases after important international events and at the beginning of a reelection campaign or at the end of the term. Since 1945, the Gallup organization has surveyed Americans about once a month to determine popular support for the president. The identical question—"Do you approve or disapprove of the way [the **incumbent**] is handling his job as president?"—has produced data that track presidents' relations with the public.

Every president enjoys a honeymoon period in which the nation gives the new chief **executive** broad, general support. Indeed, for several presidents, public support has peaked at the outset of their tenures. Such was the case for Truman, Kennedy, Johnson, Gerald R. Ford (1974–1977), and Carter. An administration's early days are considered the best time for a president to pass difficult legislation, such as Carter's energy program or Reagan's tax- and budget-cutting packages.

Political scientist Samuel Kernell has argued that a president's popularity throughout the four-year term is partly determined by the results of previous polls. Poll results do not vary much from month to month—mostly because only a small segment of the population is likely to veer very far from its original position, but also because of respondents' general unwillingness to change their opinions and the use of previous polls to judge the president. Presidents therefore have a strong base of support at the beginning of their term. The key question for the president is how quickly the support will decline.

Public opinions change between, as well as during, administrations. Political scientist Stephen Skowronek has argued that presidents live in "political time"—that is, they are forced to respond to the legacies and ideals of their most recent predecessors. To establish their own identities,

presidents must distance themselves from their predecessors. For example, George H.W. Bush offered the image of an engaged, energetic insider to contrast himself with the hands-off and forgetful Reagan. Nevertheless, the process of distancing can itself place undue importance on the previous president's legacy. In a time of constant change, Skowronek suggests, presidents can break free of their predecessors' legacies and set their own agendas. They also can avoid having to fulfill the expectations set by the previous occupants of the Oval Office and instead develop their own distinct approaches to the presidency.

Further Reading

Manza, Jeff; Cook, Fay Lomax; and Benjamin I. Page, eds. *Navigating Public Opinion: Polls, Policy, and the Future of American Democracy.* New York: Oxford University Press, 2002.

Reagan, Ronald, Administration of (1981–1989)

Government under the fortieth president of the United States. After college, Reagan worked as a sportscaster for radio stations in Davenport and Des Moines, Iowa. During a trip to California in 1937 to cover the spring training sessions of the Chicago Cubs baseball team, an agent for Warner Brothers movie studio persuaded Reagan to take a screen test. Reagan won the role of a small-town radio announcer, which started his movie career.

In 1942, Reagan entered the U.S. Army Air Corps as a second lieutenant and was assigned to make training films. He was discharged in 1945

with the rank of captain. After the World War II (1939–1945), he continued to act in movies but devoted an increasing share of his time to movie industry politics. In 1947, he was elected president of the Screen Actors Guild (SAG), a labor union representing Hollywood actors. He held that office until 1952 and was elected to another one-year term in 1959.

Until the late 1940s, Reagan had been a firm Democrat, supporting presidents Franklin D. Roosevelt (1933–1945) and Harry S. Truman (1945–1953). In the late 1940s, however, his political sympathies began to shift to the right as he became more concerned about communist subversion. He voted for Dwight Eisenhower (1953–1961) in 1952 and 1956 and Richard Nixon (1969–1974) in 1960. In 1962, Reagan officially abandoned the Democratic Party and registered as a Republican.

Political Career

In 1964, Reagan made a televised campaign speech on behalf of Republican presidential candidate Barry Goldwater. The speech established Reagan as an articulate spokesman for the **conservative** wing of the Republican Party and led California Republican leaders to ask him to run for governor. Reagan received the 1966 Republican nomination for governor after winning almost 65 percent of the vote in a five-candidate primary election. He then defeated **incumbent** Democrat Edmund G. Brown, who had beaten Richard Nixon four years before. Reagan was easily elected to a second term in 1970.

As governor, Reagan succeeded in passing a welfare reform bill that cut the number of Californians on welfare and increased the payments to the remaining welfare recipients. He campaigned for budget cuts and lower taxes, but early in his governorship he signed bills increasing taxes, because he claimed Brown had left the state in financial trouble. Reagan also harshly criticized student protesters on college campuses and cut state funds for higher education during his first term. During his second term, however, the funds were restored, and by the time he left office state support for higher education was double what it had been when he was first elected.

Reagan received some support for the presidential nomination in 1968, but the party nominated Richard Nixon. Reagan backed Nixon in 1972, but after declining to run for a third term as governor in 1974 he began campaigning for the presidency. Despite running against incumbent president Gerald R. Ford (1974–1977), Reagan came close to winning the 1976 Republican presidential nomination. Ford received 1,187 delegate votes to Reagan's 1,070 delegate votes at the Republican National Convention in Kansas City. When Ford lost the election to Democrat Jimmy Carter (1977–1981), Reagan became the favorite to receive the Republican nomination in 1980.

During the next four years, Reagan campaigned for Republican candidates and raised money for his 1980 campaign. He lost the Iowa **caucuses** to George H.W. Bush (1989–1993), but recovered with a win in the New Hampshire primary. Reagan went on to win all but four of the remaining Republican primaries. He then defeated incumbent Jimmy Carter in the general election, 489 electoral votes to 49.

Presidency

On March 30, 1981, less than three months after he became president, Reagan was shot as he was leaving the Washington Hilton Hotel, where he had spoken to a group of union officials. The assailant, John Hinckley Jr., fired six shots at Reagan. One bullet struck Reagan in the chest and lodged in his left lung. A police officer, a Secret Service agent, and presidential press secretary James Brady were also wounded in the shooting. Reagan was rushed to a nearby hospital, where surgeons removed the bullet. Reagan became the first incumbent president to be wounded by an assailant and survive. Hinckley, who declared he shot the president to impress Jodie Foster, a Hollywood actress, was found not guilty by reason of insanity and confined at St. Elizabeth's Hospital in Washington, D.C.

During 1981, the Reagan administration focused on economic policy. The president pushed a large tax cut through Congress, along with increases in the defense budget and decreases in funding for many domestic programs. Reagan claimed that the tax cut would produce an economic boom that would lower unemployment while ultimately increasing tax revenues that would balance the federal budget. A severe **recession** that began in late 1981, however, increased unemployment to the highest since the **Great Depression** of the 1930s. In early 1983, the economy began to recover. Unlike economic recoveries during the 1970s, however, the expansion was not accompanied by high inflation.

In the 1984 presidential election, with the economy prospering, Reagan overwhelmed his Democratic challenger, former vice president Walter F. Mondale, 525–13 in the electoral college. The economic expansion continued through the end of Reagan's term.

Although most Americans were satisfied with the economic recovery, critics charged that it was flawed because low-income groups had fared poorly during the Reagan years, the U.S. trade position had deteriorated, and the federal government had built up huge budget deficits. The last of these problems was particularly troublesome to Reagan, because he had promised in his 1980 campaign to balance the federal budget. Instead, Reagan's military buildup and tax cut had worsened the nation's budget deficit problem. In 1981, when Reagan entered office, the budget deficit was $78.9 billion. Two years later, it had more than doubled to $207.8 billion, and in 1986, it stood at $221.2 billion. The national debt had risen from a little more than one trillion dollars in 1981 to more than two trillion dollars in 1986. Reagan and the Democratic Congress addressed the debt problem by enacting the Gramm-Rudman-Hollings amendment in 1985. The measure mandated across-the-board spending cuts if the president and Congress could not agree on budget reductions that would reduce the deficit to specified yearly targets.

In foreign affairs, the first five years of Reagan's presidency were characterized by efforts to block communist expansion and even overturn pro-communist governments in the developing world. Reagan supported military funding to the anticommunist Nicaraguan rebels known as the "contras," who were fighting to overthrow the Marxist regime in their country. He also supported aid to anticommunist guerrillas fighting in Angola in Africa and Cambodia in Southeast Asia, as well Afghan rebels fighting Soviet forces that had invaded Afghanistan in 1979. In 1983, Reagan dispatched U.S. troops to Grenada to overthrow the Marxist government and bring stability to the tiny Caribbean island.

With the rise of Mikhail Gorbachev as the leader of the Soviet Union in 1985, however, the president softened his anticommunist rhetoric and began developing a working relationship with the Soviet leader. During his last three years in office, Reagan held five summits with Gorbachev and signed a treaty banning intermediate nuclear missiles in Europe.

The Reagan administration also took actions to strike back at terrorists in the Middle East, including a 1986 bombing raid on Libya in retaliation for alleged Libyan support for a terrorist bombing of a Berlin nightclub. Reagan's tough antiterrorist posture was undercut late in 1986 when the administration disclosed that the president had approved arms sales to Iran that appeared to be aimed at securing the release of American hostages in Lebanon held by pro-Iranian extremists.

Investigations revealed that members of the president's National Security Council staff had used the arms sales' profits to aid the contras, despite a congressional prohibition then in force against U.S. aid to the contras. Although investigators found no evidence that Reagan had been aware of the diversion of funds to the contras, the scandal led to the resignation of several administration officials. The Tower Commission, appointed by the president to investigate the Iran-contra affair, issued a report in 1987 that criticized the president's detached style of management, which allowed his subordinates to operate without his knowledge.

Despite the Iran-contra affair, Reagan remained one of the most popular presidents of the twentieth century. When Reagan's term ended in 1989, he returned to his home in Bel Air, California, and maintained a low public profile. In November 1994, Reagan announced in a handwritten note that he had been diagnosed with Alzheimer's disease, which causes progressive mental and physical deterioration. He noted that he wanted his announcement to help raise awareness about the disease. Reagan died on June 5, 2004, at the age of 93.

See also: Bush, George H.W., Administration of (1989–1993); Carter, Jimmy, Administration of (1977–1981).

Further Reading

Kengor, Paul. *The Crusader: Ronald Reagan and the Fall of Communism.* New York: Harper Perennial, 2007.

Reagan, Ronald. *The Reagan Diaries.* New York: HarperCollins, 2007.

Republican Party (1854–)

One of the two major American political parties, founded in 1854. The Republican Party dominated national politics from 1860 to the New Deal era and again from 1968 to 2006. In that year, the Democrats took control of both Houses of Congress. In 2008, they retained control of Congress and won the presidency. The party emerged in 1854–1856 out of a political conflict revolving around the expansion of slavery into the western territories. The new party was so named because

republicanism was the core value of American politics, and it seemed to be threatened by the expanding "slave power." The enemy was not so much the institution of slavery or the mistreatment of the slaves. Rather, it was that the political-economic system that controlled the South exerted disproportionate control over the national government and threatened to seize power in the new territories.

Origins

The party came into being in reaction to federal legislation—the Kansas-Nebraska Act of 1854—allowing the settlers of the Kansas Territory to decide for themselves whether to adopt slavery. This law **nullified** the Compromise of 1820, which explicitly forbade slavery there. The new party lost on this issue, but in addition to bringing in most northern Whigs, it gained support from "Free Soil" northern Democrats who opposed the expansion of slavery. Only a handful of **abolitionists** joined. The Republicans adopted most of the modernization programs of the Whigs, favoring banks, **tariffs,** and internal improvements and adding, as well, a demand for a homestead law that would provide free farms to western settlers.

The 1856 campaign was a crusade for "Free Soil, Free Labor, Free Men, and Fremont!" John C. Fremont was defeated by the Democratic candidate James Buchanan (1857–1861). By the late 1850s, the new Republican Party dominated every northern state. It controlled enough electoral votes to win the presidency, despite its almost complete lack of support in the South. In 1860, Abraham Lincoln (1861–1865), with only 40 percent of the popular vote, swept the North and easily carried the electoral college. Interpreting the Republican victory as a signal of intense, permanent Northern hostility, seven states of the Deep South immediately seceded and formed the Confederate States of America. Four additional Southern states joined the Confederacy after Lincoln's inauguration.

Lincoln proved brilliantly successful in uniting all the factions of his party to fight for the Union. Most northern Democrats were likewise supportive until fall 1862, when Lincoln added the **abolition** of slavery as a war goal. In Congress, the party passed major legislation to promote rapid modernization, including measures for a national banking system, high tariffs, homestead laws, and aid to education and agriculture.

Ulysses S. Grant (1869–1877) was elected president in 1868 with strong support from **radical Republicans** and the new Republican state governments in the South. He in turn vigorously supported a far-reaching **Reconstruction** program in the South, the Fourteenth **Amendment,** and equal civil and voting rights for the recently freed slaves. Most of all, he was the hero of the war veterans, who gave him strong support.

Late Nineteenth Century

The Compromise of 1877 resolved the disputed election of 1876 by giving the White House to the Republicans and all of the southern states to the Democrats. The Grand Old Party (GOP), as it was now nicknamed, split into "Stalwart" and "Half-Breed" factions. In 1884, "Mugwump" reformers split off and helped elect Democrat Grover Cleveland (1885–1889, 1893–1897).

In the 1888 election, for the first time since 1872, the Republicans gained control of the White House and both houses of Congress. The Republicans, relying on the loyal supporters that had always dominated the party's voting base, were badly defeated in the 1890 off-year election and the 1892 presidential contest, won by Cleveland. A severe economic **depression** struck both rural and urban America in 1893—on Cleveland's watch. The depression, combined with violent nationwide coal and railway strikes and **factionalism** inside the Democratic Party, led to a sweeping victory for the GOP in 1894.

The Republican Party seemed invincible in 1896, until the Democrats unexpectedly selected William Jennings Bryan as their presidential candidate. Bryan's hugely popular crusade against the gold standard, financiers, railroads, and industrialists—indeed, against the cities—created a crisis for Republican candidate William McKinley (1897–1901) and his campaign manager, Marc Hanna. Because of **civil service reforms,** parties could no longer finance themselves internally. Hanna solved that problem by directly obtaining $3.5 million from large corporations that felt threatened by Bryan.

McKinley promised prosperity for everyone and every group, with no governmental attacks on property or ethnic groups. The business community, factory workers, white-collar workers, and commercial farmers responded enthusiastically, becoming major components of the new Republican majority.

Early Twentieth Century

Rejuvenated by their triumphs in 1894 and 1896 and by the glamour of a highly popular short war in 1898, against Spain over Cuba, the Philippines, and other Spanish possessions, the Republicans rolled to victory after victory. However, the party had again grown too large, and factionalism increasingly tore it apart.

The break within the party came in 1912 over the issue of **progressivism.** President William Howard Taft (1909–1913) favored **conservative** reform controlled by the courts; former president Theodore Roosevelt (1901–1909) went to the grass roots, attacking Taft, political **bosses,** courts, big business, and the "malefactors of great wealth." Defeated at the convention, Roosevelt bolted and formed a **third party,** the Progressive, or Bull Moose Party. The vast majority of **progressive** politicians refused to follow Roosevelt's action, allowing conservatives to seize control of the GOP. Roosevelt's split of the party also allowed Democrat Woodrow Wilson (1913–1921) to gain the White House with only 40 percent of the vote. After Wilson's fragile coalition collapsed in 1920, the GOP won three consecutive presidential contests.

Herbert Hoover (1929–1933), elected in 1928, represented the epitome of the modernizing engineer, bringing efficiency to government and the economy. His weak political skill hardly seemed to matter when the economy boomed in the 1920s and Democrats were in disarray. However, when the **Great Depression** hit in the 1930s, his political ineffectiveness compounded the party's weaknesses.

New Deal and Democratic Dominance

The Great Depression sidelined the GOP for decades as their conservative formulas for prosperity had failed. The Democrats, by contrast, built up majorities that depended on labor unions, big city political **machines,** federal relief funds, and the mobilization of Catholics, Jews, and African Americans. However, middle-class hostility to new taxes, and fears about a repeat of the World

War I (1917–1918), eventually led to a Republican rebound.

In 1952, the issues of the war in Korea (1950–1953), communism, and corruption gave World War II (1939–1945) hero Dwight D. Eisenhower (1953–1961) a victory for Republicans, along with narrow control of Congress. However, the GOP remained a minority party and was factionalized, with a northeastern liberal element favorable to the New Deal welfare state and the policy of containing communist expansion, versus midwestern conservatives who bitterly opposed New Deal taxes, regulation, labor unions, and internationalism. Both factions used the issue of anticommunism and attacked the Democrats for harboring spies and allowing communist gains in China and Korea. New York governors Thomas E. Dewey and Nelson Rockefeller led the **liberal** wing, while Senators Robert Taft of Ohio and Barry Goldwater of Arizona spoke for the conservatives.

Richard Nixon (1969–1974), who was Eisenhower's vice president, was aligned with the eastern liberal GOP. Nominated in 1960 to succeed Eisenhower, he lost because the Democrats had a larger base of loyal supporters, especially among Catholics who turned out to support their candidate, John F. Kennedy (1961–1963). The defeat of yet another candidate sponsored by the eastern "establishment" opened the way for Goldwater's 1964 crusade against the New Deal and then-president Lyndon Johnson's (1963–1969) **Great Society** programs. Goldwater permanently weakened the eastern liberals. Goldwater in 1964 and independent George Wallace in 1968 took southern whites and many northern Catholics away from their Democratic roots, while at the same time the Democratic commitment to civil rights won over nine-tenths of all African American voters.

Republican Revival

President Johnson, who was Kennedy's vice president, succeeded him on Kennedy's assassination in 1963. Johnson won an overwhelming victory in 1964 and brought with him a large Democratic majority in Congress that enacted sweeping social programs that Johnson called the Great Society. However, support for these programs collapsed in the mid-1960s.

Richard M. Nixon seized the moment and ran again, winning narrowly in 1968. As president, he largely ignored his party—his 1972 reelection campaign was practically nonpartisan but wildly successful as he buried his Democratic opponent. Nixon was not to serve out his second term, however. The Watergate scandal, which revealed White House and presidential involvement in criminal activities, forced him to resign in the face of certain congressional **impeachment** and removal from office. Nixon's self-destruction wreaked havoc in the 1974 election, in which Democrats swept to a massive victory in off-year contests, and set the stage for the 1976 Carter victory.

Georgia governor Jimmy Carter (1977–1981) won the White House for the Democrats, but foreign affairs issues plagued his presidency. Public opinion saw failure in his policies toward the Soviet Union, the Middle Eastern nations that forced an energy crisis by withholding oil supplies, and Iranian revolutionaries that held Americans hostage for months. **Stagflation** in the economy meant a combination of high unemployment and high inflation. Most of all there was a sense of drift or, worse, of malaise. The country craved leadership.

Ronald Reagan (1981–1989) answered that need. A former movie actor and Republican governor of California, Reagan had been a supporter of Goldwater and an articulate spokesman for the conservative views that the 1964 presidential candidate set in motion. Reagan led a political revolution in 1980, capitalizing on grievances and mobilizing an entirely new voting bloc, the **religious right.**

By the time of the 1984 election, inflation had declined significantly, unemployment had eased, profits were soaring, some changes had been made in the Social Security system, and Reagan carried forty-nine states in winning reelection. Reagan pursued an aggressive cold war policy, which ultimately led to the collapse of the Soviet Union and the end of international communism in most nations. For the first time since 1932, the GOP pulled abreast of the Democrats in terms of party identification on the part of voters.

George Herbert Walker Bush (1989–1993) rode to the White House in 1988 on Reagan's popularity and could himself claim important victories in the cold war and in the Middle East, where the Persian Gulf War liberated Kuwait in

1991 after an invasion by neighboring Iraq. Yet Bush—so knowledgeable on international affairs—seemed indifferent about taxes, deficits, and other domestic issues that bothered Americans far more. Most importantly, Bush was plagued by the remains of a **recession** in 1990–1991 just as he was running for reelection in 1992, allowing Arkansas governor Bill Clinton (1993–2001) to take back the White House for the Democrats.

The 1990s was not a good decade for the Republican Party. It lost the 1992 and 1996 presidential elections to Clinton, the first time the GOP had lost successive White House elections since 1960 and 1964. However, the GOP roared back in 1994, gaining control of Congress—both the House and Senate—for the first time since 1952 as well as control of governors' mansions in nearly all the major states.

The bitter leadership of Speaker of the House Newt Gingrich soured politics in Washington, D.C. Thus, he was unable to deliver on most of his conservative program that he called the "Contract with America." The Republican image worsened when the party attempted to impeach and remove Clinton from office over a scandal that had its roots in an affair between Clinton and a young female intern in the White House that Clinton at first denied. The public, although appalled at the scandal, never showed enthusiasm for removing Clinton and the Senate refused to convict the president after the House impeached him.

Nevertheless, in the 2000 elections the Republican Party achieved success. In a hotly contested election, former president Bush's son, George W. Bush (2001–2009), defeated Democrat Al Gore, a victory—although one of the most narrow in history—that revived the GOP dominance of national level politics that began with Richard Nixon in 1968. Equally important, the GOP retained control of Congress, giving it complete control of the federal government for the first time since 1953. In 2004, George W. Bush was reelected with more than 50 percent of the popular vote, but in 2006 the Republican Party lost control of both houses of Congress—the first time since 1993.

See also: Democratic Party (1828–); Impeachment, Presidential; Watergate Scandal; Whig Party (1834–1856).

Further Reading

Gould, Lewis L. *Grand Old Party*. New York: Random House, 2003.

Rockefeller, Nelson A. (1908–1979)

See Ford, Gerald R., Administration of (1974–1977); Twenty-fifth Amendment (1967).

Roosevelt, Franklin D., Administration of (1933–1945)

Government under the thirty-second president of the United States. As a young man, Franklin D. Roosevelt entered Harvard University in 1900. He graduated in three years and became editor of the campus newspaper. Roosevelt stayed a fourth year at Harvard as a graduate student of history and economics. He then studied law at Columbia University from 1904 until 1907, but left without graduating when he passed the bar. A New York City firm hired him as a law clerk.

Early Political Career

In 1910, Roosevelt ran for the New York State Senate as a Democrat from a traditionally Republican district and surprised Democratic Party leaders when he won. He was reelected in 1912 but gave up his seat in 1913, when President Woodrow Wilson (1913–1921) appointed him assistant secretary of the navy, a post once held by his distant relative Theodore Roosevelt (1901–1909).

After World War I (1914–1918) war broke out in Europe, Roosevelt argued for greater military preparedness. When the United States entered the war in 1917, he twice asked Wilson to transfer him to active service, but the president turned him down saying he was needed where he was. Roosevelt made several trips to Europe to inspect U.S. naval forces.

In 1920, Roosevelt resigned from the Navy Department when the Democratic Party nominated him for the vice presidency on the ticket with presidential nominee James M. Cox. Democrats hoped that the promising young politician with the famous name could give the ticket a boost, but Republicans Warren Harding (1921–1923) and Calvin Coolidge (1923–1929) beat Cox and Roosevelt badly. After the defeat, Roosevelt became a partner in a New York City law firm.

In 1921, Roosevelt suffered a personal tragedy. While vacationing in New Brunswick, Canada, he was stricken with polio. The attack left him severely crippled. His mother urged him to give up politics and retire to the family estate at Hyde Park, New York. Roosevelt, however, struggled to rehabilitate himself. Over a period of years, he built up his arms and chest and eventually was able to walk short distances with the aid of crutches and braces.

On June 26, 1924, Roosevelt returned to national politics when he delivered the presidential nomination speech for New York governor Alfred E. Smith at the Democratic National Convention in New York City. Smith did not receive the nomination, but Roosevelt's courageous appearance on crutches at Madison Square Garden increased his popularity and made him a leading figure in the Democratic Party.

Al Smith, nominated for president in 1928, urged Roosevelt to run for governor in New York to give the Democratic ticket a boost. Roosevelt at first declined, saying he wanted to concentrate on rehabilitating his legs, but he finally agreed to run when he was nominated by acclamation. His vigorous campaigning, often conducted from an automobile, dispelled questions of Roosevelt's physical ability to function as governor. Roosevelt won the election.

Roosevelt's success as governor made him a leading candidate for the Democratic presidential nomination in 1932. He entered the convention with a majority of delegates, but he had fewer than the two-thirds necessary to win the nomination. After three ballots, he offered to endorse rival John Nance Garner, the Texan Speaker of the House, for vice president, if Garner released his presidential delegates. Garner, recognizing his chances of being nominated for president were

The First Hundred Days of Franklin D. Roosevelt

Franklin D. Roosevelt, sworn into office on March 4, 1933, convened the Seventy-third Congress into special session on March 9 to consider the Emergency Banking Act, which Congress passed after eight hours of debate. Roosevelt at first considered sending Congress back home after passage of the act, but the window of opportunity for even more action presented by the crisis seemed too valuable to waste. As historian Arthur M. Schlesinger Jr. later wrote, "In the three months after Roosevelt's inauguration, Congress and the country were subjected to a presidential barrage of ideas and programs unlike anything known to American history."[1]

Below are the major accomplishments of the now legendary "First Hundred Days":

March 9	Emergency Banking Act: reformed the national banking system
March 20	Economy Act: authorized cuts in federal spending
March 22	Beer and Wine Revenue Act: legalized sale of beer and wine
March 31	Civilian Conservation Corps: created employment for youths in a wide range of conservation efforts
April 19	Abandonment of gold standard: detached value of currency from gold
May 12	Federal Emergency Relief Act: created a national relief system
May 12	Agricultural Adjustment Act: established a national agricultural policy
May 12	Emergency Farm Mortgage Act: refinanced farm mortgages
May 18	Tennessee Valley Authority Act: provided for the unified development of the Tennessee Valley
May 27	Truth in Securities Act: required full disclosure of a firm's financial shape when it issued new securities
June 13	Home Owners' Loan Act: refinanced home mortgages
June 16	National Industrial Recovery Act: created a system of federally supervised industrial self-regulation and a $3.3 billion public works program
June 16	Glass-Steagall Banking Act: separated commercial and investment banking; guaranteed bank deposits
June 16	Farm Credit Act: reorganized federal farm credit programs
June 16	Emergency Railroad Transportation Act: created greater coordination in national railroad system

Note: 1. Arthur M. Schlesinger Jr., *The Age of Roosevelt: The Coming of the New Deal* (Boston: Houghton Mifflin, 1959), 20.

Franklin D. Roosevelt's (1933–1945) first one hundred days in office produced an historic amount of new legislation designed to combat the Great Depression that plagued the nation.

slim, accepted the deal and released his ninety delegates to Roosevelt, who was nominated on the fourth ballot. The convention then nominated Garner for vice president.

During the campaign of 1932, Roosevelt exuded confidence and outlined his recovery program, which he called the "New Deal." Although he faced **incumbent** Republican president Herbert Hoover (1929–1933) in the election, Roosevelt was favored to win because many voters blamed Hoover for the severity of the **Great Depression.** Roosevelt outpolled Hoover by more than seven million votes and won 472–59 in the electoral college.

Presidency

Roosevelt took office at the low point of the Depression. Most of the nation's banks were closed, industrial production was about half of what it had been in 1928, and as many as 15 million people were unemployed. Roosevelt worked with the new Democratic Congress to enact many New Deal bills during the productive opening period of his presidency, known as the First Hundred Days. He declared a four-day bank holiday to stop panic withdrawals, abandoned the gold standard, increased government loans to farmers and homeowners, and created federal bank deposit insurance. At Roosevelt's urging, Congress created the Civilian Conservation Corps (CCC), which employed tens of thousands of people on conservation projects and passed the Federal Emergency Relief Act, which provided grants to state and local governments for aid to the unemployed. Numerous other measures passed during the First Hundred Days—including the National Recovery Act (NRA) and the Agricultural Adjustment Act (AAA)—increased public confidence and stimulated the economy.

Business interests feared that the deficit spending required to finance the New Deal would lead to inflation, but injection of federal money into the economy eased the Depression. Roosevelt promoted his policies through "fireside chats," radio addresses to the nation from the White House. A second wave of New Deal programs, including Social Security, unemployment insurance, the National Labor Relations Act (Wagner Act, which recognized the rights of workers to form unions), and federal aid to dependent children, was passed in 1934 and 1935.

Roosevelt's New Deal successes made him a popular president. He defeated Kansas governor Alfred M. Landon in the 1936 presidential election in one of the largest landslides in presidential election history. Landon won only Maine and Vermont.

In 1937, Roosevelt suffered one of the biggest defeats of his presidency when he proposed to expand the Supreme Court from nine to as many as fifteen justices. Roosevelt had been frustrated by the **conservative** court, which had struck down several of his New Deal measures. If the Court were expanded, he could appoint justices who would accept his policies. Neither the public nor Congress, however, would go along with Roosevelt's court-packing effort.

In 1940, Roosevelt ran for an **unprecedented** third term against the **progressive** Republican nominee Wendell Willkie of Indiana. Roosevelt defeated Willkie 449 to 82 in the electoral college. His popular margin of victory narrowed from four years before, however, in part because some voters objected to Roosevelt's disregard of the unwritten rule that presidents should serve no more than two terms.

In September 1939, Adolf Hitler's Germany had invaded Poland, embroiling Great Britain, France, and other European nations in World

VIEWPOINTS

Uncle Sam (center) demonstrates his support for both employees and employers with the NRA—one of Roosevelt's New Deal programs. (The Granger Collection, New York)

War II (1939–1945) in Europe. Despite strong **neutral** sentiments among members of Congress and the general public, Roosevelt recognized that U.S. national security depended on Great Britain's survival. He promised to keep the United States out of the fighting, but pressed for the authority to aid Britain and other allied nations in every way short of going to war. In September 1940, Roosevelt violated two **neutrality** statutes in trading Great Britain fifty outdated destroyers for the right to lease certain British territory in the western Atlantic for U.S. naval and air bases. In March 1941, Roosevelt persuaded Congress to pass the Lend-Lease Act, which gave the president the power to supply weapons and equipment to "any country whose defense the president deems vital to the defense of the United States." In September of that year, Roosevelt ordered U.S. warships providing protection for supply convoys bound for Britain to attack German vessels on sight. Thus, Roosevelt had engaged the United States in an undeclared naval war months before the nation would officially enter the war.

On December 7, 1941, the Japanese launched a surprise attack against the U.S. fleet at Pearl Harbor, Hawaii. The next day Roosevelt asked for and received a declaration of war from Congress. Within a few days, Hitler's Germany declared war on the United States. Roosevelt shifted his focus and national resources from New Deal reforms to winning the war.

Roosevelt oversaw the development of military strategy and conferred often with British prime minister Winston Churchill. Roosevelt and Churchill met with Soviet leader Joseph Stalin at Tehran in 1943 and Yalta in 1945. At these meetings, the leaders of the three principal Allied nations not only discussed wartime strategy, they planned for the postwar order. At Yalta Roosevelt secured a Soviet promise to enter the war against Japan when Germany was defeated in return for territorial concessions in Asia. The allies also set new Polish borders, scheduled a conference in 1945 to establish the United Nations (UN), and agreed to allow occupied countries to construct new governments based on free elections after the war.

Although the strain of the wartime presidency had weakened Roosevelt, he ran for a fourth term in 1944. In a fateful move, he agreed to the suggestion of his political advisers to drop his third-term vice president Henry A. Wallace, who was considered too **liberal.** The Democrats nominated Senator Harry S. Truman from Missouri for vice president in Wallace's place. Roosevelt defeated his fourth Republican opponent, New York governor Thomas E. Dewey, 432–99 in the electoral college.

In April 1945, after returning from Yalta, Roosevelt went to Warm Springs, Georgia, for a rest before the conference on the establishment of the United Nations scheduled for later in the month in San Francisco. On April 12, while sitting for a portrait at his cottage, Roosevelt collapsed from a cerebral hemorrhage and died a few hours later. The same day in Washington, Harry S. Truman (1945–1953) was sworn in as president. The world mourned the dead president as a train carried his body back to the capital, where it lay in state at the White House. The train then resumed its journey north to Roosevelt's Hyde Park home, where he was buried.

See also: Hoover, Herbert, Administration of (1929–1933); Truman, Harry S., Administration of (1945–1953).

Further Reading

Jenkins, Roy. *Franklin D. Roosevelt.* New York: Times Books, 2003.
Smith, Jean Edward. *FDR.* New York: Random House, 2008.

Roosevelt, Theodore, Administration of (1901–1909)

Government under the twenty-sixth president of the United States. Roosevelt entered politics in 1881 when he was elected to the New York state legislature at the age of twenty-three. He led a group of reform Republicans who fought corruption in the state government. Roosevelt was reelected in 1882 and 1883 but declined to seek reelection after his wife, Alice, and his mother died within hours of each other on February 14, 1884.

In 1889, Roosevelt returned to public service when President Benjamin Harrison (1889–1893) appointed him U.S. civil service commissioner. He was reappointed in 1893 by Democrat Grover Cleveland (1893–1897) and served until 1895. As commissioner, Roosevelt fought against the spoils system, which he considered a source of corruption. He revised civil service exams, doubled the number of government positions subject to examination, and increased government employment opportunities for women.

From 1895 to 1897, Roosevelt served as president of the Police Commission of New York City. He moved to Washington, D.C., in 1897 when President William McKinley (1897–1901) appointed him assistant secretary of the navy. In this post, he fought to increase the size of the U.S. Navy and advocated war with Spain over that country's suppression of an independence movement in Cuba.

Soon after the United States declared war against Spain, Roosevelt resigned from the Navy Department so he could fight in Cuba. He secured the rank of lieutenant colonel and organized a regiment of cavalry that came to be known as the Rough Riders. Although the importance of the Rough Riders to the American victory over the Spanish in Cuba became exaggerated, Roosevelt demonstrated his courage in leading his regiment in the famous charge up one of the San Juan Hills overlooking Santiago. Despite suffering heavy casualties, the Rough Riders captured the hill.

Roosevelt's actions in Cuba made him a celebrity in the United States. In November 1898, he received the Republican nomination for governor of New York and was narrowly elected. As governor, his political independence and refusal to promote the interests of big business disturbed the power brokers of his party, particularly New York Republican **boss** Thomas Platt.

In 1900, Platt hoped to get rid of Roosevelt by promoting him as a candidate for vice president. Although Roosevelt declared he did not want the job, he was the popular choice at the Philadelphia Republican National Convention, and he accepted the nomination when it was offered to him. Party leaders had mixed feelings about Roosevelt. They recognized that his popularity could win votes for the ticket, but they feared what might happen if McKinley died. Mark Hanna, the Republican national chair who had overseen McKinley's career, warned his colleagues, "Don't any of you realize that there's only one life between this madman and the White House?"

On September 6, 1901, Roosevelt was hunting and fishing in Vermont when he learned that President McKinley had been shot. He rushed to Buffalo, where doctors said McKinley would recover from his wounds. Roosevelt wanted to demonstrate to the public that the president was in no danger of death, so he resumed his vacation on September 10. Three days later, however, Roosevelt was informed that McKinley's condition had deteriorated. The vice president arrived in Buffalo on September 14, the day McKinley died. Later in the day, he took the oath of office. At the age of forty-two, Roosevelt became the youngest person ever to serve as president.

Presidency

After McKinley's death, Roosevelt declared, "It shall be my aim to continue absolutely unbroken the policy of President McKinley for the peace, the prosperity, and the honor of our beloved country." Despite retaining McKinley's cabinet, Roosevelt promoted his own policies, which included measures to curb abuses by big business. Soon after taking office, he had directed Attorney General Philander Knox to prepare an antitrust suit against Northern Securities Company, a giant railroad trust. The suit was successful in 1904 when the Supreme Court ruled that the company should be dissolved. Although the Roosevelt administration would initiate fewer antitrust suits than the Taft administration (1909–1913), Roosevelt became known as the trust-busting president. In 1902, when a coal strike in Pennsylvania caused shortages and rising coal prices, Roosevelt threatened to take over the mines unless the mine owners submitted to **arbitration.** The mine owners backed down, and Roosevelt appointed a commission that gave the miners a 10 percent raise.

Roosevelt's most famous act during his first term was his acquisition of land for the Panama Canal. Colombia owned Panama, but in August 1903, the Colombian senate refused to approve a treaty giving the United States the rights to a canal zone six miles wide. Determined to build the canal, Roosevelt later that year supported a revolution in Panama, which, with the help of the U.S. Navy, overthrew Colombian rule. The new Panamanian government agreed to lease the zone to the United States, and construction of the canal began.

In the 1904 presidential election, Roosevelt ran against New York judge Alton B. Parker. Roosevelt received more than 56 percent of the popular vote and easily won in the electoral college, 336–140. He became the first successor president to win the White House in his own right after serving the unfinished term of his predecessor.

During his second term, Roosevelt championed many pieces of reform legislation including the Pure Food and Drug Act, the Meat Inspection Act, and the Hepburn Act, which empowered the government to set railroad rates. Roosevelt also continued his conservationist activities begun during his first term. Under Roosevelt, the government initiated thirty major federal irrigation projects, added 125 million acres to the national forest reserves, and doubled the number of national parks.

In foreign affairs, Roosevelt continued aggressively to promote U.S. interests overseas, often in a manner his critics described as **imperialistic.** In late 1904, he issued the Roosevelt Corollary to the Monroe Doctrine (1823), which declared that the United States would intervene in Latin American affairs to prevent European nations from intervening there. The following year he put the corollary into practice by taking control of the Santo Domingo customhouses to guarantee that country's European debts. In 1905, he mediated an agreement ending the Russo-Japanese War (1904–1905) and was awarded the Nobel Peace Prize for his efforts. In the face of congressional opposition, Roosevelt sent the U.S. fleet on a world cruise that lasted from late 1907 to early 1909. The show of strength was intended to impress other nations, especially Japan, with U.S. resolve to defend its interests and play an active role in world affairs.

Former President

Roosevelt's friend and secretary of war, William Howard Taft (1909–1913), was elected president in 1908 with Roosevelt's backing. During the next two years, however, Roosevelt became increasingly at odds with Taft, who he felt had abandoned his policies.

In 1912, Roosevelt declared his interest in the Republican nomination for president. He won most of the primaries, but the Republican National Convention in Chicago was controlled by supporters of President Taft, who received the nomination. **Progressive** Republicans organized the Progressive Party and persuaded Roosevelt to run. The party was dubbed the "Bull Moose" Party, because candidate Roosevelt declared that he felt "as fit as a bull moose."

On October 14, 1912, while campaigning in Milwaukee, Roosevelt was shot in the chest by an assailant. The candidate insisted on delivering a scheduled speech, which lasted almost an hour. He was then rushed from the amazed crowd to a hospital. Taft and the Democratic nominee, Woodrow Wilson (1913–1921), stopped their campaigns while Roosevelt recovered, but the former president was delivering speeches again within two weeks. Roosevelt's heroic campaigning, however, could not overcome the split he had caused among Republicans. Second-place Roosevelt and third-place Taft together received more than one million more popular votes than Wilson, but with his opposition divided, Wilson won the election.

The Progressives asked Roosevelt to run for president again in 1916, but Roosevelt declined and supported Republican Charles Evans Hughes, who lost to President Wilson. In 1916, Roosevelt had begun to make plans for raising a volunteer division to command if the United States entered World War I (1914–1918). When the United States did enter the war in 1917, he went to the White House to request authority to implement his plans, but Wilson turned him down. During the war, Roosevelt was a leading Republican spokesperson. He was hospitalized in November 1918 with a severe attack of rheumatism, an ailment from which he suffered during the last years of his life. He returned to his home at Sagamore Hill, New York, but remained ill. He died in his sleep on January 6, 1919, from a blood clot.

See also: McKinley, William, Administration of (1897–1901); Taft, William Howard, Administration of (1909–1913).

Further Reading

Auchincloss, Louis. *Theodore Roosevelt.* New York: Times Books, 2002.

Morris, Edmund. *Theodore Rex.* New York: Modern Library Classics, 2006.

A – Z

Scott, Dred

See Buchanan, James, Administration of (1857–1861).

Secret Service

Full-time personal protection for presidents and their families. While the bulk of the president's security is provided by the U.S. Secret Service, other government agencies also contribute to the effort to protect the president. Because the number of Secret Service personnel is insufficient to fill all the human resource demands of protecting the president, however, local and foreign police may be used, depending on where the president travels. The air force provides a fighter escort for *Air Force One;* the navy furnishes backup in case an emergency develops while the president flies over the ocean; the army provides communication equipment; and the Marine Corps posts a detachment to guard the Camp David presidential retreat. Finally, the General Services Administration (GSA) arranges for any renovations needed to improve security at a presidential residence.

Although all these agencies contribute to the president's safety, the central body is the Secret Service, which coordinates their activities. Any measures taken by GSA, for example, are at the request of the service, and it is the service that provides the human shield needed to protect the president.

Origins of the Secret Service

What is now known as the Secret Service was created in July 1865 to reduce the counterfeiting of U.S. currency. By the end of the Civil War (1861–1865), counterfeiting had reached such proportions that as many as one-third of all bills in circulation may have been bogus. In one of the last official acts of his life, President Abraham Lincoln (1861–1865) agreed to the creation of a unit within the Treasury Department that would have the permanent task of catching forgers and counterfeiters. The Secret Service Division proved quite successful at this task. During its first few years, it captured more than two hundred counterfeiters a year.

Because at that time the service was the only federal government agency that acted as a general law enforcement body, it found that its role expanded rapidly. By 1874, it was investigating fraud, peonage, and slavery cases, as well as the Ku Klux Klan.

Protection of the president was not part of the service's original function. For many years, presidents who wanted bodyguards had to hire them themselves, and most did without. Confronted with a would-be assassin in 1835, President Andrew Jackson (1829–1937) himself attacked his assailant and drove him off. On the night he was killed, President Lincoln was guarded by a single District of Columbia policeman; the guard had wandered off when assailant John Wilkes Booth arrived. Secret Service agents were nearby when Presidents James A. Garfield (1881) and William McKinley (1897–1901) were shot, but none of them were responsible for protecting the president. In McKinley's case, there were three agents next to him, but their only job was crowd control. Indeed, early efforts by the service to protect the president were rebuffed by Congress, and it was not until 1906 that the first presidential detail was authorized.

The coverage given by the service gradually expanded through the years, and protection became its second major function. Finally, in 1951, the Secret Service was permanently granted the job of presidential protection; until that time its authorization had to be renewed annually.

Roles of the Secret Service

With its roles of defender of the nation's currency and protector of the president, the Secret Service is in a sense two agencies in one: a criminal investigation unit and a bodyguard service.

The better-known part of the service's mission is protection of the president. That role has expanded considerably since its inception. The first White House detail, assigned to Theodore Roosevelt (1901–1909) in 1901, had only two agents. The detail expanded to ten by 1918 and to thirty-seven by 1940. In 1989, it numbered seventy. The protection has broadened as well. Originally, it included just the president, but in 1908, it was extended to the president-elect, and since 1962 has included the vice president and the vice president–elect. Protection for these four individuals is mandatory; by law, they may not refuse it. Further additions to the service's workload were made in 1965, when retired presidents, widows of presidents, and their children under age sixteen were protected. Coverage was extended to presidential candidates in 1968, to foreign heads of state in 1971, and to candidates' wives (on a limited basis) in 1976. In addition, the president in 1971 was granted the right to request protection for anyone thought to need it, as Jimmy Carter did for Edward Kennedy in 1980 before the senator became an official presidential candidate. Any of these people can refuse Secret Service protection, but few do; one of those few was Richard Nixon (1969–1974), who terminated his protection in 1985.

Protecting the President

All of the training undertaken by agents in the Secret Service's operations divisions is aimed at keeping the president alive and unharmed. The service has adopted numerous tactics to ensure the president's continued safety in a world filled with dangers.

The service prefers, of course, that the president remain in the White House, where there are numerous safeguards and a controlled environment. Although the service does not reveal any details, it is clear that White House security arrangements are elaborate. In the residence are locator boxes so that the agents can know where members of the first family are at all times. Anyone entering the mansion on business is checked; anyone working there, including presidential aides, must wear a photo badge. The service maintains a database of all visitors; it can tell how many times a given person has come to the White House, when and how long he or she was there, and who was visited. All incoming packages and visitors are also carefully monitored; bomb-sniffing dogs are available to check suspicious packages or vehicles. Armed guards and plainclothes agents keep watch around the premises, and sharpshooters are posted on the roof. The grounds are protected by reinforced fences, guardhouses, television cameras, and electronic sensors. In recent years, a bicycle patrol has been added. There is a Doppler radar system that looks directly up to detect any parachute assault, antiaircraft weapons (reportedly heat-seeking, shoulder-fired Stinger missiles), and a bomb shelter. Finally, should the president need help, there is a "panic button" under the desk in the Oval Office that can unobtrusively summon agents at any time.

When the president travels, the challenges for the service are greater because the variables that can be easily controlled are fewer. The White House detail and the field offices in the areas where the president plans to travel must make

---

Major Responsibilities of the Secret Service

Today, the Secret Service protects:

- the White House complex, the main Treasury Building and Annex, and other presidential offices
- the president and members of the immediate family
- the temporary official residence of the vice president in the District of Columbia
- the vice president and members of the immediate family
- foreign diplomatic missions in the Washington, D.C., metropolitan area and throughout the United States, and its territories and possessions, as prescribed by law

The primary focus of the Secret Service is protection of the president, the vice president, their families, and foreign heads of state visiting the United States.

An unidentified Secret Service agent, with automatic weapon drawn, yells orders to others at the scene of the Ronald Reagan assassination attempt on March 30, 1981. (AP Images, Ron Edmonds)

A - Z

extensive security arrangements. Working with the local police, they secure the airport where the president will arrive and depart. They carefully plan and survey the routes to be traveled, secure the buildings in which the president will appear, and arrange that rooftops and other overlooks be patrolled. Sharpshooters may be posted on roofs. Procedures for screening onlookers are introduced. The service's files are checked for any people known to be a possible threat to the president; some of them may be watched during the visit. Preparations extend to identifying a hospital to use in case of emergency and ensuring that it has adequate supplies of the president's blood type.

In recent years, security arrangements have not permitted publicity about the president's travel plans. Formerly, in an effort by political supporters to ensure the largest crowds possible, it was customary to publicize the president's travel route. For example, President John F.

Kennedy's (1961–1963) exact route through Dallas on November 22, 1963, was available to anyone who picked up a Dallas newspaper. This is no longer true. When the president travels today, the arrival and departure times and the itinerary are not public knowledge.

The most visible part of the presidential protection effort is the cordon of agents that surrounds the president. These agents are with the president at almost all times, even in the White House, except the family quarters. They stand guard both inside and outside of every room occupied by the president. When the president leaves the White House, the agents form (as best they can) a human shield around the chief **executive.** The service tries to maintain what it calls a "safe zone" or clear space around the president, so that the agents have a better chance to spot a potential assailant. Their efforts to keep a safe zone have sometimes led to criticism of their tactics.

Who Is Eligible for Secret Service Protection?

The Secret Service was formed in 1865 in order to suppress the making and use of counterfeit money. Yet, their responsibilities were briefly expanded in 1894 when they began giving unofficial protection to President Grover Cleveland (1885–1889, 1893–1897). It was not until after President William McKinley's (1897–1901) assassination in 1901 that executive protection became an official responsibility of the Secret Service. As the years passed, the Secret Service's executive protection responsibilities continued to increase such as in 1908 when they were given the responsibility to protect the president-elect and in 1915 when they became responsible for protecting the president's immediate family. Former presidents, vice presidents, and vice presidents-elect also fell under Secret Service protection in the early sixties.

When John F. Kennedy (1961–1963) came into office, he had two minor children who also required protection. Congress passed legislation to make this possible for the Kennedy family in 1963. In 1965, a law was passed saying that spouses of the president have protection available to them for life, while the children of the president could be protected until they turned sixteen. The 1963 assassination of President Kennedy and the 1968 assassination of Senator Robert F. Kennedy, who was seeking the Democratic presidential nomination, brought more reforms. In 1968, a law was passed providing Secret Service protection for all major presidential nominees and candidates and stipulating that widows of presidents would be given protection for

Because these agents represent the last line of defense for the president, they are under enormous pressure. Beyond watching for any known dangerous people who may be around, agents scan the crowds in search of unusual or threatening behavior: a man wearing an overcoat on a warm day, a person carrying a newspaper in a strange way, a woman too eager to get close to the president, or even a face that keeps reappearing in different places. Because the goal of the service is prevention, not retribution, agents must develop a sixth sense to anticipate trouble. An instinct for danger and quick reactions are critical to keeping the president safe.

Should an attack occur, agents shield the president first, then subdue the assailant, and finally, once the president is safely removed, secure the area and assist any injured bystanders. Agents are trained to become a human shield for the president. As he watched agents stand to practice with firearms, President Ronald Reagan (1981–1989)

commented that they made a very large target that way; he was told that that was the point. In Dallas in 1963, agent Rufus W. Youngblood covered Vice President Lyndon Johnson with his own body when the presidential motorcade came under attack. Videotapes of the 1981 assassination attempt on Reagan show agent Timothy J. McCarthy, with arms and legs spread wide, walking directly toward the assailant, John W. Hinckley Jr., thus blocking his view of the president. (McCarthy was shot, but he recovered.)

The service has encountered several serious difficulties in its efforts to protect the president, and several of these have had to do with presidents themselves. Some presidents have been quite cooperative with the service, but others have balked at its requests, generally for two reasons.

One reason is strictly political. Most presidents like crowds, and even if they do not, it is simply good politics for them to be seen mingling

SPOTLIGHT

their lifetime or until they remarry. The widow's children would still be provided with protection until they turned sixteen. In the 1970s and 1980s, more legislation was passed that allowed Secret Service protection to be provided for visiting heads of foreign governments, their spouses, and foreign diplomatic missions in the U.S. and its territories.

A major reform measure passed in 1997 shortened the term of protection provided for former presidents from a lifetime to ten years. This law only applies to presidents elected after January 1, 1997. Those elected before this date could still be provided with lifetime protection. The latest change came in 2000, giving the Secret Service the right to be involved in the security planning of major national events, also known as National Special Security Events. The executive protection responsibilities of the Secret Service could also be extended as the president saw fit.

As the Secret Service's executive protection responsibilities grew over the years, so did their law enforcement responsibilities. Along with enforcing anti-counterfeiting laws, the Secret Service became responsible for investigating incidences of fraud, espionage in the United States, law violations committed by federal financial institutions, identity theft, financial crime, and computer or technology crime. The Secret Service, which had been under the authority of the Department of the Treasury, joined the new Department of Homeland Security in 2003.

with their supporters. Thus, while the service probably would prefer that presidents spent their days in one room in the White House, political realities dictate that presidents get out and "press the flesh." The more they do that, the harder it is for the service. President Johnson (1963–1969), for example, loved to dive into crowds, much to his bodyguards' dismay. On that fateful day in Dallas in 1963, Kennedy had the protective cover removed from his limousine so that the crowds could see him better.

The second reason for the lack of cooperation with the service is the presidents' desire for privacy. Agents are a constant intrusive presence in the president's life, which may lead to presidential resentment and resistance. President Johnson complained that the service would not hesitate to occupy his bedroom, and when he was at his ranch, he would often try to lose his detail by jumping in the car and ordering his driver to drive as fast as possible. When at Kennebunkport,

Maine, President George H.W. Bush (1989–1993) would sometimes zoom off in his powerboat, leaving his guardians behind.

The Secret Service, however, has ways to get around presidents and first ladies, who may find their protection particularly burdensome. Eleanor Roosevelt, for example, the wife of Franklin Roosevelt (1933–1945), flatly refused to accept her protective detail. Finally, the service worked out a deal: if she would carry and learn to fire a handgun, the service would stop tailing her. In fact, the gun stayed in her dresser drawer, and the service put undercover agents at her every stop. Early in his term, Harry S. Truman (1945–1953) liked to walk to the bank, but the service did not like the fact that he waited on street corners for the lights to change, so agents fixed all the traffic lights on his route to turn red in all directions at once so Truman would never have to wait on a corner. He soon caught on, however, and ordered the service to stop. Richard Nixon's wife, Pat, tried to keep the number of agents with her on trips around Washington smaller than the service wanted, but her wishes were ignored. When one day she noticed the second car of agents that was accompanying her, she was reassured that it was only there in case her car had engine trouble.

Another problem the service faces is trying to identify a potential assassin, a critical step in preventing an attack on the president. The master files maintained by the service of anyone who may pose a risk to the president—for example, people who have made threats, mentally disturbed and violent people, or members of political extremist groups—are updated constantly. There is, however, no foolproof guide to help evaluate information, and truly dangerous people can be and are overlooked. In fact, none of the people who have shot at service protectees since 1960—Lee Harvey Oswald (President Kennedy, 1963), Sirhan Sirhan (Robert Kennedy, 1968), Arthur Bremer (Governor George Wallace, 1972), Lynette "Squeaky" Fromme (President Ford, 1975), Sara Jane Moore (President Ford, 1975), and John Hinckley (President Reagan, 1981)—were in the agency's files before the attack.

Complicating the service's mission further is the increased threat of foreign terrorist activity against the president, particularly after the attacks on the New York World Trade Center and the Pentagon in September 2001. Although such a threat may be mostly hypothetical, the service cannot take chances and must treat it seriously. Thus, in late 1981 it spent two months in a state of constant alert because of reports that Libya's Muammar Qaddafi had sent a "hit team" to kill President Reagan. Rumors flew about the nature and location of the team. In the end, however, nothing happened, and the hit squad may never have existed. This case indicates the additional burden thrown on the service in an era of international terrorism. Given the agency's limited resources, such a threat spreads the service thin and makes its job even more difficult.

Modern presidents frequently travel overseas, which also increases the problems for the Secret Service. The service must then coordinate its activities with those of a foreign country's security agencies; the difficulty of anticipating and spotting potential assassins is multiplied by the unfamiliar environment. That there are risks is shown in the attempt on former president George H.W. Bush's life in April 1993. While on a visit to Kuwait, Bush was the target of a car bomb that was planted by the Iraqi intelligence service, in retribution for his role in leading the Persian Gulf War in 1991. The plot failed and the bomb was never detonated, but the attempt indicates the potential danger and the difficulties of the service's job in protecting presidents and their families.

A new potential problem emerged for the service during the Bill Clinton's administration (1993–2001). When special prosecutor Kenneth Starr was investigating Clinton's alleged sexual relationship with White House intern Monica Lewinsky, Starr subpoenaed members of Clinton's protective detail to testify before the grand jury. Starr argued that, as federal employees, the agents had a legal responsibility to disclose anything they had witnessed or heard that might pertain to possible criminal activity. The White House, backed by the Treasury Department and the head of the Secret Service as well as by former president George H.W. Bush, refused to permit the agents to testify, invoking what it called the "protective function privilege." Extending the reasoning behind the principle of executive privilege, the White House argued that if members of the president's detail could be subpoenaed, the president would be unable to have frank conversations with his advisers in the presence of agents (which is virtually all the time).

Unfortunately for the service, the courts rejected the claim of protective function privilege. This rejection threatens to complicate the service's job. Knowing that members of the service may be forced to reveal anything they see or hear, presidents may try to keep their guardians as physically far away as possible, making the service's job of protecting the president much more difficult.

Further Reading

Holden, Henry. *To Be a U.S. Secret Service Agent.* Osceola, WI: Zenith Press, 2006.

Melanson, Philip H. *The Secret Service: The Hidden History of an Enigmatic Agency.* New York: Basic Books, 2005.

Separation of Powers

The division of powers between different branches of government to ensure that no one branch exercises too much authority over the others. Separation of powers is one of the key features of U.S. government.

The most basic expression of separation of powers in the U.S. government is the existence of three branches of government with distinct areas of authority. By granting certain powers exclusively to one branch or another, the Founders ensured that all three branches would be vital to the workings of government. The Founders also provided for a system of **checks and balances** between branches. Under this system, any branch that tries too assume too much power can be checked by the actions of the others.

The Constitution gives the **legislative** branch a wide range of powers including the power to make laws, collect taxes, borrow and print money, regulate **commerce,** establish courts, raise and support armies and navies, declare war, and to "make all laws necessary and proper to carry out powers granted Congress by the Constitution." The president, however, has the ability to **veto,** or reject laws passed by Congress. While Congress may raise armies and declare war, the president serves as commander-in-chief of the armed forces. The president also has the power to appoint a large number of government officials as well as all federal judges. The judiciary has no lawmaking power, but does have the authority to strike down laws it considers to be **unconstitutional.**

Separation of powers extends to the two houses of Congress as well. Both Houses must pass identical versions of a **bill** for it to become law. All bills intended to raise or spend money must originate in the House of Representatives. The Senate may accept or reject such bills, but it cannot **amend,** or formally change them in any way. The Senate, holds the power to approve or reject presidential appointees or treaties negotiated by the president. The House has no say in such matters.

One of the most important checks Congress has over the other branches is the power to **impeach,** or charge government officials with crimes while in office. This power is also divided between the two chambers. The House may bring **impeachment** charges against government officials, including judges and the president. If a majority of the House votes to impeach, the Senate holds a trial with senators sitting as jurors. If two-thirds of the senators present vote for conviction, the official is removed from office.

See also: Impeachment, Presidential; Presidency and Congress.

Spoils System

See Civil Service System.

State of the Union Address

The annual message of the president of the United States to Congress, usually delivered in January of each year. The Constitution states that the president "shall from time to time give to the Congress information of the State of the Union, and recommend to their Consideration such Measures as he shall judge necessary and expedient." From this clause developed the ritual of the president's annual message, or "State of the Union address," as it has been known since 1945.

George Washington (1789–1797) delivered the first annual message to Congress on January 8, 1790. John Adams (1797–1801), who enjoyed royal formalities, followed Washington's **precedent,** but Thomas Jefferson (1801–1809) objected to having presidents deliver their annual messages in person. Like many of his Democratic-Republican colleagues, he thought the custom, which had derived from the British monarch's speech from the throne at the opening of Parliament, had royal pretensions. As part of his effort

A – Z

Major Themes in State of the Union Addresses, 1961–2008

President	Year	Major themes
Kennedy	1961	Economy; social programs
	1962	Getting America moving; economy; military strength
	1963	Cuba; economy; tax reduction
L. Johnson	1964	JFK legacy; budget
	1965	Great Society domestic programs
	1966	Vietnam, foreign and defense policy
	1967	Maintaining previous momentum
	1968	Vietnam, foreign and defense policy
	1969	Review of achievements
Nixon	1970	Vietnam, foreign and defense policy
	1971	Vietnam; economic and social policy
	1972	Foreign and defense policy; plea for action on previous requests
	1973	Natural resources; economy; social policy
	1974	Energy; economic issues
Ford	1975	Economy; taxes; energy
	1976	Economic and energy issues
	1977	Energy; achievements
Carter	1978	Economic and energy issues
	1979	Inflation; SALT II
	1980	Foreign and defense policy
	1981	Record of progress; budget priorities
Reagan	1982	Economic and budget issues
	1983	Economic and budget issues
	1984	Federal deficit; foreign policy
	1985	Tax reform; government spending
	1986	Foreign policy; welfare reform
	1987	Foreign policy
	1988	Economic and budget issues
G. Bush	1990	Broad domestic and foreign policy issues
	1991	Support for Persian Gulf mission
	1992	Economic and budget issues
Clinton	1994	Domestic policy; jobs; crime; health reform
	1995	"Reinventing government"; domestic policy issues
	1996	Broad domestic policy issues
	1997	Balancing the federal budget; building communities; education
	1998	Spending future surpluses wisely; Social Security
	1999	Education; Social Security; health care; racial divisions
	2000	Social Security; health care; education; minimum wage

Major Themes in State of the Union Addresses, 1961–2008, *continued*

President	Year	Major themes
G. W. Bush	2002	War on terror; homeland defense; tax cuts; economic growth
	2003	Iraq; war on terror; tax cuts; Medicare reform
	2004	Iraq; homeland security; economic growth; tax cuts
	2005	Iraq; Social Security reform; homeland security; war on terror
	2006	Iraq; homeland security; entitlement program reform
	2007	War on terror; Iraq; energy; economic growth; health insurance
	2008	War on terror; Iraq; energy; heathcare; the economy; taxes

Sources: Charles O. Jones, "Presidential Negotiation with Congress," in *Both Ends of the Avenue: The Presidency, the Executive Branch, and Congress in the 1980s,* Anthony King, ed. Washington, DC: American Enterprise Institute, 1983, p. 103; *CQ Weekly,* various issues; Deborah Kalb, Gerhard Peters, and John Woolley, *State of the Union: Presidential Rhetoric from Woodrow Wilson to George W. Bush.* Washington, DC: CQ Press, 2007); John Woolley and Gerhard Peters, The American Presidency Project (online) (*presidency.ucsb.edu/ws/?pid=29643*), accessed February 2, 2007.

Since 1961, State of the Union addresses have focused on a combination of foreign and domestic policy goals.

to "put the ship of state back on its republican tack," he submitted his report to Congress in writing.

Subsequent presidents followed Jefferson's example until 1913 when Woodrow Wilson (1913–1921) took the suggestion of journalist Oliver Newman and went before Congress to read his annual message. Wilson saw the change as a way to make the address more personal and dramatic. He explained in the address that he wanted to verify

> that the President of the United States is a person, not a mere department of the Government hailing Congress from some isolated island of jealous power, sending messages, not speaking naturally and with his own voice—that he is a human being trying to cooperate with other human beings in a common service.

Some members of Congress echoed Jefferson's objections to the practice, but the response to Wilson's speech was generally favorable. It became acceptable once again for presidents to deliver the annual message in person, and every president since Franklin Roosevelt (1933–1945) has chosen to do so.

As with the president's inauguration, the symbolism of the contemporary State of the Union address reinforces the image of the president as the preeminent leader of the nation rather than the leader of one of its coequal branches. Congress, the cabinet, and the Supreme Court assemble in the House chamber and wait for the president to arrive, like courtiers awaiting a king. After being announced, the president is greeted by a standing ovation. Moreover, the event itself implies presidential preeminence, because the president's opinion of the state of the Union is the reason for the assemblage. Neither Congress nor the judiciary has a similar opportunity to address the top representatives of the entire government in a formal, ritualistic setting.

The invention of radio and television changed the primary audience of the address from Congress to the American people. Presidents still address Congress, but their remarks are intended primarily for public consumption. They have used this opportunity to put pressure on Congress to vote for their **legislative** agenda by appealing to the American public for support. Beginning in 1966, the major networks provided airtime to the opposition party after the State of the Union address. That year Senate Minority Leader Everett M. Dirksen of Illinois and House Minority Leader Gerald R. Ford of Michigan delivered the Republican response to President Lyndon B. Johnson's (1963–1969) address.

State, Department of

See Department of State.

Summit Meetings

See Chief Diplomat.

Taft, William Howard, Administration of (1909–1913)

Government under the twenty-seventh president of the United States. After becoming a lawyer in 1880, William Howard Taft was appointed assistant prosecutor of Hamilton County, Ohio, the following year. In 1882, he served briefly as collector of internal revenue for his Ohio district. In 1883, he established a law partnership in Cincinnati with a former partner of his father. In 1887, Taft was appointed to a vacancy on the state superior court, winning election to his own two-year term on the court the following year. In 1890, President Benjamin Harrison (1889–1893) appointed him U.S. solicitor general. Two years later, Harrison appointed him judge of the U.S. Circuit Court, where Taft remained for eight years. During this period, Taft also taught at the Cincinnati Law School.

In 1900, President William McKinley (1897–1901) appointed Taft president of the U.S. Philippine Commission, which was charged with establishing a civil government on the islands. Taft was reluctant to leave his judgeship, but McKinley persuaded him to go to the Philippines by offering him an eventual appointment to the Supreme Court.

Taft expected to be in the Philippines only a short time, but in 1901, McKinley appointed him governor-general of the islands. In this capacity, Taft reorganized the Filipino court system, acquired land for the Filipinos from the Catholic Church, improved roads, harbors, and schools, and encouraged limited self-government. While in the Philippines, Taft twice refused appointment to the Supreme Court, the position he coveted most, because he believed he could not abandon the people of the islands. In 1904, however, he accepted Theodore Roosevelt's (1901–1909) appointment as secretary of war under the condition that he would be able to continue supervising U.S. policy toward the Philippines.

As secretary of war, Taft's activities ranged beyond oversight of the army. He visited the Panama Canal site in 1904, negotiated a secret agreement with the Japanese in 1905 pledging noninterference with Japan's affairs in Korea in return for Japan's promise to recognize U.S. influence in the Philippines, served as temporary provisional governor of Cuba in 1906, and oversaw relief efforts after the 1906 San Francisco earthquake. By 1908, Taft's wide government experience, his close friendship with Theodore Roosevelt, and his well-known administrative abilities made him the front-runner for the **Republican** presidential nomination.

Taft was not anxious to run, but Theodore Roosevelt, Republican Party leaders, and his wife persuaded him to seek the presidency. As Roosevelt's chosen successor, Taft won the nomination at the 1908 Republican National Convention in Chicago on the first ballot. He then defeated

Democrat William Jennings Bryan 321–162 in the electoral college.

Presidency

Upon entering office, Taft urged Congress to reduce **tariffs.** The president, however, angered **progressive** Republicans, who favored lower tariffs, when he signed the Payne-Aldrich Tariff Act of 1909. The act reduced tariff rates by amounts that most progressives considered insignificant.

Taft showed stronger leadership in his pursuit of antitrust cases. Although Theodore Roosevelt is often remembered as the president who first made wide use of the Sherman Antitrust Act to break up monopolies, Taft's administration brought ninety antitrust suits in four years compared with forty-four during Roosevelt's seven-year presidency. The Standard Oil and American Tobacco companies were among those broken up by the Taft administration. Taft also successfully backed the passage of the Sixteenth **Amendment** (1913), which authorized a federal income tax.

In foreign affairs, Taft instituted a policy that came to be known as "dollar diplomacy." This policy sought to use investments and trade to expand U.S. influence abroad, especially in Latin America. Taft also was willing to use force to maintain order and to protect U.S. business interests in Latin America. He dispatched ships and troops to Honduras in 1911 and Nicaragua in 1910 and again in 1912 to protect American lives and property threatened by revolution. These interventions contributed to Latin American resentment toward the United States.

In 1911, Taft negotiated a trade reciprocity agreement with Canada, which significantly lowered tariffs between Canada and the United States, but the Canadian parliament rejected the agreement later that year. Taft suffered another foreign policy defeat in 1911 when the Senate attached crippling amendments to his treaty with Britain and France that called for international disputes between the signatories to be settled via **arbitration.** Taft withdrew the treaty rather than sign the amended version.

Theodore Roosevelt, who had been one of the harshest critics of the arbitration treaty during the **ratification** fight, also criticized Taft for what the former president considered **conservative** departures from his progressive policies toward big business and the environment.

In 1912, Taft was nominated by the Republican Party for reelection. Roosevelt, who had won most of the Republican primaries that year, protested that he had not received a fair chance to win the nomination at the Republican National Convention, which was controlled by Taft supporters. Roosevelt launched a third-party candidacy that doomed Taft's reelection bid. Roosevelt and Taft split the Republican vote, allowing Democrat Woodrow Wilson (1913–1921) to capture the presidency. Taft finished in third place with just eight electoral votes.

VIEWPOINTS

In this political cartoon, "Judge," holding a copy of Theodore Roosevelt's policies, tells President William Howard Taft (1909–1913), "You're big enough to have your own policies—and they are good enough for the American people." (Library of Congress)

Former President and Chief Justice

When Taft's term expired, he accepted a law professorship at Yale University. While teaching, Taft wrote for law journals and other publications and delivered many lectures around the country. In 1913, he was elected president of the American Bar Association. During World War I (1914–1918), which the United States entered in 1917, President Wilson named him joint chairman of the War Labor Board, which resolved wartime labor disputes.

When Chief Justice Edward White died on May 19, 1921, Taft's friend and fellow Republican Warren G. Harding (1921–1923) chose Taft to take White's place. Taft was a highly capable chief justice who usually delivered moderately conservative opinions. He improved the efficiency of the judicial system and fought successfully for passage of the Judiciary Act of 1925. This law increased the Supreme Court's discretion in choosing which cases to accept. As chief justice, Taft administered the presidential oath of office to Calvin Coolidge (1923–1929) in 1925 and Herbert Hoover (1929–1933) in 1929. Taft was in poor health when resigned from the Court on February 3, 1930. He died from heart failure on March 8.

See also: Roosevelt, Theodore, Administration of (1901–1909); Wilson, Woodrow, Administration of (1913–1921).

Further Reading

Burton, David. *William Howard Taft: Confident Peacemaker.* Philadelphia, PA: St. Joseph's University Press, 2004.

Taylor, Zachary, Administration of (1849–1850)

Government under the twelfth president of the United States. The election of Zachary Taylor in 1848 was to be the last major political success of the Whig Party, which collapsed soon thereafter. The Whigs stood for national unity, an ideal that was rendered politically irrelevant by the slavery controversy. Moreover, the Whig opposition to **executive** power was shown decisively to be unworkable by the last Whig to be elected to the executive office.

Taylor's presidency was marked by his unyielding opposition to the Compromise of 1850, which put no restrictions on slavery in territories acquired from Mexico and strengthened the fugitive slave law, angered southerners and threatened a major crisis. (The compromise also admitted California to the Union as a free state and ended the slave trade in the District of Columbia.)

Taylor stood firm in his opposition to the 1850 measure, despite the threat of some southern states to leave the Union. He told southern congressional leaders that he would take the field personally and hang rebels against the Union "with as little mercy" as he had hanged deserters and spies in Mexico. Because no president after Andrew Jackson (1829–1837) had played a hands-off role with respect to Congress, Taylor found that he could not return to the self-effacing **precedents** of James Madison (1809–1817) and James Monroe (1817–1825). The slavery controversy and Jackson's legacy had made this impossible by 1849. Taylor died suddenly in July 1850 and was succeeded by Millard Fillmore, who supported the Compromise of 1850.

Term Limits

See Twenty-Second Amendment (1951).

Terrorism

See Bush, George W., Administration of (2001–2009); Commander in Chief; Emergency Powers.

Third Parties and Presidential Elections

Occurrences when a political party other than the two major parties competes in a presidential election. The American system of elections favors a two-party competition for national offices. The electoral college, campaign finance laws, and state rules governing parties and campaigns all give a distinct advantage to the Republican and Democratic Parties.

However, the party system is not static. Third parties often enter the electoral battle. Such parties usually gain little support and die quickly. Since 1832, third parties have received more than 10 percent of the popular vote in only eight presidential elections, and more than 20 percent in only two elections. Nevertheless, recent elections have seen a resurgence of **third-party** activity.

Significance

Over the years, more than forty political parties have run candidates for president. Some scholars have defined significant third parties as those that have received more than 5.6 percent of the national popular vote, which is the average third-party vote historically cast for president. By that criterion, thirteen parties or independents qualify as significant.

Popular support does not reveal everything, however. The States' Rights Democratic (Dixiecrat) Party, for example, received 7.3 percent of the electoral vote in 1948 even though its candidate, Strom Thurmond, won only 2.4 percent of the popular vote. Conversely, John Anderson (1980) and Ross Perot (1992 and 1996), whose campaigns are deemed significant if judged by popular votes, did not receive a single electoral vote.

Even parties that receive only a small share of the popular or electoral vote can influence an election significantly. For example, the Liberty Party, an organization dedicated to the **abolition** of slavery, received only 2.3 percent of the popular vote and no electoral votes in 1844, yet Liberty candidate James G. Birney drained enough votes from the Whig Party to guarantee the election of the Democratic candidate, James K. Polk (1845–1849). The thirty-six electoral votes that Polk narrowly won in New York were particularly important. Similarly, the 97,000 votes that Green Party candidate Ralph Nader received in Florida in 2000 kept Al Gore, who lost the state by less than one thousand votes, from receiving Florida's twenty-five electoral votes and winning the election.

Third parties that do not garner many votes in the general election may also exercise influence by publicizing important issues that the major parties have ignored. Because the major parties do not want third parties to siphon away their votes, they may even adopt positions they otherwise would not adopt to keep from losing votes to third-party rivals.

In the nineteenth century, third parties tended to mirror the organization of majority parties. They ran slates of candidates for offices other than president, held nominating conventions, drew up platforms, and existed for more than one election. The American, or "Know-Nothing," Party elected seven governors, five senators, and forty-three members of the House of Representatives and controlled several state legislatures.

In contrast, third parties in the twentieth century were often personality-centered. The Progressive Party of 1912 was more a vehicle for Theodore Roosevelt's (1901–1909) than an enduring political party. Once Roosevelt ceased to be a candidate, the party died. The third-party candidacies of George Wallace in 1968, Eugene McCarthy in 1976, and John Anderson in 1980 functioned with little or no party organization. Ross Perot's personality and business background attracted followers to his 1992 and 1996 campaigns.

Each of these men sought the presidency more as an independent candidate than as a part of a broader-based third-party effort. To a large extent, they found that technological innovations in transportation and communication reduced the need for an established party organization to rally voter support.

One-Issue Parties

Dissatisfaction with the major parties often centers on their stances toward important and controversial issues. Many of the earliest third parties were formed in response to the slavery issue. The best known of these was the Free Soil Party, which was formed in 1848 as a coalition of three antislavery movements: the Liberty Party, the Barnburners, and the Conscience Whigs. At its convention in Buffalo, New York, in 1848, the Free Soil Party nominated former Democratic president Martin Van Buren (1837–1841) as its presidential candidate and Charles F. Adams, the son of former president John Quincy Adams

A – Z

(1825–1829), as his running mate. Although it lost the presidential election, the Free Soil Party succeeded in winning thirteen seats in Congress.

The American Party, better known as the Know-Nothings because its members told outsiders they knew nothing about its secret rituals and greetings, was another notable single-issue party of the 1800s. The Know-Nothings emerged in the 1850s in opposition to European immigration, which was at a pre–Civil War peak because of severe economic conditions abroad. The party was particularly hostile to Catholics. In 1854 and 1855, the Know-Nothings were extremely successful. They elected five senators, forty-three members of the House of Representatives, and seven governors and won control of six state legislatures. In 1856, the Know-Nothings nominated former Whig president Millard Fillmore (1850–1853) for president and Andrew Jackson Donelson for vice president. The party divided, however, over slavery. Most northern Know-Nothings turned to the Republican Party. Southern and border state Know-Nothings joined with former Whigs to form the Constitutional Union Party in 1860.

Factional Parties

Factional parties develop from splits in one of the major parties. They usually form to protest "the identity and philosophy of the major party's presi–dential candidate." In the twentieth century, factional parties were the most successful third parties at winning votes.

The Progressive Party was formed to support Theodore Roosevelt's efforts to regain the White House after President William Howard Taft (1909–1913) defeated Roosevelt for the nomination at the Republican convention of 1912. Dubbed the "Bull Moose" Party, the Progressives held a convention in Chicago to nominate Roosevelt for president and Hiram Johnson for vice president and to draw up a party platform. Although defeated by Woodrow Wilson (1913–1921), Roosevelt outpolled Taft, winning 27.4 percent of the national popular vote to Taft's 23.2 percent, and eighty-eight electoral votes to Taft's eight. In that same election the Bull Moosers also ran candidates in state and local races and won thirteen seats in the House of Representatives. However, their appeal to the voters was based on Roosevelt's involvement, and when he later defected the party disintegrated.

Like Theodore Roosevelt, Senator Robert M. La Follette of Wisconsin represented the **liberal** wing of the Republican Party. In 1924, he split off from the Republicans and revived the Progressive Party label. The Progressives then held a convention in Cleveland, where they nominated La Follette for president and Burton K. Wheeler for vice president. La Follette went on to receive an impressive 16.6 percent of the popular vote but only thirteen electoral votes. The party relied primarily on La Follette's personal appeal. When he died in 1925, the party collapsed.

In 1948, the Progressive Party label was revived yet again. This time, however, it split off from the liberal wing of the Democratic Party. At a convention in Philadelphia, the Progressives nominated former vice president Henry A. Wallace as at its presidential candidate and Glen H. Taylor as his running mate. That same year, southern **conservatives** split off from the Democratic Party over a dispute about President Harry S. Truman's (1945–1953) civil rights program. They walked out of the Democratic convention, formed the States' Rights Democratic ("Dixiecrat") Party, and convened in Birmingham, Alabama, where they nominated South Carolina governor Strom Thurmond for president and Mississippi governor Fielding Wright for vice president.

Although both the Progressives and the Dixiecrats received nearly the same number of popular votes (Wallace received 1.157 million votes and Thurmond 1.169 million), the Dixiecrats carried four states in the Deep South with thirty-nine electoral votes and the Progressives carried none. The Dixiecrats' success illustrates the electoral college's bias toward third parties with a regional base. Despite the fracturing of his party, Harry S. Truman managed to defeat his Republican challenger, Thomas Dewey.

In 1968, Alabama governor George Wallace bolted from the Democratic Party and formed the American Independent Party. He did not hold a convention and chose as his running mate the retired Air Force general Curtis E. LeMay. Wallace had come to national attention in 1963 when he stood in the doorway of the University of Alabama to block the court-ordered admission of two African American students. The next year he ran strongly in three Democratic presidential primaries in protest of the 1964 Civil Rights Act.

Top Vote-Winning Third Parties, 1832–2008

Party	Election year	Candidate	Popular vote (percent)	No. electoral votes
Anti-Masonic	1832	William Wirt	7.8	7
Free Soil	1848	Martin Van Buren	10.1	0
American ("Know-Nothing")	1856	Millard Fillmore	21.5	8
Southern Democrats	1860	John C. Breckinridge	18.1	72
Constitutional Union	1860	John Bell	12.6	39
Populist	1892	James B. Weaver	8.5	22
Socialist	1912	Eugene V. Debs	6.0	0
Progressive (Bull Moose)	1912	Theodore Roosevelt	27.4	88
Progressive	1924	Robert M. La Follette	16.6	13
American Independent	1968	George C. Wallace	13.5	46
Independent	1980	John B. Anderson	6.6	0
Independent	1992	H. Ross Perot	18.9	0
Reform	1996	H. Ross Perot	8.5	0

Note: These parties (or independents) received more than 5.6 percent of the popular vote, the average third-party vote historically cast for president. Daniel A. Mazmanian, *Third Parties in Presidential Elections*. Washington, D.C.: Brookings, 1974, pp. 4–5.

Source: *Guide to U.S. Elections*, 5th ed. Washington, DC: CQ Press, 2005, p. 446.

Third parties frequently have run candidates for the presidency. In 1912, Theodore Roosevelt, running on the Progressive, or Bull-Moose, ticket, won 88 electoral votes—the highest third-party winner to date.

Wallace's third-party candidacy in 1968 gained support from white blue-collar workers who were fed up with civil rights activism, antiwar demonstrations, urban riots, and the national Democratic Party's embrace of liberalism. In the general election, Wallace received 13.5 percent of the popular vote and carried five Deep South states with forty-six electoral votes. Some feared at the time that he would win enough support to throw the election into the House of Representatives, but the Republican candidate, Richard Nixon (1969–1974), managed to outpoll Wallace in enough southern states to win an electoral vote majority. Wallace returned to the Democratic Party after 1968, and the American Independent Party soon died.

Illinois representative John Anderson formed the National Unity Campaign as the vehicle for his independent candidacy in 1980 when he failed to win the Republican nomination. He chose former Wisconsin governor Patrick J. Lucey, a Democrat, as his running mate. In a year when many voters were dissatisfied with the candidates of the two major parties, Anderson received widespread publicity for his willingness to take controversial stands on issues, including proposing a steep tax on gasoline. Despite considerable support in early polls, he ultimately captured only 6.6 percent of the popular vote and no electoral votes.

The Perot Phenomenon

In 1992 and 1996, billionaire H. Ross Perot led a factional third party that, unlike most previous factional parties, drew evenly from discontented members of both major parties. A business executive with no experience in government might seem a peculiar spokesman for populist anger

POINT/COUNTERPOINT

ARE THIRD PARTIES RELEVANT?

A two-party system emerged shortly after the beginning of the government under the United States Constitution. Yet, third, or minor, parties have also been a part of the political landscape. Since 1856, the winner of every presidential election has been a member of one of the nation's two major political parties. In theses excerpts, Professor J. David Gillespie of Presbyterian College comments on the relevancy of third parties, while political science Professor Emeritus John F. Bibby of the Univeristy of Wisconsin points out some difficulties that third parties face.

Professor J. David Gillespie

I would say that the American two-party system is probably the most stable two-party system on Earth, and there are a number of reasons for that. . . . They have been part and parcel of our electoral process throughout most of American history.

   The roles that they [third parties] play in some ways overlap with the roles of the major U.S. parties, the Republicans and Democrats. They help to organize the electoral system by educating voters, and, thereby, organizing voter choices. They play some, usually, rather transitory or peripheral roles, in helping organize the government. . . . They do some very specific things . . . one of which, and it's an ironic role that they probably don't aspire to play, is that they can be sources of release of steam, so to speak. In this way, they can actually strengthen not just the two-party system, but also the government itself by giving dissidents a chance to air their grievances within the confines of the electoral process. And that, then, probably reduces the prospect of more violent or more aggressive kinds of approaches to political action in this country . . . .

   I think there are three kinds of third parties in the United States. One of those is the "continuing doctrinal party," and I would say that these are the true minor parties of the United States. They last for several decades at least. They don't have any rational reason for thinking that they're going to ever challenge the duopoly of the Democrats and the Republicans. But whether that happens or not, these people tend to find their gratification in principle and vision and that sort of thing. . . .

   These are parties where faithfulness to principle, whatever those are for that particular party, and loyalty to their vision take priority over electoral success.

   There is another kind of third party that is associated with what I believe are the most important political functions of third parties, and that would be the contribution to policy making and the potential for actually transforming the two-party system.

   These are what I would call the "short-lived party eruption." The Reform Party, which was founded by Ross Perot, an independent presidential candidate in the 1990s, was an example of that, as was the American Independent Party founded by the George Wallace for President movement in the 1960s and the early 1970s. . . .

These are parties that made the greatest contribution to what we usually think of as the most important role of third parties: the contribution to policy making.

Such change in policy usually happens because of fear that a third party is going to become either a viable alternative to a major party candidate, or will contribute negatively to the outcome of an election in a way that will most probably hurt a major party candidate by siphoning off votes from the candidate who is closer to the beliefs of that third party. Right now, for example, the Democrats fear that the third party candidacy of Ralph Nader will take away votes from their candidate in the upcoming presidential election.

What happens then is that the major party that feels threatened will appropriate certain policy positions of the third party . . . .

Professor Emeritus John F. Bibby

Public opinion surveys since the 1990s have consistently shown a high level of popular support for the concept of a third party. In the run-up to the 2000 election, a Gallup Poll found that 67 percent of Americans favored a strong third party that would run candidates for president, Congress, and state offices against Republican and Democratic nominees. It is just such sentiments, plus lavish campaign spending, that enabled Texas billionaire Perot to gain 19 percent of the popular vote for president in 1992, the highest percentage for a non-major-party candidate since Theodore Roosevelt (Progressive Party) won 27 percent in 1912.

In spite of demonstrations of potential support for a third party, imposing barriers exist to a third party's winning the presidency and even electing a substantial number of senators or representatives. In addition to those noted previously, the most significant is the fear among voters that if they vote for a third-party candidate, they will, in effect, be "wasting" their votes. Voters have been shown to engage in strategic voting by casting ballots for their second choice when they sense that a third-party candidate has no chance of winning. Thus in the 2000 election, 15 percent of voters in a pre-election survey rated Ralph Nader more highly than either George W. Bush or Al Gore, but Nader received only 2.7 percent of the popular vote. Similarly in 1992, among voters ranking Ross Perot highest, 21 percent defected to other candidates when they actually cast their ballots.

There is also the phenomenon of "protest" voting for third-party candidates. For example, Gallup Polls in 1992 revealed that 5 percent of Perot's voters said that they would not have voted for him if they thought he could win.

Third party and independent candidates would also face a potentially daunting post-election problem if they won the presidency. This, of course, is the problem of governing—staffing an administration and then working with a Congress dominated by Republicans and Democrats who would have only limited incentives to cooperate with a non-major-party president.

DOCUMENT-BASED QUESTION
What roles do third parties serve? What obstacles to winning elections do third-party candidates face?

Billionaire H. Ross Perot discusses his thoughts on running again for the presidency on the CNN show *Larry King Live*. Ultimately, Perot ran as the candidate of the Reform Party in 1996 but won no electoral votes. (AP Images, Mark J. Terrill)

against elites. Yet Perot, who made a $4 billion fortune in the computer industry, became one of the most successful third-party candidates in history when he tapped popular disillusionment with politics in the 1992 presidential race.

Perot had had a long association with Republican presidents and causes, but he had never contemplated a political career until President George H.W. Bush (1989–1993) fell in the public opinion surveys and the Democrats running to replace him failed to capture the voters' imagination. At the prodding of a television talk-show host, Perot said he would consider a race for the presidency.

Perot's campaign unofficially began when he appeared on the cable talk show *Larry King Live* on February 20, 1992. When King asked Perot whether he would seek the presidency, Perot at first was noncommittal, but then said he would run if supporters could get his name on the ballot in all fifty states. Within weeks, volunteers had gotten his name on the ballot in dozens of states. In June, a Harris poll showed Perot leading the race with 37 percent of those surveyed to Bush's 33 percent and Democratic hopeful Bill Clinton's 25 percent.

Perot's appeal stemmed from neither a strong ideology nor a bold stance on a major issue.

Instead, voters seemed attracted to his business background and folksy personality. Perot had amassed his fortune by starting his own company, Electronic Data Systems. His pithy statements on complicated issues—he vowed to "take back the country" and "clean out the barn"—contrasted with Bush and Clinton's measured and sometimes complicated pronouncements.

However, as volunteers continued to circulate petitions to put him on the ballot, Perot came under growing scrutiny from the media. Reporters investigated his business practices and personal foibles. Pundits criticized his authoritarian management style.

In response, just as the Democrats were concluding their July convention Perot stunned followers by announcing that he would not run. Perot's stated reason for dropping out was that his campaign might deadlock the election and send it to the House of Representatives. He also praised Clinton (1993–2001), the Democratic nominee, for revitalizing his party.

After this brief interruption, Perot announced on October 1 that he would run after all. He appeared at several rallies, but mostly delivered his message in television advertisements. In a series of half-hour infomercials that aired in prime time, Perot offered straightforward explanations of the economic and social ills facing the nation. Perot also appeared in three presidential debates with Bush and Clinton. He hit Bush the hardest but also jabbed Clinton. The issue Perot focused on most was the need for a balanced budget.

Like many third-party candidates, Perot forced the major parties to address important issues, especially the budget deficit and corruption in politics. In the end, however, he could not attract enough support to win any states. Perot ended up with 19 percent of the popular vote and no electoral votes.

Unlike many third-party candidates, Perot won support from a broad demographic base. He ran best among self-described independents, men under thirty, and voters who viewed their family's financial situation as getting worse. His influence on the election's outcome, however, was a matter of dispute. Exit polls showed that if Perot had not been on the ballot, one-third of his supporters would have voted for Bush, one-third would have voted for Clinton, and the remaining third would not have voted at all.

After the election, Perot sniped at Clinton's policies on free trade, welfare reform, campaign finance reform, and various foreign policy problems. In September 1995, he announced that he was forming the Reform Party. He ran again in 1996 and received 8 percent of the popular vote and no electoral votes. In contrast to his self-financed 1992 campaign, Perot paid for his 1996 effort with $29 million in federal funds. In 2000, the Reform Party nominated conservative activist Pat Buchanan for president. Buchanan received $12.6 million in federal campaign funds but won less than 1 percent of the national popular vote. Because campaign finance laws stipulate that a party must receive at least 5 percent of the popular vote in an election in order to receive federal funding four years later, Buchanan's lack of success left the future of the Reform Party in serious doubt. In 2004, the Reform Party chose to support Ralph Nader, who was running as an independent.

See also: Elections, Presidential; Presidential Campaigns.

Further Reading

Bibby, John F., and L. Sandy Meisel. *Two Parties– Or More? The American Party System* (2nd ed.). Boulder, CO: Westview Press, 2002.
Rosenstone, Steven J., Behr, Roy L., and Edward H. Lazarus. *Third Parties in America.* Princeton, NJ: Princeton University Press, 1996.

The Transition Period

The time between the election and the inauguration of a president. Some of the president's most fateful decisions are made before the administration takes the reins of power. In filling appointments, developing budget priorities, and taking command of foreign policy, the president-elect goes a long way toward determining the possibilities and limits of the new administration.

To ensure a smooth transition, the **incumbent** president invites the president-elect to the White House, and the new chief **executive** and incoming staff receive a battery of briefings on matters ranging from budget deficits to U.S. military alliances. All the while, the new president's transition team

Growth of Transition Teams and Expenditures, 1952–2001

President	Size of transition team	Expenditure dollars (millions)		
		Public funds	Public funds	Public funds
Eisenhower (1952–1953)	100	0	0.4	0.4
Kennedy (1960–1961)	50[a]	0	1.3	1.3
Nixon (1968–1969)	125–150	0.5	1.0	1.5
Carter (1976–1977)	300	1.7	0.2	1.9
Reagan (1980–1981)	1,550	2.0	1.0	3.0
G.H.W. Bush (1988–1989)	150[b]	3.5	0	3.5
Clinton (1992–1993)	450	3.5	4.8	8.3
G.W. Bush (2000–2001)	800[c]	4.2	4.3	8.5

Notes: a. Estimate based on statement by Richard Neustadt that Carter's transition staff was six times the size of Kennedy's (Richard Neustadt, *Presidential Power*. New York: Macmillan, 1980, p. 218. b. Plus 100–150 volunteers. c. Includes an unspecified number of volunteers.

Sources: Laurin L. Henry, *Presidential Transitions*. Washington, DC: Brookings, 1960; Frederick C. Mosher, W. David Clinton, and Daniel G. Lang, *Presidential Transitions and Foreign Affairs*. Baton Rouge: Louisiana State University Press, 1987; Herbert E. Alexander, *Financing the 1968 Election*. Lexington, MA: Lexington Books, 1971; *Financing the 1976 Election*. Washington, DC: CQ Press, 1979; *Financing the 1980 Election*. Lexington, MA: Lexington Books, 1983; Herbert E. Alexander and Monica Bauer, *Financing the 1988 Election*. Boulder: Westview Press, 1991; Herbert E. Alexander and Anthony Corrado, *Financing the 1992 Election*. New York: Sharpe, 1995; General Services Administration; White House Press Office.

The cost of transitioning from one administration to another has increased significantly since the 1950s.

pores over resumes and considers **legislative** strategy.

Media and academic accounts stress the cooperative nature of the transition period. Only in the United States, political analysts say, can the government be turned over to political opponents with such good cheer and cooperation. Transitions rarely involve active blame, and seldom is there a struggle over the legitimacy of the electoral outcome like the disputed contest between George W. Bush and Al Gore in 2000. The transition is a rare celebration of a stable democracy based on political parties that differ on specific policies but achieve consensus on the most important matters of state.

Until recently, presidents-elect financed their own transitions. Then in 1964 Congress passed the Presidential Transitions Act, which granted the newly elected president $450,000 and the outgoing president $450,000 to help cover their transition expenses. In 1988, Congress revised the act to grant $3.5 million to each incoming administration and $1.5 million to each outgoing adminis-

tration, with these amounts to be adjusted for inflation. The revised act also authorized the president-elect to raise money from private donors to cover any additional costs of the transition, provided that donations did not exceed $5,000 per donor and the names of the donors were disclosed publicly. Bill Clinton spent a total of $8.3 million during his transition period in 1992–1993, $4.8 million from private sources. In 2000–2001 George W. Bush spent slightly more, $8.5 million, $4.3 million from private sources. The money is used for staff salaries, travel expenses, talent searches, policy deliberations, and public relations activities. Separate federal funds are used for the inaugural ceremonies.

In many ways, the transition period is the most important phase of the new president's term. It period offers incoming presidents a chance to forge a governing strategy, aided by thorough analyses of national security and economic issues. The incoming administration of Bill Clinton (1993–2001) was especially active during the transition period. For example, the president-elect convened an economic conference in Little Rock, Arkansas, in December 1992 to address the economic and budgetary problems facing the nation. During the five weeks it took to resolve the outcome of the disputed 2000 election, George W. Bush (2001–2009) began transition planning on the assumption that he would win. Bush appointed Richard B. Cheney, his vice-presidential running mate, to oversee the transition.

New presidents often are so confident in the wake of winning the election that they pay little attention to the perils awaiting them at the White House. Presidents-elect have their own agendas and sometimes are unwilling to listen to the counsel of others. Moreover, they may underestimate the challenge.

The extent of the new president's electoral "mandate" is central to the transition period. Yet John F. Kennedy's (1961–1963) slim victory did not stop him from taking an aggressive approach to leading the nation. Kennedy stated after the election, "The margin is narrow, but the responsibility is clear. There may be difficulties with Congress, but a margin of only one vote would still be a mandate." As foreseen, Kennedy had many problems with Congress. Ronald Reagan's (1981–1989) landslide election led to more policy victories than a slimmer electoral triumph would have allowed.

Sometimes the most important transition moves are made behind the scenes. In 1992, President-elect Clinton met with Alan Greenspan, the chairman of the Federal Reserve Board, to confer about what policies would reassure financial markets enough to justify keeping interest rates low—a vital condition for economic growth. Indeed, Clinton and his wife, Hillary Rodham Clinton, nurtured a relationship with Greenspan, a Republican, to help push the president's economic plans through Congress. At the same time, Vice President-elect Al Gore sounded out Republican leaders on Capitol Hill about various deficit-cutting measures. Gore learned from these meetings that the GOP would not provide any support on budgetary and tax issues. That moved the Clinton White House toward a **partisan** approach to congressional relations.

Finally, the transition period can be crucial in determining what kind of "honeymoon" the new president is likely to have with Congress and the public. The length of the honeymoon, in turn, has a big effect on whether the new president can be a decisive and strong leader in the first term.

See also: Inaugural Address; Oath of Office.

Transportation, Department of

See Department of Transportation (DOT).

Treasury, Department of the

See Department of the Treasury.

The Treaty Power

The power of the president to negotiate treaties with other nations. The authors of the Constitution used only one clause to explain how treaties were to be made. Article II, Section 2, Clause 2, declares that the president "shall have the Power, by and with the Advice and Consent of the Senate, to make Treaties, provided two thirds of the Senators present concur." This concise statement blends responsibilities between the legislative and executive branches. Clearly, the president is responsible for conducting the actual treaty negotiations. In addition, clearly the president cannot conclude a treaty without first obtaining the consent of the Senate. The Constitution, therefore, ensures that no formal treaty can be concluded without a strong interbranch consensus, and that presidential negotiations will tend to be influenced by the Senate.

The **executive** branch has established itself as the more influential branch in treaty-making. As the sole source of communication with foreign countries, commander in chief, and head of the foreign policy bureaucracy, presidents have been equipped with the means necessary to lead in most phases of the treaty-making process. The president dominates decisions concerning whether and when treaty negotiations will be pursued. The president chooses the negotiators, develops the negotiating strategy, and submits completed draft treaties to the Senate for approval.

Moreover, the president's power to "make" treaties is interpreted as including the final power of **ratification.** Once the Senate has approved a treaty, it does not become law until the president **ratifies** it. Thus, the president has significant influence over any attempts by the Senate to **amend** a treaty. If the president decides to ratify a treaty the Senate has approved, an exchange of ratifications occurs between the signers. Then the treaty is promulgated—that is, officially proclaimed to be law—by the president. At any time, the president may stop the treaty-making process. Thus, the president has power over a treaty from its beginning to its ratification.

Creation of the Treaty Power

In the eighteenth century, treaties were considered to be the primary tool of foreign policy, and the authors of the Constitution deliberated extensively on how treaties should be made. Under the Articles of Confederation, the treaty power was completely entrusted to the legislature. It selected negotiators, wrote and revised their orders, and made the final decision on whether a treaty would be accepted or rejected. At the Constitutional Convention, delegates initially assumed that this legislative power would be given to the new Congress and specifically to the Senate, which was designed to be wiser and more stable than the House. Late in the convention's deliberations, and after the executive had been made fully independent of the legislature, the convention divided the treaty-making power between the executive and the Senate.

The Framers recognized that the president, as a single national officer, would be "the most fit agent" for making "preparations and auxiliary measures," for managing delicate and often secret negotiations, and for adapting to often rapidly changing circumstances.

Similar considerations favored the exclusion of the House from treaty deliberations. Alexander Hamilton and John Jay argued in *The Federalist Papers* that the Senate is favored by its smaller size, its wiser membership chosen by the "select assemblies" of the states, and the stability secured

by longer and overlapping terms. These features also would encourage the Senate to focus on the long-term interests of the nation as a whole. The extraordinary majority required for treaty approval in the Senate would, it was argued, ensure that no treaty would become law without high levels of scrutiny and approval.

By giving the president the power to "make" treaties "by and with the Advice and Consent of the Senate," the authors of the Constitution bolstered the prestige of the executive. They must have understood that the president's position as chief negotiator would afford him great influence over policy. However, they spoke of the Senate controlling the overall "system" of foreign policy. The Framers seemed to have expected that senatorial "Advice and Consent" would operate throughout the process and that the president would obtain "their sanction in the **progressive** stages of a treaty."

The Constitution also strengthened the legal status of treaties. One weakness of the national government under the Articles of Confederation was its dependence on the states to implement treaties. Congress could not force the states to recognize treaty provisions as law. As a result, several states had violated certain articles of the Peace Treaty of 1783 with Great Britain. The convention's answer to this problem was Article VI, Clause 2, of the Constitution, which states that "all Treaties made, or which shall be made, under the Authority of the United States, shall be the supreme Law of the Land; and the Judges in every State shall be bound thereby, any Thing in the Constitution or Laws of any State to the Contrary notwithstanding."

Presidential Primacy in Treaty Negotiations

The Constitution clearly states that both the president and the Senate have a role in treaty making, but the form of the Senate's advice on treaty matters and its influence over negotiations has changed over time.

President George Washington's (1789–1797) initial interpretation of the treaty-making clause was that "Advice" meant he was to seek Senate opinions in person before his representatives began negotiations. On August 21, 1789, Washington and his secretary of war, Henry Knox, questioned the Senate in its chambers about a treaty to be negotiated with the Creek Indians. After some debate, the Senate decided to postpone its response to Washington's questions until the following week so it could discuss the negotiations further. Washington, who had expected an immediate reply, returned on Monday, August 24, and received answers to his questions, but he was angered by the Senate's indecisiveness and doubted that he could rely on that body for timely consultations on treaty matters. He never again attempted to use it as an executive council before treaty negotiations. Nonetheless, during the early years of his presidency Washington conscientiously wrote to the Senate for advice on treaty matters before and during negotiations. He also routinely submitted the negotiators' instructions to the Senate and kept that body informed of the progress of talks.

The Senate's role in treaty negotiations would likely have been enhanced had Washington established a **precedent** of consulting with that body in person. Later presidents, however, agreed with Washington that the advice and consent of the Senate were best obtained from a distance. Several twentieth-century presidents, including Woodrow Wilson (1913–1921) and Harry S. Truman (1945–1953), went to the Senate to propose or to lobby for treaties, but no president has ever returned to the Senate chamber to seek direct advice on treaty matters.

Washington's handling of the important Jay Treaty of 1794, which avoided war with Great Britain, demonstrated that he had abandoned his initial interpretation of the Constitution's treaty-making clause. In preparation for the Jay Treaty negotiations, Washington submitted only the appointment of his negotiator, Chief Justice John

British prime minister David Lloyd George, Italian prime minister Vittorio Emanuele Orlando, French premier Georges Clemenceau, and President Woodrow Wilson (1913–1921) stand outside the palace at Versailles in France during the negotiation of the Treaty of Versailles that ended World War I (1914–1918). (The Granger Collection, New York)

Jay, to the Senate for approval. He withheld from the Senate Jay's instructions about the sensitive negotiations, and the negotiations were held in London without Senate involvement.

Rather than challenging the president's power to make a treaty independently of the Senate, that body responded by amending the completed Jay Treaty in a manner similar to the method by which it amended legislation. Washington accepted the Senate's authority to do this, and after initial protests, the British ratified the amended treaty. The Jay Treaty established a process of treaty making that subsequent administrations and Senates would follow.

The often significant influence the Senate has over treaty negotiations comes more from its power to reject a treaty than from any constitutional provision that the president should consider the

A–Z

Senate's advice when making treaties. The Senate, or a minority thereof, can intrude into negotiations by making the conditions of its final approval quite clear. Presidents have, therefore, often cooperated closely with the Senate in the negotiation of a treaty because they recognize that Senate involvement would increase the chances for approval. Excluding the Senate from the negotiating process has often led to troubles and defeats for presidents.

The Treaty-Making Process

The first step in making a treaty is negotiating with a foreign power. This stage is controlled by the president and presidential advisers and representatives. During or before this phase, members of Congress may offer advice to the president or express their views on the negotiations individually or collectively. A **resolution** communicating Congress's disapproval may cause the president to change negotiating strategies or abandon a treaty altogether. A supportive resolution, however, may contribute to the executive branch's enthusiasm for a particular treaty. In 1948, for example, the Senate's Vandenberg Resolution, which preceded the development of NATO and other alliance systems, advised the president to negotiate regional security agreements. Regardless of congressional protests or encouragement, the president and representatives of the president cannot be prevented from initiating and conducting treaty negotiations with another country.

Although the executive branch has the power to negotiate a treaty without Congress, many presidents have found that involving individual senators in the negotiating process can be a useful political tool. Such involvement can take several forms. During most treaty negotiations, influential senators are at least asked for their opinions on the proceedings, but a president also may ask senators to help select the negotiating team, observe the negotiations, follow the progress of the talks through briefings, or even be negotiators.

Once U.S. negotiators have agreed on the terms of a treaty with a foreign government, the president must decide whether to submit the draft to the Senate for consideration. If it appears that Senate opposition to a treaty will make approval unlikely, the president may decide to withdraw the treaty to avoid a political defeat. Also, international events may change the president's mind about the desirability of ratifying a treaty. President Jimmy Carter (1977–1981) withdrew a treaty to limit strategic nuclear weapons, called the SALT II treaty, from Senate consideration to protest the Soviet invasion and occupation of Afghanistan in 1979.

If the president decides to submit a treaty to the Senate for consideration, the Constitution requires that two-thirds of the Senate vote in favor of the treaty for it to be approved. The Senate is not compelled by the Constitution either to approve or to reject a treaty as it has been negotiated by the executive branch. It may attach amendments to a treaty that require the president to renegotiate its terms with the other signatories before the Senate grants its approval. In 1978, the Senate added conditions and reservations to the treaty that provided for the transfer of the Panama Canal to Panamanian control after the year 2000. The most notable of these amendments was written by Senator Dennis DeConcini (D-AZ). It claimed for the United States the right to take whatever steps were necessary, including military force, to open the canal if its operations ceased. The Panamanian government agreed to accept the Senate amendments without renegotiation.

Although such amendments can often make agreement between the United States and its negotiating partner difficult or impossible, presidents have little choice but to accept the Senate's power to force renegotiation of parts of a treaty. In effect, when the Senate gives its consent on condition that its amendments are accepted by the negotiating partner of the United States, it is rejecting the treaty while outlining a revision of the treaty to which it grants its consent in advance. Presidents in turn may decide not to renegotiate if they believe the senatorial amendments make the treaty undesirable.

See also: Presidency and Congress.

Further Reading

Matuz, Roger. *The Presidents Fact Book: A Comprehensive Handbook to the Achievements, Events, People, Triumphs, and Tragedies of Every President from George Washington to George W. Bush.* New York: Black Dog and Leventhal, 2004.

Truman, Harry S., Administration of (1945–1953)

Government under the thirty-third president of the United States. After graduating from high school, Truman held a succession of jobs, including mailroom clerk, bank teller, and bookkeeper. He wanted to go to college, but he and his family could not afford it. In 1906, when Truman was twenty-two, he took over the management of his grandmother's 600-acre farm in Grandview, Missouri. He succeeded at farming and became active in local politics and community organizations.

When the United States entered World War I (1914–1918) in 1917, Truman received a commission as a first lieutenant. He served with distinction in several campaigns as commander of an artillery battery and attained the rank of major before leaving the service in 1919.

Early Political Career

Upon returning home, Truman opened a **haberdashery** in Kansas City, Missouri, with a army friend. When the store failed in 1922, he ran for judge of the eastern district of Jackson County. He won the election with the support of the powerful Kansas City political **boss** Tom Pendergast. He failed in his bid for reelection two years later, but was elected presiding judge of the court in 1926 and was reelected in 1930. These judgeships were administrative rather than judicial positions. Truman controlled hundreds of **patronage** jobs and millions of dollars' worth of public works projects.

Truman became well known in the Kansas City area. He retained his close connections to Pendergast and the Kansas City political **machine,** but also developed a reputation for honesty. Using his Kansas City political base, Truman launched a campaign for the U.S. Senate and was elected in 1934.

In the Senate, Truman supported Franklin D. Roosevelt's (1933–1945) New Deal legislation. Despite the conviction of Tom Pendergast for income tax evasion, Truman was reelected by a narrow margin in 1940. During his second term, Truman chaired the Special Committee to Investigate the National Defense Program, which sought to eliminate waste and inefficiency among defense contractors. He also supported Roosevelt's efforts to aid the Allies in World War II (1939–1945) before United States into World War II in 1941.

In 1944, the Democratic Party was set to nominate President Franklin D. Roosevelt for his fourth term, but the vice-presidential nomination remained in doubt. Vice President Henry Wallace had alienated many Democratic Party leaders, who considered his political views too **liberal.** Robert Hannegan, national chairman of the Democratic Party, recommended to Roosevelt that Truman be nominated in place of Wallace, and the president agreed. Truman was nominated for vice president on the second ballot at the Democratic National Convention in Chicago. Roosevelt and Truman then defeated Republicans Thomas E. Dewey and John W. Bricker in the general election.

Presidency

Truman served just eighty-two days as vice president. On April 12, 1945, he was summoned to the White House and informed by First Lady Eleanor Roosevelt that the president was dead. Later in the day, he took the oath of office at the White House from Supreme Court Chief Justice Harlan F. Stone.

World events forced Truman to become an expert in foreign affairs, an area of policy in which he had little experience before becoming president. Truman's first priority was winning World War II. On May 7, Germany surrendered unconditionally to the allies. In July 1945, Truman traveled to Potsdam, Germany, to discuss the postwar world with British prime minister Winston Churchill and Soviet premier Joseph Stalin. There the three leaders agreed to divide Germany and its capital, Berlin, into occupation zones.

While at Potsdam, Truman was informed that the United States had successfully tested an atomic bomb. He authorized atomic attacks on Japanese cities to hasten the end of the war. On August 6, 1945, an atomic bomb dropped from a U.S. warplane on Hiroshima killed eighty thousand people. Three days later, another bomb destroyed the city of Nagasaki. Truman's decision to use atomic weapons has been debated by many scholars and military analysts since World War II. Before the bombs were dropped, Japan had sent signals that

On April 12, 1945, Harry S. Truman (1945–1953) took the oath of office after the death of President Franklin D. Roosevelt (1933–1945). Standing behind Truman are his wife Bess and daughter Margaret. (The Granger Collection, New York)

it might surrender, but Truman believed a quick end of the war was necessary to avoid an invasion of Japan that would cost many U.S. lives. On September 2, the Japanese surrendered, ending the war.

Despite U.S.-Soviet cooperation during World War II, differences between the two nations developed into a "cold war" by 1946. The United States objected to the Soviet Union's creation of communist governments in the eastern European states they had occupied while pushing the Nazi armies back into Germany. Truman vigorously protested Moscow's actions and resolved to contain further Soviet expansionism.

In March 1947, when Britain withdrew its assistance to Greek anticommunists for economic reasons, Truman proclaimed the Truman Doctrine and asked Congress for $400 million in economic and military aid to prevent Greece and Turkey from falling to communist insurgents. The Truman Doctrine declared that the United States would aid governments threatened by communist subversion. Later that year, Truman and Secretary of State George Marshall asked Congress to expand foreign aid dramatically by approving the Marshall Plan, a multibillion-dollar program to rebuild the economies of Western Europe. Congress gave its approval in 1948, and the Marshall Plan became one of the foremost successes of the Truman administration. Later in 1948, when the Soviets closed passage between western Germany and Berlin, which was located within the Soviet occupation zone, Truman used a massive airlift to supply the parts of the city administered by

Britain, France, and the United States. The Soviets had hoped to force the United States and its western allies to give up control of their part of Berlin, but Truman's airlift broke the blockade and the Soviets backed down without a military confrontation.

In domestic policy, Truman developed a plan to extend Franklin Roosevelt's New Deal, which the new president called the Fair Deal. Republicans and **conservative** Democrats in Congress, however, blocked many of his proposals. He also unsuccessfully backed **progressive** civil rights legislation. In 1947, Congress overrode Truman's **veto** of the Taft-Hartley Act, which he claimed unfairly weakened the bargaining power of unions. Five years later, he seized and operated steel mills shut down by a strike during the Korean War (1950–1953), a move that the Supreme Court declared **unconstitutional.** Truman battled postwar inflation with the modest tools at his disposal, but Congress rejected his proposals for more sweeping price-control legislation, and inflation continued to be the most troublesome domestic problem during Truman's years in office.

In 1948, Truman ran for reelection against Thomas E. Dewey. Truman's reelection chances appeared slim when **liberal** Democrats nominated Henry Wallace for president, and southern Democrats, who disliked Truman's strong civil rights platform, formed the "Dixiecrat" Party and nominated Senator Strom Thurmond of South Carolina. During the campaign public opinion polls indicated that Dewey would win. Truman, however, used a cross-country, whistle-stop campaign to take his message to the people and won a surprise victory, defeating Dewey 303–189 in the electoral college.

Truman's second term was dominated by the Korean War. On June 24, 1950, troops from communist North Korea invaded South Korea. Truman sent U.S. troops to Korea under the auspices of the United Nations (UN). UN forces pushed the North Koreans out of South Korea and drove into North Korea in an attempt to unify the country. Communist China entered the war on the side of the North Koreans in late 1950, however, and pushed UN forces back into South Korea. Eventually the war became deadlocked near the thirty-eighth parallel that had divided the two Koreas

before the start of the war. Truman was unable to attain a negotiated peace during his presidency.

In 1951, Truman fired General Douglas MacArthur, commander of UN forces in Korea, for insubordination. MacArthur had criticized the Truman administration's conduct of the war, publicly advocated a provocative invasion of China, interfered with Truman's diplomatic gestures, and disobeyed orders. Nevertheless, MacArthur enjoyed a large following in Congress and among the American public, and Truman's popularity sank after he fired the general.

During Truman's years in office, the country became obsessed with fears about communist subversion. Senator Joseph R. McCarthy (R-WI), led a group in Congress who claimed that communist agents had infiltrated the U.S. government, especially the State Department. McCarthy pointed to the failure of the United States to stop the communist revolution in China in 1949 as evidence of the communist sympathies of key U.S. officials. Truman denounced McCarthy, but was unable to rally public support against the senator, despite the lack of evidence backing up McCarthy's accusations. After Truman left office, McCarthy became chairman of a Senate investigative subcommittee and accused many citizens of pro-communist activities before being **censured** by the Senate in 1954.

On March 29, 1952, Truman announced that he would not run for reelection in the fall. After leaving office, he returned to his home in Independence, Missouri. Truman remained active during his retirement, delivering lectures, commenting on political developments, and overseeing construction of the Truman Library near his home. He published his two-volume memoirs in 1955 and 1956. He died in 1972 at age eighty-eight.

See also: Eisenhower, Dwight D., Administration of (1953–1961); Roosevelt, Franklin D., Administration of (1933–1945).

Further Reading

Burnes, Brian. *Harry S. Truman: His Life and Times.* Kansas City, MO: Kansas City Star Books, 2003.

Dallek, Robert. *Harry S. Truman.* New York: Times Books, 2008.

A – Z

Twelfth Amendment (1804)

Amendment that refined the way in which electors vote for the president and vice president. Paragraphs 2 through 4 of Article II, Section 1, of the Constitution, which created the electoral college method of choosing the president and vice president, were among the least controversial provisions of the Constitution, both during the late stages of the Constitutional Convention and in the state **ratification** debates that followed. "The mode of appointment of the Chief Magistrate of the United States," wrote Alexander Hamilton in *Federalist* No. 68, "is almost the only part of the system of any consequence, which has escaped without severe **censure,** or which has received the slightest mark of approbation from its opponents." It is all the more ironic, then, that the electoral college was the first institution of the new government to undergo a major constitutional overhaul.

The main effect of the Twelfth **Amendment** was to change a system in which electors cast two votes for president, with the candidate receiving the largest majority elected as president and the second-place finisher elected as vice president, to a system in which the electors were charged to vote separately for president and vice president, with a majority of electoral votes required to win each office.

The Twelfth Amendment also reduced from the five highest electoral vote recipients to the three highest the pool of candidates from which the House would elect the president in the event that no candidate received a majority of electoral votes for president. Authority to select a vice president in the event of an electoral college failure was lodged exclusively in the Senate, not partially, as in the original Constitution. The amendment empowered the Senate to choose from the two highest electoral vote recipients for vice president, with a majority vote of the entire membership of the Senate required for election. The Constitution's age, residency, and citizenship requirements for president were extended to the vice president. Finally, the amendment stated that if a vice president, but no president, is chosen by the March 4 following the election, "the Vice President shall act as President as in the case of the death or other constitutional disability of the President."

The System Breaks Down

The original electoral college was designed by the Constitutional Convention on the assumption that political parties would not arise and dominate the presidential election process. Instead, the delegates had believed that states and ad hoc groups would nominate candidates for president. The most popular and, presumably, the best-qualified candidate would be elected as president and the second most popular as vice president.

Despite the Framers' intentions, two political parties—the Federalists and the Democratic-Republicans—formed during George Washington's first term as president and, within a very few years, began nominating complete national tickets: Federalist and Democratic-Republican candidates for president and Federalist and Democratic-Republican candidates for vice president. In 1800, the inevitable happened. All seventy-three Democratic-Republican electors (a majority of the electoral college) cast one of their votes for president for Thomas Jefferson (1801–1809) and the other for Aaron Burr, the Democratic-Republican candidates. Although these electors wanted Jefferson to be elected as president and Burr as vice president, the vote was constitutionally recorded as a tie between Jefferson and Burr for the office of president. Under Article II, Section 1, Clause 3, the House of Representatives was then forced to choose between them.

Dominated by a **lame-duck** Federalist majority, the House, through thirty-five ballots, denied Jefferson the majority of state delegations that was required for election. On the thirty-sixth ballot, prodded by Hamilton to cease its mischief making, the House elected Jefferson as president and Burr as vice president.

Proposal and Ratification

Aware both of the unsuitability of the original Constitution's presidential election process to the new reality of party politics and of the Federalists' willingness to continue exploiting the process's weaknesses, the Democratic-Republican-controlled Congress voted to propose the Twelfth Amendment in December 1803. All but the most fervent Federalist states quickly **ratified** the amendment (Massachusetts finally ratified in 1961), and it became part of the Constitution in June 1804, just in time for the presidential election the following November.

Separate Balloting for President and Vice President

The Twelfth Amendment's requirement that electors vote separately for president and vice president solved the problem that had occasioned the amendment's enactment. Not since 1800 has there been any confusion about who was running for president and who for vice president. In addition, the Twelfth Amendment reinforced the unitary character of the **executive** by eliminating the possibility that the vice president would be the leader of the opposition party—as had happened in 1796 when John Adams won the presidency and Jefferson the vice presidency.

One aspect of electoral voting that emerged as an issue only much later was that of the "faithless elector." Whatever the Framers' intentions may have been, in practice electors have always been chosen to vote for the candidate supported by their state, not to exercise independent judgment in deciding whom to support. No constitutional requirement binds electors to do so, however. Twenty-four states and the District of Columbia currently have laws that require electors to support the candidates whom they are pledged to represent, but these laws may well violate the Twelfth Amendment.

Historically, less than fifteen of the more than eighteen thousand electors who have been chosen since 1789 have been "faithless," and none have been punished for violating their pledges. In no case have their votes affected the outcome of an election. Nevertheless, the frequency of faithless voting has increased from one in every twenty elections from 1789 to 1944 to more than one in every two elections from 1948 to 2004. In 2000, an elector from the District of Columbia abstained rather than vote for Al Gore, who had carried the District with 85 percent of the vote. She explained that she was protesting the District's lack of representation in Congress. No elector had ever used his or her vote in such a way. Nor had an elector ever voted faithlessly in such a close election. In 2004, one faithless elector cast a presidential bal-

lot for North Carolina senator John Edwards, the Democratic nominee for vice president.

See also: Twelfth Amendment, 1804, in the **Primary Source Library.**

Twentieth Amendment (1933)

Amendment written mainly to shorten the time between the election of the president, vice president, and members of Congress and their entry into office; also known as the "**lame-duck**" amendment. The gap for newly elected representatives and senators (unless the president called Congress into special session) had been thirteen months—from the first Tuesday after the first Monday in November (Election Day) until the first Monday in December of the following year. This date was established by Article I, Section 4, Clause 2, of the Constitution as the initial meeting day for Congress. The delay for presidents and vice presidents had been approximately four months, from Election Day until the following March 4. The source of this date for presidential inauguration was a decision by the Congress of the Articles of Confederation. After the Constitution was **ratified,** Congress had declared March 4, 1789, the date "for commencing proceedings under the said Constitution." A law passed by the House and Senate in 1792 confirmed March 4 as the starting date for future presidential terms.

Senator George W. Norris, a Republican from Nebraska, was the main author of the Twentieth Amendment. Norris sought to remedy three major flaws he saw in the traditional arrangement, which he regarded as better suited to an age when travel was difficult and time-consuming and the business of the federal government was relatively minor. The first flaw was the **biennial** lame-duck session of Congress, which typically lasted from the December after the election until the following March and which included many outgoing members of the defeated party. Second, by not having Congress begin its term before the president, existing procedures empowered the lame-duck Congress, not the most recently elected one, to choose

A – Z

the president and vice president in the event of an electoral college deadlock. This had happened in 1801 and 1825. Finally, Norris regarded four months as too long a time for the nation to have, in effect, two presidents—an outgoing **incumbent** and an incoming president-elect.

Section 1

To remedy the lame-duck and two-presidents problems, Section 1 of the Twentieth Amendment established noon on January 20 as the beginning of the president's and vice president's four-year terms and noon on January 3 as the start of the term for members of Congress. The wisdom of moving up the president's inauguration seemed vindicated when, in the last transition to take place under the old system, a nation gripped by the **Great Depression** had to endure four months of awkward stalemate between President-elect Franklin Roosevelt (1933–1945) and the incumbent president he had defeated in the 1932 election, Herbert C. Hoover (1929–1933).

Section 3

Norris also used the Twentieth Amendment as a vehicle to address two other potential problems in the presidential and vice-presidential selection process. Section 3 provides that if the president-elect dies before the start of the term, the vice president-elect would be inaugurated as president. Under Section 2 of the Twenty-fifth Amendment, which became part of the Constitution in 1967, the vice president-elect who thus succeeds to the presidency then would appoint a new vice president, pending congressional approval.

In addition to death, Section 3 also stipulates that if, by inauguration day, no presidential candidate has received the electoral vote majority or, failing that, the majority of state delegations in the House of Representatives that is required for election, the vice president-elect becomes acting president until a president is chosen. The same would be true if a president-elect is found to be unqualified under Article II, Section 1, Clause 5, by virtue of age, citizenship, or residency. The amendment also authorized Congress to legislate for the possibility that a vice president-elect might not be chosen either, whether through failure to secure an electoral vote majority or inability to win a Senate election. Congress passed such a law

in 1947, the Presidential Succession Act. The act stipulated that the Speaker of the House would serve as the acting president until a president or vice president is elected.

Section 4

The possibility that either a winning presidential or vice-presidential candidate might die before officially receiving "elect" status when Congress counts the electoral votes on January 6 underlay the writing of Section 4. The section simply calls on Congress to legislate for these contingencies. Congress never has done so, however, which means that if such a death were to occur, it would have to improvise. One of Congress's options, in counting the votes, would be to declare the dead candidate elected, thus triggering (if the presidential candidate had died) Section 1 of the amendment, under which the vice president-elect would become president, or (if the winning vice-presidential candidate had died) Section 2 of the Twenty-fifth Amendment, under which the vice-president-elect-turned-president would nominate a new vice president after being sworn in as president. Congress's other choice—less absurd than electing a dead person but politically more problematic—would be to allow the House of Representatives to elect one of the defeated presidential candidates as president.

Proposal and Ratification

The Twentieth Amendment passed easily through Congress on March 2, 1932, and was ratified without controversy on February 6, 1933. It is the only amendment in history to be ratified by every state when initially considered. The wisdom of the amendment seemed confirmed when, nine days later, an assassin shot at President-elect Franklin Roosevelt on a speaker's platform in Miami, Florida.

See also: 📖 Twentieth Amendment, 1933, in the **Primary Source Library.**

Twenty-fifth Amendment (1967)

Amendment to the United States Constitution concerning presidential disability and succession, which took effect in 1967. The **amendment** provided for continuity in carrying out the functions of the presidency in the event of presidential disability and for filling a vacancy in the vice presidency. The amendment was approved by the Senate and House in 1965 and took effect February 10, 1967, after **ratification** by thirty-eight states.

Congressional consideration of presidential disability had been prompted by President Dwight D. Eisenhower's (1953–1961) heart attack in 1955. The ambiguity of the language of the disability clause (Article II, Section 1, Clause 5) of the Constitution had caused debate ever since the Constitutional Convention of 1787. However, it never had been decided how far the term *disability* extended or who would be the judge of it.

Clause 5 provided that Congress should decide who was to succeed to the presidency if both the president and the vice president died, resigned, or became disabled. Congress enacted succession laws three times. By the Act of March 1, 1792, it provided for succession—after the vice president—of the president pro tempore of the Senate, then of the House Speaker; if those offices were vacant, states were to send electors to Washington to choose a new president.

That law stood until passage of the Presidential Succession Act of January 19, 1886, which changed the line of succession to run from the vice president to the secretary of state, secretary of the treasury, and so on through the cabinet in order of rank. Sixty-one years later the Presidential Succession Act of July 18, 1947, which is still in force, placed the Speaker of the House and the president pro tempore of the Senate ahead of cabinet officers in succession after the vice president.

Before ratification of the Twenty-fifth Amendment, no procedures were in place to cover presidential incapacity or of a vacancy in the office of vice president. Two presidents had had serious disabilities—James A. Garfield (1881), shot in 1881 and confined to his bed until he died two and a half months later, and Woodrow Wilson (1913–1921), who suffered a stroke in 1919. In each case, the vice president did not assume any duties of the presidency for fear he would appear to be taking over the powers of that office.

Ratification of the Twenty-fifth Amendment established procedures that clarified these areas of uncertainty in the Constitution. The amendment

provided that the vice president should become acting president under either one of two circumstances: (1) if the president informed Congress of inability to perform duties, the vice president would become acting president until the president could resume normal responsibilities; (2) if the vice president and a majority of the cabinet, or another body designated by Congress, found the president to be incapacitated, the vice president would become acting president until the president informed Congress that the disability had ended. Congress was given twenty-one days to resolve any dispute over the president's disability; a two-thirds vote of both chambers was required to overrule the president's declaration of being no longer incapacitated.

Vacancy in the Vice Presidency

The Twenty-fifth Amendment also specified what to do when a vacancy occurred in the office of the vice president, by death, succession to the presidency, or resignation. Under the amendment, the president nominates a replacement vice president, with the nomination subject to confirmation by a majority vote of both chambers of Congress. Within only eight years after ratification, two presidents used the power to appoint a new vice president.

In October 1973 when Vice President Agnew resigned, President Richard Nixon (1969–1974) nominated Gerald Ford as the new vice president. Ford was confirmed by both houses of Congress and sworn in December 6, 1973. After Nixon's resignation on August 9, 1974, Ford (1974–1977) succeeded to the presidency, becoming the first president in American history who was elected neither to the presidency nor to the vice presidency. Ford chose as his new vice president Nelson A. Rockefeller, former governor of New York, who was sworn in December 19, 1974.

With both the president and vice president holding office through appointment rather than election, some members of Congress and the public expressed concern about the power of a president to appoint, in effect, his own successor. Accordingly, Sen. John O. Pastore, a Rhode Island Democrat, introduced a proposed constitutional amendment February 3, 1975. This proposed amendment would provide for a special national election for president when more than one year remained in a presidential term. Hearings were held before the Senate Judiciary Subcommittee on Constitutional Amendments, but no action was taken.

See also: Presidential Succession; 📖 Twenty-fifth Amendment, 1967, in the **Primary Source Library**; Vice Presidential Vacancies.

Twenty-fourth Amendment (1964)

Bars the United States or any state from requiring citizens to pay a **poll tax** in order to vote in primary or general elections for president and Congress. The Twenty-fourth **Amendment** was proposed by Congress on August 27, 1962, and **ratified** by the states on February 4, 1964. Although once used by many southern states as a tool to **disenfranchise** blacks and poor whites, the poll tax already had been abandoned by all but five states at the time the Twenty-fourth Amendment was passed. Congress's main purpose in proposing the amendment seems to have been to make a positive gesture to the growing civil rights movement.

The Twenty-fourth Amendment says nothing about **poll taxes** for state and local elections. But in 1966, in the case of *Harper v. Virginia Board of Electors,* the Supreme Court ruled that they too were **unconstitutional** because they violated the Fourteenth Amendment's guarantee of "equal protection of the laws." In a sense, this ruling rendered the Twenty-fourth Amendment unnecessary.

See also: 📖 Twenty-fourth Amendment, 1964, in the **Primary Source Library.**

Twenty-second Amendment (1951)

Prohibits any person from being elected president more than two times. The Twenty-second **Amendment** also prevents successor presidents from being elected more than once if they have served more than two years of a departed president's four-year term. If they serve two years or less of an unexpired term, they may be elected two times on their own, for a maximum tenure of ten years. The amendment was written in such a way as to exempt Harry S. Truman (1945–1953), who was president at the time Congress was considering the matter, from its coverage.

The Two-Term "Tradition"

Thomas Jefferson (1801–1809) was the first president to argue that no president should serve more than two terms. Responding on December 10, 1807, to a letter from the Vermont state legislature urging him to run for a third term, Jefferson pointed out that George Washington (1789–1797) stepped down after two terms in office.

Jefferson's defense of a two-term limit took root quickly in presidential politics. Indeed, the Whig Party and many Democrats soon argued for a one-term limit. Andrew Jackson (1829–1837) was the last president until Abraham Lincoln (1861–1865) to be elected to two terms, and even Jackson said he would prefer a constitutional amendment barring more than one six-year presidential term. Of the first thirty presidents—Washington to Herbert Hoover (1929–1933)— twenty served one term or less.

In the late nineteenth and early twentieth centuries, the issue of a third term arose occasionally. Ulysses S. Grant (in 1876) and Woodrow Wilson (in 1920) probably would have liked to serve another four years, but were too unpopular at the end of their second terms even to be renominated by their parties. Theodore Roosevelt's (1901–1909) situation was more complicated. He was elected president only once, in 1904, but, as vice president, he had served all but six months of the term of his assassinated predecessor, William McKinley (1897–1901). In 1908, Roosevelt declined a certain renomination and, considering his great popularity, a probable reelection, calling the two-term limit a "wise custom." Four years later, however, he ran for president again, first as a Republican, then as a **third-party** candidate. That he had declined a "third cup of coffee" in 1908, Roosevelt said, did not mean that he never intended to drink coffee again. "I meant, of course, a third consecutive term," he said.

Franklin D. Roosevelt

The two-term tradition was broken by President Franklin D. Roosevelt (1933–1945) in 1940. In 1937 Roosevelt, although not flatly ruling out a third term, had declared that his "great ambition on January 20, 1941" (the day his second term would expire) was to "turn over this desk and chair in the White House" to a successor. A number of Democrats, including Postmaster General James A. Farley, Vice President John Nance Garner, and former Indiana governor Paul V. McNutt, began preparing their own presidential candidacies. As Roosevelt's second term wore on, however, he became increasingly frustrated by Congress's resistance to his policies and programs. In 1939, World War II broke out in Europe in response to German, Italian, and Soviet aggression, with little prospect that the United States would be able to remain above the fray. Waiting until the Democratic convention in July 1940, Roosevelt finally signaled his willingness to be renominated. The delegates overwhelmingly approved.

Public opinion polls had shown that the voters were deeply divided about the propriety of Roosevelt's candidacy, and Republicans took up the cry "No third term!" on behalf of their nominee, business leader Wendell Willkie. Roosevelt won the election, but by a much narrower popular vote margin than in 1936—five million votes, compared with eleven million. In 1944, with the United States and its allies nearing victory in World War II, Roosevelt won another term, by three million votes. Ill at the time of his fourth election, he died less than three months after the inauguration.

Proposing the Amendment

Congress had never been fully satisfied with the original Constitution's provision for unrestricted presidential reeligibility. Between 1789 and 1947, 270 **resolutions** to limit the president's term had been introduced in the House and Senate, sixty of them—an average of three per year—since 1928. In addition, the Roosevelt years added a **partisan** dimension to this long-standing concern. In 1932 the Republicans, who had formed the nation's majority party since 1860, were driven from power by Roosevelt's New Deal Democratic coalition. **Conservative** Democrats, mostly southern, lost control of their party to **liberals** and northerners at the national level.

In the midterm elections of 1946, the Republicans regained a majority of both houses of Congress. On February 6, 1947, less than five weeks after the opening of the Eightieth Congress, the House passed a strict two-term amendment to the Constitution by a vote of 285–121. The House **bill** provided that any president who had served one full term and even one day of another would be barred from seeking reelection. Republicans supported the amendment unanimously (238–0); Democrats opposed it by a 47–121 vote, with most of the Democratic yea votes coming from southerners. Five weeks later, on March 12, the Senate passed a slightly different version of the amendment (it allowed a president who had served one full term and less than half of another to seek an additional term) by a vote of 59–23. Republican senators, like their House colleagues, were unanimous in their support (46–0); Democrats opposed the amendment by a vote of 23–13. The differences between the two versions of the amendment were ironed out quickly in favor of the Senate's and final congressional action took place on March 24, 1947.

The debate on the Twenty-second Amendment was highly partisan. Republicans contended that a two-term limit would protect Americans against the threat of an overly personal presidency. Democrats like Representative Estes Kefauver of Tennessee noted that the people, "by a mere majority vote, have the opportunity of deciding every four years whether they want to terminate the services of the President if he stands for reelection." Little, if any, consideration was given to the Constitutional Convention's original decision to place no restrictions on presidential reeligibility. Nor did Congress foresee the beneficial political effect of the amendment on the vice presidency. With second-term presidents barred from reelection, vice presidents could openly campaign for their party's presidential nomination without jeopardizing their standing within the administration, as Richard Nixon did in 1960, George H.W. Bush did in 1988, and Al Gore did in 2000.

Ratification

Once proposed, the Twenty-second Amendment received a mixed response from the states. Only one other amendment to the Constitution has taken longer to ratify than the three years, eleven months required for the two-term limit. Eighteen

POINT/COUNTERPOINT

SHOULD THE TWENTY-SECOND AMENDMENT BE REPEALED?

After Franklin Delano Roosevelt's four-term presidency (1933–1945), the Twenty-second Amendment to the U.S. Constitution codified that which had been previously only tradition: presidents should serve no more than two terms. Some Constitutional experts, advocates of a strong executive, and many former presidents, have sought the amendment's repeal.

Repeal the Twenty-second Amendment

The two-term limit is undemocratic. If Americans want to vote for a President again after two terms, and that President is willing to serve, why should their wishes automatically be denied? The two-term convention was seized upon by a coalition of senators who wanted more power for themselves (by undermining the Presidency), FDR haters and presidential aspirants who wanted to ensure regular turnover at the top. There is no logical basis for this limitation beyond that. The effect of this scheming is damaging: it denies Americans the chance to vote for a candidate they might want to support. This amendment limits voter choice.

state legislatures—exactly half the needed number—approved the amendment in 1947, all of them in predominantly Republican states. Afterward, **ratification** proceeded slowly, with most victories coming in the South. The adoption of the Twenty-second Amendment was certified and declared part of the Constitution by Jess Larson, administrator of the General Services Administration (GSA), on February 27, 1951.

See also: 📖 Twenty-second Amendment, 1951, in the **Primary Source Library.**

Twenty-third Amendment (1961)

Gives residents of the District of Columbia electors in presidential elections. Until the Constitution was written, the location of the capital of the United States was ever changing—at various times, it moved or was forced to move to Philadelphia, Trenton, New York, and elsewhere. To prevent

this migration from happening again, the Constitutional Convention stipulated in Article I, Section 8, Clause 17, that the new capital would be a federal city, governed by Congress and carved out of territory "not exceeding ten miles square" that was **ceded** to the federal government by the states. Maryland and Virginia both donated land to the new federal city.

One result of being neither a state nor a part of a state was that the District of Columbia, or Washington, D.C., was not represented in the federal government. It lacked senators and representatives in Congress and electoral votes in the presidential election. Over the years, this became the source of much resentment among the taxpaying citizens of Washington, whose population by 1950 exceeded 800,000, making it more populous than thirteen states.

The Twenty-third **Amendment,** proposed by Congress on June 16, 1960, granted the District a "number of electors of President and Vice President . . . in no event more than the least populous state"—that is, three. The amendment passed both houses on voice votes, mostly because Democrats

Retain the Twenty-second Amendment

The Presidency is different from almost any other kind of office in the US. Senators and Congressmen don't have term limits because their voices are balanced by opposition in their respective chambers; the President has no comparable counterbalance. The nearest analogy would be with state governors—many of which have term limits, too. This is because the role of the individual in such "head of executive" functions is of such importance that pure democracy—unlimited terms—must be tempered by the fear of "elective dictatorship"—a strong President using the undoubted advantages of incumbency to win election after election. America's beginnings are based in a rejection of monarchy and of cronyism: the 22nd Amendment stops this from coming about by other means.

DOCUMENT-BASED QUESTION

What evidence does the first excerpt use to support the notion that the Twenty-second Amendment is undemocratic? Why does the second excerpt note that the president's role is unique?

A–Z

and Republicans each thought they had a chance to win the District. It was **ratified** quickly, on March 29, 1961. Overwhelmingly African American and Democratic, the District of Columbia has never given less than 75 percent of its vote to the Democratic candidate for president.

In 1978, Congress proposed a constitutional amendment to repeal the Twenty-third Amendment and expand the voting rights of District residents. The proposed amendment would have granted the District some of the electoral rights of states, such as power to ratify proposed constitutional amendments, two senators, and a number of representatives and presidential electors commensurate with its population. Mostly for **partisan** reasons, the amendment failed. Republicans realized that they had little hope of winning elections in the District. Only sixteen states—fewer than half the number needed—had ratified it by the time the seven-year deadline for state action expired.

See also: 📖 Twenty-third Amendment, 1961, in the **Primary Source Library.**

Tyler, John, Administration of (1841–1845)

Government under the tenth president of the United States. William Henry Harrison (1841), the ninth president, died after only a month in office, and Vice President John Tyler quickly took the oath of office. He thus imposed a solution on the unresolved question of the vice president's right to assume the full status of the presidency if it became vacant. Leaving absolutely no doubt that he intended to be his own man as president, Tyler went before an audience assembled in the capital on April 9, 1841, and gave an inaugural address in the manner of an elected president. Tyler's "exposition of the principles" that would govern his administration was a signal to the country that he would not be content to stand in Harrison's shadow. It was also a warning to

VIEWPOINTS

TYLER RECEIVING THE NEWS OF HARRISON'S DEATH.

John Tyler solemnly receives the news that William Henry Harrison (1841) is dead. Tyler (1841–1845) did much to establish the precedent that a vice president who succeeds to the presidential office after the death of his predecessor becomes "president" and not "acting president." Nonetheless, Tyler's critics referred to him as "His Accidency." (Library of Congress)

Whigs that Tyler did not intend to be a compliant servant to Henry Clay, Daniel Webster, and other party leaders. By acting boldly and decisively, Tyler established, in the absence of clear constitutional guidance, the firm **precedent** that an "accidental" president enjoys the same station as an elected president.

The difficulties that Tyler faced in office went beyond the constitutional doubts that surrounded his succession. His elevation to the presidency also created a political impasse. Tyler represented a faction of the Whig Party that dissented from many of the **nationalist** views preached by its leaders. Tyler's vice presidential nomination had

been a gesture of compromise from the National Republican wing of the Whig Party to the smaller southern states' rights wing. Yet in this case, ticket balancing backfired: Tyler decisively seized the reins of office after Harrison's death. He proceeded to exercise the powers of the presidency in a way that frustrated the Whig efforts to enact Clay's "American plan" for government-sponsored economic development.

Tyler's opposition to much of the Whig domestic program prompted him to cast more **vetoes** than any of his predecessors except Jackson. In 1841, he vetoed two successive **bills** that resembled the old bank legislation that Jackson had

John Tyler (1841–1845) became president upon the death of William Henry Harrison (1841), the first vice president to assume the presidential office on the death of his predecessor. (Library of Congress)

killed. The outburst of fury against Tyler after his second veto led every cabinet member except Secretary of State Daniel Webster to resign.

The bank battles were only the beginning of the struggle between Tyler and his party. His veto of a **tariff** measure a year later provoked the first attempt in history to **impeach** a president of the United States. Tyler's assertive exercise of the veto power could not be reconciled with the Whig theory of **executive** subordination to Congress. To more easily counter Tyler's vetoes, Clay even proposed a constitutional amendment that would permit Congress to override a veto by a simple majority.

Tyler claimed for the president the right to participate in the **legislative** process, as Jackson had done and defended his veto of the **tariff** bill on programmatic, not constitutional, grounds. Like Jackson, too, Tyler argued that when a conflict developed between the president and Congress, the people were to decide who was right. When the Whigs were defeated in the congressional election of 1842, Tyler believed that his defense of the executive had been vindicated.

Nothing came of the movement to impeach the president, and the proposal for a constitutional **amendment** to curb the veto power elicited only public indifference. Thus although Tyler lost his party's support and with it any chance to be re-elected in 1844, he prevented a potentially damaging setback to the executive office. As one scholar wrote, Tyler "prepared the way for the completion of the movement toward executive leadership started by Andrew Jackson."

See also: Harrison, William Henry, Administration of (1841); Polk, James, Administration of (1845–1849); Vice Presidency.

Further Reading

Crapol, Edward P. *John Tyler: The Accidental President.* Chapel Hill, NC: University of North Carolina Press, 2006.

A–Z

Van Buren, Martin, Administration of (1837–1841)

Government under the eighth president of the United States. The able and shrewd Martin Van Buren easily won the election of 1836. Soon after he took office, however, he became the first president to face a domestic crisis. No sooner had he assumed office than the economy began a downward spiral, a decline that was at least in part the legacy of Andrew Jackson's assault on the national bank. The Panic of 1837 was caused in large measure by speculation. A boom in western land, manufacturing, transportation, banking, and several other business enterprises began in 1825 and brought about an overextension of credit.

By removing the deposits from the **conservative Bank of the United States** and placing them in selected pet state banks, the Jackson administration had contributed to the **liberal** expansion of credit. Then, conscious of the problems posed by an overextended economy, Jackson issued a Treasury order, the **Specie Circular,** in July 1836, requiring that **hard currency,** or gold and silver, be used in payment for all federal lands. This order aroused concern that Jackson and his successor would do all they could to tighten the money supply, causing banks to call in loans and consequently helping to bring on the panic.

By early 1837, American mercantile houses began to fall, and riots broke out in New York over the high cost of flour. In short order, almost every bank in the country had suspended **specie** payments, and the state banking system that Jackson had set up to replace the national bank collapsed, costing the Treasury some $9 million.

Van Buren was a more pragmatic statesman than his predecessor, but he was sufficiently wedded to Jacksonian principles to resist government-sponsored solutions to the economic crisis. He rejected any notion of reviving a national institution such as the Bank of the United States to regulate currency. Similarly, he rejected the view that the Treasury ought to provide a paper medium to facilitate domestic exchange. The Treasury was to attend to its own affairs and let business do the same.

Rejecting the "constant desire" of the Whigs "to enlarge the power of government," Van Buren's response to the panic was minimal, given its

Martin Van Buren (1837–1841) was a strong supporter of Andrew Jackson's (1829–1837) policies and continued them during his presidential term. Van Buren lost his reelection bid, however, in part because of the Panic of 1837 that was caused by the federal government's removal of funds from the Bank of the United States. (Library of Congress)

severity. Van Buren's response centered on a proposal to establish an independent treasury, which would hold government funds in federal vaults instead of depositing them in state banks. The proposed subtreasury, however, was to have limited power, leaving state banks free from federal regulations. Even this modest measure was not put into effect until 1840, as it was resisted for most of Van Buren's tenure by a coalition of conservative Democrats and Whigs, most of whom favored a stronger role for the national government in the economy. Thus, the presidential election of 1840 took place in the midst of a **depression,** for which the Democratic Party was held responsible.

See also: 📖 "A Hard Road to Hoe," 1840, in the **Primary Source Library;** Harrison, William Henry, Administration of (1841); Jackson, Andrew, Administration of (1829–1837).

Further Reading

Widmer, Ted. *Martin Van Buren.* New York: Times Books, Henry Holt and Company, 2005.

Veterans Affairs, Department of

See Department of Veterans Affairs.

Veto Power

The president's power to reject legislation passed by Congress. Any bill Congress passes must go to the president, who must either sign it or **veto** it—send it back to Congress with objections. Congress can, by voting to override a veto, pass the legislation anyway if enough members in each house vote to do so.

The president may exercise either a regular veto or a "pocket veto." A pocket veto occurs when the president refuses to act on a bill until Congress **adjourns,** or temporarily suspends its activities. At that time, the bill is automatically killed. To override a veto requires the approval of two-thirds of members present and voting in each chamber.

Early History

Early American presidents saw the veto as a tool to be used only to prevent Congress from assuming powers the Constitution grants to other branches of government. Of the first six presidents, George Washington (1789–1797) vetoed only two **bills;** John Adams (1797–1801) and Thomas Jefferson (1801–1809) vetoed none; James Madison (1809–1817) and James Monroe (1817–1825) vetoed eight bills between them; and John Quincy Adams (1825–1829) also did not veto a single bill. In all but one case, presidents vetoed only bills they felt were **unconstitutional,** not merely those they opposed politically.

The concept of the veto changed dramatically under Andrew Jackson (1829–1837), who vetoed twelve bills—more than all six of his predecessors put together—mostly because he opposed their purpose. Jackson, who used the pocket veto for the first time, believed the president could reject any bill that he felt was harmful to the nation. His most noteworthy veto was of a bill to create a new charter, or founding document, for the **Bank of the United States.** The Bank's first charter had expired several years earlier. Jackson felt that the Bank existed solely to serve the interests of large business, and not those of the general public. According to one historian, Jackson's veto was "a landmark in the evolution of the presidency. For the first time in American history, a veto message was used as an instrument of party warfare. . . . Though addressed to Congress, the veto message was an appeal to the nation."

In 1867, Congress overrode President Andrew Johnson's (1865–1869) veto of a bill to protect the rights of freed slaves. This marked the first override of a presidential veto on a major issue. It was only the first of several bills passed over Johnson's veto. Others included the Tenure of Office Act, which prohibited the president from removing appointed officials from office until the Senate had confirmed their successors. When Johnson refused to abide by the provisions of the act, the House began **impeachment** proceedings against him.

Vetoes rose during the late nineteenth and early twentieth centuries. Grover Cleveland (1885–1889, 1893–1897), for example, vetoed 584 bills during his two terms of office. Franklin D. Roosevelt (1933–1945) broke Cleveland's record by

Vetoes and Vetoes Overridden, All Bills 1789–2008

President	All bills vetoed	Regular vetoes	Pocket vetoes	Vetoes overridden
Washington	2	2	0	0
J. Adams	0	0	0	0
Jefferson	0	0	0	0
Madison	7	5	2	0
Monroe	1	1	0	0
J.Q. Adams	0	0	0	0
Jackson	12	5	7	0
Van Buren	1	0	1	0
W.H. Harrison	0	0	0	0
Tyler	10	6	4	1
Polk	3	2	1	0
Taylor	0	0	0	0
Fillmore	0	0	0	0
Pierce	9	9	0	5
Buchanan	7	4	3	0
Lincoln	7	2	5	0
A. Johnson	29	21	8	15
Grant	93[a]	45	48[a]	4
Hayes	13	12	1	1
Garfield	0	0	0	0
Arthur	12	4	8	1
Cleveland (1st term)	414	304	110	2
B. Harrison	44	19	25	1
Cleveland (2d term)	170	42	128	5
McKinley	42	6	36	0
T. Roosevelt	82	42	40	1
Taft	39	30	9	1
Wilson	44	33	11	6
Harding	6	5	1	0

Vetoes and Vetoes Overridden, All Bills 1789–2008, *continued*

President	All bills vetoed	Regular vetoes	Pocket vetoes	Vetoes overridden
Coolidge	50	20	30	4
Hoover	37	21	16	3
F. Roosevelt	635	372	263	9
Truman	250	180	70	12
Eisenhower	181	73	108	2
Kennedy	21	12	9	0
L. Johnson	30	16	14	0
Nixon	43	26[b]	17	7
Ford	66	48	18	12
Carter	31	13	18	2
Reagan	78	39	39	9
G.H.W. Bush[c]	44	29	15	1
Clinton	37	36	1	2
G. W. Bush	10	10	0	3
TOTAL	**2,560**	**1,494**	**1,066**	**109**

Notes: a. Veto total listed for Grant does not include a pocket veto of a bill that apparently never was placed before him for his signature. b. Two pocket vetoes, later overturned in court, are counted as regular vetoes. c. Two pocket vetoes, attempted by Bush during intrasession periods, are not counted since Congress considered the two bills enacted into law because of Bush's failure to return them to legislation.

Source: U.S. House of Representatives, Office of the Clerk, "Historical Highlights, Presidential Vetoes, (1789–2006)" (clerk.house .gov/art_history/house_history/vetoes.html), accessed February 1, 2007.

The presidents' use of the veto has often depended on their interpretation of the power of the office as well as their support in Congress.

vetoing 635 bills between 1933 and 1944. Roosevelt's immediate successors Harry S. Truman (1945–1953) and Dwight D. Eisenhower (1953–1961) continued to make extensive use of the veto, but Presidents John F. Kennedy (1961–1963) and Lyndon B. Johnson (1963–1969) seldom had to use the veto or threaten it. They were activist presidents whose main interest lay in getting their programs through a Congress controlled by their own party. Like Eisenhower, Republican presidents Richard M. Nixon (1969–1974) and Gerald R. Ford (1974–1977) used the veto and its threat to prevent enactment of Democratic programs in the late 1960s and 1970s.

Recent History

Ronald Reagan (1981–1989) frequently threatened vetoes, but failed to follow through on many of these threats. He vetoed seventy-one bills, almost half using the pocket veto. George H. W. Bush (1989–1993), on the other hand, used vetoes and veto threats to great effect. Like other recent Republican presidents, he faced a Democratic-controlled Congress. Bush issued around 60 veto threats per year, often not to kill legislation but to stimulate serious bargaining with Congress.

Bill Clinton (1993–2001) did not veto a bill from the Democratic-controlled Congress in the first two years of his first term. This changed drastically after Republicans took over both houses of Congress in 1995. Over the course of that year, Clinton vetoed ten spending bills proposed by Republicans to reduce the size of government and balance the budget. Clinton used vetoes and the threat of vetoes to counteract what he branded the "extremism" of the new congressional leaders. George W. Bush (2001–2009), like Reagan, issued many veto threats, but vetoed just twelve bills.

See also: Impeachment, Presidential; Presidency and Congress.

Further Reading

Library of Congress Congressional Research Service, Galemore, Gary L, and G. V. Lipson, eds. *Presidential Vetoes: Challenges and Bibliography.* Hauppauge, NY: Nova Science Publishers, 2002.

Vice Presidency

Office of the person who succeeds the president, should the presidency become vacant. During the period of British rule, several colonies had lieutenant governors (known in some states as deputy governors or by another title) whose ongoing duties were minor but who stood by to serve as acting governor if the governor died, was removed from office, was ill, or was absent from the colony.

After independence, five states—New York, Connecticut, Rhode Island, Massachusetts, and South Carolina—included lieutenant governors in their constitutions. Each was elected in the same manner as the governor and was charged to act as governor when needed. New York's lieutenant governor also was the president of the state senate and was empowered to break tie votes. Other states handled the matter of gubernatorial death, absence, or inability differently. In Virginia and Georgia, for example, the head of the privy council, a cabinet-style body, was the designated gubernatorial successor; in Delaware and North Carolina, it was the speaker of the upper house of the legislature; in New Hampshire, the senior member of the state senate.

It is difficult to say whether the experience of the states had much influence on the convention's decision to create the vice presidency. No reference was made to the state lieutenant governors in the debates. Nor was any proposal made to include a vice president in the Constitution until very late in the proceedings. Indeed, the invention of the vice presidency seems to have been an afterthought of the convention.

The delegates initially had decided that the legislature should choose the **executive,** but they eventually replaced **legislative** selection with the electoral college, in which each state was to pick presidential electors, who in turn would choose the president by majority vote. A possibly fatal defect of this procedure was that the electors simply would vote for a variety of local favorites, preventing the choice of a nationally elected president. However, the committee remedied this possible problem by assigning each elector two votes for president, requiring that they cast at least one of these votes for a candidate who "shall not be an Inhabitant of the same State with themselves," and attaching a consequence to both votes—the runner-up in the election for president would be awarded the newly created office of vice president.

Thus as Hugh Williamson, a member of the Committee on Postponed Matters, testified, "Such an office as vice-President was not wanted. It was introduced only for the sake of a valuable mode of election which required two to be chosen at the same time." Having invented the vice presidency, the committee proposed that the office also be used to solve two other problems that had come forward at the convention.

Senate President

The first problem was the role of president of the Senate. Some delegates had fretted that if a senator were chosen for this position, one of two difficulties inevitably would arise. If the senator were barred from voting on legislative matters except in the event of a tie (which was customary for presiding officers because it guaranteed that tie votes would be broken), the senator's state would effectively be denied half its representation on most issues. If the senator were allowed to vote on all matters, the state would be overrepresented in the Senate, occupying two voting seats and the presiding officer's chair. The Committee on Postponed

Vice Presidents Often Attain Top Spot

Fourteen of the forty-three men who have served as president of the United States were vice presidents first, but only five of them got to the Oval Office by being elected to it. The others made it because of the death or resignation of the president.

Of the five vice presidents elevated by election, two—John Adams and Thomas Jefferson—were elected when there was no public participation in the presidential nominating process and little participation in the general election. Martin Van Buren was elected directly to the presidency in 1836, as was George H.W. Bush in 1988. Richard Nixon narrowly lost his bid to move up from the vice presidency in 1960 but was elected president eight years later.

A few other vice presidents have come close to attaining the Oval Office. Hubert H. Humphrey lost narrowly to Nixon in 1968. Walter F. Mondale won the Democratic presidential nomination in 1984, four years after his term as vice president ended, but lost to Ronald Reagan. Al Gore was defeated by Republican George W. Bush in 2000, even though Gore won a plurality of the national popular vote.

Two other vice presidents ran unsuccessfully as third-party presidential candidates. John C. Breckinridge, Democrat James Buchanan's vice president (1857–1861), was the nominee of the Southern Democrats in 1860. Henry A. Wallace, Franklin D. Roosevelt's second vice president (1941–1945), was the candidate of the Progressive Party in 1948.

Vice presidents who became president and those who won a major party presidential nomination are listed below. The party affiliation of the vice presidents and the names of the presidents under whom they served are noted.

Assumed Presidency on Death or Resignation	Year Assumed Presidency
John Tyler, Whig (W. H. Harrison)	1841
Millard Fillmore, Whig (Taylor)	1850
Andrew Johnson, D (Lincoln)	1865
Chester A. Arthur, R (Garfield)	1881
Theodore Roosevelt, R (McKinley)	1901
Calvin Coolidge, R (Harding)	1923
Harry S. Truman, D (F. Roosevelt)	1945
Lyndon B. Johnson, D (Kennedy)	1963
Gerald R. Ford, R (Nixon)	1974
Elected President Directly from Vice Presidency	**Year Elected President**
John Adams, Federalist (Washington)	1796
Thomas Jefferson, D-R (J. Adams)	1800
Martin Van Buren, D (Jackson)	1836
George H.W. Bush, R (Reagan)	1988
Elected President Later	**Year Elected President**
Richard Nixon, R (Eisenhower)	1968

(continued on next page)

A–Z

Vice Presidents Often Attain Top Spot, *continued*

Nominated for President but Lost	Year Sought Presidency
Richard Nixon, R (Eisenhower)	1960
Hubert H. Humphrey, D (L. Johnson)	1968
Walter F. Mondale, D (Carter)	1984
Al Gore, D (Clinton)	2000

Several presidents have served as vice president before obtaining the presidency—either through election or succession. The most recent vice president elected to the presidency was George H.W. Bush in 1992.

Matters recommended that, as a way around this dilemma, the vice president would serve as president of the Senate, voting only to break ties. An exception was made for impeachment trials of the president, when the chief justice of the Supreme Court would preside over the Senate.

Succession

The second loose end that the committee used the vice presidency to tie off was presidential succession. This, too, was a matter to which the convention turned rather late. The Virginia Plan and the New Jersey Plan had been silent about succession. Attention was first given to the succession question by the Committee of Detail:

In the case of his [the president's] removal as aforesaid, death, resignation, or disability to discharge the powers and duties of his office, the President of the Senate shall exercise those powers and duties, until another President of the United States be chosen, or until the disability of the President be removed.

Considerable dissatisfaction was voiced when the delegates discussed this provision of the committee's report on August 27. James Madison (1809–1817), who feared that the Senate would have an incentive to create presidential vacancies if its own president were the designated successor, suggested that "the persons composing the Council to the President" fill that role instead. Gouverneur Morris suggested the chief justice as successor. Finally, Williamson asked that the question be postponed. The convention agreed,

placing the issue in the hands of the Committee on Postponed Matters.

The committee, which reported to the convention on September 4, proposed:

In the case of his [the president's] removal as aforesaid, death, absence, resignation, or inability to discharge the powers or duties of his office the Vice President shall exercise those powers and duties until another President be chosen, or until the inability of the President be removed.

Three days later, Edmund Randolph, in an effort to supplement the committee's proposal with one that would provide a method of presidential succession if there were no vice president, moved:

The Legislature may declare by law what officer of the United States shall act as President in the case of the death, resignation, or disability of the President and Vice President; and such Officer shall act accordingly until the time of electing a President shall arrive.

Madison moved to replace the last nine words of Randolph's motion with "until such disability be removed, or a President shall be elected." The motion passed, as amended.

Madison's reason for amending Randolph's motion is clear: he wanted to allow Congress to call a special election to replace a departed president or, in his words, to permit "a supply of vacancy by an intermediate election of the

President." Other evidence from the records of the convention suggests that most of the delegates intended that the president's successor would serve only as acting president until a special election could be called. Nevertheless, sometime in the period between September 8 and 12, when the Committee of Style was working to fulfill its charge to produce a smooth, final draft of the Constitution, that intention was, probably innocently, lost. The committee took the September 4 motion of the Committee on Postponed Matters and Randolph's September 7 motion and merged them into one passage, which, with minor modification, became Clause 6 of Article II, Section 1, of the Constitution:

> In case of the Removal of the President from Office, or of his death, Resignation, or Inability to discharge the Powers and Duties of the said Office, the Same shall devolve on the Vice President, and the Congress may by law provide for the Case of Removal, Death, Resignation, or Inability, both of the President and Vice President, declaring what Officer shall then act as President, and such officer shall act accordingly, until the Disability be removed, or a President shall be elected.

Clearly, the delegates' intentions regarding succession were obscured by the Committee of Style. Grammatically, it is impossible to tell—and in its rush to **adjournment,** the convention did not notice the ambiguity—whether "the Same" in this provision refers to "the said office" (the presidency) or, as the delegates intended, only to its "powers and duties." Nor can one ascertain if "until . . . a President shall be elected" means until the end of the original four-year term or, again as intended, until a special election is held.

The vice presidency was not a very controversial issue at the Constitutional Convention. On September 4, when the delegates were considering the Committee on Postponed Matters' proposal for the electoral college, Nathaniel Gorham of Massachusetts worried that "a very obscure man with very few votes" might be elected, because the proposal required only that the vice president be runner-up in the presidential election, not the recipient of a

majority of electoral votes. Roger Sherman of Connecticut replied that any of the leading candidates for president would likely be qualified.

The role of the vice president as president of the Senate became a subject of minor controversy on September 7. Elbridge Gerry, seconded by Edmund Randolph, complained about the mixing of legislative and executive elements: "We might as well put the President himself at the head of the Legislature. The close intimacy that must subsist between the President & vice-president makes it absolutely improper." Gerry was "agst. [against] having any vice President."

Sherman replied, "if the vice-President were not to be President of the Senate, he would be without employment." He also reminded the convention that for the Senate to elect its president from among its own members probably would deprive that senator of a vote. George Mason ended the brief debate by branding the office of vice-President "an encroachment on the rights of the Senate; . . . it mixed too much the Legislative and Executive, which as well as the Judiciary departments, ought to be kept as separate as possible."

Despite these objections, the convention voted overwhelmingly to approve the vice presidency. Interestingly, the delegates gave no serious attention to the vice president's responsibilities as successor to the president.

See also: Twelfth Amendment, 1804, in the **Primary Source Library;** Twenty-fifth Amendment, 1967, in the **Primary Source Library.**

Vice Presidential Salary and Benefits

See Vice Presidency.

Vice Presidential Vacancies

When the United States is without a sitting vice president. The vice presidency becomes vacant when the vice president dies, resigns, or is **impeached** and removed, or when the vice president succeeds to the presidency after the president dies, resigns, or is impeached and removed. Such circumstances left the nation without a vice president sixteen times between 1789 and 1963: seven times because the vice president died (all of natural causes), eight times because the president died, and once because the vice president resigned.

Changing succession laws provided for the possibility of a double vacancy in the presidency and vice presidency by placing the president pro tempore of the Senate and the Speaker of the House, respectively, next in line to the presidency (pending a special presidential election) from 1792 to 1886; the secretary of state and the other department heads next in line (pending an optional special election) from 1886 to 1947; and the Speaker of the House and the Senate president pro tempore, respectively, next in line (with no special election) after 1947. So far a double vacancy has never occurred.

Addressing the Problem

Public and congressional concern about the problems of presidential disability and vice-presidential vacancy was minor and episodic through most of the first century and a half of U.S. history, usually rising for brief periods while a president was disabled, then waning when the crisis passed. From 1945 to 1963, however, a combination of events took place that placed these problems high on the nation's constitutional agenda.

The invention and spread of nuclear weapons and intercontinental ballistic missiles after 1945 heightened concern that an able president be available at all times to wield the powers of the office. Then, in rapid succession, President Dwight D. Eisenhower (1953–1961) suffered a series of disabling illnesses—a heart attack in 1955, an ileitis attack and operation in 1956, and a stroke in 1957. In 1963, the assassination of President John F. Kennedy (1961–1963) left the nation with a president, Lyndon Johnson, who had a history of heart trouble and whose legally designated successors, in the absence of a vice president, were an ailing House Speaker, John W. McCormack (D-MA), and an even more enfeebled Senate president pro tempore, Carl Hayden (D-AZ).

The first tangible result of this series of developments was a letter, released to the public on March 3, 1958, that President Eisenhower sent to Vice President Richard Nixon. The letter stated that if Eisenhower ever were disabled again, he would instruct the vice president to serve as acting president until the disability passed, at which time the president would reclaim his powers. If Eisenhower were disabled but unable to communicate with Nixon for some reason, Nixon could make the decision to assume power himself. Again, Eisenhower would determine when it was time to resume the powers of his office.

The Eisenhower letter was later adopted by President Kennedy and Vice President Johnson, President Johnson and Speaker McCormack, and (after the 1964 election) President Johnson and Vice President Hubert Humphrey. However, it hardly solved the problem of presidential disability. For one thing, a letter lacked the force of law. For another, Eisenhower's letter made no provision to relieve a president who was disabled, perhaps mentally, but who refused to admit it. Finally, the letter did not—nor could it—address the related problem of the vacant vice presidency.

Proposing the Amendment: Disability

In December 1963, less than a month after the Kennedy assassination, Senator Birch Bayh (D-IN), the chairman of the Senate Judiciary Committee's Subcommittee on Constitutional Amendments, announced that he would hold hearings in early 1964 to consider constitutional remedies to the disability and vacancy problems. Coordinating his efforts with those of a special committee of the American Bar Association, Bayh drafted an amendment that formed the basis for the subcommittee's hearings and that, with minor modifications, later entered the Constitution as the Twenty-fifth **Amendment.**

The Senate approved the amendment on September 29, 1964, by a vote of 65–0. The House did not act in 1964, perhaps because to propose an amendment to fill vice-presidential vacancies would be perceived as an insult to Speaker McCormack, who under the existing arrangement was first in line to succeed President Johnson. In 1965, however, after Humphrey's election as vice president in November 1964, the House joined the Senate (which had reaffirmed its support of the amendment by a vote of 72–0 on February 19). On April 13 the House voted its approval, 368–29.

From the beginning, most of Congress's concerns about the Twenty-fifth Amendment were directed at its disability provisions. As drafted by Bayh and enacted by Congress, three very different situations were covered by sections 3 and 4 of the amendment. In the first, the president is "unable to discharge the powers and duties of his office" and recognizes the condition, say, before or after surgery. A simple letter from the president to the Speaker of the House and the president pro tempore of the Senate is sufficient to make the vice president the acting president. A subsequent letter declaring that the disability is ended restores the president's powers.

In the second situation, the president is disabled but, having perhaps lost consciousness, is unable to say so. Should this happen, either the vice president or the head of an executive department may call a meeting of the vice president and cabinet to discuss the situation. If both the vice president and a majority of the heads of the departments declare the president disabled, the vice president becomes acting president—again, until the president writes to congressional leaders to announce an end to the disability.

Some critics of the Bayh proposal argued that it vested too much power in the executive branch to make disability determinations. Suggestions were offered to create a disability commission that included members of all three government branches, perhaps joined by a number of physicians. Bayh defended his proposal by saying that any move to strip power from the president by officials outside the administration risked violating the constitutional principle of separation of powers. In the end, both to satisfy the critics and to preclude the possibility that a president might fire the cabinet to forestall a declaration of disability, the amendment empowered Congress, at its discretion, to substitute another body for the cabinet.

The third situation covered by the disability portions of the amendment is the most troubling. It involves instances (such as questionable mental health or sudden physical disability) in which the president's ability to fulfill the office is in dispute: the president claims to be able, but the vice president and cabinet judge differently. The amendment provides that should this happen, the vice president would become acting president pending a congressional resolution of the matter. Congress would have a maximum of three weeks to decide whether or not the president is disabled, with a two-thirds vote of both the House and the Senate needed to overturn the president's judgment. The reason for the requirement of an extraordinary majority was the presumption that the president should receive the benefit of any doubt. Nevertheless, because the Twenty-fifth Amendment only transfers power to the vice president for as long as the president is disabled, a subsequent claim of restored health by the president would set the whole process in motion again.

Interestingly, the Twenty-fifth Amendment, although creating an elaborate set of procedures for disability determinations, includes no definition of *disability*. It is clear from the congressional debate that disability is not to be equated with incompetence, laziness, unpopularity, or impeachable conduct. As to what disability is, Congress thought that any definition it might write into the Constitution in 1965 would be rendered obsolete by changes in medical theory and practice.

Proposing the Amendment

Widespread agreement existed in Congress about the need to replace the vice president when the office becomes vacant, both to increase the likelihood of a smooth succession to the presidency by a member of the president's party and to ensure that the presidential disability provisions of the Twenty-fifth Amendment would always have a vice president on hand to execute them. Bayh's proposal—that the president nominate a new vice president when the office becomes vacant and that a majority of both houses of Congress, voting separately, confirm the nomination—prevailed and became Section 2 of the amendment.

Ratification

No serious opposition to the Twenty-fifth Amendment arose during the **ratification** process. The needed approval of thirty-eight state legislatures was attained on February 10, 1967, barely a year and a half after Congress proposed the amendment. In the end, all but three states voted to **ratify.**

Section 2 of the Twenty-fifth Amendment—the vice-presidential vacancy provision—was put to use rather quickly in surprising circumstances. Vice President Spiro T. Agnew, facing prosecution in federal court on a variety of bribery-related charges, resigned from office as part of a plea bargain on October 10, 1973. President Nixon nominated House Republican leader Gerald Ford to replace Agnew on October 12. After a nearly two-month-long investigation, the Senate approved Ford's nomination on November 27 by a vote of 92–3, and the House gave its approval on December 6, voting 387–35.

Barely eight months later, when President Nixon resigned on August 9, 1974, to avoid being impeached for his involvement in the Watergate cover-up, Ford became president. On August 20, he nominated Governor Nelson A. Rockefeller of New York to be vice president. Congress investigated and debated the nomination for four months before approving Rockefeller by a vote of 90–7 in the Senate on December 10, and 287–128 in the House on December 19.

Use of the Twenty-fifth Amendment's presidential disability provisions (sections 3 and 4) has, for the most part, been infrequent and grudging. No occasions of disability arose until March 30, 1981, when President Ronald Reagan (1981–1989) was wounded by a would-be assassin's bullet. Although conscious and lucid before surgery, he did not sign his powers over to Vice President George H.W. Bush. Mean-

On December 6, 1973, Gerald R. Ford was sworn in as the fortieth vice president of the United States, succeeding Spiro T. Agnew, who had resigned amid allegations of taking bribes. The following year, Ford (1974–1977) assumed the presidency upon the resignation of Richard M. Nixon (1969–1974,) who also had resigned as a result of "high crimes and misdemeanors" in the Watergate coverup. (The Granger Collection, New York)

while, presidential aides stifled discussion at the White House about the possibility of a cabinet-voted transfer. In July 1985, before undergoing cancer surgery, Reagan did sign his powers over to Bush, but only after arguing that the Twenty-fifth Amendment was not meant to apply to such brief episodes of disability.

As president (1989–1993), Bush's approach to

the matter of disability was more constructive than his predecessor's. Before entering the hospital in May 1991 because of an irregular heartbeat, Bush announced a plan to turn over power to Vice President Dan Quayle in the event that his condition required electroshock therapy. It did not, so the plan did not need to be implemented. In 2007, President George W. Bush (2001–2009) invoked the Twenty-fifth Amendment and temporarily transferred power to Vice President Richard Cheney while undergoing a medical procedure.

See also: 📖 Twenty-fifth Amendment, 1967, in the **Primary Source Library;** Vice Presidency.

Further Reading

Feerick, John D. *The Twenty-fifth Amendment: Its Complete History and Applications.* New York: Fordham University Press, 1992.

Gilbert, Robert E., ed. *Managing Crisis: Presidential Disability and the Twenty-Fifth Amendment.* New York: Fordham University Press, 2000.

Toole, James F., Robert J. Joynt, and Arthur S. Link. *Presidential Disability: Papers, Discussions, and Recommendations on the Twenty-Fifth Amendment and Issues of Inability and Disability among Presidents of the United States.* Rochester, NY: University of Rochester Press, 2001.

War Power

See Commander in Chief.

War Powers Resolution

Legislation passed in 1973 to limit the president's power to over U.S. forces abroad without congressional approval. The War Powers Resolution states that the president can commit U.S. forces in only three cases:

1. When Congress has declared war,

2. In case of an attack on the United States, its territories, or its armed forces, or

3. In any situation where the law gives the president specific authority to commit troops.

It requires the president to consult with Congress before introducing U.S. forces into hostilities and to report any such commitment to Congress within forty-eight hours. The president is required to terminate any troop commitment within sixty to ninety days unless Congress specifically approve its continuation, or if Congress is unable to meet because of an attack on the United States.

President Richard M. Nixon (1969–1974) **vetoed,** or rejected the **resolution,** saying it would impose dangerous and **unconstitutional** restrictions on presidential authority. Congress, however, overrode his veto and passed the resolution without Nixon's signature.

The War Powers Resolution was controversial when it was adopted and it has remained so. Presidents have refused to invoke the law—or even concede its constitutionality—while Congress has been reluctant to challenge the president directly.

Recent Developments

The War Powers Resolution has done little to restrain U.S. presidents from using force without explicit congressional approval. Most of the presidents who have served since passage of the resolution have deployed troops on their own authority, only later receiving official approval from Congress. These deployments often triggered clashes with Congress over the scope of the president's authority.

The most recent clash over the president's war powers involved the Authorization for Use of Military Force Against Iraq Resolution of 2002. This resolution gave President George W. Bush (2001–2009) the authority to use military force to "defend the national security of the United States against the continuing threat posed by Iraq; and enforce all relevant United Nations Security Council Resolutions regarding Iraq." President Bush cited the resolution as authority for the subsequent U.S. invasion of Iraq in 2003.

Congressional opponents of the war argued that the invasion was unauthorized because Iraq posed no credible threat to the United States. Some legislators who voted in favor of the resolution later argued they did not mean for it to be a blank check to invade Iraq. They asserted that they meant only to give the president the power to use force if necessary to protect national security. As in earlier confrontations, the president was able to maintain the U.S. military commitment in Iraq, despite the growing unpopularity of the war and opposition in Congress.

See also: Commander in Chief; Presidency and Congress.

Washington, George, Administration of (1789–1797)

Government under the first president of the United States. The election of George Washington in 1789 as the first president of the United States was never in doubt. Upon receiving word of his election on April 14 from the secretary of Congress, Charles Thomson, Washington took his time getting to New York, "lest unseemly haste suggest that he was improperly eager for the office." Because he believed that the future of the government depended largely on its acceptance by the people, he was concerned with the way his travels through the states would be received. The popular praise that greeted him during the trip made obvious his country's devotion to him. The nation's first president arrived in New York just in time to be inaugurated on April 30.

Making the Presidency Safe for Democracy

Washington's personality and popularity not only made him an vital source of unity and legitimacy to the newly formed government; it also made him seem, to people who were suspicious of strong **executive** power, extremely dangerous. Thus, many of the conflicts of Washington's administration revolved around efforts to make strong executive power compatible with representative democracy. Washington's conduct of the office revealed his great sensitivity to the task of obtaining popular support for the presidency. In addition, he understood that the activities of the executive office's first occupant were of great symbolic importance.

One controversial issue was the form of address for the new president. A committee of the House of Representatives suggested simply "the President of the United States," as in the Constitution. The Senate in May 1789, at the behest of Vice President John Adams (1797–1801), rejected the House report. Adams, believing that "titles and politically inspired elegance were essential aspects of strong government," supported the title "His Highness the President of the United States and protector of their Liberties." Washington made known his annoyance at Adams's efforts. On May 27, the Senate agreed that the chief executive should have no fancier title than "the President of the United States."

Forming the Executive Department

During Washington's first term, Congress passed **bills** setting up three major departments of government: State, Treasury, and War. The heads of these departments were nominated by the president and **ratified** by the Senate.

For secretary of state, Washington chose Thomas Jefferson (1801–1809), who as minister to France had shown himself to be an excellent diplomat. Alexander Hamilton, a recognized expert on finance and **commerce,** became head of the Treasury Department. General Henry Knox, a diligent administrator, who as chief of artillery had served Washington reliably during the Revolutionary War, was selected to be secretary of war.

Edmund Randolph of Virginia became the first attorney general. The office of attorney general did not yet possess the status of a department, but after 1792, its occupant regularly attended cabinet meetings and served as legal adviser of the president and of the department heads.

In forming the cabinet and the executive branch, the Washington administration employed highly informal procedures. In general, the administration was ad hoc and personal. The notion of a "president's cabinet" did not even take form during the early years of Washington's terms. Washington did not use the word *cabinet* until April 1793, and he did not call formal meetings of the department heads until close to the end of his first term.

Washington's appointments to minor jobs in the government also were made with attention to the need to establish the legitimacy of the fledgling national government. As the various enactments creating the major departments became law during his first term, the president found himself with nearly a thousand offices to fill. Considering these appointments important, Washington devoted an enormous amount of time to them: "no collector of customs, captain of a cutter, keeper of a lighthouse, or surveyor of revenue was appointed except after specific consideration by the President."

Presidential Supremacy

In assuming the tasks of nation building, the Washington administration established the critical **precedent** that executive authority was solely the president's. This view, held by Washington, prevailed against competing ideas of public administration that believed either the Senate or individual cabinet officers share fully in the operations of the executive department.

One controversial bill, for example, involving the creation of the State Department, raised the issue of where the power to dismiss, or fire, an executive official should lie. Opponents of a strong presidency argued that the constitutional provision that presidents could appoint officials only with Senate approval implied that they could dismiss officials only with Senate approval. Favoring a strong presidency, President Washington and James Madison (1809–1817), his chief congressional ally, argued that presidents would be weakened if they were denied the power of removal.

Madison effectively led the fight in the House against senatorial interference with presidential removals. The Senate, however, was evenly divided, and the final vote was tied. Vice President Adams, as presiding officer, broke the tie by supporting presidential supremacy over the executive department.

The eventual consent of Congress to presidential supremacy over the executive departments was a tribute to Washington's devotion to the separation of powers. Washington did make recommendations to Congress, although sparingly, but he made no special effort to get his program through, "nor did he attempt during his first term to achieve by executive orders any matter which the strictest interpretation of the Constitution could regard as within the **legislative** domain." Washington adhered to the view that the presidential **veto** power properly extended only to bills of doubtful constitutionality, not to unwise policy.

The Beginning of Party Conflict

Washington's conduct as president expressed his belief that the presidency is a nonpartisan office. Like most of the Framers of the Constitution, he disapproved of "factions" and did not see himself as the leader of any political party. Although Washington insisted on being master of the executive department, trying to influence elections or the legislative process was contrary to his principles. He believed his primary duty was to enforce the laws.

Hamilton and Jefferson

Washington's idea of the presidency did not endure, however. Party conflict grew out of the sharp differences between Hamilton and Jefferson, differences that began during Washington's first term and became incompatible during the second term. These differences first surfaced in response to Hamilton's financial measures for the "adequate support of public credit," which he proposed in a series of reports presented to Congress between 1790 and 1791. These measures called for the assumption by the national government of the war debts of the states, the creation of a national bank, and a **tariff** system designed to protect infant industries in the United States.

Jefferson did not oppose all of Hamilton's measures—for example, he approved payment of

SPOTLIGHT

Precedents Established by George Washington

As the first president of the United States, George Washington (1789–1797) was very aware of the influence that he would have on the future of the presidency. As he once wrote to James Madison, "As the first of everything, in our situation will serve to establish a Precedent, it is devoutly wished on my part, that these precedents may be fixed on true principles." He knew that he would be making choices, setting traditions, and setting policy not dictated in the Constitution that might be copied by future presidents. One of the first precedents that Washington set was the formation of the cabinet, a group of presidential advisers that became part of the executive branch. The first cabinet members included Thomas Jefferson (1801–1809), who was Washington's secretary of state, and Alexander Hamilton, Washington's secretary of the treasury and closest adviser.

Another precedent set by George Washington came in the form of foreign policy. France and Great Britain went to war during Washington's presidency. Many people believed that the newly formed United States would get involved, especially since France had been the Americans' ally in the American Revolution (1775–1783). Washington made the decision not to interfere and to remain **neutral.** Future presidents followed this precedent of **neutrality** until the United States entered World War I (1914–1918) in 1917. During his presidency, Washington also took steps to form a friendship with Britain after the Revolution. This friendship, while unsteady at first, strengthened as the United States grew as a country and is still in existence today.

Washington also set the precedent of using force to suppress those who attempted to defy the laws of the federal government. This precedent was set during the Whiskey Rebellion of 1794, during which Pennsylvania farmers launched a series of attacks on federal agents to demonstrate their opposition to an excise tax on whiskey. Washington called up the militia in order to stop the uprising. Future presidents followed this example of using the armed forces to keep order in the nation, although the responsibility of federal law enforcement has been divided and shifted among different organizations over the years.

Of course, not all of the precedents set by George Washington were intentional. One that was set by accident was the tradition of each president serving a maximum of two terms. Washington left the presidency after two terms because of personal reasons. Yet, every president after Washington, except for Franklin D. Roosevelt (1933–1945), followed this tradition. It became part of the Constitution after the **ratification** of the Twenty-Second Amendment in 1951. Upon leaving the office of the president in 1797, Washington again set a precedent by giving a farewell address, a tradition that is still followed.

the domestic and foreign debt. Jefferson, and eventually Madison, opposed Hamilton's program for a national bank. According to Jefferson and Madison, Hamilton's plan would establish national institutions and policies that go beyond the powers of Congress. Furthermore, the proposed domestic and international programs assumed a major role for the president in formulating and carrying out public policy. Thus, Jefferson and Madison believed the more decentralizing and democratic institutions—Congress and the states—would be subordinate to the chief executive. In turn, this would diminish **popular sovereignty** and push the United States toward a British-style monarchy.

The Neutrality Proclamation of 1793

The rift between Hamilton and Jefferson was aggravated by a foreign policy controversy during Washington's second term, centering on the war between Britain and France that broke out in 1793. As with domestic policy, the conflict over foreign affairs was linked to opposing views of the appropriate extent of presidential power. President Washington issued the **Neutrality** Proclamation of 1793, which declared that the duties and interests of the United States required that it "should with sincerity and good faith adopt and pursue a conduct friendly and impartial to the belligerent powers." To Americans, it prohibited "committing, aiding, or abetting hostilities against any of the said powers, or by carrying to them any of those articles which are deemed contraband by the modern usage of nations."

The precedent established during the Washington administration for the executive to voice a policy of neutrality was less important than the larger principle in the debate that took place between Washington's leading advisers. The issue was whether the president was to be limited by the letter of constitution, or be considered a sovereign head of state with discretion to act except when the Constitution specifically noted limitations.

Ultimately, this debate caused strains that made party conflict inevitable. The full implications of this conflict between the Federalists, who shared Hamilton's point of view, and the Democratic-Republicans, who shared Jefferson's, became clear during the presidency of John Adams, who took office in 1797. Still, this party conflict never became as raw and disruptive as the Framers feared

factional strife might be. The enduring limits of **factionalism** in the United States were probably attributable largely to Washington's forceful example of nonpartisanship. To some extent, Washington sought to deal with the divisive conflict between the Hamiltonians and Jeffersonians by avoiding it, by choosing to continue to "preside" rather than to lead and direct. He thereby exerted a moderating influence at a time when maintaining unity was critical to the survival of the new government. In domestic and foreign policy, Washington did take stands, usually tilting to the Hamiltonian point of view. Yet his extraordinary stature and popularity, combined with a commitment to the existence of a strong and independent legislature, restrained partisan strife as long as he presided over the nation. Moreover, Washington's renunciation of party leadership, clearly articulated in his Farewell Address, left his successors a legacy of presidential "impartiality" that has never been completely eclipsed. Thus, even after a formal party system emerged, the Washington precedent demanded that the chief executive lead the nation, not just the party that governed the nation.

The Rise of Party Politics and the Triumph of Jeffersonianism

The end of Washington's administration marked an important change in the executive office from a nonpartisan to a partisan institution. The leaders of the first great party conflicts in the United States—John Adams, Alexander Hamilton, Thomas Jefferson, and James Madison—viewed **partisanship** with great disfavor. Yet the struggles that followed Washington's terms made open party conflict a central part of the American presidency. Thereafter, presidents might attempt to rise above party, but partisanship had become an unavoidable condition of effective presidential leadership.

Washington's Retirement and the 1796 Election

As the end of 1795 approached, the paramount question for most public figures in the United States was whether Washington would accept another term as president. The Constitution originally imposed no limit on presidential terms. Washington, could have stayed in office had he chosen to do so.

Washington was anxious to return to Mount Vernon, however, and in September 1796, he announced his retirement, an event marked by the release of his Farewell Address, published without ceremony. Washington's voluntary retirement set a precedent for limiting presidents to two terms, a practice that endured for nearly 150 years. His decision eased somewhat the Jeffersonians' concerns about the dangerous use of executive power. Washington's retirement also resulted in a more partisan form of presidential politics. As long as the first president was on the scene, he was able to restrain open party conflict. This situation did not last.

See also: Adams, John, Administration of (1797–1801); Cabinet; Political Parties and the President.

Further Reading

Burns, James MacGregor, and Susan Dunn. *George Washington.* New York: Times Books, Henry Holt and Company, 2004.

Ellis, Joseph, J. *His Excellency: George Washington.* New York: Alfred A. Knopf, 2004.

Washington, Martha

See First Lady.

Watergate Scandal

A political scandal that ultimately led to the resignation of the president of the United States. The Watergate affair was perhaps the greatest political scandal in United States history. President Richard Nixon (1969–1974) resigned on August 9, 1974, when it became apparent that the House of Representatives would **impeach** him for "high crimes and misdemeanors" and the Senate would convict him. In addition, a number of Nixon aides, including his first attorney general and campaign manager, John Mitchell, would spend time in jail because of the scandal.

At its simplest, the Watergate affair was "a third-rate burglary," followed by a cover-up on the part of President Nixon and his aides. In the summer of 1972, several employees of the Committee to Re-elect the President (dubbed "CREEP"), a fundraising group for Nixon's 1972 reelection effort, were arrested after they were discovered breaking into and bugging the Democratic National Committee's offices at the Watergate Hotel and office complex in Washington, D.C. The break-in was not a major issue in the 1972 election, but the next year a Senate committee began an investigation.

During the investigation, a presidential aide revealed that Nixon had secretly taped Oval Office conversations with aides. When the Watergate special prosecutor, Archibald Cox, ordered Nixon to surrender the tapes in October 1973, Nixon ordered Cox fired. Because Nixon's attorney general, Elliot Richardson, and assistant attorney general, William D. Ruckelshaus, refused to fire Cox, the task was carried out by Solicitor General Robert Bork, igniting a constitutional crisis dubbed the "Saturday night massacre."

Nixon soon handed over the tapes Cox had sought. In the summer of 1974, the Supreme Court ruled that Nixon had to surrender even more tapes, which indicated that he had played an active role in covering up the Watergate scandal. Nixon resigned the presidency when his **impeachment** and conviction appeared certain. The impeachment articles charged him with obstruction of justice, abuse of presidential powers, and contempt of Congress.

See also: Nixon, Richard M., Administration of (1969–1974).

Further Reading

Rosen, James. *The Strong Man: John Mitchell and the Secrets of Watergate.* New York: Doubleday, 2008.

Woodward, Bob, and Carl Bernstein. *All the President's Men.* New York: Simon & Schuster, 1994.

Whig Party (1834–1856)

A political party organized to oppose the Jacksonian Democrats. Whigs were nineteenth-century modernizers who saw President Andrew Jackson

(1829–1837) as a dangerous man with strong opposition to the forces of social, economic, and moral change. As Jackson purged his opponents, **vetoed** internal improvements, and killed the **Bank of the United States,** alarmed local and influential leaders fought back.

The Whigs, led by Henry Clay, endorsed Clay's vision of the "American System." They demanded government support for a more modern, market-oriented economy, in which skill, expertise, and bank credit would count for more than physical strength or land ownership. They also sought to promote industrialization through high **tariffs,** a business-oriented money supply based on a national bank, and a vigorous program of government-funded "internal improvements," especially expansion of the road and canal systems. To help modernize Americans, the Whigs helped create public schools, private colleges, charities, and cultural institutions.

The Democrats, by contrast, harkened to the Jeffersonian ideal of an equalitarian agricultural society, insisting that traditional farm life bred **republican** simplicity, whereas modernization threatened to create a politically powerful caste of rich aristocrats who might subvert democracy. In general, the Democrats enacted their policies at the national level; the Whigs succeeded in passing modernization projects in most states.

Although the Whigs won votes in every socioeconomic class, including the poorest, they appealed especially to more prosperous Americans. The Democrats likewise won support from all groups, but they often sharpened their appeals to lower-income people by ridiculing the aristocratic airs of the Whigs. Most bankers, storekeepers, factory owners, master mechanics, clerks, and professionals favored the Whigs. Commercially oriented farmers in the North voted Whig, as did most large-scale planters in the South.

In general, the commercial and manufacturing towns and cities were heavily Whig, except for Democratic wards filled with recent Irish Catholic and German immigrants. Waves of Protestant religious revivals in the 1830s injected a moralistic element into the Whig ranks. Nonreligious individuals who found themselves the targets of moral crusades, such as calls for prohibition, denounced the Whigs as Puritans and sought refuge in the Democratic Party. Rejecting the automatic party loyalty that was the hallmark of the tight Democratic Party organization, the Whigs suffered from **factionalism.** Yet the party's superb network of newspapers provided an internal information system.

Whigs clashed with Democrats throughout what historians term the "Second American Party System." When they controlled the Senate, Whigs passed a **censure** motion in 1834 denouncing Jackson's arrogant assumption of **executive** power in the face of the true will of the people as represented by Congress. Backing Henry Clay in 1832 and then several candidates in 1836, the Whigs rallied in 1840 behind a popular general, William Henry Harrison (1841); his successful campaign proved that the national Whig Party could win. Moreover, in the 1840s Whigs won 49 percent of gubernatorial elections, with strong bases in the manufacturing Northeast and in the so-called border states further south.

Yet the party revealed limited staying power. Whigs were ready to enact their programs in 1841, but Harrison died and was succeeded by John Tyler (1841–1845), a Democrat who never believed in Whiggery and was, in fact, disowned by the party while he was president. Factionalism ruined the party's program and helped defeat Henry Clay, the Whig presidential candidate, in 1844. In 1848, opportunity beckoned as the Democrats split. By ignoring Clay and nominating a famous war hero, General Zachary Taylor (1850–1853), the Whigs papered over their deepening splits on slavery, and they won. The trend, however, was for the Democrats to gain followers and for the Whigs to lose more and more states and districts. After the close 1844 contest, the Democratic advantage widened and the Whigs could win the White House only if the Democrats split.

The Whigs were unable to deal with the slavery issue after 1850. Almost all of their southern leaders owned slaves. The northeastern Whigs, led by Daniel Webster, represented business leaders who loved the nation and the national market, but cared little about slavery. Many Whig voters in the North, however, felt slavery was incompatible with a free labor-free market economy, but no one discovered a compromise that would keep the party united.

At the same time, the growing economy made full-time careers in business or law much more attractive than public service for ambitious young Whigs. For example, the party leader in Illinois, Abraham Lincoln, simply abandoned politics for several years after 1849. When new issues of nativism, prohibition, and antislavery burst on the scene in the mid-1850s, no one looked to the fast-disintegrating Whig Party for answers. In the North, most ex-Whigs joined the new Republican Party, and in the South, they flocked to a new, short-lived American ("Know Nothing") Party. During the Lincoln administration (1861–1865), ex-Whigs enacted much of the "American System." In the end, America adopted Whig economic policies coupled with a Democratic strong presidency.

See also: Democratic Party (1828–); Republican Party (1854–).

White House

The Executive Mansion in Washington, D.C., and the home to every United States president except George Washington (1789–1797). Although he never lived there, the nation's first president was instrumental in determining the location and appearance of the White House. Under Washington's direction, French engineer and architect Pierre Charles L'Enfant mapped out the new capital city. Together, they selected the site for the presidential residence.

Washington appointed three commissioners to oversee development of the federal city and its buildings, and in 1792, they conducted a public contest to choose the design for the house. The winner was James Hoban, a self-taught, Irish-born master builder who, in addition to the honor of becoming the architect of the "President's House," as Washington called it, received a $500 gold medal and a plot of land for his personal use. The commissioners subsequently hired Hoban as general supervisor of construction.

Hoban designed a simple, three-story, boxlike structure that incorporated the harmonious proportions of late-eighteenth-century Georgian architecture. The plan called for **balustrades,** a hipped roof, and columns at the main entrance. Symmetrical, rectangular windows would provide the main exterior ornamentation: windows on the first floor would be tall, with alternating arched and triangular pediments.

Hoban's interior design included a large entrance hall with a spacious ceremonial room on the east end of the building (today's East Room) balanced by a formal dining room on the west end (the State Dining Room). Three smaller drawing rooms (the Green Room, the Blue Room, and the Red Room) would line the transverse corridor joining the East Room and the State Dining Room. Hoban's plan for these rooms on the first floor (also called the "state floor") has not been changed significantly since he designed them.

Master stonemason Collen Williamson laid the cornerstone of the President's House on October 13, 1792, eleven months before George Washington laid the cornerstone of the Capitol. The White House is, then, the oldest federal building in the District of Columbia.

Money was in short supply from the beginning, and Congress held the purse strings tightly. To cut costs, Washington instructed Hoban to eliminate the third floor. (This floor eventually was added in 1927.) Major construction took eight years and cost approximately $240,000, but much work remained to be done when President John Adams (1797–1801) and his wife, Abigail, became the first residents of the President's House in November 1800, shortly before the end of Adams's term. In fact, only six rooms in the house were usable. "Not a chamber is finished of the whole," wrote Abigail Adams of her new home. There was little firewood to warm the large, drafty rooms and no indoor bathroom. Plaster was still wet, the main staircase was unfinished, and water had to be carried to the house from a park five blocks away.

Still, Abigail Adams made the best of things in her four-month stay. She used the vast, unfinished East Room as a place to hang her laundry, and each week she and President Adams held large, formal receptions—then called "levees"—in the Oval Room (known today as the Blue Room).

Thomas Jefferson (1801–1809) introduced a different style of living when he succeeded Adams as president. Instead of large receptions, he held small dinner parties where he seated no one by importance or rank. In another change, the president adopted the more democratic gesture of shaking hands with his guests instead of bowing to them, a custom favored by his predecessors.

SPOTLIGHT

White House Renovations

Construction began on the White House in 1792 under the supervision of President George Washington (1789–1797). The architect of the building was James Hoban, an Irish immigrant, who won a $500 prize in a competition held to find a designer for the presidential home. He ultimately would be involved in many of the house's renovations and updates.

Most of the renovations of the White House have been the result of the differing tastes of the presidents and their families, although some were made necessary by fires and age. The first renovation of the White House or, as it was then called, the President's House, was undertaken after British forces burned the building during the War of 1812 (1812–1814). After the war, only the exterior shell of the building remained. Hoban was brought in to reconstruct the building, following its original design. In the 1820s, a north and south portico were added, again, under the direction of Hoban. Smaller additions and renovations completed during the 1800s included the addition of a greenhouse and conservatories (which were eventually replaced by the West Wing), and a complete redesign of the interior done by Louis C. Tiffany and commissioned by President Chester A. Arthur (1881–1885).

In 1902, Edith Roosevelt, wife of Theodore Roosevelt (1901–1909), went to architect Charles McKim to plan a renovation of the house. This renovation involved enlarging the family living quarters, building a new wing for the president and his staff, and building a new area for receiving guests. Around this time, President Roosevelt officially named the house the White House. The new office wing added by McKim became the West Wing and was remodeled during the William Howard Taft (1909–1913), Herbert Hoover (1929–1933), and Franklin D. Roosevelt (1933–1945) administrations. The Oval Office was added during the Taft renovation. Other renovations made in the early twentieth century include the addition of the Rose Garden during the Woodrow Wilson administration (1913–1921), the addition of a third floor during the Calvin Coolidge administration (1923–1929), and the addition of a new East Wing designed by Lorenzo Winslow and commissioned by Franklin D. Roosevelt in 1942.

The most recent major renovation of the White House took place during the Harry Truman's administration after it was discovered that the house had been made unstable by age and the addition of the third floor. The house was completely gutted, leaving behind only the outside walls, the third floor, and the roof. The interior of the house was then rebuilt. Subsequent renovations include he addition of a press center in the West Terrace in the 1960s and the restoration of the exterior that took place in the 1970s and 1980s. Recent renovation efforts have focused primarily on preserving the history of the house.

James Madison (1809–1817) and his wife, Dolley, a well-known hostess, succeeded Jefferson in the President's House. Congress **appropriated** $14,000 for household furnishings and $12,000 for repairs when Madison took office. Dolley Madison redecorated, under the direction of Latrobe, who designed Greek Revival furniture for the Oval Room. In 1814, during the War of 1812, the British invaded Washington and burned the Capitol, the departmental buildings, the Navy Yard, and the White House. Through a spyglass from the White House roof, Dolley Madison watched British troops approach. Just before leaving the house, she demanded that Gilbert Stuart's portrait of George Washington be saved. Fire gutted the interior. Only the sandstone exterior walls, blackened from smoke and flames, were left standing.

Renovations and Refurbishings

The White House has been hollowed out and its interior rebuilt twice—after the fire of 1814 and from 1949 to 1952 during the administration of Harry S. Truman (1945–1953), when the building was found to be structurally unsound. Major, but less encompassing, structural renovation took place during Theodore Roosevelt's (1901–1909) administration in 1902 and during Calvin Coolidge's (1923–1929) administration in 1927. Between 1817 and 1902, however, the White House underwent only minor changes in its structure, although every first family engaged in some degree of redecorating, depending on the generosity of Congress.

The White House Today

The White House contains 132 rooms, including 35 bathrooms, 28 fireplaces, and over 400 windows. The residence, which is 170 feet long and 85 feet wide, consists of four floors (referred to as the ground, first, second, and third floors) and two basements; the West and East Wings each have three floors. The ground floor, opening onto the South Portico, is visible only from the south side of the house. The five staterooms usually open for tours are on the first floor, which contains the North Portico entrance facing Pennsylvania Avenue. The second floor contains seven historic rooms and the principal living quarters. On the third floor are additional rooms for the first family, the solarium, guest bedrooms, and storage areas.

The Committee for the Preservation of the White House works closely with the White House Historical Association to acquire furniture, paintings, and decorative objects through private donations. In addition, Congress **appropriates** funds at the start of each presidential term for the president to have the family quarters painted and decorated.

White House Chief of Staff

See White House.

Wilson, Woodrow, Administration of (1913–1921)

Government under the twenty-eighth president of the United States. After finishing law school in 1882, Woodrow Wilson established a law partnership in Atlanta with a law school friend. He quit the profession in 1883, however, to enroll in Johns Hopkins University as a graduate student of history and government.

At Johns Hopkins, Wilson distinguished himself as a brilliant student. In 1885, he published his first book, *Congressional Government,* which argued that Congress had become the dominant branch of government and that it should adopt a system of governing patterned after the British Parliament. The book received critical acclaim and served as Wilson's dissertation. He was awarded his doctorate degree in 1886.

In 1890, Wilson accepted a professorship at Princeton University. Princeton's trustees unanimously elected him president of the university in 1902. Wilson regarded his new job as an opportunity to implement his ideas about education. He introduced a system providing for small scholarly discussion groups and close faculty supervision of students. Wilson became known as a crusader for democratic principles in education.

In 1910, New Jersey's Democratic Party leaders proposed to Wilson that he run for governor. They hoped the fame he had gained while president of Princeton would carry him to the New Jersey statehouse. Once in office, Wilson pushed a series of reforms through the legislature that attracted national attention, including laws establishing direct primaries, workers' compensation, and antitrust measures. His efforts also led to improved regulation of utilities and the reorganization of the public school system. By 1912, Democrats were considering him as a presidential candidate.

At the 1912 Democratic National Convention in Baltimore, Speaker of the House Champ Clark of Missouri was the favorite candidate. Although Clark led Wilson in the early ballots, he could not win a majority. On the fourteenth ballot, the Democratic leader William Jennings Bryan abandoned Clark to support Wilson. Wilson was finally nominated on the forty-sixth ballot.

Wilson's election to the presidency was virtually assured when former president Theodore Roosevelt (1901–1909) split the Republican Party by running for president as the candidate of the Progressive Party. Of the 15 million votes cast, Wilson received only 6.3 million, but Republicans divided their votes between Roosevelt and William Howard Taft (1909–1913), who was running for reelection. Wilson received 435 electoral votes, while Roosevelt received 88 and Taft 8.

Presidency

Once in office, Wilson demonstrated the same independence and innovation he had shown as governor and university president. He delivered his first annual message to Congress in person on April 8, 1913, which no president had done since John Adams (1797–1801). He also established weekly press conferences.

Wilson fulfilled a campaign promise to lower **tariffs** by signing the Underwood Tariff Act of 1913. The act cut tariff rates to their lowest levels since before the Civil War (1861–1865) and provided for the levying of the first income tax since the Sixteenth Amendment (1913) had made such taxes legal. At Wilson's urging, Congress passed the Federal Reserve Act of 1913, which created a system of regional federal banks to regulate currency and the banking industry.

He supported the establishment of the Federal Trade Commission in 1914 to ensure fair business practices. That year he also signed the Clayton Antitrust Act, which strengthened the government's powers to break up monopolies. In 1916, Congress passed the Adamson Act at Wilson's request, which established the eight-hour day for railroad workers.

When World War I (1914–1918) began, Wilson announced that the United States would stay out of the conflict. German submarines in the Atlantic Ocean, however, were not observing U.S. **neutrality.** In May 1915, a German submarine sank the British passenger ship *Lusitania* with more than 100 Americans aboard. The incident led Wilson to issue several diplomatic protests, until the Germans agreed not to prey on passenger ships and to place other restrictions on their submarine warfare.

In the 1916 presidential election, Wilson did not face a divided Republican Party as he had in 1912. The Republicans nominated Supreme Court justice Charles Evans Hughes. Wilson campaigned on his domestic accomplishments and his success in keeping the United States out of war. In one of the closest presidential elections in history, Wilson defeated Hughes 277–254 in the electoral college. Had Wilson lost any of the ten states he won that had twelve or more electoral votes he would have lost the election.

Wilson, who tried to mediate an end to the war in Europe, made a speech on January 22, 1917, that called for a "peace without victory" that would end the fighting. He also called for the establishment of a league of nations, an international body that would prevent and settle disputes between members. A week after Wilson's speech, however, the Germans, who expected the United States to enter the war, announced they would attack without warning any ship passing through a wide zone in the Atlantic Ocean. Wilson responded to the submarine offensive by severing diplomatic relations with Germany on February 3. When the Germans continued their submarine warfare in defiance of Wilson's protests, he asked Congress on April 2, 1917, for a declaration of war. Within four days, both houses had overwhelmingly passed the declaration.

Congress delegated broad emergency powers to Wilson to marshal the nation's resources, build an army, and prosecute the war. He pushed the Selective Service Act through Congress, took control of the railroads, established the War Industries Board to oversee the economy, and instituted many other emergency measures.

With the addition of U.S. troops on the Allied side, the war went badly for Germany. An **armistice** was signed on November 11, 1918. After U.S. entry into the war, Wilson had outlined a plan for the maintenance of world peace once the war was over. The basis of this plan was his Fourteen Points, which included freedom of the seas, removal of trade barriers, an end to secret treaties, and a reduction of armaments.

In December 1918, Wilson sailed to France to attend the Versailles peace conference. Europeans hailed the American president as a hero, and he dominated the deliberations of the Allies. Nevertheless, he was forced to make many concessions to European leaders to gain their endorsement of his Fourteen Points and the establishment of a League of Nations. The treaty produced by the conference imposed a harsh peace on Germany that included heavy war reparations and the loss of its colonies.

Wilson submitted the Treaty of Versailles to the Senate for approval on July 10, 1919, but he could not persuade two-thirds of the Senate to support it. A group of senators led by Republican Henry Cabot Lodge of Massachusetts objected to the provision within the treaty establishing the League of Nations. They would not vote for the treaty without attaching reservations that Wilson opposed. On September 4, 1919, Wilson launched a speaking tour of the western states to mobilize public support for the treaty. On September 26, after delivering speeches in twenty-nine cities, Wilson became ill in Pueblo, Colorado, and was forced to cancel the rest of his tour. He returned to Washington, D.C., where he suffered a severe stroke on October 2.

The stroke left the president almost entirely incapacitated for several months, and he never completely recovered his strength. While Wilson recuperated, the Senate debated the Treaty of Versailles. Wilson refused to compromise with Lodge to gain passage of the treaty and advised his supporters against accepting it with Lodge's reservations. The Senate rejected the treaty on November 19, 1919.

When Wilson left office he retired to a home on S Street in Washington, D.C. He formed a law partnership, but did not practice. He lived in near seclusion until he died on February 3, 1924, from another stroke.

Wilson married Ellen Louise Axson, the daughter of a Presbyterian minister, on June 24, 1885. They had three daughters. Ellen Wilson died on August 6, 1914, in the White House. On December 18, 1915, Wilson married Edith Bolling Galt, a forty-three-year-old widow. After Wilson suffered his stroke in 1919, Edith Wilson restricted access to her husband. During the president's convalescence, he conducted much of his presidential business through Edith. Historians have speculated that she may have made many presidential decisions for her husband.

See also: Harding, Warren, Administration of (1921–1923); Taft, William Howard, Administration of (1909–1913).

Further Reading

Brands, H. W. *Woodrow Wilson.* New York: Times Books, 2003.

Maynard, W. Barksdale. *Woodrow Wilson: Princeton to the Presidency.* New Haven, CT: Yale University Press, 2008.

PART THREE

Primary Source Library

United States Constitution, Article I, Section 7, 1789

Article I, Section 7, of the United States Constitution describes the president's responsibility to approve or veto *bills passed by Congress. It also details how Congress can override a presidential veto. This article establishes an essential part of the system of* checks *and* balances *between the* legislative *and* executive *branches of government.*

United States Constitution, Article I, Section 7

Section 7. All bills for raising Revenue shall originate in the House of Representatives; but the Senate may propose or concur with Amendments as on other Bills.

Every Bill which shall have passed the House of Representatives and the Senate, shall, before it become a Law, be presented to the President of the United States; if he approve he shall sign it, but if not he shall return it, with his Objections to that House in which it shall have originated, who shall enter the Objections at large on their Journal, and proceed to reconsider it. If after such Reconsideration two thirds of that House shall agree to pass the Bill, it shall be sent, together with the Objections, to the other House, by which it shall likewise be reconsidered, and if approved by two thirds of that House, it shall become a Law. But in all such Cases the Votes of both Houses shall be determined by Yeas and Nays, and the Names of the Persons voting for and against the Bill shall be entered on the Journal of each House respectively. If any Bill shall not be returned by the President within ten Days (Sundays excepted) after it shall have been presented to him, the Same shall be a Law, in like Manner as if he had signed it, unless the Congress by their Adjournment prevent its Return, in which case it shall not be a Law.

Every Order, Resolution, or Vote to which the Concurrence of the Senate and House of Representatives may be necessary (except on a question of Adjournment) shall be presented to the President of the United States; and before the Same shall take Effect, shall be approved by him, or being disapproved by him, shall be repassed by two thirds of the Senate and House of Representatives, according to the Rules and Limitations prescribed in the Case of a Bill.

United States Constitution, Article II, Section 3, 1789

The president is given the responsibility for presenting the State of the Union address to Congress in Article II, Section 3. It goes on to grant the president the right to recommend legislation and the authority to convene special sessions of Congress. The last clause empowers the president to ensure that the laws passed by Congress are "faithfully executed."

United States Constitution, Article II, Section 3

He shall from time to time give to the Congress information of the state of the union, and recommend to their consideration such measures as he shall judge necessary and expedient; he may, on extraordinary occasions, convene both Houses, or either of them, and in case of disagreement between them, with respect to the time of adjournment, he may **adjourn** them to such time as he shall think proper; he shall receive ambassadors and other public ministers; he shall take care that the laws be faithfully executed, and shall commission all the officers of the United States.

Twelfth Amendment, 1804

The Twelfth Amendment, ratified in 1804, replaced Article II, Section 1, Clause 3, of the Constitution. The amendment specifies that members of the electoral college cast separate ballots for president and for vice president, thus preventing a recurrence of the situation that occurred in the Election of 1800, in which Thomas Jefferson (1801–1809) and Aaron Burr each received the same number of electoral votes. The amendment also modified the procedures by which the House of Representatives chooses a president when no candidate receives an electoral vote majority.

Twelfth Amendment

The Electors shall meet in their respective states and vote by ballot for President and Vice-President, one of whom, at least, shall not be an inhabitant of the same state with themselves; they shall name in their ballots the person voted for as President, and in distinct ballots the person voted for as Vice-President, and they shall make distinct lists of all persons voted for as President, and of all persons voted for as Vice-President, and of the number of votes for each, which lists they shall sign and certify, and transmit sealed to the seat of the government of the United States, directed to the President of the Senate;

The President of the Senate shall, in the presence of the Senate and House of Representatives, open all the certificates and the votes shall then be counted;

The person having the greatest Number of votes for President, shall be the President, if such number be a majority of the whole number of Electors appointed; and if no person have such majority, then from the persons having the highest numbers not exceeding three on the list of those voted for as President, the House of Representatives shall choose immediately, by ballot, the President. But in choosing the President, the votes shall be taken by states, the representation from each state having one vote; a quorum for this purpose shall consist of a member or members from two-thirds of the states, and a majority of all the states shall be necessary to a choice. And if the House of Representatives shall not choose a President whenever the right of choice shall devolve upon them, before the fourth day of March next following, then the Vice-President shall act as President, as in the case of the death or other constitutional disability of the President.

The person having the greatest number of votes as Vice-President, shall be the Vice-President, if such number be a majority of the whole number of Electors appointed, and if no person have a majority, then from the two highest numbers on the list, the Senate shall choose the Vice-President; a quorum for the purpose shall consist of two-thirds of the whole number of Senators, and a majority of the whole number shall be necessary to a choice. But no person constitutionally ineligible to the office of President shall be eligible to that of Vice-President of the United States.

See also: Electoral College in **The Presidency A to Z.**

Thomas Jefferson Being Robbed by King George III and Napoleon, 1809

An 1809 political cartoon portrays President Thomas Jefferson (1801–1809) (center) being robbed by England's King George III (r. 1760–1820) (left) and France's Emperor Napoleon Bonaparte (r. 1804–1815) (right). England and France were at war, and the cartoon symbolizes the war's effect on United States trade.

King Andrew I, 1832

An 1832 political cartoon portrays President Andrew Jackson (1829–1837) as a king, trampling the rights guaranteed by the U.S. Constitution, a ledger of Supreme Court decisions, and the watchwords virtue, liberty, *and* independence.

A Hard Road to Hoe, 1840

An 1840 campaign cartoon shows former president Andrew Jackson (1829–1837) leading President Martin Van Buren (1837–1841) to the White House for a second term. Van Buren, known as "Old Kinderhook" after his New York home in that region, lost to the "hard cider and log cabin" candidate William Henry Harrison (1841). His partisan rallying cry "OK!" entered the language as an expression of agreement.

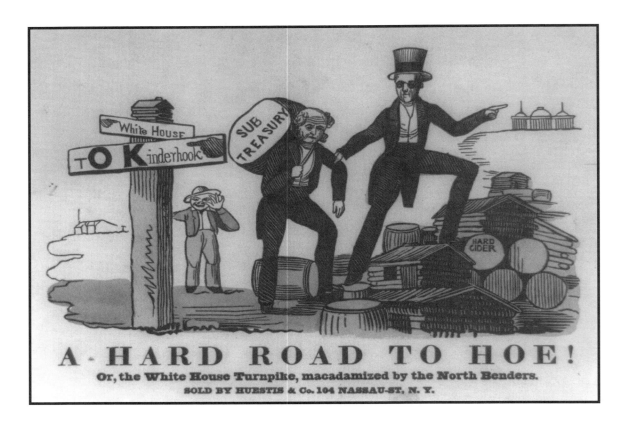

Keep the Ball Rolling, 1840

An 1840 political cartoon shows supporters of William Henry Harrison, who won the presidency, rolling a huge ball from town to town, singing, "It is the ball a-rolling on for Tippecanoe and Tyler too." Harrison's followers were referring to him as the hero of the Battle of Tippecanoe as well as his running mate John Tyler. Thus, the phrase "Keep the ball rolling" entered the language.

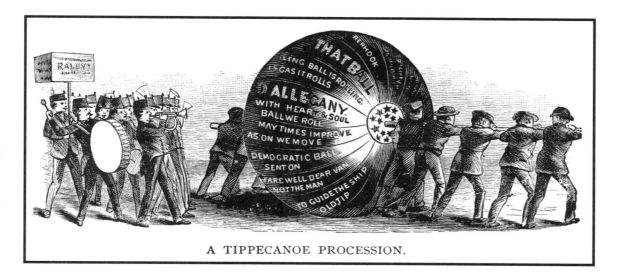

A TIPPECANOE PROCESSION.

Harrison Memorial Ribbon, 1841

One month after his inauguration, William Henry Harrison became the first president to die in office, serving the shortest presidential term—March 4, 1841 to April 4, 1841. Mourners wore ribbons such as this one to express their sorrow over the loss of the president.

James Buchanan's Inauguration, March 4, 1857

This earliest known photograph of a presidential inauguration was taken at the Capitol in Washington, D.C., on March 4, 1857, at James Buchanan's swearing in ceremony.

Union Is Dissolved! 1860

An 1860 broadside announces that the Union is dissolved after the secession of South Carolina, the first state to take such action. By the time of Abraham Lincoln's inauguration on March 4, 1861, six more Southern states had seceded and formed the Confederate States of America.

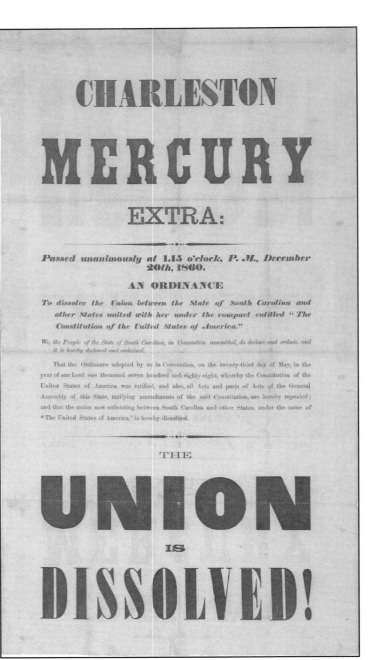

Lincoln's First Inaugural Address, 1861

With the threat of civil war looming, Abraham Lincoln, the first Republican president (1861–1865), presented a somber inaugural address in which he cautioned those who were dissatisfied with his election to move slowly before attempting to dissolve the Union. The president expressed his intention not to interfere with slavery where it already existed and noted that the United States government would not attack the South. He clearly places the issue of the pending war in the hands of the South.

Lincoln's First Inaugural Address

Fellow-Citizens of the United States:

In compliance with a custom as old as the Government itself, I appear before you to address you briefly and to take in your presence the oath prescribed by the Constitution of the United States to be taken by the President "before he enters on the execution of this office."

I do not consider it necessary at present for me to discuss those matters of administration about which there is no special anxiety or excitement.

Apprehension seems to exist among the people of the Southern States that by the accession of a Republican Administration their property and their peace and personal security are to be endangered. There has never been any reasonable cause for such apprehension. Indeed, the most ample evidence to the contrary has all the while existed and been open to their inspection. It is found in nearly all the published speeches of him who now addresses you. I do but quote from one of those speeches when I declare that—

I have no purpose, directly or indirectly, to interfere with the institution of slavery in the States where it exists. I believe I have no lawful right to do so, and I have no inclination to do so.

Those who nominated and elected me did so with full knowledge that I had made this and many similar declarations and had never recanted them; and more than this, they placed in the platform for my acceptance, and as a law to themselves and to me, the clear and emphatic resolution which I now read:

Resolved, That the maintenance inviolate of the rights of the States, and especially the right of each State to order and control its own domestic institutions according to its own judgment exclusively, is essential to that balance of power on which the perfection and endurance of our political fabric depend; and we denounce the lawless invasion by armed force of the soil of any State or Territory, no matter what pretext, as among the gravest of crimes.

My countrymen, one and all, think calmly and *well* upon this whole subject. Nothing valuable can be lost by taking time. If there be an object to *hurry* any of you in hot haste to a step which you would never take *deliberately,* that object will be frustrated by taking time; but no good object can be frustrated by it. Such of you as are now dissatisfied still have the old Constitution unimpaired, and, on the sensitive point, the laws of your own framing under it; while the new Administration will have no immediate power, if it would,

Primary Source Library

to change either. If it were admitted that you who are dissatisfied hold the right side in the dispute, there still is no single good reason for precipitate action. Intelligence, patriotism, Christianity, and a firm reliance on Him who has never yet forsaken this favored land are still competent to adjust in the best way all our present difficulty.

In *your* hands, my dissatisfied fellow-countrymen, and not in *mine,* is the momentous issue of civil war. The Government will not assail *you.* You can have no conflict without being yourselves the aggressors. *You* have no oath registered in heaven to destroy the Government, while I shall have the most solemn one to "preserve, protect, and defend it."

I am loath to close. We are not enemies, but friends. We must not be enemies. Though passion may have strained it must not break our bonds of affection. The mystic chords of memory, stretching from every battlefield and patriot grave to every living heart and hearthstone all over this broad land, will yet swell the chorus of the Union, when again touched, as surely they will be, by the better angels of our nature.

See also: Lincoln, Abraham, Administration of (1861–1865), in **The Presidency A to Z.**

Lincoln's Second Inaugural Address, 1865

As President Lincoln (1861–1865) gave his Second Inaugural Address to the nation, the Civil War was winding down and the Union's victory imminent. Lincoln called for reconciliation between the sections of the country and a lasting peace. He called on the people to bind up the nation's wounds and to care for the wounded, the widowed, and the orphaned in both North and South.

Lincoln's Second Inaugural Address

Fellow-Countrymen:
At this second appearing to take the oath of the Presidential office there is less occasion for an extended address than there was at the first. Then a statement somewhat in detail of a course to be pursued seemed fitting and proper. Now, at the expiration of four years, during which public declarations have been constantly called forth on every point and phase of the great contest which still absorbs the attention and engrosses the energies of the nation, little that is new could be presented. The progress of our arms, upon which all else chiefly depends, is as well known to the public as to myself, and it is, I trust, reasonably satisfactory and encouraging to all. With high hope for the future, no prediction in regard to it is ventured.

On the occasion corresponding to this four years ago all thoughts were anxiously directed to an impending civil war. All dreaded it, all sought to avert it. While the inaugural address was being delivered from this place, devoted altogether to *saving* the Union without war, urgent agents were in the city seeking to *destroy* it without war—

seeking to dissolve the Union and divide effects by negotiation. Both parties deprecated war, but one of them would *make* war rather than let the nation survive, and the other would *accept* war rather than let it perish, and the war came.

One-eighth of the whole population were colored slaves, not distributed generally over the Union, but localized in the southern part of it. These slaves constituted a peculiar and powerful interest. All knew that this interest was somehow the cause of the war. To strengthen, perpetuate, and extend this interest was the object for which the insurgents would rend the Union even by war, while the Government claimed no right to do more than to restrict the territorial enlargement of it. Neither party expected for the war the magnitude or the duration which it has already attained. Neither anticipated that the *cause* of the conflict might cease with or even before the conflict itself should cease. Each looked for an easier triumph, and a result less fundamental and astounding. Both read the same Bible and pray to the same God, and each invokes His aid against the other. It may seem strange that any men should dare to ask a just God's assistance in wringing their bread from the sweat of other men's faces, but let us judge not, that we be not judged. The prayers of both could not be answered. That of neither has been answered fully. The Almighty has His own purposes. "Woe unto the world because of offenses; for it must needs be that offenses come, but woe to that man by whom the offense cometh." If we shall suppose that American slavery is one of those offenses which, in the providence of God, must needs come, but which, having continued through His appointed time, He now wills to remove, and that He gives to both North and South this terrible war as the woe due to those by whom the offense came, shall we discern therein any departure from those divine attributes which the believers in a living God always ascribe to Him? Fondly do we hope, fervently do we pray, that this mighty scourge of war may speedily pass away. Yet, if God wills that it continue until all the wealth piled by the bondsman's two hundred and fifty years of unrequited toil shall be sunk, and until every drop of blood drawn with the lash shall be paid by another drawn with the sword, as was said three thousand years ago, so still it must be said "the judgments of the Lord are true and righteous altogether."

With malice toward none, with charity for all, with firmness in the right as God gives us to see the right, let us strive on to finish the work we are in, to bind up the nation's wounds, to care for him who shall have borne the battle and for his widow and his orphan, to do all which may achieve and cherish a just and lasting peace among ourselves and with all nations.

See also: Lincoln, Abraham, Administration of (1861–1865), in **The Presidency A to Z.**

Primary Source Library

Congressional Government, 1885

In 1885, Woodrow Wilson, then a graduate student at Princeton University, wrote a book titled Congressional Government, *in which he provided an overview of the entire government. He then went on to discuss the role of* checks and balances, *as well as the powers of the presidency at a time when Congress seemed to be the most powerful branch of the United States government.*

Congressional Government

It is difficult to describe any single part of a great governmental system without describing the whole of it. Governments are living things and operate as organic wholes. Moreover, governments have their natural evolution and are one thing in one age, another in another. The makers of the Constitution constructed the federal government upon a theory of checks and balances which was meant to limit the operation of each part and allow to no single part or organ of it a dominating force; but no government can be successfully conducted upon so mechanical a theory. Leadership and control must be lodged somewhere; the whole art of statesmanship is the art of bringing the several parts of government into effective cooperation for the accomplishment of particular common objects,—and party objects at that. Our study of each part of our federal system, if we are to discover our real government as it lives, must be made to disclose to us its operative coordination as a whole: its places of leadership, its method of action, how it operates, what checks it, what gives it energy and effect. Governments are what politicians make them, and it is easier to write of the President than of the presidency. . . .

One of the greatest of the President's powers I have not yet spoken of at all: his control, which is very absolute, of the foreign relations of the nation. The initiative in foreign affairs, which the President possesses without any restriction whatever, is virtually the power to control them absolutely. The President cannot conclude a treaty with a foreign power without the consent of the Senate, but he may guide every step of diplomacy, and to guide diplomacy is to determine what treaties must be made, if the faith and prestige of the government are to be maintained. He need disclose no step of negotiation until it is complete, and when in any critical matter it is completed the government is virtually committed. Whatever its disinclination, the Senate may feel itself committed also.

I have not dwelt upon this power of the President, because it has been decisively influential in determining the character and influence of the office at only two periods in our history; at the very first, when the government was young and had so to use its incipient force as to win the respect of the nations into whose family it had thrust itself, and in our own day when the results of the Spanish War, the ownership of distant possessions, and many sharp struggles for foreign trade make it necessary that we should turn our best talents to the task of dealing firmly, wisely, and justly with political and commercial rivals. The President can never again be the mere domestic figure he has been throughout so large a part of our history. The nation has risen to the first rank in power and resources. The other nations of the world look askance upon her, half in envy, half in fear, and wonder with a deep anxiety what she will do with her vast strength. They receive the frank professions of men like Mr. John Hay, whom we wholly trusted, with a grain of salt, and doubt what we were sure of, their truthfulness and sincerity, suspecting a hidden design under every utterance he makes. Our President must always, henceforth, be one of the great powers of the world, whether he act greatly and wisely or not, and the best statesmen we can produce will be needed to fill the office of Secretary of State. We have but begun to see the presidential office in this light; but it is the light which will more and more beat upon it, and more and more determine its character and its effect upon the politics of the nation. We can never hide our President again as a mere domestic officer. We can never again see him the mere **executive** he was in the thirties and forties. He must stand always at the front of our affairs, and the office will be as big and as influential as the man who occupies it. . . .

The future development of the presidency, therefore, must certainly, one would confidently predict, run along such lines as the President's later relations with his cabinet suggest. General Washington, partly out of unaffected modesty, no doubt, but also out of the sure practical instinct which he possessed in so unusual a degree, set an example which few of his successors seem to have followed in any systematic manner. He made constant and intimate use of his colleagues in every matter that he handled, seeking their assistance and advice by letter when they were at a distance and he could not obtain it in person. It is well known to all close students of our history that his greater state papers, even those which seem in some peculiar and intimate sense his personal utterances, are full of the ideas and the very phrases of the men about him whom he most trusted. His rough drafts came back to him from Mr. Hamilton and Mr. Madison in great part rephrased and rewritten, in many passages reconceived and given a new color. He thought and acted always by the light of counsel, with a will and definite choice of his own, but through the instrumentality of other minds as well as his own. The duties and responsibilities laid upon the President by the Constitution can be changed only by constitutional amendment,—a thing too difficult to attempt except upon some greater necessity than the relief of an overburdened office, even though that office be the greatest in the land; and it is to be doubted whether the deliberate opinion of the country would consent to make of the President a less powerful officer than he is. He can secure his own relief without shirking any real responsibility. Appointments, for example, he can, if he will, make more and more upon the advice and choice of his executive colleagues; every matter of detail not only, but also every minor matter of counsel or of general policy, he can more and more depend upon his chosen advisers to determine; he need reserve for himself only the larger matters of counsel and that general oversight of the

Theodore Roosevelt (1901–1909) and William Howard Taft (1909–1913) were good friends who held very different views of the office of the presidency. (Theodore Roosevelt Collection, Harvard College Library)

POINT/COUNTERPOINT

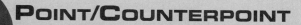

TWO VIEWS OF EXECUTIVE AUTHORITY

The Constitution's ambiguous wording concerning the presidency has stirred debate since the nation's founding. President Theodore Roosevelt (1901–1909), a loose constructionist, held very different views from his friend and successor, William Howard Taft (1909–1913).

President Theodore Roosevelt

I declined to adopt the view that what was imperatively necessary for the Nation could not be done by the President unless he could find some specific authorization to do it. My belief was that it was not only his right but his duty to do anything that the needs of the Nation demanded unless such action was forbidden by the Constitution or by the law.

President William Howard Taft

The true view of the Executive function is, as I conceive it, that the President can exercise no power which cannot be fairly and reasonably traced to some specific grant of power, or justly implied and included within such grant of power and necessary to its exercise.

DOCUMENT-BASED QUESTION

What is the major difference concerning presidential authority as described by Roosevelt and Taft?

---

business of the government and of the persons who conduct it which is not possible without intimate daily consultations, indeed, but which is possible without attempting the intolerable burden of direct control. This is, no doubt, the idea of their functions which most Presidents have entertained and which most Presidents suppose themselves to have acted on; but we have reason to believe that most of our Presidents have taken their duties too literally and have attempted the impossible. But we can safely predict that as the multitude of the President's duties increases, as it must with the growth and widening activities of the nation itself, the incumbents of the great office will more and more come to feel that they are administering it in its truest purpose and with greatest effect by re-garding themselves as less and less executive officers and more and more directors of affairs and leaders of the nation, men of counsel and of the sort of action that makes for enlightenment.

President McKinley Shot Down, 1901

The September 7, 1901, issue of The New York Press *announced that President William McKinley (1897–1901) had been struck by an assassin's bullets as he greeted well-wishers at the Pan-American Exposition in Buffalo, New York. The paper held out hope that the president would survive, but he died eight days later.*

Twentieth Amendment, 1933

The Twentieth Amendment, ratified in 1933, moved the beginning of the president's term of office from March 4 to January 20 of the year after a presidential election. It also moved the terms of a new Congress from March 4 to January 3 of the year following a congressional election. The amendment further provides for situations in which the president-elect or vice president-elect is not able to take office.

Twentieth Amendment

Section 1. The terms of the President and Vice President shall end at noon on the 20th day of January, and the terms of Senators and Representatives at noon on the 3d day of January, of the years in which such terms would have ended if this article had not been ratified; and the terms of their successors shall then begin.

Section 2. The Congress shall assemble at least once in every year, and such meeting shall begin at noon on the 3d day of January, unless they shall by law appoint a different day.

Section 3. If, at the time fixed for the beginning of the term of the President, the President elect shall have died, the Vice President elect shall become President. If a President shall not have been chosen before the time fixed for the beginning of his term, or if the President elect shall have failed to qualify, then the Vice President elect shall act as President until a President shall have qualified; and the Congress may by law provide for the case wherein neither a President elect nor a Vice President elect shall have qualified, declaring who shall then act as President, or the manner in which one who is to act shall be selected, and such person shall act accordingly until a President or Vice President shall have qualified.

Section 4. The Congress may by law provide for the case of the death of any of the persons from whom the House of Representatives may choose a President whenever the right of choice shall have devolved upon them, and for the case of the death of any of the persons from whom the Senate may choose a Vice President whenever the right of choice shall have devolved upon them.

Section 5. Sections 1 and 2 shall take effect on the 15th day of October following the **ratification** of this article.

Section 6. This article shall be inoperative unless it shall have been ratified as an amendment to the Constitution by the legislatures of three-fourths of the several states within seven years from the date of its submission.

See also: Twentieth Amendment (1933) in **The Presidency A to Z.**

Primary Source Library

Roosevelt's Four Freedoms Speech, 1941

President Franklin D. Roosevelt (1933–1945) addressed the nation on January 9, 1941—as World War II raged in Europe and about eleven months before the Japanese attack on Pearl Harbor, Hawaii. With war looming, the president set forth his vision for freedom and the state of human rights in the coming years.

Roosevelt's Four Freedoms Speech

. . . In the future days, which we seek to make secure, we look forward to a world founded upon four essential human freedoms.

The first is freedom of speech and expression—everywhere in the world.

The second is freedom of every person to worship God in his own way—everywhere in the world.

The third is freedom from want—which, translated into world terms, means economic understandings which will secure to every nation a healthy peacetime life for its inhabitants—everywhere in the world.

The fourth is freedom from fear—which, translated into world terms, means a world-wide reduction of armaments to such a point and in such a thorough fashion that no nation will be in a position to commit an act of physical aggression against any neighbor—anywhere in the world.

That is no vision of a distant millennium. It is a definite basis for a kind of world attainable in our own time and generation. That kind of world is the very antithesis of the so-called new order of **tyranny** which the dictators seek to create with the crash of a bomb.

To that new order we oppose the greater conception—the moral order. A good society is able to face schemes of world domination and foreign revolutions alike without fear.

Since the beginning of our American history, we have been engaged in change—in a perpetual peaceful revolution—a revolution which goes on steadily, quietly adjusting itself to changing conditions—without the concentration camp or the quick-lime in the ditch. The world order which we seek is the cooperation of free countries, working together in a friendly, civilized society.

This nation has placed its destiny in the hands and heads and hearts of its millions of free men and women; and its faith in freedom under the guidance of God. Freedom means the supremacy of human rights everywhere. Our support goes to those who struggle to gain those rights or keep them. Our strength is our unity of purpose. To that high concept there can be no end save victory.

FIFTH DRAFT

_—29 —18 .178_

The first is freedom of speech and expression everywhere

in the world.

The second is freedom of every person to worship God in

his own way everywhere in the world.

The third is freedom from want — which translated into

~~international~~ _world_ terms means economic understandings which will secure

to every nation ~~everywhere~~ a healthy peace time life for its

inhabitants— _everywhere in the world_

The fourth is freedom from fear — which translated into

~~international~~ _world_ terms means a world-wide reduction of armaments to such

a point and in such a thorough fashion that no nation ~~anywhere~~ will

be in a position to commit an act of physical aggression against any

neighbor.— _anywhere in the world._

_A 17 A_ That kind of a world is the very antithesis of the so-called

"new order" which the dictators seek to create ~~at the point of a gun~~ _with the crash of a_

bomb in Europe and in Asia.

To that "new order" we oppose the greater conception, the

moral order. A good society is able to face schemes of world domina-

tion and foreign revolutions alike without fear. It has no need either

for the one or for the other.

In his "Four Freedoms" speech, President Franklin D. Roosevelt envisioned freedom and democracy for the entire world. (Herbert Orth, Time Life Pictures, Getty Images)

See also: Roosevelt, Franklin D., Administration of (1933–1945), in **The Presidency A to Z.**

Twenty-second Amendment, 1951

The Twenty-second Amendment, passed by Congress in 1947 and ratified in 1951, limits the president to two terms. It came about as a response to Franklin D. Roosevelt's having been elected to four terms (1933–1945). Roosevelt is the only president to have won more than two elections.

Twenty-second Amendment

Section 1. No person shall be elected to the office of the President more than twice, and no person who has held the office of President, or acted as President, for more than two years of a term to which some other person was elected President shall be elected to the office of the President more than once. But this article shall not apply to any person holding the office of President when this article was proposed by the Congress, and shall not prevent any person who may be holding the office of President, or acting as President, during the term within which this article becomes operative from holding the office of President or acting as President during the remainder of such term.

Section 2. This article shall be inoperative unless it shall have been ratified as an amendment to the Constitution by the legislatures of three-fourths of the several states within seven years from the date of its submission to the states by the Congress.

See also: Twenty-second Amendment (1951) in **The Presidency A to Z.**

Twenty-third Amendment, 1961

The Twenty-third Amendment gave electors in the electoral college to the citizens living in the District of Columbia. Before the passage of this amendment, Washington, D.C., residents were not allowed to participate in presidential elections because the district is not a state. The amendment was passed by Congress in 1960 and ratified by the states in 1961.

Twenty-third Amendment

Section 1. The District constituting the seat of government of the United States shall appoint in such manner as the Congress may direct:

A number of electors of President and Vice President equal to the whole number of Senators and Representatives in Congress to which the District would be entitled if it were a state, but in no event more than the least populous state; they shall be in addition to those appointed by the states, but they shall be considered, for the purposes of the election of President and Vice President, to be electors appointed by a state; and they shall meet in the District and perform such duties as provided by the twelfth article of amendment.

Section 2. The Congress shall have power to enforce this article by appropriate legislation.

See also: Twenty-third Amendment (1961) in **The Presidency A to Z.**

Twenty-fourth Amendment, 1964

Proposed by Congress on August 29, 1962, the Twenty-fourth Amendment was ratified on January 23, 1964. The amendment removed poll taxes, which had been used to keep poor African Americans from voting, as a requirement for voting in federal elections. In 1966, the Supreme Court declared in Harper v. Virginia Board of Elections that poll taxes applied to state elections violated the equal protection clause of the Fourteenth Amendment.

Twenty-fourth Amendment

Section 1. The right of citizens of the United States to vote in any primary or other election for President or Vice President, for electors for President or Vice President, or for Senator or Representative in Congress, shall not be denied or abridged by the United States or any state by reason of failure to pay any poll tax or other tax.

Section 2. The Congress shall have power to enforce this article by appropriate legislation.

See also: Twenty-fourth Amendment (1964) in **The Presidency A to Z.**

Gulf of Tonkin Resolution, 1964

On August 7, 1964, the United States House of Representatives and Senate overwhelmingly passed a joint resolution authorizing President Lyndon B. Johnson (1963–1969) to take all necessary steps to protect the United States and its allies in Southeast Asia. As a result, American involvement in the Vietnam War (1964–1975) increased without a formal declaration of war.

Gulf of Tonkin Resolution

Resolved by the Senate and House of Representatives of the United States of America in Congress assembled,

That the Congress approves and supports the determination of the President, as Commander in Chief, to take all necessary measures to repel any armed attack against the forces of the United States and to prevent further aggression.

Section 2. The United States regards as vital to its national interest and to world peace the maintenance of international peace and security in southeast Asia. Consonant with the Constitution of the United States and the Charter of the United Nations and in accordance with its obligations under the Southeast Asia Collective Defense Treaty, the United States is, therefore, prepared, as the President determines, to take all necessary steps, including the use of armed force, to assist any member or protocol state of the Southeast Asia Collective Defense Treaty requesting assistance in defense of its freedom.

Primary Source Library

Section 3. This resolution shall expire when the President shall determine that the peace and security of the area is reasonably assured by international conditions created by action of the United Nations or otherwise, except that it may be terminated earlier by concurrent resolution of the Congress.

With the signing of the Gulf of Tonkin Resolution, President Lyndon B. Johnson (1963–1969) was given sweeping, widespread power to conduct the Vietnam War. (MPI, Getty Images)

Twenty-fifth Amendment, 1967

Proposed by Congress in 1966 and ratified by the states in 1967, the Twenty-fifth Amendment outlines the process by which a vice-presidential vacancy is filled. Section 2 of the amendment has been used twice—with the nomination and approval of Gerald R. Ford (1974–1977) as vice president in 1973 and again with his successor, Nelson Rockefeller, in 1974. Section 3 of the amendment provides guidance to the vice president and Congress in case of presidential disability. It has been invoked when a president is temporarily incapacitated during surgery or other medical procedures.

Twenty-fifth Amendment

Section 1. In case of the removal of the President from office or of his death or resignation, the Vice President shall become President.

Section 2. Whenever there is a vacancy in the office of the Vice President, the President shall nominate a Vice President who shall take office upon confirmation by a majority vote of both Houses of Congress.

Section 3. Whenever the President transmits to the President pro tempore of the Senate and the Speaker of the House of Representatives his written declaration that he is unable to discharge the powers and duties of his office, and until he transmits to them a written declaration to the contrary, such powers and duties shall be discharged by the Vice President as Acting President.

The appointment of Gerald R. Ford to the vice presidency in 1973, and Ford's nomination of Nelson A. Rockefeller in 1974 (after Ford succeeded Richard M. Nixon, who had resigned) demonstrates the processes outlined in the Twenty-fifth Amendment (1967). (AP Images)

Primary Source Library

Section 4. Whenever the Vice President and a majority of either the principal officers of the **executive** departments or of such other body as Congress may by law provide, transmit to the President pro tempore of the Senate and the Speaker of the House of Representatives their written declaration that the President is unable to discharge the powers and duties of his office, the Vice President shall immediately assume the powers and duties of the office as Acting President.

Thereafter, when the President transmits to the President pro tempore of the Senate and the Speaker of the House of Representatives his written declaration that no inability exists, he shall resume the powers and duties of his office unless the Vice President and a majority of either the principal officers of the executive department or of such other body as Congress may by law provide, transmit within four days to the President pro tempore of the Senate and the Speaker of the House of Representatives their written declaration that the President is unable to discharge the powers and duties of his office. Thereupon Congress shall decide the issue, assembling within forty-eight hours for that purpose if not in session. If the Congress, within twenty-one days after receipt of the latter written declaration, or, if Congress is not in session, within twenty-one days after Congress is required to assemble, determines by two-thirds vote of both Houses that the President is unable to discharge the powers and duties of his office, the Vice President shall continue to discharge the same as Acting President; otherwise, the President shall resume the powers and duties of his office.

See also: Twenty-fifth Amendment (1967) in **The Presidency A to Z.**

Vice President Spiro T. Agnew Resigns, 1973

On October 10, 1973, Spiro T. Agnew resigned the office of the vice presidency, becoming the second vice president in history to do so. The resignation came after months of allegations of scandal and of the vice president's accepting bribes while he was governor of Maryland. Below are the letter of resignation that Vice President Agnew submitted to Secretary of State Henry A. Kissinger, the letter that the vice president sent to President Richard M. Nixon (1969– 1974), followed by the president's reply to the vice president. The letter is addressed to "Ted," stemming from the vice president's middle name, "Theodore."

Vice President Spiro T. Agnew's Letter of Resignation

Dear Mr. Secretary:

I hereby resign the Office of Vice President of the United States, effective immediately.

Sincerely,

SPIRO T. AGNEW

In 1973, Spiro Agnew became the second vice president in United States history to resign from office. Back in 1832, John. C. Calhoun had resigned the vice presidency, but under different conditions; he resigned in order to accept a Senate seat from his home state of South Carolina. (AP Images, File)

Primary Source Library

Vice President Spiro T. Agnew's letter to President Richard M. Nixon

Dear Mr. President:

As you are aware, the accusations against me cannot be resolved without a long, divisive and debilitating struggle in the Congress and in the Courts. I have concluded that, painful as it is to me and to my family, it is in the best interests of the Nation that I relinquish the Vice Presidency.

Accordingly, I have today resigned the Office of Vice President of the United States. A copy of the instrument of resignation is enclosed.

It has been a privilege to serve with you. May I express to the American people, through you, my deep gratitude for their confidence in twice electing me to be Vice President.

Sincerely,

SPIRO T. AGNEW

President Richard M. Nixon's reply to the vice president

Dear Ted:

The most difficult decisions are often those that are the most personal, and I know your decision to resign as Vice President has been as difficult as any facing a man in public life could be. Your departure from the Administration leaves me with a great sense of personal loss. You have been a valued associate throughout these nearly five years that we have served together. However, I respect your decision, and I also respect the concern for the national interest that led you to conclude that a resolution of the matter in this way, rather than through an extended battle in the Courts and the Congress, was advisable in order to prevent a protracted period of national division and uncertainty.

As Vice President, you have addressed the great issues of our times with courage and candor. Your strong patriotism, and your profound dedication to the welfare of the Nation, have been an inspiration to all who have served with you as well as to millions of others throughout the country.

I have been deeply saddened by this whole course of events, and I hope that you and your family will be sustained in the days ahead by a well-justified pride in all that you have contributed to the Nation by your years of service as Vice President.

Sincerely,

RICHARD NIXON

President Richard Nixon's Letter of Resignation, August 9, 1974

During the evening of August 8, 1974, President Richard M. Nixon (1969–1974) went on national television and announced that he had resigned from the presidency effective at noon the next day, August 9. Nixon presented his official letter of resignation to Secretary of State Henry Kissinger. Nixon is the only president to have resigned from office.

THE WHITE HOUSE

WASHINGTON

August 9, 1974

Dear Mr. Secretary:

I hereby resign the Office of President of the United States.

Sincerely,

Richard Nixon

11.35 AM

HK

The Honorable Henry A. Kissinger
The Secretary of State
Washington, D. C. 20520

See also: Nixon, Richard M., Administration of (1969–1974), in **The Presidency A to Z.**

Gerald R. Ford's Pardon of Richard Nixon, 1974

On September 8, 1974—one month after Richard Nixon (1969–1974) resigned the presidency in disgrace—President Gerald R. Ford (1974–1977) granted "a full, free, and absolute pardon unto Richard Nixon for all offenses against the United States which he, Richard Nixon, has committed or may have committed." Ford's pardon was controversial; many people believed that Nixon should have gone to trial for breaking the law during the Watergate scandal.

Gerald R. Ford's
Pardon of
Richard Nixon

By the President of the United States of America a Proclamation

Richard Nixon became the thirty-seventh President of the United States on January 20, 1969 and was reelected in 1972 for a second term by the electors of forty-nine of the fifty states. His term in office continued until his resignation on August 9, 1974.

Pursuant to **resolutions** of the House of Representatives, its Committee on the Judiciary conducted an inquiry and investigation on the **impeachment** of the President extending over more than eight months. The hearings of the Committee and its deliberations, which received wide national publicity over television, radio, and in printed media, resulted in votes adverse to Richard Nixon on recommended Articles of Impeachment.

As a result of certain acts or omissions occurring before his resignation from the Office of President, Richard Nixon has become liable to possible indictment and trial for offenses against the United States. Whether or not he shall be so prosecuted depends on findings of the appropriate grand jury and on the discretion of the authorized prosecutor. Should an indictment ensue, the accused shall then be entitled to a fair trial by an impartial jury, as guaranteed to every individual by the Constitution.

It is believed that a trial of Richard Nixon, if it became necessary, could not fairly begin until a year or more has elapsed. In the meantime, the tranquility to which this nation has been restored by the events of recent weeks could be irreparably lost by the prospects of bringing to trial a former President of the United States. The prospects of such trial will cause prolonged and divisive debate over the propriety of exposing to further punishment and degradation a man who has already paid the **unprecedented** penalty of relinquishing the highest elective office of the United States.

Now, THEREFORE, I, GERALD R. FORD, President of the United States, pursuant to the pardon power conferred upon me by Article II, Section 2, of the Constitution, have granted and by these presents do grant a full, free, and absolute pardon unto Richard Nixon for all offenses against the United States which he, Richard Nixon, has committed or may have committed or taken part in during the period from January 20, 1969 through August 9, 1974.

IN WITNESS WHEREOF, I have hereunto set my hand this eighth day of September, in the year of our Lord nineteen hundred and seventy-four, and of the Independence of the United States of America the one hundred and ninety-ninth.

GERALD R. FORD

See also: Ford, Gerald R., Administration of (1974–1977), in **The Presidency A to Z.**

Primary Source Library

George W. Bush's Speech, September 11, 2001

After the devastating assault on the nation, President George W. Bush (2001–2009) went on national television to acknowledge the deadly terror attacks, offer his condolences to the victims, and reassure Americans that the nation remained strong and would fight back against the attack on democracy and the American way of life. He also noted that the terrorists failed to frighten the nation into submission.

George W. Bush's Speech, September 11, 2001

Good evening.

Today, our fellow citizens, our way of life, our very freedom came under attack in a series of deliberate and deadly terrorist acts.

The victims were in airplanes or in their offices—secretaries, businessmen and women, military and federal workers. Moms and dads. Friends and neighbors.

Thousands of lives were suddenly ended by evil, despicable acts of terror.

The pictures of airplanes flying into buildings, fires burning, huge structures collapsing, have filled us with disbelief, terrible sadness and a quiet, unyielding anger.

These acts of mass murder were intended to frighten our nation into chaos and retreat. But they have failed. Our country is strong. A great people has been moved to defend a great nation.

Terrorist attacks can shake the foundations of our biggest buildings, but they cannot touch the foundation of America. These acts shatter steel, but they cannot dent the steel of American resolve.

America was targeted for attack because we're the brightest beacon for freedom and opportunity in the world. And no one will keep that light from shining.

Today, our nation saw evil, the very worst of human nature, and we responded with the best of America, with the daring of our rescue workers, with the caring for strangers and neighbors who came to give blood and help in any way they could.

Immediately following the first attack, I implemented our government's emergency response plans. Our military is powerful, and it's prepared. Our emergency teams are working in New York City and Washington, D.C., to help with local rescue efforts.

Our first priority is to get help to those who have been injured and to take every precaution to protect our citizens at home and around the world from further attacks.

The functions of our government continue without interruption. Federal agencies in Washington which had to be evacuated today are reopening for essential personnel tonight and will be open for business tomorrow.

President George W. Bush (2001–2009) addresses the American people after the devastating terrorist attacks on the nation on September 11, 2001. (AP Images, Doug Mills)

Our financial institutions remain strong, and the American economy will be open for business as well.

The search is underway for those who are behind these evil acts. I've directed the full resources for our intelligence and law enforcement communities to find those responsible and bring them to justice. We will make no distinction between the terrorists who committed these acts and those who harbor them.

I appreciate so very much the members of Congress who have joined me in strongly condemning these attacks. And on behalf of the American people, I thank the many world leaders who have called to offer their condolences and assistance.

America and our friends and allies join with all those who want peace and security in the world and we stand together to win the war against terrorism.

Tonight I ask for your prayers for all those who grieve, for the children whose worlds have been shattered, for all whose sense of safety and security has been threatened. And I pray they will be comforted by a power greater than any of us spoken through the ages in Psalm 23: "Even though I walk through the valley of the shadow of death, I fear no evil, for You are with me."

This is a day when all Americans from every walk of life unite in our resolve for justice and peace. America has stood down enemies before, and we will do so this time.

None of us will ever forget this day, yet we go forward to defend freedom and all that is good and just in our world.

Thank you. Good night and God bless America.

See also: Bush, George W., Administration of (2001–2009), in **The Presidency A to Z.**

State of the Union Address, 2008

On January 28, 2008, as required by the Constitution, President George W. Bush (2001–2009) gave his annual State of the Union Address to a joint session of Congress and to the nation. The president spoke on many subjects, among them the nation's economy, education, the wars in Afghanistan and Iraq, and the ongoing war on terrorism.

State of the Union Address

Madam Speaker, Vice President Cheney, members of Congress, distinguished guests, and fellow citizens: Seven years have passed since I first stood before you at this rostrum. In that time, our country has been tested in ways none of us could have imagined. We faced hard decisions about peace and war, rising competition in the world economy, and the health and welfare of our citizens. These issues call for vigorous debate, and I think it's fair to say we've answered the call. Yet history will record that amid our differences, we acted with purpose. And together, we showed the world the power and resilience of American self-government.

All of us were sent to Washington to carry out the people's business. That is the purpose of this body. It is the meaning of our oath. It remains our charge to keep.

The actions of the 110th Congress will affect the security and prosperity of our nation long after this session has ended. In this election year, let us show our fellow Americans that we recognize our responsibilities and are determined to meet them. Let us show them that Republicans and Democrats can compete for votes and cooperate for results at the same time. (Applause.) . . .

To build a prosperous future, we must trust people with their own money and empower them to grow our economy. As we meet tonight, our economy is undergoing a period of uncertainty. America has added jobs for a record 52 straight months, but jobs are now growing at a slower pace. Wages are up, but so are prices for food and gas. Exports are rising, but the housing market has declined. At kitchen tables across our country, there is a concern about our economic future.

In the long run, Americans can be confident about our economic growth. But in the short run, we can all see that that growth is slowing. So last week, my administration reached agreement with Speaker Pelosi and Republican Leader Boehner on a robust growth package that includes tax relief for individuals and families and incentives for business investment. The temptation will be to load up the bill. That would delay it or derail it, and neither option is acceptable. (Applause.) This is a good agreement that will keep our economy growing and our people working. And this Congress must pass it as soon as possible. (Applause.) . . .

On education, we must trust students to learn if given the chance, and empower parents to demand results from our schools. In neighborhoods across our country, there are boys and girls with dreams—and a decent education is their only hope of achieving them.

Six years ago, we came together to pass the No Child Left Behind Act, and today no one can deny its results. Last year, fourth and eighth graders achieved the highest math scores on record. Reading scores are on the rise. African American and Hispanic students posted all-time highs. (Applause.) Now we must work together to increase accountability, add flexibility for states and districts, reduce the number of high school dropouts, provide extra help for struggling schools.

Members of Congress: The No Child Left Behind Act is a **bipartisan** achievement. It is succeeding. And we owe it to America's children, their parents, and their teachers to strengthen this good law. (Applause.) . . .

Our foreign policy is based on a clear premise: We trust that people, when given the chance, will choose a future of freedom and peace. In the last seven years, we have witnessed stirring moments in the history of liberty. We've seen citizens in Georgia and Ukraine stand up for their right to free and fair elections. We've seen people in Lebanon take to the streets to demand their independence. We've seen Afghans emerge from the **tyranny** of the Taliban and choose a new president and a new parliament. We've seen jubilant Iraqis holding up ink-stained fingers and celebrating their freedom. These images of liberty have inspired us. (Applause.)

In the past seven years, we've also seen images that have sobered us. We've watched throngs of mourners in Lebanon and Pakistan carrying the caskets of beloved leaders taken by the assassin's hand. We've seen wedding guests in blood-soaked finery staggering from a hotel in Jordan, Afghans and Iraqis blown up in mosques and markets, and trains in London and Madrid ripped apart by bombs. On a clear September day, we saw thousands of our fellow citizens taken from us in an instant. These horrific images serve as a grim reminder: The advance of liberty is opposed by terrorists and extremists—evil men who despise freedom, despise America, and aim to subject millions to their violent rule.

Since 9/11, we have taken the fight to these terrorists and extremists. We will stay on the offense, we will keep up the pressure, and we will deliver justice to our enemies. (Applause.)

We are engaged in the defining ideological struggle of the 21st century. The terrorists oppose every principle of humanity and decency that we hold dear. Yet in this war on terror, there is one thing we and our enemies agree on: In the long run, men and women who are free to determine their own destinies will reject terror and refuse to live in tyranny. And that is why the terrorists are fighting to deny this choice to the people in Lebanon, Iraq, Afghanistan, Pakistan, and the Palestinian Territories. And that is why, for the security of America and the peace of the world, we are spreading the hope of freedom. (Applause.)

In Afghanistan, America, our 25 NATO allies, and 15 partner nations are helping the Afghan people defend their freedom and rebuild their country. Thanks to the courage of these military and civilian personnel, a nation that was once a safe haven for al Qaeda is now a young democracy where boys and girls are going to school, new roads and hospitals are being built, and people are looking to the future with new hope. These successes must continue, so we're adding 3,200 Marines to our forces in Afghanistan, where they will fight the terrorists and train the Afghan Army and police. Defeating the Taliban and al Qaeda is critical to our security, and I thank the Congress for supporting America's vital mission in Afghanistan. (Applause.)

In Iraq, the terrorists and extremists are fighting to deny a proud people their liberty, and fighting to establish safe havens for attacks across the world. One year ago, our enemies were succeeding in their efforts to plunge Iraq into chaos. So we reviewed our strategy and changed course. We launched a surge of American forces into Iraq. We gave our troops a new mission: Work with the Iraqi forces to protect the Iraqi people, pursue the enemy in its strongholds, and deny the terrorists sanctuary anywhere in the country.

The Iraqi people quickly realized that something dramatic had happened. Those who had worried that America was preparing to abandon them instead saw tens of thousands of American forces flowing into their country. They saw our forces moving into neighborhoods, clearing out the terrorists, and staying behind to ensure the enemy did not return. And they saw our troops, along with Provincial Reconstruction. Teams that include Foreign Service officers and other skilled public servants, coming in to ensure that improved security was followed by improvements in daily life. Our military and civilians in Iraq are performing with courage and distinction, and they have the gratitude of our whole nation. (Applause.)

On the home front, we will continue to take every lawful and effective measure to protect our country. This is our most solemn duty. We are grateful that there has not been another attack on our soil since 9/11. This is not for the lack of desire or effort on the part of the enemy. In the past six years, we've stopped numerous attacks, including a plot to fly a plane into the tallest building in Los Angeles and another to blow up passenger jets bound for America over the Atlantic. Dedicated men and women in our government toil day and night to stop the terrorists from carrying out their plans. These good citizens are saving American lives, and everyone in this chamber owes them our thanks. (Applause.)

And we owe them something more: We owe them the tools they need to keep our people safe. And one of the most important tools we can give them is the ability to monitor terrorist communications. To protect America, we need to know who the terrorists are talking to, what they are saying, and what they're planning. Last year, Congress passed legislation to help us do that. Unfortunately, Congress set the legislation to expire on February the 1st. That means if you don't act by Friday, our ability to track terrorist threats would be weakened and our citizens will be in greater danger. Congress must ensure the flow of vital intelligence is not disrupted. Congress must pass liability protection for companies believed to have assisted in the efforts to defend America. We've had ample time for debate. The time to act is now. (Applause.)

Protecting our nation from the dangers of a new century requires more than good intelligence and a strong military. It also requires changing the conditions that breed resentment and allow extremists to prey on despair. So America is using its influence to build a freer, more hopeful, and more compassionate world. This is a reflection of our national interest; it is the calling of our conscience. . . .

The strength—the secret of our strength, the miracle of America, is that our greatness lies not in our government, but in the spirit and determination of our people. (Applause.) When the Federal Convention met in Philadelphia in 1787, our nation was bound by the Articles of Confederation, which began with the words, "We the undersigned delegates." When Gouverneur Morris was asked to draft a preamble to our new Constitution, he offered an important revision and opened with words that changed the course of our nation and the history of the world: "We the people."

By trusting the people, our Founders wagered that a great and noble nation could be built on the liberty that resides in the hearts of all men and women. By trusting the people, succeeding generations transformed our fragile young democracy into the most powerful nation on Earth and a beacon of hope for millions. And so long as we continue to trust the people, our nation will prosper, our liberty will be secure, and the state of our Union will remain strong. (Applause.)

So tonight, with confidence in freedom's power, and trust in the people, let us set forth to do their business. God bless America. (Applause.)

See also: State of the Union Address in **The Presidency A to Z.**

President George W. Bush (2001–2009) gives the annual State of the Union address. The annual address to Congress and the nation fulfills a constitutional requirement of the presidential office. (Scott J. Ferrell, CQ)

Primary Source Library

Using Primary Sources

Researching With Primary and Secondary Sources

A primary source is first-hand information or data. A primary source has not been subject to analysis by someone else. Typical primary sources—such as the Twelfth Amendment, Abraham Lincoln's First Inaugural Address, and excerpts from *Bush v. Gore* (2000)—are eyewitness accounts of an event, letters, diary entries, photographs, and documents. In the Primary Source Library, Part Three of this volume, there is a variety of primary sources, especially useful when researching the presidency and the **executive** branch of government.

In contrast, a secondary source is information that has been reviewed and analyzed by someone else. For example, historian David McCullough's biography of the second U.S. president John Adams is a secondary source. The author (McCullough) has reviewed and analyzed a variety of primary and secondary sources to present a biography of his subject (Adams). Most magazine articles, books, and Internet sources are secondary sources.

Developing Research Questions

When you are assigned a report and select a topic for research, it is important to begin with a clear sense of direction. Ask yourself several questions that will help you limit your topic. For example, for a report on the importance of the growth of presidential power, you will likely be able to find hundreds of primary and secondary sources. However, to help narrow the topic, ask yourself the following questions:

- What powers does the Constitution provide to the president?
- Which presidents strengthened the office?
- What circumstances lead to a stronger presidency?
- How do international affairs affect the American presidency?
- What crises or emergencies lead to an increase in presidential power?

With answers to these questions, you will have the focus you need to begin further research.

Identifying Sources of Information

You likely will begin looking for information in your school or local library or on the Internet. You can also locate other sources of information within your community, such as local government sources, newspaper offices, historical societies, and museums. All of these sources can provide valuable information. However, you must determine if the information will be useful to your research topic. Evaluate and decide on the usefulness of the source. Useful sources should have the following characteristics:

- **Pertinent and appropriate** Is the information related to your topic? Skim the book, and check the table of contents and the index.

- **Trustworthy and dependable** Is the source objective? Does it seem accurate? What sources did the author of the book or article use?

- **Current and recent** How old is the source? Is the information out of date? Keep in mind that historical documents such as the U.S. Constitution and topics such as the growth of presidential power are researched and evaluated by political scientists and historians. Be sure that some of your sources are current analyses.

- **Typical and representative** Be certain to find balanced or unbiased sources. If you are writing about a controversial topic, such as the election of 2000, be sure to use sources that represent both sides of the issue.

Planning and Organizing

As you gather various primary and secondary sources, you begin to develop a plan for your report. This might include a preliminary outline with headings and subheadings that will help you organize your resources and report. With this plan, you can decide what information to include in your notes.

Thorough note taking is essential; you will want to document all the information you have gathered for your report. Following are useful tips for taking notes:

- Use ruled index cards.
- Use a separate card for each item of information.
- Use a separate card for each source.

Use the following techniques to record information:

- **Quote** Copy the information exactly as it appears in the source. Use quotation marks to indicate a direct quote.
- **Paraphrase** Rewrite the information in your own words.
- **Summarize** Condense the information, noting essential material and key ideas.

Documenting Sources for the Bibliography

On index cards, keep a record of the books, newspaper or magazine articles, Internet sites, and other sources you have consulted. As you locate useful sources, record the publishing data on your index cards, so you can easily find the information later. This data will be essential for compiling the bibliography at the end of your report.

Citing Sources

All writers must identify the sources of the words, facts, and thoughts that they find in other works. Noting your sources allows your reader to check those sources and determine how reliable or important a particular piece of information is.

What You Should Document

- Someone's exact words
- A close paraphrase of another's ideas or several ideas
- Information on the topic that is not found in most books on the subject or that is not generally known

What You Do Not Have To Document

- Simple definitions, commonly used sayings, or famous quotations
- Information that is common knowledge or that is easily found in most sources

Author and Publication Information

Author information should always appear at the beginning of your citation, with the author's last name first.

- For books with two authors, reverse only the first author's name, followed by a comma and the second author's name.
- If no author is noted, list the editor; if no editor is identified, start with the title of the work.
- Should you use more than one work by the same author, you do not need to list the author information each time. Use three hyphens followed by a period to begin the line.
- The name of the work (underlined or in italics) appears next, followed by a period.

Publication information follows the author and title of the work. You also may need to include the editor's name, volume or edition number, and a series name.

Citing Internet Sources

When citing Internet sources, you likely will not be able to include all the information in the list that follows. Many on-line sources do not provide all this information. Therefore, provide as much information as possible.

- Author or editor of the source
- Title of a book (underlined or in italics)
- Title of an article, short work, or poem (in quotation marks)
- Publication information for any print version of the source
- Title of the database, scholarly project, periodical, or professional site (underlined or in italics)
- Version number of the source or journal; volume number, issue number, or other identifier
- Date of the electronic version or last update

Using the Primary Source Library in This Volume

In Part Three of this volume you will find a wealth of primary sources useful for various research topics. In chronological order, important source documents appear that are related to or that have affected the presidency and the executive branch. To help you find out about the growth of presidential power, for example, the following primary sources will likely be useful:

- United States Constitution, Article I, Section 7, 1789
- United States Constitution, Article II, Section 3, 1789
- Lincoln's First Inaugural Address, 1861
- Gulf of Tonkin Resolution, 1964
- George W. Bush's Speech, September 11, 2001

For more information about doing research with authoritative sources, consult your local librarian, teacher, or one of numerous available publications.

abolition A social movement that emerged before the Civil War (1861–1865) which demanded an end to slavery; practiced by **abolitionists**

adjourn To suspend until a later stated time

aerial reconnaissance photography Scouting or spy photographs taken by high-flying aircraft

Alien and Sedition Acts of 1798 Laws passed by the Federalist-controlled Congress that were designed to increase the time for foreigners to become American citizens and limit criticism of the federal government

amend To improve something by changing or modifying it

amendment A change to the Constitution

amphibious Able to move about both on land and on water

anarchist One who believes in the doctrine that all forms of government are oppressive and should be abolished

annex To append, attach, or absorb

appropriate To set aside something, such as funds, for a specific use

appropriations Resources or funds set apart for a particular use

arbitration Negotiations to end a dispute

armistice A cease-fire during wartime prior to the signing of a formal peace treaty

balustrades In architecture, a rail and the row of posts that support it, as along the front of a gallery

Bank of the United States One of the two official national banks of the United States. The First Bank of the United States existed from 1791 to 1811; the Second Bank of the United States existed from 1816 to 1836, when its federal charter expired; President Andrew Jackson (1829–1837) almost destroyed the bank when he ordered the Department of the Treasury to stop depositing the nation's money into the bank.

bicameral Consisting of a two-house legislature

biennial Occurring every two years

bills Proposed laws

bipartisan Involving members of two political parties

bosses Powerful political party leaders

caucus Organized group of legislatures with a common background or goals; also, a closed meeting of party members within a legislative body to decide on questions of policy or leadership

cedes; ceded Yields or grants

censure An official rebuke

chads Small pieces of paper that voters are supposed to punch out from voting cards

checks and balances A system in which each branch of the government exercises some control over the other branches

civil service reform The changing of the administrative service of the government, exclusive of the armed forces

commerce Exchange of goods, ideas, or opinions

commodity prices A physical substance, such as food, grains, or metals, which investors buy or sell. In a market economy, the price of the commodity is subject to the forces of supply and demand

conservative Someone who believes that the role of the government should be very limited and that individuals should be responsible for their own well-being

dark-horse candidate A little known candidate who does better than expected

depression A period of extended and severe decline in a nation's economy, marked by low production and high unemployment

despotic having the characteristics or behavior of a cruel or tyrannical ruler or leader

disenfranchised Deprived of the right to vote

disenfranchisement The deprivation of the right to vote; being **disenfranchised** deprives one of the right to vote

embargo A country's banning of the export and import of goods to and from another country

ensign in the U.S. Navy, a person holding the lowest commissioned rank, below a lieutenant

ethnic cleansing the deliberate execution of an ethnic group within a specific geographic area

executive the chief office of a government, state, or other political entity

factionalism The existence of interest groups within a country's political parties

fascism A strongly nationalistic ideology, named for the Fascist Party of Italy; a government characterized by racism and militarism; a repressive one-party dictatorship

favorite sons Candidates with strong support from one state or region of the country

franchise The right to vote

Great Depression In United States history, a serious economic downturn that began with the crash of the stock market in 1929 and ended after the nation entered World War II (1939–1945) in 1941

Great Society A series of federal social programs sponsored by President Lyndon B. Johnson (1963–1969)

habeas corpus (writ of) One of a variety of formal legal documents that may be issued to bring a party before a court or judge; serves to release the party from unlawful restraint

haberdashery A store that sells men's hats, apparel, and other furnishings

hard currency Currency consisting of gold or silver coins as opposed to paper money

Hartford Convention A meeting of Federalist Party members opposed to the War of 1812. The convention called for a number of amendments that would weaken the federal government; it also raised the issue of secession

impeach To formally accuse a public official of misconduct while in office

impeachment The formal accusation of misconduct in office against a public official

imperialist Extending power and authority to gain control over the political and economic lives of others

impound Refuse to spend funds appropriated by Congress

incumbent Politician running for the office that she or he is currently holding

inflation In an economy, the overall general upward price movement of goods and services

isolationism The avoidance of involvement in world affairs; an **isolationist** supports this type of foreign policy

joint session A concurrent meeting of the United States Senate and the United States House of Representatives

judicial review The power of the United States Supreme Court to declare laws passed by Congress and signed by the president to be unconstitutional

jurisdiction The right and power of a court to interpret and apply the law

lame-duck A politician who, at the end of his or her current term, will be succeeded either due to choice or to term limits

legislative Of or relating to a lawmaking body or the power to make law

liberal In the modern era, someone who believes the national government should be active in helping individuals and communities promote health, education, justice, and equal opportunity

loophole primary A type of primary election in which voters express a preference for a presidential nominee, but also elect convention delegates who are then to support the winner of the presidential preference vote at the nominating convention

machine A highly organized political group under the leadership of a boss or small clique

merit system A method in which individuals are hired or promoted based on talent or skill, rather than seniority or special treatment

military-industrial complex Term first used by President Dwight D. Eisenhower (1953–1961) to describe the close relationship between the nation's armed forces and its manufacturers

nationalism A strong feeling of pride in one's nation, culture, or heritage

nationalist An individual who strongly supports the policies of his or her nation

neutral Not taking part in either side of a dispute, such as a war

neutrality The state or policy of being neutral, or not taking sides, especially nonparticipation in war

nullification The process by which a law is declared null and void

nullified To have made something of no consequence or value

partisan Devoted to or biased in favor of one political party

partisanship Having the characteristics of a partisan, that is, being devoted to or biased in favor of one political party over another

patronage The practice of gaining favors to reward party loyalty

philanthropist One who practices goodwill to others, especially through gifts to charitable or humanitarian organizations

poll taxes Money paid in order to vote

popular sovereignty The concept that citizens in a region should vote to decide an issue, often used before the Civil War (1861–1865) to mean that the voters in the states should determine whether to allow slavery

precedent An established course of action in a given situation

progressive A term used, especially in the late 1800s and early 1900s, to describe someone interested in social, economic, and governmental reforms

progressivism The principles, beliefs, or practices of progressives

public enemies High-profile, violent criminals who are a threat to society

Radical Republicans Members of the Republican party who advocated extreme measures to bring about change in the South during and after the Civil War (1861–1865)

ratification A formal approval or confirmation (of an amendment or treaty)

ratified Approved

reapportion To reallocate, as in the allotment of representatives among the states

recession A period of declining productivity and reduced economic activity

Reconstruction The period in United States history when the former Confederate States were brought back into the Union, lasting from about 1865 until 1877

religious right Beginning in 1980, a term used to describe those groups of citizens who, because of their conservative religious beliefs, vote for conservative political candidates

republican Relating to a republic, a form of government in which the people rule through elected representatives

resolutions Statements of issues that are relevant to only one house of Congress and are passed only by the house to which they apply

revenue bills Proposed legislation designed to raise money

secession The act of leaving or withdrawing from a nation or other political entity

segregation The practice of keeping groups apart or separate based on a characteristic, such as race, religion, or ethnicity

segregationist A person who believes in or practices segregation (especially of races)

soft money Political donations made to avoid federal campaign laws, such as a donation to a political organization rather than directly to a candidate

sortie A flight of a combat aircraft on a mission

sovereignty Complete independence and self-government

specie Coinage, as opposed to paper currency

Specie Circular Executive order issued in 1836 by President Andrew Jackson (1829–1837) requiring that payment for purchases of public lands be made with gold or silver, rather than with paper money

stagflation An unusual economic condition characterized by both a stagnant economy and rising prices

strict construction The interpretation of the Unites States Constitution which holds that the government is permitted to carry out only those functions that are specifically identified in the document; Thomas Jefferson's Democratic Republicans held **strict constructionist** views

suffrage The right to vote

surplus An extra amount of a good or product

tariff Tax on imported goods

temperance laws Laws that restrict the sale, use, or consumption of alcoholic beverages

third party In a two-party political system, as in the United States, any political party other than the two main parties—Democratic and Republican

triumvirate A government that is led by three persons ruling jointly

tyranny Of or relating to a cruel ruler with absolute power

unconstitutional In violation of the Constitution

unified commands Military groups with broad continuing missions under a single commander and composed of forces from two or more military departments

unprecedented Having no previous occurrence or example

veto Rejection of a bill

wage and price controls Laws or policies that restrict the amount of wages workers can earn and that prevent increases in the prices of goods and services

war hawks Political figures who favor engaging in military conflicts

writ of mandamus An order issued to a public official to do his or her duty as required by law

Aaseng, Nathan. *Famous Trials—The Impeachment of Bill Clinton.* Farmington Hills, MI: Lucent, 1999.

Ackerman, Bruce. *Bush v. Gore: The Question of Legitimacy.* New Haven, CT: Yale University Press, 2002.

Ackerman, Kenneth D. *Dark Horse: The Surprise Election and Political Murder of President James A. Garfield.* Jackson, TN: Da Capo Press, 2004.

Adams, John, National Park. http://www.nps.gov/adam/

Adkins, Randall E., ed. *The Evolution of Political Parties, Campaigns, and Elections: Landmark Documents, 1787–2008.* Washington, DC: CQ Press, 2008.

Appleby, Joyce. *Thomas Jefferson.* New York: Times Books, Henry Holt and Company, 2003.

Articles of Confederation. http://www.loc.gov/rr/program/bib/ourdocs/articles.html.

Bartels, Larry M. *Presidential Primaries and the Dynamics of Public Choice.* Princeton, NJ: Princeton University Press, 1988.

Benedict, Michael Les. *The Impeachment and Trial of Andrew Johnson.* New York: W.W. Norton, 1999.

Black, Conrad. *Richard Nixon: A Life in Full.* New York: PublicAffairs Books, 2007.

Boller, Paul F. *Presidential Campaigns: From George Washington to George W. Bush.* New York: Oxford University Press, 2004.

Boller, Paul F. *Presidential Inaugurations.* Orlando, FL: Harcourt, 2001.

Boller, Paul F., Jr., *Presidential Wives: An Anecdotal History.* New York: Oxford University Press, 1988.

Brinkley, Douglas. *Gerald R. Ford.* New York: Times Books, 2007.

Brinkley, Douglas G. *The Unfinished Presidency: Jimmy Carter's Journey Beyond the White House.* New York: Penguin, 1999.

Bunting, Josiah III. *Ulysses S. Grant.* New York: Times Books, 2004.

Burner, David. *Herbert Hoover: A Public Life.* Newtown, CT: American Political Biography Press, 2005.

Bush, George H.W. *All the Best, George Bush: My Life in Letters and Other Writings.* New York: Scribner, 2000.

Calabresi, Steven G., and Christopher S. Yoo. *The Unitary Executive: Presidential Power from Washington to Bush.* New Haven, CT: Yale University Press, 2008.

Calhoun, Charles W. *Benjamin Harrison.* New York: Times Books, 2005.

Campbell, Colin, and Bert A. Rockman, eds. *The George W. Bush Presidency: Appraisals and Prospects.* Washington, DC: CQ Press, 2003.

Campbell, James E. *The American Campaign: U.S. Presidential Campaigns and the National Vote.* College Station, TX: Texas A&M University Press, 2008.

Clinton, Bill. *My Life.* New York: Knopf, 2004.

Cohen, Jeffrey E. *The Presidency in the Era of 24-Hour News.* Princeton, NJ: Princeton University Press, 2008.

Cohen, Jeffrey E. *Presidential Responsiveness and Public Policy-Making: The Publics and the Policies that Presidents Choose.* Ann Arbor, MI: University of Michigan Press, 1999.

Constitution, United States. http://www.archives.gov/exhibits/charters/constitution.html.

Cook, Rhodes. *United States Presidential Primary Elections 2000–2004: A Handbook of Election Statistics.* Washington, DC: CQ Press, 2006.

Crapol, Edward P. *John Tyler: The Accidental President.* Chapel Hill, NC: University of North Carolina Press, 2006.

Crenson, Matthew, and Benjamin Ginsburg. *Presidential Power: Unchecked and Unbalanced.* New York: W.W. Norton, 2007.

CQ Press. *National Party Conventions, 1831–2004.* Washington, DC: CQ Press, 2005.

CQ Press. *Presidential Elections, 1789–2004.* Washington, DC: CQ Press, 2005.

Dallek, Robert. *Lyndon Johnson: Portrait of a President.* New York: Oxford University Press, 2005.

Dallek, Robert. *An Unfinished Life: John F. Kennedy, 1917–1963.* Boston: Back Bay Books, 2004.

Davis, Barbara J. *The Teapot Dome Scandal: Corruption Rocks 1920s America.* Mankato, MN: Compass Point, 2008.

Dean, John W. *Warren Harding.* New York: Times Books, 2004.

Diggins, John Patrick. *John Adams.* New York: Times Books, Henry Holt and Company, 2003.

Ditchfield, Christin. *Condoleezza Rice: National Security Advisor.* New York: Franklin Watts, 2003.

Donald, David Herbert. *Lincoln.* New York: Simon and Schuster, 1995.

Drew, Elizabeth. *Richard M. Nixon.* New York: Times Books, 2007.

Ellis, Richard J., and Michael Nelson, eds. *Debating the Presidency: Conflicting Perspectives on the American Executive.* Washington, DC: CQ Press, 2006.

Feerick, John D. *The Twenty-fifth Amendment: Its Complete History and Applications.* New York: Fordham University Press, 1992.

Felzenberg, Alvin S. *The Leaders We Deserved (and a Few We Didn't): Rethinking the Presidential Rating Game.* Jackson, TN: Basic Books, 2008.

Ferling, John. *Adams vs. Jefferson: The Tumultuous Election of 1800.* New York: Oxford University Press, 2004.

Fisher, Louis. *Presidential War Power.* Lawrence, KS: University of Kansas Press, 2004.

Freeman, Michael. *Freedom or Security: The Consequences for Democracies Using Emergency Powers to Fight Terror.* Westport: CT: Praeger, 2003.

Genovese, Michael A. *The Power of the American Presidency: 1789–2000.* New York: Oxford University Press, 2000.

Gilbert, Robert E. *Managing Crisis: Presidential Disability and the Twenty-Fifth Amendment.* New York: Fordham University Press, 2000.

Graff, Henry F. *Grover Cleveland.* New York: Times Books, 2002.

Grant, James. *John Adams: Party of One.* New York: Farrar, Straus and Giroux, 2005.

Grant, Ulysses S. *The Personal Memoirs of Ulysses S. Grant.* New York: Cosimo Classics, 2007.

Greenberg, David. *Calvin Coolidge.* New York: Times Books, 2006.

Harris, John F. *The Survivor: Bill Clinton in the White House.* New York: Random House, 2006.

Harris, William C. *Lincoln's Rise to the Presidency.* Lawrence, KS: University of Kansas Press, 2007.

Hart, Gary. *James Monroe.* New York: Times Books, Henry Holt and Company, 2005.

Havelin, Kate. *Andrew Johnson.* Minneapolis, MN: Lerner Publications, 2004.

Hermitage. http://www.thehermitage.com/

Herrnson, Paul S., Ronald G. Shaiko, and Clyde Wilcox, eds. *The Interest Group Connection: Electioneering, Lobbying, and Policymaking in Washington,* 2nd edition. Washington, DC: CQ Press, 2002.

Historic Hyde Park. http://www.historichydepark.org/common/11050/?clientID=11050

Hook, Stephen W. *U.S. Foreign Policy: The Paradox of World Power,* 2nd edition. Washington, DC: CQ Press, 2007.

Hopkins, David A. *Presidential Elections: Strategies and Structures of American Politics.* Lanham, MD: Roman and Littlefield, 2007.

Inderfurth, Karl F., and Loch K. Johnson, eds. *Fateful Decisions: Inside the National Security Council.* New York: Oxford University Press, 2004.

Jeffers, H.P. *An Honest President: The Life and Presidencies of Grover Cleveland.* New York: Harper Perennial, 2002.

Johnson, Lyndon B., National Park. http://www.nps.gov/lyjo/

Karabell, Zachary. *Chester Alan Arthur.* New York: Times Books, 2004.

Kaufman, Burton I., and Scott Kaufman. *The Presidency of James Earl Carter, Jr.,* 2nd edition. Lawrence, KS: The University of Kansas Press, 2006.

Kengor, Paul. *The Crusader: Ronald Reagan and the Fall of Communism.* New York: Harper Perennial, 2007.

Kennedy, John F., Presidential Library and Musum. http://www.jfklibrary.org/

Kennerly, David Hume. *Extraordinary Circumstances: The Presidency of Gerald R. Ford.* Austin, TX: The Center for American History, the University of Texas at Austin, 2007.

Kernell, Samuel. *Going Public: New Strategies of Presidential Leadership,* 4th edition. Washington, DC: CQ Press, 2006.

Korda, Michael. *Ike: An American Hero.* New York: Harper Perennial, 2008.

Leuchtenburg, William E. *Herbert Hoover.* New York: Times Books, 2009.

Levy, Debbie. *Rutherford B. Hayes.* Minneapolis, MN: Lerner Books, 2006.

Lincoln, Abraham, Papers at the Library of Congress. http://lcweb2.loc.gov/ammem/alhtml/malhome.html

Lubunski, Richard. *James Madison and the Struggle for the Bill of Rights.* New York: Oxford University Press, 2008.

Manza, Jeff, Fay Lomax Cook, and Benjamin I. Page, eds. *Navigating Public Opinion: Polls, Policy, and the Future of American Democracy.* New York: Oxford University Press, 2002.

McCartney, Laton. *The Teapot Dome Scandal: How Big Oil Bought the Harding White House and Tried to Steal the Country.* New York: Random House, 2008.

McCullough, David. *John Adams.* New York: Simon and Schuster, 2001.

Means, Howard. *The Avenger Takes His Place: Andrew Johnson and the 45 Days That Changed the Nation.* Orlando, FL: Harcourt, 2006.

Milkis, Sidney M., and Michael Nelson. *The American Presidency: Origins and Development, 1776–2002.* Washington, DC: CQ Press, 2003.

Minow, Newton N., and Craig L. LaMay. *Inside the Presidential Debates: Their Improbable Past and Promising Future.* Chicago: University of Chicago Press, 2008.

Monticello. http://www.monticello.org/

Montpelier. http://www.montpelier.org/

Moore, Anne Chieko. *Benjamin Harrison: Centennial President.* Hauppauge, NY: Nova, 2008.

Morgan, H. Wayne. *William McKinley and His America.* Kent, OH: Kent State University Press, 2004.

Moss, Kenneth B. *Undeclared War and the Future of U.S. Foreign Policy.* Baltimore, MD: Johns Hopkins University Press, 2008.

Mount Vernon. http://www.mountvernon.org/

Naftali, Timothy. *George H.W. Bush.* New York: Times Books, 2007.

O'Brien, Michael. *John F. Kennedy: A Biography.* New York: St. Martin's Griffin, 2006.

Panogoupolis, Costas. *Rewiring Politics: Presidential Nominating Conventions in the Media Age.* Baton Rouge, LA: Louisiana State University Press, 2007.

Patrick, John J. *The Bill of Rights: A History in Documents.* New York: Oxford University Press, 2003.

Pfiffner, James P., and Douglas A. Brook, eds. *The Future of Merit: Twenty Years After the Civil Service Reform Act.* Baltimore, MD: Johns Hopkins University Press, 2000.

Phillips, Kevin. *William McKinley.* New York: Times Books, 2003.

Ponder, Stephen. *Managing the Press: Origins of the Media Presidency, 1897–1933.* New York: Palgrave Macmillan, 2000.

POTUS Presidents of the United States. http://www.potus.com/

Presidential Libraries. http://www.archives.gov/presidential-libraries/

Rauchway, Eric. *Murdering McKinley.* New York: Hill and Wang, 2003.

Reagan, Ronald. *The Reagan Diaries.* New York: HarperCollins, 2007.

Reagan, Ronald W., Presidential Library and Museum. http://www.reaganlibrary.net/

Reich, Cary. *The Life of Nelson A. Rockefeller: Worlds to Conquer, 1908–1958.* New York: Doubleday, 1996.

Remini, Robert V. *John Quincy Adams.* New York: Times Books, Henry Holt and Company, 2002.

Roberts, John B., II, *Rating the First Ladies*. New York: Citadel Press, 2003.

Roleff, Tamara L. *What Limits Should Be Placed on Presidential Powers?* Farmington Hills, MI: Greenhaven, 2006.

Rosen, Jeffrey. *The Supreme Court: The Personalities and Rivalries That Defined America*. New York: Holt, 2007.

Ross, Tara. *Enlightened Democracy: The Case for the Electoral College*. Dallas, TX: Colonial Press, 2005.

Rozell, Mark J., Clyde Wilcox, and David Madland. *Interest Groups in American Campaigns: The New Face of Electioneering*, 2nd edition. Washington, DC: CQ Press, 2005.

Rutkow, Ira. *James A. Garfield*. New York: Times Books, 2006.

Samples, John. *The Fallacy of Campaign Finance Reform*. Chicago: University of Chicago Press, 2006.

Schislinger, Galbraith. *Of the People: The 200 Year History of the Democratic Party*. North York, ON: Stoddart, 1992.

Schlesinger, Arthur. M., Jr. *The Age of Jackson*. Old Saybrook, CT: Konecky and Konecky, 1971.

Schroeder, Alan. *The Presidential Debates: Fifty Years of High Risk TV*. New York: Columbia University Press, 2008.

Schulman, Bruce J. *Lyndon Johnson and American Liberalism: A Brief Biography with Documents*, 2nd edition. New York: Palgrave Macmillan, 2006.

Schumaker, Paul D., and Burdett A. Loomis, eds. *Choosing a President: The Electoral College and Beyond*. Washington, DC: CQ Press, 2002.

Seigenthaler, John. *James K. Polk*. New York: Times Books, Henry Holt and Company, 2004.

Sergis, Diana K. *Bush v. Gore: Controversial Presidential Election Case*. Berkeley Heights, NJ: Enslow, 2003.

Stewart, David O. *The Summer of 1787: The Men Who Invented the Constitution*. New York: Simon and Schuster, 2007.

Swanson, James L. *Manhunt: The 12-Day Chase for Lincoln's Killer*. New York: William Morrow, 2006.

Trefousse, Hans. *Rutherford B. Hayes*. New York: Times Books, 2002.

Thurber, James A. *Rivals for Power: Presidential-Congressional Relations*. Lanham, MD: Rowman & Littlefield, 2005.

Turque, Bill. *Inventing Al Gore: A Biography*. Boston: Houghton Mifflin, 2000.

Updegrove, Mark K. *Second Acts: Presidential Lives and Legacies after the White House*. Guilford, CT: The Lyons Press, 2006.

Wagner, Heather Lehr. *Henry Kissinger*. New York: Chelsea House, 2006.

Wagner, Heather Lehr. *The History of the Democratic Party*. New York: Chelsea House Publications, 2007.

Walsh, Kenneth T. *Air Force One: A History of the Presidents and Their Planes*. New York: Hyperion, 2003.

The Warren Report: The Official Report on the Assassination of President John F. Kennedy. New York: The Associated Press, 1964.

Wheelan, Joseph. *Mr. Adams's Last Crusade*. New York: Public Affairs, 2008.

White House. http://www.whitehouse.gov/

Whittington, Keith E. *Political Foundations of Judicial Supremacy: The Presidency, the Supreme Court, and Constitutional Leadership in U.S. History*. Princeton, NJ: Princeton University Press, 2007.

Wicker, Tom. *Dwight D. Eisenhower*. New York: Times Books, 2002.

Widmer, Ted. *Martin Van Buren*. New York: Times Books, Henry Holt and Company, 2005.

Wilentz, Sean. *Andrew Jackson*. New York: Times Books, Henry Holt and Company, 2005.

Wills, Gary. *James Madison*. New York: Times Books, Henry Holt and Company, 2002.

Witcover, Jules. *Party of the People: A History of the Democrats*. New York: Random House, 2003.

Yoo, John. *The Powers of War and Peace: The Constitution and Foreign Affairs after 9/11*. Chicago: University of Chicago Press, 2006.

Zelden, Charles L. *Bush v. Gore: Exposing the Hidden Crisis in American Democracy*. Lawrence, KS: University Press of Kansas, 2008.

General Index

Note: Page numbers in *bold italic* type indicate main encyclopedia entries. Page numbers in *italic* type indicate illustrations, figures, tables, or maps. Page numbers in **bold** type refer to terms that are highlighted in bold in the text and also defined in the Glossary.